The West in Global Context

The West in Global Context

FROM 1500 TO THE PRESENT

Editors

George B. Kirsch

Frederick M. Schweitzer

Wolodymyr Stojko

George L. Mahoney
History Department, Manhattan College

Prentice Hall, *Upper Saddle River, New Jersey 07458*

Library of Congress Cataloging-in-Publication Data

The West in global context : from 1500 to the present / editors,
   George B. Kirsch ... [et al.].
      p.   cm.
   ISBN 0-13-485210-9
   1.   History, Modern—Sources.   I. Kirsch, George B.
D5W47   1997
909.08—dc20   96-4586
                                                     CIP

Acquisitions editor: Sally Constable
Production editor: Judy Winthrop
Copy editor: Rene Lynch
Cover designer: Wendy Alling Judy
Manufacturing buyer: Lynn Pearlman
Editorial assistant: Justin Belinski

This book was set in 10/12 Palatino by Compset, Inc.
and was printed and bound by RR Donnelley & Sons Company.
The cover was printed by Phoenix Color Corp.

Printed in the United States of America
10   9   8   7   6   5   4   3   2   1

ISBN 0-13-485210-9

Prentice-Hall International (UK) Limited, *London*
Prentice-Hall of Australia Pty. Limited, *Sydney*
Prentice-Hall Canada Inc., *Toronto*
Prentice-Hall Hispanoamericana, S. A., *Mexico*
Prentice-Hall of India Private Limited, *New Delhi*
Prentice-Hall of Japan, Inc., *Tokyo*
Simon & Schuster Asia Pte. Ltd., *Singapore*
Editora Prentice-Hall do Brasil, Ltda., *Rio de Janeiro*

To the Students Enrolled in "Roots of the Modern Age—History"
Manhattan College

Contents

INTRODUCTION TO UNIT FOUR

Nationalism and Imperialism — 175

INTRODUCTION TO UNIT FIVE

World War I and Its Aftermath _____ 245

INTRODUCTION TO UNIT SIX

World War II and Its Consequences _____ 297

INTRODUCTION TO UNIT SEVEN

The New World Order _____ 365

Preface

The documents in this collection are designed for use in a course in the history of Western Civilization from early modern times to the present. This volume focuses on seven major topics: The Age of Exploration and Discovery, the Age of Democratic Revolutions, the Industrial Revolution, Nationalism and Imperialism, World War I and Its Aftermath, World War II and Its Consequences, and the New World Order. It highlights the *interaction* of the peoples of Europe and the United States with other peoples and cultures around the globe. As a result we have reduced the space allotted to the internal political developments in Western nations in order to pay more attention to the effects of European and United States colonization and imperialism on the native cultures of Africa, the Americas, and Asia. We also consider the reactions of those peoples to westerners. Many of the following documents reveal the impact of modernization and westernization on traditional societies, and they also present the views and actions of leaders who struggled to meet the challenges presented by foreigners.

In this anthology each introduction to a unit contains a concise narrative of the leading issues and events for its subject. While we feel that a standard history textbook should be assigned along with the sources, we also believe that a brief review of the background material for each unit will be very beneficial for students. Each selection begins with a headnote and review questions for class discussion and/or written assignments.

We have chosen the documents to emphasize certain special features of our course, especially the nature and impact of European (and later United States) colonization and imperialism, comparative revolutions in England, France, the United States, the Soviet Union, and the emerging nations of the Third World, the Industrial Revolution, the significance of the world wars of the twentieth century, and recent political, social, and cultural trends. The anthology reflects our efforts to blend elements of European, United States, and world history into a coherent examination of the past 500 years. We also aim to help our students gain a clearer understanding of the complex contemporary world. Some of the documents treat the most important political, constitutional, and diplomatic events, while others provide interesting and entertaining insights into the cultures of men and women of all races around the world.

We would like to thank our colleagues in the History Department and the School of Arts and Social Sciences for their helpful suggestions and cooperation in this project—especially Professors Julie Leininger Pycior, Claire E. Nolte, and Michael E. Antolik. Winsome A. Downie and Thomas S. Ferguson also supplied us with important materials. Finally, we are deeply grateful for the help provided by the librarians at Manhattan College, Fordham University, and Columbia University.

George B. Kirsch
Frederick M. Schweitzer
Wolodymyr Stojko
George L. Mahoney

The West in Global Context

The Age of Exploration and Discovery

In the fifteenth century Portugal and Spain launched a series of voyages of exploration and discovery that brought Europeans to the shores of Africa, North and South America, and Asia. These Portuguese and Spanish adventurers would soon be joined by the Dutch, French, and English; together they established a European hegemony that lasted nearly five centuries, until the shocks of both world wars opened a new era in world history.

Religion played a major role in the contest for empire among the European nations. One of the original impulses for Europe's outward thrust came from the crusading spirit of the medieval Christian holy wars against the Islamic peoples of the Mediterranean, Eastern Europe, and the Near East. As the adventurers conquered and explored new lands, they carried with them both the sword and the cross as they struggled to impose their will and their beliefs on native peoples. By the sixteenth century the turmoil created by the Reformation intensified the competition among the Europeans, as Protestants battled Catholics for supremacy in the New World and Asia.

The lure of wealth also attracted westerners to the Orient. For many years the products of the East had reached European markets through land routes, but now oceanic travel raised new possibilities for bringing spices, silks, cotton cloth, precious stones, and other valuable commodities to the West in greater quantities and at lower prices. Imperial rivalries and internal political and social pressures also motivated the European powers to compete with each other for dominance throughout the world. By the late 1400s they had acquired the necessary scientific, technical, and military tools required for navigation on the high seas and the conquest of peoples of foreign lands. The race for empire was now on; the world would witness profound changes as the Europeans encountered and interacted with diverse cultures around the globe.

The failure of the land campaigns against the Muslims moved Christian kings to seek ways to outflank or attack them at the periphery of their power. In 1418 Prince Henry the Navigator of Portugal started expeditions along the

African coast. In 1499 Vasco da Gama returned from a successful voyage around that continent to India. During the sixteenth century Portugal seized several key points in India and China as bases for trade, and also reached Japan. In the New World it founded the colony of Brazil in South America. But Portuguese power waned by the next century, because of increased competition and domination by Spain, trade difficulties, and the inability of the Crown to control its agents halfway across the globe.

The Spanish empire in the New World began in 1492, when King Ferdinand of Aragon and Queen Isabella of Castile financed Christopher Columbus's first attempt to sail west to reach the Orient. Columbus explored part of the Caribbean and South America, but he died believing that he had reached islands off the coast of Asia. It took the efforts of Amerigo Vespucci, Vasco Nuñez de Balboa, and Ferdinand Magellan during the early 1500s to prove that a vast continent stood between Europe and the Far East.

During the sixteenth and seventeenth centuries, Spain sent soldiers, missionaries, and administrators to Central and South America and the Caribbean. The main goals of the invaders were to organize and exploit Indian labor, convert the indigenous peoples to Catholicism, and develop a thriving trade based on mining precious minerals. The conquests of the Aztec Empire by Hernando Cortés (see Document 1) and the Inca Empire by Francisco Pizarro yielded fortunes in gold and silver for Spain. This influx of Europeans had a catastrophic impact on the Indians, as epidemic diseases killed vast numbers of natives, while others became casualties of war. Most of the survivors abandoned their traditional religion and embraced the faith of the conquerors, but the resulting New World brand of Catholicism included native pre-Columbian elements. During the sixteenth century Bartolomé de las Casas and other Spanish priests inaugurated a humanitarian campaign in defense of the indigenous peoples. Las Casas wrote a detailed narrative of the atrocities committed by the Spanish and also called for reforms. But although the Church and the Crown did issue orders that prohibited the outright enslavement of the natives and increased their rights, the new rules did little to alleviate their suffering. Millions died as a result of their encounter with the Spanish, while most of those who remained alive mixed with the newcomers to create a new race of Hispanic Americans.

During the 1500s Spain extended its empire as far as the Philippines in the Pacific, building an elaborate trading network that linked Asia, Central and South America, the Caribbean, and the mother country. But while Spain subjugated local peoples and carried off much gold and silver, it could not supply its colonies with sufficient goods at competitive prices. Its possessions in the New World offered tempting trade opportunities for pirates, privateers, slavers, smugglers, and illegal traders from other empires. Dutch, French, and English competition pressed hard upon Spanish holdings, especially in the Caribbean and north of Florida. Moreover, Spain's involvement in religious and dynastic wars throughout Europe and its construction of monumental palaces in the homeland drained the imperial treasury. By the 1600s Spain's rulers were deeply in debt to foreign creditors.

During the sixteenth century the Dutch and the French also joined the race for empire. The Dutch established colonies in South America, the East and West Indies, and North America. With the port of New Amsterdam (later New York City) on the Hudson River and stations in the Caribbean, they were well positioned to reap profits in trade with their own colonies and through illicit commerce with those of their rivals. Their skill in finance, shipping, and business made them a major commercial power in Europe, on the Atlantic, and in the Caribbean. Meanwhile the French entered the scramble for colonies in 1534 when Jacques Cartier began a series of voyages to Newfoundland and the St. Lawrence River region. By the 1600s France had settlements along the St. Lawrence in the interior of North America, as well as in the Caribbean. Unlike the Spanish and Portuguese, the French found no precious metals and did not exploit native labor. They lived on subsistence agriculture, fishing, and the fur trade in Canada, and founded tobacco and sugar plantations in the Caribbean.

The English were latecomers in the race for empire in the New World. Despite the early expeditions of John and Sebastian Cabot in 1497–1498 and 1508–1509, England waited until the end of the sixteenth century to begin colonization of North America. The political and religious instability of Tudor England and the effort to consolidate control over Scotland, Wales, and Ireland explain the delay. During the 1580s propagandists such as Richard Hakluyt and adventurers such as Humphrey Gilbert and Walter Raleigh urged Queen Elizabeth to support plantations in the New World (see Document 2). But England's expansion first required the successful subjugation of the natives of Ireland. The conquest of that island and its settlement by Englishmen constituted the first phase in Great Britain's westward course of empire (see Document 3). Next came the founding of the Jamestown colony in 1607, when the Virginia Company sent John Smith and his companions to the Chesapeake Bay region (see Document 4). The first Virginians barely survived starvation and conflict with natives, until a tobacco boom saved the colony in the 1620s. Meanwhile English Protestant dissenters organized several plantations in New England. The Pilgrims settled Plymouth Plantation in 1620, while a much more numerous expedition of Puritans launched the Massachusetts Bay experiment in 1630.

Relations between the English and the natives of North America differed markedly from the racial encounters of the Spanish with the peoples of Central and South America and the Caribbean. Although large numbers of North American Indians died as a result of their exposure to new diseases, those who survived did not supply a large labor pool for the invaders, nor did they convert to Protestantism in significant numbers. Instead, the English pursued a policy of racial separatism toward the Indians. At the same time, their western expansion from the Atlantic coast brought them into increasing conflict with the powerful interior tribes. In addition, since the English (unlike the Spanish) also generally brought women with them to the New World, they were far less likely to intermix with the natives. The result was a much lower rate of miscegenation in the English colonies than was the case in the rest of the New World.

In pursuing the goal of enhanced national strength, all the European colonial powers were guided by the economic philosophy of mercantilism, or what some economic historians prefer to call "national economics." As theory and practice, mercantilism was based on the understanding, as old as Thucydides, that wealth is power. The stronger a nation-state's economy and tax base, the greater was its capacity to defend itself, expand its frontiers and annex territory, control trade routes and markets, and become dominant in diplomatic negotiations and the formation of alliances. During the reign of Louis XIV of France, the mercantilist minister of finance, Jean Baptiste Colbert, sought to promote economic growth and expansion in order to increase the state treasury's revenues and tax returns. A characteristic expedient was the chartering of a company by the Crown, such as the Hudson's Bay Company, created by England in 1670. Sometimes the government itself functioned as the entrepreneur in establishing industries to produce woolen cloth for uniforms or iron for cannon, as in Prussia. More usually, compacts were worked out between government and productive elements, whether agricultural producers, merchants, or industrialists. Since agriculture remained the principal source of wealth in the heyday of mercantilism, 1400–1800, state policies sought to enhance productivity. But because agriculture tends to be tradition-bound, with an uncertain and limited return on investment, and a perishable and relatively inconvertible yield, mercantilists preferred to give their attention to trade and industry. Here the dividend was about twice that of agriculture, more predictable, and readily convertible into artillery, warships, the salaries of royal bureaucrats, and other instruments of state power. Because mercantilists defined wealth as bullion, they believed that in every transaction one party won and the other lost, depending upon who paid out the gold or silver. Hence they interpreted trade as a form of warfare, fought many commercial wars, and sought to attain economic self-sufficiency (autarky). The familiar mercantilist policies follow from these premises: favorable balance of trade; acquisition of colonies to provide raw materials and guaranteed markets; subsidizing merchant marines; building ports, canals, and turnpikes; underwriting research for new productive techniques; establishing agricultural and mechanical colleges; offering patents and monopolies; and much else of a similar nature. Many governments today follow neomercantilist policies.

As the Europeans began to develop the commercial potential of the western hemisphere, they also looked eastward to Asia during the sixteenth and seventeenth centuries. The Portuguese had established contact with China and Japan, and by the late 1500s Jesuit missionaries were introducing Catholicism to those nations. The activities of Matteo Ricci and others brought mixed success at best in converting the Chinese, but Jesuit reports on the customs of the people stimulated great interest in the Orient back in Europe (see Document 5). In the Celestial Empire the new Manchu rulers barely tolerated the foreigners as "south sea barbarians." Meanwhile the Muscovites' capture of Kazan and Astrakhan had opened the road to the Ural Mountains. The fall of the trans-Ural khanate of Sibir at the end of the sixteenth century marked the beginning of Muscovy's northward and eastward Asian expansion. The conquests proceeded in the name of the Tsar or on his orders. The Muscovites' firearms, better organization, and supporting forces prevailed over the obstinate resistance of the native peoples. The invaders utilized waterways and advanced from one river basin to another, establishing smaller and larger forts until they reached the Sea of Okhotsk in 1639. The forts served both as centers to secure control and collect tribute from natives and also as bases for further conquests. By the end of the 1600s the Muscovites had streamed across Siberia, subjugating local tribes and establishing towns along a 5,000-mile stretch of territory that extended to the Pacific Ocean (see Document 6). The Japanese at first welcomed the Europeans, but internal strife and fear of Christian influence moved the Tokugawa shoguns to persecute and expel the Europeans. They closed Japan to the West during the 1630s (see Document 7).

Each group of Europeans that established colonies in the New World faced shortages of labor as they attempted to capitalize on the commercial potential of their respective settlements. While the Spanish had some success in mobilizing the native peoples of Central and South America, the Dutch, Portuguese, French, and English depended more on the exploitation of African slaves for their sugar, tobacco, and rice plantations. The institution of slavery dated back to biblical times and was familiar to both Europeans and Africans at the dawn of the age of discovery and was widely practiced in Muslim societies. Westerners simply adapted ancient practices to the needs of the Atlantic economy.

The Portuguese inaugurated the modern era of the slave trade in 1472 and monopolized it for the next century, until the Dutch and English increased their shares of the market. The Europeans came to the coast of tropical Africa, where native sellers exchanged gold, ivory, and slaves for guns, bars of iron and copper, brass pots, beads, rum, and textiles. As the development of commercial agriculture increased the demand for slaves, African kings intensified their efforts to acquire the "black gold" that was needed to work the plantations of the New World. They organized raiding parties into the heart of Africa that seized prisoners and marched them to the coast, where they were packed on board slave ships for the dreaded "middle passage" to the West Indies. There some were reshipped to other destinations. Conditions on board these vessels were horrendous, and a large percentage of Africans died on their way to the Americas (see Document 8). But the multitudes that did survive played a critical role in the economic and cultural development of the Western world. Over the course of four centuries the forced migration of Africans brought approximately eleven million people to the Americas. Their labor provided the foundation for the wealth that later financed the Industrial Revolution. Their interaction with Europeans and Amerindians provided one of the central forces that shaped the acculturation of the three races that converged in the New World.

The great European explorations, discoveries, and colonial enterprises brought momentous political, economic, social, and cultural consequences for the entire world. The competition for empire fostered and intensified national and imperial rivalries that broke out into intermittent warfare for centuries. The invasion of the Americas also led directly to the extermination or subjugation of the indigenous peoples of the New World, as well as the forced migration of millions of African slaves. The gold and silver carried off to Europe contributed to an inflation of prices that transformed the Western economy. The spread of New World crops such as tobacco, maize, and potatoes revolutionized the diet and food supply of Europe and Africa, while the introduction of tools, textiles, weapons, alcohol, horses, and domesticated livestock in turn dramatically altered the lifestyles of native Americans. Perhaps most significantly, the coming of the Europeans drastically affected demographic patterns for all peoples. The introduction of European diseases annihilated large numbers of Indians, while varying degrees of miscegenation mixed white, red, and black populations. In the long run, the exploration and colonization of the Americas brought about an acculturation of peoples that continues today, five centuries after the Europeans first reached the shores of the New World.

1. Two Accounts of the Spanish Encounter with the Aztecs, 1519

Bernal Díaz del Castillo (1492–1584) was born in Castile, Spain, the same year that Christopher Columbus launched the first Spanish voyages of discovery to the New World. In 1514 he sailed on an expedition to Central America in search of fabulous wealth rumored to be located in the region of the isthmus of Panama. In 1518 he joined the army of Hernando Cortés as a foot soldier. He survived several serious wounds received in combat and he escaped from captivity during his adventures under Cortés's command. After the conquest of the Aztecs he joined parties of Spaniards seeking mines and Indian subjects, but he failed to enrich himself. Disappointed with his inability to reap great rewards in the New World, in 1539 he returned to Spain in the hopes of obtaining an office in Mexico City. His request for a prized position was denied, but he did receive a lesser place in Guatemala. There he remained from 1541 until his death, raising a family and serving his community as a magistrate. During the 1560s Díaz del Castillo wrote his *True History of the Conquest of New Spain,* which was not published until 1632. The excerpt which appears here (Part A) describes the Spaniards' first impressions of the Aztec ruler, Montezuma, and the society and customs of the people of the capital city of Tenochtitlán. This selection reflects the influence on the author of romances of chivalry that were popular during the sixteenth century. It also reveals the writer's lively and colloquial style, his admiration for certain characteristics of Aztec society, and his disgust for other features of their culture.

Shortly after their arrival in the Aztec capital of Tenochtitlán, Cortés and his Spanish forces placed Montezuma under guard and began seizing the natives' treasures. Cortés then left the city to turn back a challenge from a rival Spaniard who had orders from the governor of Cuba to arrest him. While he was away his deputy, Pedro de Alvarado, authorized the murder of young warriors and others who were celebrating the fiesta of Toxcatl, in honor of the god Huitzilopochtli. According to the Spanish historian and missionary, Bernardino de Sahagún, that holiday was a spring festival comparable in importance to the Christian observance of Easter. Part B of this document presents excerpts from the *General History of the Things of New Spain*, compiled in about 1585 by Sahagún and native Indian informants from a variety of indigenous sources. These included written codices (which contained pictures, symbols, and characters) and songs and narratives passed down through the oral tradition for generations after the Conquest. Sahagún and other missionaries devised a system of writing the native language of Nahuatl using the Latin alphabet.

QUESTIONS

1. How did the Aztecs organize their political life? What role did Montezuma play in their government?
2. What does this document reveal about the economic life of the Aztecs, especially their agriculture, arts, and crafts?
3. What does this document tell you about the Aztecs' religious and spiritual life? What was Cortés's reaction to their religion?
4. Did Bernal Díaz del Castillo consider the Aztecs to be a civilized people? What impressed the author most about Aztec society? What disturbed him the most?
5. Describe and analyze the Aztecs' celebration of the Fiesta of Toxcatl. Compare the accounts of the Aztecs' religious beliefs and rituals presented in both parts of this document.
6. Why did the Spaniards choose this occasion to attack and massacre the Aztecs?
7. What was Montezuma's response to this massacre? How did the surviving Aztecs react to his message? Describe and explain their behavior after the massacre.

A. Memoirs of the Conquistador Bernal Díaz del Castillo

When it was announced to Cortés that Montezuma himself was approaching, he alighted from his horse and advanced to meet him. Many compliments were now passed on both sides. Montezuma bid Cortés welcome, who, through Marina, said, in return, he hoped his majesty was in good health. If I still remember rightly, Cortés, who had Marina next to him, wished to concede the place of honour to the monarch, who, however, would not accept of it, but conceded it to Cortés, who now brought forth a necklace of precious stones, of the most beautiful colours and shapes, strung upon gold wire, and perfumed with musk, which he hung about the neck of Montezuma. Our commander was then going to embrace him, but the grandees by whom he was surrounded held back his arms, as they considered it improper. Our general then desired Marina to tell the monarch how exceedingly he congratulated himself upon his good fortune of having seen such a powerful monarch face to face, and of the honour he had done us by coming out to meet us himself. To all this Montezuma answered in very appropriate terms, and ordered his two nephews, the princes of Tetzuco and Conohuacan, to conduct us to our quarters. He himself returned to the city, accompanied by his two other relatives, the princes of Cuitlahuac and Tlacupa, with the other grandees of his numerous suite. As they passed by, we perceived how all those who composed his majesty's retinue held their heads bent forward, no one daring to lift up his eyes in his presence; and altogether what deep veneration was paid him.

The road before us now became less crowded, and yet who could have been able to count the vast numbers of men, women, and children who filled the streets, crowded the balconies, and the canoes in the canals, merely to gaze upon us? . . .

We were quartered in a large building where there was room enough for us all, and which had been occupied by Axayacatl, father of Montezuma, during his life-time. Here the latter had likewise a secret room full of treasures, and where the gold he had inherited from his father was hid, which he had never touched up to this moment. Near this building there were temples and Mexican idols, and this place had been purposely selected for us because we were termed teules, or were thought to be such, and that we might dwell among the latter as among our equals. The apartments and halls were very spacious and those set apart for our

general were furnished with carpets. There were separate beds for each of us, which could not have been better fitted up for a gentleman of the first rank. Every place was swept clean, and the walls had been newly plastered and decorated.

When we had arrived in the great court-yard adjoining this palace, Montezuma came up to Cortés, and, taking him by the hand, conducted him himself into the apartments where he was to lodge, which had been beautifully decorated after the fashion of the country. He then hung about his neck a chaste necklace of gold, most curiously worked with figures all representing crabs. The Mexican grandees were greatly astonished at all these uncommon favours which their monarch bestowed upon our general.

Cortés returned the monarch many thanks for so much kindness, and the latter took leave of him with these words: "Malinche, you and your brothers must now do as if you were at home, and take some rest after the fatigues of the journey," then returned to his own palace, which was close at hand.

We allotted the apartments according to the several companies, placed our cannon in an advantageous position, and made such arrangements that our cavalry, as well as the infantry, might be ready at a moment's notice. We then sat down to a plentiful repast, which had been previously spread out for us, and made a sumptuous meal.

This our bold and memorable entry into the large city of Tenochtitlán Mexico took place on the 8th of November, 1519. Praise be to the Lord Jesus Christ for all this. . . .

The mighty Montezuma may have been about this time in the fortieth year of his age. He was tall of stature, of slender make, and rather thin, but the symmetry of his body was beautiful. His complexion was not very brown, merely approaching to that of the inhabitants in general. The hair of his head was not very long, excepting where it hung thickly down over his ears, which were quite hidden by it. His black beard, though thin, looked handsome. His countenance was rather of an elongated form, but cheerful; and his fine eyes had the expression of love or severity, at the proper moments. He was particularly clean in his person, and took a bath every evening. Besides a number of concubines, who were all daughters of persons of rank and quality, he had two lawful wives of royal extraction, whom, however, he visited secretly without any one daring to observe it, save his most confidential servants. He was perfectly innocent of any unnatural crimes. The dress he had on one day was not worn again until four days had elapsed. In the halls adjoining his own private apartments there was always a guard of 2000 men of quality, in waiting; with whom, however, he never held any conversation unless to give them orders or to receive some intelligence from them. Whenever for this purpose they entered his apartment, they had first to take off their rich costumes and put on meaner garments, though these were always neat and clean; and were only allowed to enter into his presence barefooted, with eyes cast down. No person durst look at him full in the face, and during the three prostrations which they were obliged to make before they could approach him, they pronounced these words: "Lord! my Lord! sublime Lord!" Everything that was communicated to him was to be said in few words, the eyes of the speaker being constantly cast down, and on leaving the monarch's presence he walked backwards out of the room. I also remarked that even princes and other great personages who come to Mexico respecting law-suits, or on other business from the interior of the country, always took off their

shoes and changed their whole dress for one of a meaner appearance when they entered his palace. Neither were they allowed to enter the palace straightaway, but had to show themselves for a considerable time outside the doors; as it would have been considered want of respect to the monarch if this had been omitted.

Above 300 kinds of dishes were served up for Montezuma's dinner from his kitchen, underneath which were placed pans of porcelain filled with fire, to keep them warm. Three hundred dishes of various kinds were served up for him alone, and above 1000 for the persons in waiting. He sometimes, but very seldom, accompanied by the chief officers of his household, ordered the dinner himself, and desired that the best dishes and various kinds of birds should be called over to him. We were told that the flesh of young children as a very dainty bit, were also set before him sometimes by way of a relish. Whether there was any truth in this we could not possibly discover; on account of the great variety of dishes, consisting in fowls, turkeys, pheasants, partridges, quails, tame and wild geese, venison, musk swine, pigeons, hares, rabbits, and of numerous other birds and beasts; besides which there were various other kinds of provisions, indeed it would have been no easy task to call them all over by name.

I had almost forgotten to mention, that during dinner-time, two other young women of great beauty brought the monarch small cakes, as white as snow, made of eggs and other very nourishing ingredients, on plates covered with clean napkins; also a kind of long-shaped bread, likewise made of very substantial things, and some pachol, which is a kind of wafer-cake. They then presented him with three beautifully painted and gilt tubes, which were filled with liquid amber, and a herb called by the Indians tobacco. After the dinner had been cleared away and the singing and dancing done, one of these tubes was lighted, and the monarch took the smoke into his mouth, and after he had done this a short time, he fell asleep.

About this time a celebrated cazique, whom we called Tapia, was Montezuma's chief steward: he kept an account of the whole of Montezuma's revenue, in large books of paper which the Mexicans call am-atl. A whole house was filled with such large books of accounts.

Montezuma had also two arsenals filled with arms of every description, of which many were ornamented with gold and precious stones. These arms consisted of shields of different sizes, sabres, and a species of broadsword, which is wielded with both hands, the edge furnished with flint stones, so extremely sharp that they cut much better than our Spanish swords; further, lances of greater length than ours, with spikes at their end, full one fathom in length, likewise furnished with several sharp flint stones. The pikes are so very sharp and hard that they will pierce the strongest shield, and cut like a razor; so that the Mexicans even shave themselves with these stones. Then there were excellent bows and arrows, pikes with single and double points, and the proper thongs to throw them with; slings with round stones purposely made for them; also a species of large shield, so ingeniously constructed that it could be rolled up when not wanted: they are only unrolled on the field of battle, and completely cover the whole body from the head to the feet. Further, we saw here a great variety of cuirasses made of quilted cotton, which were outwardly adorned with soft feathers of different colours, and looked like uniforms. . . .

I will now, however, turn to another subject, and rather acquaint my readers with the skillful arts practised among the Mexicans: among which I will first mention the sculptors, and the gold- and silver-smiths, who were clever in working and smelting gold, and would have astonished the most celebrated of our Spanish gold-smiths: the number of these was very great, and the most skillful lived at a place called Ezcapuzalco, about four miles from Mexico. After these came the very skillful masters in cutting and polishing precious stones, and the calchihuis, which resemble the emerald. Then followed the great masters in painting, and decorators in feathers, and the wonderful sculptors. Even at this day there are living in Mexico three Indian artists, named Marcos de Aguino, Juan de la Cruz, and El Crespello, who have severally reached to such great proficiency in the art of painting and sculpture, that they may be compared to an Apelles, or our contemporaries Michael Angelo and Berruguete. . . .

The powerful Montezuma had also a number of dancers and clowns: some danced in stilts, tumbled, and performed a variety of other antics for the monarch's entertainment: a whole quarter of the city was inhabited by these performers, and their only occupation consisted in such like performances. Lastly, Montezuma had in his service great numbers of stone cutters, masons, and carpenters, who were solely employed in the royal palaces. Above all, I must not forget to mention here his gardens for the culture of flowers, trees, and vegetables, of which there were various kinds. In these gardens were also numerous baths, wells, basins, and ponds full of limpid water, which regularly ebbed and flowed. All this was enlivened by endless varieties of small birds, which sang among the trees. Also the plantations of medical plants and vegetables are well worthy of our notice: these were kept in proper order by a large body of gardeners. All the baths, wells, ponds, and buildings were substantially constructed of stonework, as also the theatres where the singers and dancers performed. There were upon the whole so many remarkable things for my observation in these gardens and throughout the whole town, that I can scarcely find words to express the astonishment I felt at the pomp and splendour of the Mexican monarch. . . .

We had already been four days in the city of Mexico, and neither our commander nor any of us had, during that time, left our quarters, excepting to visit the gardens and buildings adjoining the palace. Cortés now, therefore, determined to view the city, and visit the great market, and the chief temple of Huitzilopochtli. . . .

The moment we arrived in this immense market, we were perfectly astonished at the vast numbers of people, the profusion of merchandise which was there exposed for sale, and at the good police and order that reigned throughout. The grandees who accompanied us drew our attention to the smallest circumstance, and gave us full explanation of all we saw. Every species of merchandise had a separate spot for its sale. We first of all visited those divisions of the market appropriated for the sale of gold and silver wares, of jewels, of cloths interwoven with feathers, and of other manufactured goods; besides slaves of both sexes. This slave market was upon as great a scale as the Portuguese market for negro slaves at Guinea. To prevent these from running away, they were fastened with halters about their neck, though some were allowed to walk at large. Next to these came the dealers in coarser wares—cotton, twisted thread, and cacao. In short, every species of goods which New Spain produces were here to be found; and everything put me in mind of my native town Medina del Campo during fair time, where every merchandise has a separate street assigned for its sale. . . .

What can I further add? If I am to note everything down, I must also mention human excrements, which were exposed for sale in canoes lying in the canals near this square, and is used for the tanning of leather; for, according to the assurances of the Mexicans, it is impossible to tan well without it. I can easily imagine that many of my readers will laugh at this; however, what I have stated is a fact, and, as further proof of this, I must acquaint the reader that along every road accommodations were built of reeds, straw, or grass, by which those who made use of them were hidden from the view of the passers-by, so that great care was taken that none of the last-mentioned treasures should be lost. But why should I so minutely detail every article exposed for sale in this great market? If I had to enumerate everything singly, I should not so easily get to the end. . . . The variety was so great that it would occupy more space than I can well spare to note them down in; besides which, the market was so crowded with people, and the thronging so excessive in the porticoes, that it was quite impossible to see all in one day. . . .

Before we mounted the steps of the great temple, Montezuma, who was sacrificing on the top to his idols, sent six papas and two of his principal officers to conduct Cortés up the steps. There were 114 steps to the summit. . . . Indeed, this infernal temple, from its great height, commanded a view of the whole surrounding neighbourhood. From this place we could likewise see the three causeways which led into Mexico,— that from Iztapalapan, by which we had entered the city four days ago; that from Tlacupa, along which we took our flight eight months after, when we were beaten out of the city by the new monarch Cuitlahuatzin; the third was that of Tepeaquilla. We also observed the aqueduct which ran from Chapultepec, and provided the whole town with sweet water. We could also distinctly see the bridges across the openings, by which these causeways were intersected, and through which the waters of the lake ebbed and flowed. The lake itself was crowded with canoes, which were bringing provisions, manufactures, and other merchandise to the city. From here we also discovered that the only communication of the houses in this city, and of all the other towns built in the lake, was by means of drawbridges or canoes. In all these towns the beautiful white plastered temples rose above the smaller ones, like so many towers and castles in our Spanish towns, and this, it may be imagined, was a splendid sight.

After we had sufficiently gazed upon this magnificent picture, we again turned our eyes toward the great market, and beheld the vast numbers of buyers and sellers who thronged there. The bustle and noise occasioned by this multitude of human beings was so great that it could be heard at a distance of more than four miles. Some of our men, who had been at Constantinople and Rome, and travelled through the whole of Italy, said that they never had seen a marketplace of such large dimensions, or which was so well regulated or so crowded with people as this one at Mexico.

On this occasion Cortés said to Father Olmedo, who had accompanied us: "I have just been thinking that we should take this opportunity, and apply to Montezuma for permission to build a church here."

To which Father Olmedo replied, that it would, no doubt, be an excellent thing if the monarch would grant this; but that it would be acting overhasty to make a proposition of that nature to him now, whose consent would not easily be gained at any time.

Cortés then turned to Montezuma, and said to him, by means of our interpreter, Doña Marina: "Your majesty is, indeed, a great monarch, and you merit to be still greater! It has been a real delight to us to view all your cities. I have now one favour to beg of you, that you would allow us to see your gods and teules."

To which Montezuma answered, that he must first consult the chief papas, to whom he then addressed a few words. Upon this, we were led into a kind of small tower, with one room, in which we saw two basements resembling altars, decked with coverings of extreme beauty. On each of these basements stood a gigantic, fat-looking figure, of which the one on the right hand represented the god of war Huitzilopochtli. This idol had a very broad face, with distorted and furious-looking eyes, and was covered all over with jewels, gold, and pearls, which were stuck to it by means of a species of paste, which, in this country, is prepared from a certain root. Large serpents, likewise, covered with gold and precious stones, wound round the body of this monster, which held in one hand a bow, and in the other a bunch of arrows. Another small idol which stood by its side, representing its page, carried this monster's short spear, and its golden shield studded with precious stones. Around Huitzilopochtli's neck were figures representing human faces and hearts made of gold and silver, and decorated with blue stones. In front of him stood perfuming pans with copal, the incense of the country; also the hearts of three Indians, who had that day been slaughtered, were now consuming before him as a burnt-offering. Every wall of this chapel and the whole floor had become almost black with human blood, and the stench was abominable.

Respecting the abominable human sacrifices of these people, the following was communicated to us: The breast of the unhappy victim destined to be sacrificed was ripped open with a knife made of sharp flint; the throbbing heart was then torn out, and immediately offered to the idol-god in whose honour the sacrifice had been instituted. After this, the head, arms, and legs were cut off and eaten at their banquets, with the exception of the head, which was saved, and hung to a beam appropriated for that purpose. No other part of the body was eaten, but the remainder was thrown to the beasts which were kept in those abominable dens, in which there were also vipers and other poisonous serpents, and, among the latter in particular, a species at the end of whose tail there was a kind of rattle. This last mentioned serpent, which is the most dangerous, was kept in a cabin of a diversified form, in which a quantity of feathers had been strewed: here it laid its eggs, and it was fed with the flesh of dogs and of human beings who had been sacrificed. We were positively told that, after we had been beaten out of the city of Mexico, and had lost 850 of our men, these horrible beasts were fed on many successive days with the bodies of our unfortunate countrymen. Indeed, when all the tigers and lions roared together, with the howlings of the jackals and foxes, and hissing of the serpents, it was quite fearful, and you could not suppose otherwise than that you were in hell. . . .

Our commander here said smilingly, to Montezuma: "I cannot imagine that such a powerful and wise monarch as you are, should not have yourself discovered by this time that these idols are not divinities, but evil spirits, called devils. In order that you may be convinced of this, and that your papas may satisfy themselves of this truth, allow me to erect a cross on the summit of this temple; and, in the chapel, where stand your Huitzilopochtli and Tetzcatlipuca, give us a small space that I may place there the image of the holy Virgin; then you will see what terror will seize these idols by which you have been so long deluded."

Montezuma knew what the image of the Virgin Mary was, yet he was very much displeased with Cortés's offer, and replied, in presence of two papas, whose anger was not less conspicuous, "Malinche, could I have conjectured that you would have used such reviling language as you have just done, I would certainly not have shown you my gods. In our eyes these are good divinities: they preserve our lives, give us nourishment, water, and good harvests, healthy and growing weather, and victory whenever we pray to them for it. Therefore we offer up our prayers to them, and make them sacrifices. I earnestly beg of you not to say another word to insult the profound veneration in which we hold these gods."

As soon as Cortés heard these words and perceived the great excitement under which they were pronounced, he said nothing in return, but merely remarked to the monarch with a cheerful smile: "It is time for us both to depart hence." To which Montezuma answered, that he would not detain him any longer, but he himself was now obliged to stay some time to atone to his gods by prayer and sacrifice for having committed *gratlatlacol,* by allowing us to ascend the great temple, and thereby occasioning the affronts which we had offered them. . . .

Now as there was a rumour and we had heard the story that Montezuma kept the treasure of his father Axayaca in that building, it was suspected that it might be in this chamber which had been closed up and cemented only a few days before. Yanes spoke about it to Juan Valasquez de Leon and Francisco de Lugo, and those Captains told the story to Cortés, and the door was secretly opened. When it was opened Cortés and some of his Captains went in first, and they saw such a number of jewels and slabs and plates of gold and figures of goddesses and other great riches, that they were quite carried away and did not know what to say about such wealth. The news soon spread among all the other captains and soldiers, and very secretly we went in to see it. When I saw it I marvelled, and as at that time I was a youth and had never seen such riches as those in my life before, I took it for certain that there could not be another such store of wealth in the whole world. It was decided by all our captains and soldiers, that we should not dream of touching a particle of it, but that the stones should immediately be put back in the doorway and it should be sealed up and cemented just as we found it, and that it should not be spoken about, lest it should reach Montezuma's ears, until times should alter.

B. An Aztec Account of the Massacre in the Main Temple

The Preparations for the Fiesta of Toxcatl

The Aztecs begged permission of their king to hold the fiesta to learn how it was celebrated. A delegation of the celebrants came to the palace where Montezuma was a prisoner, and when their spokesman asked his permission, he granted it to them.

As soon as the delegation returned, the women began to grind seeds of the *chicalote* [an edible plant, also used in medicines]. These women had fasted for a whole year. They ground the seeds in the patio of the temple. The Spaniards came out of the palace together, dressed in armor and carrying their weapons with them. They stalked among the women and looked at them one by one; they stared into the faces of the women who were grinding seeds. After this cold inspection, they went back into the palace. It is said that they planned to kill the celebrants if the men entered the patio.

The Statue of Huitzilopochtli

On the evening before the fiesta of Toxcatl, the celebrants began to model a statue of Huitzilopochtli. They gave it such a human appearance that it seemed the body of a living man. Yet they made the statue with nothing but a paste made of the ground seeds of the *chicalote*, which they shaped over an armature of sticks.

When the statue was finished, they dressed it in rich feathers, and they painted crossbars over and under its eyes. They also clipped on its earrings of turquoise mosaic; these were in the shape of serpents, with gold rings hanging from them. Its nose plug, in the shape of an arrow, was made of gold and was inlaid with fine stones. They placed the magic headdress of humming-bird feathers on its head. They also adorned it with an *anecuyotl*, which was a belt made of feathers, with a cone at the back. Then they hung around its neck an ornament of yellow parrot feathers, fringed like the locks of a young boy. Over this they put its nettle-leaf cape, which was painted black and decorated with five clusters of eagle feathers. Next they wrapped it in its cloak, which was painted with skulls and bones, and over this they fastened its vest. The vest was painted with dismembered human parts: skulls, ears, hearts, intestines, torsos, breasts, hands, and feet. They also put on its *maxtlatl*, or loin-cloth, which was decorated with images of dissevered limbs and fringed with amate paper. This *maxtlatl* was painted with vertical stripes of bright blue. They fastened a red paper flag at its shoulder and placed on its head what looked like a sacrificial flint knife. This too was made of red paper; it seemed to have been steeped in blood. The statue carried a *tehuehuelli*, a bamboo shield decorated with four clusters of fine eagle feathers. The pendant of this shield was blood-red, like the knife and the shoulder flag. The statue also carried four arrows. Finally, they put the wristbands on its arms. These bands, made of coyote skin, were fringed with paper cut into little strips.

The Beginning of the Fiesta

Early the next morning, the statue's face was uncovered by those who had been chosen for that ceremony. They gathered in front of the idol in single file and offered it gifts of food, such as round seedcakes or perhaps human flesh. But they did not carry it up to its temple on top of the pyramid. All the young warriors were eager for the fiesta to begin. They had sworn to dance and sing with all their hearts, so that the Spaniards would marvel at the beauty of the rituals.

The procession began, and the celebrants filed into the temple patio to dance the Dance of the Serpent. When they were all together in the patio, the songs and the dance began. Those who had fasted for twenty days and those who had fasted for a year were in command of the others; they kept the dancers in file with pine wands. (If anyone wished to urinate, he did not stop dancing, but simply opened his clothing at the hips and separated his clusters of heron feathers.) If anyone disobeyed the leaders or was not in proper place they struck him on the hips and shoulders. Then they drove him out of the patio, beating him and shoving him from behind. They pushed him so hard that he sprawled to the ground, and they dragged him outside by the ears. No one dared to say a word about his punishment, for those who had fasted during the year were feared and venerated; they had earned the exclusive title "Brothers of Huitzilopochtli."

The great captains, the bravest warriors, danced at the head of the files to guide the others. The youths followed at a slight distance. Some of the youths wore their hair gathered into large locks, a sign that they had never taken any captives. Others carried their headdresses on their shoulders; they had taken captives, but only with help. Then came the recruits, who were called "the young warriors." They had each captured an enemy or two. The others called to them: "Come, comrades, show us how brave you are! Dance with all your hearts!"

The Spaniards Attack the Celebrants

At this moment in the fiesta, when the dance was loveliest and when song was linked to song, the Spaniards were seized with an urge to kill the celebrants. They all ran forward, armed as if for battle. They closed the entrances and the passageways, all the gates of the patio: the Eagle Gate in the lesser palace, the Gate of the Canestalk and the Gate of the Serpent of Mirrors. They posted guards so that no one could escape, and then rushed into the Sacred Patio to slaughter the celebrants. They came on foot, carrying their swords and their wooden or metal shields. They ran in among the dancers, forcing their way to the place the drums were played. They attacked the man who was drumming and cut off his arms. Then they cut off his head, and it rolled across the floor. They attacked all the celebrants, stabbing them, spearing them, striking them with their swords. They attacked some of them from behind, and these fell instantly to the ground with their entrails hanging out. Others they beheaded: they cut off their heads, or split their heads to pieces. They struck others in the shoulders, and their arms were torn from their bodies. They wounded some in the thigh and some in the calf. They slashed others in the abdomen, and their entrails all spilled to the ground. Some attempted to run away, but their intestines dragged as they ran; they seemed to tangle their feet in their own entrails. No matter how they tried to save themselves, they could find no escape. Some attempted to force their way out, but the Spaniards murdered them at the gates. Others climbed the walls, but they could not save themselves. Those who ran into the communal houses were safe there for a while; so were those who lay down among the victims and pretended to be dead. But if they stood up again, the Spaniards saw them and killed them. The blood of the warriors flowed like water and gathered into pools. The pools widened, and the stench of blood and entrails filled the air. The Spaniards ran into the communal houses to kill those who were hiding. They ran everywhere and searched everywhere, they invaded every room, hunting and killing.

The Aztecs Retaliate

When the news of this massacre was heard outside the Sacred Patio, a great cry went up: "Mexicanos, come running! Bring your spears and shields! The strangers have murdered our warriors!" This cry was answered with a roar of grief and anger: the people shouted and wailed and beat their palms against their mouths. The captains assembled at once, as if the hour had been determined in advance. They all carried their spears and shields. Then the battle began. The Aztecs attacked with javelins and arrows, even with the light spears that are used for hunting birds. They hurled their javelins with all their strength, and the cloud of missiles spread out over the Spaniards like a yellow cloak. The Spaniards immediately took refuge in the palace. They began to shoot at the Mexicans with their iron arrows and to fire their cannons and arquebuses. And they shackled Montezuma in chains.

The Lament for the Dead

The Mexicans who had died in the massacre were taken out of the patio one by one and inquiries were made to discover their names. The fathers and mothers of the dead wept and lamented. Each victim was taken first to his own house and then to the Sacred Patio, where all the dead were brought together. Some of the bodies were later burned in the place called the Eagle Urn, and others in the House of the Young Men.

Montezuma's Message

At sunset, Itzcuauhtzin climbed onto the roof of the palace and shouted this proclamation: "Mexicanos! Tlatelolcas! Your king, the lord Montezuma, has sent me to speak for him. Mexicanos, hear me, for these are his words to you: `We must not fight them. We are not their equals in battle. Put down your shields and arrows.' He tells you this because it is the aged who will suffer most, and they deserve your pity. The humblest classes will also suffer, and so will the innocent children who still crawl on all fours, who still sleep in their cradles. Therefore your king says: `We are not strong enough to defeat them. Stop fighting, and return to your homes.' Mexicanos, they have put your king in chains; his feet are bound with chains."

When Itzcuauhtzin had finished speaking, there was a great uproar among the people. They shouted insults at him in their fury, and cried: "Who is Montezuma to give us orders? We are no longer his slaves!" The Spanish quickly hid Montezuma and Itzcuauhtzin behind their shields so that the arrows would not find them. The Mexicans were enraged because the attack on the captains had been so treacherous: their warriors had been killed without the slightest warning. Now they refused to go away or to put down their arms.

The Spaniards Are Besieged

The royal palace was placed under siege. The Mexicans kept a close watch to prevent anyone from stealing in with food for the Spaniards. They also stopped delivering supplies: they brought them absolutely nothing, and waited for them to die of hunger. A few people attempted to communicate with the Spaniards. They hoped to win their favor by giving them advice and information or by secretly bringing them food. But the guards found them and killed them on the spot; they broke their necks or stoned them to death. Once a group of porters was discovered bringing rabbit skins into the city. They let slip the fact that other persons had been hiding in their midst. Therefore strict orders were issued to maintain a watch over all the roads and causeways leading to the city. The porters themselves had been sent by the chiefs of Ayotzintepec and Chinantlan. They were only performing their duties, but the guards seized them and put them to death for no reason. They would shout: "Here is another one!" and then kill him. And if they happened to see one of Montezuma's servants with his glass lip plug, they slaughtered him at once, claiming: "He was bringing food to Montezuma." They seized anyone who was dressed like a porter or any other servant. "Here is another traitor," they would say. "He is bringing news to Montezuma." The prisoner would try to save his life by pleading with them: "What are you doing, Mexicanos? I am not a traitor!" But they would answer: "Yes, you are. We know you are one of his servants." And they would immediately put him to death. They stopped and examined everyone in the same way, studying each man's face and questioning him about his work. No one could walk out of doors without being arrested and accused. They sentenced a great many people for imaginary crimes; the victims were executed for acts they had never committed. The other servants, therefore, went home and hid themselves. They were afraid to be seen in public; they knew what would happen to them if they fell into the hands of the guards or the other warriors.

2. A Discourse Concerning Western Planting, 1584

Richard Hakluyt

Richard Hakluyt (1551 or 1552–1616) was probably born in London. As a teenager he became enthralled with the excitement of geography and exploration. His interest was probably kindled by his cousin, who shared his name and who was an enthusiast for English expansion. The younger Hakluyt earned degrees at Oxford during the 1570s, and was then ordained as a clergyman in the Church of England. During the next decade he joined those English merchants, navigators, adventurers, and geographers who were advocating an active national program of exploration and colonization of the New World. That enterprise raised a challenge to the power of Spain and France. Hakluyt and his fellow propagandists urged Queen Elizabeth to compete with Protestant England's Catholic rivals for power, wealth, and spiritual supremacy in North America. Although the Queen did not respond favorably to their requests, Hakluyt's years of labor finally yielded some rewards in 1606, under the reign of James I, when he was one of four London patentees in the first charter of the Virginia Company.

To publicize and promote his scheme of empire Hakluyt wrote a number of tracts, including *A Discourse Concerning Western Planting*, which appeared in 1584. He composed this treatise at the request of Sir Walter Raleigh as a private appeal to the Queen for financial support for Raleigh's colonization program. The excerpt that appears here outlines the political, diplomatic, economic, religious, and social reasons for competition with Spain and an English empire in the New World.

QUESTIONS

1. What audience is Hakluyt addressing?
2. What are the most important arguments that Hakluyt presents in urging England to plant colonies in the New World? How central are the religious aims? Is Hakluyt a mercantilist?
3. What does this document reveal about the relations between England and Spain during the late sixteenth century?
4. How does Hakluyt view the native peoples of the New World?
5. How does Hakluyt link the domestic situation within England to the proposed experiment of planting colonies in the New World?

I

Seeing that the people of that part of America from 30 degrees in Florida northward unto 63 degrees (which is yet in no Christian prince's actual possession) are idolaters; . . . and yet notwithstanding they are very easy to be persuaded, . . . it remaineth to be . . . considered by what means and by whom this most godly and Christian work may be performed of enlarging the glorious gospel of Christ, and reducing infinite multitudes of these simple people that are in error into the right and perfect way of their salvation . . . Now the Kings and Queens of England have the name of Defenders of the Faith. By which title I think they are not only charged to maintain and patronize the faith of Christ, but also to enlarge and advance the same. Neither ought this to be their last work, but rather the principal and chief of all others, according to the commandment of our Saviour. . . . And this enterprise the princes of the [reformed] religion (among whom her Majesty is principal) ought the rather to take in hand, because the papists . . . have been the only converters of many millions of infidels to Christianity. . . .

IV

It is well worth the observation to see and consider what the like voyages of discovery and planting in the East and West Indies hath wrought in the kingdoms of Portingale and Spain; both which realms, being of themselves poor and barren and hardly able to sustain their inhabitants, by . . . these, their new discoveries, . . . have so many honest ways to set them on work, as they rather want men than means to employ them. But we, for all the statutes that hitherto can be devised, and the sharp execution of the same in punishing idle and lazy persons, for want of sufficient occasion of honest employment, cannot deliver our commonwealth from multitudes of loiterers and idle vagabonds. Truth it is, that through our long peace and seldom sickness (two singular blessings of Almighty God), we are grown more populous than ever heretofore; so that now there are of every art and science so many, that they can hardly live one by another, nay rather they are ready to eat up one another. Yea many thousands of idle persons are within this realm, which, having no way to be set on work, . . . often fall to pilfering and thieving and other lewdness, whereby all the prisons of the land are daily pestered and stuffed full of them. . . .

Whereas if this voyage were put in execution, these petty thieves might be condemned for certain years in the western parts, especially in Newfoundland, in sawing and felling of timber for masts of ships, . . . in burning of the firs and pine trees to make pitch, tar, resin, and soap ashes; in beating and working of hemp for cordage; and, in the more southern parts, in setting them to work in mines of gold, silver, copper, lead, and iron; . . . in planting of sugar canes, as the Portingales have done in Madeira; in maintenance and increasing of silk worms for silk; . . . in gathering of cotton whereof there is plenty; . . . in dressing of vines whereof there is great abundance for wine; olives, whereof the soil is capable for oil; trees for oranges, lemons, almonds, figs, and other fruits, all which are found to grow there already; . . . in fishing, salting, and drying of ling, cod, salmon, herring. . . .

And seeing the savages of . . . Canada . . . are greatly delighted with any cap or garment made of coarse woolen cloth, their country being cold and sharp in the winter, it is manifest we shall find great utterance of our cloths, especially of our coarsest and basest; . . . whereby all occupations belonging to clothing and knitting shall be freshly set on work. . . .

In sum, this enterprise will minister matter for all sorts and states of men to work upon. . . .

V

We are moreover to understand that the savages of Florida are the Spaniards' mortal enemies, and will be ready to join with us against them. . . . And this is the greatest fear that the Spaniards have, to wit, our planting in those parts and joining with those savages, their neighbours, in Florida. . . . Which thing an English gentleman, Captain Moffett, who is now in France, told . . . that when he was in Spain, prisoner, not long since he heard the treasurer of the West Indies say, that there was no such way to hinder his master, as to plant upon the coast near unto Florida. . . .

VII

And entering into the consideration of the way how this Philip [King of Spain] may be abased, I mean first to begin with the West Indies, as there to lay a chief foundation for his overthrow. And like as the foundation of the strongest hold undermined and removed, the mightiest and strongest walls fall flat to the earth; so this prince, spoiled or intercepted for a while of his treasure, occasion by lack of the same is given that all his territories in Europe out of Spain slide from him, and the Moors enter into Spain itself, and the people revolt in every foreign territory of his, and cut the throats of the proud, hateful Spaniards, their governours. . . . And this weighed, we are to know what Philip is in the West Indies; and that we be not abused with Spanish brags. . . . And therefore we are to understand that Philip rather governeth in the West Indies by opinion, than by might; for the small manred of Spain, of itself being always at the best slenderly peopled, was never able to rule so many regions, or to keep in subjection such worlds of people as be there, were it not for the error of the Indian people, that . . . do imagine that Philip hath a thousand Spaniards for every single natural subject that he hath there. . . . So as in truth the Spaniard is very weak there. . . .

If you touch him in the Indies, you touch the apple of his eye; for take away his treasure, which is *nervus belli,* and which he hath almost out of his West Indies, his old bands of soldiers will soon be dissolved, his purposes defeated, his power and strength diminished, his pride abated, and his tyranny utterly suppressed. . . .

XIII

The manifold testimonies . . . of . . . Ribaut, . . . Verrazzano, which all were the discoverers of the coast and inland of America between 30 and 63 degrees, prove infallibly unto us that gold, silver, copper, pearls, precious stones, and turquoises, and emeralds, and many other commodities, have been by them found in those regions. . . . Now the fifth part of all these aforenamed commodities cannot choose but amount to a great matter, being yearly reserved unto her Majesty. . . . What gains this imposition may turn unto the Crown of England in short time we may more than guess, having but an eye to the King of Spain's revenues, which he now hath out of all his dominions in all the West Indies. . . .

XX

A brief collection of certain reasons to induce her Majesty and the state to take in hand the western voyage and the planting there.

1. The soil yieldeth . . . all the several commodities of Europe, and of all kingdoms . . . and territories that England tradeth with, that by trade of merchandise cometh into this realm.

2. The passage thither and home is neither too long nor too short, but easy and to be made twice in the year.

3. The passage cutteth not near the trade of any prince, nor near any of their countries or territories, and is a safe passage, and not easy to be annoyed by prince or potentate whatsoever.

4. The passage is to be performed at all times of the year. . . .

6. This enterprise may stay the Spanish King from flowing over all the face of that waste firm of America, if we seat and plant there in time. . . . How easy a matter may it be to this realm, swarming at this day with valiant youths, . . . to be lords of all those seas, and to spoil Philip's Indian navy, and

to deprive him of yearly passage of his treasure into Europe, and consequently to cut off the common mischiefs that come to all Europe by the peculiar abundance of his Indian treasure, and this without difficulty. . . .

7. This voyage, albeit it may be accomplished by bark or smallest pinnace, . . . yet . . . the merchant will not for profit's sake use it but by ships of great burden; so as this realm shall have by that means ships of great burden and of great strength for the defense of this realm. . . .

10. By this course . . . foreign princes' customs are avoided, and the foreign commodities cheaply purchased, to the common benefit of the people, and to the saving of great treasure in the realm. . . .

11. At the first traffic with the people of those parts, the subjects of this realm for many years shall change many cheap commodities of these parts for things of high value there not esteemed. . . .

13. By making of ships and by preparing of things for the same, . . . by planting of vines and olive trees, and by making of wine and oil, by husbandry, and by thousands of things there to be done, infinite numbers of the English nation may be set on work, to the unburdening of the realm with many that now live chargeable to the state at home. . . .

16. We shall by planting there enlarge the glory of the gospel, and from England plant sincere religion, and provide a safe and a sure place to receive people from all parts of the world that are forced to flee for the truth of God's word. . . .

18. The Spaniards govern in the Indies with all pride and tyranny; . . . so no doubt whensoever the Queen of England, a prince of such clemency, shall seat upon that firm of America, and shall be reported throughout all that tract to use the natural people there with all humanity, courtesy, and freedom, they will yield themselves to her government, and revolt clean from the Spaniard. . . .

20. Many men of excellent wits and divers singular gifts, overthrown by suertiship (civil litigation), by sea, or by some folly of youth, that are not able to live in England, may there be raised again, and do their country a good service. . . .

21. Many soldiers and servitors, in the end of the wars, . . . may there be unladen, to the common profit and quiet of this realm. . . .

22. The fry (offspring) of the wandering beggars of England, that grow up idly, and hurtful and burdenous to this realm, may there be unladen, better bred up, and may people waste countries to the home and foreign benefit, and to their own more happy state.

3. A View of the Present State of Ireland, 1596

Edmund Spenser

Edmund Spenser, c. 1552–1599, author of the *Faerie Queene,* is one of the great English poets. But his literary reputation as a friend of truth, love, generosity, pity, justice, and responsibility is hard to square with his career as a civil servant in Ireland from 1580 to 1596. For two years he was secretary to Lord Edward Grey, the lord deputy of Ireland; thereafter he served in various capacities in chancery court, commissioner of musters in county Kildare, deputy clerk to the council for Munster, and thus saw civil and military matters close up. In the aftermath of the Desmond rebellion, 1579–1583, and as part of "the plantation of Munster," Spenser acquired a 3,000 acre estate, Kilcolman, from land forfeited by the rebels. During the O'Neill rebellion of 1598 Kilcolman castle was pillaged and burned to the ground by the rebels. The Spensers barely escaped with their lives. "A View of the Present State of Ireland" shows to what lengths religious hatred can be carried and illuminates the Anglo-Irish conflict that persists in Northern Ireland. Spenser's hatred for the Old English who settled in Ireland before the Reformation and who remained Catholic is more extreme than his animosity toward the Gaelic Irish.

Ireland was "the first colony" and many of the techniques of "plantation" as well as contempt for the "natives" developed there. In sum, Spenser's solution for England's Irish problem is totalitarian: garrison, dragoon, deport, decimate, cultural genocide. His views and attitudes were not peculiar to Spenser but were shared by Elizabethan soldiers and civil servants who dealt with Ireland. Among them the "View" circulated extensively; it long remained popular among the New English settlers. Many of Spenser's recommendations were put into practice by James I and Cromwell.

QUESTIONS

1. Who was Edmund Spenser?
2. What problems does the colonial governor in Ireland have?
3. What English stereotype of the Irish is developed here?
4. Who are the Anglo-Irish? According to the author, what is wrong with the Anglo-Irish?
5. What policies does Spenser propose for English rule in Ireland?
6. What significance might attach to the reference to Machiavelli in the last sentence?
7. What roots of the present "troubles" in Northern Ireland can be traced here?

If that country of Ireland . . . be so goodly and commodious a soil, . . . I wonder that no course is taken thereof to good uses, and reducing that savage nation to better government and civility.

There have been diverse plots devised and wise counsels cast already about reformation of that realm, but they say it is the fatal destiny of that land, that no purposes whatsoever are meant for her good will prosper or take good effect; which whether it proceed from the very genius of the soil, or influence of the stars, or that Almighty God hath not yet appointed the time of her reformation, or that He reserveth her in this unquiet state still, for some secret scourge which shall by her come unto England, it is hard to be known but yet much to be feared.

I . . . declare the evils which seem to be most hurtful to the common weale of that land, and first those which I said were most ancient and long grown; and they are also of three kinds: the first in the laws, the second in customs, and last in religion.

Ireland . . . is a nation ever acquainted with wars though but amongst themselves, and in their own kind of military discipline trained up even from their youths, which they have never yet been taught to lay aside, nor made to learn obedience unto law, scarcely to know the name of law, but instead thereof have always preserved and kept their own law which is the Brehon law. It is a certain rule of right unwritten, but delivered by tradition from one to another, in which often there appeareth great show of equity in determining the right between party and party, but in many things repugning quite both to God's law and man's, as for example, in the case of murder, the Brehon that is their judge will compound between murderer and the friends of the party murdered which prosecute the action, that the malefactor shall give unto them, or to the child or wife of him that is slain, a recompense which they call an Iriach, by which vile law of theirs many murders are amongst them made up and smothered. This is a most wicked law indeed, but it is not now used in Ireland, since the kings of England have had the absolute dominion thereof and established their own laws there. [But] there are many wide countries in Ireland in which the laws of England were never established, nor any acknowledgement of subjugation made, and also even in those which are subdued, and seem to acknowledge subjugation, yet the same Brehon law is privily practised amongst themselves, by reason that dwelling as they do whole nations and septs of the Irish to-

gether without any Englishman amongst them, they may do what they list, and compound or altogether conceal amongst themselves their own crimes, of which no notice can be had by them which could and might amend the same by the rule of the laws of England.

The kings of England conquered all the realm and thereby assumed and invested all the right of that land to themselves and their heirs and successors forever, so as nothing was left. It is in the power of the conqueror to take upon himself what title he will over his dominions conquered. For all is the conqueror's, as Tully to Brutus saith; and therefore . . . all the Irish . . . are now tied, their lives, their lands, and their liberties are in his [the king's] free power to appoint what tenures, what laws, what conditions he would over them, which are all his, against which there could be no rightful resistance.

Regard and moderation ought to be had in tempering and managing this stubborn nation of the Irish, to bring them from their delight of licentious barbarism unto the love of goodness and civility. . . . In Ireland there are many civil brawls, . . . many tumultuous rebellions, that even hazard oftentimes the whole safety of the kingdom, . . . no laws, penalties can restrain, but that they do in the violence of that fury tread down and trample underfoot all . . . divine and human things, and the laws themselves they do specially rage at and rend in their pieces as most repugnant to their liberty and natural freedom, which in their madness they effect. So it is with Ireland continually, for the sword was never yet out of their hand, but when they are weary with wars and brought down to extreme wretchedness; then they creep a little perhaps and sue for grace, till they have gotten new breath and recovered strength again: so it is vain to speak of planting of laws and plotting of policies till they be altogether subdued.

Out of Spain certainly they came, that do all the Irish chronicles agree, [but] the histories of ancient times . . . those Irish chronicles . . . are most fabulous and forged; no monument remaineth of their beginnings and inhabiting there; specially having been always without letters [the Irish have] only bare traditions of times and remembrances of bards, which they use to forge and falsify everything. . . . The Irish themselves, through their ignorance in matters of learning, and deep judgement, do most constantly believe and avouch them.

Earl Strongbow, having conquered that land, delivered up the same unto the hands of Henry the Second, then King, who sent over [1170s] great store of gentlemen and other warlike people amongst whom he distributed the land and settled such a strong colony therein as never since could with all the subtle practices of the Irish be routed out, but abide still a mighty people of so many as remain English of them. Why are not they that were once English abiding English still? The most part of them are degenerated and grown almost mere Irish, yea and more malicious to the English than the very Irish themselves. And is it possible that an Englishman brought up naturally in such sweet civility as England affords could find such liking in that barbarous rudeness that he should forget his own name and forgo his own nation?

The Gauls used to drink their enemies' blood and to paint themselves therewith, so also they write that the Old Irish were wont; and so have I seen some of the Irish do but not their enemies' but friends' blood, as namely at the execution of a notable traitor at Limerick called Murrogh O'Briend, I saw an old woman which was his foster mother took up his head whilst he was quartered and sucked up all the blood running there

out, saying that the earth was not worth to drink it, and therewith also steeped her face and breast, and tore her hair, crying and shrieking out more terribly.

The chiefest abuses which are now in that realm of Ireland are grown from the Old English [who] are now more licentious and lawless than the very wild Irish. . . . they are now grown to be almost as lewd as the Irish; I mean of such English as were planted above towards the west, for the English Pale hath preserved itself through nearness of their state in reasonable civility, but the rest which dwell above in Connaught and Munster, which is the sweetest soul of Ireland, and some in Leinster and Ulster, are degenerate and grown to be as very patchocks as the wild Irish, yea and some of them have quite shaken off their English names and put on Irish, that they might be altogether Irish. . . . Other great houses there be of the old English in Ireland, which through licentious conversing with the Irish, or marrying and fostering with them, or lack of meet nurture, or other such unhappy occasions, have degenerated from their ancient dignities and are now grown as Irish as O'Hanlon's breech (as the proverb there is), of which sort there are two most pitiful ensamples above the rest, to wit the Lord Bremingham, who being the most ancient Baron I think in England, is now waxen the most savage Irish, naming himself, Irishlike, Maccorish; and the other is the great Mortimer, who is forgetting how great he was once in England, or English at all, is now become the most barbarous of them all, and is called Macnemarra; and not much better than he is the old Courcie, who having lewdly wasted all the lands and signories that he had and aliened them unto the Irish is himself also now grown quite Irish.

It is strange . . . that the English [in Ireland] should take more delight to speak that language than their own, whereas they should . . . rather take scorn to acquaint their tongues thereto, for it hath been ever the use of the conqueror to despise the language of the conquered, and to force him by all means to learn his. So did the Romans always. . . . I suppose that the chief cause of bringing in the Irish language amongst them was especially their fostering and marrying with the Irish, which are two most dangerous infections, for first the child that sucketh the milk of the nurse must of necessity learn his first speech of her, the which being the first that is enured to his tongue is ever after most pleasing to him, insomuch as though he afterwards be taught English, yet the smack of the first will always abide with him, and not only of the speech, but of the manners and conditions. For besides the young children be like apes, which will affect and imitate what they see done before them, specially by their nurses whom they love so well. They moreover draw into themselves together with their suck, even the nature and disposition of their nurses, for the mind followeth much the temperature of the body; and also the words are the image of the mind, so as they, proceeding from the mind, the mind must be the needs effected with the words; so that the speech being Irish, the heart must needs be Irish, for out of the abundance of the heart the tongue speaketh. The next is the marrying with the Irish, which how dangerous a thing it is in all commonwealths appeareth to every simplest sense . . . ; and indeed how can such matching but bring forth an evil race, seeing that commonly the child taketh most of his nature of the mother, besides speech, manners, inclination, which are for the most part agreeable to the conditions of their mothers, for by them they are first framed and fashioned, so as they receive anything from them, they will hardly forgo. Therefore are these two evil customs, of fos-

tering and marrying with the Irish most carefully to be restrained, for of them two, the third, that is the evil custom of language which I spake of chiefly proceedeth.

The fault I find in [their] religion is but one, but the same universal throughout all that country, that is that they are all Papists by their profession, but in the same so blindly and brutishly informed, for the most part as would rather think them atheists or infidels; but not one amongst an hundred knoweth any ground of religion or article of his faith, but can perhaps say his pater noster or his Ave Maria, without any knowledge or understanding what one word meaneth. This is truly most pitiful, . . . that so many souls should fall into the Devil's hands at once . . . but lie weltering in such spiritual darkness, hard by hell's mouth, and ready to fall in. . . . The general fault cometh not of any late abuse either in the people or their priests, who can teach no better than they know, nor show no more light than they have seen but in the first institution and planting of religion in all that realm, which was (as I read), in the time of Pope Celestine; who, as it was written, did first send over thither Palladius, who there deceasing, he afterwards sent over St. Patrick, being by nation a Briton, who converted the people, being then infidels, from paganism, and christened them; in which Pope's time and long before, it is certain that religion was generally corrupted with their Popish trumpery. Therefore, what other could they learn than such trash as was taught to them, and drink of that cup of fornication, with which the purple harlot had then made all nations drunken? . . . They drunk not of the pure spring of life, but only tasted of such troubled waters as were brought unto them, the dregs thereof have brought great contagion in their souls, the which daily increasing and being still more augmented with their own lewd lives and filthy conversation, hath now bred in them this general disease, that cannot but only with very strong purgations be cleansed and carried away, . . . and so old [religion] must be removed. To begin all as it were anew and to alter the whole form of the government is a dangerous thing to attempt. All change is to be shunned, where the affairs stand in such state as that they are, but that in the realm of Ireland we see much otherwise, for every day we perceive the troubles growing more upon us, and one evil growing upon another, insomuch as there is no part sound nor ascertained, but all have their ears upright, waiting when the watchword shall come that they should all rise generally in rebellion and cast away English subjection to which there now little wanteth, for I think the word be already given and there wanteth nothing but opportunity. . . . And therefore all the realm is first to be reformed [by the sword] and laws are afterward to be made, for keeping and continuing it in that reformed estate, . . . by the sword, for all those evils must first be cut away with a strong hand before any good can be planted, like as the corrupt branches and the unwholesome boughs are first to be pruned, and the foul moss cleansed or scraped away, before the tree can bring forth any good fruit.

The first thing must be to send over into that realm such a strong power of men as that shall perforce bring in all that rebellious rout of loose people . . . not above 10,000 footmen and 1,000 horse, and all those not above the space of one year and a half. Would you lead forth your army against the enemy and seek him where he is to fight? No, for it is well known that he is a flying enemy, hiding himself in woods and bogs, from whence he will not draw forth but into some strait passage or perilous ford where he knows the army must needs pass, there will he lie in wait, and if he find the advantage fit, will dangerously hazard the troubled soldier, therefore to seek him out that still flyeth, and follow him that can hardly be found were vain and bootless. . . . I would divide my men in garrison upon his country, in such places as I should think might most annoy him. And these garrisons, issuing forth at such convenient times as they shall have intelligence or espial upon the enemy, will so drive him from one stead to another, and tennis him amongst them, that he shall find nowhere safe to keep his creet nor hide himself, but flying from the fire shall fall into the water, and out of one danger into another, that in short time his creet [cattle], which is his most sustenance, shall be wasted with preying, or killed with driving, or starved for want of pasture in the woods, and he himself brought so low that he shall have no heart nor ability to endure his wretchedness; the which will surely come to pass in very short space, for one winter's well following of him will so pluck him on his knees that he will never be able to stand up again . . . for it is not with Ireland as with other countries, where the wars flame most in summer, and the helmets glister brightest in the fair sunshine, but in Ireland the winter yieldeth best services, for then the trees are bare and naked, which use both to clothe and house the kerne [soldier], the ground is cold and wet which useth to be his bedding, the air is sharp and bitter which useth to blow through his naked sides and legs, the kine are barren and without milk, which useth to be his only food; neither if he kill them, then will they yield him flesh, nor if he keeps them will they give him food, besides then being all in calf, for the most part they will through much chasing and driving, cast all their calves and lose all their milk which should relieve him the next summer after; . . . but the open enemy having all his country wasted, what by himself and what by the soldier, findeth then succour in no place, towns there are none of which he may get spoil, they are all burnt, country houses and farmers there are none, they be all fled, bread he hath none, he ploughed not in summer, flesh he hath, but if he kill it in the winter he shall want milk in the summer. Therefore, if they be well followed but one winter ye shall have little work with them [ever again].

[After the reformation by conquest] I would devise, that six thousand soldiers of these whom I have now employed in the service, and made thoroughly acquainted both with the state of the country and manners of the people, should henceforth be still continued for ever maintained of the country [as peasant-soldiers] without any charge to Her Majesty. And the rest that either are old and unable to serve longer or willing should be placed in part of the lands by them won. [Second] I wish that there be a general proclamation made, that whatsoever outlaws will freely come in and submit themselves to Her Majesty's mercy shall have liberty so to do, some men to remain in hostage one of another, and some other for the rest. I would have them first unarmed utterly, and stripped quite of all their warlike weapons, and then these conditions set down and made known unto them, that they shall be brought and removed with such creet as they have [to the west], where they shall be placed, and have land given to them to occupy and live upon in such sort as shall become good subjects to labor thenceforth for their living. Special regard shall be had, that in no place under any landlord there shall be many of them planted together, but dispersed wide from their acquaintances, and scattered far abroad through all the country. For that is the evil which I now find in all Ireland, that the Irish dwell altogether by their septs and several nations, so as they may practise or conspire

what they will, whereas if there were English shed amongst them and placed over them they should not be able once to stir or murmur, but that it should be known, and they shortened according to their demerits. And the want of this ordinance in the first conquest of Ireland, by Henry the Second, was the cause of the so short decay of the government, and the quick recovery again of the Irish. Therefore, by all means it is to be provided for.

Moreover for the breaking up of these heads and septs which is . . . one of the greatest strengthes of the Irish, methinks it should do very well to renew that old statute . . . by which it was commanded that whereas all men then used to be called by the name of their septs . . . and had no surnames at all, that from thenceforth each one should take unto himself a . . . surname, either of his trade or faculty or of some quality of his body or mind, or of the place where he dwelt, so as everyone should be distinguished from others or from most. . . . He shall in short time learn quite to forget his Irish nation. And herewithal would I also wish all the Oes and the Macs which the heads of septs have taken to their names to be utterly forbidden and extinguished, for that the same being as old manner (as some sayth) first made by O'Brien for the strengthening of the Irish, the abrogating thereof will as much enfeeble them.

I . . . wish that there were some ordinance made amongst them, that whatsoever keepeth 20 kine should keep a plough going, for otherwise all men would fall to pasturage and none to husbandry, which is . . . a cause of the usual stealths now in Ireland; for look into all countries that live in such sort by keeping of cattle, and you shall find that they are both very barbarous and uncivil and also greatly given to war. . . . And therefore since now we purpose to draw the Irish from desire of wars and tumults to the love of peace and civility, it is expedient to abridge their great custom of herding and augment there more trade of tilling and husbandry. As for other occupations and trades they need not to be enforced to, but every man bound only to follow one that he thinks himself aptest for . . . But learning and bringing up in liberal sciences will not come of itself, but must be drawn on with strait laws and ordinances; and therefore it were meet that . . . an act were ordained, that all the sons of lords and gentlemen and such others as are able to bring them up in learning should be trained up herein from their childhoods, and for that end every parish should be forced to keep one petty schoolmaster, adjoining unto the [Anglican] parish church, to be the more in view, which would bring up their children in the first rudiments of letters; and that in every country or barony they should keep another able schoolmaster, which should instruct them in [English] grammar and in the principles of sciences, to whom they should be compelled to send their youth to be disciplined, whereby they will in short time grow up to that civil conversation, that . . . the children will loathe the former rudeness in which they were bred, . . . for learning hath that wonderful power of itself that it can soften

and temper the most stern and savage nature.

[It is most necessary to bring about the reformation of religion among them to abandon Papism and adopt Protestantism. Anglican missionaries] and some discreet ministers of their own countrymen ought to be sent amongst them. . . . It is great wonder to see the odds which is between the zeal of the Popish priests and ministers of the gospel, for they spare not to come out of Spain, from Rome, from Rheims, by long toil and dangerous travel hither, where they know peril of death awaiteth them and no reward nor riches is to be found, only to draw the people to the church of Rome. [Nothing good will come of all our efforts, however, until the Irish] be restrained from sending their young men abroad to other universities beyond seas as Rheims, Douai, Louvaine and the like, and that others from abroad be restrained from coming unto them; for they, lurking secretly in their houses and in corners of the country, do more hurt and hindrance to religion with their private persuasions than all the others can do good with their public instructions. . . . And this I remember is worthily observed by Machiavel in his discourse. . . .

4. Narrative of Early Virginia, 1607–1609

John Smith

Soldier of fortune, adventurer, explorer, colonizer, and propagandist, John Smith (1579 or 1580–1631) was born in Willoughby, Lincolnshire, England. As a young man he enlisted with English Protestants fighting the forces of Philip II, the Catholic King of Spain. Next he joined in combat with Christians who were battling Islamic soldiers in Eastern Europe. After being wounded, captured, and enslaved by the Turks, he escaped to further excitement in Russia and off the coast of North Africa. He returned to England in 1604, and three years later he sailed with the Virginia Company's expedition to North America. He spent two years with the Jamestown colony before returning to England. Smith also visited and explored New England in 1614. His descriptions and maps of that region proved to be useful to the Plymouth Company that launched the Pilgrim expedition to Massachusetts Bay. During the 1620s he was a prominent critic of the Virginia Company and a historian of early British America.

Smith's narratives of his exploits in Virginia combined his own testimony with depositions written by fellow colonizers. While he certainly embellished his story of his exploits in the New World, it appears that despite some obvious exaggeration his testimony is generally accurate. The selection from Smith's writings that appears below presents his defense of the actions he took in early Jamestown to keep the struggling settlement alive during its trials of internal dissension, conflict with natives, economic failure, and disease.

QUESTIONS

1. How well prepared were Smith and his men for establishing a colony in Virginia?
2. How did the founders of Jamestown organize their political system, and how well did it work?
3. Describe the economy of early Virginia, and discuss the problems that the settlers faced in supporting themselves. How well did they solve these problems?
4. Describe and analyze the relations between the English colonists and the natives. How did they view each other? How did they interact?
5. Compare the culture of the natives of Virginia with that of the Aztecs.
6. According to the conclusion of this narrative, what were the most important differences between the results of the English founding of Virginia and the Spanish and Portugese colonization of the New World? What explains the different outcomes?

Chapter One

On the 19th of December, 1606, we set sail from Blackwall, but by unprosperous winds, were kept six weeks in the sight of England. . . .

The first land they made they called Cape Henry; where thirty of them recreating themselves on shore, were assaulted by five savages, who hurt two of the English very dangerously.

That night was the box opened, and the orders read, in which Bartholomew Gosnold, John Smith, Edward Wingfield, Christopher Newport, John Ratcliffe, John Martine, and George Kendall were named to be the Council, and to choose a President amongst them for a year, who with the

Council should govern. Matters of moment were to be examined by a jury, but determined by the major part of the Council, in which the President had two votes.

Until the 13th of May, 1607 they sought a place to plant in; then the Council was sworne, Master Wingfield was chosen President, and an oration made, why Captain Smith was not admitted of the Council as the rest.

Now falleth every man to work, the Council contrive the fort, the rest cut down trees to make place to pitch their tents; some provide clapboard to relade the ships, some make gardens, some nets, etc. The savages often visited us kindly. The President's overweening jealousy would admit no exercises at arms, or fortification but the boughs of trees cast together in the form of a half moon by the extraordinary pains and diligence of Captain Kendall. Newport, Smith, and twenty others were sent to discover the head of the river; by divers small habitations they passed, in six days they arrived at a town called Powhatan, consisting of some twelve houses, pleasantly seated on a hill; before it three fertile isles, about it many of their cornfields, the place is very pleasant and strong by nature; of this place the Prince is called Powhatan, and his people Powhatans. To this place the river is navigable; but higher within a mile, by reason of the rocks and isles, there is not passage for a small boat, this they call the falls. The people in all parts kindly treated them, till being returned within twenty miles of James town, they gave just cause of jealousy: but had God not blessed the discoverers other wise than those at the fort, there had then been an end of that plantation, for at the fort, where they arrived the next day, they found 17 men hurt, and a boy slain by the savages, and had it not chanced a cross bar shot from the ships struck down a bough

from a tree amongst them, that caused them to retire, our men had all been slain, being securely all at work, and their arms in dry fats.

Hereupon the President was contented the fort should be pallisaded, the ordnance mounted, his men armed and exercised; for many were the assaults, and ambushes of the savages, and our men by their disorderly straggling were often hurt, when the savages by the nimbleness of their heels well escaped.

What toil we had, with so small a power to guard our workmen at days, watch all night, resist our enemies, and effect our business, to relade the ships, cut down trees, and prepare the ground to plant our corn, etc., I refer to the reader's consideration.

[Smith next relates how he was at first held prisoner because of suspicions that he plotted to usurp the government, murder the Council, and make himself King. But in June, 1607 he was cleared of these charges and was admitted to the Council. In that month the natives made peace overtures and Captain Newport returned to England, leaving about one hundred men in Virginia.]

Chapter Two

Being thus left to our fortunes, it fortuned that within ten days scarce ten amongst us could either go, or well stand, such extreme weakness and sickness oppressed us. And threat none need marvel, if they consider the cause and reason, which was this. While the ships stayed, our allowance was somewhat bettered by a daily proportion of bisket, which the sailors would pilfer to sell, give, or exchange with us, for money, sassafras, furs, or loue. But when they departed, there remained neither tavern, beer house, nor place of relief, but the common kettell. Had we been as free from all sins as gluttony, and drunkenness, we might have been canonized for saints; but our President (Wingfield) would never had been admitted, for ingrossing to his private use, oatmeal, sack, oil, aquavita, beef, eggs, or what not, but the Kettell; that indeed he allowed equally to be distributed, and that was half a pint of wheat, and as much barley boiled with water for a man a day, and this fried some 26 weeks in the ships hold, contained as many worms as grains; so that we might truly call it rather so much bran than corn, our drink was water, our lodgings castles in the air.

With this lodging and diet, our extreme toil in bearing and planting pallisades, so strained and bruised us, and our continual labour in the extremity of the heat had so weakened us, as were cause sufficient to have made us as miserable in our native country, or any other place in the world.

From May to September 1607 those that escaped lived upon sturgeon, and sea-crabs, fifty in this time we buried, the rest seeing the President's projects to escape these miseries in our Pinnace by flight (who all this time had neither felt want nor sickness) so moved our dead spirits, as we deposed him; and established Ratcliffe in his place, Gosnol being dead, Kendall deposed. Smith newly recovered, Martin and Ratcliffe was by his care preserved and relieved, and the most of the soldiers recovered with the skillful diligence of Master Thomas Wotton, our surgeon general.

But now was all our provision spent, the Sturgeon gone, all helps abandoned, each hour expecting the fury of the savages; when God the patron of all good endeavors, in that desperate extremity so changed the hearts of the savages, that they brought such plenty of their fruits, and provision, as no man wanted.

And now where some affirmed it was ill done of the Council to send forth men so badly provided, this incontradictable reason will show them plainly they are too ill advised to nourish such ill conceits; first, the fault of our going was our own, what could be thought fitting or necessary we had; but what we should find, or want, or where we should be, we were all ignorant, and supposing to make our passage in two months, with victual to live, and the advantage of the spring to work; we were at sea five months, where we spent our victual and lost the opportunity of the time and season to plant, by the unskillfull presumption of our ignorant transporters, that understood not at all, what they undertook. . . .

The new President (Ratcliffe) and Martin, being little beloved, of weak judgement in dangers, and less industry in peace, committed the managing of all things abroad to Captain Smith; who by his own example, good works, and fair promises, set some to mow, others to bind thatch, some to build houses, others to thatch them, himself always bearing the greatest task for his own share, so that in short time he provided most of them lodgings, neglecting any for himself. . . .

[Smith next relates how he negotiated with the natives for provisions, and put down a plot by a few of the deposed councilors to abandon the settlement and flee.]

The Spaniard never more greedily desired gold than Smith victual; nor his soldiers more to abandon the Country, than he to keep it. But he found plenty of corn in the river of Chickahamania, where hundreds of savages in divers places stood with baskets expecting his coming.

And now the winter approaching, the rivers became so covered with swans, geese, ducks, and cranes, that we daily feasted with good bread, Virginia peas, pumpkins, and putchamins, fish, fowl, and diverse sorts of wild beasts as fat as we could eat them; so that none of our Tuftaffaty humorists desired to go for England.

But our comedies never endured long without a tragedy, some idle exceptions being muttered against Captain Smith, for not discovering the head of Chickahamania river, and being taxed by the Council, to be too slow in so worthy an attempt. The next voyage he proceeded so far that with much labor by cutting of trees insunder he made his passage; but when his barge could pass no farther he left her in a broad bay out of danger of shot, commanding none should go a shore till his return; himself with two English and two savages went up higher in a canoe; but he was not long absent, but his men went a shore, whose want of government gave both occasion and opportunity to the savages to surprise one George Cassen, whom they slew, and much failed not to have cut off the boat and all the rest.

Smith little dreaming of that accident, being got to the marshes at the rivers head, twenty miles in the desert, had his two men slain (as is supposed) sleeping by the canoe, whilst himself by fowling sought them victual; who finding he was beset with 200 savages, two of them he slew, still defending himself with the aid of savage his guide, whom he bound to his arm with his garters, and used him as a buckler, yet he was shot in his thigh a little, and had many arrows that stuck in his clothes but no great hurt, till at last they took him prisoner.

When this news came to James town, much was their sorrow for his loss, few expecting what ensued. For a few weeks those barbarians kept him prisoner, many strange triumphs and conjurations they made of him, yet he so demeaned himself amongst them, as he not only diverted them from surprising the fort, but procured his own liberty, and got himself and his company

such estimation amongst them, that those savages admired him more than their own Quiyouckosucks. The manner how they used and delivered him, is as follows. . . .

Smith demanding for their Captain, they showed him Opechankanough, King of the Pamavnkee, to whom he gave a round Ivory double compass Dial. Much they marveled at the playing of the fly and needle, which they could see so plainly, and yet not touch it, because of the glass that covered them. But when he demonstrated by that globe-like jewell, the roundness of the earth, and skies, the sphere of the sun, moon, and stars, and how the sun did chase the night round about the world continually; the greatness of the land and sea, the diversity of nations, variety of complexions, and we were to them antipodes, and many other such like matters, they all stood as amazed with admiration.

Notwithstanding, within an hour after they tied him to a tree, and as many as could stand about him prepared to shoot him; but the King holding up the compass in his hand, they all laid down their bows and arrows, and in a triumphant manner led him to Orapaks, where he was after their manner kindly feasted, and used. . . .

Two days after a man would have slain him (but that the guard prevented it) for the death of his son, to whom they conducted him to recover the poor man then breathing his last. Smith told them that at James town he had a water would do it, if they would let him fetch it, but they would not permit that; but made all the preparations they could to assault James town, craving his advice; and for recompence he should have life, liberty, and women. In part of a table book he writ his mind to them at the fort, what was intended, how they should follow that direction to affright the messengers, and without fail send him such things as he writ for. And an inventory with them. The difficulty and danger he told the savages, of the mines, great guns, and other engines exceedingly affrighted them, yet according to his request they went to James town, in as bitter weather as could be of frost and snow, and within three days returned with an answer.

But when they came to James town, seeing men sally out as he had told them they would, they fled; yet in the night they came again to the same place where he had told them they should receive an answer, and such things as he had promised them; which they found accordingly, and with which they returned with no small expedition, to the wonder of them all that heard it, that he could either divine, or the paper could speak. . . .

At last they brought Smith to Meronocomoco (January 5, 1608), where was Powhatan their Emperor. Here more than two hundred of those grim courtiers stood wondering at him, as he had been a monster; till Powhatan and his train had put themselves in their greatest braveries. Before a fire upon a seat like a bedstead, he sat covered with a great robe, made of Rarowcun skins, and all the tails hanging by. On either hand did sit a young wench of 16 or 18 years, and along on each side the house, two rows of men, and behind them as many women, with all their heads and shoulders painted red; many of their heads bedecked with something; and a great chain of white beads about their necks.

At his entrance before the King, all the people gave a great shout. The Queen of Appamatuck was appointed to bring him a bunch of feathers, instead of a towel to dry them; having feasted him after their best barbarous manner they could, a long consultation was held, but the conclusion was, two great stones were brought before Powhatan; then as many as could laid hands on him, dragged him to them, and thereon laid his head, and being ready with their clubs, to beat out his brains, Pocahontas the King's dearest daughter, when no entreaty could prevail, got his head in her arms, and laid her own upon his to save him from death; whereat the Emperor was contented he should live to make him hatchets, and her bells, beads, and copper; for they thought him as well of all occupations as themselves. For the King himself will make his own robes, shoes, bows, arrows, pots; plant, hunt, or do anything so well as the rest.

Two days after Powhatan having disguised himself in the most fearfullest manner he could, caused Captain Smith to be brought forth to a great house in the woods, and there upon a mat by the fire to be left alone. Not long after from behind a mat that divided the house was made the most dolefullest noise he ever heard; then Powhatan more like a devil than a man, with some two hundred more as black as himself, came unto him and told him now they were friends, and presently he should go to James town, to send him two great guns, and a grindstone, for which he would give him the country of Capahowosick, and for ever esteem him as his son Nantaquoud.

So to James town with 12 guides Powhatan sent him. That night (January 7, 1608) they quartered in the woods, he still expecting (as he had done all this long time of his imprisonment) every hour to be put to one death or other, for all their feasting. But almighty God (by his divine providence) had mollified the hearts of those stern Barbarians with compassion. The next morning betimes they came to the fort, where Smith having used the savages with what kindness he could, he showed Rawhunt, Powhatan's trusty servant, two demi-culverins and a millstone to carry Powhatan; they found them somewhat too heavy; but when they did see him discharge them, being loaded with stones, among the boughs of a great tree loaded with isicles, the ice and branches came so tumbling down, that the poor savages ran away half dead with fear. But at last we regained some conference with them, and gave them such toys, and sent to Powhatan, his women, and children such presents, as gave them in general full content.

Now in James town they were all in combustion, the strongest preparing once more to run away with the Pinnace; which with the hazard of his life, with sakrefalcon and musket shot, Smith forced now the third time to stay or sink.

Some no better than they should be, had plotted the President (Ratcliffe) the next day to have put him to death by the Levitical law, for the lives of Robinson and Emry; pretending the fault was his that had led them to their ends; but he quickly took such order with such lawyers, that he laid them by the heels till he sent some of them prisoners for England.

Now every once in four or five days, Pocahontas with her attendants brought him so much provision, that saved many of their lives, that else for all this had starved with hunger. . . .

Chapter Three

[Smith next tells of the arrival of Captain Newport's supply ship and the meetings and feasts held with Powhatan and himself and Captain Newport. He also complains about how his men wasted the provisions brought by Newport.]

But the worst was our guilded refiners with their golden promises made all men their slaves in hope of recompence; there was no talk, no hope, no work, but dig gold, wash gold, refine gold, load gold, such a bruit of gold that one mad fellow desired to be buried in the sands lest they should by their art make gold of his bones; little need

there was and less reason, the ship should stay, their wages run on, our victuals consume 14 weeks, that the mariners might say, they did help to build such golden church that we can say the rain washed to nothing in 14 days.

Were it that Captain Smith would not applaud all those golden adventures, because they admitted him not to the sight of their trials nor golden consultations, I know not; but I have heard him often question with Captain Martin and tell him, except he could show him a more substantial trial, he was not enamoured with their dirty skill, breathing out these and many other passions, never anything did more torment him, than to see all necessary business neglected, to fraught such a drunken ship with so much guilded dirt. . . .

[The narrative then relates more adventures with the natives, including how Pocahontas warned Smith about a plot by Powhatan to murder him. In 1609 several of Smith's men wrote the following apology for the first planters of Virginia.]

Those temporizing proceedings to some may seem too charitable, to such a daily daring treacherous people; to others not pleasing, that we washed not the ground with their blood, nor showed such strange inventions in mangling, murdering, ransacking, and destroying (as did the Spaniards) the simple bodies of such ignorant souls; not delightful, because not stuffed with relations of heaps and mines of gold and silver, nor such rare commodities, as the Portuguese and Spaniards found in the East and West Indies. The want whereof hath begot us (that were the first undertakers) no less scorn and contempt, than the noble conquests and valiant adventures beautified with it, praise and honor. Too much I confess the world cannot attribute to their ever memorable merit; and to clear us from the blind world's ignorant censure, these few words may suffice any reasonable understanding.

It was the Spaniard's good hap to happen in those parts where were infinite numbers of people, who had manured the ground with that providence, it afforded victuals of all times. And time had brought them to that perfection, they had the use of gold and silver, and the most of such commodities as those countries afforded; so that, what the Spaniard got was chiefly the spoil and pillage of those country people, and not the labors of their own hands. But had those fruitful countries been as savage, as barbarous, as ill peopled, as little planted, labored, and manured, as Virginia, their proper labors it is likely would have produced as small profit as ours.

But had Virginia been peopled, planted, manured, and adorned with such store of precious jewels, and rich commodities as was the Indies; then had we not gotten and done as much as by their examples might be expected from us, the world might then have traduced us and our merits, and have made shame and infamy over recompence and reward.

But we chanced in a Land even as God made it, where we found only an idle, improvident, scattered people, ignorant of the knowledge of gold and silver, or any commodities, and careless of any thing but from hand to mouth, except baubles of no worth; to encourage us, but what accidently we found Nature afforded. Which ere we could bring to recompence our pains, defray our charges, and satisfy our adventurers; we were to discover the country, subdue the people, bring them to be tractable, civil, and industrious, and teach them trades, that the fruits of their labors might make us some recompence; or plant such colonies of our own, that must first make provision how to live of themselves, ere they can bring to perfection the commodities of the country; which doubtless will be as commodious for England as the West Indies for Spain, if rightly managed; notwithstanding all our home-bred opinions, that will argue the contrary, as formerly some have done against the Spaniards and Portuguese. But to conclude, against all rumor of opinion, I only say this, for those that the three first years began this plantation; notwithstanding all their factions, mutinies, and miseries, so gently corrected, and well prevented, peruse the Spanish Decades, the relations of Master Hakluyt, and tell me how many ever with such small means as a barge of two tons, sometimes with seven, eight, or nine, or but at most twelve or sixteen men, did ever discover so many fair and navigable rivers, subject so many several kings, people, and nations, to obedience and contribution, with so little bloodshed.

And if in the search of those countries we had happened where wealth had been, we had as surely had it as obedience and contribution; but if we have overskipped it we will not envy them that shall find it; yet can we not but lament, it was our fortunes to end when we had only learned how to begin, and found the right course how to proceed.

5. Jesuit Report on Sixteenth-Century China

Matteo Ricci

Matteo Ricci (1552–1610) was born in Italy and studied at a Jesuit college and joined the Society of Jesus in 1571. He embarked for India in 1578, and remained there for four years, until he was assigned to a missionary position in China. For nearly three decades Ricci labored in Nanking, Peking, and other cities to spread the gospel of Christianity in China. His method was to try to convert the masses by first gaining the favor of the educated and ruling classes. He was able to gain entry into the higher ranks of Chinese society by learning their language and by teaching them European science, mathematics, and geography. He also adopted the dress and customs of the Chinese monks and philosophers. He became well known in China as a learned thinker, commentator on Confucius, scientist, and teacher of the Christian religion.

Ricci's diary was edited and translated from Italian into Latin by Father Nicola Trigault and first published in 1615. The appearance of that text opened a new era in Europe's relations with China. Ricci's account of Chinese society stimulated great interest in that country within the literary, scientific, philosophical, religious, and mercantile communities of the western world. In particular it introduced Confucius to Europeans and led to increased political, economic, and cultural contacts between the West and the Orient. The passage from his diary that is reprinted below presents a few of Ricci's impressions of China's size, natural resources, products, people, and institutions.

QUESTIONS

1. What impresses Ricci so much about China?
2. What specific comparisons does he make between the people and products of China and European nations?
3. What does Ricci tell us about the agriculture and crafts of China?
4. What is Ricci's view of the political system of China?
5. On the basis of Ricci's observations, what is the Chinese national character or psychology?

This most distant empire of the Far East has been known to Europeans under various names. The most ancient of these appellations is Sina, by which it was known in the time of Ptolemy. In later days it was called Cathay by Marco Polo, the Venetian traveler who first made Europeans fairly well acquainted with the empire. The most widely known name, however, China, was given by the Portuguese who reached this kingdom after vast maritime explorations and who even today carry on their trade in the southeastern province of Canton. The name, China, was slightly modified by the Italians and by some other European nations, due to their lack of familiarity with the Spanish pronunciation which differs somewhat from the Latin. China is pronounced by all Spaniards in the same way in which the Italians pronounce Cina.

In my judgment there can be little doubt that this is the country which is called the land of the Hippophagi, the horse eaters, for even to this very day, in this vast empire, the flesh of horse is eaten much in the same way as we eat the flesh of oxen. Nor again have I any doubt that this is the country referred to as the Land of Silk (Serrica regio), for nowhere in the Far East except in China is silk found in such abundance that it is not only worn by all the inhabitants of the country, the poor as well as the rich, but it is also exported in great quantities to the most distant parts of the earth. There is no other staple of commerce with which the Portuguese prefer to lade their ships than Chinese silks, which they carry to Japan and India where it finds a ready market. The Spaniards, too, who dwell in the Philippine Islands, freight their trading vessels with Chinese silks for exportation to New Spain and other parts of the world. In the annals of the Chinese Empire, I find mention of the art of silk weaving as far back as the year 2636 before Christ, and it appears that the knowledge of this art was carried to the rest of Asia, to Europe, and even to Africa from the Chinese Empire.

It does not appear strange to us that the Chinese should never have heard of the variety of names given to their country by outsiders and that they should be entirely unaware of their existence. No vestige of these names is to be found among them nor is there any cause to explain the multiplicity of names. The Chinese themselves in the past have given many different names to their country and perhaps will impose others in the future. It is a custom of immemor-

ial age in this country, that as often as the right to govern passes from one family to another, the country itself must be given a new name by the sovereign whose rule is about to begin. This the new ruler does by imposing some appropriate name according to his own good pleasure. . . .

He whose authority extends over this immense kingdom is called Lord of the Universe, because the Chinese are of the opinion that the extent of their vast dominion is to all intents and purposes coterminous with the borders of the universe. The few kingdoms contiguous to their state, of which they had any knowledge before they learned of the existence of Europe, were, in their estimation, hardly worthy of consideration. If this idea of assumed jurisdiction should seem strange to a European, let him consider that it would have seemed equally strange to the Chinese, if they had known that so many of our own rulers applied this same title to themselves, without at the same time having any jurisdiction over the vast expanse of China. So much then for the name of the kingdom known as China.

Relative to the extent of China, it is not without good reason that the writers of all times have added the prefix great to its name. Considering its vast stretches and the boundaries of its lands, it would at present surpass all the kingdoms of the earth, taken as one, and as far as I am aware, it has surpassed them during all previous ages. . . .

Referring again to the enormous extent and renown of this empire, it should be observed that it is quite well protected on all sides, by defenses supplied by both nature and science. To the south and the east it is washed by the sea, and the coast is dotted with so many small islands that it would be difficult for a hostile fleet to approach the mainland. To the north the country is defended against hostile Tartar raids by precipitous hills, which are joined into an unbroken line of defense with a tremendous wall four hundred and five miles long. To the northwest it is flanked by a great desert of many days' march, which either deters an advancing army from attacking the Chinese border or becomes the burial place of those who attempt the attack. Beyond the mountain range which hems in the kingdom to the west, there exist only impoverished countries to which the Chinese pay little or no attention, as they neither fear them nor consider them worth while annexing.

Due to the great extent of this country north and south as well as east and west, it can be safely asserted that nowhere else in the world is found such a variety of plant and animal life within the confines of a single kingdom. The wide range of climatic conditions in China gives rise to a great diversity of vegetable products, some of which are most readily grown in tropical countries, others in arctic, and others again in the temperate zones. The Chinese themselves, in their geographies, give us detailed accounts of the fertility of the various provinces and of the variety of their products. It hardly falls within the scope of my present treatise to enter into a comprehensive discussion of these matters. Generally speaking, it may be said with truth that all of these writers are correct when they say that everything which the people need for their well-being and sustenance, whether it be for food or clothing or even delicacies and superfluities, is abundantly produced within the borders of the kingdom and not imported from foreign climes. I would even venture to say that practically everything which is grown in Europe is likewise found in China. If not, then what is missing here is abundantly supplied by various other products unknown to Europeans. To begin with, the soil of China supplies its people with every species of grain—barley, millet, winter wheat, and similar grains.

Rice, which is the staple article of Chinese diet, is produced here in far greater abundance than in Europe. Vegetables, especially beans, and the like, all of which are used not only as food for the people but also as fodder for cattle and beasts of burden, are grown in unlimited variety. The Chinese harvest two and sometimes three crops of such plants every year, owing not only to the fertility of the soil and the mildness of the climate but in great measure to the industry of the people. With the exception of olives and almonds, all the principal fruits known in Europe grow also in China, while the real fig tree, which, by the way, our Fathers introduced into China, yields in nothing to its European progenitors. The Chinese, moreover, possess a variety of fruits unknown in Europe which are found exclusively in the province of Canton and in the southern parts of China. These fruits are called licya and longana by the natives and for the most part they are very pleasing to the taste. The Indian nut-bearing palm tree and other Indian fruits are found here, and there is a species of fruit called the Chinese fig, a very sweet and appetizing fruit which the Portuguese call sucusina. This particular fruit can be eaten only after it is dried, hence the Portuguese call it a fig. It has nothing in common with the real fig, however, since it resembles a large Persian apple (probably the peach), only it is red, and lacks the soft down and the pit. Here, too, we find oranges and other citrus fruits and every kind of fruit that grows on thornbushes, in a larger variety and possessing a finer flavor than the same fruits grown in other countries.

Much of the same can be said of the variety and quality of table vegetables and the cultivation of garden herbs, all of which the Chinese use in far greater quantities than is common among the people of Europe. In fact, there are many among the common folk who live entirely upon a vegetable diet through the whole course of their lives, either because they are forced to do so by reason of poverty or because they embrace this course of life for some religious motive. The profusion of flowering plants really leaves nothing to be desired, as the Chinese have many species unknown to us which make a deep appeal to the aesthetic sense and show forth the lavish bounty of the Creator. . . .

All of the known metals without exception are to be found in China. Besides brass and ordinary copper alloys, the Chinese manufacture another metal which is an imitation silver but which costs no more than yellow brass. From molten iron they fashion many more articles than we do, for example, cauldrons, pots, bells, gongs, mortars, gratings, furnaces, martial weapons, instruments of torture, and a great number of other things, all but equal in workmanship to our own metal-craft. Gold is considered to be a precious metal, but they do not appraise it as highly as we do. Silver is used as a currency and, whether by weight or in stamped coins, is used as legal tender in all commercial transactions. This, of course, gives rise to difficulties, such as the fluctuating value of silver, which must always be taken into account when paying bills, and the ease of counterfeiting, which is not at all infrequent. In many places a small brass coin, which is struck off in a public mint, is used for smaller purchases. Silver vessels, and, among the very rich, even vessels of gold are used, but rather more sparingly than in Europe. Here, as elsewhere, much silver and gold is used to fashion head-dresses and ornaments for womenfolk. The ordinary tableware of the Chinese is clay pottery. It is not quite clear to me why it is called porcelain in the West. There is nothing like it in European pottery either from the standpoint of the material itself or its thin and fragile construction. The finest specimens of porcelain are made from clay found in the province of Kiam, and these are shipped not only to every part of China but even to the remotest corners of Europe where they are highly prized by those who appreciate elegance at their banquets rather than pompous display. This porcelain, too, will bear the heat of hot foods without cracking and, what is more to be wondered at, if it is broken and sewed with a brass wire it will hold liquids without any leakage. These people have also acquired the art of glass blowing but their workmanship here falls far short of what we see at home. . . .

It is a matter of common knowledge, borne out by our own experience, that the Chinese are a most industrious people. . . . They have all sorts of raw material and they are endowed by nature with a talent for trading, both of which are potent factors in bringing about a high development of the mechanical arts. It will suffice to illustrate the versatility of this people by touching upon those phases only, of the arts in question, in which the practice of the Chinese seems to differ most widely from that of our own artisans. It should be noted that because these people are accustomed to live sparingly, the Chinese craftsman does not strive to reach a perfection of workmanship in the object he creates, with a view to obtaining a higher price for it. His labor is guided rather by the demand of the purchaser who is usually satisfied with a less finished product. Consequently they frequently sacrifice quality in their productions, and rest content with a superficial finish intended to catch the eye of the purchaser. This seems to be particularly noticeable when they toil for the magistrates who pay the craftsmen according to their own whims without any regard to the real value of what they buy. At times, too, they compel the artisans to design things for which they have no genius or aptitude.

Chinese architecture is in every way inferior to that of Europe with respect to the style and the durability of their buildings. In fact, it is dubious just which of these two qualities is the weaker. When they set about building, they seem to gauge things by the span of human life, building for themselves rather than for posterity. Whereas, Europeans in accordance with the urge of their civilization seem to strive for the eternal. This trait of theirs makes it impossible for them to appreciate the magnificence of our architecture as it appears in public and in private buildings, or even to give credence to what we tell them about it. They seem to be utterly at a loss for expression when we tell them that many of our buildings have withstood the elements for the space of a hundred years and some even for one or two thousand years. When they question this and we tell them that the reason for this durability is the depth and massiveness of the foundations which are able to carry the superstructure unshaken for such an extent of time, they merely stare at us in blank amazement. This, however, is not to be wondered at, because they themselves do not dig into the ground to build up foundations but merely place large stones on an unbroken surface of the ground, or, if they do dig foundations, these do not go deeper than a yard or two even though the walls or towers are to be built up to a great height. The result is that their buildings and fortifications cannot even weather the storms of a century without the need of frequent repairs. We have stated already, as one will recall, that most of their buildings are constructed of wood, or if made in masonry they are covered in by roofs supported on wooden columns. The advantage of this latter method of construction is that the walls can be renovated at any time, while the rest of the building remains intact, since the roof

is supported by the columns and is not carried by the walls.

The art of printing was practiced in China at a date somewhat earlier than that assigned to the beginning of printing in Europe, which was about 1405. It is quite certain that the Chinese knew the art of printing at least five centuries ago, and some of them assert that printing was known to their people before the beginning of the Christian era, about 50 B.C. Their method of printing differs widely from that employed in Europe, and our method would be quite impracticable for them because of the exceedingly large number of Chinese characters and symbols. At present they cut their characters in a reverse position and in a simplified form, on a comparatively small table made for the most part from the wood of the pear tree or the apple tree, although at times the wood of the jujube tree is also used for this purpose.

Their method of making printed books is quite ingenious. The text is written in ink, with a brush made of very fine hair, on a sheet of paper which is inverted and pasted on a wooden tablet. When the paper has become thoroughly dry, its surface is scraped off quickly and with great skill, until nothing but a fine tissue bearing the characters remains on the wooden tablet. Then, with a steel graver, the workman cuts away the surface following the outlines of the characters until these alone stand out in low relief. From such a block a skilled printer can make copies with incredible speed, turning out as many as fifteen hundred copies in a single day. Chinese printers are so skilled in engraving these blocks, that no more time is consumed in making one of them than would be required by one of our printers in setting up a form of type and making the necessary corrections. This scheme of engraving wood on blocks is well adapted for the large and complex nature of the Chinese characters, but I do not think it would lend itself very aptly to our European type which could hardly be engraved upon wood because of its small dimensions. . . .

The extent of their kingdom is so vast, its borders so distant, and their utter lack of knowledge of a transmaritime world is so complete that the Chinese imagine the whole world as included in their kingdom. Even now, as from time beyond recording, they call their emperor, Thiencu, the son of Heaven, and because they worship heaven as the Supreme Being, the Son of Heaven and the Son of God are one and the same. In ordinary speech, he is referred to as *Hoamsi,* meaning supreme ruler or monarch, while other and subordinate rulers are called by the much inferior title of *Guam.* . . .

Only such as have earned a doctor's degree or that of licentiate are admitted to take part in the government of the kingdom, and due to the interest of the magistrates and of the king himself there is no lack of such candidates. Every public office is therefore fortified with and dependent upon the attested science, prudence, and diplomacy of the person assigned to it, whether he be taking office for the first time or is already experienced in the conduct of civil life. . . .

. . . it seems to be quite remarkable when we stop to consider it, that in a kingdom of almost limitless expanse and innumerable population, and abounding in copious supplies of every description, though they have a well-equipped army and navy that could easily conquer the neighboring nations, neither the King nor his people ever think of waging a war of aggression. They are quite content with what they have and are not ambitious of conquest. In this respect they are much different from the people of Europe, who are frequently discontented with their own governments and covetous of what others enjoy. While the nations of the West seem to be entirely consumed with the idea of supreme domination, they cannot even preserve what their ancestors have bequeathed them, as the Chinese have done through a period of some thousands of years. . . .

Another remarkable fact and quite worthy of note as marking a difference from the West, is that the entire kingdom is administered by the Order of the Learned, commonly known as The Philosophers. The responsibility for orderly management of the entire realm is wholly and completely committed to their charge and care. The army, both officers and soldiers, hold them in high respect and show them the promptest obedience and deference, and not infrequently the military are disciplined by them as a schoolboy might be punished by his master. Policies of war are formulated and military questions are decided by the Philosophers only, and their advice and counsel has more weight with the King than that of the military leaders. In fact very few of these, and only on rare occasions, are admitted to war consultations. Hence it follows that those who aspire to be cultured frown upon war and would prefer the lowest rank in the philosophical order to the highest in the military, realizing that the Philosophers far excel military leaders in the good will and the respect of the people and in opportunities of acquiring wealth. What is still more surprising to strangers is that these same Philosophers, as they are called, with respect to nobility of sentiment and in contempt of danger and death, where fidelity to King and country is concerned, surpass even those whose particular profession is the defense of the fatherland. Perhaps this sentiment has its origin in the fact that the mind of man is ennobled by the study of letters. Or again, it may have developed from the fact that from the beginning and foundation of this empire the study of letters was always more acceptable to the people than the profession of arms, as being more suitable to a people who had little or no interest in the extension of the empire.

The order and harmony that prevails among magistrates, both high and low, in the provinces and in the regal Curia is also worthy of admiration. Their attitude toward the King, in exact obedience and in external ceremony, is a cause of wonderment to a foreigner.

6. Muscovy's Conquests in Asia, Seventeenth Century

During the seventeenth century Muscovites carried the rule of their Tsar north and east of the Ural Mountains across Siberia. Rumors about the riches of the Amur region attracted several adventurers, including Erofei P. Khabarov. Born around 1610, he came to that area as a veteran of several earlier expeditions along the rivers of Siberia. After his first penetration along the Amur river in 1649–1650 he requested support for a new mission. The aid was granted, and he was ordered by the voevoda of Iakutsk to conquer the Amur peoples and to force them to submit to the Tsar of Muscovy (see part A). He described his efforts and the resistance of the natives in his report to the voevoda [commander] of Iakutsk (see part B). He soon learned that the natives were paying iasak (tribute) to the "Bogdoi tsar" (Chinese emperor). The confrontation with the Chinese in Siberia led to the Treaty of Nerchinsk (1689) by which the Chinese reasserted their control over the Amur region. Russian expansion began anew in that area in the mid-nineteenth century.

QUESTIONS

1. Who was Erofei P. Khabarov and what kind of instructions was he given in regard to his expedition into the land of the Daurs?
2. How did the peoples on the Amur River react to the Khabarov expedition? Why were they so easily and repeatedly beaten? In what relation do the Bogdoi and Daur peoples stand to each other?
3. What were the techniques employed by the Russians in order to control the conquered peoples? Did they hold out any inducements to persuade the various peoples to submit? How successful do you think the expedition was?

A. Between March 6, 1649 and May, 1651 Instructions from the Voevoda of Iakutsk, Dmitrii Frantsbekov, to the Explorer Erofei Khabarov, Regarding His Expedition into the Land of the Daurs

On March 6, 1649, the veteran explorer, Erofei P. Khabarov, reported to the Sovereign Tsar and Grand Prince Aleksei Mikhailovich of all Russia. In his report he stated that in accordance with the Sovereign's ukaz [edict, statute, or administrative decree], during the past years he had been sent on government service against [princes] Lavkai and Botogo, under the administration of the stolnik [high ranking official] and voevoda Petr Petrovich Golovin, and the pismennaia golova [writing chief] Enalei Bakhteiarov. Seventy servitors [vassals, semi-free] were sent with him, but they did not reach these princes. . . .

He now asks that the Sovereign again grant him, Erofei, permission to go, together with volunteer servitors and promyshlenniks [traders or hunters], however many may choose to go, and this time without being given government supplies. He wants about 150 men, or as many as possible, and he would provision them himself. He would provide their food and all supplies, including boats and equipment, and, the Sovereign's luck permitting, he would bring Lavkai and Botogo under the Sovereign Tsar's mighty hand, as well as any other transmontane non-iasak [non-tribute paying] people, from whom the Sovereign would receive considerable benefit from the collection of iasak [tribute]. . . .

They will go along the Olekma and Tugur rivers to the Shilka portage and thence along the Shilka; they will put down any indigenous people who are disobedient and disloyal and will not pay iasak either for themselves or on behalf of their ulus [village communities] inhabitants. They are also to force Lavkai and Botogo and their ulus people and other transmontane non-iasak people to submit, on behalf of the Sovereign Tsar and Grand Prince Aleksei Mikhailovich of all Russia. They will collect iasak and explore new territories. They are instructed to proceed with care, taking due precautions; they are to post sentries wherever they stop so the natives will not harm them in any way.

They are to follow the Olekma River and the Tugur River to the portage, or to the Shilka; they are to ascertain where it would be most advantageous to build an ostrozhek [blockhouse], and then they are to build it and protect it with all possible fortifications so this ostrozhek can provide complete safety and security against attack by hostile non-iasak people for persons who may be sent there in the future to collect the Sovereign's iasak.

Erofei is to go out from this ostrog with the volunteer servitors and promyshlenniks who go with him, against Lavkai and Botogo and other non-iasak transmontane people who are disobedient and insubordinate to His Imperial Majesty. He is to persuade them to submit in eternal iasak servitude under the mighty hand of the Sovereign Tsar and Grand Prince Aleksei Mikhailovich of all Russia, and to pay iasak for themselves, Lavkai and Botogo, and for all their ulus subjects. . . .

If these newly contacted people, Lavkai and Botogo, and their ulus subjects, and other non-iasak transmontane people are obedient and submissive and willing to come under the mighty hand of the Sovereign Tsar and Grand Prince Aleksei Mikhailovich of all Russia, and pay iasak from themselves and from their ulus subjects, for all eternity, then Lavkai and Botogo and their ulus people can live in their previous nomadic grounds, without fear, and the Sovereign will order that his government troops protect them.

Lavkai and Botogo and other leaders are to be induced to take the oath, according to their religious faith, so that henceforth they and all of their relatives and their ulus subjects will be forever, undeviatingly, in direct iasak servitude. . . . The names of the leaders are to be written down in the books. And when he persuades them to take the oath of allegiance, he is to take their leaders as hostages, so that in the future these tribes will pay the Sovereign's iasak and pominki [gifts or bribes] for all time to come.

Lavkai and Botogo and their ulus subjects and other transmontane non-iasak-paying people are to be given firm orders and threatened with punishment from the Sovereign, including death, if they steal from the merchants and promyshlenniks or kill them or harm them. . . . Depending on the situation at the time, all measures are to be used to establish complete control over the inhabitants of new territories, Lavkai and Botogo and other non-iasak people, and every effort is to be made, and no mistakes are to be committed, in order to bring substantial profit to the Sovereign's iasak treasury, so that it will be stable and constant in the future. In return for this service they are to receive compensation from the Sovereign.

You, Erofei, are personally entrusted with the government assignment to pacify and bring under the suzerainty [political control] of the Sovereign both Lavkai and Botogo as well as non-iasak people who are not paying iasak to the Sovereign. Invoke God's aid, and use force, either war or surprise attacks.

You are to collect iasak for the Sovereign from them, which is to be made up of sables, sable shubas [cloaks], neck pieces, sable backs, sable bellies, black foxes, black-brown foxes, brown foxes, cross foxes, red foxes, ermine shubas, beavers and otters. Since there are no sables, foxes, beavers or otters in the steppe, then from those non-iasak people who live in the steppe rather than in the forest, you are to collect any other kind of animal pelt, or whatever precious goods the land may offer, such as gold, silver, silk or precious stones, depending on what is available. They must not think that because there is a scarcity of animals for iasak that they will not come under the Sovereign's mighty hand. . . .

If Lavkai and Botogo will not pay iasak from themselves and from their ulus people, and will not willingly come under the mighty hand of the Sovereign Tsar and Grand Prince Aleksei Mikhailovich of all Russia, in eternal servitude, then invoking God's aid, the voevoda Dmitrii Andreevich Frantsbekov and the diak [secretary] Osip Stepanov will personally assemble and head a large force and will attack Lavkai and Botogo and all the other non-iasak people.

Some will be hanged, and others will be ruined. After they have totally destroyed them, they will take their wives and children into captivity. But if the non-iasak people bow down and are in every way obedient to the Sovereign, then in accordance with their religious practices, these people are to be brought to swear allegiance so that they will be personally under the Sovereign Tsar's mighty hand in eternal iasak servitude, for all time, undeviatingly, and pay iasak for themselves and for their ulus subjects without interruption. . . .

Erofei, you are to send as many men as possible with the government iasak treasury and the pominki to Iakutsk ostrog [fort], and you are also to enter the names of the iasak people into the iasak books. Prepare a chart of the rivers, noting where there are large numbers of persons living along the rivers and to what tribes they belong. Send this information in writing to the Prikaz [central government department] office at Iakutsk ostrog, to the voevoda Dmitrii Andreevich Frantsbekov and the diak Osip Stepanov.

Erofei, you are to make a thorough investigation of any merchants or promyshlenniks who are on the Olekma for their own trade and hunting. Look into their belongings, and if you find any furs which they have acquired from the Tungus, make a record of that fact and send those persons under guard to Iakutsk ostrog so that they will not pass through into any other towns. . . .

B. August 1652 A Report from Erofei Khabarov to the Voevoda of Iakutsk, Dmitrii Frantsbekov, Concerning His Expedition on the Amur River

The humble servant of the Sovereign Tsar and Grand Prince Aleksei Mikhailovich of all Russia, the prikashchik [special agent] Erofei Pavlovich Khabarov, with the servitors, volunteers and newly recruited Daur servitors, report from the great Amur River and from the mouth of the Zeia River and Kokorei's ulus to the voevoda Dmitrii Andreevich Frantsbekov and the diak Osip Stepanov.

I, the humble servant of the Sovereign, lived with the servitors and volunteers on the great Amur River in the town of Albazin. All the adventures that befell us have been written for the Sovereign in my reports to you, Dmitrii Andreevich and Osip Stepanov.

On June 2, having built both large and small boats, and having asked mercy of God and of the Almighty Merciful Savior, we set out from the town of Albazin. We sailed for two days, and on the second day reached a town which belongs to Prince Dasaul. This town and its iurts had been burned to the ground; only two small iurts [camps] remained. We did not find any people there. From that town we sailed until midday, when we came upon iurts, but there were no people in the iurts. The people had fled on horseback. These are Daur people, and they had all run away from us. We were only able to capture an old Daur woman who said that all the Daur people live in uluses. We immediately went aboard the Lena boats and went swiftly downriver and found two iurts. All the Daur people were in those iurts. When they sighted us, they mounted their horses and rode off. We captured only one prisoner. The rest stayed in another ulus and began to deliver iasak to the town. They burned their iurts and raised a cloud of smoke.

That same day we went on to Guigudar's town, using the Lena boats . . . (missing). Prince Guigudar had two other princes with him as well as the Bogdoi ulus people. These men all stood on the shore in front of us and would not let us land. We fired our guns at them from the boats and killed about twenty Daur people. The princes, Guigudar, Olgemza and Lotodii, and their ulus people, were afraid of the Tsar's wrath and fled from shore. We quickly disembarked from our boats onto the shore and went after them. Princes Guigudar, Olgemza and Lotodii and their ulus people fortified themselves in their towns. They have three new towns which are protected by an earthen wall made of clay on top. The towns are side by side, with only walls separating them. There are tunnels without gates under these walls, and deep excavations have been made in these towns where both livestock and prisoners are kept. There are two moats one sazhen [seven feet] deep around these towns, and these moats are very close to the walls. Formerly there were uluses around these towns, but they had been burned.

When the princes encamped in the town, the Bogdoi people did not camp together with the Daur people; rather, they went on into the open country. With God's mercy and the luck of the Tsar, and for your pleasure, Dmitrii Andreevich and Osip Stepanovich, and with my ingenuity, prikashchik Erofei Pavlovich, and with the servitors and volunteers, we immediately laid siege to the town and the Daur people shot arrows at us from the towers. I, the prikashchik, told the interpreters to say that the Tsarist Majesty, our Sovereign Tsar and Grand Prince Aleksei Mikhailovich of all Russia, is fearful and awesome, that he possesses many realms, and that no horde can stand up against our Sovereign Tsar and Grand Prince Aleksei Mikhailovich of all Russia in battle. Therefore, I said, princes Guigudar and Olgodii (Olgemza) and Lotodii must be obedient and humble before our Sovereign Tsar and Grand Prince Aleksei Mikhailovich of all Russia. They must surrender without a struggle and give whatever they could in the way of iasak to our Sovereign and allow our Sovereign to protect them from hordes more powerful than theirs.

Guigudar replied, "We pay iasak to the Bogdoi Tsar Shamshakan. And as for the iasak which you are asking us to give, it would be like giving up our last child."

Then, asking God's mercy and the Sovereign's luck, we began the Sovereign's service with the usual military action. We ordered large cannon to be fired, and began to fire at the towers from the lower part of town. We fired on the people in the town with our small arms such as muskets and harquebuses. The Daur people fired back at us from the town, and their arrows flew at us from town without cease. The Daurs who were in the town fired so many arrows on us in the field that it looked like grain before the harvest.

We fought with the Daur people all night long until early dawn the next day. We broke through the wall near a tower. Those of us who were wearing armor, and other servitors who were protected with shields, took the wall and entered the town one by one. Thanks to the fortune of the Sovereign, we captured the lower town. The Daurs assembled in the other two towns, and at noon we servitors fought the Daurs of the second town from this town. All of these fierce Daurs then gathered in one town, and we fired at them without cease, from large and small arms, and in these sorties we killed 214 Daur men.

These fierce Daurs could not withstand the Sovereign's wrath and our attack. About fifteen of them managed to break through, but they were the only ones who escaped from the town. The rest of the Daurs were defeated and burned with the city. The battle was fierce and brutal for us cossacks, but with God's mercy and the luck of the Sovereign, we killed all of these Daurs, one after another. In this fearful battle we killed 427 Daur men and boys. The total number of Daurs killed, including the ones who had gathered and those who took part in the attack, was 661 men and boys. Only four of our cossacks were killed by the Daurs. Here in the town, the Daurs wounded 45 of our cossacks, but they all recovered from their wounds.

With the luck of the Sovereign we took this town, with livestock and prisoners. The total number of prisoners taken, partly old women and the rest young girls, was 243. There were 118 young prisoners. We also captured 237 horses, both large and small, from the Daurs; and we also took 113 head of cattle. While the fighting was going on the Bogdoi people circled the field and watched, but did not fire on our cossacks. We asked the prisoners about these Bogdoi people, "Why did these Bogdoi people come to you? How many Bogdoi people are there?" And the prisoners told us, "Fifty of these Bogdoi people live here all the time to collect iasak and other goods, until they are replaced by their own people." Then we asked the old women, "Why did they not come with you into the town? Why did they not join you?" And the prisoners replied, "Our Daur people, our prince Guigudar and his men, took them to the town to help, but the Bogdoi people told him, `Guigudar! Our tsar Shamshakan has forbidden us to fight with the Russians!' " . . .

---

7. Edict Closing Japan, 1636

In 1543 Portuguese traders reached an island off the coast of Japan, and six years later one of their ships brought the Jesuit missionary, St. Francis Xavier. The early Europeans experienced great success in their initial contacts with the Japanese. Warlords eagerly sought the firearms and cannons imported by the foreigners, and their introduction led to the unification of Japan and the concentration of power into the hands of a single de facto ruler. Converts to Christianity reached the hundreds of thousands as Jesuits founded more than 200 churches. But in 1587 a new leader, Toyotomi Hideyoshi, reversed his predecessor's tolerant policy toward the missionaries. In 1603 his successor, Tokugawa Ieyasu, intensified the persecution of Christians. Over the next few decades the Tokugawa shoguns became increasingly suspicious of European activities, which they saw as subversive and incompatible with their system of government and society. Fearing an alliance between Japanese dissidents and foreigners, they decided to expel the Portuguese, eradicate all Christian influences, and close Japan to the outside world. By 1639 they had ridden themselves of the outsiders, although they did allow the Dutch and the Chinese minimal trading rights. Japan remained shut off from the western world for more than two centuries, until the American Matthew Perry forced the nation to open its doors once again in 1854.

QUESTIONS

1. What are the assumptions and motives that explain the policies outlined in this document? What kind of a government enacts such policies?
2. What precisely is enacted here? Is Japan sealed off entirely?
3. Who are the Southern Barbarians?

1. No Japanese ships may leave for foreign countries.
2. No Japanese may go abroad secretly. If anybody tries to do this, he will be killed, and the ship and owner(s) will be placed under arrest whilst higher authority is informed.

3. Any Japanese now living abroad who tries to return to Japan will be put to death.

4. If any Kirishitan (Christian) believer is discovered, you two (Nagasaki bugyo, or governors) will make a full investigation.

5. Any informer(s) revealing the whereabouts of a bateren (Jesuit father) will be paid 200 or 300 pieces of silver. If any other categories of Kirishitans are discovered, the informer(s) will be paid at your discretion as hitherto.

6. On the arrival of foreign ships, arrangements will be made to have them guarded by ships provided by the Omura clan whilst report is being made to Yedo, as hitherto.

7. Any foreigners who help the bateren or other criminal foreigners will be imprisoned at Omura as hitherto.

8. Strict search will be made for bateren on all incoming ships.

9. No offspring of Southern Barbarians will be allowed to remain. Anyone violating this order will be killed, and all relatives punished according to the gravity of the offence.

10. If any Japanese have adopted the offspring of Southern Barbarians they deserve to die. Nevertheless, such adopted children and their foster parents will be handed over to the Southern Barbarians for deportation.

11. If any deportees should try to return or to communicate with Japan by letter or otherwise, they will of course be killed if they are caught, whilst their relatives will be severely dealt with, according to the gravity of the offence.

12. Samurai are not allowed to have direct commercial dealings with either foreign or Chinese shipping at Nagasaki.

13. Nobody other than those of the five places (Yedo, Kyoto, Osaka, Sakai and Nagasaki) is allowed to participate in the allocation of ito-wappu (bulk marketing of silk imports from Macao in China) and the fixing of silk import prices.

14. Purchases can only be made after the ito-wappu is fixed. However, as the Chinese ships are small, you will not be too rigorous with them. Only twenty days are allowed for the sale.

15. The twentieth day of the ninth month is the deadline for the return of foreign ships, but latecomers will be allowed fifty days grace from the date of their arrival. Chinese ships will be allowed to leave a little after the departure of the (Portuguese) galliots.

16. Unsold goods cannot be left in charge of Japanese for storage or safe-keeping.

17. Representatives of the five (shogunal) cities should arrive at Nagasaki not later than the fifth day of the long month. Late arrivals will not be allowed to participate in the silk allocation and purchase.

18. Ships arriving at Hirado will not be allowed to transact business until after the price allocations have been fixed at Nagasaki.

---

8. Narrative of the Life of Olaudah Equiano

Olaudah Equiano (1745?–1800?) was born in the interior of Africa in what is now eastern Nigeria. Captured with his sister by local raiders, he was carried down the Niger river to the sea, where slavers bought him and shipped him off to the West Indies. He was then transferred to North America and eventually he became the property of Captain Michael Pascal, who called him Gustavus Vassa. He was known by that name for the rest of his life. He served Pascal during several campaigns of the Seven Years War, then lived for a while in England and received some schooling. His second master, a Philadelphia Quaker merchant named Robert King, put him to work as a shipping clerk and amateur navigator on vessels that sailed between America and the West Indies. He continued his education during his bondage, and in 1766 he was able to purchase his freedom from King for forty pounds sterling. As a free man he toured the Mediterranean, the Arctic, and the Mosquito coast of Central America. He also embraced the Calvinist faith and devoted the remainder of his life to the cause of antislavery. In 1789 Equiano published his autobiography, *The Interesting Narrative of the Life of Olaudah Equiano, or Gustavus Vassa the African, written by himself.* The book sold very well in Great Britain and the United States, in part because its author travelled widely promoting his tract and making speeches against the slave trade. The selections from that work reprinted below present Equiano's descriptions of his early life in Africa, his kidnapping, and his "middle passage" across the Atlantic.

QUESTIONS

1. Describe the chief economic and social characteristics of Equiano's African village.
2. Describe the nature of slavery as it was practiced by Africans. Discuss Equiano's views on the role of both Africans and Europeans in the system of slavery.
3. Discuss Equiano's description of the conditions on board the slave ship during the "middle passage" to the West Indies.
4. What does Equiano mean by his reference to "nominal Christians"?
5. How do you explain the treatment of slaves described in this document? Is it genocide?

My Early Life in Eboe

As we live in a country where nature is prodigal of her favours, our wants are few and easily supplied; of course we have few manufactures. They consist for the most part of calicoes, earthenware, ornaments, and instruments of war and husbandry. But these make no part of our commerce, the principal articles of which, as I have observed, are provisions. In such a state money is of little use; however we have some small pieces of coin, if I may call them such. They are made something like an anchor, but I do not remember either their value or denomination. We have also markets, at which I have been frequently with my mother. These are sometimes visited by stout mahogany-coloured men from the south-west of us; we call them *Oye-Eboe*, which term signifies red men living at a distance. They generally bring us fire-arms, gunpowder, hats, beads, and dried fish. The last we esteemed a great rarity as our waters were only brooks and springs. These articles they barter with us for odoriferous woods and earth, and our salt of wood ashes. They always carry slaves through our land, but the strictest account is exacted of their manner of procuring them before they are suffered to pass. Sometimes indeed we sold slaves to them, but they were only prisoners of war, or such among us as had been convicted of kidnapping, or adultery, and some other crimes which we esteemed heinous. This practice of kidnapping induces me to think that, notwithstanding all our strictness, their principal business among us was to trepan [trick] our people. I remember too they carried great sacks along with them, which not long after I had an opportunity of fatally seeing applied to that infamous purpose.

Our land is uncommonly rich and fruitful, and produces all kinds of vegetables in great abundance. We have plenty of Indian corn, and vast quantities of cotton and tobacco. Our pineapples grow without culture; they are about the size of the largest sugar-loaf and finely flavoured. We have also spices of different kinds, particularly pepper, and a variety of delicious fruits which I have never seen in Europe, together with gums of various kinds and honey in abundance. All our industry is exerted to improve those blessings of nature. Agriculture is our chief employment, and everyone, even the children and women, are engaged in it. Thus we are all habituated to labor from our earliest years. Everyone contributes something to the common stock, and as we are unacquainted with idleness we have no beggars. The benefits of such a mode of living are obvious. The West India planters prefer the slaves of Benin or Eboe to those of any other part of Guinea for their hardiness, intelligence, integrity, and zeal. Those benefits are felt by us in the general healthiness of the people, and in their vigour and activity. I might have added too in their comeliness. . . . Our women too were in my eyes at least uncommonly graceful, alert, and modest to a degree of bashfulness; nor do I remember to have ever heard of an instance of incontinence amongst them before marriage. They are also remarkably cheerful. Indeed cheerfulness and affability are two of the leading characteristics of our nation.

Our tillage is exercised in a large plain or common, some hours walk from our dwellings, and all the neighbors resort thither in a body. . . . This common is often the theatre of war, and therefore when our people go out to till their land they not only go in a body but generally take their arms with them for fear of a surprise, and when they apprehend an invasion they guard the avenues to their dwellings by driving sticks into the ground, which are so sharp at one end as to pierce the foot and are generally dipped in poison. From what I can recollect of these battles, they appear to have been irruptions of one little state or district on the other to obtain prisoners or booty. Perhaps they were incited to this by those traders who brought the European goods I mentioned amongst us. Such a mode of obtaining slaves in Africa is common, and I believe more are procured this way and by kidnapping than any other. When a trader wants slaves he applies to a chief for them and tempts him with his wares. It is not extraordinary if on this occasion he yields to the temptation with as little firmness, and accepts the price of his fellow creatures' liberty with as little reluctance as the enlightened merchant. Accordingly he falls on his neighbours and a desperate battle ensues. If he prevails and takes prisoners, he gratifies his avarice by selling them; but if his party be vanquished and he falls into the hands of the enemy, he is put to death; for as he has been known to foment their quarrels it is thought dangerous to let him survive, and no ransom can save him, though all other prisoners may be redeemed. We have fire-arms, bows and arrows, broad two-edged swords and javelins; we have shields also which cover a man from head to foot. All are taught the use of these weapons; even our women are warriors and march boldly out to fight along with the men. Our whole district is a kind of militia; on a certain signal given, such as the firing of a gun at night, they all rise in arms and rush upon their enemy. It is perhaps something remarkable that when our people march to the field a red flag or banner is borne before them. I was once a witness to a battle in our common. . . . After fighting for a considerable time and with great fury and after many had been killed, our people obtained the victory and took their enemy's Chief prisoner. He was carried off in great triumph, and though he offered a large ransom for his life he was put to death. . . . Those prisoners which were not sold we kept as slaves: but how different was their condition from that of the slaves in the West Indies! With us they do no more work than other members of the community, even their master; their food, clothing and lodging were nearly the same as theirs (except that they were not permitted to eat with those who were freeborn), and there was scarce any other difference between them than a superior degree of importance which the head of a family possesses in our state, and that authority which, as such, he exercises over every part of his household. Some of these slaves have even slaves under them as their own property and for their own use. . . .

Kidnapped

My father, besides many slaves, had a numerous family of which seven lived to grow up, including myself and a sister who was the only daughter. As I was the youngest of the sons I became, of course, the greatest favourite with my mother and was always with her; and she used to take particular pains to form my mind. I was trained up from my earliest years in the art of war, my daily exercise was shooting and throwing javelins, and my mother adorned me with emblems after the manner of our greatest warriors. In this way I grew up till I was turned the age of 11, when an end was put to my happiness in the following manner. Generally when the grown people in the neighborhood were gone far in the fields to labour, the children assembled together in some of the neighbours' premises to play, and commonly some of us used to get up a tree to look out for any assailant or kidnapper that might come upon us, for they sometimes took those opportunities of our parents' absence to attack and carry off as many as they could seize. One day, as I was watching at the top of a tree in our yard, I saw one of those people come into the yard of our next neighbour but one to kidnap, there being many stout young people in it. Immediately on this I gave the alarm of the rogue and he was surrounded by the stoutest of them, who entangled him with cords so that he could not escape till some of the grown people came and secured him. But alas! ere long it was my fate to be thus attacked and to be carried off when none of the grown people were nigh. One day, when all our people were gone out to their works as usual and only I and my dear sister were left to mind the house, two men and a woman got over our walls, and in a moment seized us both, and without giving us time to cry out or make resistance they stopped our mouths and ran off with us into the nearest wood. Here they tied our hands and continued to carry us as far as they could till night came on, when we reached a small house where the robbers halted for refreshment and spent the night. We were then unbound but were unable to take any food, and being quite overpowered by fatigue and grief, our only relief was some sleep, which allayed our misfortune for a short time. The next morning we left the house and continued travelling all the day. For a long time we had kept to the woods, but at last we came into a road which I believed I knew. I had now some hopes of being delivered, for we had advanced but a little way before I discovered some people at a distance, on which I began to cry out for their assistance: but my cries had no other effect than to make them tie me faster and stop my mouth, and then they put me into a large sack. They also stopped my sister's mouth and tied her hands, and in this manner we proceeded till we were out of the sight of these people. When we went to rest the following night they offered us some victuals, but we refused it, and the only comfort we had was in being in one another's arms all that night and bathing each other with our tears. But alas! we were soon deprived of even the small comfort of weeping together. The next day proved a day of greater sorrow than I had yet experienced, for my sister and I were then separated while we lay clasped in each other's arms. It was in vain that we besought them not to part us; she was torn from me and immediately carried away, while I was left in a state of distraction not to be described. I cried and grieved continually, and for several days I did not eat anything but what they forced into my mouth. . . .

The Slave Ship

The first object which saluted my eyes when I arrived on the coast was the sea, and a slave ship, which was then riding at anchor, and waiting for its cargo. These filled me with astonishment, which was soon converted into terror, which I am yet at a loss to describe, nor the then feelings of my mind. When I was carried on board I was immediately handled, and tossed up, to see if I were sound, by some of the crew; and I was now persuaded that I had gotten into a world of bad spirits, and that they were going to kill me. Their complexions too differing so much from ours, their long hair, and the language they spoke, which was very different from any I had ever heard, united to confirm me in this belief. Indeed, such were the horrors of my views and fears at the moment, that, if ten thousand worlds had been my own, I would have freely parted with them all to have exchanged my condition with that of the meanest slave in my own country. When I looked round the ship too, and saw a large furnace of copper boiling, and a multitude of black people of every description chained together, every one of their countenances expressing dejection and sorrow, I no longer doubted of my fate; and, quite overpowered with horror and anguish, I fell motionless on the deck and fainted. When I recovered a little, I found some black people about me, who I believed were some of those who brought me on board, and had been receiving their pay; they talked to me in order to cheer me, but all in vain. I asked them if we were not to be eaten by those white men with horrible looks, red faces, and long hair. They told me I was not. . . . Soon after this, the blacks who brought me on board went off, and left me abandoned to despair.

   I now saw myself deprived of all chance of returning to my native country, or even the least glimpse of hope of gaining the shore, which I now considered as friendly; and I even wished for my former slavery, in preference to my present situation, which was filled with horrors of every kind, still heightened by my ignorance of what I was to undergo. I was not long suffered to indulge my grief; I was soon put down under the decks, and there I received such a salutation in my nostrils as I had never experienced in my life; so that, with the loathsomeness of the stench, and crying together, I became so sick and low that I was not able to eat, nor had I the least desire to taste any thing. I now wished for the last friend, death, to relieve me; but soon, to my grief, two of the white men offered me eatables; and, on my refusing to eat, one of them held me fast by the hands, and laid me across, I think, the windlass, and tied my feet while the other flogged me severely. I had never experienced any thing of this kind before; and, although not being used to the water, I naturally feared that element the first time I saw it; yet, nevertheless, could I have got over the nettings, I would have jumped over the side; but I could not; and, besides, the crew used to watch us very closely who were not chained down to the decks, lest we should leap into the water: and I have seen some of these poor African prisoners most severely cut for attempting to do so, and hourly whipped for not eating. This indeed was often the case with myself. In a little time after, amongst the poor chained men I found some of my own nation, which in a small degree gave ease to my mind. I inquired of these what was to be done with us; they gave me to understand we were to be carried to these white people's country to work for them. I then was a little relieved, and thought if it were no worse than working, my situation was not so desperate; but still I feared I should be put to death, the white people looked and acted, as I thought, in so savage a manner; for I had never seen among my people such instances of brutal cruelty, and this not only shewn towards us blacks but also to some of the whites themselves. One white man in particular I saw, when we were permitted to be on deck, flogged so unmercifully with a large rope near the foremast, that he died in consequence of it, and they tossed him over the side as they would have done a brute. This made me fear these people the more; and I expected nothing less than to be treated in the same manner. . . .

. . . At last, when the ship we were in had got in all her cargo . . . we were all put under deck. . . . The closeness of the place, and the heat of the climate, added to the number in the ship, which was so crowded that each had scarcely room to turn himself, almost suffocated us. This produced copious perspirations, so that the air soon became unfit for respiration, from a variety of loathsome smells, and brought on a sickness amongst the slaves, of which many died, thus falling victims to the improvident avarice, as I may call it, of their purchasers. This wretched situation was again aggravated by the galling of the chains, now become insupportable; and the filth of the necessary tubs, into which the children often fell, and were almost suffocated. The shrieks of the women, and the groans of the dying, rendered the whole a scene of horror almost inconceivable. Happily perhaps for myself I was soon reduced so low here that it was thought necessary to keep me almost always on deck; and from my extreme youth I was not put in fetters. In this situation I expected every hour to share the fate of my companions, some of whom were almost daily brought upon deck at the point of death, which I began to hope would soon put an end to my miseries. Often did I think many of the inhabitants of the deep much more happy than myself; I envied them the freedom they enjoyed, and as often wished I could change my condition for theirs. Every circumstance I met with served only to render my state more painful, and heighten my apprehensions and my opinion of the cruelty of the whites. . . .

. . . One day, when we had a smooth sea and moderate wind, two of my wearied countrymen who were chained together (I was near them at the time), preferring death to such a life of misery, somehow made through the nettings and jumped into the sea: immediately another dejected fellow, who on account of his illness was suffered to be out of irons, also followed their example; and I believe many more would very soon have done the same if they had not been prevented by the ship's crew, who were instantly alarmed. Those of us that were the most active were in a moment put down under the deck, and there was such a noise and confusion amongst the people of the ship as I never heard before, to stop her and get the boat out to go after the slaves. However two of the wretches were drowned, but they got the other and afterwards flogged him unmercifully for thus attempting to prefer death to slavery. . . .

. . . At last we came in sight of the island of Barbados, at which the whites on board gave a great shout and made many signs of joy to us. We did not know what to think of this, but as the vessel drew nearer we plainly saw the harbour and other ships of different kinds and sizes, and we soon anchored amongst them off Bridgetown. Many merchants and planters now came on board, though it was in the evening. They put us in separate parcels and examined us attentively. They also made us jump, and pointed to the land, signifying we were to go there. We thought by this we should be eaten by these ugly men, as they appeared to us; and

when soon after we were all put down under the deck again, there was much dread and trembling among us, and nothing but bitter cries to be heard all the night from these apprehensions, insomuch that at last the white people got some old slaves from the land to pacify us. They told us we were not to be eaten, but to work, and were soon to go on land where we should see many of our country people. This report eased us much; and sure enough, soon after we landed, there came to us Africans of all languages. We were conducted immediately to the merchant's yard, where we were all pent up together like so many sheep in a fold, without regard to sex or age. As every object was new to me, everything I saw filled me with surprise. What struck me first was, that the houses were built with bricks, in stories, and in every other respect different from those I have seen in Africa: but I was still more astonished on seeing people on horseback. I did not know what this could mean; and indeed I thought these people were full of nothing but magical arts. While I was in this astonishment, one of my fellow prisoners spoke to a countryman of his about the horses, who said they were the same kind they had in their country. . . . We were not many days in the merchant's custody, before we were sold after their usual manner, which is this: on a signal given (as the beat of a drum), the buyers rush at once into the yard where the slaves are confined, and make choice of that parcel they like best. The noise and clamour with which this is attended, and the eagerness visible in the countenances of the buyers, serve not a little to increase the apprehension of the terrified Africans, who may well be supposed to consider them as the ministers of that destruction to which they think themselves devoted. In this manner, without scruple, are relations and friends separated, most of them never to see each other again. I remember in the vessel in which I was brought over, in the men's apartment, there were several brothers who, in the sale, were sold in different lots; and it was very moving on this occasion to see and hear their cries at parting. O, ye nominal Christians! might not an African ask you, learned you this from your God? who says unto you, Do unto all men as you would men should do unto you. Is it not enough that we are torn from our country and friends to toil for your luxury and lust of gain? Must every tender feeling be likewise sacrificed to your avarice? Are the dearest friends and relations, now rendered more dear by their separation from their kindred, still to be parted from each other, and thus prevented from cheering the gloom of slavery with the small comfort of being together, and mingling their sufferings and sorrows? Why are parents to lose their children, brothers their sisters, or husbands their wives? Surely this is a new refinement in cruelty, which, while it has no advantage to atone for it, thus aggravates distress, and adds fresh horrors even to the wretchedness of slavery.

INTRODUCTION TO UNIT TWO

The Age of Democratic Revolutions

Although this unit concentrates on the English, American, and French revolutions, "the age of democratic revolutions" ushered in momentous forces which transformed every European country. In a sense it began with the Dutch Revolt of 1567, which was a full-fledged revolution against the monarchy of Philip II and a war of independence against Spain, a rebellion against taxation and the mercantilist hamstringing of Dutch trade, as well as defiance of the monopoly position of the established Catholic church and the Spanish Inquisition's persecution of Protestants. The Dutch struggle, which ran on until 1648, was a particularly contagious example for England. The United Netherlands Act of Abjuration of 1581 anticipates the United States Declaration of Independence in that it contains a long list of grievances, proclaims sovereign independence as the only possible resolution, and justifies its action by the contract theory of government. It states: "All mankind know that a prince is appointed by God to cherish his subjects, just as a shepherd to guard his sheep. When, therefore, the prince does not fulfil his duty as protector; when he oppresses his subjects, destroys their ancient liberties, and treats them as slaves, he is to be considered, not a prince, but a tyrant. As such, the estates of the land may lawfully and reasonably depose him, and elect another in his place."

During the seventeenth and eighteenth centuries a series of religious, financial, and political crises rocked England, her American colonies, and France. First came the English Civil War and the rule of Parliament and Oliver Cromwell during the 1640s and 1650s, followed by the Glorious Revolution of 1688 that brought William and Mary to the throne. Those momentous events profoundly shaped the constitutional development of both Britain and her settlements in North America. When representatives of thirteen colonies revolted in 1776 to form the United States, they borrowed heavily from the experience of the mother country during the preceding century. The American Revolution in turn contributed to the French Revolution, which toppled Louis XVI and brought a succession of republican regimes to France during the 1790s. By 1800 England, the

United States, and France had passed through profound political and social transformations. These three nations created new models of radical change whose influence would be felt around the world over the next two hundred years.

In the seventeenth century England began its spectacular rise to the status of one of the great powers of the world. It accomplished this achievement by creating a stable political system that successfully coped with three problems inherited from the reign of Queen Elizabeth. These sources of tensions were inextricably linked, and together they brought civil war and a series of political upheavals that swept away two kings. The first challenge concerned finding a workable balance of power between the Crown and Parliament. The second involved raising a revenue that would allow the King to govern effectively at home and to expand a growing colonial empire abroad. The third entailed establishing a national religion that could satisfy a majority of Protestants who had rejected allegiance to Rome but who disagreed on church liturgy, polity, and theology. For one hundred years these issues nearly tore England apart, but by 1700 it had attained a stable form of government—parliamentary monarchy—and the country was prepared to dominate first the British isles and then much of the rest of the world.

England's road to revolution began when James VI of Scotland inherited the throne and established the Stuart dynasty as James I of England in 1603. A philosopher of royal absolutism, he believed that kings drew their power from God, and were responsible to God alone. His faith in the divine right of monarchs to rule independent of Parliament alienated those who controlled the legislature. Lawyers, landowners, merchants, townsmen, and noblemen defended their ancient rights and refused to grant the King adequate funds. Under his reign Puritan dissenters also rejected the practices of the Anglican church, organizing independent congregations and holding services in violation of law.

When Charles I became king in 1625, he maintained his father's policies but soon became deadlocked with the House of Commons and House of Lords. In 1629 he suspended Parliament and refused to convene it again until 1640, when a Scottish rebellion threatened his regime. The new legislature became known as the Long Parliament because it lasted in various forms for twenty years. Its Puritan leaders soon challenged Charles I, and in 1642 open warfare broke out between its forces (Roundheads) and those of the Crown (Cavaliers). The victory of the Roundheads under Oliver Cromwell signaled the supremacy of Parliament and the Nonconformists and sealed the fate of the King. Cromwell purged Parliament down to a "rump" group of men, and a high court of justice (67 appointees) tried and sentenced Charles I to be beheaded in 1649.

For the next decade Cromwell and his supporters tried to rule England and the rest of the British isles as a republic and "commonwealth." He first crushed a rebellion in Scotland and then suppressed a rising in Ireland. Next he massacred Catholics and sent Protestant landlords to rule over the natives in Ireland. At home in England he resisted a radical democratic movement (the Levellers), abolished the Rump Parliament, and attempted to govern as Lord Protector under a new written constitution, the Instrument of Government (see Document 9).

But the new system failed, and Cromwell's regime became a military dictatorship until he died in 1658. After two years of anarchy Charles II was invited to reclaim the throne of England, Scotland, and Ireland. Parliament and the Anglican church were revived. The Restoration ended two decades of bloodshed and political turmoil and brought back much of the old order, but it did not resolve the conflicts that had plunged the nation into civil war.

During the twenty-five-year reign of Charles II, the King and Parliament worked out a constitutional arrangement that permitted the legislature to share power and to control revenues by raising or lowering taxes. But trouble returned over the issue of religion, for Charles II and his brother and heir, James, favored Catholicism. At first some in Parliament tried to exclude James from the succession. After he became James II in 1685 he antagonized Anglicans by pressing for a general religious toleration for all Protestant dissenters as well as Roman Catholics. Fearing an alliance between James II and France, prominent leaders of Parliament, Anglican officials, and spokesmen for Protestant dissenters joined to force a change in government. They invited James's Protestant daughter, Mary, and her husband, William of Orange, a Dutch leader, to replace him. When William invaded the kingdom with an army in 1688, James fled to France.

The following year Parliament enacted the Bill of Rights, which listed the privileges of the legislature and the people and excluded Catholics from becoming monarchs of England (see Document 10). Soon thereafter Parliament passed a Toleration Act, which allowed Protestant dissenters freedom of religion but which still barred them from political life. That ended the Glorious Revolution, which laid the foundation for the nation's spectacular rise to power in the next century. In 1707 England and Scotland joined to form the United Kingdom of Great Britain, with the new order providing a strong and flexible constitutional and financial system. With Wales and Ireland already conquered and with a thriving empire in the New World, the British were poised for new rounds of domestic development and foreign expansion.

During the eighteenth century Great Britain clashed with her archrival, France, as both powers struggled for supremacy in North America, the Caribbean, and India. By 1763 the British had driven the French out of Canada, but during the next two decades this magnificent victory turned to bitterness and humiliation. Thirteen North American colonies revolted against the rule of George III and Parliament and fought a civil war that established a new nation, the United States of America. In so doing they drew heavily upon the heritage of English constitutional history and especially the Glorious Revolution of 1688.

The road to the American Revolution began with the British conquest of Canada in 1761. The war against the French had been costly, and now Britain needed more money to protect and administer the land won from the French. George III and his ministers believed that the American colonists had benefited enormously from the removal of the French from their borderlands. They also were certain that the settlers could afford to pay their fair share of the increased expenses of the British empire. Thus, with the approval of the King, Parliament passed legislation that raised a revenue and that tightened the enforcement of laws regulating trade between the mother country and the colonies. In particular, in 1764 the Sugar Act imposed new taxes on American imports of foreign molasses. In 1765 the Stamp Act enacted an excise tax on printed materials, legal documents, and other items.

The American reaction to the Stamp Act was explosive. Mobs halted its implementation through attacks on the property of several British officials. Patriot radicals, organized as "Sons of Liberty," also applied economic coercion by organizing the boycott of British imported goods. These violent and other more peaceful forms of pressure also triggered an intense debate over the proper constitutional relations between England and her colonies. Colonial leaders insisted that only the provincial legislatures held the right to tax the people of America. They argued that Parliament could continue to regulate the external trade of the colonies but could not levy any tariffs or internal taxes for the explicit purpose of raising revenue. The crisis ended when Parliament repealed the Stamp Act in 1766, but the King and his ministers refused to concede the principle of their absolute sovereignty over the colonies. The Declaratory Act stated that Parliament reserved the right to legislate and to tax "in all cases whatsoever."

Parliament renewed its effort to raise an American revenue in 1767, when it passed the Townshend Acts. This legislation levied tariffs on glass, lead, paper, tea, and other products imported into the provinces. The new taxes sparked another round of protests, as radicals again intimidated officials, organized nonimportation agreements, and drafted pamphlets and petitions that challenged the legality of the laws. Once again the British backed down; in 1770 Parliament repealed all of the Townshend duties except the tax on tea. Relations remained quiet for three years, until the Tea Act revived the dispute. That law was designed to save the failing English East India Company and to force the colonists to import and pay the required taxes on English tea. Patriot bands responded by dumping the tea into the waters of Boston harbor and by preventing its importation at other seaports. Upon hearing the news of these "tea parties," the King and his ministers decided to punish the provincials. The Coercive Acts of 1774 shut down Boston harbor and restricted the political rights of the people of Massachusetts. The colonists responded in turn by the calling of the First Continental Congress, which cut off trade with England and prepared for the final confrontation with the King and Parliament.

After the Revolutionary War began at Lexington and Concord in April 1775, the Continental Congress waited nearly fifteen months before deciding in favor of independence. By this time the Patriots had totally rejected the authority of Parliament over the colonies, and were fighting British troops and German mercenaries. Yet public opinion stopped short of a final break with the Crown. Many Americans remained loyal to George III, who was the last link connecting the colonies with the British empire. In early 1776 Tom Paine's electrifying pamphlet Common Sense persuaded many to support the final move toward independence (see Document 11). In July Congress approved Thomas Jefferson's draft of the Declaration of Independence, which proclaimed the United States to be free of British rule and a new member of the family of nations of the world (see Document 12).

In 1776 Congress also adopted the Articles of Confederation—the first constitution of the United States. Under that charter the national government negotiated a commercial and military alliance with France, won the Revolutionary War, and acquired western lands as far as the Mississippi River from Great Britain in the 1783 Treaty of Paris. After the war Congress planned for the settlement of the west through the Land Ordinance of 1785 and the Northwest Ordinance of 1787. But throughout this period financial problems plagued the federal government, since the Articles reserved the power to tax to the states. Without an adequate and dependable revenue, Congress could not raise sufficient funds to pay for the costs of the war. A ruinous inflation undermined Continental currency and made it virtually impossible for the United States to borrow money from abroad. In addition the federal government shared the power to regulate interstate commerce with the states. That prevented the nation from formulating a uniform trade policy with other nations. The system was also deficient in the area of foreign policy, for under the Articles there was no independent executive branch that could conduct diplomacy efficiently with other nations.

In order to remedy these defects Congress authorized a commercial convention to be held at Annapolis, Maryland in the fall of 1786. That body in turn decided to call another meeting to consider sweeping revisions of the Articles of Confederation. When the Constitutional Convention met in the summer of 1787 at Philadelphia it scrapped the Articles completely and drafted a new scheme, the Constitution of the United States (see Document 13). That document, with ten amendments added in 1791 as the Bill of Rights, became the blueprint for the nation. The United States of America, an experiment in republicanism born out of the British empire, now challenged the monarchies of Europe with an alternative model of government based on the principles of popular sovereignty, an elected executive, and the consent of the governed.

The age of democratic change climaxed with the French Revolution, which proved to be more radical than the English or the American upheavals. Eighteenth-century France was a prosperous and powerful nation that exerted great cultural influence throughout Europe. But its political, financial, and social systems were deeply flawed. The King, Louis XVI, ruled a country that had been united by his predecessors; nationalism in France was far more developed than in any of her continental rivals. But the King could not effectively mobilize his people, because of his personal failings as a leader and because the royal bureaucracy could not extract funds from the recalcitrant nobility. The French economy was thriving, as industrial production and foreign trade increased steadily. But the nation's wealth was very unevenly distributed among its social classes. While the landowners, clergy, nobility, and merchants grew rich, city artisans and wage earners suffered a decline in purchasing power. Rural peasants were burdened with heavy church and feudal dues and taxes and suffered hardships during periodic recessions and poor harvests, especially during the late 1780s.

Social tensions compounded France's problems during this time, for its class system retained many remnants of medieval feudalism. An individual's personal status and legal rights, privileges, and obligations were prescribed by membership in one of three estates. The first was the clergy of the Catholic church, which owned between 5 and 10 percent of all of the nation's land, and which took a tithe (a tax of 10 percent) on agricultural produce. The second order was the nobility, who monopolized the highest political, military, and religious offices and who limited the power of the King. The third category included all others—wealthy bourgeois landowners and merchants, professionals, artisans, wage earners, small farmers, and peasants. Affluent, middle-class, and poor members of the Third Estate increasingly resented the privileges of the other two ranks of society. They presented their grievances at the outset of the rebellion, and played a critical role as it progressed through its more extreme stages (see Documents 14 and 15).

A financial crisis precipitated the first phase of the French Revolution, as was the case with the American Revolution. Old war debts and current expenses to maintain the army and navy could not be paid because of tax exemptions and evasions by privileged people. A call for financial reforms by the King moved leading nobles to suggest the summoning of an Estates General in 1789, which brought the three orders together to solve the financial problem. That gathering took it upon itself to establish a new system of government for France as well. But when disagreements over the procedures and organization of that body prevented progress, representatives of the Third Estate took advantage of the situation to assert their position and proclaimed themselves the National Assembly (also known as the Constituent Assembly) of France. The King at first favored the nobility's plan to keep the three groups separate, but then he yielded and ordered the other two estates to join in the deliberations of the National Assembly. The storming of the Bastille prison on July 14 and the outbreak of rural violence led to the renunciation of feudal obligations, fees, and tithes by landowners in early August.

The momentum of the rebellion was now irresistible, and over the next few years the National Assembly legislated a series of sweeping changes in French society. First, it drafted the Declaration of the Rights of Man and Citizen. That proclamation echoed the philosophy of natural laws and natural rights expressed in Jefferson's Declaration of Independence and the Bill of Rights in the United States Constitution. The Constitution of 1791 reaffirmed the basic principles of the revolution and established a constitutional monarchy with a king and an elected legislature. It allowed the King a limited royal veto over laws and gave suffrage to property holders (see Document 16). The National Assembly also thoroughly reorganized local government and raised money by confiscating the land of the Catholic church, which it used to back a newly issued currency. Finally, in a new Civil Constitution of the Clergy, it denied Papal authority over the Church and took responsibility for appointing and paying priests and bishops.

France's system of constitutional monarchy lasted only until the fall of 1792. Louis XVI never fully accepted many of the changes enacted by the National Assembly, and he was deeply offended by the attacks on the Catholic church. He turned to émigrés who had fled the country and who were trying to organize resistance to the new regime both inside France and abroad. While the great events in France had stirred many who were sympathetic to the principles of the rebellion, others feared the French assaults on traditional privileges of the King, the nobility, and the Church. Conservatives such as the Irishman Edmund Burke criticized the revolutionaries for tearing down a structure that had served France for centuries (see Document 17). The King hoped for foreign intervention by Austria and Prussia and attempted to escape in June 1791. But he was caught near the border and became a prisoner of the Assembly and of the Paris mob. In the assembly revolutionary factions were aiming for a French republic and were pressing for a war that they believed would consolidate the revolution in France, liberate the oppressed people of Europe, and spread the revolutionary message of France across the continent. The Assembly then declared war on the Habsburg emperor in April 1792. That in turn resulted in a crisis which led to the execution of Louis XVI in January 1793. A French republic now faced the emergency of war against most of the powers of Europe and widespread rebellion at home.

The National Convention that met in September 1792 soon split into factions, with a new radical group, nicknamed "The Mountain," taking control. In 1793 one of its leaders, Maximilien Robespierre, inaugurated a program that aimed to win the war, suppress internal opposition, and establish a new model society, a "republic of virtue," for France (see Documents 18 and 19). The Reign of Terror followed, as special tribunals executed between 30,000 and 50,000 people in an effort to purge the nation of its enemies. Many of those victims died on the guillotine. The Terror resulted from many factors, including the desperation of the foreign war, class tensions, utopian impulses, and mass fear. It lasted until 1794, when moderates in the Convention ousted and guillotined Robespierre.

The final phase of the revolution began in 1795, when the Convention wrote a new constitution that created a two-chamber legislature and an executive of five directors. The new system, called the Directory, lasted only four years. It proved to be ineffective in solving the nation's economic problems, inept in conducting war, and politically corrupt. Challenged by both conservative royalist forces and radical democrats, the Directory became more dependent upon the army and more dictatorial. The stage was now set for a military coup d'état. General Napoleon Bonaparte, a popular hero of campaigns in Italy and Egypt, seized his opportunity to take power by force. In late 1799 he drove the legislators from their chambers, abolished the Directory, and proclaimed a new republic, the Consulate. With himself as First Consul, Bonaparte began a rule that would witness new rounds of international warfare and sweeping political changes in France for the next fifteen years.

The rise of Napoleon Bonaparte ended the first great age of democratic revolutions. In England, America, and France popular forces had dethroned kings and had instituted forms of republicanism based on representation of the people. Great Britain had restored the Crown and had developed a system of constitutional monarchy. The United States experimented with a federal system of states under a national government composed of President, Congress, and Supreme Court. France had passed from constitutional monarchy to a series of republics to dictatorship. But in each case the new regimes had ushered in the triumph of liberal capitalism. In varying degrees each nation witnessed the ascendancy of the bourgeoisie—merchants, lawyers, small farmers, artisans, and other entrepreneurs who demanded liberty, protection of private property, and a voice in the political system.

Finally, each revolution demonstrated the power of popular demonstrations, mob action, and civil disobedience. The three rebellions left a legacy that threatened the ruling classes of nineteenth-century Europe and gave later radicals models of successful assaults on privilege and power. The American example, because it was so resoundingly successful, inspired opponents of the old regime in Holland, Belgium (which was under Austrian Habsburg rule), Ireland (under English rule), and Poland to bestir themselves, although uniformly unsuccessfully. The tremors from across the Atlantic turned into a tidal wave, however, emanating from France, and most especially after 1792, with the creation of a democratic republic and the onset of the wars between France and much of Europe that lasted until Napoleon's defeat in 1815. Demands for liberty, equality, and self-government appeared in the Spanish, French, and Portuguese colonies, the seeds of those wars of independence and revolution that created the Latin American republics in the years after 1810 (see Document 20). A dramatic episode was the abolition of slavery in 1794 by the French Government (the Convention) in what eventually became Haiti. Under the leadership of a former slave, Toussaint L'Ouverture, an attempt was made to create an island republic against great odds and with much bloodshed. Haiti remains memorable as the first society of the New World to abolish slavery; its people rejected white supremacy for racial equality and struggled to create a black republic on the French revolutionary model. Echoes of this age ultimately reached Asia, where Japanese statesmen studied the democratic upheavals for models they could follow as they revised their own political system (see Document 22).

While the age of democratic revolutions could be said to have continued on after Napoleon's defeat—into the 1820s with the Greek revolt and the Latin American wars of independence, or the Revolution of 1830, or that of 1848, or that it continues on ever more widely to the present, the decisive turning point was 1799, when Napoleon came to power in a coup d'état that overthrew the Republic. By then the democratic revolution had permanently succeeded in portions of Europe, and, as the historian R. R. Palmer put it, "The line between a liberal West and an autocratic East in Europe in effect dates from the events symbolized by 1789." It is interesting to note that the communist revolutions of the twentieth century were most successful in those areas where the democratic revolution had the least effect and no permanent result—so at least, one could say, until the momentous events of 1989–1991, which may ultimately be interpreted as the vindication of the democratic revolution.

What was fundamentally at stake in the last third of the eighteenth century was a conception of society, the idea of the national community. The program contested by the opposing groups—the "democrats" versus the "aristocrats" as the terms were from the 1790s on—was "liberty and equality," the watchwords by which the revolutionary movement everywhere proclaimed itself. What was meant was essentially political liberty and legal equality. The motto did not necessarily mean one man, one vote; socialism or a welfare state and society; or the abolition of monarchy. It did mean the rule of law and written constitutions, declarations of civil rights, the abolition of hereditary rank and privilege, the sovereignty of the people or nation rather than monarchy or the nobility or parliament; that representative bodies were to be elected in frequent elections for equal districts and governed by majority rule; that all public officials were responsible and removable; that social distinctions and privileges were not ruled out so long as they were earned and in the public interest; that property rights were guaranteed rather than infringed; that the special privileges of established churches were abolished and all connection between religious affiliation and qualification for citizenship was severed. For example, many countries emancipated their Jewish populations from legal burdens and restrictions, as freedom of religion, ideas, and opinion gained ground. The notion of divine right or religion-sanctioned government yielded to new notions of rule by consent of the people. Edmund Burke, although speaking in castigation of the French Revolution, was quite right when he pronounced that there had been "nothing like it in Europe since the Reformation."

Finally, the tidal wave of change ultimately brought women into greater participation in the world of politics, as champions of equal rights for females drew on the principles of this era. But the struggle was long and difficult. Throughout the nineteenth century, women's emancipation, whether in legal or psychological terms, progressed slowly throughout the Western world. While peasants, religious dissenters, slaves, workers, and other groups made significant gains in civil and political rights, women were shunted aside by the great liberating forces of the age. The English philosopher John Stuart Mill (1806–1873) introduced the first woman's suffrage bill in Parliament in 1870. In his writings he argued that the institution of marriage had originated in force and had become a form of "slavery" that was perpetuated by custom and tradition. He also questioned contemporary ideas about the "nature" of women, who were supposedly radically different from males and who were thought to be incapable of any tasks other than those which served husbands and children. In the United States Elizabeth Cady Stanton was one of the pioneers in the crusade for better treatment and greater opportunities and rights for women (see Document 21).

9. The Instrument of Government, 1653

The English constitutional struggle was continuous from the 1590s, the last decade of Elizabeth I's reign, through those of James I and Charles I, against whom civil war broke out in 1642, until the eventual victory of Parliament and the Roundheads over the Crown and Cavaliers. Then the real problem arose: what kind of government would replace the ancient constitution.

The Heads of Proposals, 1647, was a moderate document which would have preserved the monarchy but with its prerogatives distinctly limited. Since it was rejected by Charles I it was never implemented. An Agreement of the People, 1649, was a radical document drawn up by the democratic Levellers: it abolished the monarchy and the House of Lords, promulgated the sovereignty of the people, spelled out limits of state power, and prescribed a list of man's "natural and inalienable rights." Since it was rejected by Cromwell and the army leadership the Agreement never took effect.

The Instrument of Government was in some respects an averaging out of the differences between these two attempts at a written constitution. It came in the wake of the trial and execution of Charles I, the abolition of the monarchy and the House of Lords, and the unchallengeable ascendancy of Cromwell and the army, and reflected the views of the more moderate Independents and the army council. It was intended to resolve the prolonged impasse between Cromwell and the Rump, Barebone's Parliament. The Instrument of Government was a genuine attempt to establish an ethical basis for government, but it did not resolve the fundamental question: in a government that balanced the legislative and executive arms, how were disputes to be dealt with? The Instrument of Government does not authorize any mode or institution to resolve such quarrels, thus opening the way to resort to force.

QUESTIONS

1. This is the first written constitution in history: What might have induced the framers to attempt to issue a definitive set of rules on how the government is to be conducted?
2. What form of government is provided for here? To what extent does it provide for a separation of powers?
3. How democratic or undemocratic is it?
4. This constitution did not work and was abrogated after a few years; are there elements or omissions that suggest why it failed?

The government of the Commonwealth of England, Scotland and Ireland, and the dominions thereunto belonging:

1. That the supreme legislative authority of the Commonwealth of England, Scotland and Ireland, and the dominions thereunto

belonging, shall be and reside in one person and the people assembled in Parliament; the style of which person shall be the Lord Protector of the Commonwealth of England, Scotland and Ireland.

2. That the exercise of the chief magistracy and the administration of the government over the said countries and dominions, and the people thereof, shall be in the Lord Protector, assisted with a Council, the number whereof shall not exceed twenty-one nor be less than thirteen.

3. That all writs, process, commissions, patents, grants and other things, which now run in the name and style of the Keepers of the Liberty of England by Authority of Parliament, shall run in the name and style of the Lord Protector, from whom, for the future, shall be derived all magistracy and honors in these three nations. And (he shall) have the power of pardons, except in case of murders and treason, and benefit of all forfeitures for the public use; and shall govern the said countries and dominions in all things by the advice of the Council, and according to these presents and the laws.

4. That the Lord Protector, the Parliament sitting, shall dispose and order the militia and forces, both by sea and land, for the peace and good of the three nations by consent of Parliament; and that the Lord Protector, with the advice and consent of the major part of the Council, shall dispose and order the militia for the ends aforesaid in the intervals of Parliament.

5. That the Lord Protector, by the advice aforesaid, shall direct in all things concerning the keeping and holding of a good correspondence with foreign kings, princes and states; and also with the consent of the major part of the Council, have the power of war and peace.

6. That the laws shall not be altered, suspended, abrogated or repealed, nor any new law made, nor any tax, charge or imposition laid upon the people, but by common consent in Parliament. . . .

7. That there shall be a Parliament summoned to meet at Westminster upon the 3d day of September 1654, and that successively a Parliament shall be summoned once in every third year. . . .

8. That neither the Parliament to be next summoned nor any successive Parliaments shall, during the time of five months to be accounted from the day of their first meeting, be adjourned, prorogued or dissolved without their own consent.

9. That as well the next as all other successive Parliaments shall be summoned and elected in manner hereafter expressed: that is to say, the persons to be chosen within England, Wales, the isles of Jersey, Guernsey and the town of Berwick-upon-Tweed to sit and serve in Parliament shall be, and not exceed, the number of 400; the persons to be chosen within Scotland . . . the number of 30; and the persons to be chosen . . . for Ireland . . . the number of 30. . . .

14. That all and every person and persons who have aided, advised, assisted or abetted in any war against Parliament since the first day of January 1641—unless they have been since in the service of the Parliament and given signal testimony of their good affection thereunto—shall be disabled and incapable to be elected or to give any vote in the election of any members to serve in the next Parliament or in the three succeeding triennial Parliaments.

15. That all such who have advised, assisted or abetted the rebellion of Ireland shall be disabled and incapable forever to be elected or give any vote in the election of any member to serve in Parliament; as also all such who do or shall profess the Roman Catholic religion. . . .

17. That the persons who shall be elected to serve in Parliament shall be such . . . as are persons of known integrity, fearing God,

and of good conversation, and being of the age of twenty-one years.

18. That all and every person and persons seised or possessed to his own use of any estate, real or personal, to the value of £200, and not within the aforesaid exceptions, shall be capable to elect members to serve in Parliament for counties. . . .

24. That all bills agreed unto by the Parliament shall be presented to the Lord Protector for his consent; and in case he shall not give his consent thereto within twenty days after they shall be presented to him, or give satisfaction to the Parliament within the time limited, that then, upon declaration of the Parliament that the Lord Protector hath not consented nor given satisfaction, such bills shall pass into and become laws, . . . provided such bills contain nothing in them contrary to the matters contained in these presents.

25. That Henry Lawrence (with 14 others) . . . , or any seven of them, shall be a Council for the purposes expressed in this writing. And upon the death or other removal of any of them, the Parliament shall nominate six persons of ability, integrity, and fearing God, for every one that is dead or removed, out of which the major part of the Council shall elect two, and present them to the Lord Protector, of whom he shall elect one. . . .

26. That the Lord Protector and the major part of the Council aforesaid may, at any time before the meeting of the next Parliament, add to the Council such persons as they shall think fit, provided the number of the Council be not made thereby to exceed twenty-one. . . .

27. That a constant yearly revenue shall be raised, settled and established for maintaining of 10,000 horse and dragoons and 20,000 foot in England, Scotland and Ireland, for the defense and security thereof; and also for a convenient number of ships for guarding of the seas; besides £200,000 per annum for defraying the other necessary charges of administration of justice and other expenses of the government—which revenue shall be raised by the customs, and such other ways and means as shall be agreed upon by the Lord Protector and the Council, and shall not be taken away or diminished, nor the way agreed upon for raising the same altered, but by the consent of the Lord Protector and the Parliament.

32. That the office of Lord Protector over these nations shall be elective and not hereditary and, upon the death of the Lord Protector, another fit person shall be forthwith elected to succeed him in the government; which election shall be by the Council. . . .

33. That Oliver Cromwell, Captain-General of the forces of England, Scotland and Ireland, shall be and is hereby declared to be Lord Protector of the Commonwealth of England, Scotland and Ireland, and the dominions thereto belonging, for his life.

34. That the chancellor, keeper or commissioners of the great seal, the treasurer, admiral, chief governors of Ireland and Scotland, and the chief justices of both the benches, shall be chosen by the approbation of Parliament; and in the intervals of Parliament, by the approbation of the major part of the Council, to be afterwards approved by the Parliament.

35. That the Christian religion, as contained in the Scriptures, be held forth and recommended as the public profession of these nations; and that, as soon as may be, a provision less subject to scruple and contention, and more certain than the present, be made for the encouragement and maintenance of able and painful teachers, for instructing the people and for discovery and confutation of error, heresy and whatever is contrary to sound doctrine; and that, until such provision be made, the present maintenance shall not be taken away nor impeached.

36. That to the public profession held forth none shall be compelled by penalties or otherwise, but that endeavors be used to win them by sound doctrine and the example of a good conversation.

37. That such as profess faith in God by Jesus Christ, though differing in judgment from the doctrine, worship or discipline publicly held forth, shall not be restrained from, but shall be protected in, the profession of the faith and exercise of their religion; so as they abuse not this liberty to the civil injury of others and to the actual disturbance of the public peace on their parts; provided this liberty be not extended to popery nor prelacy, nor to such as, under the profession of Christ, hold forth and practice licentiousness. . . .

41. That every successive Lord Protector over these nations shall take and subscribe a solemn oath, in the presence of the Council and such others as they shall call to them, that he will seek the peace, quiet and welfare of these nations, cause law and justice to be equally administered, and that he will not violate or infringe the matters and things contained in this writing, and in all other things will, to his power and to the best of his understanding, govern these nations according to the laws, statutes and customs thereof. . . .

10. The English Bill of Rights, 1689

The English Revolution of 1688–1689 was "bloodless" and "glorious." It witnessed the overthrow or abdication of James II in favor of his son-in-law and daughter, William III and Mary. It was adroitly managed, partly because all leaders remembered and wished to avoid the horrors of civil war. It was a revolution to preserve and restore the constitution rather than to reform it. The Bill of Rights rehearses and forbids all the violations of the constitution by James II, and it recapitulates much of the conflict of the preceding century. The terms of the offer of the crown to William are those of a contract, and they reflect the ideas of John Locke.

By the Bill of Rights English monarchs ceased to hold the throne by divine right. Parliament elected William and Mary and bestowed succession on their Protestant heirs. Since they had none it was bestowed on Mary's sister Anne and descendants; since she had none Parliament turned to the Hanoverians (descendants of James I's daughter Elizabeth). It has been hereditary in the Hanover house ever since. Parliament's sovereignty was only implicit in the settlement, since the king still retained the prerogative to choose his own ministers and form a government. But after nearly a century of conflict, both crown and parliament were found to be indispensable to the workings of government. They were now fused together in an organic balance. Yet it took until 1834 to finally establish that the monarch could not form or sustain a government against the wishes of parliament.

QUESTIONS

1. Compare the balance of legislative and executive powers with that of the Instrument of Government.
2. What historical event does this document deal with?
3. What familiar individual rights are granted here? Which are left out?

Whereas the . . . late King James the Second having abdicated the government and the throne being thereby vacant, his Highness the Prince of Orange (whom it has pleased almighty God to make the glorious instrument of delivering this kingdom from popery and arbitrary power) did (by the advice of the Lords Spiritual and Temporal and divers principal persons of the Commons) cause letters to be written to the Lords Spiritual and Temporal being Protestants, and other letters to the several counties, cities, universities, boroughs and cinque ports, for the choosing of such persons to represent them as were of right to be sent to Parliament, to meet and sit at Westminster upon the two and twentieth day of January in this year, in order to such an establishment as that their religion, laws and liberties might not again be in danger of being subverted, upon which letters elections having been accordingly made:

And thereupon the said Lords Spiritual and Temporal and Commons, . . . being now assembled in a full and free representative of this nation, taking into their most serious consideration the best means for attaining the ends aforesaid, do in the first place (as their ancestors in like case have usually done) for the vindicating and asserting their ancient rights and liberties declare:

That the pretended power of suspending of laws or the execution of laws by regal authority without consent of Parliament is illegal.

That the pretended power of dispensing with laws or the execution of laws by regal authority without consent of Parliament is illegal.

That the commission for erecting the late Court of Commissioners for Ecclesiastical Causes, and all other commissions and courts of like nature, are illegal and pernicious.

That levying money for or to the use of the crown by pretense of perogative without grant of Parliament, for longer time or in other manner than the same is or shall be granted, is illegal.

That it is the right of the subjects to petition the King, and all commitments and prosecutions for such petitioning are illegal.

That the raising or keeping a standing army within the kingdom in time of peace, unless it be with consent of Parliament, is against law.

That the subjects which are Protestants may have arms for their defense, suitable to their conditions and as allowed by law.

That election of members of Parliament ought to be free.

That the freedom of speech and debates or proceedings in Parliament ought not to be impeached or questioned in any court or place out of Parliament.

That excessive bail ought not to be required, nor excessive fines imposed, nor cruel and unusual punishments inflicted.

That jurors ought to be duly impanelled and returned, and jurors which pass upon men in trials for high treason ought to be freeholders.

That all grants and promises of fines and forfeitures of particular persons before conviction are illegal and void.

And that for redress of all grievances, and for the amending, strengthening and preserving of the laws, Parliament ought to be held frequently.

And they do claim, demand and insist upon all and singular the premises as their undoubted rights and liberties, and that no declarations, judgments, doings or proceedings to the prejudice of the people in any of the said premises ought in any wise to be drawn hereafter into consequence or example; to which demand of their rights they are particularly encouraged by the declaration of his Highness the Prince of Orange as being the only means for obtaining a full redress and remedy therein. Having therefore an entire confidence that his said Highness . . . will perfect the deliverance so far advanced by him, and will still preserve them from the violation of their rights which they have here asserted, and from all other attempts upon their religion, rights and liberties, the said Lords Spiritual and Temporal and Commons assembled at Westminster do resolve that William and Mary, Prince and Princess of Orange, be and be declared King and Queen of England, France and Ireland and the dominions thereunto belonging, to hold the crown and royal dignity of the said kingdoms and dominions to them . . . during their lives and the life of the survivor of them, and that the sole and full exercise of the regal power be only in and executed by the said Prince of Orange in the names of the said Prince and Princess during their joint lives, and after their deceases the said crown and royal dignity . . . to be to the heirs of the body of the said Princess, and for default of such issue to the Princess

Anne of Denmark and the heirs of her body, and for default of such issue to the heirs of the body of the said Prince of Orange. And the Lords Spiritual and Temporal and Commons do pray the said Prince and Princess to accept the same accordingly.

And that the oaths hereafter mentioned be taken by all persons of whom the oaths of allegiance and supremacy might be required by law, instead of them; and that the said oaths of allegiance and supremacy be abrogated.

I, A. B., do sincerely promise and swear that I will be faithful and bear true allegiance to their Majesties King William and Queen Mary. So help me God.

I, A. B., do swear that I do from my heart abhor, detest and adjure as impious and heretical this damnable doctrine and position that princes excommunicated or deprived by the Pope or any authority of the See of Rome may be deposed or murdered by their subjects or any other whatsoever. And I do declare that no foreign prince, person, prelate, state or potentate hath or ought to have any jurisdiction, power, superiority, pre-eminence or authority, ecclesiastical or spiritual, within this realm. So help me God.

Upon which their said Majesties did accept the crown and royal dignity of the Kingdom of England, France and Ireland, and the dominions thereunto belonging, according to the resolution and desire of the said Lords and Commons contained in the said declaration. And thereupon their majesties were pleased that the said Lords . . . and Commons, being the two houses of Parliament, should continue to sit, and with their Majesties' royal concurrence make effectual provision for the settlement of the religion, laws and liberties of this Kingdom, so that the same for the future might not be in danger again of being subverted, to which the said Lords . . . and Commons did agree, and proceed to act accordingly. Now in pursuance of the premises the said Lords . . . do pray that it may be delcared and enacted that all and singular the rights and liberties asserted and claimed in the said declaration are the true, ancient and indubitable rights and liberties of the people of this kingdom, and so shall be esteemed, allowed, adjudged, deemed and taken to be; and that all and every the particulars aforesaid shall be firmly and strictly holden and observed as they are expressed in the said declaration, and all officers and ministers whatsoever shall serve their Majesties and their successors according to the same in all times to come. And the said Lords . . . and Commons do hereby recognize, acknowledge and declare that King James II having abdicated the government, and their Majesties having accepted the Crown and royal dignity as aforesaid, their said Majesties did become . . . and of right ought to be by the laws of this realm our sovereign liege lord and lady, King and Queen of England, France and Ireland and the dominions thereunto belonging, in and to whose princely persons the royal state, crown and dignity of the said realms with all honors, styles, titles, regalities, prerogatives, powers, jurisdictions and authorities to the same belonging and appertaining are most fully, rightfully and entirely invested and incorporated, united and annexed. . . . And the said Lords . . . and Commons do in the name of all the people . . . most humbly and faithfully submit themselves, their heirs and posterities forever, and do faithfully promise that they will stand to, maintain and defend their said Majesties, and also the limitation and succession of the Crown herein specified and contained, to the utmost of their powers and their lives and estates against all persons whatsoever

that shall attempt anything to the contrary. And whereas it has been found by experience that it is inconsistent with the safety and welfare of this Protestant Kingdom to be governed by a popish prince, or by any King or Queen marrying a papist, the said Lords all and every person and persons that is, are or shall be reconciled to or shall hold communion with the See or Church of Rome, or shall profess the popish religion, or shall marry a papist, shall be excluded and be forever incapable to inherit, possess or enjoy the Crown and government of this Realm . . . or to have, use or exercise any regal power, authority or jurisdiction within the same; and in all and every such case or cases the people of these Realms shall be and are hereby absolved of their allegiance; and the said Crown and government shall from time to time descend to and be enjoyed by such person or persons being Protestants as should have inherited and enjoyed the same in case the said person or persons so reconciled, holding communion or professing or marrying as aforesaid were naturally dead; and that every King and Queen of this realm who at any time hereafter shall come to and succeed in the imperial Crown of this Kingdom shall on the first day of the meeting of the first Parliament next after his or her coming to the Crown, sitting in his or her throne in the House of Peers in the presence of the Lords and Commons therein assembled, or at his or her coronation before such person or persons who shall administer the coronation oath to him or her . . . make, subscribe and audibly repeat the declaration mentioned in the statute made in the thirtieth year of the reign of King Charles II entitled, "An Act for the More Effectual Preserving the King's Person and Government by Disabling Papists from Sitting in Either House of Parliament."

11. Common Sense, 1776

Thomas Paine

Thomas Paine (1737–1809) was born into a Quaker family in England. As a young man he struggled through several troubled years as a staymaker, teacher, and excise tax officer for the British government. Dismissed from his last position and bankrupt, he sailed for America, settling in Philadelphia in 1774. In January 1776 he published the classic pamphlet, *Common Sense*. After the Declaration of Independence Paine joined the Patriot army, and penned a series of essays known as The American Crisis. He returned to Europe in 1787, but was outlawed by the British government for the radical philosophy expressed in his book, *The Rights of Man*, and for his support for the French Revolution. He then fled to France, but his latest plunge into radical politics landed him in jail for nearly a year. After his release he wrote *The Age of Reason*, a critical assault on Christian revelation. Paine died in poverty and obscurity in New York City.

In *Common Sense* Paine challenged traditional assumptions that most British-Americans had taken for granted. The following selection presents a sample of his stirring, angry and lyrical prose. In this text Paine denies that England was the true "mother country" to the colonies. His powerful, relentless argument proclaims the political, diplomatic, economic and practical disadvantages of America's connection with the British empire. *Common Sense* became a runaway best seller and contributed greatly to the final decision for American independence. But its publication did not enrich its author, for Paine gave away his copyright claim as his contribution to American independence.

QUESTIONS

1. According to Paine, who is the parent country to America? Why?
2. According to Paine, what are the major disadvantages that affect the American colonies through their connection with Great Britain?
3. Explain Paine's major objections to a reconciliation between Britain and her American colonies.
4. Why does Paine urge the colonists to announce their independence without further delay in 1776?

In the following pages I offer nothing more than simple facts, plain arguments, and common sense: and have no other preliminaries to settle with the reader, than that he will divest himself of prejudice and prepossession, and suffer his reason and his feelings to determine for themselves: that he will put on, or rather that he will not put off, the true character of a man, and generously enlarge his views beyond the present day.

Volumes have been written on the subject of the struggle between England and America. Men of all ranks have embarked in the controversy, from different motives, and with various designs; but all have been ineffectual, and the period of debate is closed. Arms as the last resource decide the contest; the appeal was the choice of the King, and the Continent has accepted the challenge. . . .

The Sun never shined on a cause of greater worth. 'Tis not the affair of a City, a County, a Province, or a Kingdom; but of a Continent—of at least one eighth part of the habitable Globe. 'Tis not the concern of a day, a year, or an age; posterity are virtually involved in the contest, and will be more or less affected even to the end of time, by the proceedings now. Now is the seed-time of the Continental union, faith and honour. The least fracture now will be like a name engraved with the point of a pin on the tender rind of a young oak; the wound would enlarge with the tree, and posterity read it in full grown characters.

By referring the matter from argument to arms, a new area for politics is struck—a new method of thinking hath arisen. All plans, proposals, &c. prior to the nineteenth of April [1775], *i.e.* to the commencement of hostilities, are like the almanacks of the last year; which tho' proper then, are superceded and useless now. Whatever was advanced by the advocates on either side of the question then, terminated in one and the same point, *viz.* a union with Great Britain; the only difference between the parties was the method of effecting it; the one proposing force, the other friendship; but it hath so far happened that the first hath failed, and the second hath withdrawn her influence.

As much hath been said of the advantages of reconciliation which, like an agreeable dream, hath passed away and left us as we were, it is but right that we should examine the contrary side of the argument, and

enquire into some of the many material injuries which these Colonies sustain, and always will sustain by being connected with and dependent on Great Britain. To examine that connection and dependence, on the principles of nature and common sense, to see what we have to trust to, if separated, and what we are to expect, if dependent.

I have heard it asserted by some, that as America has flourished under her former connection with Great Britain, the same connection is necessary towards her future happiness, and will always have the same effect. Nothing can be more fallacious than this kind of argument. We may as well assert that because a child has thrived upon milk, that it is never to have meat, or that the first twenty years of our lives is to become a precedent for the next twenty. But even this is admitting more than is true; for I answer roundly, that America would have flourished as much, and probably much more, had no European power taken any notice of her. The commerce by which she hath enriched herself are the necessaries of life, and will always have a market while eating is the custom of Europe.

But she had protected us, say some. That she hath engrossed us is true, and defended the Continent at our expense as well as her own, is admitted; and she would have defended Turkey from the same motive, *viz.* for the sake of trade and dominion.

Alas! we have been long led away by ancient prejudices and made large sacrifices to superstition. We have boasted the protection of Great Britain, without considering that her motive was *interest* not *attachment*; and that she did not protect us from *our enemies* on *our account*; but from *her enemies* on *her own account*, and who will always be our enemies on the *same* account. Let Britain waive her pretensions to the Continent, or the Continent throw off the dependence, and we should be at peace with France and

Spain, were they at war with Britain. The miseries of Hanover's last war ought to warn us against connections.

It hath lately been asserted in parliament, that the Colonies have no relation to each other but through the Parent Country, *i.e.*, that Pennsylvania and the Jerseys, and so on for the rest are sister Colonies by the way of England; this is certainly a very roundabout way of proving relationship, but it is the nearest and only true way of proving enmity (or enemyship, if I may so call it). France and Spain never were, nor perhaps ever will be, our enemies as *Americans*, but as our being the *subjects of Great Britain*.

But Britain is the parent country say some. Then the more shame upon her conduct. Even brutes do not devour their young, nor savages make war upon their families. Wherefore, the assertion, if true, turns to her reproach; but it happens not to be true, or only partly so, and the phrase *parent* or *mother country* hath been jesuitically adopted by the King and his parasites, with a low papistical design of gaining an unfair bias on the credulous weakness of our minds. Europe, not England is the parent country of America. This new World hath been the asylum for the persecuted lovers of civil and religious liberty from *every part* of Europe. Hither have they fled, not from the tender embraces of the mother, but from the cruelty of the monster; and it is so far true of England, that the same tyranny which drove the first emigrants from home, pursues their descendants still. . . .

But, admitting that we were all of English descent, what does it amount to? Nothing. Britain, being now an open enemy, extinguished every other name and title: and to say that reconciliation is our duty, is truly farcical. The first king of England, of the present line (William the Conqueror) was a Frenchman, and half the peers of England are descendants from the same country; wherefore, by the same method of reasoning, England ought to be governed by France.

Much hath been said of the united strength of Britain and the Colonies, that in conjunction they might bid defiance to the world: But this is mere presumption; the fate of war is uncertain, neither do the expressions mean any thing; for this Continent would never suffer itself to be drained of inhabitants, to support the British arms in either Asia, Africa, or Europe.

Besides, what have we to do with setting the world at defiance? Our plan is commerce, and that, well attended to, will secure us the peace and friendship of all Europe; because it is the interest of all Europe to have America a free port. Her trade will always be a protection, and her barrenness of gold and silver secure her from invaders.

I challenge the warmest advocate for reconciliation to show a single advantage that this Continent can reap by being connected with Great Britain. I repeat the challenge; not a single advantage is derived. Our corn will fetch its price in any market in Europe, and our imported goods must be paid for buy them where we will.

But the injuries and disadvantages which we sustain by that connection, are without number; and our duty to mankind at large, as well as to ourselves, instruct us to renounce the alliance: because, any submission to, or dependence on, Great Britain, tends directly to involve this Continent in European wars and quarrels, and set us at variance with nations who would otherwise seek our friendship, and against whom we have neither anger nor complaint. As Europe is our market for trade, we ought to form no partial connection with any part of it. It is the true interest of America to steer clear of European contentions, which she never can do, while, by her dependence on

Britain, she is made the make-weight in the scale of British politics.

Europe is too thickly planted with Kingdoms to be at peace, and whenever a war breaks out between England and any foreign power, the trade of America goes to ruin, *because of her connection with Britain.* The next war may not turn out like the last, and should it not, the advocates for reconciliation now will be wishing for separation then, because neutrality in that case would be a safer convoy than a man of war. Every thing that is right or reasonable pleads for separation. The blood of the slain, the weeping voice of nature cries, 'TIS TIME TO PART. Even the distance at which the Almighty hath placed England and America is a strong and natural proof that the authority of the one over the other, was never the design of Heaven. The time likewise at which the Continent was discovered, adds weight to the argument, and the manner in which it was peopled, increases the force of it. The Reformation was preceded by the discovery of America: As if the Almighty graciously meant to open a sanctuary to the persecuted in future years, when home should afford neither friendship nor safety.

The authority of Great Britain over this Continent, is a form of government, which sooner or later must have an end: And a serious mind can draw no true pleasure by looking forward, under the painful and positive conviction that what he calls "the present constitution" is merely temporary. As parents, we can have no joy, knowing that this government is not sufficiently lasting to ensure any thing which we may bequeath to posterity: And by a plain method of argument, as we are running the next generation into debt, we ought to do the work of it, otherwise we use them meanly and pitifully. In order to discover the line of our duty rightly, we should take our children in our hand, and fix our station a few years farther into life; that eminence will present a prospect which a few present fears and prejudices conceal from our sight.

Men of passive tempers look somewhat lightly over the offences of Great Britain, and, still hoping for the best, are apt to call out, *Come, come, we shall be friends again for all this.* But examine the passions and feelings of mankind: bring the doctrine of reconciliation to the touchstone of nature, and then tell me whether you can hereafter love, honour, and faithfully serve the power that hath carried fire and sword into your land? If you cannot do all these, then are you only deceiving yourselves, and by your delay bringing ruin upon posterity. Your future connection with Britain, whom you can neither love nor honour, will be forced and unnatural, and being formed only on the plan of present convenience, will in a little time fall into a relapse more wretched than the first. But if you say, you can still pass the violations over, then I ask, hath your house been burnt? Hath your property been destroyed before your face? Are your wife and children destitute of a bed to lie on, or bread to live on? Have you lost a parent or a child by their hands, and yourself the ruined and wretched survivor? If you have not, then are you not a judge of those who have? But if you have, and can still shake hands with the murderers, then are you unworthy the name of husband, father, friend, or lover, and whatever may be your rank or title in life, you have the heart of a coward, and the spirit of a sycophant.

As to government matters, 'tis not in the power of Britain to do this Continent justice: the business of it will soon be too weighty and intricate to be managed with any tolerable degree of convenience, by a power so distant from us, and so very ignorant of us; for if they cannot conquer us, they cannot govern us. To be always running three or four thousand miles with a tale or a petition, waiting four or five months for an answer, which, when obtained, requires five or six more to explain it in, will in a few years be looked upon as folly and childishness. There was a time when it was proper, and there is a proper time for it to cease.

Small islands not capable of protecting themselves are the proper objects for government to take under their care; but there is something absurd, in supposing a Continent to be perpetually governed by an island. In no instance hath nature made the satellite larger than its primary plant; and as England and America, with respect to each other, reverse the common order of nature, it is evident that they belong to different systems. England to Europe: America to itself. . . .

But admitting that matters were now made up, what would be the event? I answer, the ruin of the Continent. And that for several reasons.

First. The powers of governing still remaining in the hands of the King, he will have a negative over the whole legislation of this Continent. And as he hath shown himself such an inveterate enemy to liberty, and discovered such a thirst for arbitrary power, is he, or is he not a proper person to say to these colonies, *You shall make no laws but what I please!?* And is there any inhabitant of America so ignorant as not to know, that according to what is called the *present constitution,* this Continent can make no laws but what the King gives leave to; and is there any man so unwise as not to see, that (considering what has happened) he will suffer no law to be made here but such as suits *his* purpose? We may be as effectually enslaved by the want of laws in America, as by submitting to laws made for us in England. After matters are made up (as it is called) can there be any doubt, but

the whole power of the crown will be exerted to keep this Continent as low and humble as possible? Instead of going forward we shall go backward, or be perpetually quarrelling, or ridiculously petitioning. We are already greater than the King wishes us to be, and will he not hereafter endeavor to make us less? To bring the matter to one point, Is the power who is jealous of our prosperity, a proper power to govern us? Whoever says *No* to this question, is an Independent for independency means no more than this, whether we shall make our own laws, or, whether the King, the greatest enemy this Continent hath, or can have, shall tell us *there shall be no laws but such as I like.* . . .

Secondly. That as even the best terms which we can expect to obtain can amount to no more than a temporary expedient, or a kind of government by guardianship, which can last no longer than till the Colonies come of age, so the general face and state of things in the interim will be unsettled and unpromising. Emigrants of property will not choose to come to a country whose form of government hangs but by a thread, and who is every day tottering on the brink of commotion and disturbance; and numbers of the present inhabitants would lay hold of the interval to dispose of their effects, and quit the Continent.

But the most powerful of all arguments is, that nothing but independence, i.e. a Continental form of government, can keep the peace of the Continent and preserve it inviolate from civil wars. I dread the event of a reconciliation with Britain now, as it is more than probable that it will be followed by a revolt some where or other, the consequences of which may be far more fatal than all the malice of Britain. . . .

TO CONCLUDE, however strange it may appear to some, or however unwilling they may be to think so, matters not, but many strong and striking reasons may be given to show, that nothing can settle our affairs so expeditiously as an open and determined declaration for independence. Some of which are,

First—It is the custom of Nations, when any two are at war, for some other powers, not engaged in the quarrel, to step in as mediators, and bring about the preliminaries of a peace: But while America calls herself the subject of Great Britain, no power, however well disposed she may be, can offer her mediation. Wherefore, in our present state we may quarrel on for ever.

Secondly—It is unreasonable to suppose, that France or Spain will give us any kind of assistance for the purpose of repairing the breach, and strengthening the connection between Britain and America; because, those powers would be sufferers by the consequences.

Thirdly—While we profess ourselves the subjects of Britain, we must, in the eyes of foreign nations, be considered as Rebels. The precedent is somewhat dangerous to their peace, for men to be in arms under the name of subjects: we, on the spot, can solve the paradox; but to unite resistance and subjection, requires an idea much too refined for common understanding.

Fourthly—Were a manifesto to be published, and despatched to foreign Courts, setting forth the miseries we have endured, and the peaceful methods which we have ineffectually used for redress; declaring at the same time, that not being able any longer to live happily or safely under the cruel disposition of the British Court, we had been driven to the necessity of breaking off all connections with her; at the same time, assuring all such Courts of our peaceable disposition towards them, and of our desire of entering into trade with them: such a memorial would produce more good effects to this Continent, than if a ship were freighted with petitions to Britain.

Under our present denomination of British subjects, we can neither be received nor heard abroad: the custom of all Courts is against us, and will be so, until by an independence we take rank with other nations.

These proceedings may at first seem strange and difficult, but like all other steps which we have already passed over, will in a little time become familiar and agreeable: and until an independence is declared, the Continent will feel itself like a man who continues putting off some unpleasant business from day to day, yet knows it must be done, hates to set about it, wishes it over, and is continually haunted with the thoughts of its necessity. . . .

O ye that love mankind! Ye that dare to oppose not only the tyranny but the tyrant, stand forth! Every spot of the old world is overrun with oppression. Freedom hath been hunted round the globe. Asia and Africa have long expelled her. Europe regards her like a stranger, and England hath given her warning to depart. O! receive the fugitive, and prepare in time an asylum for mankind.

12. The Declaration of Independence in Congress, July 4, 1776

Philosopher, statesman, diplomat, party leader, architect, and third President of the United States, Thomas Jefferson (1743–1826) was born in Albemarle County, Virginia. A graduate of William and Mary College in 1762, he studied and practiced law as a young man while he managed his tobacco plantation. He began his political career in Virginia's House of Burgesses, and in 1774 he published his first political pamphlet, *A Summary View of the Rights of British America.* In June of 1776 he became chairman of the committee appointed by the Second Continental Congress to write a formal statement explaining the reasons for the American separation from Great Britain. Congress officially adopted Jefferson's draft with some revisions on July 4, 1776. He next served his state as Governor and his nation as minister to France, Secretary of State, Vice President, and President of the United States. After leaving office in 1809 he retired to his home at Monticello and founded the University of Virginia. He died on the fiftieth anniversary of the signing of the Declaration of Independence.

The Declaration of Independence consists of three parts. In the first section Jefferson justifies revolution on the grounds of natural laws and the natural rights of the American people for "life, liberty, and the pursuit of happiness." The second part presents a long list of charges against King George III (not Parliament). The conclusion formally proclaims American independence and invites recognition and support from foreign powers.

QUESTIONS

1. What does Jefferson mean by his reference to "the laws of nature and of nature's God"?
2. What does Jefferson mean when he states that "all men are created equal"? What are their "unalienable rights"?
3. What general theory and justification of revolution does he present? How does he justify the American Revolution in particular?
4. Whom does Jefferson blame for causing the troubles between Great Britain and her colonies? What part of the British government is not directly mentioned in his list of charges? Why is it excluded?
5. Is Jefferson's indictment a fair one? Is it convincing?
6. Explain the purpose of the last paragraph.

When in the course of human events, it becomes necessary for one people to dissolve the political bands which have connected them with another, and to assume, among the powers of the earth, the separate and equal station to which the laws of nature and of nature's God entitle them, a decent respect to the opinions of mankind requires that they should declare the causes which impel them to the separation.

We hold these truths to be self-evident: That all men are created equal; that they are endowed by their Creator with certain unalienable rights; that among these are life, liberty, and the pursuit of happiness; that, to secure these rights, governments are instituted among men, deriving their just powers from the consent of the governed; that whenever any form of government becomes destructive of these ends, it is the right of the people to alter or abolish it, and to institute new government, laying its foundation on such principles, and organizing its powers in such form, as to them shall seem most likely to effect their safety and happiness. Prudence, indeed, will dictate that governments long established should not be changed for light or transient causes; and accordingly all experience hath shown that mankind are more disposed to suffer, while evils are sufferable, than to right themselves by abolishing the forms to which they are accustomed. But when a long train of abuses and usurpations, pursuing invariably the same object, evinces a design to reduce them under absolute despotism, it is their right, it is their duty, to throw off such government, and to provide new guards for their future security. Such has been that patient sufferance of these colonies; and such is now the necessity which constrains them to alter their former systems of government. The history of the present King of Great Britain is a history of repeated injuries and usurpations, all having in direct object the establishment of an absolute tyranny over these states. To prove this, let facts be submitted to a candid world.

He has refused his assent to laws, the most wholesome and necessary for the public good.

He has forbidden his governors to pass laws of immediate and pressing importance, unless suspended in their operation till his assent should be obtained; and, when so suspended, he has utterly neglected to attend them.

He has refused to pass other laws for the accommodation of large districts of people, unless those people would relinquish the right of representation in the legislature, a right inestimable to them, and formidable to tyrants only.

He has dissolved representative houses repeatedly, for opposing, with manly firmness, his invasions on the rights of the people.

He has refused for a long time, after such dissolutions, to cause others to be elected; whereby the legislative powers, incapable of annihilation, have returned to the people at large for their exercise; the state remaining, in the mean time, exposed to all the dangers of invasions from without and convulsions within.

He has endeavored to prevent the population of these states; for that purpose obstructing the laws for naturalization of foreigners; refusing to pass others to encourage their migration hither, and raising the conditions of new appropriations of lands.

He has obstructed the administration of justice, by refusing his assent to laws for establishing judiciary powers.

He has made judges dependent on his will alone, for the tenure of their offices, and the amount and payment of their salaries.

He has erected a multitude of new offices, and sent hither swarms of officers to harass our people and eat out their substance.

He has kept among us, in times of peace, standing armies, without consent of our legislatures.

He has affected to render the military independent of, and superior to, the civil power.

He has combined with others to subject us to a jurisdiction foreign to our constitution, and unacknowledged by our laws, giving his assent to their acts of pretended legislation:

For quartering large bodies of armed troops among us;

For protecting them, by a mock trial, from punishment for any murders which they should commit on the inhabitants of these states;

For cutting off our trade with all parts of the world;

For imposing taxes on us without our consent;

For depriving us, in many cases, of the benefits of trial by jury;

For transporting us beyond seas, to be tried for pretended offences;

For abolishing the free system of English laws in a neighboring province, establishing therein an arbitrary government, and enlarging its boundaries, so as to render it at once an example and fit instrument for introducing the same absolute rule into these colonies;

For taking away our charters, abolishing our most valuable laws, and altering fundamentally the forms of our governments;

For suspending our own legislatures, and declaring themselves invested with power to legislate for us in all cases whatsoever.

He has abdicated government here, by declaring us out of his protection and waging war against us.

He has plundered our seas, ravaged our coasts, burned our towns, and destroyed the lives of our people.

He is at this time transporting large armies of foreign mercenaries to complete the works of death, desolation, and tyranny already begun with circumstances of cruelty and perfidy scarcely paralleled in the most barbarous ages, and totally unworthy the head of a civilized nation.

He has constrained our fellow-citizens, taken captive on the high seas, to bear arms against their country, to become the executioners of their friends and brethren, or to fall themselves by their hands.

He has excited domestic insurrection among us, and has endeavored to bring on the inhabitants of our frontiers the merciless Indian savages, whose known rule of warfare is an undistinguished destruction of all ages, sexes, and conditions.

In every stage of these oppressions we have petitioned for redress in the most humble terms; our repeated petitions have been answered only by repeated injury. A prince, whose character is thus marked by every act which may define a tyrant, is unfit to be the ruler of a free people.

Nor have we been wanting in our attentions to our British brethren. We have warned them, from time to time, of attempts by their legislature to extend an unwarrantable jurisdiction over us. We have reminded them of the circumstances of our emigration and settlement here. We have appealed to their native justice and magnanimity; and we have conjured them, by the ties of our common kindred, to disavow these usurpations, which would inevitably interrupt our connections and correspondence. They, too, have been deaf to the voice of justice and of consanguinity. We must, therefore, acquiesce in the necessity which denounces our separation, and hold them, as we hold the rest of mankind, enemies in war, in peace friends.

We, therefore, the representatives of the United States of America, in General Congress assembled, appealing to the Supreme Judge of the world for the rectitude of our intentions, do, in the name and by the authority of the good people of the colonies, solemnly publish and declare, that these United Colonies are, and of right ought to be, FREE AND INDEPENDENT STATES; that they are absolved from all allegiance to the British crown, and that all political connection between them and the state of Great Britain is, and ought to be, totally dissolved; and that, as free and independent states, they have full power to levy war, conclude peace, contract alliances, establish commerce, and do all other acts and things which independent states may of right do. And for the support of this declaration, with a firm reliance on the protection of Divine Providence, we mutually pledge to each other our lives, our fortunes, and our sacred honor.

John Hancock [President] [and fifty-five others]

13. The Constitution of the United States, 1787

On May 25, 1787 a gathering of delegates from the United States of America convened in Philadelphia to write a constitution for the new republic. Over the course of a hot summer fifty-five men representing every state except Rhode Island labored to replace the first American charter, the Articles of Confederation, with a new plan of government. After nearly four months of draining debate and hard compromise the statesmen constructed a document that has endured the strains and challenges of many tests over two centuries.

The framers of the United States Constitution solved three major problems that had plagued the country under the Articles of Confederation. These concerned the powers to be exercised by the national government and the states, the structure of the national government, and the status of slavery in the nation. The Constitution created a republican form of government for the United States and became the highest law in the land. It solved the vexing issue of sovereignty by granting all power to the people of the United States as a whole, who then delegated specific powers to the federal and state governments as spelled out in the document. It protected the liberty of the people through its system of separation of powers and checks and balances, and through the Bill of Rights, added by the first Congress. Finally, it temporarily solved the problem of slavery through compromises on counting slaves for the purposes of taxation and representation, on the return of fugitive slaves, and on banning the importation of slaves.

QUESTIONS

1. According to this document, where does ultimate sovereignty reside in the United States of America?
2. What are the most important powers that are exclusively reserved for the national government? Which powers are reserved to the states? Which are shared by both levels of government?

3. What are the major powers and functions of the President?
4. Why did the framers of this Constitution establish three separate branches of government?
5. What are the major compromises on the issue of slavery?
6. Compare the American Bill of Rights with the English Bill of Rights.

Preamble

We the people of the United States, in order to form a more perfect Union, establish justice, insure domestic tranquility, provide for the common defense, promote the general welfare, and secure the blessings of liberty to ourselves and our posterity, do ordain and establish this Constitution for the United States of America.

Article I

Section I

All legislative powers herein granted shall be vested in a Congress of the United States, which shall consist of a Senate and a House of Representatives. . . .

Section II

Representatives and direct taxes shall be apportioned among the several States which may be included within this Union, according to their respective numbers, which shall be determined by adding to the whole number of free persons, including those bound to service for a term of years and excluding Indians not taxed, three-fifths of all other persons. . . .

Section VII

Every bill which shall have passed the House of Representatives and the Senate, shall, before it become a law, be presented to the President of the United States; if he approve he shall sign it, but if not he shall return it with objections to that house in which it originated, who shall enter the objections at large on their journal, and proceed to reconsider it. If after such reconsideration two-thirds of that house shall agree to pass the bill, it shall be sent, together with the objections, to the other house, by which it shall likewise be reconsidered, and, if approved by two-thirds of that house, it shall become a law. But in all such cases the votes of both houses shall be determined by yeas and nays, and the names of the persons voting for and against the bill shall be entered on the journal of each house respectively. If any bill shall not be returned by the President within ten days (Sundays excepted) after it shall have been presented to him, the same shall be a law, in like manner as if he had signed it, unless the Congress by their adjournment prevent its return, in which case it shall not be a law.

Every order, resolution, or vote to which the concurrence of the Senate and House of Representatives may be necessary (except on a question of adjournment) shall be presented to the President of the United States; and before the same shall take effect, shall be approved by him, or being disapproved by him, shall be repassed by two-thirds of the Senate and House of Representatives, according to the rules and limitations prescribed in the case of a bill.

Section VIII

The Congress shall have the power

To lay and collect taxes, duties, imposts, and excises, to pay the debts and provide for the common defense and general welfare of the United States; but all duties, imposts and excises shall be uniform throughout the United States;

To borrow money on the credit of the United States;

To regulate commerce with foreign nations, and among the several States, and with the Indian tribes;

To establish an uniform rule of naturalization, and uniform laws on the subject of bankruptcies throughout the United States;

To coin money, regulate the value thereof, and of foreign coin, and fix the standard of weights and measures;

To provide for the punishment of counterfeiting the securities and current coin of the United States;

To establish post offices and post roads;

To promote the progress of science and useful arts by securing for limited times to authors and inventors the exclusive right to their respective writings and discoveries;

To constitute tribunals inferior to the Supreme Court;

To define and punish piracies and felonies committed on the high seas and offenses against the law of nations;

To raise and support armies, but no appropriation of money to that use shall be for a longer term than two years;

To make rules for the government and regulation of the land and naval forces;

To provide for calling forth the militia to execute the laws of the Union, suppress insurrections, and repel invasions;

To provide for organizing, arming, and disciplining the militia, and for governing such part of them as may be employed in the service of the United States, reserving to the States respectively the appointment of the officers, and the authority of training the militia according to the discipline prescribed by Congress;

To exercise exclusive legislation in all cases whatsoever, over such district (not exceeding ten miles square) as may, by cession of particular States, and the acceptance of Congress, become the seat of government of the United States, and to exercise like authority over all places purchased by the consent of the legislature of the State, in which the same shall be, for the erections of forts, magazines, arsenals, dock-yards, and other needful buildings;—and

To make all laws which shall be necessary and proper for carrying into execution the foregoing powers, and all other powers vested by this Constitution in the government of the United States, or in any department or officer thereof.

Section IX

The migration or importation of such persons as any of the States now existing shall think proper to admit shall not be prohibited by the Congress prior to the year 1808; but a tax or duty may be imposed on such importation, not exceeding $10 for each person.

Section X

No state shall enter into any treaty, alliance, or confederation; grant letters of marque and reprisal; coin money; emit bills of credit; make anything but gold and silver coin a tender in payment of debts; pass any bill of attainer, ex post facto law, or law impairing the obligation of contracts, or grant any title of nobility.

No State shall, without the consent of Congress, lay any imposts or duties on imports or exports, except what may be absolutely necessary for executing its inspection laws: and the net produce of all duties and imposts, laid by any States on imports or exports, shall be for the use of the treasury of the United States; and all such laws shall be subject to the revision and control of the Congress. . . .

Article II

Section I

The executive power shall be vested in a President of the United States of America. He shall hold his office during the term of four years. . . .

Section II

The President shall be commander in chief of the army and navy of the United States, and of the militia of the several States, when called into the actual service of the United States; he may require the opinion, in writing, of the principal officer in each of the executive departments, upon any subject relating to the duties of their respective offices, and he shall have power to grant reprieves and pardons for offenses against the United States, except in cases of impeachment.

He shall have power, by and with the advice and consent of the Senate, to make treaties, provided two-thirds of the Senators present concur; and he shall nominate, and by and with the advice and consent of the Senate, shall appoint ambassadors, other public ministers and consuls, judges of the Supreme Court, and all other officers of the United States, whose appointments are not herein otherwise provided for, and which shall be established by law; but Congress may by law vest the appointment of such inferior officers, as they think proper, in the President alone, in the courts of law, or in the heads of departments. . . .

Amendments (Bill of Rights) (1791)

Article I

Congress shall make no law respecting an establishment of religion, or prohibiting the free exercise thereof; or abridging the freedom of speech, or of the press; or the right of the people peaceably to assemble, and to petition the government for a redress of grievances.

Article II

A well-regulated militia being necessary to the security of a free State, the right of the people to keep and bear arms shall not be infringed.

Article III

No soldier shall, in time of peace, be quartered in any house without the consent of the owner, nor in time of war, but in a manner to be prescribed by law.

Article IV

The right of the people to be secure in their persons, houses, papers, and effects, against unreasonable searches and seizures, shall not be violated, and no warrants shall issue but upon probable cause, supported by oath or affirmation, and particularly describing the place to be searched, and the persons or things to be seized.

Article V

No person shall be held to answer for a capital, or otherwise infamous crime, unless on a presentment or indictment of a grand jury, except in cases arising in the land or naval forces, or in the militia, when in actual service in time of war or public danger; nor shall any person be subject for the same offense to be twice put in jeopardy of life or limb; nor shall be compelled in any criminal case to be a witness against himself, nor be deprived of life, liberty, or property, without due process of law; nor shall private property be taken for public use without just compensation.

Article VI

In all criminal prosecutions, the accused shall enjoy the right to a speedy and public trial, by an impartial jury of the State and district wherein the crime shall have been committed, which district shall have been previously ascertained by law, and to be informed of the nature and cause of the accusation; to be confronted with the witnesses against him; to have compulsory process for obtaining witnesses in his favor, and to have the assistance of counsel for his defense.

Article VII

In suits at common law, where the value in controversy shall exceed twenty dollars, the right of trial by jury shall be preserved, and no fact tried by a jury shall be otherwise reexamined in any court of the United States, than according to the rules of the common law.

Article VIII

Excessive bail shall not be required, nor excessive fines imposed, nor cruel and unusual punishments inflicted.

Article IX

The enumeration in the Constitution, of certain rights, shall not be construed to deny or disparage others retained by the people.

Article X

The powers not delegated to the United States by the Constitution, nor prohibited by it to the States, are reserved to the States respectively, or to the people.

14. What Is the Third Estate? 1789

Emmanuel Joseph Sieyès

As the French people prepared to choose deputies to the meeting of the Estates General in 1789, hundreds of writers published pamphlets that discussed the upcoming elections. One of the most important of these publications was *What Is the Third Estate?*, which was written by a clergyman who was steeped in the ideas of the Enlightenment, Emmanuel Joseph Sieyès (1748–1836), and which appeared in January 1789. This piece had a critical impact in stirring the political consciousness and in promoting the interests of many members of the third estate.

Sieyès's authorship of this essay propelled him into political prominence. Although as a cleric he was a member of the first estate, he was chosen by the electors of Paris to represent the third estate. He played a prominent role in the establishment of the National Assembly as a sovereign body, and soon became one of its leaders. He was active in drafting the Declaration of the Rights of Man and Citizen. He survived the Reign of Terror, served as one of the Directors during the late 1790s, and took part in the coup d'état that brought Napoleon Bonaparte to power.

QUESTIONS

1. How did Sieyès define the French nation? What did he believe were the roles and contributions of the Third Estate and the privileged order?
2. According to Sieyès, how did the political system in France discriminate against the Third Estate? What specific political reforms does he advocate?

The plan of this pamphlet is very simple. We have three questions to ask: 1st. What is the third estate? Everything. 2nd. What has it been heretofore in the political order? Nothing. 3rd. What does it demand: To become something therein. . . .

Chapter I The Third Estate Is a Complete Nation

What are the essentials of national existence and prosperity? *Private* enterprise and *public* functions.

Private enterprise may be divided into four classes: 1st. Since earth and water furnish the raw material for man's needs, the first class will comprise all families engaged in agricultural pursuits. 2nd. Between the original sale of materials and their consumption or use, further workmanship, more or less manifold, adds to these materials a second value, more or less compounded.

Human industry thus succeeds in perfecting the benefits of nature and in increasing the gross produce twofold, tenfold, one hundredfold in value. Such is the work of the second class. 3rd. Between production and consumption, as well as among the different degrees of production, a group of intermediate agents, useful to producers as well as to consumers, comes into being; these are the dealers and merchants. . . . 4th. In addition to these three classes of industrious and useful citizens concerned with goods for consumption and use, a society needs many private undertakings and endeavors which are *directly* useful or agreeable to the *individual*. This fourth class includes from the most distinguished scientific and liberal professions to the least esteemed domestic services. Such are the labors which sustain society. Who performs them? The third estate.

Public functions likewise under present circumstances may be classified under four well known headings: the Sword, the Robe, the Church, and the Administration. It is unnecessary to discuss them in detail in order to demonstrate that the third estate everywhere constitutes nineteenth-twentieths of them, except that it is burdened with all that is really arduous, with all the tasks that the privileged order refuses to perform. Only the lucrative and honorary positions are held by members of the privileged order . . . nevertheless they have dared lay the order of the third estate under an interdict. They had said to it: "Whatever be your services, whatever your talents, you shall do thus far and no farther. It is not fitting that you be honored."

. . . It suffices here to have revealed that the alleged utility of a privileged order to public service is only a chimera; that without it, all that is arduous in such service is performed by the third estate; that without it, the higher positions would be infinitely better filled; that they naturally ought to be the lot of and reward for talents and recognized services; and that if the privileged classes have succeeded in usurping all the lucrative and honorary positions, it is both an odious injustice to the majority of citizens and a treason to the commonwealth.

Who, then would dare to say that the third estate has not within itself all that is necessary to constitute a complete nation? It is the strong and robust man whose one arm remains enchained. If the privileged order were abolished, the nation would be not something less but something more. Thus, what is the third estate? Everything; but an everything shackled and oppressed. What would it be without the privileged order? Everything; but an everything free and flourishing. Nothing can progress without it; everything would proceed infinitely better without the others. It is not sufficient to have demonstrated that the privileged classes, far from being useful to the nation,

can only enfeeble and injure it; it is necessary, moreover, to prove that the nobility does not belong to the social organization at all; that, indeed, it may be a *burden* upon the nation, but that it would not know how to constitute a part thereof. . . .

What is a nation? a body of associates living under a common law and represented by the same *legislature.*

Is it not exceedingly clear that the noble order has privileges, exemptions, even rights separate from the rights of the majority of citizens? Thus it deviates from the common order, from the common law. Thus its civil rights already render it a people apart in a great nation. It is indeed *imperium in imperio.*

Also, it enjoys its political rights separately. It has its own representatives, who are by no means charged with representing the people. Its deputation sits apart; and when it is assembled in the same room with the deputies of ordinary citizens, it is equally true that its representation is essentially distinct and separate; it is foreign to the nation in principle, since its mandate does not emanate from the people, and in aim, since its purpose is to defend not the general but a special interest.

The third estate, then, comprises everything appertaining to the nation; and whatever is not the third estate may not be regarded as being of the nation. What is the third estate? Everything!

Chapter II What Has the Third Estate Been Heretofore? Nothing

. . . The third estate must be understood to mean the mass of the citizens belonging to the common order. Legalized privilege in any form deviates from the common order, constitutes an exception to the common law, and consequently, does not appertain to the third estate at all. We repeat, a common law and a common representation are what constitute one nation. It is only too true that one is *nothing* in France when one has only the protection of the common law; if one does not possess some privilege, one must resign oneself to enduring contempt, injury, and vexations of every sort. . . .

But here we have to consider the order of the third estate less in its civil status than in its relation with the constitution. Let us examine its position in the Estates General.

Who have been its so-called representatives: The ennobled or those privileged for a period of years. These false deputies have not even been always freely elected by the people. Sometimes in the Estates General, and almost always in the provincial Estates, the representation of the people has been regarded as perquisite of certain posts or offices. . . . Add to this appalling truth that, in one manner or another, all branches of the executive power also have fallen to the caste which furnishes the Church, the Robe, and the Sword. A sort of spirit of brotherhood causes the nobles to prefer themselves . . . to the rest of the nation. Usurpation is complete; in truth, they reign.

. . . it is a great error to believe that France is subject to a monarchical regime. . . . It is the court, and not the monarch, that has reigned. It is the court that makes and unmakes, appoints and discharges ministers, creates and dispenses positions, etc. And what is the court if not the head of this immense aristocracy which overruns all parts of France; which through its members attains all and everywhere does whatever is essential in all parts of the commonwealth? . . .

Let us sum up: the third estate has not heretofore had real representatives in the Estates General. Thus its political rights are null.

Chapter III What Does the Third Estate Demand?

To Become Something

. . . The true petitions of this order may be appreciated only through the authentic claims directed to the government by the large municipalities of the kingdom. What is indicated therein? That the people wishes to be *something,* and, in truth, the very least that is possible. It wishes to have real representatives in the Estates General, that is to say deputies *drawn from its order,* who are competent to be interpreters of its will and defenders of its interests. But what will it avail it to be present at the Estates General if the predominating interest there is contrary to its own! Its presence would only consecrate the oppression of which it would be the eternal victim. Thus, it is indeed certain that it cannot come to vote at the Estates General unless it is to have in that body an *influence at least equal to that of the privileged classes;* and it demands a number of representatives equal to that of the first two orders together. Finally, this equality of representation would become completely illusory if every chamber voted separately. The third estate demands, then, that votes be taken *by head and not by order.* This is the essence of those claims so alarming to the privileged classes, because they believe that thereby the reform of abuses would become inevitable. The real intention of the third estate is to have an influence in the Estates General equal to that of the privileged classes. I repeat, can it ask less? And is it not clear that if its influence therein is less than equality, it cannot be expected to emerge from its political nullity and become *something?*

15. Grievances of the Third Estate, 1789

During the spring of 1789 the three estates of France held elections to choose delegates who would attend the meeting of the Estates General. At the same time each group drew up lists of grievances (*cahiers de doléances*) that would be discussed at that gathering. All three orders of society called for a new system of constitutional monarchy with an elected legislature. But while the clergy and the nobility stressed the preservation of their ancient privileges and rights, the representatives of the third estate demanded sweeping reforms in most areas of French life and government. The following presents the proposals of the common people of Dourdan, in the district of Orleans.

QUESTIONS

1. What basic principles pervade this Cahier of the Third Estate of Dourdan?
2. What are the most radical reform proposals made in this statement of grievances?
3. What attitude toward the King is conveyed in this document?
4. Compare this document with the selection from Sieyès's *What Is the Third Estate?* What common themes appear in both?

The order of the third estate of the City, *Bailliage* [judicial district], and County of Dourdan, imbued with gratitude prompted by the paternal kindness of the King, who deigns to restore its former rights and its former constitution, forgets at this moment its misfortunes and impotence, to harken only to its foremost sentiment and its foremost duty, that of sacrificing everything to the glory of the *Patrie* and the service of His Majesty. It supplicates him to accept the grievances, complaints, and remonstrances which it is permitted to bring to the foot of the throne, and to see therein only the expression of its zeal and the homage of its obedience.

It wishes:

1. That his subjects of the third estate, equal by such status to all other citizens, present themselves before the common father without other distinction which might degrade them.

2. That all the orders, already united by duty and a common desire to contribute equally to the needs of the State, also deliberate in common concerning its needs.

3. That no citizen lose his liberty except according to law; that, consequently, no one be arrested by virtue of special orders, or, if imperative circumstances necessitate such orders, that the prisoner be handed over to the regular courts of justice within forty-eight hours at the latest.

4. That no letters or writings intercepted in the post be the cause of the detention of any citizen, or be produced in court against him, except in case of conspiracy or undertaking against the State.

5. That the property of all citizens be inviolable, and that no one be required to make sacrifice thereof for the public welfare, except

upon assurance of indemnification based upon the statement of freely selected appraisers. . . .

12. That every tax, direct or indirect, be granted only for a limited time, and that every collection beyond such term be regarded as peculation [taking of public funds for private gain], and punished as such. . . .

15. That every personal tax be abolished; that thus the *capitation* and the *taille* and its accessories be merged with the *vingtièmes* in a tax on land and real or nominal property.

16. That such tax be borne equally, without distinction, by all classes of citizens and by all kinds of property, even feudal and contingent rights. . . .

18. That provincial Estates, subordinate to the Estates General, be established and charged with the assessment and levying of subsidies, with their deposit in the national treasury, with the administration of all public works, and with the examination of all projects conducive to the prosperity of lands situated within the limits of their jurisdiction.

19. That such Estates be composed of freely elected deputies of the three orders from the cities, boroughs, and parishes subject to their administration, and in the proportion established for the next session of the Estates General.

Justice

1. That the administration of justice be reformed, either by restoring strict execution of ordinances, or by reforming the sections thereof that are contrary to the dispatch and welfare of justice. . . .

7. That venality [sale] of offices be suppressed by successive reimbursement in proportion to their disestablishment; that, accordingly, a fund be constituted forthwith to effect such reimbursement.

8. That the excessive number of offices in the necessary courts be reduced in just measure, and that no one be given an office of magistracy if he is not at least twenty-five years of age, and until after a substantial public examination has verified his morality, integrity, and ability. . . .

11. That a body of general customary law be drafted of all articles common to all the customs of the several provinces and *bailliages,* and that the customs of the several provinces and *bailliages* thereafter contain only articles which are in exception to the general custom.

12. That deliberations of courts and companies of magistracy which tend to prevent entry of the third estate thereto be rescinded and annulled as injurious to the citizens of that order, in contempt of the authority of the King, whose choice they limit, and contrary to the welfare of justice, the administration of which would become the patrimony of those of noble birth instead of being entrusted to merit, enlightenment, and virtue.

13. That military ordinances which restrict entrance to the service to those possessing nobility be reformed.

That naval ordinances establishing a degrading distinction between officers born into the order of nobility and those born into that of the third estate be revoked, as thoroughly injurious to an order of citizens and destructive of the competition so necessary to the glory and prosperity of the State.

Finances

1. That if the Estates General considers it necessary to preserve the fees of *aides* [tax on commodities], such fees be made uniform throughout the entire kingdom and reduced to a single denomination. . . .

2. That the tax of the *gabelle* [tax on salt] be eliminated if possible, or that it be regulated among the several provinces of the kingdom. . . .

3. That the taxes on hides, which have totally destroyed that branch of commerce and caused it to go abroad, be suppressed forever.

4. That . . . all useless offices, either in police or in the administration of justice, be abolished and suppressed.

Agriculture

15. That the militia, which devastates the country, takes workers away from husbandry, produces premature and illmatched marriages, and imposes secret and arbitrary taxes upon those who are subject thereto, be suppressed and replaced by voluntary enlistment at the expense of the provinces.

Commerce

1. That every regulation which tends to impede the business of citizens be revoked.

3. That all toll rights and other similar ones be suppressed throughout the interior of the kingdom, that customhouses be moved back to the frontiers. . . .

Morals

1. That in the chief town of every *bailliage* a public school be established, where young citizens may be brought up in the principles of religion and provided with the necessary education by methods authorized by His Majesty on the request of the nation.

2. That in cities and villages schools be established where the poor will be admitted without cost, and instructed in whatever is necessary for them concerning either morals or their individual interests.

3. That livings and benefices for the care of souls henceforth be granted only by competitive examination.

4. That prelates and *curés* be subject to perpetual residence, under penalty of loss of the fruits of their benefices. . . .

7. That every lottery, the effect of which is to corrupt public morals, every loan involving the element of chance, the effect of which is to encourage speculation and divert funds destined for agriculture and commerce, be proscribed forever.

8. That every community be required to provide for the maintenance of its invalid poor; that, accordingly, all private alms be strictly forbidden; that in every district a charity workshop be established, the funds for which shall be composed of voluntary contributions of individuals and sums which the provincial Estates shall designate therefor, in order to assure constant work for the able-bodied poor.

---

16. Declarations of Rights and Preamble to French Constitution

Once the National Assembly (also known as the Constituent Assembly) was established with the three estates consolidated together, it addressed the problem of formulating a constitution. At first there were differences of opinion on the question of whether the members should first prepare a statement of general principles. Some deputies were concerned that such a pronouncement might limit the options of the Assembly. But those who wished to emulate the American example of the Declaration of Independence and the Bill of Rights prevailed. The Declaration of the Rights of Man and Citizen was adopted on August 26, 1789. It reflected the ideas of the era, and laid the foundations of the new order. Relying heavily on British and American precedents, it also gave expression to French experience and needs. It recognized the existence of certain "natural rights" to be enjoyed by all citizens equally, and it established the principle that sovereignty belonged to the entire nation. Yet it was also silent on some rights, as for example the rights of assembly and petition.

The second selection that appears below is a manifesto of women's rights written by Olympe de Gouges (1743–1793). The daughter of a butcher, she was self-educated and a playwright and author of pamphlets who argued that men could never be free so long as women were oppressed. She lobbied against the traditional dowry system and in favor of the extension of educational opportunities for women, who she believed should also have equal property rights and access to government employment. While her Declaration is clearly modelled on the National Assembly's Declaration of the Rights of Man and Citizen, often simply substituting "Woman" for "Man," it goes beyond it in her assertions that women have the same natural rights as men and that motherhood is an additional source of rights for women in civil society. She was torn between her loyalty to the monarchy (she had volunteered to serve as defense counsel at Louis XVI's trial) and to constitutionalism. She fell afoul of Robespierre and the Jacobins; she was tried under the Terror and guillotined in November, 1793. Despite her efforts the Revolution brought only very modest gains for women in France. The cahiers of grievances (see Document 15) make very little reference to women, except for some pleas for women's education and the exclusion of men from such women's occupations as embroidery. Actual legislation was limited to an act in 1790 that restricted the right of the eldest male in inheritance; in 1792 divorce was legalized but it had little importance owing to women's lack of economic independence.

The final piece that follows below is the preamble to the Constitution of 1791, the first of about a dozen that the French people adopted over the next two centuries. The full document contains 207 articles, many of them statements of abstract principles. It created a constitutional monarchy with a strong unicameral legislature that had the prerogative solely to initiate legislation and allotted the king only a suspensive veto through two legislative sessions. However, perhaps inevitably, much of the royal government and administration—long in place and functioning—was carried over under the new system. The document required all citizens to swear allegiance to the nation, the law, and the king. The Constitution distinguished between "active" and "passive" citizens on the basis of a property qualification. "Active" citizens paid an annual tax equivalent to three days' wages and could sit in local assemblies to choose "electors" (who qualified by a tax equal to ten days' wages) who then elected "deputies" (they met a much higher property qualification) for a two-year term in the Assembly.

"Passive" citizens sat on the sidelines, having the right to protection of their persons, their liberty, and their property. There was no ratification process beyond the king's accepting the Constitution and taking the oath to it.

QUESTIONS

1. What purpose did the writers of the Declaration of Rights intend the document to have? Was it supposed to describe reality as it was? Was it a law to be obeyed? Was it a standard against which to measure reality?
2. According to the Declaration, what do all men share by birth and what makes it possible for them to differ from one another in public life?
3. What does the Declaration say about the nature of political liberty? What are its limits, and how are they determined?
4. How does the Declaration show the influence of the American Declaration of Independence?
5. On what basis does Gouges demand equal rights for women? What does she call for women to do?
6. Why might the revolution have contributed so little to women's emancipation?
7. What is the balance of negative and positive provisions in the Constitution of 1791? Why so much "demolition"? Is it bourgeois? democratic, moderate, or conservative?

A. Declaration of the Rights of Man and Citizen, 1789

The Representatives of the French people, organized in National Assembly, considering that ignorance, forgetfulness, or contempt of rights of man are the sole causes of public misfortunes and of the corruption of governments, have resolved to set forth in a solemn declaration the natural, inalienable, and sacred rights of man, in order that such declaration, continually before all members of the social body, may be a perpetual reminder of their rights and duties; in order that the acts of the legislative power and those of the executive power may constantly be compared with the aim of every political institution and may accordingly be more respected; in order that the demands of the citizens, founded henceforth upon simple and incontestable principles, may always be directed towards the maintenance of the Constitution and the welfare of all.

Accordingly, the National Assembly recognizes and proclaims, in the presence and under the auspices of the Supreme Being, the following rights of man and citizen.

1. Men are born and remain free and equal in rights; social distinctions may be based only upon general usefulness.
2. The aim of every political association is the preservation of the natural and inalienable rights of man; these rights are liberty, property, security, and resistance to oppression.
3. The source of all sovereignty resides essentially in the nation; no group, no individual may exercise authority not emanating expressly therefrom.

4. Liberty consists in the power of doing whatever is not injurious to others; thus the enjoyment of the natural rights of every man has for its limits only those that assure other members of society the enjoyment of those same rights; such limits may be determined only by law.

5. The law has the right to forbid only actions which are injurious to society. What is not forbidden may not be prevented, and no one may be constrained to do what it does not prescribe.

6. Law is the expression of the general will; all citizens have the right to concur personally, or through their representatives, in its formation; it must be the same for all, whether it protects or punishes. All citizens, being equal before it, are equally admissible to all public offices, positions, and employments, according to their capacity, and without other distinction than that of virtues and talents.

7. No man may be accused, arrested, or detained except in the cases determined by law, and according to forms prescribed thereby. Whoever solicit, expedite, or execute arbitrary orders, or have them executed, must be punished; but every citizen summoned or apprehended in pursuance of the law must obey immediately; he renders himself culpable by resistance.

8. The law is to establish only penalties that are absolutely and obviously necessary; and no one may be punished except by virtue of a law established and promulgated prior to the offence and legally applied.

9. Since every man is presumed innocent until declared guilty, if arrest be deemed indispensable, all unnecessary severity for securing the person of the accused must be severely repressed by law.

10. No one is to be disquieted because of his opinions, even religious, provided their manifestation does not disturb the public order established by law.

11. Free communication of ideas and opinions is one of the most precious of the rights of man. Consequently, every citizen may speak, write, and print freely, subject to responsibility for the abuse of such liberty in the cases determined by law.

12. The guarantee of the rights of man and citizen necessitates a public force; such a force, therefore, is instituted for the advantage of all and not for the particular benefit of those to whom it is entrusted.

13. For the maintenance of the public force and for the expenses of administration a common tax is indispensable; it must be assessed equally on all citizens in proportion to their means.

14. Citizens have the right to ascertain, by themselves or through their representatives, the necessity of the public tax, to consent to it freely, to supervise its use, and to determine its quota, assessment, payment, and duration.

15. Society has the right to require of every public agent an accounting of his administration.

16. Every society in which the guarantee of rights is not assured or the separation of powers not determined has no constitution at all.

17. Since property is a sacred and inviolable right, no one may be deprived thereof unless a legally established public necessity obviously requires it, and upon condition of a just and previous indemnity.

B. Declaration of the Rights of Woman and Citizen, 1791

Olympe de Gouges

The mothers, daughters, sisters, representatives of the nation, ask to constitute a National Assembly. Considering that ignorance, forgetfulness or contempt of the rights of women are the sole causes of public miseries, and of corruption of governments, they have resolved to set forth in a solemn declaration, the natural, unalterable and sacred rights of woman, so that this declaration, being ever present to all members of the social body, may unceasingly remind them of their rights and their duties; in order that the acts of woman's power, as well as those of men, may be judged constantly against the aim of all political institutions, and thereby be more respected for it, in order that the complaints of women citizens, based henceforth on simple and indisputable principles, may always take the direction of maintaining the Constitution, good morals and the welfare of all.

In consequence, the sex superior in beauty and in courage in maternal suffering recognizes and declares, in the presence of the Supreme Being, the following rights of woman and of the woman citizen. . . .

Article IV—Liberty and Justice consist in giving back to others all that belongs to them; thus the only limits on the exercise of woman's natural rights are the perpetual tyranny by which man opposes her; these limits must be reformed by the laws of nature and of reason. . . .

Article X—No one ought to be disturbed for one's opinions, however fundamental they are; since a woman has the right to mount the scaffold, she must also have the right to mount the tribune, provided her interventions do not disturb the public order as it has been established by law.

Article XI—The free communication of ideas and opinions is one of the most precious rights of woman, since this freedom ensures the legitimacy of fathers toward their children. Every woman citizen can

therefore say freely: I am the mother of a child that belongs to you, without being forced to conceal the truth because of a barbaric prejudice; except to be answerable for abuses of this liberty as determined by law. . . .

Article XIII—For the upkeep of public forces and for administrative expenses, the contributions of woman and man are equal; a woman shares in all the labors required by law, in the painful tasks; she must therefore have an equal share in the distribution of offices, employments, trusts, dignities and work.

Article XVII—Ownership of property is for both sexes, mutually and separately; it is for each a sacred and inviolable right; no one can be deprived of it as a true patrimony from nature, unless a public necessity, legally established, evidently demands it, and with the condition of a just and prior indemnity.

Afterword

Woman, wake up! The alarm bell of reason is making itself heard throughout the universe; recognize your rights. The powerful empire of nature is no longer beset by prejudices, fanaticism, superstition and lies. The torch of truth has dispelled all clouds of stupidity and usurpation. The enslaved man multiplied his forces but has had to resort to yours to break his chains. Once free he became unjust to his female companion. O women! women, when will you stop being blind? What advantages have you received from the Revolution? A more pronounced scorn, a more marked contempt? During the centuries of corruption, your only power was over the weaknesses of men. Your empire is destroyed, what then is left to you? The conviction that men are unjust. The claiming of your patrimony based on the wise laws of nature. The good word of the Lawgiver of the Marriage at Cana? Are you afraid that our French lawmakers, correctors of this morality, so long tied up with the politics which is no longer in style, will say to you: "Women, what is there in common between you and us?"—Everything, you would have to reply. If they persisted in their weakness, in putting forth this inconsistency which is a contradiction of their principles, you should courageously oppose these hale pretensions of superiority with the force of reason; unite under the banner of philosophy, unfold all the energy of your character and you will soon see these proud men, your servile adorers, crawling at your feet. . . . Whatever the obstacles that oppose us may be, it is in your power to free us, you have only to will it. . . . Since it is now a question of national education, let us see if our wise lawmakers will think wisely about the education of women.

C. Preamble to the French Constitution of 1791

The National Assembly, wishing to establish the French constitution on the principles it has just recognized and declared, abolishes irrevocably the institutions which were injurious to liberty and equality of rights.

Neither nobility, nor peerage, nor hereditary distinctions, nor distinctions of orders, nor feudal regime, nor patrimonial courts, nor any titles, denominations or prerogatives derived therefrom, nor any order of knighthood, nor any corporations or decorations requiring proofs of nobility or implying distinctions of birth, nor any superiority other than that of public functionaries in the performance of their duties any longer exists.

Neither venality nor inheritance of any public office any longer exists.

Neither privilege nor exception to the law common to all Frenchmen any longer exists for any part of the nation or for any individual.

Neither *jurands* [guilds] nor corporations of professions, arts and crafts any longer exist.

The law no longer recognizes religious vows or any other obligation contrary to natural rights or the Constitution.

Title I: Fundamental Provisions Guaranteed by the Constitution

The Constitution guarantees as natural and civil rights:

1st, That all citizens are admissible to all offices and employments without other distinction than virtues and talents.

2nd, That all taxes shall be assessed equally upon all citizens, in proportion to their means.

3rd, That similar offences shall be punished with similar penalties, without any distinction of persons.

The Constitution guarantees likewise as natural and civil rights:

Liberty to every man to come and go without being subject to arrest or detention, except according to the forms determined by the Constitution;

Liberty to every man to speak, write, print, and publish his opinions without having his writings subject to any censorship or inspection before their publication, and to worship as he pleases;

Liberty to citizens to assemble peacefully and without arms in accordance with police regulations;

Liberty to address individually signed petitions to the constituted authorities.

The legislative power may not make any laws which infringe upon or obstruct the exercise of the natural and civil rights recorded in the present title and guaranteed by the Constitution; but, since liberty consists of being able to do only whatever is not injurious to the rights of others or to public security, the law may establish penalties for acts which, assailing either public security or the rights of others, might be injurious to society.

The Constitution guarantees the inviolability of property, or a just and previous indemnity for that of which a legally established public necessity requires the sacrifice.

Property reserved for the expenses of worship and for all services of public benefit belongs to the nation, and is at its disposal at all times.

The Constitution guarantees conveyances which have been or may be made according to the forms established by law.

Citizens have the right to elect or choose the ministers of their religions.

A general establishment for *public relief* shall be created and organized to raise foundlings, relieve the infirm poor, and furnish work for the able-bodied poor who have been unable to procure it for themselves.

Public instruction for all citizens, free of charge in those branches of education which are indispensable to all men, shall be constituted and organized, and the establishments thereof shall be apportioned gradually, in accordance with the division of the kingdom.

National festivals shall be instituted to preserve the memory of the French Revolution, to maintain fraternity among the citizens, and to bind them to the Constitution, the *Patrie,* and the laws.

A code of civil law common to the entire kingdom shall be drafted.

---

17. Reflections on the Revolution in France, 1790

Edmund Burke

Born in Ireland, Burke (1729–1797) was the son of a Protestant father and Catholic mother. He made a political career in England as secretary to the Whig leader, the Marquis of Rockingham, and as a member of Parliament 1765–1795. A member of one of the most memorable opposition parties in the history of Parliament, he was well known as an eloquent liberal and reformer. He supported the colonists during the American revolution and flayed the government of George III and Lord North. Burke himself also attacked British misrule in Ireland and India. The central question about Burke is his consistency or inconsistency, after he had supported the American revolution and other similar causes, in condemning the French revolution. He did so as early as 1790 during that rebellion's moderate stage. He did not confine himself to an attack on its extremism and violence; he also extended his analysis to a searching attack on the philosophical justification of such radical and rapid change. He predicted the cycle in France of a reign of terror that would end with a military despotism. Burke was not specially knowledgeable about events in France, and his fundamental concern was with Britain. Within a year of the publication of his *Reflections* (1790) the Whig party split into two factions. One side pleaded that the cause of liberty was advanced despite that great upheaval's excesses and crimes, while Burke opposed the revolt. Once war broke out between France and Britain in 1793, Burke's views became orthodox and widespread and greatly influenced government policy. He became the toast of his old enemies, the Tories, and George III praised the *Reflections,* recommending that everyone read it; Louis XVI is reported to have translated it and Catherine of Russia congratulated Burke. Burke has had many followers and is seen as the fountainhead of the philosophy of conservatism.

QUESTIONS

1. Make the case either for Burke's consistency or inconsistency in his views on the American and French revolutions. Why did Burke so detest the French revolution? Was he opposed to all change? Explain your answer.
2. Describe Burke's concept of society, of government, and of history.
3. What is Burke's attitude toward majority rule, reason, natural rights, and the philosophes of the Enlightenment?

It appears to me as if I were in a great crisis, not of the affairs of France alone, but of all Europe, perhaps of more than Europe. All circumstances taken together, the French Revolution is the most astonishing that has hitherto happened in the world. . . . In viewing this monstrous tragi-comic scene, the most opposite passions necessarily succeed, and sometimes mix with each other in the mind; alternate contempt and indignation; alternate laughter and tears; alternate scorn and horror.

It cannot, however, be denied, that to some [such as Richard Price] this strange scene . . . . inspired no other sentiments than those of exultation and rapture. They saw nothing in what has been done in France, but a firm and temperate exertion of freedom . . . . [The principles of the French revolution and the English revolution of 1688, according to them, are the same:]

1. "To choose our own governors."
2. "To cashier them for misconduct."
3. "To frame a government for ourselves."

This new, and hitherto unheard of, bill of rights, though made in the name of the whole people, belongs to those gentlemen and their faction only. . . . It is necessary that we should separate what they confound. We must recall their erring fancies to the *acts* of the Revolution [of 1688] which we revere, for the discovery of its true *principles*. If the true *principles* of the Revolution of 1688 are anywhere to be found, it is in the statute called the Declaration of Right. In that most wise, sober, and considerate declaration, drawn up by great lawyers and great statesmen, and not by warm and inexperienced enthusiasts, not one word is said, not one suggestion made, of a general right "to choose our own *governors; to cashier them for misconduct; and to *form* a government for ourselves."* . . .

You will observe that from Magna Carta [1215] to the Declaration of Right [1689], it has been the uniform policy of our constitution to claim and assert our liberties, as an *entailed inheritance* derived to us from our forefathers, and to be transmitted to our posterity; as an estate specially belonging to the people of this kingdom, without any reference whatever to any more general or prior right. By this means our constitution preserves a unity in so great a diversity of its parts. We have an inheritable crown; an inheritable peerage; and a House of Commons and a people inheriting privileges, franchises, and liberties, from a long line of ancestors.

This policy appears to me to be the result of profound reflection; or rather the happy effect of following nature, which is wisdom without reflection, and above it. A spirit of innovation is generally the result of a selfish temper and confined views. People will not look forward to posterity, who never look backward to their ancestors. Besides, the people of England will know, that the idea of inheritance furnishes a sure principle of conservation and a sure principle of transmission; without at all excluding a principle of improvement. . . .

In this choice of inheritance we have given to our frame of polity the image of a relation in blood; binding up the constitution of our country with our dearest domestic ties; adopting our fundamental laws into the bosoms of our family affections; keeping inseparable, and cherishing with the warmth of all their combined and mutually reflected charities, our state, our hearths, our sepulchres, and our altars.

Compute your gains [Frenchmen]: see what is got by those extravagant and presumptuous speculations which have taught your leaders to despise all their predecessors, and all their contemporaries, and even to despise themselves, until the moment in which they became truly despicable. By following those false lights, France has brought undisguised calamities at a higher price than any nation has purchased the most unequivocal blessings! France has bought poverty by crime! France has not sacrificed her virtue to her interest, but she has abandoned her interest, that she might prostitute her virtue. . . . France, when she let loose the reins of regal authority, doubled the license of a ferocious dissoluteness in manners, and of an insolent irreligion in opinions and practices; and has extended through all ranks of life, as if she were communicating some privilege, or laying open some secluded benefit, all the unhappy corruptions that usually were the disease of wealth and power. This is one of the new principles of equality in France. . . .

[T]he constitution of a state, and the due distribution of its powers, [are] a matter of the most delicate and complicated skill. It requires a deep knowledge of human nature and human necessities, and of the things which facilitate or obstruct the various ends, which are to be pursued by the mechanism of civil institutions. . . .

The science of constructing a commonwealth, or renovating it, or reforming it, is like every other experimental science, not to be taught *a priori*. Nor is it a short experience that can instruct us in that practical science; because the real effects of moral causes are not always immediate; but that which in the first instance is prejudicial may be excellent in its remoter operation; and its excellence may arise even from the ill effects it produces in the beginning. The reverse also happens; and very plausible schemes, with very pleasing commencements, have often shameful and lamentable conclusions. In states there are often some obscure and almost latent causes, things which appear at first view of little moment, on which a very great part of its prosperity or adversity may most essentially depend. The science of government being therefore so practical in itself, and intended for such practical purposes, a matter which requires experience, and even more experience than any person can in his whole life, however sagacious and observing he may be, it is with infinite caution that any man ought to venture upon pulling down an edifice, which has answered in any tolerable degree for ages the common purposes of society, or on building it up again, without having models and patterns of approved utility before his eyes.

Your literary men, and your politicians [of France] have no respect for the wisdom of others; but they pay it off by a very full measure of confidence in their own. With them it is a sufficient motive to destroy an old scheme of things, because it is an old one. As to the new, they are in no sort of fear with regard to the duration of a building run up in haste; because duration is no object to those who think little or nothing has been done before their time, and who place all their hopes in discovery. They conceive, very systematically, that all things which give perpetuity are mischievous, and therefore they are at inexpiable war with all establishments. . . . Their attachment to their country itself is only so far as it agrees with some of their fleeting projects. . . . We are resolved to keep an established church, an established monarchy, and an established aristocracy, and an established democracy, each in its degree, and in no greater. . . .

Society is indeed a contract. Subordinate contracts for objects of mere occasional interest may be dissolved at pleasure—but the state ought not to be considered as nothing better than a partnership agreement in a trade of pepper and coffee, calico or tobacco, or some other such low concern, to be taken up for a little temporary interest, and to be dissolved by the fancy of the parties. It is to be looked upon with . . . reverence; because it is not a partnership in things subservient only to the gross animal existence of a temporary and perishable nature. It is a partnership in all science; a partnership in all art; a partnership in every virtue, and in all perfection. As the ends of such a partnership cannot be obtained in many generations, it becomes a partnership not only between those who are living, but between those who are living, those who are dead, and those who are to be born.

We do not draw the moral lessons we might from history. On the contrary, without care it may be used to vitiate our minds and to destroy our happiness. In history a great volume is unrolled for our instruction, drawing the materials of future wisdom from the past errors and infirmities of mankind. It may, in the perversion, serve for a magazine, furnishing offensive and defensive weapons for parties in church and state, and supplying the means of keeping alive, or reviving animosities, and adding fuel to civil fury. History consists, for the greater part, of the miseries brought upon the world by pride, ambition, avarice, revenge, lust, sedition, hypocrisy, ungoverned zeal, and all the train of disorderly appetites, which shake the public with the same "troublous storms that toss/The private state, and render life unsweet. . . ."

18. Levée en Masse and Law of Suspects, 1793

During the summer and fall of 1793 foreign invasion and internal rebellion threatened the new French Republic and its legislative body, the National Convention. Faced with a desperate situation, in August the Convention issued the *levée en masse*, which created a national conscript army. The order was originally intended to call forth a spontaneous burst of martial enthusiasm among citizen-soldiers who were backed by an aroused civilian population. These new raw recruits were mostly peasants who joined the existing professional army and prepared to repel the outsiders and crush the domestic dissidents. In September the Convention inaugurated the Reign of Terror with its charter document—the Law of Suspects. This act gave the Committee of Public Safety and its representatives the power to arrest and punish those who were deemed to be dangerous counterrevolutionaries. The criteria for detention were so elastic that within a few months the jails of the Republic were swollen with political prisoners.

QUESTIONS

1. When the Levée was presented to the Convention, the members were so enthusiastic they asked to have it read out several times over: Why all the excitement?
2. The Levée has been called "the birth certificate of the nation-state": How so? Would the designation apply to the Law of Suspects also?
3. The Law of Suspects is not "normal justice." What kind of justice is it? Is it justifiable?
4. What do the two documents, "Levée en Masse" and the "Law of Suspects," suggest about the nature of the governments that issued them?

**From the Levée en Masse
(August 23, 1793)**

1. Henceforth, until the enemies have been driven from the territory of the Republic, the French people are in permanent requisition for army service.

The young men shall go to battle; the married men shall forge arms and transport provisions; the women shall make tents and clothes, and shall serve in the hospitals; the children shall turn old linen into lint; the old men shall repair to the public places, to stimulate the courage of the warriors and preach the unity of the Republic and hatred of kings.

2. National buildings shall be converted into barracks; public places into armament workshops; the soil of cellars shall be washed in lye to extract saltpeter therefrom.

3. Arms of caliber shall be turned over exclusively to those who march against the enemy; the service of the interior shall be carried on with fowling pieces and sabers.

4. Saddle horses are called for to complete the cavalry corps; draught horses, other than

those employed in agriculture, shall haul artillery and provisions.

5. The Committee of Public Safety is charged with taking all measures necessary for establishing, without delay, a special manufacture of arms of all kinds, in harmony with the *élan* and the energy of the French people. Accordingly, it is authorized to constitute all establishments, manufactories, workshops, and factories deemed necessary for the execution of such works, as well as to requisition for such purpose, throughout the entire extent of the Republic, the artists and workmen who may contribute to their success. For such purpose a sum of 30,000,000, taken from the 498,200,000 *livres* in *assignats* in reserve in the "Fund of the Three Keys," shall be placed at the disposal of the Minister of War. The central establishment of said special manufacture shall be established at Paris.

6. The representatives of the people dispatched for the execution of the present law shall have similar authority in their respective *arrondissements*, acting in concert with the Committee of Public Safety; they are invested with the unlimited powers attributed to the representatives of the people with the armies.

7. No one may obtain a substitute in the service to which he is summoned. The public functionaries shall remain at their posts.

8. The levy shall be general. Unmarried citizens or childless widowers, from eighteen to twenty-five years, shall go first; they shall meet, without delay, at the chief town of their districts, where they shall practice manual exercise daily, while awaiting the hour of departure.

9. The representatives of the people shall regulate the musters and marches so as to have armed citizens arrive at the points of assembling only in so far as supplies, munitions, and all that constitutes the material part of the army exist in sufficient proportion. . . .

11. The battalion organized in each district shall be united under a banner bearing the inscription: *The French people risen against tyrants*. . . .

13. In order to collect supplies in sufficient quantity, the farmers and managers of national property shall deposit the produce of such property, in the form of grain, in the chief town of their respective districts.

14. Owners, farmers, and others possessing grain shall be required to pay, in kind, arrears of taxes, even the two-thirds of those of 1793, on the tolls which have served to effect the last payment. . . .

17. The Minister of War is responsible for taking all measures necessary for the prompt execution of the present decree; a sum of 50,000, from the 498,200,000 *livres* in *assignats* in the "Fund of the Three Keys," shall be placed at his disposal by the National Treasury.

From the Law of Suspects (September 17, 1793)

1. Immediately after the publication of the present decree, all suspected persons within the territory of the Republic and still at liberty shall be placed in custody.

2. The following are deemed suspected persons: 1st, those who, by their conduct, associations, talk, or writings have shown themselves partisans of tyranny or federalism and enemies of liberty; 2nd, those who are unable to justify, in the manner prescribed by the decree of 21 March last, their means of existence and the performance of their civic duties; 3rd, those to whom certificates of patriotism have been refused; 4th, public functionaries suspended or dismissed from their positions by the National Con-

vention or by its commissioners, and not re-instated, especially those who have been or are to be dismissed by virtue of the decree of 14 August last; 5th, those former nobles, husbands, wives, fathers, mothers, sons or daughters, brothers or sisters, and agents of the émigrés, who have not steadily manifested their devotion to the Republic; 6th, those who have emigrated during the interval between 1 July, 1789, and the publication of the decree of 30 March–8 April, 1792, even though they may have returned to France within the period established by said decree or prior thereto.

3. The Watch Committees established according to the decree of 21 March last, or those substituted therefor, either by orders of the representatives of the people dispatched to the armies and the departments, or by virtue of particular decrees of the National Convention, are charged with drafting, each in its own *arrondissement*, a list of suspected persons, with issuing warrants of arrest against them, and with having seals placed on their papers. Commanders of the public force to whom such warrants are remitted shall be required to put them into effect immediately, under penalty of dismissal.

4. The members of the committee may order the arrest of any individual only if seven are present, and only by absolute majority of votes.

5. Individuals arrested as suspects shall be taken first to the jails of the place of their detention; in default of jails, they shall be kept under surveillance in their respective dwellings.

6. Within the following week, they shall be transferred to national buildings, which the departmental administrations shall be required to designate and to have prepared for such purpose immediately after the receipt of the present decree.

7. The prisoners may have their absolutely essential belongings brought into said buildings; they shall remain there under guard until the peace.

8. The expenses of custody shall be charged to the prisoners, and shall be divided among them equally; such custody shall be confided preferably to fathers of families and to the relatives of citizens who are at or may go to the frontiers. The salary therefor is established, for each man of the guard, at the value of one and one-half days of labor.

9. The Watch Committee shall dispatch to the Committee of General Security of the National Convention, without delay, the list of persons whom they have arrested, with the reasons for their arrest and with the papers they have seized in such connection.

10. If there is occasion, the civil and criminal courts may have detained, in custody, and dispatched to the jails above stated, those who are accused of offences with regard to which it has been declared that there was no occasion for indictment or who have been acquitted of charges brought against them.

19. On Revolutionary Government, 1793

Maximilien Robespierre

Maximilien Robespierre (1758–1794) was the son of a lawyer. He earned a scholarship to attend one of the most famous colleges in Paris. Elected to the Estates-General in 1789, he rose from being an obscure delegate to a leading Jacobin who championed a moral style of politics. A follower of Rousseau and a student of Roman history, he passionately argued that the French Republic should become a great school for democracy, good citizenship, patriotism, and virtue. He played a pivotal role in the Reign of Terror, which he supported because he believed that it was necessary to save the nation and the revolution from destruction. He himself became a victim of the violence. After an apparent attempt at suicide he was guillotined.

QUESTIONS

1. According to Robespierre, how did constitutional and revolutionary governments differ?
2. Whom does Robespierre identify as the foreign and domestic enemies of the French Revolution?
3. Explain Robespierre's justification of the use of terror.

The Defenders of the Republic must adopt Caesar's maxim, for they believe that *nothing has been done as long as anything remains to be done.* Enough dangers still face us to engage all our efforts.

It has not fully extended the valor of our Republican soldiers to conquer a few Englishmen and a few traitors. A task no less important, and one more difficult, now awaits us: to sustain an energy sufficient to defeat the constant intrigues of all the enemies of our freedom and to bring to a triumphant realization the principles that must be the cornerstone of the public welfare.

Such are the first duties that you have imposed on your Committee of Public Safety.

We shall first outline the principles and the needs underlying the creation of a revolutionary government; next we shall expound the cause that threatens to throttle it at birth.

The theory of revolutionary government is as new as the Revolution that created it. It is as pointless to seek its origins in the books of the political theorists, who failed to foresee this revolution, as in the laws of the tyrants, who are happy enough to abuse their exercise of authority without seeking out its legal justification. And so this phrase is for the aristocracy a mere subject of terror or a term of slander, for tyrants an outrage and for many an enigma. It behooves us to explain it to all in order that we may rally good citizens, at least, in support of the principles governing the public interest.

It is the function of government to guide the moral and physical energies of the nation toward the purposes for which it was established.

The object of constitutional government is to preserve the Republic; the object of revolutionary government is to establish it.

Revolution is the war waged by liberty against its enemies; a constitution is that which crowns the edifice of freedom once victory has been won and the nation is at peace.

The revolutionary government has to summon extraordinary activity to its aid precisely because it is at war. It is subjected to less binding and less uniform regulations, because the circumstances in which it finds itself are tempestuous and shifting, above all because it is compelled to deploy, swiftly and incessantly, new resources to meet new and pressing dangers.

The principal concern of constitutional government is civil liberty; that of revolutionary government, public liberty. Under a constitutional government little more is required than to protect the individual against abuses by the state, whereas revolutionary government is obliged to defend the state itself against the factions that assail it from every quarter.

To good citizens revolutionary government owes the full protection of the state; to the enemies of the people it owes only death.

These ideas are in themselves sufficient to explain the origin and the nature of the laws that we term revolutionary. Those who call them arbitrary or tyrannical are foolish or perverse sophists who seek to reconcile white with black and black with white: they prescribe the same system for peace and war, for health and sickness; or rather their only object is to resurrect tyranny and to destroy the fatherland. When they invoke the literal application of constitutional principles, it is only to violate them with impunity. They are cowardly assassins who, in order to strangle the Republic in its infancy without danger to themselves, try to throttle it with vague maxims which they have no intention of observing.

The ship of the constitution was certainly not built to remain on the ways forever; but should we launch it at the moment when the storm is at its height and the winds are driving most furiously against us? This was the demand of the tyrants and the slaves who, in the first place, resisted its construction; but the people of France has commanded you to wait till the calm returns. Its unanimous wish and its command, drowning the clamor of aristocrats and federalists, is that you first deliver it from all its enemies.

The temples of the gods were not created to serve as a refuge for the sacrilegious to profane, nor was the constitution designed as a cover for the conspiracies of the tyrants who seek to destroy it.

Is a revolutionary government the less just and the less legitimate because it must be more vigorous in its actions and freer in its movements than an ordinary government? No! for it rests on the most sacred of all laws, the safety of the people, and on necessity, which is the most indisputable of all rights.

It also has its rules, all based on justice and on public order. It has nothing in common with anarchy or disorder; on the contrary, its purpose is to repress them and to establish and consolidate the rule of law. It has nothing in common with arbitrary rule; it is public interest that governs it and not the whims of private individuals. . . .

Thanks to five years of treason and tyranny, thanks to our credulity and lack of foresight and to the pusillanimity that followed too brief an exercise of vigor, Austria and England, Russia, Prussia and Italy have had time to set up in our country a secret government to challenge the authority of our own. They have also their committees, their treasury and their undercover agents. This government assumes whatever strength we deny to ours; it has the unity which ours has lacked, the policies that we have been too often willing to forego, the sense of continuity and concert whose need we have too often failed to appreciate.

Thus the courts of Europe have been able to spew over France all the artful rogues enlisted in their service. Their agents still infect our armies. . . . They deliberate within our organs of administration and within the meetings of our Sections; they enter our revolutionary clubs and have even held seats in the santuary of Parliament itself; and they direct, and will continue to direct, the counterrevolution by these and similar means. . . .

Yes, these perfidious emissaries that speak to us and flatter us are the brothers and accomplices of the savage satellites who have taken over French ships and cities sold to their masters, who have massacred our brothers, our wives and children, and the nation's representatives. Yet the monsters who have committed these crimes are a thousand times less detestable than the wretches who secretly devour our entrails; and yet they still live and conspire against us with impunity.

All they need in order to rally is leaders, and they hope to find them within this Assembly. Their principal purpose is to set us at each other's throats. Such a disastrous struggle would raise the hopes of the aristocracy and revive the federalist conspiracy; it would revenge the Girondin faction for the law that punished their crimes; it would punish the Mountain for its exemplary devotion, for it is the Mountain—or rather it is the Convention—that is being attacked by dividing it and destroying its work.

As for us, we shall make war only on the English, the Prussians, the Austrians and their accomplices. It is only by exterminating them that we shall reply to their slanders. We hate no one but the enemies of our country. We shall strike terror, not in the hearts of patriots or of the weak and humble, but in the haunts of the foreign brigands, where they divide out the spoils and drink the blood of the people of France.

---

20. Address to the Second National Congress of Venezuela, 1819

Simón Bolívar

Simón Bolívar (1783–1830) was one of the great leaders of the cause of Latin American independence from the Spanish Empire. Born into a wealthy creole family in what later became Venezuela, as a young man he made several journeys to Europe. There he embraced the doctrines of Locke, Hobbes, Rousseau, and other philosophers of the Enlightenment. He began his revolutionary activity at his home in Caracas in 1808, and over the next two decades he earned his fame as a conquering general in his native Venezuela, Colombia, Ecuador, Peru, and Upper Peru, which was renamed Bolivia in his honor. Sometimes called "the Liberator" or "the George Washington of South America," Bolívar also distinguished himself as a political and constitutional theorist and a champion of union among the new Latin American states. Although at times he held dictatorial power over the lands which he liberated from Spanish rule, as a native of the New World he passionately supported democratic and republican institutions which were properly designed to reflect the racial, political, and cultural heritage of the peoples of South America. Although he died disappointed at the failure of his dream of a united South America, his legacy did inspire the founding of the present day Organization of American States. The following excerpt from a speech he delivered to a national congress in Venezuela suggests his concern for the creation of a constitution which would truly embody both the spirit of democracy and the traditions of its citizens.

QUESTIONS

1. What position did Bolívar hold in Venezuela? What was the purpose of this address?
2. According to Bolívar, what were the most important factors which shaped the political heritage of the people of Latin America? What is the significance of that political heritage for the task at hand for the legislators?
3. What racial factors does Bolívar identify as important elements in Venezuelan culture?
4. Explain and discuss Bolívar's comparison of the proposed Venezuelan Constitution and the United States Constitution.
5. Describe and explain his criticism of the proposed Venezuelan Constitution.
6. Explain Bolívar's views on equality.
7. How does this document reflect themes of the Age of Democratic Revolutions?

Gentlemen:

Fortunate is the citizen, who, under the emblem of his command, has convoked this assembly of the national sovereignty so that it may exercise its absoute will! I, therefore, place myself among those most favored by Divine Providence, for I have had the honor of uniting the representatives of the people of Venezuela in this august Congress, the source of legitimate authority, the custodian of the sovereign will, and the arbiter of the Nation's destiny.

In returning to the representatives of the people the Supreme Power which was entrusted to me, I gratify not only my own innermost desires but also those of my fellow-citizens and of future generations, who trust to your wisdom, rectitude, and prudence in all things. Upon the fulfillment of this grateful obligation, I shall be released from the immense authority with which I have been burdened and from the unlimited responsibility which has weighed so heavily upon my slender resources. Only the force of necessity, coupled with the imperious will of the people, compelled me to assume the fearful and dangerous post of *Dictator and Supreme Chief of the Republic.* But now I can breathe more freely, for I am returning to you this authority which I have succeeded in maintaining at the price of so much danger, hardship, and suffering, amidst the worst tribulations suffered by any society. . . .

Legislators! I deliver into your hands the supreme rule of Venezuela. Yours is now the august duty of consecrating yourselves to the achievement of felicity of the Republic; your hands hold the scales of our destiny, the measures of our glory. They shall seal the decrees that will insure our liberty. At this moment the Supreme Chief of the Republic is no more than just a plain citizen, and such he wishes to remain until death. I shall, however, serve as a soldier so long as any foe remains in Venezuela. Our country has a multitude of worthy sons who are capable of directing her progress. . . .

The continuance of authority in the same individual has frequently meant the end of democratic governments. Repeated elections are essential in popular systems of government, for nothing is more perilous than to permit one citizen to retain power for an extended period. The people become accustomed to obeying him, and he forms the habit of commanding them; herein lie the origins of usurpation and tyranny. A just zeal is the guarantee of republican liberty. Our citizens must with good reason learn to fear lest the magistrate who has governed them long will govern them forever.

Since, therefore, by this profession of mine in support of Venezuela's freedom I may aspire to the glory of being reckoned among her most faithful sons, allow me, Gentlemen, to expound, with the frankness of a true republican, my respectful opinion on a *Plan of a Constitution*, which I take the liberty of submitting to you as testimony of the candor and sincerity of my sentiments. As this plan concerns the welfare of all, I venture to assume that I have the right to be heard by the representatives of the people. I well know that your wisdom needs no counsel, and I know also that my plan may perhaps appear to be mistaken and impracticable. But I implore you, Gentlemen, receive this work with benevolence, for it is more a tribute of my sincere deference to the Congress than an act of presumption. Moreover, as your function is to create a body politic, or, it might be said, to create an entire society while surrounded by every obstacle that a most peculiar and difficult situation can present, perhaps the voice of one citizen may reveal the presence of a hidden or unknown danger.

Let us review the past to discover the base upon which the republic of Venezuela is founded.

America, in separating from the Spanish monarchy, found herself in a situation similar to that of the Roman Empire when its enormous framework fell to pieces in the midst of the ancient world. Each Roman division then formed an independent nation in keeping with its location or interests; but this situation differed from America's in that those members proceeded to reestablish their former associations. We, on the contrary, do not even retain the vestiges of our original being. We are not Europeans; we are not Indians; we are but a mixed species of aborigines and Spaniards. Americans by birth and Europeans by law, we find ourselves engaged in a dual conflict: we are disputing with the natives for titles of ownership, and at the same time we are struggling to maintain ourselves in the country that gave us birth against the opposition of the invaders. Thus our position is most extraordinary and complicated. But there is more. As our role has always been strictly passive and our political existence nil, we find that our quest for liberty is now even more difficult of accomplishment; for we, having been placed in a state lower than slavery, had been robbed not only of our freedom but also of the right to exercise an active domestic tyranny. Permit me to explain this paradox.

In absolute systems, the central power is unlimited. The will of the despot is the supreme law, arbitrarily enforced by subordinates who take part in the organized oppression in proportion to the authority that they wield. They are charged with civil, political, military, and religious functions; but, in the final analysis, the satraps of Persia are Persian, the pashas of the Grand Turk are Turks, and the sultans of Tartary are Tartars. China does not seek her mandarins in the homeland of Genghis Kahn, her conqueror. America, on the contrary, received everything from Spain, who, in effect, deprived her of the experience that she would have gained from the exercise of an active tyranny by not allowing her to take part in her own domestic affairs and administration. This exclusion made it impossible for us to acquaint ourselves with the management of public affairs; nor did we enjoy that personal consideration, of such great value in major revolutions, that the brilliance of power inspires in the eyes of the multitude. In brief, Gentlemen, we were deliberately kept in ignorance and cut off from the world in all matters relating to the science of government.

Subject to the threefold yoke of ignorance, tyranny, and vice, the American people have been unable to acquire knowledge, power, or [civic] virtue. The lessons we received and the models we studied, as pupils of such pernicious teachers, were most destructive. We have been ruled more by deceit than by force, and we have been degraded more by vice than by superstition. Slavery is the daughter of Darkness: an ignorant people is a blind instrument of its own destruction. Ambition and intrigue abuse the credulity and experience of men lacking all political, economic, and civic knowledge; they adopt pure illusion as reality; they take licence for liberty, treachery for patriotism, and vengeance for justice. This situation is similar to that of the robust blind man who, beguiled by his strength, strides forward with all the assurance of one who can see, but, upon hitting every variety of obstacle, finds himself unable to retrace his steps.

If a people, perverted by their training, succeed in achieving their liberty, they will soon lose it, for it would be of no avail to endeavor to explain to them that happiness consists in the practise of virtue; that the rule of law is more powerful than the rule of tyrants, because, as the laws are more inflexible, everyone should submit to their beneficent austerity; that to practise justice is to practise liberty. Therefore, Legislators, your work is so much the more arduous, inasmuch as you have to reeducate men who have been corrupted by erroneous illusions and false incentives. Liberty, says Rousseau, is a succulent morsel, but one difficult to digest. Our weak fellow-citizens will have to strengthen their spirit greatly before they can digest the wholesome nutriment of freedom. Their limbs benumbed by chains, their sight dimmed by the darkness of dungeons, and their strength sapped by the pestilence of servitude, are they capable of marching toward the august temple of Liberty without faltering? Can they come near enough to bask in its brilliant rays and to breathe freely the pure air which reigns therein?

Legislators, meditate well before you choose. Forget not that you are to lay the political foundation for a newly born nation which can rise to the heights of greatness that Nature has marked out for it if you but proportion this foundation in keeping with the high plane that it aspires to attain. Unless your choice is based upon the peculiar tutelary experience of the Venezuelan people—a factor that should guide you in determining the nature and form of government you are about to adopt for the well-being of the people—and, I repeat, unless you happen upon the right type of government, the result of our reforms will be slavery. . . .

. . . I experience a surge of joy when I witness the great advances that our Republic has made since it began its noble career. Loving what is most useful, animated by what is most just, and aspiring to what is most perfect, Venezuela, on breaking away from Spain, has recovered her independence, her freedom, her equality, and her national sovereignty. By establishing a democratic republic, she has proscribed monarchy, distinctions, nobility, prerogatives, and privileges. She has declared for the rights of man and freedom of action, thought, speech, and press. These eminently liberal acts, because of the sincerity that has inspired them, will never cease to be admired. The first Congress of Venezuela has indelibly stamped upon the annals of our laws the majesty of the people, and, in placing its seal upon the social document best calculated to develop the well-being of the nation, that Congress has fittingly given expression to this thought.

I am forced to gather all my strength and to exert every effort of which I am capable in order to perceive the supreme good embodied in this immortal Code of our rights and laws. But how can I venture to say it! Shall I dare, by my criticism, to profane the sacred tablets of our laws . . . [sic]? There are some feelings that a true patriot cannot retain in his heart. They overflow, forced out by their own violence, and in spite of one's efforts to restrain them an inner force will make them known. I am thoroughly imbued with the idea that the government of Venezuela should be reformed; and, although many prominent citizens

think as I do, not all of them possess the courage necessary to recommend publicly the adoption of new principles. This consideration obliges me to take the initiative in a matter of the greatest importance—a matter in which the utmost audacity is required—the offering of advice to the councilors of the people.

The more I admire the excellence of the federal Constitution of Venezuela, the more I am convinced of the impossibility of its application to our state. And, to my way of thinking, it is a marvel that its prototype in North America endures so successfully and has not been overthrown at the first sign of adversity or danger. Although the people of North America are a singular model of political virtue and moral rectitude; although the nation was cradled in liberty, reared on freedom, and maintained by liberty alone; and—I must reveal everything—although those people, so lacking in many respects, are unique in the history of mankind, it is a marvel, I repeat, that so weak and complicated a government as the federal system has managed to govern them in the difficult and trying circumstances of their past. But, regardless of the effectiveness of this form of government with respect to North America, I must say that it has never for a moment entered my mind to compare the position and character of two states as dissimilar as the English-American and the Spanish-American. Would it not be most difficult to apply to Spain the English system of political, civil, and religious liberty? Hence, it would be even more difficult to adapt to Venezuela the laws of North America. Does not [Montesquieu's] *L'Esprit des lois* state that laws should be suited to the people for whom they are made; that it would be a major coincidence if those of one nation could be adapted to another; that laws must take into account the physical conditions of the country, climate, character of the land, location, size, and mode of living of the people; that they should be in keeping with the degree of liberty that the Constitution can sanction respecting the religion of the inhabitants, their inclinations, resources, number, commerce, habits, and customs? This is the code we must consult, not the code of Washington!

The Venezuelan Constitution, although based upon the most perfect of constitutions from the stand point of the correctness of its principles and the beneficent effects of its administration, differed fundamentally from the North American Constitution on one cardinal point, and, without doubt, the most important point. The Congress of Venezuela, like the North American legislative body, participates in some of the duties vested in the executive power. We, however, have subdivided the executive power by vesting it in a collective body. Consequently, this executive body has been subject to the disadvantages resulting from the periodic existence of a government which is suspended and dissolved whenever its members adjourn. Our executive triumvirate lacks, so to speak, unity, continuity, and individual responsibility. It is deprived of prompt action, continuous existence, true uniformity, and direct responsibility. The government that does not possess these things which give it a morality of its own must be deemed a nonentity.

Although the powers of the President of the United States are limited by numerous restrictions, he alone exercises all the governmental functions which the Constitution has delegated to him; thus there is no doubt but that his administration must be uniform, constant, and more truly his own than an administration wherein the power is divided among a number of persons, a grouping that is nothing less than a monstrosity. The judicial power in Venezuela is similar to that of North America: its duration is not defined; it is temporary and not

for life; and it enjoys all the independence proper to the judiciary.

The first Congress, in its federal Constitution, responded more to the spirit of the provinces than to the sound idea of creating an indivisible and centralized republic. In this instance, our legislators yielded to the ill-considered pleadings of those men from the provinces who were captivated by the apparent brilliance of the happiness of the North American people, believing that the blessings they enjoy result exclusively from their form of government rather than from the character and customs of the citizens. In effect, the United States' example, because of their remarkable prosperity, was one too tempting not to be followed. Who could resist the powerful attraction of full and absolute enjoyment of sovereignty, independence, and freedom? Who could resist the devotion inspired by an intelligent government that has not only blended public and private rights but has also based its supreme law respecting the desires of the individual upon common consent? Who could resist the rule of a beneficent government which, with a skilled, dextrous, and powerful hand always and in all regions, directs its resources toward social perfection, the sole aim of human institutions?

But no matter how tempting this magnificent federative system might have appeared, and regardless of its possible effect, the Venezuelans were not prepared to enjoy it immediately upon casting off their chains. We were not prepared for such good, for good, like evil, results in death when it is sudden and excessive. Our moral fibre did not then possess the stability necessary to derive benefits from a wholly representative government; a government so sublime, in fact, that it might more nearly befit a republic of saints. . . .

Permit me to call the attention of the Congress to a matter that may be of vital importance. We must keep in mind that our people are neither European nor North American; rather, they are a mixture of African and the Americans who originated in Europe. Even Spain herself has ceased to be European because of her African blood, her institutions, and her character. It is impossible to determine with any degree of accuracy where we belong in the human family. The greater portion of the native Indians has been annihilated; Spaniards have mixed with Americans and Africans, and Africans with Indians and Spaniards. While we have all been born of the same mother, our fathers, different in origin and in blood, are foreigners, and all differ visibly as to the color of their skin: a dissimilarity which places upon us an obligation of the greatest importance.

Under the Constitution, which interprets the laws of Nature, all citizens of Venezuela enjoy complete political equality. Although equality may not have been the political dogma of Athens, France, or North America, we must consecrate it here in order to correct the disparity that apparently exists. My opinion, Legislators, is that the fundamental basis of our political system hinges directly and exclusively upon the establishment and practise of equality in Venezuela. Most wise men concede that men are born with equal rights to share the benefits of society, but it does not follow that all men are born equally gifted to attain every rank. All men should practise virtue, but not all do; all ought to be courageous, but not all are; all should possess talents, but not everyone does. Herein are the real distinctions which can be observed among individuals even in the most liberally constituted society. If the principle of political equality is generally recognized, so also must be the principle of physical and moral inequality. Nature makes men unequal in intelligence, temperament, strength, and character. Laws correct this disparity by so placing the individual within society that education, industry, arts, services, and virtues give him a fictitious equality that is properly termed political and social. The idea of a classless state, wherein diversity increases in proportion to the rise in population, was an eminently beneficial inspiration. By this step alone, cruel discord has been completely eliminated. How much jealousy, rivalry, and hate have thus been averted!

21. Equal Rights for Women in the United States, 1848

Elizabeth Cady Stanton

Elizabeth Cady Stanton (1815–1902) was one of the pioneers of the women's rights movement in the United States. The daughter of a prominent New York judge, she was a graduate of Emma Willard's Troy Female Seminary. She and her husband, Henry B. Stanton, were active abolitionists who attended the World Anti-Slavery Convention in London in 1840. After that body voted to exclude women from its deliberations she intensified her efforts for feminist causes. In 1848 she joined with Lucretia Mott to organize the first women's rights convention in the United States, which met in Seneca Falls, New York. For that gathering she drafted the Declaration of Sentiments (Part A), which she modeled on Jefferson's Declaration of Independence. Part B presents excerpts from an address she delivered at Seneca Falls and Rochester, N.Y. on July 19 and August 2, 1848. Over the next fifteen years she labored for both the end of slavery and the extension of women's rights. After the abolition of slavery she dedicated the rest of her life to feminist issues, especially the right to vote.

QUESTIONS

1. Why did Stanton choose to use Jefferson's Declaration of Independence as a model for her Declaration of Sentiments? What does she list as the most important "injuries and usurpations on the part of man toward woman"?
2. Explain her argument in Part B for the intellectual equality of the sexes.
3. How does Stanton compare the rights of women and lower-class white males and foreigners? Discuss her references to those groups in both parts of this document.

A. Declaration of Sentiments at Seneca Falls Convention

When, in the course of human events, it becomes necessary for one portion of the family of man to assume among the people of the earth a position different from that which they have hitherto occupied, but one to which the laws of nature and of nature's God entitle them, a decent respect to the opinions of mankind requires that they should declare the causes that impel them to such a course.

We hold these truths to be self-evident: that all men and women are created equal; that they are endowed by their Creator with certain inalienable rights; that among these are life, liberty, and the pursuit of happiness; that to secure these rights governments are instituted, deriving their just powers from the consent of the governed. Whenever any form of government becomes destructive of these ends, it is the right of those who suffer from it to refuse allegiance to it, and to insist upon the institution of a new government, laying its foundation on such principles, and organizing its powers in such form, as to them shall seem most likely to effect their safety and happiness. Prudence, indeed, will dictate that governments long established should not be changed for light and transient causes; and accordingly all experience hath shown that mankind are more disposed to suffer, while evils are sufferable, than to right themselves by abolishing the forms to which they were accustomed. But when a long train of abuses and usurpations, pursuing invariably the same object evinces a design to reduce them under absolute despotism, it is their duty to throw off such government, and to provide new guards for their future security. Such has been the patient sufferance of the women under this government, and such is now the necessity which constrains them to demand the equal station to which they are entitled.

The history of mankind is a history of repeated injuries and usurpations on the part of man toward woman, having in direct object the establishment of an absolute tyranny over her. To prove this, let facts be submitted to a candid world.

He has never permitted her to exercise her inalienable right to the elective franchise.

He has compelled her to submit to laws, in the formation of which she had no voice.

He has withheld from her rights which are given to the most ignorant and degraded men—both natives and foreigners.

Having deprived her of this first right of a citizen, the elective franchise, thereby leaving her without representation in the halls of legislation, he has oppressed her on all sides.

He has made her, if married, in the eye of the law, civilly dead.

He has taken from her all right of property, even to the wages she earns.

He has made her, morally, an irresponsible being, as she can commit many crimes with impunity, provided they be done in the presence of her husband. In the covenant of marriage, she is compelled to promise obedience to her husband, he becoming, to all intents and purposes, her master—the law giving him power to deprive her of her liberty, and to administer chastisement.

He has so framed the laws of divorce, as to what shall be the proper causes, and in case of separation, to whom the guardianship of the children shall be given, as to be wholly regardless of the happiness of women—the law, in all cases, going upon a false supposition of the supremacy of man, and giving all power into his hands.

After depriving her of all rights as a married woman, if single, and the owner of property, he has taxed her to support a government which recognizes her only when her property can be made profitable to it.

He has monopolized nearly all the profitable employments, and from those she is permitted to follow, she receives but a scanty remuneration. He closes against her all the avenues to wealth and distinction which he considers most honorable to himself. As a teacher of theology, medicine, or law, she is not known.

He has denied her the facilities for obtaining a thorough education, all colleges being closed against her.

He allows her in Church, as well as State, but a subordinate position, claiming Apostolic authority for her exclusion from the ministry, and with some exceptions, from any public participation in the affairs of the Church.

He has created a false public sentiment by giving to the world a different code of morals for men and women, by which moral delinquencies which exclude women from society, are not only tolerated, but deemed of little account in man.

He has usurped the prerogative of Jehovah himself, claiming it as his right to assign for her a sphere of action, when that belongs to her conscience and to her God.

He has endeavored, in every way that he could, to destroy her confidence in her own powers, to lessen her self-respect, and to make her willing to lead a dependent and abject life.

Now, in view of this entire disfranchisement of one-half the people of this country, their social and religious degradation—in view of the unjust laws above mentioned, and because women do feel themselves aggrieved, oppressed, and fraudulently deprived of their most sacred rights, we insist that they have immediate admission to all the rights and privileges which belong to them as citizens of the United States.

In entering upon the great work before us, we anticipate no small amount of misconception, misrepresentation, and ridicule; but we shall use every instrumentality within our power to effect our object. We shall employ agents, circulate tracts, petition the State and National legislatures, and endeavor to enlist the pulpit and the press in our behalf. We hope this Convention will be followed by a series of Conventions embracing every part of the country.

B. "The Right Is Ours"

. . . Every allusion to the degraded and inferior position occupied by women all over the world has been met by scorn and abuse. From the man of highest mental cultivation to the most degraded wretch who staggers in the streets do we meet ridicule, and coarse jests, freely bestowed upon those who dare assert that woman stands by the side of man, his equal, placed here by her God, to enjoy with him the beautiful earth, which is her home as it is his, having the same sense of right and wrong, and looking to the same Being for guidance and support. So long has man exercised tyranny over her, injurious to himself and benumbing to her faculties, that few can nerve themselves to meet the storm; and so long has the chain been about her that she knows not there is a remedy. . . .

Man's intellectual superiority cannot be a question until woman has had a fair trial. When we shall have had our freedom to find out our own sphere, when we shall have had our colleges, our professions, our trades, for a century, a comparison then may be justly instituted. When woman . . . shall first educate herself, when she shall be just to herself before she is generous to others; improving the talents God has given her, and leaving her neighbor to do the same for himself, we shall not then hear so much about this boasted superiority. How often now, we see young men carelessly throwing away the intellectual food their sisters crave.

A little music, that she may while an hour away pleasantly, a little French, a smattering of the sciences, and in rare instances, some slight classical knowledge, and woman is considered highly educated. She leaves her books and studies just as a young man is entering thoroughly into his. Then comes the gay routine of fashionable life, courtship and marriage, the perplexities of house and children, and she knows nothing beside. Her sphere is home. And whatever yearning her spirit may have felt for a higher existence, whatever may have been the capacity she well knew she possessed for more elevated enjoyments, enjoyments which would not conflict with those holy duties, but add new lustre to them, all, all is buried beneath the weight of these undivided cares. . . .

We have met here to-day to discuss our rights and wrongs, civil and political, and not, as some have supposed, to go into the detail of social life alone. We do not propose to petition the legislature to make our husbands just, generous and courteous, to seat every man at the head of a cradle, and to clothe every woman in male attire. . . . But we are assembled to protest against a form of government, existing without the consent of the governed—to declare our right to be free as man is free, to be represented in the government which we are taxed to support, to have such disgraceful laws as give man the power to chastise and imprison his wife, to take the wages which she earns, the property which she inherits, and, in case of separation, the children of her love; laws which made her the mere dependent on his bounty. . . . And, strange as it may seem to many, we now demand our right to vote according to the declaration of the government under which we live. This right no one pretends to deny. We need not prove ourselves equal to Daniel Webster to enjoy this privilege, for the ignorant Irishman in the ditch has all the civil rights he has. We need not prove our muscular power equal to this same Irishman to enjoy this privilege, for the most tiny, weak, ill-shaped stripling of twenty-one, has all the civil rights of the Irishman. . . . All white men in this country have the same rights, however they may differ in mind, body or estate. The right is ours. The question now is, how shall we get possession of what rightfully belongs to us. . . . to have drunkards, idiots, horse-racing, rumselling rowdies, ignorant foreigners and silly boys fully recognized, while we ourselves are thrust out from all the rights that belong to citizens, it is too grossly insulting to the dignity of woman to be longer quietly submitted to. The right is ours. Have it, we must. Use it, we will. The pens, the tongues, the fortunes, the indomitable wills of many women are already pledged to secure this right. The great truth, that no just government can be formed without the consent of the governed, we shall echo and re-

echo in the ears of the unjust judge, until by continual coming we shall weary him. . . .

Let woman live as she should. Let her feel her accountability to her Maker. Let her know that her spirit is fitted for as high a sphere as man's and that her soul requires food as pure and exalted as his. Let her live *first* for God, and she will not make imperfect man an object of reverence and awe. Teach her her responsibility as a being of conscience and reason, that all earthly support is weak and unstable, that her only safe dependence is the arm of omnipotence, and that true happiness springs from duty accomplished. Thus will she learn the lesson of individual responsibility for time and eternity. That neither father, husband, brother or son, however willing they may be, can discharge her high duties of life, or stand in her stead when called in the presence of the great Searcher of Hearts at the last day.

22. Constitutional Government in Japan

Ito Hirobumi

Prince Ito Hirobumi (1841–1909) was a Japanese statesman who played a pivotal role in the transformation of Japan into a formidable world power. Born into a family of humble social status but of samurai descent, he was a "barefoot boy" who endured a rigorous samurai training for the life of a footsoldier. In 1863 he defied Tokugawa seclusion laws and sailed to Europe as a deckhand on an English ship. That trip introduced him to the West and convinced him that Japan should reform itself by incorporating elements of Western political and economic life into its society. After supporting the 1868 Meiji Restoration and overthrow of the shogunate, he rose to high rank, serving as prime minister four times between 1885 and 1901. In 1895 he negotiated the treaty of Shimonoseki, which ended the Sino-Japanese War and granted Korea its independence. He also was instrumental in securing Japan's alliance with Great Britain in 1902. After Japan took control of Korea in 1905, Ito was appointed resident-general of that country, where he served until he was assassinated by a Korean nationalist in Manchuria. One of his greatest achievements was his drafting of a new constitution for Japan, in effect from 1889 until 1945, which was modeled on Bismarck's charter for the new German empire. For Ito the new system was "a voluntary gift of the Emperor to his subjects." The following selections present his thoughts on Japan's new governmental order.

QUESTIONS

1. According to Ito, what changes did the Japanese undertake in their culture that enabled them to meet the challenges of the modern world?
2. What traditions did the Japanese draw upon in their heritage which proved useful in the modernization of their society? What "peculiar features" and "emotional elements" of Japanese culture does he identify? What problems did they present for the period of transition into a constitutional system?
3. Describe the constitutional system which he outlines in these passages. What role did the emperor play in the new regime? How democratic was it?
4. How does the Japanese political experience during the late nineteenth century reflect the influence of the earlier democratic revolutions in Western Europe and the United States?
5. What indications here foreshadow Japan's remarkable success in adopting foreign modes and practices, while preserving its traditional way of life?

Speech on the Restoration and Constitutional Government, 1899

When our enlightened emperor decided to accept the open-door principle as an imperial policy . . . it became a matter of urgent necessity to develop the intellectual faculties of our people and to increase their business activities. This led to the abolition of the feudal system and made it possible for the Japanese people to live in a new political environment and to have diverse freedoms. . . . The first of these freedoms was the freedom of movement, followed by the freedom to pursue an occupation of one's own choosing. Moreover, the freedom to study at any place of one's choosing was given to all. There was also granted freedom of speech in political affairs. Thus, the Japanese today enjoy freedom, each according to his desires, within the limits of the law. These rights belong to the people who live in civilized government. If these rights are withheld and their enjoyment refused, a people cannot develop. And if the people cannot develop, the nation's wealth and the nation's strength cannot develop. . . . But the fact is that because of the imperial policy of the open-door, we have established a government which is civilized. And as we have advanced to such a position, it has become necessary to establish a fixed definition of the fundamental laws. That, in short, is the reason for the establishment of constitutional government.

A constitutional government makes a clear distinction between the realms of the ruler and the ruled, and thereby defines what the people and the sovereign should do; that is, the rights which the sovereign should exercise and the rights which the people should enjoy, followed by the procedure for the management of the government. According to the Constitution the people have the right to participate in government, but this right is at once an important obligation as well as a right. Government is a prerogative of the emperor. As you will be participating in government—which is the emperor's prerogative—you must regard this right as the responsibility of the people, the honor of the people. It is therefore a matter of the greatest importance.

In this connection what all Japanese must bear in mind is Japan's national polity [*kokutai*]. It is history which defines the national polity; thus the Japanese people have the duty to know their history. . . . The national polity of the various countries differs one from another, but it is the testimony of the history of Japan to this day that the unification of the country was achieved around the Imperial House. So I say that the understanding of the national polity of Japan is the first important duty of our people.

Reminiscences on the Drafting of the New Constitution, 1908

The advent of Commodore Perry, followed by a rigid succession of great events too well known to be repeated here, roughly awakened us to the consciousness of mighty forces at work to change the face of the outside world. We were ill-prepared to bear the brunt of these forces, but once awakened to the need, were not slow to grapple with them. So, first of all, the whole fabric of the feudal system, which with its obsolete shackles and formalities hindered us in every branch of free development, had to be up-

rooted and destroyed. The annihilation of centrifugal forces taking the form of autocratic feudal provinces was a necessary step to the unification of the country under a strong central government, without which we would not have been able to offer a united front to the outside forces or stand up as a united whole to maintain the country's very existence.

Sources of Japanese Civilization and Culture

I must, however, disabuse my readers of the very common illusion that there was no education and an entire absence of public spirit during feudal times. It is this false impression which has led superficial observers to believe that our civilization has been so recent that its continuance is doubtful—in short, that our civilization is nothing but a hastily donned, superficial veneer. On the contrary, I am not exaggerating when I say that, for generations and centuries, we have been enjoying a moral education of the highest type. The great ideals, offered by philosophy and by historical examples of the golden ages of China and India, Japanicized in the form of a "crust of customs," developed and sanctioned by the continual usage of centuries under the comprehensive name of *bushido* [the samurai code of conduct], offered us splendid standards of morality, rigorously enforced in the everyday life of the educated classes. The result, as everyone who is acquainted with Old Japan knows, was an education which aspired to the attainment of Stoic heroism, a rustic simplicity and a self-sacrificing spirit unsurpassed in Sparta, and the aesthetic culture and intellectual refinement of Athens. Art, delicacy of sentiment, higher types of valor and chivalry—all these we have tried to combine in the man as he ought to be. We laid great stress on the harmonious combination of all known accomplishments of a developed human being, and it is only since the introduction of modern technical sciences that we have been obliged to pay more attention to specialized technical attainments than to the harmonious development of the whole. Let me remark, *en passant,* that the humanitarian efforts which in the course of the recent [Russo-Japanese] war were so much in evidence and which so much surprised Western nations were not, as might have been thought, the products of the new civilization, but survivals of our ancient feudal chivalry. If further instance were needed, we may direct attention to the numbers of our renowned warriors and statesmen who have left behind them works of religious and moral devotions, of philosophical contemplations, as well as splendid specimens of calligraphy, painting, and poetry, to an extent probably unparalleled in the feudalism of other nations.

Thus it will be seen that what was lacking in our countrymen of the feudal era was not mental or moral fiber, but the scientific, technical, and materialistic side of modern civilization. Our present condition is not the result of the ingrafting of a civilization entirely different from our own, as foreign observers are apt to believe, but simply a different training and nursing of a strongly vital character already existent. . . .

Peculiar Features
of the National Life

It was evident from the outset that mere imitation of foreign models would not suffice, for there were historical peculiarities of our country which had to be taken into consideration. For example, the Crown was, with us, an institution far more deeply rooted in the national sentiment and in our history than in other countries. It was indeed the very essence of a once theocratic

State, so that in formulating the restrictions on its prerogatives in the new Constitution, we had to take care to safeguard the future realness or vitality of these prerogatives, and not to let the institution degenerate into an ornamental crowning piece of edifice. At the same time, it was also evident that any form of constitutional regime was impossible without full and extended protection of honor, liberty, property, and personal security of citizens, entailing necessarily many important restrictions on the powers of the Crown.

Emotional Elements in Social Life
of People

On the other hand, there was one peculiarity of our social conditions that is without parallel in any other civilized country. Homogeneous in race, language, religion, and sentiments, so long secluded from the outside world, with the centuries-long traditions and inertia of the feudal system, in which the family and quasi-family ties permeated and formed the essence of every social organization, and moreover with such moral and religious tenets as laid undue stress on duties of fraternal aid and mutual succor, we had during the course of our seclusion unconsciously become a vast village community where cold intellect and calculation of public events were always restrained and even often hindered by warm emotions between man and man. Those who have closely observed the effects of the commercial crises of our country—that is, of the events wherein cold-blooded calculation ought to have the precedence of every other factor—and compared them with those of other countries, must have observed a remarkable distinction between them. In other countries they serve in a certain measure as the scavengers of the commercial world, the solid undertakings surviving the shock, while enterprises founded solely on speculative bases are sure to vanish thereafter. But, generally speaking, this is not the case in our country. Moral and emotional factors come into play. Solid undertakings are dragged into the whirlpool, and the speculative ones are saved from the abyss—the general standard of prosperity is lowered for the moment, but the commercial fabric escapes violent shocks. In industry, also, in spite of the recent enormous development of manufactures in our country, our laborers have not yet degenerated into spiritless machines and toiling beasts. There still survives the bond of patron and protegé between them and the capitalist employers. It must, of course, be admitted that this social peculiarity is not without beneficial influences. It mitigates the conflict, serves as the lubricator of social organisms, and tends generally to act as a powerful lever for the practical application of the moral principle of mutual assistance between fellow citizens. But unless curbed and held in restraint, it too may exercise baneful influences on society, for in a village community, where feelings and emotions hold a higher place than intellect, free discussion is apt to be smothered, attainment and transference of power liable to become a family question of a powerful oligarchy, and the realization of such a regime as constitutional monarchy to become an impossibility, simply because in any representative regime free discussion is a matter of prime necessity, because emotions and passions have to be stopped for the sake of the cool calculation of national welfare, and even the best of friends have often to be sacrificed if the best abilities and highest intellects are to guide the helm. Besides, the dissensions between brothers and relatives, deprived as they usually are of safety-valves for giving free and hearty vent to their own opinions or discontents, are apt to degenerate into passionate quarrels and

overstep the bounds of simple differences of opinion. The good side of this social peculiarity had to be retained as much as possible, while its baneful influences had to be safeguarded. These and many other peculiarities had to be taken into account in order to have a constitution adapted to the actual condition of the country.

Conflict Between the Old and New Thoughts

Another difficulty equally grave had to be taken into consideration. We were just then in an age of transition. The opinions prevailing in the country were extremely heterogenous, and often diametrically opposed to each other. We had survivors of former generations who were still full of theocratic ideas, and who believed that any attempt to restrict an imperial prerogative amounted to something like high treason. On the other hand there was a large and powerful body of the younger generation educated at the time when the Manchester theory [of laissez-faire individualism] was in vogue, and who in consequence were ultra-radical in their ideas of freedom. Members of the bureaucracy were prone to lend willing ears to the German doctrinaires of the reactionary period, while, on the other hand, the educated politicians among the people having not yet tasted the bitter significance of administrative responsibility were liable to be more influenced by the dazzling words and lucid theories of Montesquieu, Rousseau, and other similar French writers. A work entitled *History of Civilization*, by Buckle, which denounced every form of government as unnecessary evil, became the great favorite of students of all higher schools, including the Imperial University. On the other hand, these same students would not have dared to expound the theories of Buckle before their own conservative fathers. At the time we had not yet arrived at the stage of distinguishing clearly between political opposition on the one hand, and treason to the established order of things on the other. The virtues necessary for the smooth working of any constitution, such as love of freedom of speech, love of publicity of proceedings, the spirit of tolerance for opinions opposed to one's own, etc., had yet to be learned by long experience.

INTRODUCTION TO UNIT THREE

The Industrial Revolution

No historical term has given rise to more discussion or lent itself to worse misinterpretations in textbooks than "the Industrial Revolution," which first gained currency from Arnold Toynbee's *The Industrial Revolution*, posthumously published in 1884. Some substitutes for the term have been economic "take off stage" or "breakthrough." A frequent use of the phrase has been to apply it to a single industry, as in "the industrial revolution of the thirteenth century," when wind and water power were applied in the processing of wool cloth. "The first industrial revolution" has been used to characterize developments in the British coal industry and the manufacture of such things as glass in the century 1540–1640. The "second industrial revolution" often designates the period after 1870 and the resort to electricity, chemistry, steel, and the gasoline engine; the "third industrial revolution" to atomic energy, automation, and computers. Still others have argued that the pace of change was too slow and protracted to be called a revolution at all.

Nevertheless, "industrial revolution" is still a justifiable term, since significant political changes often occur within a short period of time, but economic transformations are normally long term, measured in decades, generations, or centuries. There is no doubt that the industrial revolution had momentous effects. In one century humankind's productive capacity was extended more than had occurred in the previous 5,000 to 10,000 years of recorded and unrecorded history. Moreover, the character of social life changed equally radically, both quantitatively and qualitatively. More specifically, the transition from handicraft to machine industry and from an agricultural to an industrial society profoundly altered the material existence of Western civilization, the nature of its society, and its relationship to the non-Western world.

At the center of the industrial revolution was an intertwined series of technological and social developments. Mechanical contrivances were substituted for human skills, and steam power replaced human, animal, wind, and water energy. Greater efficiency was achieved in extracting and working raw materials that utilized metallurgical and chemical processes; new systems of factory organization and discipline and an ever-extending division of labor brought class differentiation, consciousness, and conflict. The owner, employer, capital source, marketer (often the same person) now faced the worker who no longer could own his tools or means of production. The employee was landless and became a mere "hand" swallowed up in the ocean of proletarians. Fewer and fewer workmen produced more and more—and often better—goods at such a rate of increase that a rise in real wages and in the standard of living occurred despite the tripling of the British population between 1750 and 1850.

The industrial revolution began in England in the textile industry, especially cotton. Not one but a concatenation of factors triggered the breakthrough. These included a strong demand for cheap goods at home and abroad, a balanced supply of natural resources (especially of coal and iron); efficient agriculture (which had itself undergone a "revolution") that provided enough food, labor, markets, capital; increasing population that raised prices, created a labor glut, and enhanced demand; efficient transport in a small, insular, unified country where distances were short, coastal shipping was feasible, and no inland customs barriers held things up and raised costs; efficient financial institutions provided by the Bank of England and many country banks which mobilized capital accumulated in agriculture and commerce for investment in industry at low rates of interest; no costly standing army to drain away resources; long-term stability and reliability afforded by the government's fiscal structure and sound national debt; an environment hospitable to technological change and social mobility.

The industrial revolution did not occur in a vacuum, but rather within the global economy, which had been expanding since the discoveries of Columbus and da Gama and is, much extended, still with us. Oceanic communications had brought Europe into contact with Africa, America, and Asia. The first beneficiaries were the Spanish and Portuguese, followed by the Dutch, French, and British, who after 1715 enjoyed a triple monopoly of international trade, merchant marine, and naval power. Britain owed her increasing wealth to the trade her empire and the global economy opened up to her as well as to the domestic manufacturing of her handicrafts and cottage industries under the putting out/gathering in system. Trade with Asia was problematic since there was no market for European goods, with the consequence that the massive imports of spices, tea, rugs, china, cotton cloth (madras, calico, muslin, gingham) had to be paid in gold, which continued to drain out of Europe to Asia as it had done since antiquity. Mercantilist legislation to restrict or prohibit imports was ineffective; Daniel Defoe noted in 1708 that everyone wore cotton cloth and it has "crept into our houses, our closets and bed chambers; curtains, cushions, chairs and at last beds themselves were nothing but calicos or Indian stuffs."

Much of the gold to pay for these Asian products came from the African Gold Coast, as did slaves. British trade with America mounted, especially sugar, and after 1800 and the cotton gin, raw cotton. The slave trade remained immensely profitable, however, and was largely in British and New England hands. Liverpool rose from an obscure fishing village to a flourishing seaport on the trade in slaves and slave-produced goods. Capital formation in Western Europe drew heavily on the outside world: African slave labor and gold, Asian resources and skills, and American natural resources. Britain in particular drew much of the sinews of the industrial revolution from overseas.

Hence the industrial revolution in Britain occurred within, and depended upon, a European and, particularly, a global context. The woolen and worsted industry had been England's great staple in the Middle Ages and had made England the richest nation per capita since the later sixteenth century. Unlike continental countries, Britain never had a very potent guild system controlling woolen cloth production; thus the weavers in most of the kingdom were organized in the putting out system, while in Yorkshire they were independent entrepreneurs. Such freedom, unhampered by quotas or regulations as to methods and techniques, put a premium on efficiency and innovation.

According to one contemporary source of the 1730s, nearly half the British population was "engaged in manufactures," and about half of them, mostly part time, many of them women and children, were engaged in cloth making, working at home as wage earners for merchant capitalists under the putting out system. This arrangement, in which the workers had possession of the material they processed, lent itself to embezzlement and recalcitrance, which were especially rife at times of expanding demand, when the "putter out" had less leverage in inducing workers to deliver. Factory methods were adopted in part to deal with the losses and breakdown of discipline in the putting out system under the spur of accelerating demand.

Some of the new textile machines had been invented for wool production but were applied to cotton because those fibers were more tractable to mechanization. Wool was an old industry and hence tradition-bound in some degree; demand for cotton was greater and soared as costs fell (to one-twentieth from 1760 to 1840). Hence it was the cotton industry that took off. Yet, as has been said, "cotton was a lonely hare in an industrial world of tortoises," for the pace of mechanization was slow rather than fast. Nevertheless, cotton dragged others along with it. Its need particularly for steam power and metal production turned the development of the cotton industry into a system of production common to all manufacturing. Power was preeminent. The climax of the epic of power—once the problems were solved of putting the engine on wheels and the wheels on tracks—was the railroad. By 1850 private entrepreneurs had built 6,500 miles of railroads, thereby promoting and substantially completing Britain's industrial development. The Great Exhibition of 1851, first of the international world's fairs, opened in the Crystal Palace, a grand pavilion of glass and iron erected in Hyde Park in London, to celebrate "the industry of all nations," but above all it heralded Britain's industrial triumph. Thereafter a period of stasis set in.

Textbooks have long canonized seven names under the rubric of the industrial revolution: four Lancashire men (John Kay, James Hargreaves, Richard Arkwright, and Samuel Crompton), two Scots (Adam Smith and James Watt), and one Episcopal minister (Edmund Cartwright). Kay, Hargreaves, Arkwright, Crompton, and Cartwright invented textile machines; Watt improved the steam engine; and Smith wrote *The Wealth of Nations* (see Document 23). To let it go at that is to ignore the important fact that the inventors and entrepreneurs of the industrial revolution were drawn from all walks of life: from the aristocracy came the canal-building duke of Bridgewater, from the nameless "labouring poor" came some who rose to be mill owners like the Matthew Crabtree of Document 27. This phenomenon reflects the relative homogeneity of British society, and can also be seen in the wide social range from which the inventors were drawn: Kay was the son of a yeoman, Crompton's father was a farmer who produced cloth on the side, Cartwright was an Oxford graduate and clergyman, Watt was the son of a failed merchant, Arkwright was a barber and wig dyer, and John Roebuck was a chemist who developed bleaching material and had studied at Edinburgh and Leyden.

As early as 1750 continental powers began to realize that they were falling behind Britain in manufacturing techniques, and so they began to send experts, businessmen, and other types of spies to inspect and report. Their reports are a principal source for the historian of the industrial revolution, and seem to serve the historian far better than they did the governments that commissioned them. Whereas the continental societies were often superior to Britain in science and education, and imported and copied the machines (as they did workmen, prohibitions notwithstanding) soon after their invention, it was not until the 1840s that the European powers made serious efforts to try to catch up with the British. It took another century or more to actually do so. Immaterial factors were not so easily transplanted. Class-ridden continental society looked down upon pursuits in trade and industry, and a characteristic pattern was for the successful entrepreneur to flee as soon as he could to join the rural aristocracy, acquire a landed estate, and purchase a title of nobility. As for "the rising bourgeoisie" canonized by generations of textbooks, the most successful bourgeois did not so much rise as disappear into the ranks of the nobility.

The continent's typical business organization was the family firm, like Thomas Mann's Buddenbrooks, which was tradition-bound and incapable of taking advantage of untraditional opportunities. Transport and communication were over longer distances and more formidable topography, punctuated by numerous boundaries and tolls, and made for less efficiency and greater costs. Since timber remained in ample supply, there was less incentive to resort to coal and coke. As always, war bedeviled the continent, whereas Britain had been free from Armageddon since the mid-seventeenth century. Especially in the revolutionary and Napoleonic period, the continent suffered a generation of war's turmoil, destruction, blockade, etc. and had to start all over in 1815, whereas Britain had progressed in organization and technology, and was financially stronger than ever. Especially critical on the continent was guild organization. In the few favored places where it was weak, enterprise flourished by accident; generally, the guilds functioned effectively to restrict competition and inhibit innovation. State intervention, as Adam Smith argued, often misfired and did not succeed in promoting industrial development, despite importing entrepreneurs and skilled workers as well as machines, subsidized production, guaranteed markets, awards of patents and monopolies, etc.

After 1825 and despite the law, British workmen and machines were imported to the continent. In the 1820s about 2,000 skilled Britons were to be found in Belgium and France. They taught industrial skills and built railways, roads, canals, and bridges. In the 1830s a second wave, this time of French and Belgian workers, swept into Germany to engage in the same kind of educational and construction undertakings. Thereafter, in France and especially in Germany, technical and engineering schools and polytechnics were erected. These paid off after 1870 when technical and industrial development became more dependent upon theoretical and applied science than upon empirical rule of thumb. Public support for technical education in Britain had to wait until 1891, by which time Britain was faltering in the industrial race.

Belgium, which became independent of Holland in 1830, was heir to the tradition of Flemish cloth making in the Middle Ages. For many centuries its economic development had been stymied by Holland's blockade of the Scheldt River and Antwerp. It gained greatly during the revolutionary wars owing to French annexation in 1793 and the opening up thereby of a large market. Well endowed with coal and iron, Belgium is small and tied together by waterways; by 1844 the government had built more than 300 miles of railroads linking up local lines, thus making the country the turntable of railway traffic on the continent. In 1799 Belgian entrepreneurs hired the British machinist William Cockerill and learned to build spinning and weaving machines for wool; in 1817 (after setting up a woolen factory in Berlin) he and his sons established the largest iron foundry and machine plant on the continent. With the organizing and mechanical genius of a Henry Ford, they built textile machinery, steam engines, locomotives, steamboats, and armaments, which they supplied to France, Germany, Russia, Spain, and Italy. Industrialization proceeded rapidly in Belgium, facilitated by joint-stock investment banks (which were slow to develop on the continent). With a rising output of coal, iron, and, later, steel, Belgium became one of the most densely industrialized areas of the globe.

In contrast to Belgium, French industrialization was much slower, partly owing to distance and high transport costs, which meant that France remained divided into several large, economically autonomous areas. The French national railway system was not complete until the 1850s, and its economy remained diversified and strongly agricultural.

Germany was fragmented among many petty states, but was left by the Napoleonic wars and the peace settlement somewhat consolidated in a confederation. The most powerful of the German states, Prussia, was so stung by its humiliating defeat by Napoleon in 1806 that it vowed to attain national unity and strength. 1818 witnessed the start of the end of trade barriers within Prussia; the *Zollverein* or customs union was initiated in 1834 and gradually incorporated most of the German states. It was reinforced by a unified railway system in the 1830s, the first in Europe. During this period the German economist Friedrich

List opposed the free trade ideas of Adam Smith and lobbied for protectionism and a more modern transportation system for his homeland (see Document 24). All this was prelude to the German industrial revolution, which came in the wake of unification after 1870 and paralleled that of the United States following the Civil War. The only other country before 1850 to adopt elements of the new technology and organization of industry was Switzerland; Holland remained a great commercial and financial center but did not embark on the course of industrialization. As for Russia, Tsar Nicholas I objected to railways on the grounds that they promoted vagrancy; when it was decided to build a line from St. Petersburg to Moscow, the rails were ordered from a state-owned factory which could not make them and in the end almost all of the rails came from Britain. The rolling stock was built in a state-owned factory run by Americans, who imported the parts and just assembled the locomotives and wagons!

Most accounts of the industrial revolution concentrate on its consequences rather than its origins. Ironically, the earliest students of the subject, Adam Smith (see Document 23) and the classical economists such as Thomas Malthus (see Document 25), were unaware of or indifferent to industrialization; they seem to have taken it for granted, seeing in it only quantitative change in the form of economic growth rather than a fundamental change from an agrarian to an industrialized society. Assessments that portray the industrial revolution as grim in its course and consequences began with Engels's *Condition of the Working Class in England in 1844* and continued through Marx's *Capital,* and their *Manifesto of the Communist Party* (see Document 30). This view was reinforced by Victorian novelists such as Charles Dickens. Examples of the negative effects of industrialization appear in Documents 26 and 27, which contain reports on long hours and low wages, poor working conditions, miserable housing and food, and abuse of women and children. Document 29 presents a light account of a group who were trying to escape from the consequences of the industrial revolution through communal living.

From the start the industrial revolution had its defenders and apologists who saw in it a great and beneficent transformation. After World War I the pessimistic view was challenged by economic historians, who offer evidence that real wages and the standard of living rose between 1815 and 1850, when even the unskilled enjoyed an abundance of cotton clothing, dishes, pots and pans, cutlery, tea and sugar, etc. The revisionist school has roots that can be traced back to contemporary accounts such as the one by Andrew Ure, reprinted here in Document 28.

Some points can be made not to resolve but to impart focus to the debate. *First,* there is no abstract necessity that large investment in industrial growth must result in a fall in the living standard of the population at large by diminishing consumption. The evidence indicates that in Britain increased productivity kept ahead of industrialization; by contrast, many countries, such as the Soviet Union, embarked on state-directed industrialization at the price of sharp contractions of consumption and declining living standards.

Second, every industrial revolution in history has produced slums. Yet the new factory towns were in some respects more attractive places to live than the rural areas many workers (especially the numerous Irish and Scottish immigrants) had left but to which few returned. It is true that family life tended to disintegrate, with whole families living in single rooms. The industrial revolution in the form of cheap bricks, water and sewer pipes, house fixtures, etc. did not catch up with the building trade until the 1880s or later, while governmental responsibility for housing provision had to wait until the twentieth century.

Third, one has to distinguish the evil effects that stemmed from industrialization from those that did not, e.g., the dislocations emanating from the frequent wars, especially 1793 to 1815, rapidly growing population, urbanization, ignorance of public health, etc. In Ireland there was no industrial revolution at a time of extraordinary population growth, which ended disastrously in the potato famine of the 1840s. Dublin, like many unindustrialized cities, teemed with slums and squalor.

Fourth, most of the social evils attributed to the industrial revolution were not new, were not as dire or widespread as alleged, and had little to do with industrialization. Mining, smelting, sugar refining, cloth finishing, ship building and sail making, and the manufacture of glass, bricks, paper, leather, cannon, gunpowder, etc. were conducted in factories or work places outside the home long before 1760. Fixed hours, long hours, child labor, exploitation of women, low wages, unemployment whether chronic or periodic, and slums—all had very long histories. Some women found the factory liberating, freeing them from parental domination or employment as housemaids. Cruelty was certainly known in factories but was not confined to them, for it was rampant throughout society, in prisons, schools, the army and navy as well as in the parents' cottage and domestic workshop. What might be called civilizing the beast of industrialized society went on apace 1820–1850: factory acts, legalization of labor unions, emancipation of slaves, Protestant dissenters, and Roman Catholics, reform of Parliament, the poor law, and municipal government, reorganization of the banking system, abolition of the Navigation Acts, and enactment of free trade.

Fifth, industrialization, which generated wealth and services for all, sharpened the age-old cleavage between employer and employee: while the industrial revolution did not create the first industrial proletariat in history, the numerous and concentrated industrial workers of the eighteenth and nineteenth centuries became more and more class conscious, organized themselves into labor unions and political parties with radical programs, and fought the capitalist bourgeoisie.

Sixth, the capitalist bourgeoisie—two of the most abused terms in our vocabulary—was not spawned by the industrial revolution either, but developed on a scale unprecedented in numbers and strength; yet it was neither monolithic nor "dominant." In effect, the bourgeoisie emerged abreast of the old nobility as the industrial workers emerged abreast of the ancient peasantry, the result being a complex, richly variegated society. The industrial revolution afforded opportunities to acquire wealth and rise in social status that had never existed before.

Seventh, the industrial revolution effected a drastic shift in the international balance of power. Military strength hinged less on numbers and tactical leadership, more on the industrial capacity to produce armaments and transport them efficiently. Western power and domination, ascending since the fifteenth century, reached their zenith and carried on unchecked till Third World societies underwent their own industrial revolutions and began to attain countervailing power.

Eighth, needless to say, the industrial revolution is not over and will not stop in the foreseeable future. Science and technology, its leading edge, continue the human harvest of achievement and disappointment, creation and destruction, healing and suffering, promise and danger.

23. The Wealth of Nations, 1776

Adam Smith

Adam Smith (1723–1790) was one of the great figures of the Enlightenment and the principal creator of economics as a scientific discipline, a kind of Newtonian system in which all the elements of the economic universe—price, production, wages, population, rent, capital, etc.—are kept in their orbits by mutual counterpoise and interaction. He attended Oxford and held a professorship at Glasgow University. While travelling in France he met many of the Physiocrats, whose views confirmed rather than influenced his own; their famous slogan, *laissez-faire, laissez-passer,* Smith's motto as well, never actually appears in his publications. He was more decidedly influenced by his fellow Scotsman, the philosopher and historian David Hume, many of whose ideas, though much more fully developed, resonate in *The Wealth of Nations.* These include the concept of world peace through world trade and economic interdependence, free trade, greater economic equality, and a higher standard of living for workmen. Smith did not invent capitalism, which is age-old; he speaks frequently of capital but not at all of capitalism, a term which did not come into use until about 1850. Nevertheless, the idea is central to his conception of economics and can be defined as the assembly by management or owners of raw materials, tools and techniques, and labor so as to produce increased wealth which constitutes profit; capitalism can take the form, variously, of private enterprise, corporate enterprise, state enterprise (as under socialism or communism) or a combination of these modes of organization. Smith placed great emphasis on private ownership of property and on individual freedom. In 1778 Smith was appointed a commissioner of customs for Scotland, a kind of sinecure necessary in an age when there was little provision for pensions or retirement benefits.

QUESTIONS

1. According to Smith, what are the economic advantages and human disadvantages of the division of labor?
2. What was mercantilism? According to Smith, what was wrong with it?
3. Define "the invisible hand" and suggest a word or phrase that could be substituted for it. How is the public good provided for?
4. How rational do individuals have to be for Smith's economic structure to function? Are individuals more rational, knowledgeable, or reliable than governments?
5. Why does Smith oppose giving "the monopoly of the home market" to domestic producers?
6. What is "natural" in economic matters, according to Smith? By logical extension, what would he call "unnatural"?
7. What policies and actions might the state pursue as a "duty" under category three of the government's role? Might these conflict with the principle he enunciated with regard to commerce?
8. On the basis of this reading, argue whether Smith favored *laissez-faire*, capitalism, and the division of labor.

Of Systems of Political Economy

Political economy, considered as a branch of the science of a statesman or legislator, proposes two distinct objects: first, to provide a plentiful revenue or subsistence for the people, or more properly to enable them to provide such a revenue or subsistence for themselves; and secondly, to supply the state or commonwealth with a revenue sufficient for the public services. It proposes to enrich both the people and the sovereign.

Of the Division of Labour

The greatest improvement in the productive powers of labour, and the greater part of the skill, dexterity, and judgment with which it is any where directed, or applied, seem to have been the effects of the division of labour. . . .

To take an example, therefore, from a very trifling manufacturer; but one in which the division of labour has been very often taken notice of, the trade of the pin-maker; a workman not educated to this business (which the division of labour has rendered a distinct trade) nor acquainted with the use of the machinery employed in it (to the invention of which the same division of labour has probably given occasion), could scarce, perhaps, with his utmost industry, make one pin in a day, and certainly could not make twenty. But in the way in which this business is now carried on, not only the whole work is a peculiar trade, but it is divided into a number of branches, of which the greater part are likewise peculiar trades. One man draws out the wire, another straights it, a third cuts it, a fourth points it, a fifth grinds it at the top for receiving the head; to make the head requires two or three distinct operations; to put it on, is a peculiar business, to whiten the pins is another; it is even a trade by itself to put them into the paper; and the important business of making a pin is, in this manner, divided into about eighteen distinct operations, which, in some manufactories, are all performed by distinct hands, though in others the same man will sometimes perform two or three of them. I have seen a small manufactory of this kind where ten men only were employed, and where some of them consequently performed two or three distinct operations. But though they were very poor, and therefore but indifferently accommodated with the necessary machinery, they could, when they exerted themselves, make among them about twelve pounds of pins in a day. There are in a pound upwards of four thousand pins of a middling size. Those ten persons, therefore, could make among them upwards of forty-eight thousand pins in a day. Each person, therefore, making a tenth part of forty-eight thousand pins, might be considered as making four thousand eight hundred pins in a day. But if they had all wrought separately and independently, and without any of them having been educated to this peculiar business, they certainly could not each of them have made twenty, perhaps not one pin in a day; that is, certainly, not the two hundred and fortieth, perhaps not the four thousand eight hundredth part of what they are at present capable of performing, in consequence of a proper division and combination of their different operations.

This great increase of the quantity of work, which, in consequence of the division of labour, the same number of people are capable of performing, is owing to three different circumstances; first, to the increase of dexterity in every particular workman; secondly, to the saving of the time which is commonly lost in passing from one species of work to another; and lastly, to the invention of a great number of machines which facilitate and abridge labour, and enable one man to do the work of many. . . .

The labour too which is necessary to produce any one complete manufacture, is almost always divided among a great number of hands. How many different trades are employed in each branch of the linen and woolen manufactures, from the growers of the flax and the wool, to the bleachers and smoothers of the linen, or to the dyers and dressers of the cloth! The nature of agriculture, indeed, does not admit of so many subdivisions of labour, nor of so complete a separation of one business from another, as manufactures. . . . The spinner is almost always a distinct person from the weaver; but the ploughman, the harrower, the sower of the seed, and the reaper of the corn, are often the same. . . . This impossibility of making so complete and entire a separation of all the different branches of labour employed in agriculture, is perhaps the reason why the improvement of the productive powers of labour in this art, does not always keep pace with their improvement in manufactures. . . .

In the progress of the division of labour, the employment of the far greater part of those who live by labour, that is, of the great body of the people, comes to be confined to a few very simple operations, frequently to one or two. But the understandings of the greater part of men are necessarily formed by the ordinary employments. The man whose whole life is spent in performing a few simple operations, of which the effects too are, perhaps, always the same, or very nearly the same, has no occasion to exert his understanding, or to exercise his invention in finding out expedients for removing difficulties which never occur. He naturally loses, therefore, the habit of such exertion, and generally becomes as stupid and ignorant as it is possible for a human creature to become. The torpor of his mind renders him, not only incapable of relishing or bearing a part in any rational conversation, but of conceiving any generous, noble, or tender sentiment, and consequently of forming any just judgment concerning many even of the ordinary duties of private life. Of the great and extensive interests of his country he is altogether incapable of judging and unless very particular pains have been taken to render him otherwise, he is equally incapable of defending his country in war. The uniformity of his stationary life naturally corrupts the courage of his mind. . . .

Workmen, when they are liberally paid by the piece, are very apt to over-work themselves, and to ruin their health and constitution in a few years. A carpenter in London, and in some other places, is not supposed to last in his utmost vigour above eight years. Something of the same kind happens in many other trades, in which the workmen are paid by the piece; as they generally are in manufactures, and even in country labour, wherever wages are higher than ordinary. Almost every class of artificers is subject to some peculiar infirmity occasioned by excessive application to their peculiar species of work. Ramuzzini, an eminent Italian physician, has written a particular book concerning such diseases. . . . If masters would always listen to the dictates of reason and humanity, they have frequently occasion rather to moderate, than to animate the application of many of their workmen. It will be found, I believe, in every sort of trade, that the man who works so moderately, as to be able to work constantly, not only preserves his health the longest, but, in the course of the year, executes the greatest quantity of work. . . .

Of the Wages of Labour

What are the common wages of labour, depends every where upon the contract usually made between those two parties, whose interests are by no means the same. The workmen desire to get as much, the masters to give as little as possible. The former are disposed to combine in order to raise, the latter in order to lower the wages of labour.

It is not, however, difficult to foresee which of the two parties must, upon all ordinary occasions, have the advantage in the dispute, and force the other into a compliance with their terms. The masters, being fewer in number, can combine much more easily; and the law, besides, authorises, or at least does not prohibit their combinations, while it prohibits those of the workmen. We have no acts of parliament against combining to lower the price of work; but many against combining to raise it. In all such disputes the masters can hold out much longer. . . . In the long-run the workman may be as necessary to his master as his master is to him, but the necessity is not so immediate.

We rarely hear, it has been said, of the combinations of masters, though frequently of those of workmen. But whoever imagines, upon this account, that masters rarely combine, is as ignorant of the world as of the subject. Masters are always and every where in a sort of tacit, but constant and uniform combination, not to raise the wages of labour above their actual rate. To violate this combination is every where a most unpopular action, and a sort of reproach to a master among his neighbours and equals. We seldom, indeed, hear of this combination, because it is the usual, and one may say, the natural state of things which nobody ever hears of. Masters too sometimes enter into particular combinations to sink the wages of labour even below this rate. These are always conducted with the utmost silence and secrecy, till the moment of execution, and when the workmen yield, as they sometimes do, without resistance, though severely felt by them, they are never heard of by other people. Such combinations, however, are frequently resisted by a contrary defensive combination of the workmen; who sometimes too, without any provocation of this kind, combine of their own accord to raise the price of their labour. Their usual pretences are, sometimes the high price of provisions; sometimes the great profit which their masters make by their work. But whether their combinations be offensive or defensive, they are always abundantly heard of. In order to bring the point to a speedy decision, they have always recourse to the loudest clamour, and sometimes to the most shocking violence and outrage. They are desperate, and act with the folly and extravagance of desperate men, who must either starve, or frighten their masters into an immediate compliance with their demands.

Of the Mercantile System [Mercantilism]

[Through Mercantilism the] nations have been taught that their interest consisted in beggaring all their neighbours. Each nation has been made to look with an invidious eye upon the prosperity of all the nations with which it trades, and to consider their gain as its own loss. Commerce, which ought naturally to be, among nations, as among individuals, a bond of union and friendship, has become the most fertile source of discord and animosity. The capricious ambition of kings and ministers has not, during the present and the preceding century, been more fatal to the repose of Europe, than the impertinent jealousy of merchants and manufacturers. . . .

That it was the spirit of monopoly which originally both invented and propagated this doctrine, cannot be doubted. . . . In every country it always is and must be the in-

terest of the great body of the people to buy whatever they want of those who sell it cheapest. The proposition is so very manifest, that it seems ridiculous to take any pains to prove it; nor could it ever have been called in question, had not the interested sophistry of merchants and manufacturers confounded the common sense of mankind. . . .

There is no commercial country in Europe of which the approaching ruin has not frequently been foretold by the pretended doctors of this system, from an unfavourable balance of trade. After all the anxiety, however, which they have excited about this, after all the vain attempts of almost all trading nations to turn that balance in their own favour and against their neighbours, it does not appear that any one nation in Europe has been in any respect impoverished by this cause. Every town and country, on the contrary, in proportion as they have opened their ports to all nations, instead of being ruined by this free trade, as the principles of the [mercantilist] system would lead us to expect, have been enriched by it. . . .

There is another balance, indeed, . . . very different from the balance of trade, and which, according as it happens to be either favourable or unfavourable, necessarily occasions the prosperity or decay of every nation. This is the balance of the annual produce and consumption. If the exchangeable value of the annual produce, it has already been observed, exceeds that of the annual consumption, the capital of the society must annually increase in proportion to this excess. . . .

The balance of produce and consumption may be constantly in favour of a nation, though what is called the balance of trade be generally against it. A nation may import to a greater value than it exports for half a century, perhaps, together; the gold and silver which comes into it during all this time may be all immediately sent out of it; its circulating coin may gradually decay, different sorts of paper money being substituted in its place, and even the debts too which it contracts in the principal nations with whom it deals, may be gradually increasing; and yet its real wealth, the exchangeable value of the annual produce of its lands and labour, may, during the same period, have been increasing in a much greater proportion. The state of our North American colonies, and of the trade which they carried on with Great Britain, before the commencement of the present disturbances, may serve as a proof that this is by no means an impossible supposition.

The Invisible Hand

Every individual is continually exerting himself to find out the most advantageous employment for whatever capital he can command. It is his own advantage, indeed, and not that of society, which he has in view. But the study of his own advantage, naturally, or rather necessarily, leads him to prefer that employment which is most advantageous to society. . . .

As every individual . . . endeavors as much as he can both to employ his capital in the support of domestic industry, and so to direct that industry that its produce may be of the greatest value; every individual necessarily labours to render the annual revenue of the society as great as he can. He generally, indeed, neither intends to promote the public interest, nor knows how much he is promoting it. By preferring the support of domestic to that of foreign industry, he intends only his own gain, and he is in this, as in many other cases, led by an invisible hand to promote an end which was no part of his intention. Nor is it always the worse for the society that it was no part of it.

By pursuing his own interest he frequently promotes that of the society more effectually than when he really intends to promote it. I have never known much good done by those who affected to trade for the public good. It is an affectation, indeed, not very common among merchants, and very few words need be employed in dissuading them from it.

What is the species of domestic industry which his capital can employ, and of which the produce is likely to be of the greatest value, every individual, it is evident, can, in his local situation, judge much better than any statesman or lawgiver can do for him. The statesman, who should attempt to direct private people in what manner they ought to employ their capitals, would not only load himself with a most unnecessary attention, but assume an authority which could safely be trusted, not only to no single person, but to no council or senate whatever, and which would nowhere be so dangerous as in the hands of a man who had folly and presumption enough to fancy himself fit to exercise it.

To give the monopoly of the home market to the produce of domestic industry, in any particular art or manufacture, is in some measure to direct private people in what manner they ought to employ their capitals, and must, in almost all cases, be either a useless or a hurtful regulation. If the produce of domestic can be bought there as cheap as that of foreign industry, the regulation is evidently useless. If it cannot, it must generally be hurtful. It is the maxim of every prudent master of a family never to attempt to make at home what it will cost him more to make than to buy. The taylor does not attempt to make his own shoes, but buys them of the shoemaker. The shoemaker does not attempt to make his own clothes, but employs a taylor. The farmer attempts to make neither the one nor the other, but employs those different artificers. All of them find it for their interest to employ their whole industry in a way in which they have some advantage over their neighbors, and to purchase with a part of its produce, or what is the same thing, with the price of a part of it, whatever else they have occasion for.

What is prudence in the conduct of every private family, can scarce be folly in that of a great kingdom. If a foreign country can supply us with a commodity cheaper than we ourselves can make it, better buy it of them with some part of the produce of our own industry, employed in a way in which we have some advantage. The general industry of the country, being always in proportion to the capital which employs it will not thereby be diminished, no more than that of the above-mentioned artificers; but only left to find out the way in which it can be employed to the greatest advantage, when it is thus directed towards an object which it can buy cheaper than it can make. The value of its annual produce is certainly more or less diminished, when it is thus turned away from producing commodities evidently of more value than the commodity which it is directed to produce. According to the supposition, that commodity could be purchased from foreign countries cheaper than it can be made at home. It could, therefore, have been purchased with a part only of the commodities, or, what is the same thing, with a part only of the price of the commodities, which the industry employed by an equal capital would have produced at home, had it been left to follow its natural course. The industry of the country therefore, is thus turned away from a more, to a less advantageous employment, and the exchangeable value of its annual produce, instead of being increased, according to the intention of the lawgiver, must necessarily be diminished by every such regulation. . . .

The Role of Government

All systems either of preference or of restraint, therefore, being thus completely taken away, the obvious and simple system of natural liberty establishes itself of its own accord. Every man, as long as he does not violate the laws of justice, is left perfectly free to pursue his own interest his own way, and to bring both his industry and capital into competition with those of any other man, or order of men. The sovereign is completely discharged from a duty, in the attempting to perform which he must always be exposed to innumerable delusions, and for the proper performance of which no human wisdom or knowledge could ever be sufficient; the duty of superintending the industry of private people, and of directing it towards the employments most suitable to the interest of the society. According to the system of natural liberty, the sovereign has only three duties to attend to; three duties of great importance, indeed, but plain and intelligible to common understanding: first, the duty of protecting the society from the violence and invasion of other independent societies; secondly, the duty of protecting, as far as possible, every member of the society from the injustice or oppression of every other member of it, or the duty of establishing an exact administration of justice; and, thirdly, the duty of erecting and maintaining certain public works and certain public institutions, which it can never be for the interest of any individual, or small number of individuals, to erect and maintain; because the profit could never repay the expence to any individual or small number of individuals, though it may frequently do much more than repay it to a great society. . . .

24. The National System of Political Economy, 1841–1844

Friedrich List

Friedrich List (1789–1846) was a German economist, professor, journalist, politician and businessman who spent a lifetime attacking Adam Smith's economic theories. Largely self-educated, he was a liberal constitutionalist and polemical critic of bureaucratic absolutism. His views cost him his seat in the legislative assembly of his native Wurttemberg and his professorship. After being sentenced to jail he fled to the United States, where during the years between 1825 and 1832 he developed most of his ideas and engaged extensively in the debate over protectionism and tariff reform. President Andrew Jackson appointed him consul at Leipzig and he returned to Germany; there he resumed his activities as leading publicist and organizer of the Zollverein (the German customs and commercial union headed by Prussia and the foundation of German political unification that came a generation later under Bismarck). Like many Germans of succeeding generations, List resented Britain's naval, commercial, and manufacturing power. He viewed Smith's free trade policy as a British conspiracy especially against Germany. He ceaselessly advocated creation of a national system of railways, turnpikes, rivers and canals unified under Zollverein direction, a German navy and merchant marine, consular offices worldwide, a national flag, and colonies in southeast Europe, South America, Australia, and New Zealand. Despite his Anglophobia, he admired Britain for its parliamentary government, security of person and property, and general freedom, which he regarded as necessary for sound economic development. His neo-mercantilist ideas have been especially influential in Germany, the United States, and to some degree in France. List had a keen sense of the economic foundations of military power as well as the strategic significance of railways and steamships around the world. Depressed with illness and overwork, he committed suicide just when his ideas and proposals began to find an audience.

QUESTIONS

1. Define national economics on the basis of List's exposition.
2. What relationship does List postulate between economics and war?
3. What elements of later German national ambition does List reveal?
4. What part in economic life does List ascribe to the individual?
5. Defend or rebut the assertion that List was a mercantilist.
6. What does List mean by "productive powers"?
7. What are the fundamental differences between List and Adam Smith? What features of Smith's analysis does List accept?

Introduction

In national economic development we must distinguish the following stages: the savage, the pastoral, the agricultural, the agricultural and manufacturing, the agricultural, manufacturing, and commercial. . . . Every nation, which attaches any value to its independence and continued existence, must strive to pass with all speed from a lower stage of culture to a higher, and to combine within its own territory agriculture, manufactures, shipping, and commerce. The transition from savagery to the pastoral state, and from the latter to the agricultural state, are best effected by free trade with civilized, that is, manufacturing and commercial nations. The transition from an agricultural community into the class of agricultural, commercial, and manufacturing nations, could only take place under free trade if the same process of development occurred simultaneously in all nations destined to manufactures, if nations put no hindrance in the way of one another's economic development, if they did not check one another's progress through war and tariffs. But since individual nations, through specially favorable circumstances, gained an advantage over others in manufactures, trade, and shipping, and since they early understood the best means of getting and maintaining through these advantages political ascendancy, they have accordingly invented a policy which aimed, and still aims, at obtaining a monopoly in manufactures and trade, and at checking the progress of less advanced nations. The combination of the details of this policy (prohibition of imports, import duties, restrictions on shipping, bounties on exports) is known as the tariff system. . . .

Hence there is a cosmopolitan and a political economy, a theory of exchange values and a theory of productive powers [or capacities], two doctrines which are essentially distinct and which must be developed independently. The productive powers of a nation are not only limited by the industry, thrift, morality, and intelligence of its individual members, and by its natural resources or material capital, but also by its social, political, and municipal laws and institutions, and especially by the securities for the continued existence, independence, and power of the nationality. However industrious, thrifty, enterprising, moral, and intelligent the individuals may be, without national unity, national division of labor, and national co-operation of productive powers the nation will never reach a high level of prosperity and power, or ensure to itself the lasting possession of its intellectual, social, and material goods. . . .

A nation which desires to pass from a non-protective policy to protection must . . . begin with low [import] taxes, which increase gradually upon a predetermined scale. Taxes pre-determined in this way must be maintained intact by statesmen. They must not lower the taxes before the time, though they may raise them if they seem insufficient. Excessively high import duties, which entirely cut off foreign competition, injure the country which imposes them, since its manufacturers are not forced to compete with foreigners, and indolence is fostered. If home manufactures do not prosper under moderate and gradually increasing duties, this is a proof that the country has not the necessary qualifications for the development of its own manufacturing system. . . .

The loss which a nation incurs by protection is only one of *values*, but it gains *powers* by which it is enabled to go on producing permanently inestimable amounts of value. This loss in value should be regarded merely as the price paid for the industrial education of the nation. . . . Moderate protection does not grant a monopoly to home manufactures, only a guarantee against loss for those individuals who have devoted their capital, talent, and labor to new and untried industries. There can be no monopoly since home competition takes the place of foreign, and it is open to each member of the state to share in the benefits it offers to individuals. . . .

History affords striking examples of whole nations falling into ruin because they did not know how to undertake at the right moment the great task of planting their own manufactures, and a powerful industry and commerce, by which they could insure to themselves intellectual, economic, and political independence. . . . At a time when technical and mechanical science exercise such immense influence on the methods of warfare, when all warlike operations depend so much on the condition of the national revenue, where successful defense greatly depends on . . . whether it [the nation] can muster many or but few defenders of the country—at such times, more than ever before, must the value of manufactures be estimated from a political point of view.

Condemnation of Adam Smith and Laissez-Faire

Adam Smith's doctrine . . . ignores the very nature of nationalities, seems almost entirely to exclude politics and the power of the state, presupposes the existence of a state of perpetual peace and of universal union, underrates the value of a national manufacturing power, and the means of obtaining it, and demands absolute freedom of trade.

Adam Smith fell into these fundamental errors . . . by regarding absolute freedom in international trade as an axiom assent to which is demanded by common sense, and by not investigating to the bottom how far history supports this idea.

[According to Smith] the power of the state can and ought to do nothing, except to allow justice to be administered, to impose as little taxation as possible. Statesmen who attempt to found a manufacturing power, to promote navigation, to extend foreign trade, to protect it by naval power, and to found or acquire colonies, are in his opinion project makers who only hinder the progress of the community. For him no *nation* exists, but merely a community, i.e. a number of individuals dwelling together.

The mistake has been simply, that this system at bottom is nothing else than a system of the private economy of all the individual persons in a country, or of the individuals of the whole human race, as that economy would develop and shape itself, under a state of things in which there were no distinct nations, nationalities, or national interests—no distinctive political constitutions of degrees of civilization—no wars or national animosities; that it is nothing more than a theory of values; a mere shopkeeper's or individual merchant's theory—not a scientific doctrine, showing how the productive powers of an entire nation can be called into existence, increased, maintained, and preserved—for the special benefit of its civilization, welfare, might, continuance, and independence.

This system regards everything from the shopkeeper's point of view. The value of anything is wealth, according to it, so its sole object is to gain values. The establishment of powers of production, it leaves to chance, to nature, or to the providence of God (whichever you please), only the state must have nothing at all to do with it, nor must politics venture to meddle with the business of accumulating exchangeable values. It is resolved to buy wherever it can find the cheapest articles. . . .

We now see into what extraordinary mistakes and contradictions the [Smithite] school has fallen in making material wealth or value of exchange the sole object of investigations, and by regarding mere bodily labor as the sole productive power: The man who breeds pigs is . . . a productive member of the community, but he who educates men is a mere non-productive. The maker of bagpipes or jews-harps for sale is a productive, while the great composers and virtuosos are non-productive simply because that which they play cannot be brought into the market. The physician who saves the lives of his patients does not belong to the productive class, but on the contrary the chemist's boy does so, although the values of exchange (viz. the pills) which he produces may exist only for a few minutes before they pass into a valueless condition. A Newton, a Watt, or a Kepler is not so productive as a donkey, a horse, or a draught-ox.

We must say . . . that *political* economy is not, in our opinion, that science which teaches only how values in exchange are produced by individuals, distributed among them, and consumed by them; we say . . . that a statesman will know and must know, over and above that, how the *productive powers* of a whole nation can be awakened, increased, and protected, and how on the other hand they are weakened, laid to sleep, or utterly destroyed; and how by means of those national productive powers the national resources can be utilized in the wisest and best manner so as to produce national existence, national independence, national prosperity, national strength, national culture, and a national future.

Power is more important than wealth. That is indeed the fact. Power is more important than wealth. And why? Simply because national power is a dynamic force by which new productive resources are opened out, and because the forces of production are the tree on which wealth grows, and because the tree which bears the fruit is of greater value than the fruit itself. Power is of more importance than wealth because a nation, by means of power, is enabled not only to open up new productive forces, but to maintain itself in possession of former and of recently acquired wealth, and because the reverse of power—namely, feebleness—leads to the relinquishment of all that we possess, not of acquired wealth alone, but of powers of production, of our civilization, of our freedom, nay, even of our national independence, into the hands of those who surpass us in might, as is abundantly attested by the history of the Italian republics, of the Hanseatic League, of the Belgians, the Dutch, the Spaniards, and the Portuguese.

National Economics

Between each individual and entire humanity . . . stands THE NATION, with its special language and literature, with its peculiar origin and history, with its special manners and customs, laws and institutions, with the claims of all these for existence, independence, perfection, and continuance for the future, and with its separate territory; a society which, united by a thousand ties of mind and of interests, combines itself into one independent whole, which recognizes the law of right for and within itself, and in its united character is still opposed to other societies of a similar kind in their national liberty, and consequently can only under the existing conditions of the world maintain self-existence and independence by its own power and resources. As the individual chiefly obtains by means of the nation and in the nation mental culture, power of production, security, and prosperity, so is the civilization of the human race only conceivable and possible by means of the civilization and development of the individual nations.

Meanwhile, however, an infinite difference exists in the condition and circumstances of the various nations: we observe among them giants and dwarfs, well-formed bodies and cripples, civilized, half-civilized, and barbarous nations; but in all of them, as in the individual human being, exists the impulse of self-preservation, the striving for improvement which is implanted by nature. It is the task of politics to civilize the barbarous nationalities, to make the small and weak ones great and strong, but, above all, to secure to them existence and continuance. It is the task of national economy to accomplish the economical development of the nation, and to prepare it for admission into the universal society of the future. . . .

A large population, and an extensive territory endowed with manifold national resources, are essential requirements of the normal nationality; they are the fundamental conditions of mental cultivation as well as of material development and political power. A nation restricted in the number of its population and in territory, especially if it has a separate language, can only possess a crippled literature, crippled institutions for promoting art and science. A small state can never bring to complete perfection within its territory the various branches of production. . . . A nation not bounded by seas and chains of mountains lies open to the attacks of foreign nations, and can only by great sacrifices, and in any case only very imperfectly, establish and maintain a separate tariff system of its own.

Territorial deficiencies of the nation can be remedied either by means of hereditary succession, as in the case of England and Scotland; or by purchase, as in the case of Florida and Louisiana; or by conquests,

as in the case of Great Britain and Ireland. . . . It must not be ignored that rectification of territory must be reckoned among the most important requirements of the nations, that striving to attain it is legitimate, that indeed in many cases it is a justifiable reason for war.

In modern times a fourth means has been adopted, which leads to this object in manner much more in accordance with justice and with the prosperity of nations than conquest, and which is not so dependent on accidents as hereditary succession, namely, the union of the interests of various states by means of free conventions.

By its Zollverein, the German nation first obtained one of the most important attributes of its nationality. But this measure cannot be considered complete so long as it does not extend over the whole coast, from the mouth of the Rhine to the frontier of Poland, including Holland and Denmark. A natural consequence of this union must be the admission of both these countries into the German Bund [the Germanic Confederation set up in 1815, replacing the Holy Roman Empire], and consequently into the German nationality, whereby the latter will at once obtain what it is now in need of, namely, fisheries and naval power, maritime commerce and colonies. Besides, both these nations belong, as respects their descent and whole character, to the German nationality. . . . Holland is in reference to its geographical position, as well as in respect to its commercial and industrial circumstances, and the origin and language of its inhabitants, a German province, which has been separated from Germany at a period of German national disunion, without whose reincorporation in the German Union Germany may be compared to a house the door of which belongs to a stranger. . . . The Germans . . . will have it in their power to compel Holland to join the Zollverein. . . . Belgium [which joined the Zollverein in 1844] can only remedy by means of confederation with a neighboring larger nation her needs which are inseparable from her restricted territory and population. . . . [The] central part of Europe constitutes at present the apple of discord for which the east and west contend, while each party hopes to draw to its own side this middle power, which is weakened by want of national unity, and is always uncertainly wavering hither and thither. If . . . Germany could constitute itself with the maritime territories which appertain to it, with Holland, Belgium, and Switzerland, as a powerful commercial and political whole . . . then Germany could secure peace to the continent of Europe for a long time.

---

25. On the Principles of Population, 1798, 1803

Thomas Robert Malthus

In his own view Thomas Malthus's (1766–1834) two life-long concerns were the obstacles thwarting improvement of the human condition and the factors that can limit or overcome those obstacles. He was professor of history and political economy at the East India Company's College (founded to train recruits for its administration of India) at Haileybury near London. He was a graduate of Cambridge University with honors in mathematics, an Anglican priest, and one of the founders of what became the Royal Statistical Society. The starting point of Malthus's work was his rebuttal of what he took to be the Enlightenment's excessive optimism. He knew well the specter of over-population as well as wartime shortages, bad harvests, breakdowns in the poor relief system, and the Irish Rising of 1798. In the second edition of his *Essay on Population* (1803) Malthus sought to prove his thesis by many instances and examples buttressed with statistics. He also softened his pessimistic assessment considerably by his argument that a rising standard of living would induce "moral restraint," because the well-to-do have smaller families since they want a better life for their children and more comfort for themselves. His concept of the pressure of population on food supply, land, rent, and resources generally gave rise to what was later called "the iron law of wages." As developed by David Ricardo, it was so grim that later generations dubbed economics "the dismal science." That is perhaps unfair to Malthus's reputation, since his goal was the happiness and wealth of all. Malthus's writings had a profound influence on English poor laws, the early movement for birth control, and Darwin's theories of natural selection.

QUESTIONS

1. According to Thomas Malthus, what natural laws govern the relationship between population growth and food supply?
2. Define what Malthus means by preventive and positive checks to population growth.
3. Is Malthus optimistic or pessimistic about the future of mankind? Explain.
4. What does he suggest about the study of the lower classes?

Population's Effects on Society, 1798

I have read some of the speculations on the perfectibility of man and of society with great pleasure. I have been warmed and delighted with the enchanting picture which they hold forth. I ardently wish for such happy improvements. But I see great and, to my understanding, unconquerable difficulties in the way to them. These difficulties it is my present purpose to state, declaring, at the same time, that so far from exulting in them, as a cause of triumphing over the friends of innovation, nothing would give me greater pleasure than to see them completely removed. . . .

[These difficulties are] First, That food is necessary to the existence of man. Secondly, That the passion between the sexes is necessary and will remain nearly in its present state.

These two laws, ever since we have had any knowledge of mankind, appear to have been fixed laws of our nature; and as we have not hitherto seen any alteration in them, we have no right to conclude that they will ever cease to be what they are now, without an immediate act of power in that Being who first arranged the system of the universe, and for the advantage of His creatures, still executes, according to fixed laws, all its various operations. . . .

Assuming, then, my postulata as granted, I say that the power of population is indefinitely greater than the power in the earth to produce subsistence for man.

Population, when unchecked, increases in a geometrical ratio. Subsistence only increases in an arithmetical ratio. A slight acquaintance with numbers will show the immensity of the first power in comparison of the second.

By that law of our nature which makes food necessary to the life of man, the effects of these two unequal powers may be kept equal.

This implies a strong and constantly operating check on population from the difficulty of subsistence. This difficulty must fall somewhere and must necessarily be severely felt by a large portion of mankind. . . .

This natural inequality of the two powers of population and of production in the earth, and that great law of our nature which must constantly keep their efforts equal, form the great difficulty that to me appears insurmountable in the way to the perfectibility of society. . . .

Consequently, if the premises are just, the argument is conclusive against the perfectibility of the mass of mankind.

Population's Effects on Human Happiness, 1803

The ultimate check to population appears then to be a want of food, arising necessarily from the different ratios according to which population and food increase. But this ultimate check is never the immediate check, except in cases of actual famine.

The immediate check may be stated to consist in all those customs, and all those diseases, which seem to be generated by a scarcity of the means of subsistence; and all those causes, independent of this scarcity, which tend prematurely to weaken and destroy the human frame.

These checks to population, which are constantly operating with more or less force in every society, and keep down the number to the level of the means of subsistence, may be classed under two general heads—the preventive and the positive checks.

The preventive check, as far as it is voluntary, is peculiar to man, and arises from that distinctive superiority in his reasoning faculties which enables him to calculate distant consequences. Man cannot look around him and see the distress which frequently presses upon those who have large families; he cannot contemplate his present possessions or earnings which he now nearly consumes himself, and calculate the amount of each share, when with a little addition they must be divided, perhaps, among seven or eight, without feeling a doubt whether, if he follow the bent of his inclinations, he may be able to support the offspring which he will probably bring into the world. . . .

The conditions are calculated to prevent, and certainly do prevent, a great number of persons in all civilized nations from pursuing the dictate of nature in an early attachment to one woman. . . .

The positive checks to population are extremely various, and include every cause, whether arising from vice or misery, which in any degree contributes to shorten the natural duration of human life. Under this head, therefore, may be enumerated all unwholesome occupations, severe labor and

exposure to the seasons, extreme poverty, bad nursing of children, great towns, excesses of all kinds, the whole train of common diseases and epidemics, wars, plague, and famine. . . .

Of the General Checks to Population

In every country some of these checks are, with more or less force, in constant operation; yet, notwithstanding their general prevalence, there are few states in which there is not a constant effort in the population to increase beyond the means of subsistence. This constant effort as constantly tends to subject the lower classes of society to distress, and to prevent any great permanent melioration of their condition.

These effects, in the present state of society, seem to be produced in the following manner. We will suppose the means of subsistence in any country just equal to the easy support of its inhabitants. The constant effort towards population, which is found to act even in the most vicious societies, increases the number of people before the means of subsistence are increased. The food, therefore, which before supported eleven millions, must now be divided among eleven millions and a half. The poor consequently must live much worse, and many of them be reduced to severe distress. The number of labourers also being above the proportion of work in the market, the price of labour must tend to fall, while the price of provisions would at the same time tend to rise. The labourer therefore must do more work to earn the same as he did before. During this season of distress, the discouragements to marriage and the difficulty of rearing a family are so great that the progress of population is retarded. In the meantime, the cheapness of labour, the plenty of labourers, and the necessity of an increased industry among them, encourage cultivators to employ more labour upon their land, to turn up fresh soil, and to manure and improve more completely what is already in tillage, till ultimately the means of subsistence may become in the same proportion to the population as at the period from which we set out. The situation of the labourer being then again tolerably comfortable, the restraints to population are in some degree loosened; and, after a short period, the same retrograde and progressive movements, with respect to happiness, are repeated.

This sort of oscillation will not probably be obvious to common view; and it may be difficult even for the most attentive observer to calculate its periods. Yet that, in the generality of old states, some alternation of this kind does exist though in a much less marked, and in a much more irregular manner, than I have described it, no reflecting man, who considers the subject deeply, can well doubt.

One principal reason why this oscillation has been less remarked, and less decidedly confirmed by experience than might naturally be expected, is, that the histories of mankind which we possess are, in general, histories only of the higher classes. We have not many accounts that can be depended upon of the manners and customs of that part of mankind where these retrograde and progressive movements chiefly take place. A satisfactory history of this kind, of one people and of one period, would require the constant and minute attention of many observing minds in local and general remarks on the state of the lower classes of society, and the causes that influenced it; and to draw accurate inferences upon this subject, a succession of such historians for some centuries would be necessary. This branch of statistical knowledge has, of late years, been attended to in some countries, and we may promise ourselves a clearer insight into the internal structure of human society from the progress of these inquiries. But the science may be said yet to be in its infancy. . . .

26. Regulations of the Foundry and Engineering Works of the Royal Overseas Trading Company, 1844

Berlin

As much an invention of the age as the steam engine, the factory, a main building with machinery where workmen congregated for a stipulated time span, began to emerge in England after 1760. Factory discipline, also a product of the era, required that workmen arrive on time and work steadily, since the machines were demanding and could not stand idle without loss or damage. Factory organization initiated an unprecedented degree of separation between employer, foreman, and employee. It imposed regimentation that was unimaginable to previous generations of workers, utilizing fines and blacklisting for infractions. Such "industrial discipline" must have been especially difficult for the first generation of mill people, many of whom were women or children, and generally poor, uneducated, and often unruly. One of the most significant results was a new consciousness of time, of which railroad timetables were perhaps the most striking example. Marx drew attention to the division of the working day into chunks, making time a marketable commodity. Friedrich List argued that the value of time was recognized much more in manufacturing than in agricultural nations. He noted the English saying, "Time is money." Below are the regulations of a German factory in the Moabit section of Berlin. It is a typical code in that it seeks to establish proper conduct beyond the confines of the factory, no doubt to imbue workers with the capitalist virtues that were good for business, but also those of a good parent and citizen.

QUESTIONS

1. Describe the time-discipline imposed on workers in this factory in Berlin.
2. How was the personal behavior of the workers regulated in this factory?
3. What methods did the management of this factory use to enforce these rules?
4. How did the work schedule described in this document differ from labor routines in preindustrial towns and farms?

In every large works, and in the co-ordination of any large number of workmen, good order and harmony must be looked upon as the fundamentals of success, and therefore the following rules shall be strictly observed.

Every man employed in the concern named below shall receive a copy of these rules, so that no one can plead ignorance. Its acceptance shall be deemed to mean consent to submit to its regulations.

1. The normal working day begins at all seasons at 6 a.m. precisely and ends, after the usual break of half an hour for breakfast, an hour for dinner and half an hour for tea, at 7 p.m., and it shall be strictly observed.

Five minutes before the beginning of the stated hours of work until their actual commencement, a bell shall ring and indicate that every worker employed in the concern has to proceed to his place of work, in order to start as soon as the bell stops.

The doorkeeper shall lock the door punctually at 6 a.m., 8:30 a.m., 1 p.m. and 4:30 p.m.

Workers arriving 2 minutes late shall lose half an hour's wages; whoever is more than 2 minutes late may not start work until after the next break, or at least shall lose his wages until then. Any disputes about the correct time shall be settled by the clock mounted above the gatekeeper's lodge.

These rules are valid both for time- and for piece-workers, and in cases of breaches of these rules, workmen shall be fined in proportion to their earnings. The deductions from the wage shall be entered in the wage-book of the gatekeeper whose duty they are; they shall be unconditionally accepted as it will not be possible to enter into any discussions about them.

2. When the bell is rung to denote the end of the working day, every workman, both on piece- and on day-wage, shall leave

his workshop and the yard, but is not allowed to make preparations for his departure before the bell rings. Every breach of this rule shall lead to a fine of five silver groschen [pennies] to the sick fund. Only those who have obtained special permission by the overseer may stay on in the workshop in order to work.—If a workman has worked beyond the closing bell, he must give his name to the gatekeeper on leaving, on pain of losing his payment for the overtime.

3. No workman, whether employed by time or piece, may leave before the end of the working day, without having first received permission from the overseer and having given his name to the gatekeeper. Omission of these two actions shall lead to a fine of ten silver groschen payable to the sick fund.

4. Repeated irregular arrival at work shall lead to dismissal. This shall also apply to those who are found idling by an official or overseer, and refuse to obey their order to resume work.

5. Entry to the firm's property by any but the designated gateway, and exit by any prohibited route, e.g. by climbing fences or walls, or by crossing the Spree, shall be punished by a fine of fifteen silver groschen to the sick fund for the first offences, and dismissal for the second.

6. No worker may leave his place of work otherwise than for reasons connected with his work.

7. All conversation with fellow-workers is prohibited; if any worker requires information about his work, he must turn to the overseer, or to the particular fellow-worker designated for the purpose.

8. Smoking in the workshops or in the yard is prohibited during working hours; anyone caught smoking shall be fined five silver groschen for the sick fund for every such offence.

9. Every worker is responsible for cleaning up his space in the workshop, and if in doubt, he is to turn to his overseer.—All tools must always be kept in good condition, and must be cleaned after use. This applies particularly to the turner, regarding his lathe.

10. Natural functions must be performed at the appropriate places, and whoever is found soiling walls, fences, squares, etc., and similarly, whoever is found washing his face and hands in the workshop and not in the places assigned for the purpose, shall be fined five silver groschen for the sick fund.

11. On completion of his piece of work, every workman must hand it over at once to his foreman or superior, in order to receive a fresh piece of work. Pattern makers must on no account hand over their patterns to the foundry without express order of their supervisors. No workman may take over work from his fellow-workman without instruction to that effect by the foreman.

12. It goes without saying that all overseers and officials of the firm shall be obeyed without question, and shall be treated with due deference. Disobedience will be punished by dismissal.

13. Immediate dismissal shall also be the fate of anyone found drunk in any of the workshops.

14. Untrue allegations against superiors or officials of the concern shall lead to stern reprimand, and may lead to dismissal. The same punishment shall be meted out to those who knowingly allow errors to slip through when supervising or stocktaking.

15. Every workman is obliged to report to his superiors any acts of dishonesty or embezzlement on the part of his fellow workmen. If he omits to do so, and it is shown after subsequent discovery of a misdemeanour that he knew about it at the time, he shall be liable to be taken to court as an accessory after the fact and the wage due to him shall be retained as punishment. Con-

versely, anyone denouncing a theft in such a way as to allow conviction of the thief shall receive a reward of two Thaler and, if necessary, his name shall be kept confidential.— Further, the gatekeeper and the watchman, as well as every official, are entitled to search the baskets, parcels, aprons etc. of the women and children who are taking the dinners into the works, on their departure, as well as search any worker suspected of stealing any article whatever. . . .

18. Advances shall be granted only to the older workers, and even to them only in exceptional circumstances. As long as he is working by the piece, the workman is entitled merely to his fixed weekly wage as sub-sistence pay; the extra earnings shall be paid out only on completion of the whole piece contract. If a workman leaves before his piece contract is completed, either of his own free will, or on being dismissed as punishment, or because of illness, the partly completed work shall be valued by the general manager with the help of two overseers, and he will be paid accordingly. There is no appeal against the decision of these experts.

19. A free copy of these rules is handed to every workman, but whoever loses it and requires a new one, or cannot produce it on leaving, shall be fined 2 1/2 silver groschen, payable to the sick fund.

27. Parliamentary Inquiries into Working Conditions, 1832, 1842

The following documents are typical examples of public reaction in Britain to industrialization. There were hundreds of royal and parliamentary commissions and committees of inquiry into the working conditions of the laboring classes. They followed a characteristic pattern: a conscience-driven person or small group made accusations; these were denied; a committee or commission was appointed to hear evidence and report with recommendations; the published reports—Blue Books—gave rise to public outcry and demands that something be done; reform legislation followed. In short, the sequence was private initiative, inquiry, publicity, scandal, reform.

Michael Thomas Sadler (1780–1835), and Anthony Ashley Cooper, 7th Earl of Shaftesbury (1801–1885), are examples of social reformers who were evangelical Anglicans. They illustrate the noblesse oblige that animated some members of the old landed aristocracy. Sadler was a Tory member of Parliament and an economist who was highly critical of the classical school of Adam Smith, Malthus, and Ricardo, whom he condemned as "pests of society and the persecutors of the poor." His involvement in the linen business drew him to the cause of alleviating poverty in Ireland, but he also vehemently opposed Catholic emancipation. In 1831 his bill to limit the working hours of children ran into stout opposition and was referred to the committee whose report is excerpted below. It met 43 times and heard 89 witnesses, about half of whom were workers. Sadler exhausted himself in doing most of the work and, when he failed of re-election, his place as sponsor of the ten hours bill was taken by Ashley. The legislation limiting the work day of children did not pass until 1847. Ashley was a philanthropist, social reformer, and statesman who devoted most of his life to a parliamentary career, first as a Tory, then—deserting his party on the issue of free trade—as a Whig. He was the prime mover of a great deal of reform legislation and philanthropic efforts affecting the insane, factory workers, chimney sweeps, the penal system for juvenile offenders, education, housing, and much else. The Mines Commission and the subsequent Mines Act of 1842 (barring all women and boys under 13 from employment in mines) are typical episodes of his career.

QUESTIONS

1. According to these documents, what were the ages of the children who worked in the factories and mines? What were their hours for a typical work day?
2. Why did the managers of these establishments employ children? What was the role and viewpoint of their parents in their employment?
3. How did the supervisors keep children alert at their tasks?
4. Why did Sadler question Matthew Crabtree concerning the state of morality in the factory where he worked? What was the witness's response?
5. What conditions of work prevail in the mines? Is there any way out? Why do you think the Ashley Mines Commission was appointed?
6. What kind of family life do the witnesses have? Do they live a civilized life?
7. What view does the owner of one of the mines take? What inconsistency is there in his position?

Sadler Commission Report on Child Labor, 1832

Committee on Factories Bill:
Minutes of Evidence.

[April 12,] 1832.
Michael Thomas Sadler, Esquire, in the Chair.
William Cooper, called in; and Examined.

What is your business?—I follow the cloth-dressing at present.

What is your age?—I was eight-and-twenty last February.

When did you first begin to work in mills or factories?—When I was about 10 years of age.

With whom did you first work?—At Mr. Benyon's Flax mills, in Meadowlane, Leeds.

What were your usual hours of working?—We began at five, and gave over at nine; at five o'clock in the morning.

And you gave over at nine o'clock?—At nine at night.

At what distance might you have lived from the mill?—About a mile and a half.

At what time had you to get up in the morning to attend to your labour?—I had to be up soon after four o'clock.

Every morning?—Every morning.

What intermissions had you for meals?—When we began at five in the morning, we went on until noon, and then we had 40 minutes for dinner.

Had you no time for breakfast?—No, we got it as we could, while we were working.

Had you any time for an afternoon refreshment, or what is called in Yorkshire your "drinking?"—No; when we began at noon, we went on till night; there was only one stoppage, the 40 minutes for dinner.

Then as you had to get your breakfast, and what is called "drinking" in that manner, you had to put it on one side?—Yes, we had to put it on one side; and when we got our frames doffed, we ate two or three mouthfuls, and then put it by again.

Is there not considerable dust in a flax mill?—A flax mill is very dusty indeed.

Was not your food therefore frequently spoiled?—Yes, at times with the dust; sometimes we could not eat it, when it had got a lot of dust on.

What were you when you were ten years old?—What is called a bobbin-doffer; when the frames are quite full, we have to doff them.

Then as you lived so far from home, you took your dinner to the mill?—We took all our meals with us, living so far off.

During the 40 minutes which you were allowed for dinner, had you ever to employ that time in your turn in cleaning the machinery?—At times we had to stop to clean the machinery, and then we got our dinner as well as we could; they paid us for that. . . .

Did you ever work even later than the time you have mentioned?—I cannot say that I worked later there. I had a sister who worked up stairs, and she worked till 11 at night, in what they call the cardroom.

At what time in the morning did she begin work?—At the same time as myself.

And they kept her there till 11 at night?—Till 11 at night.

You say that your sister was in the cardroom?—Yes.

Is not that a very dusty department?—Yes, very dusty indeed.

She had to be at the mill at five, and was kept at work till eleven at night?—Yes.

During the whole time she was there?—During the whole time; there was only 40 minutes allowed at dinner out of that.

To keep you at your work for such a length of time, and especially towards the termination of such a day's labour as that, what means were taken to keep you awake and attentive?—They strapped [beat] us at times, when we were not quite ready to be doffing the frame when it was full.

Were you frequently strapped?—At times we were frequently strapped.

What sort of strap was it?—About this length (describing it).

What was it made of?—Of leather.

Were you occasionally very considerably hurt with the strap?—Sometimes it hurt us very much, and sometimes they did not lay on so hard as they did at others.

Were the girls strapped in that sort of way?—They did not strap what they called the grown-up women.

Were any of the female children strapped?—Yes, they were strapped in the same way as the lesser boys.

What were your wages at 10 years old at Mr. Benyon's?—I think it was 4 s. [shillings] a week.

[May 18,] 1832.
Michael Thomas Sadler, Esquire, in the chair.

Mr. Matthew Crabtree, called in; and Examined.

What age are you?—Twenty-two.

What is your occupation?—A blanket manufacturer.

Have you ever been employed in a factory?—Yes.

At what age did you first go to work in one?—Eight.

How long did you continue in that occupation?—Four years.

Will you state the hours of labour at the period when you first went to the factory, in ordinary times?—From 6 in the morning to 8 at night.

Fourteen hours?—Yes.

With what intervals for refreshment and rest?—An hour at noon.

Then you had no resting time allowed in which to take your breakfast, or what is in Yorkshire called your "drinking"?—No.

When trade was brisk what were your hours?—From 5 in the morning to 9 in the evening.

Sixteen hours?—Yes.

With what intervals at dinner?—An hour.

How far did you live from the mill?—About two miles.

Was there any time allowed for you to get your breakfast in the mill?—No.

Did you take it before you left home?—Generally.

During those long hours of labour could you be punctual, how did you awake?—I seldom did awake spontaneously. I was most generally awoke or lifted out of bed, sometimes asleep, by my parents.

Were you always in time?—No.

What was the consequence if you had been too late?—I was most commonly beaten.

Severely?—Very severely, I thought.

In whose factory was this?—Messrs. Hague & Cook's, of Dewsbury.

Will you state the effect that those long hours had upon the state of your health and feelings?—I was, when working those long hours, commonly very much fatigued at night, when I left my work, so much so that I sometimes should have slept as I walked if I had not stumbled and started awake again, and so sick often that I could not eat, and what I did eat I vomited.

Did this labour destroy your appetite?—It did.

In what situation were you in that mill?—I was a piecener.

Will you state to the Committee whether pieceening is a very laborious employment for children, or not?—It is a very laborious employment. Pieceners are continually running to and fro, and on their feet the whole day.

The duty of the piecener is to take the cardings from one part of the machinery, and to place them on another?—Yes.

So that the labour is not only continual, but it is unabated to the last?—It is unabated to the last.

Do you not think, from your own experience, that the speed of the machinery is so calculated as to demand the utmost exertions of a child, supposing the hours were moderate?—It is as much as they could do at the best; they are always upon the stretch, and it is commonly very difficult to keep up with their work.

State the condition of the children towards the latter part of the day, who have thus to keep up with the machinery?—It is as much as they can do when they are not very much fatigued to keep up with their work, and towards the close of the day, when they come to be more fatigued, they cannot keep up with it very well, and the consequence is that they are beaten to spur them on.

Were you beaten under those circumstances?—Yes.

And is it your belief that if you had not been so beaten, you should not have got through the work?—I should not if I had not been kept up to it by some means.

Does beating then principally occur at the latter end of the day, when the children are exceedingly fatigued?—It does at the latter end of the day, and in the morning sometimes, when they are very drowsy, and have not got rid of the fatigue of the day before.

What were you beaten with principally?—A strap.

Any thing else?—Yes, a stick sometimes; and there is a kind of roller which runs on the top of the machine called a billy, perhaps two or three yards in length, and perhaps an inch and a half, or more, in diameter; the circumference would be four or five inches, I cannot speak exactly.

Were you beaten with that instrument?—Yes.

Have you yourself been beaten, and have you seen other children struck severely with that roller?—I have been struck very severely with it myself, so much so as to knock me down, and I have seen other children have their heads broken with it.

You think that it is a general practice to beat the children with the roller?—It is.

You do not think then that you were worse treated than other children in the mill?—No, I was not, perhaps not so bad as some were. . . .

Can you speak as to the effect of this labour in the mills and factories on the morals of the children, as far as you have observed?—As far as I have observed with regard to morals in the mills, there is every thing about them that is disgusting to every one conscious of correct morality.

Do you find that the children, the females especially, are very early demoralized in them?—They are.

Is their language indecent?—Very indecent; and both sexes take great familiarities with each other in the mills, without at all being ashamed of their conduct.

Do you connect their immorality of language and conduct with their excessive labour?—It may be somewhat connected with it, for it is to be observed that most of that goes on towards night, when they begin to be drowsy; it is a kind of stimulus which they use to keep them awake; they say some pert thing or other to keep themselves from drowsiness, and it generally happens to be some obscene language.

Have not a considerable number of the females employed in mills illegitimate children very early in life?—I believe there are; I have known some of them have illegitimate children when they were between 16 and 17 years of age.

How many grown up females had you in the mill?—I cannot speak to the exact number that were grown up; perhaps there might be thirty-four or so that worked in the mill at that time.

How many of those had illegitimate children?—A great many of them, eighteen or nineteen of them, I think.

Did they generally marry the men by whom they had the children?—No, it sometimes happens that young women have children by married men, and I have known an instance, a few weeks since, where one of the young women had a child by a married man.

Evidence Given Before Lord Ashley's Mines Commission, 1842

Sarah Gooder, aged 8 years

I'm a trapper in the Gawber pit. It does not tire men, but I have to trap without a light and I'm scared. I go at four and half past. I never go to sleep. Sometimes I sing when I've light, but not in the dark; I dare not sing then. I don't like being in the pit. I am very sleepy when I go sometimes in the morning. I go to Sunday-schools and read *Reading made Easy.* She knows her letters and can read little words. They teach me to pray. She repeated the Lord's Prayer, not very perfectly, and ran on with the following addition:—"God bless my father and mother, and sister and brother, uncles and aunts and cousins, and everybody else, and God bless me and make me a good servant. Amen. I have heard tell of Jesus many a time. I don't know why he came on earth, I'm sure, and I don't know why he died, but he had stones for his head to rest on. I would like to be at school far better than in the pit."

Thomas Wilson, Esq., of the Banks, Silkstone, owner of three collieries

The employment of females of any age in and about the mines is most objectionable, and I should rejoice to see it put an end to; but in the present feeling of the colliers, no individual would succeed in stopping it in a neighborhood where it prevailed, because the men would immediately go to those pits where their daughters would be employed. The only way effectually to put an end to this and other evils in the present colliery system is to elevate the minds of the men; and the only means to attain this is to combine sound moral and religious training and industrial habits with a system of intellectual culture much more perfect than can at present be obtained by them.

I object on general principles to government interference in the conduct of any trade, and I am satisfied that in mines it would be productive of the greatest injury and injustice. The art of mining is not so perfectly understood as to admit of the way in which a colliery shall be conducted being dictated by any person, however experienced, with such certainty as would warrant an interference with the management of private business. I should also most decidedly object to placing collieries under the present provisions of the Factory Act with respect to the education of children employed therein. First, because, if it is contended that coal-owners, as employers of children, are bound to attend to their education, this obligation extends equally to all other employers, and therefore it is unjust to single out one class only; secondly, because, if the legislature asserts a right to interfere to secure education, it is bound to make that interference general; and thirdly, because the mining population is in this neighborhood so intermixed with other classes, and is in such small bodies in any one place, that it would be impossible to provide separate schools for them.

Isabella Read, 12 years old, coal-bearer

Works on mother's account, as father has been dead two years. Mother bides at home, she is troubled with bad breath, and is very weak in her body from early labor. I am wrought with sister and brother, it is very sore work; cannot say how many rakes or journeys I make from pit's bottom to wall face and back, thinks about 30 or 25 on the average; the distance varies from 100 to 250 fathom.

I carry about 1 cwt. [hundred weight] and a quarter on my back; have to stoop much and creep through water, which is frequently up to the calves of my legs. When first down, fell frequently asleep while waiting for coal from heat and fatigue.

I do not like the work, nor do the lassies, but they are made to like it. When the weather is warm there is difficulty in breathing, and frequently the lights go out.

Isabel Wilson, 38 years old, coal-putter

When women have children thick (fast) they are compelled to take them down early, I have been married 19 years and have had 10 born; seven are in life. When on Sir John's work was a carrier of coals, which caused me to miscarry five times from the strains, and was ill after each. Putting is not so oppressive; last child was born on Saturday morning, and I was at work on the Friday night.

Once met with an accident; a coal broke my cheek-bone, which kept me idle some weeks.

I have wrought below 30 years, and so has the guid man; he is getting touched in the breath now.

None of the children read; as the work is not regular. I did read once, but not able to attend to it now; when I go below lassie 10 years of age keeps house and makes the broth or stir-about.

Nine sleep in two bedsteads; there did not appear to be any beds, and the whole of the other furniture consisted of two chairs, three stools, a table, a kail-pot and a few broken basins and cups. Upon asking if the furniture was all they had, the guid wife said, furniture was of no use, as it was so troublesome to flit with.

Patience Kershaw, aged 17

My father has been dead about a year; my mother is living and has ten children, five lads and five lasses; the oldest is about thirty, the youngest is four; three lasses go to mill; all the lads are colliers, two getters and three hurriers; one lives at home and does nothing; mother does nought but look after home.

All my sisters have been hurriers, but three went to the mill. Alice went because her legs swelled from hurrying in cold water when she was hot. I never went to day-school; I go to Sunday-school, but I cannot read or write; I go to pit at five o'clock in the morning and come out at five in the evening; I get my breakfast of porridge and milk first; I take my dinner with me, a cake, and I eat as I go; I do not stop or rest any time for the purpose; I get nothing else until I get home, and then have potatoes and meat, not every day meat. I hurry in the clothes I have now got on, trousers and ragged jacket; the bald place on my head is made by thrusting the corves; my legs have never swelled, but sisters' did when they got to the mill; I hurry the corves a mile and more under ground and back; they weigh 300 cwt.; I hurry 11 a day; I wear a belt and chain at the workings to get the corves out; the getters that I work when I go up; sometimes they beat me, if I am not quick enough, with their hands; they strike upon my back; the boys take liberties with me; sometimes they pull me about; I am the only girl in the pit; there are about 20 boys and 15 men; all the men are naked; I would rather work in the mill than in coal-pit.

Mary Barrett, age 14, June 15

I have worked down in the pit five years; father is working in next pit; I have 12 brothers and sisters—all of them but one live at home; they weave, and wind, and hurry, and one is a counter, one of them can read, none of the rest can, or write; they never went to day-school, but three of them go to Sunday-school; I hurry for my brother John, and come down at seven o'clock about; I go up at six, sometimes seven; I do not like working in the pit, but I am obliged to get a living; I work always without stockings, or shoes, or trousers; I wear nothing but my chemise; I have to go to the headings with the men; they are all naked there; I am get well used to that, and don't care now much about it; I was afraid at first, and did not like it; they never behave rudely to me; I cannot read or write.

---

28. The Philosophy of Manufactures, 1835

Andrew Ure

Andrew Ure (1778–1857) was a Scottish professor of chemistry, medical doctor, and writer on scientific subjects who became a student and propagandist of industrialization as well as a trenchant defender of the factory system. He authored a celebratory work on *The Cotton Manufactures of Great Britain*, 1836. Ure was also a pioneer of scientific management who lobbied for the efficient co-ordination of capital, labor, raw materials, marketing finished products, and utilizing sophisticated accounting methods. He was a staunch advocate of the development and administration of a strict code of factory discipline that would retrain workers who were accustomed to premodern patterns of labor. As director of the Glasgow Observatory Ure introduced popular science classes for workingmen. The excerpt that follows is from his best known work, *The Philosophy of Manufactures*, 1835.

QUESTIONS

1. According to Andrew Ure, what were the working conditions for children in English factories? Summarize his view of their attitudes and their behavior at work.
2. According to his view, how did the lives of children who worked in factories compare with the lives of their counterparts in agricultural districts?
3. Compare Ure's interpretation of factory life with the evidence presented in the preceding document. Is it possible to reconcile the contrasting perspectives presented in these sources?

No master would wish to have any wayward children to work within the walls of his factory, who do not mind their business without beating, and he therefore usually fines or turns away any spinners who are known to maltreat their assistants. Hence, ill-usage of any kind is a very rare occurrence. I have visited many factories, both in Manchester and in the surrounding districts, during a period of several months, entering the spinning rooms, unexpectedly, and often alone, at different times of the day, and I never saw a single instance of corporal chastisement inflicted on a child, nor indeed did I ever see children in ill-humour. They seemed to be always cheerful and alert, taking pleasure in the light play of their muscles,—enjoying the mobility natural to their age. The scene of industry, so far from exciting sad emotions in my mind, was always exhilarating. It was delightful to observe the nimbleness with which they pieced the broken ends, as the mule-carriage began to recede from the fixed roller-beam, and to see them at leisure, after a few seconds exercise of their tiny fingers, to amuse themselves in any attitude they chose, till the stretch and winding-on were once more completed. The work of these lively elves seemed to resemble a sport, in which habit gave them a pleasing dexterity. Conscious of their skill, they were delighted to show it off to any stranger. As to exhaustion by the day's work, they evinced no trace of it on emerging from the mill in the evening; for they immediately began to skip about any neighbouring play-ground, and to commence their little amusements with the same alacrity as boys issuing from a school. It is moreover my firm conviction, that if children are not ill-used by bad parents or guardians, but receive in food and raiment the full benefit of what they earn, they would thrive better when employed in our modern factories, than if left at home in apartments too often ill-aired, damp, and cold. . . .

It is certain, then, that the reason which was so prominently put before the public in favour of the ten-hour bill is altogether groundless—that children in cotton-mills are not injured by their labours, and are not in general overworked. The notion of their being so is wholly repudiated in the greatest manufacturing district of England. . . .

It seems established by a body of incontestable evidence, that the wages of our factory work-people, if prudently spent, would enable them to live in a comfortable manner, and decidedly better than formerly, in consequence of the relative diminution in the price of food, fuel, lodgings, and clothing. But the manufacturers fear that, from the lower rate of wages, and the less expensive style of living among the working people on the Continent, and in the United States, their foreign rivals may, ere long, be able to bring forward many descriptions of cotton goods more cheaply than they can continue to do, if competition advances in the same ratio as it has done for several years. . . .

. . . Of all the common prejudices that exist with regard to factory labour, there is none more unfounded than that which ascribes to it excessive tedium and irksomeness above other occupations, owing to its being carried on in conjunction with the "unceasing motion of the steam-engine." In an establishment for spinning or weaving cotton, all the hard work is performed by the steam-engine which leaves for the attendant no hard labour at all, and literally nothing to do in general; but at intervals to perform some delicate operation, such as joining the threads that break, taking the cops off the spindles, &c. And it is so far from being true that the work in a factory is incessant, because the motion of the steam-engine is incessant, that the fact is, that the labour is not incessant on that very account, because it is performed in conjunction with the steam-engine. Of all manufacturing employments, those are by far the most irksome and incessant in which steam-engines are not employed, as in lace-running and stocking-weaving; and the way to prevent an employment from being incessant, is to introduce a steam-engine into it. These remarks certainly apply more especially to the labour of children in factories. Three-fourths of the children so employed are engaged in piecing at the mules. "When the carriages of these have receded a foot and a half or two feet from the rollers," says Mr. Tufnell, "nothing is to be done, not even attention is required from either spinner or piecer." Both of them stand idle for a time, and in fine spinning particularly, for three-quarters of a minute, or more. Consequently, if a child remains at this business twelve hours daily, he has nine hours of inaction. And though he attends two mules, he has still six hours of non-exertion. Spinners sometimes dedicate these intervals to the perusal of books. The scavengers, who in Mr. Sadler's report have been described as being "constantly in a state of grief, always in terror, and every moment they have to spare stretched all their length upon the floor in a state of perspiration," may be observed in cotton-factories idle for four minutes at a time, or moving about in a sportive mood, utterly unconscious of the tragical scenes in which they were dramatized.

Occupations which are assisted by steam-engines require for the most part a higher, or at least a steadier species of labour, than those which are not; the exercise of the mind being then partially substituted for that of the muscles, constituting skilled labour, which is always paid more highly than unskilled. On this principle we can readily account for the comparatively high wages which the inmates of a factory, whether children or adults, obtain. . . .

What I have myself witnessed at several times, both on Sundays and working-days, has convinced me that the population of Belper is, in reference to health, domestic comfort, and religious culture, in a truly enviable state, compared with the average of our agricultural villages. The factory rooms are well aired, and as clean as any gentleman's parlour. The children are well-com-

plexioned, and work with cheerful dexterity at their respective occupations.

At Quarry Bank, near Wilmslow, in Cheshire, is situated the oldest of the five establishments belonging to the great firm of Messrs. Greg and Sons, of Manchester, who work up the one-hundredth part of all the cotton consumed in Great Britain. It is driven by an elegant water-wheel, 32 feet in diameter, and 24 feet broad, equivalent in power to 120 horses. The country round is beautiful, and presents a succession of picturesque wooded dells interspersed with richly cultivated fields. At a little distance from the factory, on a sunny slope, stands a handsome house, two stories high, built for the accommodation of the female apprentices. Here are well fed, clothed, educated, and lodged, under kind superintendence, sixty young girls, who by their deportment at the mill, as well as in Wilmslow Church on Sunday, where I saw them assembled, evince a degree of comfort most creditable to the humane and intelligent proprietors. The Sunday scholars, equally numerous, belonging to the rural population, appeared to great disadvantage alongside of the factory children, the former being worse clad and worse looking than the latter, and worse behaved during divine service. . . .

Sufficient evidence has been adduced to convince the candid mind, that factories, more especially cotton-mills, are so organized as to afford as easy and comfortable occupation as anywhere can fall to the lot of the labouring classes.

What a pity it is that the party who lately declaimed so loudly about the inmates of factories being universally victims of oppression, misery, and vice, did not, from their rural or civic retreats, examine first of all into the relative condition of their own rustic operatives, and dispassionately see how the balance stood betwixt them! . . . It is, in fact, in the factory districts alone that the demoralizing agency of pauperism has been effectually resisted, and a noble spirit of industry, enterprise, and intelligence, called forth. What a contrast is there at this day, between the torpor and brutality which pervade very many of the farming parishes, as delineated in the official reports, and the beneficent activity which animates all the cotton factory towns, villages, and hamlets!

The regularity required in mills is such as to render persons who are in the habit of getting intoxicated unfit to be employed there, and all respectable manufacturers object to employ persons guilty of that vice; and thus mill-work tends to check drunkenness. Mr. Marshall, M.P. of Leeds, thinks that the health of persons employed in mills is better from the regularity of their habits, than of those employed at home in weaving.

29. Transcendental Wild Oats

Louisa May Alcott

A number of cooperative communities were founded in the United States prior to the Civil War. Some were religious in origin, while others were secular. The participants in these experiments hoped to establish model societies that featured simple living and spiritual fulfillment. These settlements were designed to offer an alternative way of life to the competitive individualism and materialism of the northern states. Fruitlands was the brainchild of Amos Bronson Alcott (1799–1888), and it reflected the Transcendentalist philosophy promulgated by such New England intellectuals as Ralph Waldo Emerson and Henry David Thoreau. In 1844 Alcott led his family and followers to a ninety acre tract located in a beautiful valley near the village of Harvard, Massachusetts, thirty miles south of Boston. But Alcott proved to be far more interested in philosophy than in the practical matters of building a viable community. The reform experiment lasted only six months. Thirty years later Louisa May Alcott (1832–1888) wrote a humorous account of her family's misadventures. Best known for her novel *Little Women,* she wrote the following essay to highlight the good intentions of the leaders of the expedition, even as she satirized their deeds. Soon Marxists and other reformers derisively labeled Fruitlands and similar settlements as examples of "Utopian Socialism."

QUESTIONS

1. What "picture" is Louisa May Alcott drawing of the entrance into Fruitlands?
2. Describe the character of Sister Hope.
3. What role does the food diet play? What role would it play today?

4. Does Louisa May Alcott see any value in sowing transcendental wild oats?
5. How would this Utopian Socialist scheme be regarded today?
6. Could this happen only in America?

On the first day of June, 184–, a large wagon drawn by a small horse and containing a motley load went lumbering over certain New England hills, with the pleasing accompaniments of wind, rain, and hail. A serene man with a serene child upon his knee was driving or rather being driven, for the small horse had it all his own way. A brown boy with a William Penn style of countenance sat beside him, firmly embracing a bust of Socrates. Behind them was an energetic-looking woman with a benevolent brow, satirical mouth, and eyes brimful of hope and courage. A baby reposed upon her lap, a mirror leaned against her knee, and a basket of provisions danced about at her feet, as she struggled with a large, unruly umbrella. Two blue-eyed little girls with hands full of childish treasures sat under one old shawl, chatting happily together.

In front of this lively party stalked a tall, sharp-featured man in a long blue cloak; and a fourth small girl trudged along beside him through the mud as if she rather enjoyed it.

The wind whistled over the bleak hills; the rain fell in a despondent drizzle; and twilight began to fall. But the calm man gazed as tranquilly into the fog as if he beheld a radiant bow of promise spanning the gray sky. The cheery woman tried to cover every one but herself with the big umbrella. The brown boy pillowed his head on the bald pate of Socrates and slumbered peacefully. The little girls sang lullabies to their dolls in soft, maternal murmurs. The sharp-nosed pedestrian marched steadily on, with the blue cloak streaming out behind him like a banner; and the lively infant splashed through the puddles with a duck-like satisfaction pleasant to behold.

Thus these modern pilgrims journeyed hopefully out of the old world, to found a new one in the wilderness. This prospective Eden at present consisted of an old red farmhouse, a dilapidated barn, many acres of meadowland, and a grove. Ten ancient apple trees were all the "chaste supply" which the place offered as yet; but, in the firm belief that plenteous orchards were soon to be evoked from their inner consciousness, these sanguine founders had christened their domain Fruitlands.

Here Timon Lion intended to found a colony of latter-day saints, who, under his patriarchal sway, should regenerate the world and glorify his name for ever. Here Abel Lamb [Bronson Alcott], with the devoutest faith in the high ideal which was to him a living truth, desired to plant a Paradise, where Beauty, Virtue, Justice, and Love might live happily together, without the possibility of a serpent entering in. And here his wife, unconverted but faithful to the end, hoped, after many wanderings over the face of the earth, to find rest for herself and a home for her children.

"There is our new abode," announced the enthusiast, smiling with a satisfaction quite undamped by the drops dripping from his hatbrim, as they turned at length into a cart path that wound along a steep hillside into a barren-looking valley.

"A little difficult of access," observed his practical wife, as she endeavored to keep her various household goods from going overboard with every lurch of the laden ark.

"Like all good things. But those who earnestly desire and patiently seek will soon find us," placidly responded the philosopher from the mud, through which he was now endeavoring to pilot the much-enduring horse.

"Truth lies at the bottom of a well, Sister Hope," said Brother Timon, pausing to detach his small comrade from a gate whereon she was perched for a clearer gaze into futurity.

"That's the reason we so seldom get at it, I suppose," replied Sister Hope, making a vain clutch at the mirror, which a sudden jolt sent flying out of her hands.

"We want no false reflections here," said Timon with a grim smile, as he crunched the fragments underfoot in his onward march.

Sister Hope held her peace and looked wistfully through the mist at her promised home. The old red house with a hospitable glimmer at its windows cheered her eyes, and, considering the weather, was a fitter refuge than the sylvan bowers some of the more ardent souls might have preferred.

The newcomers were welcomed by one of the elect—a regenerate farmer, whose idea of reform consisted chiefly in wearing white cotton raiment and shoes of untanned leather. This costume, with a snowy beard, gave him a venerable and at the same time a somewhat bridal appearance.

The goods and chattels of the Society not having arrived, the weary family reposed before the fire on blocks of wood, while Brother Moses White regaled them with roasted potatoes, brown bread, and water, in two plates, a tin pan, and one mug, his table service being limited. But, having cast the forms and vanities of a depraved world behind them, the elders welcomed hardship with the enthusiasm of new pioneers, and the children heartily enjoyed this foretaste of what they believed was to be a sort of perpetual picnic.

During the progress of this frugal meal, two more brothers appeared. One was a dark, melancholy man, clad in homespun, whose peculiar mission was to turn his name hind part before and use as few words as possible. The other was a bland, bearded Englishman, who expected to be saved by eating uncooked food and going without clothes. He had not yet adopted the primitive costume, however, but contented himself with meditatively chewing dry beans out of a basket.

"Every meal should be a sacrament, and the vessels used should be beautiful and symbolical," observed Brother Lamb, mildly, righting the tin pan slipping about on his knees. "I priced a silver service when in town, but it was too costly; so I got some graceful cups and vases of Britannia ware."

"Hardest things in the world to keep bright. Will whiting be allowed in the community?" inquired Sister Hope, with a housewife's interest in labor-saving institutions.

"Such trival questions will be discussed at a more fitting time," answered Brother Timon sharply, as he burnt his fingers with a very hot potato. "Neither sugar, molasses, milk, butter, cheese, nor flesh are to be used among us, for nothing is to be admitted which has caused wrong or death to man or beast."

"Our garments are to be linen till we learn to raise our own cotton or some substitute for woolen fabrics," added Brother Abel, blissfully basking in an imaginary future as warm and brilliant as the generous fire before him.

"Haou abaout shoes?" asked Brother Moses, surveying his own with interest.

"We must yield that point till we can manufacture an innocent substitute for leather. Bark, wood, or some durable fabric will be invented in time. Meanwhile, those who desire to carry out our idea to the fullest extent can go barefooted," said Lion, who liked extreme measures.

"I never will, nor let my girls," murmured rebellious Sister Hope, under her breath.

"Haou do you cattle'ate to treat the ten-acre lot? Ef things ain't 'tended to right smart, we shan't hev no crops," observed the practical patriarch in cotton.

"We shall spade it," replied Abel, in such perfect good faith that Moses said no more, though he indulged in a shake of the head as he glanced at hands that had held nothing heavier than a pen for years. He was a paternal old soul and regarded the younger men as promising boys on a new sort of lark.

"What shall we do for lamps if we cannot use any animal substance? I do hope light of some sort is to be thrown upon the enterprise," said Mrs. Lamb with anxiety, for in those days kerosene and camphene were not, and gas was unknown in the wilderness.

"We shall go without till we have discovered some vegetable oil or wax to serve us," replied Brother Timon, in a decided tone, which caused Sister Hope to resolve that her private lamp should be always trimmed, if not burning.

"Each member is to perform the work for which experience, strength, and taste best fit him," continued Dictator Lion. "Thus drudgery and disorder will be avoided and harmony prevail. We shall rise at dawn, begin the day by bathing, followed by music, and then a chaste repast of fruit and bread. Each one finds congenial occupation till the meridian meal, when some deep-searching conversation gives rest to the body and development to the mind. Healthful labor again engages us till the last meal, when we assemble in social communion, prolonged till sunset, when we retire to sweet repose, ready for the next day's activity."

"What part of the work do you incline to yourself?" asked Sister Hope, with a humorous glimmer in her keen eyes.

"I shall wait till it is made clear to me. Being in preference to doing is the great aim, and this comes to us rather by a resigned willingness than a wilful activity, which is a check to all divine growth," responded Brother Timon.

"I thought so." And Mrs. Lamb sighed audibly, for during the year he had spent in her family Brother Timon had so faithfully carried out his idea of "being, not doing," that she had found his "divine growth" both an expensive and unsatisfactory process. . . .

The furniture arrived next day, and was soon bestowed, for the principal property of the community consisted in books. To this rare library was devoted the best room in the house, and the few busts and pictures that still survived many flittings were added to beautify the sanctuary, for here the family was to meet for amusement, instruction, and worship.

Any housewife can imagine the emotions of Sister Hope when she took possession of a large dilapidated kitchen, containing an old stove and the peculiar stores out of which food was to be evolved for her little family of eleven—cakes of maple sugar, dried peas and beans, barley and hominy, meal of all sorts, potatoes, and dried fruit. No milk, butter, cheese, tea, or meat appeared. Even salt was considered a useless luxury and spice entirely forbidden by these lovers of Spartan simplicity. Her ten years' experience of vegetarian vagaries had been good training for this new freak, and her sense of the ludicrous supported her through many trying scenes.

Unleavened bread, porridge, and water for breakfast; bread, vegetables, and water for dinner; bread, fruit, and water for supper was the bill of fare ordained by the elders. No teapot profaned that sacred stove, no gory steak cried aloud for vengeance from her chaste gridiron; and only a brave woman's taste, time, and temper were sacrificed on that domestic altar.

The vexed question of light was settled by buying a quantity of bayberry wax for candles, and (when it was discovered) that no one knew how to make them, pine knots were introduced, to be used when absolutely necessary. [As it was] summer, the evenings were not long, and the weary fraternity found it no great hardship to retire with the birds. The inner light was sufficient for most of them. But Mrs. Lamb rebelled. Evening was the only time she had to herself; and while the tired feet rested, the skillful hands mended torn frocks and little stockings, or the anxious heart forgot its burden in a book.

So "mother's lamp" burned steadily, while the philosophers built a new heaven and earth by moonlight; and through all the metaphysical mists and philanthropic pyrotechnics of that period Sister Hope played her own little game of "throwing light," and none but the moths were the worse for it.

Such farming probably was never seen before since Adam delved. The band of brothers began by spading garden and field, but a few days of it lessened their ardor amazingly. Blistered hands and aching backs suggested the expediency of permitting the use of cattle till the workers were better fitted for noble toil by a summer of the new life.

The sowing was equally peculiar, for, owing to some mistake, the three brethren who devoted themselves to this graceful task found, when about half through the job, that each had been sowing a different sort of grain in the same field, a mistake which caused much perplexity, as it could not be remedied. But after a long consultation and a good deal of laughter, it was decided to say nothing and see what would come of it.

Slowly things got into order and rapidly rumors of the new experiment went abroad, causing many strange spirits to flock thither, for in those days communities were the fashion and transcendentalism raged wildly. Some came to look on and laugh, some to be supported in poetic idleness, a few to believe sincerely and work heartily. Each member was allowed to mount his favorite hobby and ride it to his heart's content. Very queer were some of the riders, and very rampant some of the hobbies.

One youth, believing that language was of little consequence if the spirit was only right, startled newcomers by blandly greeting them with "Good morning, damn you," and other remarks of an equally mixed order. A second irrepressible being held that all the emotions of the soul should be freely expressed, and illustrated his theory by antics that would have sent him to a lunatic asylum, if, as an unregenerate wag said, he were not already in one. When his spirit soared, he climbed trees and shouted; when doubt assailed him, he lay upon the floor and groaned lamentably. At joyful periods he raced, leaped, and sang; when sad, he wept aloud; and when a great thought burst upon him in the watches of the night, he crowed like a jocund cockerel, to the great delight of the children and the great annoyance of the elders. One musical brother fiddled whenever so moved, sang sentimentally to the four little girls, and put a music box on the wall when he hoed corn.

Transcendental wild oats were sown broadcast that year, and the fame thereof has not yet ceased in the land; for, futile as this crop seemed to outsiders, it bore an invisible harvest, worth much to those who planted it in earnest.

A new dress was invented, since cotton, silk, and wool were forbidden as the products of slave labor, worm slaughter, and sheep robbery. Tunics and trousers of brown linen were the only wear. The women's shirts were longer and their straw hatbrims wider than the men's, and this was the only difference. Some persecution lent a charm to the costume, and the long-haired, linen-clad reformers quite enjoyed the mild martyrdom they endured when they left home.

Money was abjured as the root of all evil. The produce of the land was to supply most of their wants or be exchanged for the few things they could not grow. This idea had its inconveniences, but self-denial was the fashion, and it was surprising how many things one can do without. When they desired to travel, they walked, if possible, begged the loan of a vehicle, or boldly entered car or coach and, stating their principles to the officials, took the consequences. Usually their dress, their earnest frankness, and gentle resolution won them a passage; but now and then they met with hard usage and had the satisfaction of suffering for their principles.

They preached vegetarianism everywhere and resisted all temptations of the flesh, contentedly eating apples and bread at well-spread tables and much afflicting hospitable hostesses by denouncing their food and taking away their appetites, discussing the "horrors of shambles," the "incorporation of the brute in man," and "on elegant abstinence the sign of a pure soul." But when the perplexed or offended ladies asked what they should eat, they got in reply a bill of fare consisting of "bowls of sunrise for breakfast," "solar seeds of the sphere," "dishes from Plutarch's chaste table," and other viands equally hard to find in any modern market.

Reform conventions of all sorts were haunted by these brethren, who said many wise things and did many foolish ones. Unfortunately, these wanderings interfered with their harvest at home; but the rule was to do what the spirit moved, so they left their crops to Providence and went a-reaping in wider and, let us hope, more fruitful fields than their own. . . .

This attempt at regeneration had its tragic as well as its comic side, though the world saw only the former.

---

30. Manifesto of the Communist Party, 1848

Karl Marx and Friedrich Engels

Karl Marx (1818–1883), son of a well-to-do German lawyer, studied law and philosophy at the University of Bonn and Berlin. His career in journalism was short due to his radical views. He lived in Paris and then Brussels before he eventually settled down in London. While enduring considerable hardships he expounded his brand of socialism or communism while he promoted radical movements that aimed at social revolution. In developing his doctrines of "scientific socialism" and in formulating his "laws of history" he borrowed ideas from such authors as Adam Smith, Georg W. F. Hegel, and others. His works include *The Poverty of Philosophy* (1847), *A Contribution to the Critique of Political Economy* (1859), and *Capital* (in three volumes—1867, 1885, 1894).

Friedrich Engels (1820–1895), son of a wealthy manufacturer, was employed at his family's cotton mill in Manchester, England, where he moved from Germany. He met Marx in the early 1840s and became his life-long collaborator and benefactor. His best known works include *The Condition of the Working Class in England in 1844* (1845), *The Origin of the Family, Private Property and the State* (1884), and *Socialism, Utopian and Scientific.*

The most important work that the two produced jointly was *The Communist Manifesto.* It was published in 1848 as a platform of the Communist League, a small radical German workingmen's association. This document, written in a stirring, combative style, expresses most of the major beliefs of Marxism. The selections below are from parts I, II, and IV. Part III, which is omitted here, contains criticism of other forms of socialism.

QUESTIONS

1. Why, according to Marx, was the specter of communism "haunting Europe"?
2. What are the bases of class differences and the sources of change in society, according to Marx?
3. What lies at the bottom of the class struggle, according to Marx, and who is going to come out victorious?
4. What does Marx mean by "bourgeois" and what role in history does he ascribe to the bourgeoisie?
5. What is Marx's philosophy of history?
6. Why is it appropriate that this document is designated as a "Manifesto"? Is this document prophetic?
7. Does Marx agree or disagree with Adam Smith on the significance of the division of labor? With Friedrich List on free trade? Explain.

A specter is haunting Europe—the specter of Communism. All the powers of Old Europe have entered into a holy alliance to exorcise this specter; Pope and Czar, Metternich and Guizot, French Radicals and German police-spies.

Where is the party in opposition that has not been decried as communistic by its opponents in power? Where the opposition that has not hurled back the branding reproach of Communism, against the more advanced opposition parties, as well as against reactionary adversaries?

Two things result from this fact.

I. Communism is already acknowledged by all European powers to be in itself a power.

II. It is high time that Communists should openly, in the face of the whole world, publish their views, their aims, their tendencies, and meet this nursery tale of the specter of Communism with a Manifesto of the Party itself.

To this end Communists of various nationalities have assembled in London, and sketched the following Manifesto to be published in the English, French, German, Italian, Flemish and Danish languages.

I Bourgeois and Proletarians

The history of all hitherto existing society is the history of class struggles.

Freeman and slave, patrician and plebeian, lord and serf, guild-master and journeyman, in a word, oppressor and oppressed, stood in constant opposition to one another, carried on an uninterrupted, now hidden, now open fight, that each time ended, either in a revolutionary reconstruction of society at large, or in the common ruin of the contending classes.

In the earlier epochs of history we find almost everywhere a complicated arrangement of society into various orders, a manifold gradation of social rank. In ancient Rome we have patricians, knights, plebeians, slaves; in the middle ages, feudal lord, vassals, guild masters, journeymen, apprentices, serfs; in almost all of these classes, again, subordinate gradations.

The modern bourgeois society that has sprouted from the ruins of feudal society, has not done away with class antagonisms. It has but established new classes, new conditions of oppression, new forms of struggle in place of the old ones.

Our epoch, the epoch of the bourgeoisie, possesses, however, this distinctive feature; it has simplified the class antagonisms. Society as a whole is more and more splitting up into two great hostile camps,

into two great classes directly facing each other: Bourgeoisie and Proletariat.

From the serfs of the Middle Ages sprang the chartered burghers of the earliest towns. From these burgesses the first elements of the bourgeoisie were developed.

The discovery of America, the rounding of the Cape, opened up fresh ground for the rising bourgeoisie. The East-Indian and Chinese markets, the colonization of America, trade with the colonies, the increase in the means of exchange and in commodities generally, gave to commerce, to navigation, to industry, an impulse never before known, and thereby, to the revolutionary element in the tottering feudal society, a rapid development.

The feudal system of industry, under which industrial production was monopolized by closed guilds, now no longer sufficed for the growing wants of the new market. The manufacturing system took its place. The guild-masters were pushed on one side by the manufacturing middle class; division of labor between the different corporate guilds vanished in the face of division of labor in each single group.

Meantime markets kept ever growing, the demand ever rising. Even manufacture no longer sufficed. Thereupon steam and machinery revolutionized industrial production. The place of manufacture was taken by the giant, Modern Industry, the place of the industrial middle class, by industrial millionaires, the leaders of whole industrial armies, the modern bourgeois.

Modern Industry has established the world's market, for which the discovery of America paved the way. This market has given immense development to commerce, to navigation, to communication by land. This development has, in its turn, reacted on the extension of industry; and in proportion as industry, commerce, navigation, railways extended, in the same proportion, the bourgeoisie developed, increased its capital, and pushed into the background every class handed down from the Middle Ages.

We see, therefore, how the modern bourgeoisie is itself the product of a long course of development, of a series of revolutions in the modes of production and exchange.

Each step in the development of the bourgeoisie was accompanied by a corresponding political advance of that class. An oppressed class under the sway of the feudal nobility, an armed and self-governing association in the medieval commune, here independent urban republic (as in Italy and Germany), there taxable "third estate" of the monarchy (as in France), afterwards, in the period of manufacture proper, serving either the semi-feudal or the absolute monarchy as a counterpoise against the nobility, and, in fact, corner-stone of the great monarchies in general, the bourgeoisie has at last, since the establishment of Modern Industry and of the world's market, conquered for itself, in the modern representative State, exclusive political sway. The executive of the modern State is but a committee for managing the common affairs of the whole bourgeoisie.

The bourgeoisie, wherever it has got the upper hand, has put an end to all feudal, patriarchal, idyllic relations. It has pitilessly torn asunder the motley feudal ties that bound man to his "natural superiors," and has left remaining no other nexus between man and man than naked self-interest, than callous "cash payment." It has drowned the most heavenly ecstasies of religious fervor, of chivalrous enthusiasm, of Philistine sentimentalism, in the icy water of egotistical calculation. It has resolved personal worth into exchange value, and in place of the numberless indefeasible chartered freedoms, has set up that single, unconscionable freedom—Free Trade. In one word, for ex-

ploitation, veiled by religious and political illusions, it has substituted naked shameless, direct, brutal exploitation. . . .

The bourgeoisie cannot exist without constantly revolutionizing the instruments of production, and thereby the relations of production, and with them the whole relations of society. Conservation of the old modes of production in unaltered form, was, on the contrary, the first condition of existence for all earlier industrial classes. Constant revolutionizing of production, uninterrupted disturbance of all social conditions, everlasting uncertainty and agitation, distinguish the bourgeois epoch from the earlier one. All fixed, fast frozen relations, with their train of ancient and venerable prejudices and opinions, are swept away; all new-formed ones become antiquated before they can ossify. All that is solid melts into air, all that is holy is profaned, and man is at last compelled to face with sober senses his real conditions of life, and his relations with his kind.

The need of a constantly expanding market for its products chases the bourgeoisie over the whole surface of the globe. It must nestle everywhere, settle everywhere, establish connections everywhere. . . .

The bourgeoisie has subjected the country to the rule of the towns. It has created enormous cities, has greatly increased the urban population as compared with the rural, and has thus rescued a considerable part of the population from the idiocy of rural life. Just as it has made the country dependent on the towns, so it has made barbarian and semi-barbarian countries dependent on the civilized ones, nations of peasants on nations of bourgeois, the East on the West. . . .

Modern bourgeois society with its relations of production, of exchange, and of property, a society that has conjured up such gigantic means of production and of exchange, is like the sorcerer, who is no longer able to control the powers of the nether world whom he has called up by his spells. For many a decade past the history of industry and commerce is but the history of the revolt of modern productive forces against modern conditions of production, against the property relations that are the conditions for the existence of the bourgeoisie and of its rule. It is enough to mention the commercial crises that by their periodical return put on its trial, each time more threateningly, the existence of the bourgeois society. In these crises a great part not only of the existing products, but also of the previously created productive forces, is periodically destroyed. In these crises there breaks out an epidemic that, in all earlier epochs, would have seemed an absurdity—the epidemic of overproduction. Society suddenly finds itself put back into a state of momentary barbarism; it appears as if a famine, a universal war of devastation, had cut off the supply of every means of subsistence; industry and commerce seem to be destroyed; and why? because there is too much civilization, too much means of subsistence, too much industry, too much commerce. The productive forces at the disposal of society no longer tend to further the development of the conditions of the bourgeoisie property; on the contrary; they have become too powerful for these conditions, by which they are fettered, and as soon as they overcome these fetters, they bring disorder into the whole bourgeoisie society, endanger the existence of bourgeoisie property. The conditions of bourgeois society are too narrow to comprise the wealth created by them. And how does the bourgeoisie get over these crises? On the one hand by enforced destruction of a mass of productive forces; on the other, by the conquest of new markets, and by the more thorough exploitation of the old ones. That is to say, by paving the way for more extensive and more destructive crises, and by diminishing the means whereby crises are prevented.

The weapons with which the bourgeoisie felled feudalism to the ground are now turned against the bourgeoisie itself.

But not only has the bourgeoisie forged the weapons that bring death to itself; it has also called into existence the men who are to wield those weapons—the modern working class—the proletarians.

In proportion as the bourgeoisie, i.e., capital, is developed, in the same proportion is the proletariat, the modern working class, developed; a class of laborers, who live only so long as they find work, and who find work so long as their labor increases capital. These laborers, who must sell themselves piecemeal, are a commodity, like every other article of commerce, and are consequently exposed to all the vicissitudes of competition, to all the fluctuations of the market.

Owing to the extensive use of machinery and to division of labor, the work of the proletarians has lost all individual character, and, consequently, all charm for the workman. He becomes an appendage of the machine, and it is only the most simple, most monotonous, and most easily acquired knack, that is required of him. Hence, the cost of production of a workman is restricted almost entirely to the means of subsistence that he requires for his maintenance, and for the propagation of his race. But the price of a commodity, and therefore so of labor, is equal to its costs of production. In proportion, therefore, as the repulsiveness of the work increases, the wage decreases. Nay, more, in proportion as the use of machinery and division of labor increases, in the same proportion the burden of toil also increases, whether by prolongation of the working hours, by increase of the work enacted in a given time, or by increased speed of the machinery, etc.

Modern industry has converted the little workshop of the patriarchal master into the great factory of the industrial capitalist. Masses of laborers, crowded into factories, are organized like soldiers. As privates of the industrial army they are placed under the command of a perfect hierarchy of officers and sergeants. Not only are they the slaves of the bourgeois class, and of the bourgeois State, they are daily and hourly enslaved by the machine, by the overlooker, and above all, by the individual bourgeois manufacturer himself. The more openly the despotism proclaims gain to be its end and aim, the more petty, the more hateful, and the more embittering it is. . . .

The less skill and exertion of strength implied in manual labor, in other words, the more modern industry becomes developed, the more is the labor of men superseded by that of women. Difference of age and sex have no longer any distinctive social validity for the working class. All are instruments of labor, more or less expensive to use, according to age and sex.

No sooner is the exploitation of the laborer by the manufacturer, so far at an end, that he receives his wages in cash, than he is set upon by the other portions of the bourgeoisie, the landlord, the shopkeeper, the pawnbroker, etc.

The lower strata of the Middle Class— the small tradespeople, shopkeepers, and retired tradesmen generally, the handicraftsmen and peasant—all these sink gradually into the proletariat, partly because their diminutive capital does not suffice for the scale on which modern industry is carried on, and is swamped in the competition with the large capitalists, partly because their specialized skill is rendered worthless by new methods of production. Thus the proletarian is recruited from all classes of the population. . . .

But with the development of industry the proletariat not only increases in number; it becomes concentrated in greater masses, its strength grows and it feels that strength more. The various interests and conditions of life within the ranks of the proletariat are more and more equalized, in proportion as machinery obliterates all distinctions of labor, and nearly everywhere reduces wages to the same low level. The growing competition among the bourgeois, and the resulting commercial crises, make the wages of the workers even more fluctuating. The unceasing improvement of machinery, ever more rapidly developing, makes their livelihood more and more precarious; the collisions between individual workmen and individual bourgeois take more and more the character of collisions between two classes. Thereupon the workers begin to form combinations against the bourgeois; they club together in order to keep up the rate of wages; they found permanent associations in order to make provision beforehand for these occasional revolts. Here and there the contest breaks out into riots.

Now and then the workers are victorious, but only for a time. The real fruit of their battles lies not in the immediate result but in the ever-improved means of communication that are created by modern industry, and that place the workers of different localities in contact with one another. It was just this contact that was needed to centralize the numerous local struggles, all of the same character, into one national struggle between classes. But every class struggle is a political struggle. And that union, to attain which the burghers of the Middle Ages, with their miserable highways, required centuries, the modern proletarians, thanks to railways, achieve in a few years.

This organization of the proletarians into a class, and consequently into a political party, is continually being upset again by the competition between the workers themselves. But it ever rises up again; stronger, firmer, mightier. It compels legislative recognition of particular interests of the workers, by taking advantage of the divisions among the bourgeoisie itself. Thus the ten-hours' bill in England was carried. . . .

Finally, in time when the class struggle nears the decisive hour, the process of dissolution going on within the ruling class, in fact, within the whole range of an old society, assumes such a violent, glaring character, that a small section of the ruling class cuts itself adrift, and joins the revolutionary class, the class that holds the future in its hands. Just as, therefore, at an earlier period, a section of the nobility went over to the bourgeoisie, so now a portion of the bourgeoisie goes over to the proletariat, and in particular, a portion of the bourgeois ideologists, who have raised themselves to the level of comprehending theoretically the historical movement as a whole.

Of all the classes that stand face to face with the bourgeoisie today the proletariat alone is a really revolutionary class. The other classes decay and finally disappear in the face of modern industry; the proletariat is its special and essential product. . . .

All previous historical movements were movements of minorities, or in the interest of minorities. The proletarian movement is the self-conscious, independent movement of the immense majority. The proletariat, the lowest stratum of our present society, cannot stir, cannot raise itself up, without the whole super-incumbent strata of official society being sprung into the air.

Though not in substance, yet in form, the struggle of the proletariat with the bourgeoisie is at first a national struggle. The proletariat of each country must, of course, first of all settle matters with its own bourgeoisie. . . .

II Proletarians and Communists

In what relation do the Communists stand to the proletarians as a whole?

The Communists do not form a separate party opposed to other working class parties.

They have no interests separate and apart from those of the proletariat as a whole. . . .

They do not set up any sectarian principles of their own by which to shape and mould the proletarian movement. . . .

The distinguishing feature of Communism is not the abolition of property generally, but the abolition of bourgeois property. But modern bourgeois private property is the final and most complete expression of the system of producing and appropriating products, that is based on class antagonisms, on the exploitation of the many by the few.

In this sense the theory of the Communists may be summed up in the single sentence: Abolition of private property. . . .

To be a capitalist, is to have not only a purely personal, but a social status in production. Capital is a collective product, and only by the united action of many members, nay, in the last resort, only by the united action of all members of society, can it be set in motion.

Capital is therefore not a personal, it is a social power.

When, therefore, capital is converted into common property, into the property of all members of society, personal property is not thereby transformed into social property. It is only the social character of the property that is changed. It loses its class character.

Let us now take wage-labor.

The average price of wage-labor is the minimum wage, i.e., that quantum of the means of subsistence, which is absolutely requisite to keep the laborer in bare existence as a laborer. What, therefore, the wage-laborer appropriates by means of his labor, merely suffices to prolong and reproduce a bare existence. We by no means intend to abolish this personal appropriation of the products of labor, an appropriation that is made for the maintenance and reproduction of human life, and that leaves no surplus wherewith to command the labor of others. All that we want to do away with, is the miserable character of this appropriation, under which the laborer lives merely to increase capital, and is allowed to live only in so far as the interest of the ruling class requires it. . . .

You are horrified at our intending to do away with private property. But in your existing society private property is already done away with for nine-tenths of the population; its existence for the few is solely due to its non-existence in the hands of those nine-tenths. You reproach us, therefore, with intending to do away with a form of property, the necessary condition for whose existence is, the non-existence of any property for the immense majority of society.

In one word, you reproach us with intending to do away with your property. Precisely so: that is just what we intend. . . .

Abolition of the family! even the most radical flare up at this infamous proposal of the Communists.

On what foundation is the present family, the bourgeois family based? On capital, on private gain. In its completely developed form this family exists only among the bourgeoisie. But this state of things finds its complement in the practical absence of the family among the proletarians, and in public prostitution.

The bourgeois family will vanish as a matter of course when its complement vanishes, and both will vanish with the vanishing of capital.

Do you charge us with wanting to stop the exploitation of children by their parents? To this crime we plead guilty.

But you will say, we destroy the most hallowed of relations, when we replace home education by social.

And your education! Is not that also social, and determined by the social conditions under which you educate, by the intervention, direct or indirect, of society by means of schools, etc.? The Communists have not invented the intervention of society in education; they do but seek to alter the character of that intervention, and to rescue education from the influence of the ruling class.

The bourgeois clap-trap about the family and education, about the hallowed correlation of parent and child becomes all the more disgusting, as, by the action of modern industry, all family ties among the proletarians are torn asunder and their children transformed into simple articles of commerce and instruments of labor.

But you Communists would introduce community of women, screams the whole bourgeoisie in chorus.

The bourgeois sees in his wife a mere instrument of production. He hears that the instruments of production are to be exploited in common, and, naturally, can come to no other conclusion then that the lot of being common to all will likewise fall to the women.

He has not even a suspicion that the real point aimed at is to do away with the status of women as mere instruments of production.

For the rest nothing is more ridiculous than the virtuous indignation of our bourgeois at the community of women which, they pretend, is to be openly and officially established by the Communists. The Communists have no need to introduce community of women; it has existed almost from time immemorial.

Our bourgeois, not content with having the wives and daughters of their proletarians at their disposal, not to speak of common prostitutes, take the greatest pleasure in seducing each others' wives.

Bourgeois marriage is in reality a system of wives in common and thus, at the most, what the Communists might possibly be reproached with, is that they desire to introduce, in substitution for a hypocritically concealed, an openly legalized community of women. For the rest it is self-evident that the abolition of the present system of production must bring with it the abolition of the community of women springing from that system, i.e., of prostitution both public and private.

The Communists are further reproached with desiring to abolish countries and nationality.

The workingmen have no country. We cannot take from them what they have not got. Since the proletariat must first of all acquire political supremacy, must rise to be the leading class of the nation, must constitute itself the nation, it is, so far, itself national, though not in the bourgeois sense of the word. . . .

Political power, properly so called, is merely the organized power of one class for oppressing another. If the proletariat during its contest with the bourgeoisie is compelled, by the force of circumstances, to organize itself as a class, if, by means of a revolution, it makes itself the ruling class, and, as such, sweeps away by force the old conditions of production, then it will, along with these conditions, have swept away the conditions

for the existence of class antagonism, and of classes generally, and will thereby have abolished its own supremacy as a class.

In place of the old bourgeois society with its classes and class antagonisms we shall have an association in which the free development of each is the condition for the free development of all. . . .

IV Positions of the Communists in Relation to the Various Existing Opposition Parties

The Communists fight for the attainment of the immediate aims, for the enforcement of the momentary interest of the working class; but in the movement of the present they also represent and take care of the future of that movement.

In short, the Communists everywhere support every revolutionary movement against the existing social and political order of things.

In all these movements they bring to the front, as the leading question in each, the property question, no matter what its degree of development at the time.

Finally, they labor everywhere for the union and agreement of the democratic parties of all countries.

The Communists disdain to conceal their views and aims. They openly declare that their ends can be attained only by the forcible overthrow of all existing social conditions. Let the ruling class tremble at a Communistic revolution. The proletarians have nothing but their chains. They have a world to win.

Working men of all countries, unite!

31. Proposals for the Economic Development of Argentina, 1852

Juan Bautista Alberdi

Juan Bautista Alberdi (1810–1884) was a journalist and diplomat who wrote a pamphlet which influenced the delegates who drafted a constitution for Argentina in 1853 after the fall of the dictator Juan Manual Rosas. The new charter was modeled in part on the United States Constitution, especially in its establishment of a federal republic with an elected president and a bicameral legislative. Alberdi recognized that the prospects for the success of the new system depended to a great extent on a sound economic base for Argentina. The following excerpts from his work, *Bases and Points of Departure for the Political Organization of the Argentine Republic,* present Alberdi's call for a liberal economic plan for his country.

QUESTIONS

1. According to Alberdi, what is the importance of transportation for Argentina? What special significance does he give to railroads?
2. Compare his views with those of Adam Smith and Friedrich List.
3. What does he mean when he writes: "Independent America is called upon to complete the work begun and left unfinished by the Spain of 1450"?

Our youth should be trained for industrial life, and therefore should be educated in the arts and sciences that would prepare them for industry. The South American type of man should be one formed for the conquest of the great and oppressive enemies of our progress: the desert, material backwardness; the brutal and primitive nature of this continent.

We should therefore endeavor to draw our youth away from the cities of the interior, where the old order with its habits of idleness, conceit, and dissipation prevails, and to attract them to the coastal towns so that they may obtain inspiration from Europe, which extends to our shores, and from the spirit of modern life. . . .

Industry is the grand means of promoting morality. By furnishing men with the means of getting a living you keep them from crime, which is generally the fruit of misery and idleness. You will find it useless to fill the minds of youths with abstract notions about religion if you leave them idle and poor. Unless they take monastic vows they will be corrupt and fanatical at the same time. England and the United States have arrived at religious morality by way of industry; Spain has failed to acquire industry and liberty by means of religion alone. Spain has never been guilty of irreligion, but that did not save her from poverty, corruption, and despotism. . . .

The railroad offers the means of righting the topsy-turvy order that Spain established on this continent. She placed the heads of our states where the feet should be.

For her ends of isolation and monopoly this was a wise system; for our aims of commercial expansion and freedom it is disastrous. We must bring our capitals to the coast, or rather bring the coast into the interior of the continent. The railroad and the electric telegraph, the conquerors of space, work this wonder better than all the potentates on earth. The railroad changes, reforms, and solves the most difficult problems without decrees or mob violence.

It will forge the unity of the Argentine Republic better than all our congresses. The congresses may declare it "one and indivisible," but without the railroad to connect its most remote regions it will always remain divided and divisible, despite all the legislative decrees.

Without the railroad you will not have political unity in lands where distance nullifies the action of the central government. Do you want the government, the legislators, the courts of the coast capital to legislate and judge concerning the affairs of the provinces of San Juan and Mendoza, for example? Bring the coast to those regions with the railroad, or vice versa; place those widely separated points within three days' travel of each other, at least. But to have the metropolis or capital a twenty days' journey away is better than having it in Spain, as it was under the old system, which we overthrew for presenting precisely this absurdity. Political unity, then, should begin with territorial unity, and only the railroad can make a single region of two regions separated by five hundred leagues.

Nor can you bring the interior of our lands within reach of Europe's immigrants, who today are regenerating our coasts, except with the powerful aid of the railroads. They are or will be to the life of our interior territories what the great arteries are to the inferior extremities of the human body: sources of life. . . .

The means of securing railroads abound in these lands. Negotiate loans abroad, pledge your national revenues and properties for enterprises that will make them prosper and multiply. It would be childish to hope that ordinary revenues may suffice for such large expenditures; invert that order, begin with expenditures, and you will have revenues. If we had waited until we had sufficient revenues to bear the cost of the War of Independence against Spain, we would still be colonists. With loans we obtained cannons, guns, ships, and soldiers, and we won our independence. What we did to emerge from slavery, we should do to emerge from backwardness, which is the same as slavery; there is no greater title to glory than civilization.

But you will not obtain loans if you do not have national credit—that is, a credit based on the united securities and obligations of all the towns of the state. With the credits of town councils and provinces you will not secure railroads or anything notable. From a national body, consolidate the securities of your present and future revenues and wealth, and you will find lenders who will make available millions for your local and general needs; for if you lack money today, you will have the means of becoming opulent tomorrow. Dispersed and divided, expect nothing but poverty and scorn. . . .

The great rivers, those "moving roads," as Pascal called them, are yet another means of introducing the civilizing action of Europe into the interior of our continent by means of her immigrants. But rivers that are not navigated do not, for practical purposes, exist. To place them under the exclusive domination of our poor banners is to close them to navigation. If they are to achieve the destiny assigned to them by God of populating the interior of the continent, we must place them under the law of the sea—that is, open them to an absolute freedom of navigation. . . .

Let the light of the world penetrate every corner of our republics. By what right do we maintain our most beautiful regions in perpetual brutality? Let us grant to European civilization what our ancient masters denied. In order to exercise their monopoly, the essence of their system, they gave only one port to the Argentine Republic; and we have preserved the exclusivism of the colonial system in the name of patriotism. No more exclusion or closure, whatever be the pretext that is invoked. No more exclusivism in the name of the Fatherland. . . .

What name will you give a land with 200,000 leagues of territory and a population of 800,000? A desert. What name will you give the constitution of that country? The constitution is a desert. Very well, the Argentine Republic is that country—and whatever its constitution, for many years it will be nothing more than the constitution of a desert.

But what constitution best fits a desert? One that will help to make it disappear: one that will enable it in the shortest possible time to cease being a desert and become a populated country. This, then, should and must be the political aim of the Argentine constitution and in general of all South American constitutions. The constitutions of unpopulated countries can have no other serious and rational end, at present and for many years to come, than to give the solitary and abandoned countryside the population it requires, as a fundamental condition for its development and progress.

Independent America is called upon to complete the work begun and left unfinished by the Spain of 1450. The colonization, the settlement of this world, new to this day despite the three hundred years that have passed since its discovery, must be completed by the sovereign and independent American states. The work is the same; only its authors are different. At that time Spain settled our lands; today we settle them ourselves. All our constitutions must be aimed at this great end. We need constitutions, we need a policy of creation, of settlement, of conquest of the solitude and the desert. . . .

The end of constitutional policy and government in America, then, is essentially economic. In America, to govern is to populate.

INTRODUCTION TO UNIT FOUR

Nationalism and Imperialism

Over the last two centuries nationalism became and remains one of the most powerful forces acting in the world—perhaps the most significant emotional factor in public life. Nationalism touches all kinds of popular feelings and prejudices: personal, social, racial, religious, and ethnic. It falls between the two extremes of particularism and cosmopolitanism, exalting the nation as a sacred entity and the supreme sanction for its members. This means that the historically more familiar and understandable sense of membership in and consciousness of other communities fade, whether it was one's city-state or province or multinational empire such as ancient Rome, or of Christianity as a universal religion, Western civilization, or of the entire human race. All are eclipsed by national consciousness. There is still no precise definition of nationalism, nor is it agreed whether it is a good or a bad thing, still less whether the nation-state is one of the supreme creations of Western civilization or a pathological instrument that will be fatal to that civilization and the world's peace, or even whether it is a permanent or passing feature of history.

"Nation" derives from Latin *natio,* meaning birth or race, belonging to a tribe or social group of the same kinship and language. Since the seventeenth century it has generally meant the population of a sovereign state. Because "nation" had become so ambiguous a designation, the term "nationality" began to come into use in the early nineteenth century and meant a society speaking the same language, living according to the same customs, sharing a historical tradition, and identifying itself as a distinct culture. Such a cultural definition stemmed largely from the writings of Johann Herder (see Document 32) and did not necessarily entail political unity or an organized sovereign state of its own. At about the same time or shortly after, "nationalism" and "nationalist" appeared, and they could refer to any of the following: the historical process by which an independent nation-state was created; the work of a political party or pressure group seeking national aims; the philosophy, theory, or ideals of the nation-state; the emotional attachment of members of a nationality, which they exalted, believing in its superiority to all others and in its unique identity and "mission." So defined, nationalism is a modern fusion of two age-old entities: patriotism (the love of the "rocks and rills" of one's home) and nationality (one's group, tribe, or city-state, distinguished from others by blood, language, history, tradition, etc.). That fusion was effected in the crucible of the French Revolution and Napoleonic wars, 1789–1815.

Historians still disagree over a proper definition of a "nation." Perhaps the best description is a group of people living according to the same customs, identifying itself as a distinct culture, and sharing a historical tradition and a belief in a common destiny. In Europe a further distinction must be made between the western and eastern lands. In the former region citizenship in a political unit or state (usually a voluntary act) determined membership in a nation. But in Eastern Europe one was born into an ethnic community. That fact determined a person's national identity, regardless of any political allegiance to any state.

A pivotal development in the emergence of nationalism was the growth—institutional and territorial—of "national monarchies" in France, Spain, Portugal, England, Denmark, Sweden, and for a time also in Bohemia (the Czech Republic), Poland, and Hungary. Concomitant with the growing political differentiation among the European peoples as distinct national monarchies came economic differentiation as well, for each monarchy pursued mercantilist (more accurately, national economic) policies that set it apart from its neighbors and rivals. With the Reformation came religious and ecclesiastical differentiation, as various Protestant denominations and national churches emerged, such as the Anglican in England, the Gallican in France, and the Lutheran in Sweden. Analogous was the cultural differentiation emerging from the development of national literatures and the resort to vernacular languages in place of medieval Latin. In sum, from the fourteenth century to 1789, we find mounting political, economic, religious, and cultural differentiation among many European nationalities, but we do not find nationalism.

The French revolutionaries took the decisive steps. To be sure, their program of Liberty, Equality, and Fraternity was a cosmopolitan one that derived from the Enlightenment of the previous age. Yet the vehicle for carrying out the grand transformation of humanity was to be the French nation. Although a universal system of harmonious nation-states was hardly the result, it was toward such ideal ends that the French revolutionaries proclaimed the people to be sovereign and the nation independent (what came to be called national self-determination). All class privileges as well as local and regional distinctions were abolished, swallowed up in the national whole. All French-speakers were incorporated into France; all Frenchmen had to speak French, thus, e.g., the requirement that French replace Breton in Brittany. The church as a rival community and rival allegiance was greatly diminished by converting the clergy into a "civil body" allegiant to the government, confiscating church lands and property, and taking over and secularizing church-provided schools and other social welfare functions. Fervid loyalty to the new nation-state was assured by the radical reorganization of state and society: a democratic republic, whose citizens participate in politics and govern themselves, is much more likely to identify itself with the state than the subjects of the old regime who were expected only to obey and to pay. The subject people became the sovereign citizenry. The identification of people (nation) and state soon manifested itself in the national flag (the Tricolor), the national hymn (the "Marseillaise"), and the national holiday (Bastille Day). The French revolutionaries transformed nationalism into a surrogate religion. France was the chosen, the providential instrument. The Constitution of 1791 was itself treated as holy writ; the solemn oath which was sworn to the Declaration of the Rights of Man and Citizen conferred citizenship on all—even foreigners like Citizen Tom Paine—while refusal cut one off from the sacred body, a kind of civic excommunication.

Napoleon became the chief evangelist of nationalism and champion of the emancipated French nation; utilizing the device of plebiscites to tap the national will, he was the first popular dictator of a kind all too familiar ever since. As the beneficiary of the political and social transformation that came in the wake of the revolution, Napoleon's France demonstrated the great power and efficiency attained by mobilizing the manpower and resources and the will of the nation-state. By reaction to or in emulation of him, the Corsican adventurer inspired nationalism in many other countries of Europe and even in Egypt (see his national appeal to Egyptians in Document 36). But it was, or soon became, a conservative, antimodernist nationalism that rejected the revolutionary program of which Napoleon was the bearer and symbol and treasured native ways, royal authority, aristocratic rule, etc. This alternative to popular, liberal nationalism is foreshadowed in Burke's *Reflections* (see Document 17); it was the brand of nationalism that exalted tradition and was espoused particularly in Germany, but also in Spain, to a lesser degree in Italy and Poland, and, as the nineteenth century proceeded, in Russia.

The Romantic movement in literature and thought was the next stage in the development of nationalism. Romantic nationalism—a much used if somewhat vague term—focused much attention on folkways, folk language, folk literature, folk history—all of them so many "heartbeats of nationality." The great nationalists of the period were poets, historians, literary historians, philologists, and folklorists who celebrated the unique "spirit" or "genius" of the nation (from Herder's concept of the *Volksgeist* as expressed in its history and literature). They greatly intensified national consciousness by their exalted emotional commitment to the nation. To Herder all nationalities were equal, a concept he conveyed by his metaphor of nationalities as plants in a garden or flowers in a bouquet, all equally precious and beautiful. That ideal did not survive the revolutionary and Napoleonic wars nor the ardor of the Romantic authors, who introduced passionate ideas of national superiority, uniqueness, sacredness, and exclusiveness, and did so particularly by linking nationality with race. Thus were sown the dragon's teeth of intolerance toward minorities within the nation-state and hostility against the nations across its frontiers.

After the revolutions of 1848, and especially from 1870 on, in politics the two dominant trends, which can be traced back to the French Revolution, were democratization and the growth in the power of the state. Both intensified nationalism as a force and as a sentiment. This growing fusion of nation and state, together with the extension of the nation-state's power, are decisive—some would say lethal—factors in the history of the last hundred years. That century has seen a growing identity of state and society, of government and citizenry, accompanied by steady progress toward democracy and the widening of political and civil rights and popular participation in government. Of great significance was the growth of mass political parties, which became major forces in the United States during the late 1820s and 1830s. They took root in England in the wake of the extension of the franchise in the reform acts of 1867 and 1884 (paralleled in 1871 by universal suffrage in France and Germany), in order to mobilize the new electorates. The resulting "nationalizing of the masses" was part of the nationalizing of politics. Politics had traditionally been local or provincial in scope: the independent member of parliament financed his campaign and ran on his own ticket. That kind of self-help and small scale gave way to a national party, institutionalized with its own secretariat and treasury and dedicated to a national program that was strictly enforced on all members by party discipline, granting or withholding campaign funds, etc. In one generation politics was transposed from a local into a national key.

In these same decades the industrial revolution, popular education, and national armies contributed mightily to uniting and vastly strengthening the nation-state. Instrumental were new systems of transportation, communication, military and naval armaments, mechanized publication, and others. The newspapers, which were produced cheaply on rotating cylinders and transported by rail everywhere in the country overnight, helped create a national market as well as a national mind. Great economic growth and production of wealth emboldened the middle classes and the masses to demand political rights. National systems of education appeared: mandatory, free, universal, and largely secular in state-supported and state-managed elementary schools, followed in the years before 1914 by the beginnings of secondary school systems. What had been the privilege of the few became the duty of the many. Mass literacy appeared for the first time in history, a phenomenon that has had an incalculable effect on Europe and the wider world. State control over the schools bound the citizenry ever closer to the state, in part by severing ties with the Church, which was often expelled from education and welfare provision, two of its traditional functions. State schools became the temples of the land wherein was taught the new secular faith, a creed which varied from country to country, but whose common denominator beyond the Three Rs was patriotism. The state's schools became the nation's *alma mater.*

The new mass or national armies after 1870 were on the Prussian-German model, itself inspired by Napoleon and the *levée en masse.* Following Prussia's defeat of France in 1870–1871, all the European powers fell in step with Prussia—partly out of fear of the new Germany and partly out of emulation. Nationalism had been steeped in militarism and the celebration of military glory since 1793; by 1914 this was universally the case and more intensely so than ever.

Armies had become immensely popular as emblems of national pride, and soldiers were respectable as never before in European history. Above all, economic and technological developments made it possible to approximate more fully than previously the revolutionary principle of the nation in arms. All the nation's blood, treasure, and will were enlisted and mobilized in the national cause, according to the famous formulation of General Clausewitz. The capacity of governments to extend the degree of mobilization—materially and psychologically—has continued to the present, and with it the closeness of the bond between nation and state.

The passing of *laissez-faire* and free trade are also significant in the intensification of nationalism that occurred in the half century prior to 1914. Increased state regulation and intervention in the economy to promote national industries (what is traditionally and accurately designated "economic nationalism") tightened the bonds between nation and state. From factory acts concerned to regulate hours, conditions, safety, child and women labor, etc., governments adopted semisocialist, welfare legislation, such as Bismarck's pioneering program of social insurance in the 1880s, providing sickness and accident coverage and old age pensions. All this economic regulation and policy making (including building and running railways, clearing slums, redistributing income, breaking strikes, and much else) made the state an economic actor, often a paternalistic one, which directly and profoundly affected the welfare of its people, drawing them into the embrace of the state and away from that of the Church and all other associations as the matrix of their lives. A British cabinet minister registered many of these trends when he acknowledged to Parliament in 1894, "We are all socialists now."

During the nineteenth century romantic nationalism, illiberal and chauvinistic, came to the fore. The tendency, both popular and scholarly, to equate nationality with race was abetted by generations of anthropologists and philologists who equated race and language with nationality. They thus reinforced its exclusiveness and intolerance, undergirding the common assertion that "foreigners," especially Jews, could not be nationalized because they were unassimilable. It was only late in the century, but to very little avail, that social scientists began to deny all connection between race, language, and nationality. It should be noted that the nationalism exported from the West included this racial strain and that it made non-Western nationalism—especially in Japan—that much more intolerant and virulent.

The organization of Europe along nationalist lines loomed up more and more as one of the great goals of the epoch. Earlier the independence of the Latin American republics, Greece, and Belgium, which separated from Holland in the revolution of 1830, was seen as vindication of the national principle. The British government in Palmerston's time (down to 1865) supported insurgent nationalities, and Napoleon III of France espoused the cause of submerged nationalities (such as the Italian, successfully, and the Polish, unsuccessfully) and proposed the reorganization of the European state system on the basis of nationality. It was the fond hope of theorists of nationalism such as Mazzini that a submerged

nationality which vindicated its claim to national self-determination and thereupon redeemed its irredenta would live happily ever after in peace and benevolence toward all other nationalities and nation-states (see Document 33). The
weakening and eventual dismemberment of multinational Austria signaled the
triumph of nationalism in Eastern Europe: after the revolution of 1848 that
Humpty-Dumpty was put back together again. Defeated by Napoleon III in
1859, it lost its Italian lands to the new Italy. Smashed by Bismarck's Prussia in
1866, as the "Dual Monarchy" it had to give way the next year to Hungarian national demands by which Austria (Germans) and Hungary (Magyars) enjoyed
virtual independence but collaborated to repress Czech, South Slav, and other
subjected nationalities (until 1918). But it was Bismarck's unification of Germany
at the expense of France in 1870–1871 that was the most portentous triumph of
nationalism. He had captured and stolen away the liberal program of nationalism, democracy, free trade, etc. for the cause of conservatism, utilizing them to
preserve and give a new lease on life to monarchical authoritarianism and aristocratic predominance in the manner of Burke.

The revolutions of 1848 had been a critical turning point, as they marked
the commandeering by conservatives of the 1789 revolutionary liberal program,
which they saw could be made to serve conservative, illiberal ends. Especially
adroit in carrying off this heist were Napoleon III of France, to a considerable degree Cavour in uniting Italy, and most of all Bismarck in Germany. The Russian
tsars also asserted their authority and expanded their rule during the mid-nineteenth century, but they did not employ democratic ideals to achieve their ends
(see Documents 34 and 37).

The outcome of the American Civil War in 1865 registered another resounding triumph for the national principle, although by frustrating that of the
Confederacy (see Document 35). In the case of the United States two rival ideologies clashed over control of the western territories. The North championed a system of free labor, urbanization, industrialization, and entrepreneurial capitalism,
while the South fought for an extension of slavery, aristocracy, and agrarianism.
The victory for the Union and the abolition of slavery ensured that the northern
way of life would prevail in a new South and in the American West. The results
of the Civil War gave a huge boost to American nationalism and guaranteed that
the United States would become a major world power.

In the nineteenth century triumphant nationalism often swelled into imperialism, which may be best defined as an aggressive form and an extension of nationalism. It entails the exercise of authority by a people or government over
alien peoples or territories, whether in the form of the planting of colonies of
one's own nationals or the imposition of one's government and culture on other
nationalities, and it always involves the use of force. As such it is a constant in
history (Europe was the victim of Ottoman Turk imperialism in the fourteenth
through the seventeenth centuries), and, unlike nationalism, it is not a European
invention.

The term "imperialism" first came into wide use as a satirical description of
the policies and government of Napoleon III in France. It was taken up as a party

epithet in parliamentary debate between Liberals and Tories in Britain. Its pejorative associations today make it difficult to use as a neutral descriptive term, but it is helpful to identify the major motives and aims for modern imperialism. First, it expressed an extreme nationalism or jingoism, which saw in empire-building the expression of one nation's superiority over all others. Each empire competed with its rivals for strategic advantage, territory, power, glory, and the means to realize its historic mission in the world. Secondly, it involved the economic quest to acquire raw materials, cheap labor, markets, and new fields for capital investment, thus making imperialism "the highest stage of capitalism," according to Lenin. Thirdly, imperialism also emphasized the benefits of expansion for the working classes through economic growth and increased employment, which also brought social reform. Finally, it incorporated the ideological urge to spread the gospels of civilization and Christianity across the globe. This missionary impulse was often accompanied by expressions of humanitarianism such as the idea of the "white man's burden," but it also carried the darker theme of a Darwinian struggle for existence and the natural superiority of those empires which were the most fit to rule (see Documents 38 and 40). No one of these factors was determinative; rather, all four, in varying proportions at different times and places, constitute the motives and aims of imperialism.

Informal imperialism, sometimes called "the imperialism of free trade," appears to fit none of these categories. It dispenses with political control as long as commercial entry and economic rights (and sometimes missionary rights) are retained by the imperial power that regards a particular area as its sphere of influence. The British policy toward China in the mid-nineteenth century is a case in point. When Chinese officials protested the imposition of the opium trade, the English used force to assert their dominance (see Document 41). Britain, other European powers, and the United States forced greater economic concessions upon the Chinese, until a powerful nationalist movement protested both foreign interference and imperial rule (see Document 43). Another interesting example is American and British policy in the nineteenth century toward Latin America, under the Monroe and Canning doctrine (see Document 45). The United States and Great Britain agreed to dominate the Caribbean, Central America, and South America, using occasional military intervention to keep the region stable and dependent. In 1898 the United States secured Cuban independence from Spain through war, but chose not to annex that island (see Document 46). Natives of those lands increasingly resented the power of the "Colossus of the North," and some reformers fought for political and economic reforms and fairer treatment for their people (see Document 47).

The history of European imperialism often exhibited a progression from informal control when possible to formal rule if and when that approach became necessary. In those cases the establishment of imperial domination involved a gradual process of encroachment. At first indirect rule utilizing native elites, partly coerced and partly voluntary, sufficed. But often the outbreak or threat of rebellion or competition with rival powers induced an imperial government to establish formal, direct rule through its own administrators and officials. This was the pattern generally in Asia (see Document 42 for the British experience in India), whereas in Latin America informal arrangements persisted owing to Anglo-American agreement.

British policy in Africa in the Victorian age was motivated by a variety of impulses. These included extinguishing both slavery and the slave trade from that continent, abolishing human sacrifices and other "evil customs," bringing Christianity and "civilization" to Africa, and opening the continent to free trade. Englishmen did not come to Africa to acquire new territories to rule at great trouble and defend at great expense. Military expeditions were sent out to open or reopen trade routes, punish rapine and interdict slaving, pacify territories for missionary or trader but not to annex. This was, in short, the imperialism of free trade. Unless an area lapsed into chaos, took on strategic importance, or was likely to be taken by a rival like France, British imperial authorities preferred to exercise power through moral suasion, influence, informal or indirect rule, external paramountcy (as exerted by the navy), or the establishment of protectorates (see Document 44).

There is no example of a pure system of colonial rule, informal or formal, for in various ways all the imperial powers enlisted indigenous institutions and collaborating elites, progressively Europeanizing them. To some observers, while the old European empires have disappeared, elements of informal rule persist, especially economically and culturally, and most notably among those former colonies that retain membership in the British Commonwealth of Nations or the *Union Française.*

A decisive turn of events for the onset of the great wave of formal imperialism in the decades before 1914 was the Franco-Prussian war of 1870–1871, when, as a British observer remarked, "Europe has lost a mistress and won a master." The upset of the traditional balance of power in Europe by Germany prompted France's attempt to regain national strength and greatness in Africa and Southeast Asia (see Document 39), necessarily, since any recouping of power within Europe was impossible. Thus was triggered a race to obtain overseas possessions and to secure those on which one already had some hold. One power could not let her traditional rivals get ahead of her, and so Britain, Italy, Belgium, and eventually Germany joined France in the scramble, as did the United States and Japan. Formal imperialism intensified during the three decades after that pivotal war of 1870–1871.

While there were many collisions in the overseas domains, they (unlike those in Europe) were resolved peaceably in negotiations and there was no war between European powers over colonial spoils. It came close to that, however, at Fashoda between France and Britain in 1898, and the United States did declare war on Spain that year (see Document 46). Many historians have interpreted imperialism as a major factor in the intensification of the lethal national and economic competition that exploded into war in 1914. Yet imperialism functioned in those decades as an emollient, a great safety valve relieving the fierce pressures generated by national conflict in Europe, by affording space for expansion and scope for compromise outside Europe. One supposes that consumption of European energies abroad also reduced friction at home. On the other hand, the European and Western ascendancy, the partitioning of Africa and nearly so of China, and the easy domination of most of the world resulted less from Western strength than from non-Western weakness. Despite the stimulus of blows which the Europeans had been exerting since 1492, little or no transformation or modernization in the non-Western world had occurred. Thus victimization by the imperial powers was the price that was paid for centuries of stagnation and complacency. Japan is the one example of a society that did respond to that stimulus of blows, and it too followed the trajectory of nation-state to imperial power.

One of the great ironies in the history of nationalism is that it was the destroyer of the old empires, such as the Austrian, Russian, and Ottoman in the 1919 peace settlement. But it was also the progenitor, or "a most devoted helpmate," of the new imperialism—after 1870—when the United States and European powers carved up most of the remaining free areas of the world. Nationalistic imperialists believed in the superiority of their nation over all others and therefore its right to have dominion over "palm and pine" as a matter of "manifest destiny." Another powerful force was national honor, the wine and poetry of nationalism, which has been called "jingoism" and compared to the honor of the dueling nobility that had to have "satisfaction." As the prestige element of nationalism, the national honor had to be vindicated when it was challenged by a real or imagined affront. European nationalism fueled imperialism and thus thwarted and repressed national self-determination outside Europe.

It is often observed that the nation-state is obsolete as an economic unit, because industry and finance are more and more international and multinational; it is as though all the world's stock markets are plugged into the same computer. Since the eighteenth century, the Unbound Prometheus of economic development has driven on relentlessly, creating one great world economy and generating some sense of interdependence and cooperation among the nation-states, transcending national boundaries and setting some limits to national egotism and rivalry. Until the twentieth century there was no international authority that transcended the nation-state, and no body of international law enforced by an international military force. Nevertheless, the Concert of Europe, an informal diplomatic arrangement among the great powers that dated from the settlement of the wars with Napoleon in 1815, was often effective in restoring or preserving peace, as in 1856, 1878, 1885–1886, and 1897. As late as 1912–1913 it succeeded in negotiating a settlement that created Albania. Examples of international cooperation were the establishment in 1856 of an international commission to regulate navigation on much of the Danube River and the Geneva Convention of 1864, which led to the founding of the International Red Cross. Part of the Geneva Convention dealt with the usages and laws of war and proclaimed the rights of prisoners of war, the wounded and ill, and noncombatants. These provisions were extended in scope in 1909 and again in 1929, when the United States and forty-six other powers signed on. Other agreements include the Universal Telegraph and Postal Unions in the 1870s, and the Berne Conventions in the 1880s on patents and on copyright. The Hague Conferences of 1899 and 1907 failed to do much toward disarmament and universal peace. They did, however, establish international courts, to which disputes between nation-states can be (and are) submitted, and undertook other efforts which can be seen as anticipations of the League of Nations and the United Nations. In any event, there were some organizations and diplomatic activity which mitigated national egotism and stimulated a degree of international consciousness and conscience. Yet for the foreseeable future the nation-state will march on as triumphant as ever and remain the normal mode for organizing a people's life.

32. The Cultural Basis of Nationality

Johann Gottfried Herder

Johann Gottfried Herder (1744–1803) was a German historian, philosopher, literary critic, and progenitor of cultural nationalism. Born into a humble, impoverished family in the borderland regions of rural Prussia, he studied Latin, Greek, and Hebrew as a child and became a Lutheran minister. As a youth he was also schooled in the Enlightenment. From 1776 on he was court preacher to the duke of Weimar and part of its circle of famous writers that included Goethe and Schiller, two of Germany's greatest poets. At the price of some censorship he finally escaped penury and his native Prussia, which he detested for its despotism and militarism, and especially their incarnation, King Frederick the Great and his francophile culture.

In his *Essay on the Origin of Language,* 1772 (see Part A), Herder was a pioneer on the nature and function of language. His contemporary, the English philologist William Jones, resided as a jurist in British India where he made fundamental discoveries of the close relationships of Sanskrit to classical Greek and Latin, thus laying the basis for the Indo-European language group (linking the Greek, Latin-Romance, Celtic, Germanic, Slavic, Baltic, Iranian, and Indic language clusters). Such developments in philology and linguistics were decisively shaped by European contacts with the outside world since 1492 and have gone on ever since. Herder anticipated some recent linguistic and genetic research that theorizes that all peoples and their languages descend from a small, original grouping of humans who, plausibly, would have spoken a single ancient mother tongue some twelve millennia ago. Herder, the "high priest of humanity" who characteristically invoked the unity of all mankind, became an inspired translator and interpreter of ancient and modern folk literatures in many languages. These interests were the source of his concept of nationality, a community defined by its culture. As a student of world history he was sensitive to all peoples and cultures, cultivating an attitude of imaginative sympathy.

Throughout his life Herder was fascinated by Jewish history, both in the biblical period and after in their dispersal. Unlike almost all his contemporaries and quite exceptional for a Christian clergyman, he did not seek and in fact opposed as illegitimate their conversion to Christianity. To Herder the Jews were a nationality, "the oldest and most excellent example," and it is likely that his concept of what a nationality is originated in his reflections on the Jewish example. He explained the survival of the Jews by five factors: the bond of the people to the land of Israel; the law and constitution given by God to Moses and accepted voluntarily by the nation; the common language, folklore, and historical tradition; the social cohesion that radiates outward from the family; the reverence for the fathers and forefathers. A close student of the Old Testament as history (rather than theology or the literal word of God), what he called the national library of the Hebrew nation, Herder saw Jewish history as central to and a model for a grand synthesis of world history. Parts B and C of the following excerpts are from his best-known work, *Ideas for a Philosophy of the History of Mankind*, 1784–1791.

QUESTIONS

1. Summarize and explain the significance of Herder's four laws concerning human beings and language. How does he use the biblical story of the Tower of Babel?
2. Does Herder's argument support the theory of cultural unity or cultural diversity throughout the world? Explain.
3. What is Herder's definition of nationality? What does he include? Exclude? What is the present definition of nationality?
4. What difficulties or dangers may lie in Herder's conception of nationality, given the circumstances prevailing in Europe in his lifetime?
5. Compare Herder's presentation of the Jews and Slavs. What elements does he single out as important? What makes them important?
6. Do the Slavs constitute a nationality, according to Herder? Assuming that they do not, what do they—or any people—need in order to become such?
7. What is the usury of which Herder speaks? Does he explain Jewish prominence in economic activity or does he indulge in stereotypes?
8. What is the relationship of one nationality to another supposed to be, according to Herder? Has it been that way? Why?

A. On the Origin of Language

Let us now examine more closely some of the circumstances and concerns which induced man to develop a language for himself upon entering the world, equipped as he was with the best disposition for language. Since these circumstances and concerns were many and varied, I propose to subsume them under certain principal laws governing the nature of man and his species.

FIRST LAW: Man is a free, thinking, and creative being whose faculties operate in a continuous progression: hence he is predisposed for language. [Herder develops the contrast between humans and animals which learn but not cumulatively and without passing on knowledge by education to their offspring: "no animal has ever evinced remembrance by an act which would improve conditions for its whole species and would generalize experiences in order to make use of them in the future"; man has this capacity and therefore language, and culture generally, are built up cumulatively and transmitted in a never ending chain.]

SECOND LAW: Man is by nature a gregarious creature, born to live in society; hence the development of language is both natural and essential for him. What a contrast there is between the natures of man and beast. Man comes into the world in a state of weakness and deficiency, deprived of instincts and natural aptitudes as no animal is, in order to receive a training and education as no animal does, and thereby develop into an intricately connected whole in a manner unknown to any animal species. . . .

THIRD LAW: Since the whole human race is not one single homogeneous group, it does not speak one and the same language. The formation of diverse national languages, therefore, is a natural corollary of human diversity. Properly speaking, no two human beings speak exactly the same language. Even father and son, husband and wife, never speak exactly alike. Just as there are no two men absolutely identical in their features and physical make-up, so there are no two words even in one language ever spoken in quite the same way by two different people.

Each generation develops in its language a specific or family idiom: this is the beginning of a dialect at least as far as pronunciation is concerned. Climate, air and water, food and drink, influence the vocal organs and of course also the language. Social conventions and the mighty goddess of fashion will introduce through gestures and polite forms this or that peculiarity or variation. So far we have chiefly had pronunciation in mind. But what vast possibilities become apparent when we consider the very soul of language, the meaning of words. . . . The more living a language and the closer it is to its origin, the more changeable it is. A language existing only in books, studied by rules, in use only by scholars and not in real intercourse, denoting a definite number of articles of objects and meaning, its vocabulary being complete and limited, its grammar systematized, its application fixed: such a language may remain virtually unaltered. But a language of a wild and roving life in the midst of the great boundless universe, devoid of well-formulated rules, of books and letter symbols, of classical masterpieces, deficient and incomplete so as to need daily enrichment, which is so young and supple that it admits of daily additions at the first perception, at the first call or sensation: such a language must undergo changes in every new world which it encounters, with every new mode of thought or reasoning.

[The biblical story of the Tower of Babel] supports by its rather poetic legend what has since been observed about many nations in all parts of the world. For it has been found that languages did not gradually change following migrations. The process resembled far more the poetic tale of the Hebrews. "Once upon a time all the world spoke a single language and the same words. Peoples assembled to erect a great edifice with its top in the heavens and to fashion a name for themselves in order not to be dispersed all over the earth. Then came disaster and they reeled under a confusion of tongues. They ceased to build the tower and scattered to the four corners of the earth." Is it not conceivable that so great an undertaking gave ample opportunity for dissension and bitterness, that some slight offense could have aroused family bias, kindling the spark of discord? Discord, in turn, could have given rise to separation and accomplished the very thing which their tower was designed to prevent: the diversification of their language, the basis of their common origin.

FOURTH LAW: Since mankind in all probability forms one progressive totality, originating from one common origin within one universal order, all languages and, with them, the whole chain of culture, derive from one common source. Many have attempted genealogies of languages: I shall not do so. There are many incidental causes which escape the etymologist, which, however, palpably increase the difficulties in tracing the genealogical tree of a language. Among travellers and missionaries there have been so few expert philologists capable of reporting on the spirit and characteristics of tribal languages that we are still on the whole left very much in the dark. What we get in most instances is a list of words. This, clearly, is not a good enough basis for a science of comparative languages. All that can be said with a degree of assurance, therefore, is that the process of language formation and language transmission is inseparable from the general development of human society.

Have we Germans not learned most of what we know as a "civilized nation" from other peoples? Indeed we have. In this and in many other such cases nature has forged a new chain of transmission, from nation to nation. Arts, sciences, languages, the totality of social cultures, have been developed and refined in a powerful progression in this very manner. We Germans would still be living contentedly in our forests, waging wars as heroes, if the chain of foreign cultures had not pressed in upon us and, with the impact of centuries, had not forced us to join in. Ro-man civilization hailed from Greece; Greece owed its culture to Asia and Egypt; Egypt to Asia, China perhaps to Egypt, and so on; thus the chain extends from its first link to the last and will one day encircle perhaps the whole world. . . . Some modern nations merely carried on and developed the heritage handed down to them. Others . . . arrived on the scene to destroy and lay waste what the former had created. Yet this only helped to stimulate new activity and new creations upon the debris of the old.

B. The Hebrews

Their country was small; and the part they acted on the stage of the world, both in and out of this country, was insignificant, as they seldom appeared in the character of conquerors. Yet through the will of fate, and a series of events, the causes of which are easy to be traced, they have had more influence on other nations than any people of Asia; nay in some degree, through the mediums of Christianity and Islam, they have been the ground work of enlightening the greater part of the world.

That the Hebrews had written annals of their actions, at a time in which most of the now enlightened nations were totally ignorant of writing, annals which they ventured to carry back to the beginning of the world, distinguishes them in an eminent manner. . . . Their account is taken merely from family chronicles, and interwoven with historical tales or poems; and its value as history is evidently increased by this simplicity of form. This account, too, derives singular weight from its having been preserved for some thousands of years, with almost superstitious scrupulosity. . . . I scruple not, therefore, to take the history of the Hebrews, as related by themselves [in the Bible], for my groundwork.

Thus . . . their progenitor [Abraham] passed the Euphrates as sheik of a wandering horde, and at last arrived in Palestine. Here he found room without opposition, to pursue the pastoral life of his ancestors, and worship the God of his fathers after the manner of his tribe. His posterity of the third generation was led into Egypt . . . till, it is not exactly known in what generation, they were emancipated by their future legislator [Moses] from the contempt and oppression . . . and conducted into Arabia. Here the great man, the greatest these people had ever had, completed his work; and gave them a constitution, founded on the religion and mode of life of their fathers it is true, but so intermingled with Egyptian polity, as on the one hand to raise them from a wandering horde to the state of a cultivated nation, yet on the other to wean them completely from Egypt, so that they were never after desirous of treading the swarthy soil. All the laws of Moses evince wonderful reflection: they extend from the greatest to the smallest things, to sway the spirit of the nation in every circumstance of life, and to be, as Moses frequently repeats, an everlasting law.

This profound system of laws was by no means the production of a moment: the legislator added to it as circumstances required, and before his death bound the whole nation to the observance of its future political constitution. For forty years he exacted a strict obedience to his injunctions: perhaps so long a time was consumed by the people in the deserts of Arabia, that, the first stubborn generation being dead, a people brought up to these customs might settle in the land of its fathers properly qualified for their exercise.

But the wish of this patriotic man was not fulfilled. The aged Moses died on the confines of the land he sought; and when his successor [Joshua] entered it, he enjoyed not sufficient authority and respect to follow completely the plan of the lawgiver. . . .

The leaders that necessity raised up [after Moses] were for the most part to be considered only as successful partisans: and when at length the people came to be governed by kings, these had so much to do with their land divided into tribes, that the third was the last [king] who reigned over the whole of the disjointed realm. Ten of the tribes withdrew from his successor; and how could two such feeble governments subsist in the neighborhood of powerful enemies, to whose attacks they were incessantly exposed? The kingdom of Israel had properly no regular constitution. . . . they wallowed in the most wretched imitation of foreign manners and customs, till the king of Assyria came, and plundered the little realm, as a boy would rob a bird's nest. The other kingdom, which at least had the support of the ancient constitution, established by two potent kings and a fortified capital, held out for some time longer; though only till a more powerful victor thought it worth his attention. The spoiler Nebuchadnezzar came, and made its feeble monarchs first tributaries, and lastly, after they revolted, slaves. The country was ravaged, the capital was razed, and Judah led to Babylon in as disgraceful captivity as Israel had been to Assyria. Thus, considered as a state, scarcely any nation exhibits a more contemptible figure in history than this, the reigns of two of its kings excepted.

What was the cause of all this? In my opinion it is clear, from the course of the narrative itself: for it was impossible that a nation with such a defective constitution, both internally and externally, should prosper in this part of the world. If David overran the desert as far as the banks of the Euphrates, and thereby only stirred up only greater enemies against his successor, could he thus give the nation the stability it wanted? . . . [Foreign ways, commerce, luxury, etc., were pernicious to the kingdom.] For the rest, since the time of Moses no second legislator had been found among the people, who was capable of bringing back the state, shattered from its beginning, to a fundamental constitution suitable to the times. The learned class soon declined; they who were zealous for the laws of the land had voice but not the arm of power; the kings were for the most part either effeminate, or creatures of the priests. Thus two things diametrically opposite, the refined nomocracy, on which Moses had settled the constitution, and a sort of theocratic monarchy, such as prevailed among all the nations of this region of despotism, contended together: and thus the law of Moses became a law of bondage to a people, to whom it was intended to have been a law of political liberty.

In the course of time the case became altered but not improved. When the Jews, set at liberty by [the Persian king] Cyrus, returned from bondage, much diminished in number, they had learned many other things, but no genuine political constitution. How, indeed, was such a constitution to have been acquired in Assyria or Chaldea? Their sentiments fluctuated between monarchical and sacerdotal government: they rebuilt a temple, as if this would have revived the times of Moses and Solomon. . . . Thus they lived and suffered for some centuries, under the Greeks of Syria, the Idumeans, and the Romans; till at length, through an animosity, to which history scarcely exhibits a parallel, both the capital and the rest of the country were destroyed [in 66–74], in a manner that grieved the humane emperor [Titus] himself. On this they were dispersed through all the territories of the Roman Empire; and with the dispersion such an influence of the Jews upon the human race commenced as could hardly have been conceived from a land of such small extent. . . . Shortly before the downfall of the Jewish state, Christianity arose in the heart of it, and in the beginning not only retained its connection with Judaism, and consequently admitted the sacred writings of the Jews to its canon, but even rested principally on these the divine mission of its Messiah. Thus through Christianity the books of the Jews were introduced to every nation that embraced the Christian doctrines; and according to the manner in which they have been understood, and the use that has been made of them, they have benefited or injured the whole Christian world. Their effect was good, so far as in them Moses made the doctrine of one god, creator of the world, the basis of all religion and philosophy, and, in many poems and precepts throughout these writings, spoke of this God with a dignity and importance, a gratitude and resignation, of which few examples are to be found in any other human work. . . . It was gratifying also to the curiosity of the human mind, to find in these books such popular answers to the questions respecting the age and creation of the world, the origin of evil, and the like, as every man could understand and comprehend: to say nothing of the instructive history of the nation, and the pure morality of several books in the collection. . . . the Jewish computation of time . . . afforded a received and general standard, and a thread with which to connect the events of universal history. . . .

With all these advantages, however, it is equally incontestable, that the misconception and abuse of these writings have been detrimental to the human mind in various respects; and the more as they have operated upon it under the claim of being divine. How many absurd cosmogonies have been framed from the simple and sublime history of the creation given by Moses! How many rigid doctrines, and unsatisfactory hypotheses, have been spun from his serpent and apple! . . .

The nation of the Jews itself, since its dispersion, has done service or injury by its presence to the people of the earth, according as they have treated it. In the early ages Christians were considered to be Jews, and despised or oppressed in common with them; they rendering themselves liable to many of the reproaches of the Jews, pride, superstition, and antipathy to other nations. Afterwards, when the Christians themselves became oppressors of the Jews, they almost everywhere gave them an opportunity of engrossing the internal trade of the country, particularly that in money, by their industriousness as individuals, and the manner in which they were spread abroad as a people; so that the less civilized nations of Europe voluntarily became the slaves of their usury. The system of exchange was not invented by them, it is true, but they soon brought it to perfection; their insecurity in Islamic and Christian countries rendering it indispensable to them. Thus this widely diffused republic of cunning usurers unquestionably restrained many nations of Europe for a long time from exercising their own industry in trade; for these thought themselves above a Jewish occupation, and were . . . little inclined to learn this intelligent and refined species of industry from the servile treasurers of Christendom. . . . Should anyone collect a history of the Jews from all the countries into which they have been dispersed, he would exhibit a picture of mankind, equally remarkable in a natural and political view: for no people upon earth have been spread abroad like these; no people upon earth remained so distinguishable and active in all climates.

Let no one, however, from this, superstitiously infer a revolution, at some period or other to be wrought by these people on all the nations of the earth. . . . neither in the people themselves, nor in historical analogy, can we discover the least foundation of any other [revolution that would touch all peoples]. The continuation of the Jews is as naturally to be explained as that of the Brahmins, Parsees, or Gypsies.

No one, in the mean time, will deny to a people, that has been such an active instrument in the hands of fate, those great qualities, which are conspicuous in its whole history. Ingenious, adroit, and laborious, the Jews have always borne themselves up under the severest oppression from other nations. . . . They have not wanted warlike courage also; as the times of David and the Maccabees show, and still more the last and most dreadful downfall of their state [at the hands of the Romans in 66–74]. . . . In short, they were a people spoiled in their [political] education, because they never arrived at a maturity of political cultivation on their own soil, and consequently not to any sentiment of [national] liberty and honor . . . their situation has almost ever denied them the virtues of a patriot.

C. Slavic Nations

The figure made by the Slavian nations in history is far from proportionate to the extent of country they occupied; one reason of which, among others, is, that they dwelt so remote from the Romans. We first discern them on the Don, among the Goths, afterwards, on the Danube, amid the Huns and Bulgarians; with whom they frequently disturbed the Roman Empire, though chiefly as associates, auxiliaries, or vassals. Notwithstanding their occasional achievements, they were never enterprising warriors or adventurers, like the Germans; these they for the most part followed quietly, occupying the places the Germans evacuated, till at length they were in possession of the vast territory extending from the Don to the Elbe, and from the Adriatic Sea to the Baltic. On this side of the Carpathian mountains their settlements extended from Luneburg over Mecklenburg, Pomerania, Brandenburg, Saxony, Lusatia, Bohemia, Moravia, Silesia, Poland, and Russia; beyond them, where at an early period they had settled in Wallachia and Moldavia, they were continually spreading farther and farther, assisted by various circumstances, till the emperor Heraclitus admitted them into Dalmatia, and the kingdoms of Slavonia, Bosnia, Servia, and Dalmatia, were founded by them. In Pannonia they were equally numerous; they possessed all the southeastern angle of Germany from Friuli, so that their domains terminated with Styria, Carinthia, and Carniola: an immense region, the European part of which is even now inhabited chiefly by one nation.

Everywhere they settled on lands, that others had relinguished, cultivating or enjoying them as colonists, husbandmen, or shepherds: so that their noiseless industry was of infinite advantage to countries, from which other nations had migrated, or which they had passed over and plundered. They were fond of agriculture, stores of corn and cattle, and various domestic arts; and everywhere opened a beneficial trade with the produce of the land and their industry. Along the Baltic, from Luebeck, they built seaport towns, among which Vineta, in the island of Rugen, was the Amsterdam of the Slavians; thus they maintained an intercourse with the Prussians, Courlanders, and Lettonians, as the language of these people shows. On the Dnieper they built Kiev, on the Wolcoff, Novgorod; which soon became flourishing commercial towns, uniting the Black Sea with the Baltic, and conveying the productions of Asia to the north and west of Europe. In Germany they followed the working of mines, understood the smelting and casting of metals, manufactured salt, fabricated linen, brewed mead, planted fruit trees, and led, after their fashion, a gay and musical life. They were liberal, hospitable to excess, lovers of pastoral freedom, but submissive and obedient, enemies to spoil and rapine. All this preserved them not from oppression; nay it contributed to their being oppressed. For, as they were never ambitious of sovereignty, had among them no hereditary princes addicted to war, and thought little of paying tribute, if only they could enjoy their lands in peace; many nations, chiefly of German origin, injuriously oppressed them.

Already under Charlemagne were carried on these oppressive wars, the object of which was evidently commercial advantages, though the Christian religion was their pretext; as it was unquestionably very commodious for the heroic Franks to treat an industrious nation, addicted to trade and agriculture, as vassals, instead of learning and pursuing these arts themselves. What the Franks began, the German Saxons completed: in whole provinces the Slavians were extirpated, or made bondsmen, and their lands divided among bishops and nobles. Northern Germans ruined their commerce on the Baltic; the Danes brought their Vineta to a melancholy end; and their remains in Germany were reduced to that state, to which the Incans and Aztecs were subjected by the Spaniards. Is it to be wondered, that, after this nation had borne the yoke for centuries, and cherished the bitterest animosity against their Christian lords and robbers, its gentle character should have sunk into the artful, cruel insolence of a slave? Yet still, particularly in lands where they enjoy any degree of freedom, their ancient stamp is universally perceptible. It was unfortunate for these people, that their love of quiet and domestic industry was incompatible with any permanent military establishment, though they were not defective in valour in the heat of resistance: unfortunate, that their situation brought them so near to the Germans on one side, and on the other left them exposed to the attacks of the Tartars from the east, from whom, particularly from the Mongols, they had much to suffer, and much they patiently bore.

The wheel of changing Time, however, revolves without ceasing; and as these nations inhabit for the most part the finest country of Europe, if it were completely cultivated, and its trade opened; while it cannot be supposed, but that legislation and politics, instead of a military spirit, must and will more and more promote quiet industry, and peaceful commerce between different states; these now deeply sunk, but once industrious and happy people, will at length awake from their long and heavy slumber, shake off the chains of slavery, enjoy the possession of their lands from the Adriatic sea to the Carpathian mountains, from the Don to the Moldow, and celebrate on them their ancient festivals of peaceful trade and industry.

As we have elegant and useful materials for the history of these people from different regions, it is to be wished that their deficiencies would be supplied from other sources; the continually decaying remains of their customs, songs, and traditions must be collected; and such a general history of this race ultimately completed, as the picture of mankind requires.

33. Young Italy, 1831

Giuseppe Mazzini

After the Congress of Vienna, Italy was a fragmented country—a geographical expression. Inspired by past glories, nationalists wanted to end foreign occupation and unite the Italian peninsula. Giuseppe Mazzini (1805–1872) was a leading figure in the struggle for Italian nationhood, the Risorgimento. Known as the "soul" of that movement, he worked to establish a united and republican Italy. Born in Genoa, Mazzini joined the Carbonari (Charcoal Burners) in the 1820s. It was a secret society dedicated to Italian national unity along republican lines. After several failed attempts the organization was absorbed into "Young Italy" in March 1831. Mazzini established this new revolutionary society and dedicated it to unifying Italy through a general uprising. "Young Italy" and Mazzini were successful in liberating Milan in 1848. In 1849 he became head of the triumvirate that functioned as the executive authority for the short-lived "Roman Republic." But when Rome fell, Mazzini went back into exile and never again regained the same prestige or position. In 1872, disguised as an Englishman, he returned to his homeland and died at Pisa.

Although it failed to secure an Italian republic, the nationalist-patriotic and liberal ideas of Mazzini's organization were important factors in Italian developments from 1831 to 1870. It is estimated that at least 50,000 men under forty years of age were enrolled in "Young Italy." The selection that follows includes the oath taken by members.

QUESTIONS

1. What is Mazzini's view of the political situation in Italy in 1831? What role does he envisage for the masses?
2. What does Mazzini mean when he writes that "Young Italy is *Republican and Unitarian*"? Compare his theory of republicanism to the political thought of the French Revolution.
3. Mazzini has often been described as a nationalist and a romantic. What evidence is there of those characteristics in this document?
4. What tactics does Mazzini advocate to achieve his goals? What are his attitudes toward foreign assistance and the use of force?

Manifesto of Young Italy

Great revolutions are the work rather of the principles than of bayonets, and are achieved first in the moral, and afterwards in the material sphere. Bayonets are truly powerful only when they assert or maintain a right; the rights and duties of society spring from a profound moral sense which has taken root in the majority. Blind brute force may create victors, victims, and martyrs; but tyranny results from its triumph, whether it crown the brow of prince or tribune, if achieved in antagonism to the will of the majority. . . .

In Italy, as in every country aspiring towards a new life, there is a clash of opposing elements, of passions assuming every variety of form, and of desires tending in fact towards one sole aim, but through modifications almost infinite.

There are many men in Italy full of lofty and indignant hatred to the foreigner, who shout for liberty simply because it is the foreigner who withholds it.

There are others, having at heart the union of Italy before all things, who would gladly unite her divided children under any strong will, whether of native or foreign tyrant.

Others again, fearful of all violent commotions, and doubtful of the possibility of suddenly subduing the shock of private interests, and the jealousies of different provinces, shrink from the idea of absolute union, and are ready to accept any new partition diminishing the number of sections into which the country is divided.

Few appear to understand that a fatal necessity will impede all true progress in Italy, until every effort at emancipation shall proceed upon the three inseparable bases of unity, liberty, and independence. . . .

Love of country, abhorrence of Austria, and a burning desire to throw off her yoke, are passions now universally diffused, and the *compromises* inculcated by fear, or a mistaken notion of tactics and diplomacy, will be abandoned, and vanish before the majesty of the national will. In this respect, therefore, the question may be regarded as lying between tyranny driven to its last and most desperate struggle, and those resolved to bravely dare its overthrow.

The question as to the means by which to reach our aim, and convert the insurrection into a lasting and fruitful victory, is by no means so simple.

Italy does know that there is no true war without the masses; that the secret of raising the masses lies in the hands of those who show themselves ready to fight and conquer at their head; that new circumstances call for new men—men untrammelled by old habits and systems, with souls virgin of interest or greed, and in whom the Idea is incarnate; that the secret of power is faith; that true virtue is sacrifice, and true policy to be and to prove oneself strong.

Young Italy knows these things. It feels the greatness of its mission and will fulfill it. We swear it by the thousands of victims that have fallen during the last ten years to prove that persecutions do not crush, but fortify conviction; we swear it by the human soul that aspires to progress.

The ideas and aspirations now scattered and disseminated among our ranks require to be organized and reduced to a system. This new and powerful element of life, which is urging Young Italy towards her regeneration, has need of purification from every servile habit, from every unworthy affection.

And we, with the help of the Italians, will undertake this task, and strive to make ourselves the true interpreters of the various desires, sufferings, and aspirations that constitute Italy of the nineteenth century.

The Aim of Young Italy

Young Italy is a brotherhood of Italians who believe in a law of *Progress* and *Duty*, and are convinced that Italy is destined to become one nation,—convinced also that she possesses sufficient strength within herself to become one, and that the ill success of her former efforts is to be attributed not to the weakness, but to the misdirection of the revolutionary elements within her,—that the secret of force lies in constancy and unity of effort. They join this association in the firm intent of consecrating both thought and action to the great aim of reconstituting Italy as one independent sovereign nation of free men and equals.

Young Italy is *Republican and Unitarian.*

Republican,—Because theoretically every nation is destined, by the law of God and humanity, to form a free and equal community of brothers; and the republican is the only form of government that insures this future.

Because all true sovereignty resides essentially in the nation, the sole progressive and continuous interpreter of the supreme moral law.

Because, whatever be the form of privilege that constitutes the apex of the social edifice, its tendency is to spread among the other classes, and by undermining the equality of the citizens, to endanger the liberty of the country.

Because, when the sovereignty is recognized as existing not in the whole body, but in several distinct powers, the path to usurpation is laid open, and the struggle for supremacy between these powers is inevitable; distrust and organized hostility take the place of harmony, which is society's law of life.

Because the monarchical element being incapable of sustaining itself alone by the side of the popular element, it necessarily involves the existence of the intermediate element of an aristocracy—the source of inequality and corruption to the whole nation.

Because both history and the nature of things teach us that elective monarchy tends to general anarchy; and hereditary monarchy tends to general despotism.

Because, when monarchy is not—as in the middle ages—based upon the belief now extinct in right divine, it becomes too weak to be a bond of unity and authority in the state.

Because our Italian tradition is essentially republican; our great memories are republican; the whole history of our national progress is republican; whereas the introduction of monarchy amongst us was coeval with our decay, and consummated our ruin by its constant servility to the foreigner, and the antagonism to the people, as well as to the unity of the nation.

Young Italy is *Unitarian*—

Because, without unity, there is no true nation.

Because, without unity, there is no real strength; and Italy, surrounded as she is by powerful, united, and jealous nations, has need of strength before all things.

Because federalism, by reducing her to the political impotence of Switzerland, would necessarily place her under the influence of one of the neighboring nations.

Because federalism, by reviving the local rivalries now extinct, would throw Italy back upon the middle ages.

Because federalism would divide the great national arena into a number of smaller arenas; and by thus opening a path for every paltry ambition, become a source of aristocracy.

Because federalism, by destroying the unity of the great Italian family, would strike at the root of the great mission Italy is destined to accomplish towards humanity.

Because Europe is undergoing a progressive series of transformations, which are gradually and irresistably guiding European society to form itself into vast and united masses.

Because the entire work of international civilization in Italy will be seen, if rightly studied, as to have been tending for ages to the formation of unity.

Because all objections raised against the unitarian system do but apply, in fact, to a system of administrative centralization and despotism, which has really nothing in common with unity.

National unity, as understood by Young Italy, does not imply the despotism of any, but the association and concord of all. The life inherent in each locality is sacred. Young Italy would have the *administrative* organization designed upon a broad basis of religious respect for the liberty of each commune, but the *political* organization, destined to represent the nation in Europe, should be one and central.

Without unity of religious belief, and unity of social pact; without unity of civil, political, and penal legislation, there is no true nation. . . .

The Oath of Young Italy

Each member will, upon his initiation into the association of Young Italy, pronounce the following form of oath, in the presence of the initiator:

In the name of God and of Italy—

In the name of all the martyrs of the holy Italian cause who have fallen beneath foreign and domestic tyranny—

By the duties which bind me to the land wherein God has placed me, and to the brothers whom God has given me;

By the love—innate in all men—I bear to the country that gave my mother birth, and will be the home of my children;

By the hatred—innate in all men—I bear to evil, injustice, usurpation, and arbitrary rule—

By the blush that rises to my brow when I stand before the citizens of other lands, to know that I have no rights of citizenship, no country, and no national flag—

By the aspiration that thrills my soul towards that liberty for which it was created, and is impotent to exert; towards the good it was created to strive after, and is impotent to achieve in the silence and isolation of slavery—

By the memory of our former greatness, and the sense of our present degradation—

By the tears of Italian mothers for their sons dead on the scaffold, in prison, or in exile—

I, A. B.

Believing in the mission entrusted by God to Italy, and the duty of every Italian to strive to attempt its fulfilment—

Convinced that where God has ordained that a nation shall be, He has given the requisite power to create it; that the people are the depositories of that power, and that in its right direction for the people, and by the people, lies the secret of victory; convinced that virtue consists in action and sacrifice, and strength in union and constancy of purpose: I give my name to Young Italy, an association of men holding the same faith, and swear—

To dedicate myself wholly and forever to the endeavor with them to constitute Italy *one, free, independent, republican nation;*

To promote by every means in my power—whether by written or spoken word, or by action—the education of my Italian brothers towards the aim of Young Italy; towards association, the sole means of its accomplishment, and to virtue, which alone can render the conquest lasting—

To abstain from enrolling myself in any other association from this time forth—

To obey all the instructions, in conformity with the spirit of Young Italy, given me by those who represent with me the union of my Italian brothers; and to keep the secret of these instructions, even at the cost of my life; to assist my brothers of the association both by action and counsel—

NOW AND FOREVER.

This do I swear, invoking upon my head the wrath of God, the abhorrence of man, and the infamy of the perjurer, if I ever betray the whole or a part of this my oath.

The Programme of Young Italy

The means by which Young Italy proposes to reach its aim are—education and insurrection, to be adopted simultaneously, and made to harmonize with each other.

Education must ever be directed to teach by example, word, and pen the necessity of insurrection. Insurrection, whenever it can be realized, must be so conducted as to render it a means of national education.

The character of the insurrection must be national; the programme of the insurrection must contain the germ of the programme of future Italian nationality. Wheresoever the initiative of insurrection shall take place, the flag raised, and the aim proposed, will be Italian. . . .

Convinced that Italy is strong enough to free herself without external help; that, in order to found a nationality, it is necessary that the feeling and consciousness of nationality should exist; and that it can never be created by any revolution, however triumphant, if achieved by foreign arms; convinced, moreover, that every insurrection that looks abroad for assistance, must remain dependant upon the state of things abroad, and can therefore never be certain of victory;—Young Italy is determined that while it will ever be ready to profit by the favourable course of events abroad, it will neither allow the character of the insurrection nor the choice of the moment to be governed by them.

Insurrection—by means of guerrilla bands—is the true method of warfare for all nations desirous of emancipating themselves from a foreign yoke. This method of warfare supplies the want—inevitable at the commencement of the insurrection—of a regular army; it calls the greatest number of elements into the field, and yet may be sustained by the smallest number. It forms the military education of the people, and consecrates every foot of the native soil by the memory of some warlike deed.

All members of Young Italy will exert themselves to diffuse these principles of insurrection.

---

34. The Theory of Official Nationality

S. S. Uvarov

In the era of Tsar Nicholas I (1825–1855) principles of autocracy were firmly asserted in Russia and any manifestation of liberalism was mercilessly suppressed. The man who formulated the doctrine of "Official Nationality" was Count S. S. Uvarov (1786–1855). He was known as "the best educated man in Russia." In his early years he held liberal views and was a religious skeptic, but he changed his viewpoint when he became a successful bureaucrat. Uvarov was President of the Imperial Academy of Sciences from 1818 to 1855 and in 1833 he was appointed Minister of National Education, a post he held until 1849. These positions gave him great influence in directing intellectual developments in Russia. The ideology of Tsardom and of the imperial, aggressive Russian nationalism was based on the three principles of orthodoxy, autocracy, and nationality. The numerous exponents of this creed propounded it with varying degrees of intensity to the end of the tsarist regime.

QUESTION

1. How does Uvarov justify his formula of the official ideology of tsarism—
   "Orthodoxy, Autocracy, and Nationality"?

Amid the rapid decline of religious and civilian institutions in Europe and the universal dissemination of destructive concepts, and in view of the sad occurrences surrounding us on every side, it becomes necessary to strengthen the fatherland on the firm foundations which are the basis of the prosperity, strength, and life of the people; to discover the principles that are the distinguishing marks of the Russian character and that belong to it exclusively; to assemble into one whole the sacred remnants of its nationality and on them to anchor our salvation. Fortunately, Russia has preserved a warm faith in the salutary principles without which she cannot prosper, become strong, or live.

Sincerely and profoundly attached to the church of his fathers, the Russian from time immemorial has regarded it as the guarantee of social and family happiness.

Without love for the faith of its ancestors, a people no less than an individual must perish. The Russian, devoted to the fatherland, is no more likely to consent to the loss of one of the dogmas of our *Orthodoxy* than to the theft of even one pearl from the crown of Monomakh. [According to a Muscovite legend, this crown had been bestowed on the Grand Prince of Kiev by the Byzantine emperor Constantine Monomarcus during the eleventh century. Thus the Russian rulers believed that they shared in the power of the Caesars.]

Autocracy constitutes the condition of Russia's political existence. The Russian colossus rests upon it as upon the cornerstone of its greatness. This truth is felt by the overwhelming majority of Your Majesty's subjects. They feel it in full measure, although they come from various walks of life and differ in education, as well as in their relations to the government.

The salutary conviction that Russia lives and is preserved by the spirit of a strong, humane, and enlightened autocracy must permeate the people's education and develop with it.

Along with these two national principles, there is a third, no less important, no less powerful—that of *Nationality*. The question of nationality lacks the unity of the former; but both emanate from the same source and are interwoven with every page of the history of Russian Tsardom. As regards nationality, the only difficulty consists of bringing into harmony the ancient and new concepts; but nationality does not compel us to retrogress or to stand still; it does not demand immobility in ideas. The governmental structure, like the human body, changes its outward aspect in proportion to its age. Its features alter with the years, but its physiognomy must not change.

---

35. Inaugural Addresses and Gettysburg Address

Abraham Lincoln

On November 6, 1860, Abraham Lincoln (1809–1865) was elected the sixteenth President of the United States. As the candidate of the Republican party he had received slightly less than forty percent of the popular vote, and he had not carried a single southern slave state. His large majority in the northern free states had earned him a victory in the Electoral College. During the four months that followed his election seven southern states seceded from the Union. Representatives from these states formed a provisional government for the Confederate States of America. The Republic of the United States was thus *de facto*, if not *de jure*, divided. As president-elect Lincoln refrained from exercising an active public role, and thus the nation anxiously awaited his inaugural address, which he delivered on March 4, 1861. On that occasion he spoke as an American nationalist, stressing the importance of preserving the Union as he reviewed the issues of secession, slavery, the nature of the federal government, and the crisis that resulted from his election. Two and a half years later Lincoln delivered some brief remarks at the dedication of a national cemetery at Gettysburg, Pennsylvania. Although afterward he characterized his speech as a "flat failure," in fact his Gettysburg Address ultimately was celebrated as one of the greatest statements of American democratic ideals. In it he struggled to reconcile the tremendous human cost of the Civil War with national survival and the rebirth of freedom and republicanism. His Second Inaugural Address is a religious meditation on the higher purpose of the Civil War. It was delivered on March 4, 1865, just a little more than a month before his assassination. Here Lincoln highlighted slavery as the principal cause of the conflict, but he also placed responsibility for the system of bondage on all parties in the nation. He accepted the punishment inflicted by Divine Providence, but he also looked forward to the end of the war and a healing peace administered "with malice toward none, with charity for all."

This document concludes with three amendments to the United States Constitution that were passed during the Reconstruction era that followed the Civil War. Principally designed to aid former slaves, they also enhanced the power of the federal government at the expense of the states. In particular, the Thirteenth Amendment abolished slavery, while the Fourteenth and Fifteenth Amendments defined citizenship and protected individual rights from encroachment by the states. These amendments were the fruits of the northern victory in the Civil War and the political power of the radical faction of the Republican party during the postwar era. Their passage completed the transformation of the United States from a union of states to a nation where the rights of all the people were protected by law.

QUESTIONS

1. According to Lincoln, was the South justified in seceding from the Union? Explain.
2. Explain Lincoln's views on the question of whether the United States was formed by the states or by the American people.
3. According to Lincoln, what was the correct way of resolving the crisis that faced the nation in 1861?
4. What was Lincoln's purpose in writing the Gettysburg Address? Why is it considered a "sacred text" in the American tradition?
5. How does Lincoln's Second Inaugural Address differ from the First Inaugural? Explain his interpretation of the causes and the significance of the Civil War.
6. What issues of the Civil War were addressed in the Reconstruction Amendments? Which of these issues were settled by the Civil War, and which ones remained unresolved into the twentieth century?

First Inaugural Address, 1861

Apprehension seems to exist, among the people of the Southern States, that by the accession of a Republican Administration their property and their peace and personal security are to be endangered. There has never been any reasonable cause for such apprehension. Indeed, the most ample evidence to the contrary has all the while existed and been open to their inspection. It is found in nearly all the published speeches of him who now addresses you. I do but quote from one of those speeches when I declare that "I have no purpose, directly or indirectly, to interfere with the institution of slavery in the States where it exists. I believe I have no lawful right to do so, and I have no inclination to do so." Those who nominated and elected me do so with full knowledge that I had made this and many similar declarations, and had never recanted them. And more than this they placed in the platform for my acceptance, and as a law to themselves and to me, the clear and emphatic resolution which I now read:

"*Resolved*, That the maintenance inviolate of the rights of the States, and especially the right of each State to order and control its own domestic institutions according to its own judgement exclusively, is essential to the balance of power on which the perfection and endurance of our political fabric depend, and we denounce the lawless invasion by armed force of the soil of any state or Territory, no matter under what pretext, as among the gravest of crimes."

I now reiterate these sentiments; and in doing so, I only press upon the public attention the most conclusive evidence of which the case is susceptible, that the property, peace, and security of no section are to be in anywise endangered by the now incoming Administration. I add, too, that all the protection which, consistently with the Constitution and the laws, can be given, will be cheerfully given to all the States, when lawfully demanded, for whatever cause—as cheerfully given to all the States, when lawfully demanded, for whatever cause—as cheerfully to one section as to another.

There is much controversy about the delivering up of fugitives from service or labor. The clause I now read is as plainly written in the Constitution as any other of its provisions:—

"No person held to service or labor in one State, under the laws thereof, escaping into another, shall, in consequence of any law or regulation therein, be discharged from such service or labor, but shall be delivered up on claim of the party to whom such service or labor may be due."

It is scarcely questioned that this provision was intended by those who made it for the reclaiming of what we call fugitive slaves; and the intention of the lawgiver is the law. All members of Congress swear their support to the whole Constitution—to this provision as much as any other. To the proposition, then, that slaves, whose cases come within the terms of this clause, "shall be delivered up," their oaths are unanimous. Now, if they would make the effort in good temper, could they not, with nearly equal unanimity frame and pass a law by means of which to keep good that unanimous oath? . . .

It is seventy-two years since the first inauguration of a President under our National Constitution. During that period, fifteen different and greatly distinguished citizens have, in succession, administered the Executive branch of the Government. They have conducted it through many perils, and generally with great success. Yet, with all this scope for precedent, I now enter upon the same task for the brief constitutional term of four years, under great and peculiar difficulty. A disruption of the Federal Union, heretofore only menaced, is now formidably attempted.

I hold that, in contemplation of universal law, and of the Constitution, the Union of these States is perpetual. Perpetuity is implied, if not expressed, in the fundamental law of all National Governments. It is safe to assert that no government proper ever had a provision in its organic law for its own termination. Continue to execute all the express provisions of our National Government, and the Union will endure forever—it being impossible to destroy it, except by some action not provided for in the instrument itself.

Again, if the United States be not a Government proper, but an association of States in the nature of contract merely, can it, as a contract, be peaceably unmade by less than all the parties who made it? One party to a contract may violate it—break it, so to speak; but does it not require all to lawfully rescind it?

Descending from these general principles, we find the proposition that, in legal contemplation, the Union is perpetual, confirmed by the history of the Union itself. The Union is much older than the Constitution. It was formed, in fact, by the Articles of Association in 1774. It was matured and continued by the Declaration of Independence in 1776. It was further matured, and the faith of all the then Thirteen States expressly plighted and engaged that it should be perpetual, by the Articles of Confederation in 1778. And, finally, in 1787, one of the declared objects for ordaining and establishing the Constitution was "to form a more perfect union."

But if destruction of the Union, by one, or by a part only of the States, be lawfully possible, the Union is less perfect than before, the Constitution having lost the vital element of perpetuity.

It follows, from these views, that no State, upon its own mere motion, can law-fully get out of the Union; that resolves and ordinances to that effect are legally void; and that acts of violence within any State or States, against the authority of the United States, are insurrectionary or revolutionary, according to circumstances.

I, therefore, consider that, in view of the Constitution and the laws, the Union is unbroken, and to the extent of my ability I shall take care, as the Constitution itself expressly enjoins upon me, that the laws of the Union be faithfully executed in all States. Doing this I deem to be only a simple duty on my part; and I shall perform it, so far as practicable, unless my rightful masters, the American people, shall withhold the requisite means, or, in some authoritative manner, direct the contrary. I trust this will not be regarded as a menace, but only as the declared purpose of the Union that it will Constitutionally defend and maintain itself.

In doing this there need be no bloodshed or violence; and there shall be none, unless it be forced upon the National authority. The power confided to me will be used to hold, occupy, and possess the property and places belonging to the Government, and to collect the duties and imposts; but beyond what may be but necessary for these objects, there will be no invasion, no using of force against or among the people anywhere. Where hostility to the United States, in any interior locality, shall be so great and universal, as to prevent competent resident citizens from holding the Federal offices, there will be no attempt to force obnoxious strangers among the people for that object. While the strict legal right may exist in the government to enforce the exercise of these offices, the attempt to do so would be so irritating, and so nearly impracticable withal, I deem it better to forego, for the time, the uses of such offices.

The mails, unless repelled, will continue to be furnished in all parts of the

Union. So far as possible, the people everywhere shall have that sense of perfect security which is most favorable to calm thought and reflection. The course here indicated will be followed, unless current events and experience shall show a modification or change to be proper, and in every case and exigency my best discretion will be exercised, according to circumstances actually existing, and with a view and a hope of a peaceful solution of the National troubles, and the restoration of fraternal sympathies and affections.

That there are persons in one section or another who seek to destroy the Union at all events, and are glad of any pretext to do it, I will neither affirm nor deny; but if there be such, I need address no word to them. To those, however, who really love the Union, may I not speak? . . .

Plainly, the central idea of secession is the essence of anarchy. A majority held in restraint by constitutional checks and limitations, and always changing easily with deliberate changes of popular opinions and sentiments, is the only true sovereign of a free people. Whoever rejects it does, of necessity, fly to anarchy or to despotism. Unanimity is impossible; the rule of a minority, as a permanent arrangement, is wholly unadmissable; so that, rejecting the majority principle, anarchy or despotism, in some form, is all that is left. . . .

Physically speaking, we cannot separate. We cannot remove our respective sections from each other, nor build an impassable wall between them. A husband and wife may be divorced, and go out of the presence and beyond the reach of each other; but the different parts of our country cannot do this. They cannot but remain face to face; and intercourse, either amicable or hostile, must continue between them. It is impossible, then, to make that intercourse more advantageous or more satisfactory after separation than before. Can aliens make treaties easier than friends can make laws? Can treaties be more faithfully enforced between aliens than laws can among friends? Suppose you go to war, you cannot fight always; and when, after much loss on both sides, and no gain on either, you cease fighting, the identical old question, as to terms of intercourse, are again upon you.

This country, with its institutions, belongs to the people who inhabit it. Whenever they shall grow weary of the existing Government, they can exercise their constitutional right to dismember or overthrow it. I cannot be ignorant of the fact that many worthy and patriotic citizens are desirous of having the National Constitution amended. While I make no recommendation of amendments, I fully recognize the rightful authority of the people over the whole subject, to be exercised in either of the modes prescribed in the instrument itself; and I should under existing circumstances, favor, rather than oppose, a fair opportunity being afforded the people to act upon it. I will venture to add, that to me the convention mode seems preferable, in that it allows amendments to originate with the people themselves, instead of only permitting them to take or reject propositions originated by others, not especially chosen for the purpose, and which might not be precisely such as they would wish to either accept or refuse. I understand a proposed amendment to the Constitution—which amendment, however, I have not seen—has passed Congress, to the effect that the Federal Government shall never interfere with the domestic institutions of the States, including that of the person held to service. To avoid misconstruction of what I have said, I depart from my purpose not to speak of particular amendments, so far as to say that, holding such a provision now to be implied constitutional law, I have no objections to its being made express and irrevocable.

The Chief Magistrate derives all his authority from the people, and they have conferred none upon him to fix terms for the separation of the States. The people themselves can do this also if they choose; but the Executive, as such, has nothing to do with it. His duty is to administer the present Government as it came to his hands, and to transmit it, unimpaired by him, to his successor.

Why should there not be a patient confidence in the ultimate justice of the people? Is there any better or equal hope in the world? In our present differences, is either party without faith of being in the right? If the Almighty Ruler of Nations, with his eternal truth and justice, be on your side of the North, or on yours of the South, that truth and that justice will surely prevail, by the judgement of this great tribunal of the American people.

By the frame of the Government under which we live, the same people have wisely given their public servants but little power for mischief, and have, with equal wisdom, provided for the return of that little to their own hands at very short intervals.

While the people retain their virtue and vigilance, no Administration, by any extreme of wickedness or folly, can very seriously injure the Government in the short space of four years.

My countrymen, one and all, think calmly and well upon this whole subject. Nothing valuable can be lost by taking time. If there be an object to hurry any of you in hot haste to a step which you would never take deliberately, that object will be frustrated by taking time; but no good object can be frustrated by it. Such of you as are now dissatisfied still have the old Constitution unimpaired, and, on the sensitive point, the laws of your own framing under it; while the new Administration will have no immediate power, if it would, to change either. If it were admitted that you who are dissatisfied hold the right side in the dispute, there still is no single good reason for precipitate action. Intelligence, patriotism, Christianity, and a firm reliance on Him who has never yet forsaken this favored land, are still competent to adjust, in the best way, all our present difficulty.

In *your* hands, my dissatisfied fellow-countrymen, and not in *mine,* is the momentous issue of civil war. The Government will not assail *you.* You have no conflict without being yourselves the aggressors. You have no oath registered in heaven to destroy the Government; while I shall have the most solemn one to "preserve, protect, and defend" it.

I am loath to close. We are not enemies, but friends. We must not be enemies. Though passions may have strained, it must not break our bonds of affection.

The mystic cord of memory, stretching from every battle-field and patriot grave to every living heart and hearthstone all over this broad land, will yet swell the chorus of the Union, when again touched, as surely they will be, by the better angels of our nature.

The Gettysburg Address, 1863

Four-score and seven years ago, our fathers brought forth on this continent a new nation, conceived in liberty, and dedicated to the proposition that all men are created equal. Now we are engaged in a great civil war, testing whether the nation, or any nation so conceived and so dedicated, can long endure. We are met on a great battle-field of that war. We have come to dedicate a portion of that field as a final resting place for those who here gave their lives that that nation might live. It is altogether fitting and proper that we should do this.

But, in a larger sense, we cannot dedicate—we cannot consecrate—we cannot hallow this ground. The brave men who struggled here have consecrated it far above our poor power to add or detract. The world will little note nor long remember what we *say* here, but it can never forget what they *did* here. It is for us, the living, rather to be dedicated here to the unfinished work which they who fought here have thus far so nobly advanced. It is, rather, for us to be here dedicated to the great task remaining before us, that from these honored dead we take increased devotion to that cause for which they gave the last full measure of devotion; that we here highly resolve that these dead shall not have died in vain; that this nation, under God, shall have a new birth of freedom; and that government of the people, by the people, for the people, shall not perish from the earth.

Second Inaugural Address, 1865

Fellow-Countrymen: At this second appearing to take the oath of the Presidential office, there is less occasion for an extended address than there was at the first. Then a statement somewhat in detail of a course to be pursued seemed very fitting and proper. Now, at the expiration of four years, during which public declarations have been constantly called forth on every point and phase of the great contest which still absorbs the attention and engrosses the energies of the nation, little that is new could be presented.

The progress of our arms, upon which all else chiefly depends, is as well known to the public as to myself, and it is, I trust, reasonably satisfactory and encouraging to all. With high hope for the future, no prediction in regard to it is ventured.

On the occasion corresponding to this four years ago, all thoughts were anxiously directed to an impending civil war. All dreaded it, all sought to avoid it. While the inaugural address was being delivered from this place, devoted altogether to *saving* the Union without war, insurgent agents were in the city seeking to *destroy* it without war—seeking to dissolve the Union, and divide effects, by negotiation. Both parties deprecated war, but one of them would *make* war rather than let the nation survive, and the other would *accept* war rather than let it perish, and the war came. One-eighth of the whole population were colored slaves, not distributed generally over the Union, but localized in the Southern part of it. These slaves constituted a peculiar and powerful interest. All knew that this interest was somehow the cause of the war. To strengthen, perpetuate, and extend this interest was the object for which the insurgents would rend the Union by war, while the Government claimed no right to do more than to restrict the territorial enlargement of it.

Neither party expected for the war the magnitude or the duration which it has already attained. Neither anticipated that the cause of the conflict might cease with, or even before, the conflict itself should cease. Each looked for an easier triumph, and a result less fundamental and astounding.

Both read the same Bible and pray to the same God, and each invokes His aid against the other. It may seem strange that any men should dare to ask a just God's assistance in wringing their bread from the sweat of other men's faces, but let us judge not, that we be not judged. The prayers of both could not be answered. That of neither has been answered fully. The Almighty has His own purposes. "Woe unto the world because of offences, for it must needs be that offences come, but woe to that man by whom the offence cometh." If we shall suppose that American slavery is one of these offences which, in the providence of God, must needs come, but which having continued through

His appointed time, He now wills to remove, and that He gives to both North and South this terrible war as the woe due to those by whom the offence came, shall we discern there any departure from those Divine attributes which the believers in a living God always ascribe to Him? Fondly do we hope, fervently do we pray, that this mighty scourge of war may speedily pass away. Yet if God wills that it continue until all the wealth piled by the bondsman's two hundred and fifty years of unrequited toil shall be sunk, and until every drop of blood drawn with the lash shall be paid by another drawn with the sword, as was said three thousand years ago, so, still it must be said that the judgements of the Lord are true and righteous altogether.

With malice towards none, with charity for all, with firmness in the right as God gives us to see the right, let us finish the work we are in, to bind up the nation's wounds, to care for him who shall have borne the battle, and for his widow and his orphans, to do all which may achieve and cherish a just and lasting peace among ourselves and with all nations.

Reconstruction Amendments to the United States Constitution

Thirteenth Amendment (1865)

1. Neither slavery nor involuntary servitude, except as a punishment for crime whereof the party shall have been duly convicted, shall exist within the United States, or any place subject to their jurisdiction. . . .

Fourteenth Amendment (1868)

1. All persons born or naturalized in the United States, and subject to the jurisdiction thereof, are citizens of the United States and of the State wherein they reside. No State shall make or enforce any law which shall abridge the privileges or immunities of citizens of the United States; nor shall any State deprive any person of life, liberty, or property, without due process of law; nor deny to any person within its jurisdiction the equal protection of the laws.

2. Representatives shall be apportioned among the several States according to their respective numbers, counting the whole number of persons in each State, excluding Indians not taxed. . . .

3. No person shall be a Senator or Representative in Congress, or Elector of President and Vice-President, or hold any office, civil or military, under the United States, or under any State, who, having previously taken an oath, as a member of Congress, or as an officer of the United States, or as a member of any State legislature, or as an executive or judicial officer of any State, to support the Constitution of the United States, shall have engaged in insurrection or rebellion against the same, or given aid or comfort to the enemies therof. But Congress may, by a vote of two-thirds of each house, remove such disability.

4. The validity of the public debt of the United States, authorized by law, including debts incurred for payment of pensions and bounties for services in suppressing insurrection or rebellion, shall not be questioned. But neither the United States nor any State shall assume or pay any debt or obligation incurred in aid of insurrection or rebellion against the United States, or any claim for the loss or emancipation of any slave; but all such debts, obligations, and claims shall be held illegal and void. . . .

Fifteenth Amendment (1870)

1. The right of citizens of the United States to vote shall not be denied or abridged by the United States or any State on account of race, color, or previous condition of servitude. . . .

36. Napoleon's Proclamation to the Egyptians, 1798

Napoleon Bonaparte (1769–1821) went to Egypt as Caesar had gone to Gaul, in pursuit of the star of his ambition. He took with him a great library and over a hundred scholars, scientists, engineers, architects, writers, and interpreters. He thought of himself as a new Alexander the Great, who had envisioned the conquest of Egypt as a means to link Africa and Asia with Europe. Napoleon intended to establish a French colony in Africa for growing sugar and cotton, cut a Suez canal, and gain control of the eastern Mediterranean by taking Malta. He also wished to dominate the Red Sea to secure a strategic base to launch a grand expedition to India. He would then expel the British from the subcontinent and undermine their dominant position in world trade. His campaign with an army of 30,000 went well until Admiral Nelson destroyed the French fleet in Aboukir Bay and the Ottoman Turkish empire declared war upon him. Nevertheless, he won the battle of the pyramids and occupied most of Egypt. There he clashed with the Mamelukes, who had ruled Egypt during the Middle Ages before being conquered by the Ottoman Turks. Next he launched an invasion of Syria during which he took El Arish, Gaza, Jaffa, and other towns memorable in antiquity and in the crusades. But he was stymied at the siege of Acre because the British still controlled the sea and had captured the siege guns he was bringing by ship from Egypt. Even though he still defeated the Turks in two spectacular land battles, Mount Tabor near Nazareth and Aboukir, he had lost the initiative, and deserted his troops to return to France and confine his amazing career to Europe.

QUESTIONS

1. What is Napoleon promising the Egyptians? Whom is he blaming for the bad relations between Egypt and the French Republic?
2. Describe and explain Napoleon's attitude toward the Ottoman Sultan.
3. Is Napoleon deceiving the Egyptians?

In the name of God, the Merciful and Compassionate; there is no God but God; In the name of the French Republic; based upon the foundations of Liberty and Equality, Bonaparte, the Commander-in-Chief of the French Forces, informs all the population of Egypt:

For a long time, those in power in Egypt have insulted the French Nation and unfairly treated her merchants by various deceitful and aggressive tactics. Now, the hour of their punishment has arrived.

For many decades, these Mamelukes, who were brought in from the Caucasus and Georgia, have been corrupting the best region of the whole world. But God, the Omnipotent, the Master of the Universe, has now made the destruction of their state imperative.

People of Egypt, some may say to you that I did not come except to obliterate your religion. That is an outright lie; do not believe it. Tell those fabricators that I came only to rescue your rights from the oppressors. And that I worship Almighty God, and respect his prophet Muhammad and the glorious *Koran* more than the Mamelukes do. Tell them also that all people are equal before God.

The only grounds for distinctions among them are reason, virtue and knowledge. [But] what virtue, reason and knowledge distinguish the Mamelukes from others which would give them exclusive rights over everything that makes life sweet? Wherever there is fertile land, it belongs to the Mamelukes; so also do they exclusively possess the most beautiful maids, horses, and houses.

If the Egyptian land has been bestowed on them, let them produce the Title which God wrote for them. But God, the Master of the Universe, is compassionate and just with his people. With God's help, from now on, no Egyptian will be barred from entering the highest positions [of the State] and from acquiring the most elevated status. The intelligent, virtuous and learned men will take charge of affairs and thus the plight of the entire nation will improve.

Formerly, there were great cities, wide canals, and thriving commerce in Egypt, all of which have disappeared as a result of the Mamelukes' greed and oppression.

Judges, Sheiks [chiefs], Imams [priests], officers and notables of the country, inform your people that the French are faithful Muslims. As proof of this, they attacked Great Rome, where they destroyed the Papal Throne, which was always urging the Christians to fight the Muslims. Then they went to Malta from which they expelled the Knights who allege that Almighty God asked them to fight the Muslims. In addition, the French at every time have been the most faithful friend of the Ottoman Sultan and the enemy of his enemies, may God preserve his reign, and destroy the Mamelukes who refuse to obey him and heed his orders. They [Mamelukes] only obeyed him originally to advance their personal greed.

Blessings and happiness to the Egyptian people who agree with us promptly, thus improving their own condition and elevating their status. Happiness also to those who remain at home, taking no side in the fighting; they will hasten to our side when they know us better.

But woe to those who join the Mamelukes and aid them in the war against us; they will find no way to escape and no trace of them will be left.

Article I

All villages situated within a three-hour circumference of the areas through which the French Forces pass must send delegates to the commander of the troops, informing him of their obedience to the French Forces and that they have raised the tri-color flag.

Article II

Any village which takes up arms against the French forces will be burned.

Article III

Any village which obeys the French Forces will also raise the flag of our friend, the Ottoman Sultan, may God prolong his existence.

Article IV

The sheiks in each village will put under seal immediately the houses and properties of all those who collaborate with the Mamelukes. They should be extremely diligent so that no losses occur.

Article V

All the sheiks, scholars, jurists and imams (the functionaries of the state, that is) must continue their duties. Each inhabitant must remain safely at home. Also, all prayers will be conducted as usual in the Mosque. All Egyptians should be grateful to God for the destruction of the Mamelukes, praying aloud "May God conserve the glory of the Ottoman Sultan! May God preserve the glory of the French Forces! God's curse on the Mamelukes! May God improve the condition of the Egyptian Nation."

37. Russia and the Eastern Question, 1876

General R. A. Fadeyev

Russian designs on the Straits (Dardanelles and the Bosphorus), and Constantinople had a long history prior to 1800. Both Peter I and Catherine II aspired to expand into the Balkans, but both failed. Peter I had undertaken an unsuccessful crusade to liberate the Balkan Slavs, and while Catherine II achieved some gains in her wars with the Ottoman Empire, she could not grasp control over Constantinople and the Straits. These attempts failed in part because the expected revolts by the Balkan peoples against their Ottoman rulers did not materialize. The acquisition of those strategic places became an especially important goal in the tsars' foreign policy after the annexation of Ukraine gave the Russians control of the northern coast of the Black Sea. During the mid-nineteenth century Russian ambitions had to take into account the interest in the region of other powers, especially Austria-Hungary and Great Britain. The following document presents the perspective on the "Eastern Question" of General R. A. Fadeyev (1824–1883). He served in the Caucasus, the Balkans, and also in Egypt, where he was in charge of the khedive's [ruler's] army. Reprinted below is (A) his memorandum of May 28, 1876 to the Minister of Foreign Affairs, N. K. Giers., and (B) the memorandum of November 20, 1876 on the "Bulgarian Affair" to the minister of war, D. A. Miliutin.

QUESTIONS

1. In the opinion of General Fadeyev, why is it necessary for the Russian Empire to occupy the Dardanelles?
2. According to Fadeyev, what is the interest of England and the Turks in the Dardanelles?

3. What is Fadeyev's view of the strategic importance of Constantinople?
4. Would Fadeyev have been satisfied with the course and outcome of the Russo-Turkish war of 1877–1878?

A. Everybody understands that Constantinople alone is nothing, that the Eastern Question is the question of the Dardanelles and only the Dardanelles, and without exception everything connected with the great question—both the soundness of its solution and the procedure in regard to the Turkish line of succession—depends solely on who secures a firm footing at the Dardanelles.

Thinking people in the East, both official and private, understand distinctly that the age-old question is now drawing swiftly and inevitably to a head, that the very essence of it lies in the possession of the Dardanelles, that there are only two competitors for possession of it—Russia and the sea powers (who lay hands on the Straits in the name of Europe, but under the Greek flag—in other words, this kind of protection would become for them an eternal apple of discord), and that Russia cannot retreat in this matter without repudiating herself; they are also aware that possession of the Straits, separating Europe from Asia, at once decides the Eastern Question in one or the other, but in a completely definite sense.

For us Russians, at least one side of the affair must be absolutely clear: We must have open communication with the southern seas, without interference from any direction whatsoever. Without it, we cannot exist. For 150 years since Peter the Great, history has compelled the Russian sovereign to solve in the south the very question which the first reformer solved in the Twenty Years' War in the north. At that time, Russia consisted basically of the northern half of the country, from the Oka [a river tributary to the Volga River] to the Arctic Ocean, and therefore the vital question was the opening of the route to the Baltic Sea; now the center of gravity has shifted, and the majority of the Russian population and the greater part of our productive forces, lie between the Oka and the Black Sea, which, without possession of the Straits amounts to no more than the Caspian Sea. Russia, deprived forever of free entry into the Mediterranean Sea, would come to resemble a bird with one wing.

We could somehow get along with the Bosphorus in foreign hands, as long as it remains in the hands of the Turks, deprived of justice and rights before every consular agent; but it is difficult to have even an approximate idea of those innumerable adversities and the periodically perilous and constantly humiliating situations which would fall to our lot in the event of the final transfer of the Straits into the hands of any other ruler, no matter how weak, who is protected by full European rights. We should be literally behind bars; and meanwhile the most durable occupation of the Straits sufficient to oppose any alliance, requires no more than one-third of the forces necessary for the protection of the Black Sea coast from Poti to the Danube. The Dardanelles position is invincible under good artillery defense and with 60,000 troops in the field. But the occupation of the Straits can only be attained when the fall of Turkey is imminent, or never. . . .

B. It is still necessary to regard the Bulgarian Affair from the point of view of the final solution of the Eastern Question. England's desire for the transfer of Constantinople, together with the Straits, to some third party in the event of the final fall of Turkey would be a measure fundamentally hostile to us, on which no further comment is needed. But the elimination of this measure leaves only one way of solving the Eastern Question. . . . Our final goal could be nothing other than the completely decisive occupation of the Dardanelles, with or without the destruction of the sultanate, depending on circumstances.

The inevitability of this goal in the relatively near future, long understood by Russian representatives in the East, is beginning to enter into the consciousness of the majority of landowners and capitalists in the southern half of Russia, for whom the fortuitous closure of the Straits, or even the rumor of it, each time threatens complete ruin; and besides it constantly hampers them, paralyzing any nautical and coastal industrial enterprise on the Black Sea. Even the peasants of south Russia will grasp the necessity for the occupation of the Straits at all costs, since there will soon be a new political regime on the coast of the Sea of Marmara, as conceived by England, with its manifest consequences. For political and also for military people, it is impossible not to see the tremendous significance of such a denouement, which permits the blocking of our southern boundary by one corps by turning its available forces to the western boundary. . . .

38. Confession of Faith, 1877

Cecil Rhodes

British imperialist and business tycoon and son of an Anglican clergyman, Cecil Rhodes (1853–1902) pursued business ventures from the age of eighteen in South Africa in cotton, diamonds, gold, and much else. After having made a fortune he went to Oxford in 1873, but business and imperial entanglements delayed his degree until 1881. As director of the British South Africa Company he stalked additional lands, carrying the flag across frontiers and inducing a sometimes reluctant British government to extend its control over more and more of Africa at the expense of the Dutch Boers and African tribes. He dreamed of a continuous band of British held territory from "the Cape to Cairo." Nicknamed the "Colossus," he was prime minister and virtual dictator of the Cape Colony from 1890 to 1896, when he was forced to resign for his part in the 1895 Jameson Raid. That adventure was a filibustering incursion into the Boer republic of Transvaal which aimed at its annexation to the Cape. Thereafter he busied himself with the development of Rhodesia, now the independent state of Zimbabwe. He commanded a force of troops at Kimberley in the South African war, 1899–1902, which he had done so much to trigger. His enormous fortune of £6 million he left almost entirely for public use, notably to endow the Rhodes scholarships at Oxford. An extraordinary mixture of virtue and guile, of grand vision and slipshod implementation, he caught the British public's imagination and thereby did much to make the new imperialism popular. One of his sayings was that he would "annex the planets if he could reach them"; another was: "If you do not want to be a socialist, you have to be an imperialist."

QUESTIONS

1. Summarize the basic assumptions of Cecil Rhodes's "Confession of Faith."
2. Discuss how the themes of nationality, race, and class appear in this document.
3. Describe and evaluate the theme of mission in Rhodes's thought.
4. Explain Rhodes's views on the separation of the United States from the British Empire.

It often strikes a man to inquire what is the chief good in life; to one the thought comes that it is a happy marriage, to another great wealth, and as each seizes on his idea, for that he more or less works for the rest of his existence. To myself thinking over the same question the wish came to render myself useful to my country. I then asked myself how could I and after reviewing the various methods I have felt that at the present day we are actually limiting our children and perhaps bringing into the world half the human beings we might owing to the lack of country for them to inhabit that if we had retained America there would at this moment be millions more of English living. I contend that we are the finest race in the world and that the more of the world we inhabit the better it is for the human race. Just fancy those parts that are at present inhabited by the most despicable specimens of human beings what an alteration there would be if they were brought under Anglo-Saxon influence, look again at the extra employment a new country added to our dominions gives. I contend that every acre added to our territory means in the future birth to some more of the English race who otherwise would not be brought into existence. Added to this the absorption of the greater portion of the world under our rule simply means the end of all wars, at this moment had we not lost America I believe we could have stopped the Russian-Turkish war by merely refusing money and supplies. Having these ideas what scheme could we think of to forward this object. I look into history and I read the story of the Jesuits I see what they were able to do in a bad cause and I might say under bad leaders.

In the present day I become a member in the Masonic order I see the wealth and power they possess the influence they hold and I think over their ceremonies and I wonder that a large body of men can devote themselves to what at times appear the most ridiculous and absurd rites without an object and without an end.

The idea gleaming and dancing before one's eyes like a will-of-the-wisp at last frames itself into a plan. Why should we not form a secret society with but one object—the furtherance of the British Empire and the bringing of the whole uncivilised world under British rule, for the recovery of the United States, for the making the Anglo-Saxon race but one Empire. What a dream, but yet it is probable, it is possible. I once heard it argued by a fellow in my own college, I am sorry to own it by an Englishman, that it was a good thing for us that we have lost the United States. There are some subjects on which there can be no arguments, and to an Englishman this is one of them, but even from an American's point of view just picture what they have lost, look at their government, are not the frauds that yearly came before the public view a disgrace to any country and especially their's which is the finest in the world. Would they have occurred had they remained under English rule great as they have become, how infinitely greater they would have been with the softening and elevating influences of English rule, think of those countless 000's [thousands] of Englishmen that during the last 100 years would have crossed the Atlantic and settled and populated the United States. Would they have not made without any prejudice a finer country of it than the low class Irish and German emigrants? All this we have lost and that country loses owing to whom? Owing to two or three ignorant pig-headed statesmen of the last century, at their door lies the blame. Do you ever feel mad? do you ever feel murderous. I think I do with those men. I bring facts to prove my assertion. Does an English father when his sons wish to emigrate ever think of suggesting emigration to a country under another flag, never—it would seem a disgrace to suggest such a thing. I think that we all think that poverty is better under our own flag than wealth under a foreign one.

Put your mind into another train of thought. Fancy Australia discovered and colonised under the French flag, what would it mean merely several millions of English unborn that at present exist we learn from the past and to form our future. We learn from having lost to cling to what we possess. We know the size of the world, we know the total extent. Africa is still lying ready for us; it is our duty to take it. It is our duty to seize every opportunity of acquiring more territory and we should keep this one idea steadily before our eyes, that more territory simply means more of the Anglo-Saxon race, more of the best the most human, most honourable race the world possesses.

To forward such a scheme what a splendid help a secret society would be, a society not openly acknowledged, but who would work in secret for such an object.

I contend that there are at the present moment numbers of the ablest men in the world who would devote their whole lives to it. . . . What has been the main cause of the success of the Romish Church? The fact that every enthusiast, call it if you like every madman finds employment in it. Let us form the same kind of society, a Church for the extension of the British Empire. A society which should have its members in every part of the British Empire working with one object and one idea we should have its members placed at our universities and our schools and should watch the English youth passing through their hands just one perhaps in every thousand would have the mind and feelings for such an object, he should be tried in every way, he should be tested whether he is endurant, possessed of eloquence, disregardful of the petty details of life, and if found to be such, then elected and bound by oath to serve for the rest of his life in his Country. He should then be supported if without means by the Society and sent to that part of the Empire where it was felt he was needed. . . .

(In every Colonial legislature the Society should attempt to have its members prepared at all times to vote or speak and advocate the closer union of England and the colonies, to crush all disloyalty and every movement for the severance of our Empire. The Society should inspire and even own portions of the press, for the press rules the mind of the people. The Society should always be searching for members who might by their position in the world by their energies or character forward the object, but the ballot and test for admittance should be severe.)

Once make it common and it fails. Take a man of great wealth who is bereft of his children perhaps having his mind soured by some bitter disappointment who shuts himself up separate from his neighbours and makes up his mind to a miserable existence. To such men as these the society should gradually disclose the greatness of their scheme and entreat him to throw in his life and property with them for this object. I think that there are thousands now existing who would eagerly grasp at the opportunity. Such are the heads of my scheme.

For fear that death might cut me off before the time for attempting its development I leave all my worldly goods in trust to S. G. Shippard and the Secretary for the Colonies at the time of my death to try to form such a Society with such an object.

---

39. Speech to the French Chamber of Deputies, 1883

Jules Ferry

Jules Ferry (1832–1893) was a lawyer, newspaper editor, and statesman of the left in the French Third Republic. A member of the government of National Defense in the aftermath of the French defeat by Germany in 1870–1871, he served two terms as premier in 1880–1881 and 1883–1885. As minister of education he re-organized the national system of primary education, making it free, compulsory, and secular; he also promoted women's education. As an imperialist he was ambitious to build up a great colonial empire as compensation for France's loss of continental position in the Franco-German war. Bismarck cooperated with him, realizing that if the French consumed their energies in empire building they would be less troublesome in Europe. Under Ferry's leadership France acquired Tunis, Tonking-Annam, and Madagascar, and penetrated deeper into Africa in the areas of the Niger and the Congo. On the pretext of the assassination of the French naval commander in Indo-China in 1884, Ferry induced the Chamber of Deputies to approve a resolution to support the conquest of Tonking. But his opponents argued against this scheme on the grounds that war with China might result, the cost was too great, and the military effort was misplaced. Ferry's enemies subordinated Indo-China to Europe and called for a war of revenge to recapture Alsace-Lorraine from Germany. His government fell, and after several attempts at a political comeback he was assassinated by a religious fanatic, apparently in revenge for his anti-clerical educational policies.

QUESTIONS

1. What varied motives for empire-building does Ferry invoke? To what classes or elements in French society does he appeal? How much do these motives coincide and how much do they differ from those of the sixteenth century, e.g., Hakluyt.
2. Why should the issue be a nonpartisan or nonpolitical one?
3. A century later, are any of Ferry's prophecies borne out?

From the beginning I have felt, gentlemen, that the debate in which we are engaged rests far above ministerial interests and questions of personal ambition. So I shall confine myself to introducing . . . just what it is that is involved in the dispute between the parties. . . .

It is not I who have gotten us into an undertaking whose foundations lie in national traditions—traditions already more than a century old—military expeditions glorious for France; two treaties; the exploits, the marvelous adventure of Francis Garnier; and finally the treaty of 1874, ratified by the National Assembly. It is not I who involved us either in the expedition or the expense, as you claim. . . .

From beginning to end it has been a French affair, and a question of the Fatherland. . . .

And why has there been any Tongking question? Ah, gentlemen, let me tell you that we have had to obey two sentiments which republicans and courageous men can and must associate.

The first of these sentiments is the care and respect for our continental forces; it is the preoccupation with the necessary concentration which we must avoid diminishing in the slightest.

But is France solely a continental power? Is it not also the second naval power in the world?

Does not France, in order to maintain her maritime position, support a large and burdensome budget? France, then, has a variety of duties to accomplish—duties which a vigilant and patriotic government must know how to harmonize. . . .

I am explaining why France needs a colonial policy. I am indicating within what limits this policy must be maintained. . . .

We say then, that all the portions of the colonial domain, its least shreds, must be sacred to us, first, because it is a legacy from the past, and next, because it is a reserve for the future. Must the Republic have an ephemeral policy, a short-sighted policy, preoccupied only with living from day to day? Must it not, like every other government, consider from a somewhat higher point of view, the future of generations which are confided to it, the future of this great democracy of labor, industry, and trade, whose care is intrusted to it?

So you, gentlemen, who have regard for this future, who truly recognize that it belongs to those who work for it, and who are courageous, cast your eyes on the map of the world and see with what watchfulness, with what eagerness, the great nations who are your friends or your rivals are reserving outlets for themselves. It is not a question of the future of tomorrow, but the future of 50 years or 100 years, of the future of even the Fatherland, of what will be the inheritance of our children, the livelihood of our workers. . . .

Yes indeed, see with what eagerness all the industrial peoples—rightly concerned with this grave question of markets which is a vital question for every producing nation—see, I say, with what eagerness they struggle to carve out places for themselves in the still unexplored world, in that Africa, in that Asia which holds so many riches, and particularly in the immense Chinese Empire. It is not a question, of course, and no one has thought so, of wishing to conquer this great Chinese Empire! . . .

The European nations have recognized for a long time that the conquest of China, of those 400 millions of consumers, must be done only by European products and producers. But one has to be at the gateway of this region in order to undertake the peaceful conquest. And that is why I admire and why I am grateful for the farsightedness, the wisdom, or the profound instinct which pushed our predecessors toward the mouth of the Red River, and which showed them the end to be achieved—the possession of Tongking. That, gentlemen, is what constitutes the great interest of this undertaking; that, permit me to repeat, is what raises this debate above mere questions of ministerial position. That, to my way of thinking, is what shows, by the most astounding and decisive example, that it is impossible, that it would be detestable, un-French, to forbid the Republic to have a colonial policy. . . .

The only part of the Tongking which we propose to occupy is the delta of the [Red River]; we do not intend to go beyond Bac-Ninh and Hung-Hoa, near the confluence of the Clear River, save, however, on the coast, the points whose occupation may appear necessary. . . .

40. National Life from the Standpoint of Science, 1901

Karl Pearson

Educated at Cambridge, Heidelberg, and Berlin, Karl Pearson (1857–1936) renounced a very successful career as a lawyer to become a mathematician and biologist. He was a disciple of Francis Galton, who was the cousin of Charles Darwin and author of two once-famous books, *Hereditary Genius* and *Natural Inheritance,* which made heredity paramount over environment. In 1911 Pearson became the first holder of the Galton Chair for Eugenics at the University of London. He followed in the footsteps of Galton in seeking to quantify biological phenomena, particularly in the areas of evolution and heredity, which he called "biometrics," apparently minting the term himself. Much of his lab research was undertaken to confirm the theories of Darwin, whom he revered. In 1901 he founded and edited the journal *Biometrika,* and he was the author of numerous books about science and a three volume biography of Galton. Although Darwin and Galton did not attempt to apply their ideas to human society, Pearson did subscribe to theories of racial superiority and the inevitability of racial wars. He differed from most of the "social Darwinists" of his era in that his training was in physical rather than social science.

QUESTIONS

1. How does Karl Pearson's argument reflect the influence of Darwinian natural science?
2. According to Pearson, what are the main differences between the "superior" and "inferior" races?
3. How does Pearson use the example of North America to support his theory?
4. According to Pearson, what policies should the most advanced races adopt toward other races?
5. What is Pearson's view of the effects of racial competition on international relations?
6. Is Pearson sympathetic to the plight of the peoples of the world whom he labels as "inferior"?

What I have said about bad stock seems to me to hold for the lower races of man. How many centuries, how many thousands of years, have the Kaffir and the Negro held large districts in Africa undisturbed by the white man? Yet their inter-tribal struggles have not yet produced a civilization in the least comparable with the Aryan. Educate and nurture them as you will, I do not believe that you will succeed in modifying the stock. History shows me one way, and one way only, in which a high state of civilization has been produced, namely, the struggle of race with race, and the survival of the physically and mentally fitter race. If you want to know whether the lower races of man can evolve a higher type, I fear the only course is to leave them to fight it out among themselves, and even then the struggle for existence between individual and individual, between tribe and tribe, may not be supported by that physical selection due to a particular climate on which probably so much of the Aryan's success depended.

If you bring the white man into contact with the black, you too often suspend the very process of natural selection on which the evolution of a higher type depends. You get superior and inferior races living on the same soil, and that co-existence is demoralizing for both. They naturally sink into the position of master and servant, if not admittedly or covertly into that of slave-owner and slave. Frequently they intercross, and if the bad stock be raised the good is lowered. Even in the cases of Eurasians, of whom I have met mentally and physically fine specimens, I have felt how much better they would have been had they been pure Asiatics or pure Europeans. Thus it comes about that when the struggle for existence between races is suspended, the solution of great problems may be unnaturally postponed; instead of the slow, stern processes of evolution, cataclysmal solutions are prepared for the future. Such problems in suspense, it appears to me, are to be found in the negro population of the Southern States of America, in the large admixture of Indian blood in some of the South American races, but above all, in the Kaffir factor in South Africa.

You may possibly think that I am straying from my subject, but I want to justify natural selection to you. I want you to see selection as something which renders the inexorable law of heredity a source of progress, which produces the good through suffering, an infinitely greater good which far outbalances the very obvious pain and evil. Let us suppose the alternative were possible. Let us suppose we could prevent the white man, if we liked, from going to lands of which the agricultural and mineral resources are not worked to the full; then I should say a thousand times better for him that he should not go than that he should settle down and live alongside the inferior race. The only healthy alternative is that he should go and completely drive out the inferior race. That is practically what the white man has done in North America. We sometimes forget the light that chapter of history throws on more recent experiences. Some 250 years ago there was a man who fought in our country against taxation without representation, and another man who did not mind going to prison for the sake of his religious opinions. As Englishmen we are proud of them both, but we sometimes forget that they were both considerable capitalists for their age, and started chartered companies in another continent. Well, a good deal went on in the plantations they founded, if not with their knowledge, with that at least of their servants and of their successors, which would shock us at the present day. But I venture to say that no man calmly judging will wish either that the whites had never gone to America, or would desire that whites and Red Indians were to-day living alongside each other as negro and white in the Southern States, as Kaffir and European in South Africa, still less that

they had mixed their blood as Spaniard and Indian in South America. The civilization of the white man is a civilization dependent upon free white labour, and when that element of stability is removed it will collapse like those of Greece and Rome. I venture to assert, then, that the struggle for existence between white and red man, painful and even terrible as it was in its details, has given us a good far outbalancing its immediate evil. In place of the red man, contributing practically nothing to the work and thought of the world, we have a great nation, mistress of many arts, and able, with its youthful imagination and fresh, untrammelled impulses, to contribute much to the common stock of civilized man. Against that you have only to put the romantic sympathy for the Red Indian generated by the novels of Cooper and the poems of Longfellow, and then—see how little it weighs in the balance!

But America is but one case in which we have to mark a masterful human progress following an inter-racial struggle. The Australian nation is another case of great civilization supplanting a lower race unable to work to the full the land and its resources. Further back in history you find the same tale with almost every European nation. Sometimes when the conquering race is not too diverse in civilization and in type of energy there is an amalgamation of races, as when Norman and Anglo-Saxon ultimately blended; at other times the inferior race is driven out before the superior, as the Celt drove out the Iberian. The struggle means suffering, intense suffering, while it is in progress; but that struggle and that suffering have been the stages by which the white man has reached his present stage of development, and they account for the fact that he no longer lives in caves and feeds on roots and nuts. This dependence of progress on the survival of the fitter race, terribly black as it may seem to some of you, gives the struggle for existence its redeeming features; it is the fiery crucible out of which comes the finer metal. You may hope for a time when the sword shall be turned into the plough-share, when American and German and English traders shall no longer compete in the markets of the world for their raw material and for their food supply, when the white man and the dark shall share the soil between them, and each till it as he lists. But, believe me, when that day comes mankind will no longer progress; there will be nothing to check the fertility of inferior stock; the relentless law of heredity will not be controlled and guided by natural selection. Man will stagnate; and unless he ceases to multiply, the catastrophe will come again; famine and pestilence, as we see them in the East, physical selection—instead of the struggle of race against race, will do the work more relentlessly, and, to judge from India and China, far less efficiently than of old. . . .

The . . . great function of science in national life . . . is to show us what national life means, and how the nation is a vast organism subject as much to the great forces of evolution as any other gregarious type of life. There is a struggle of race against race and of nation against nation. In the early days of that struggle it was a blind, unconscious struggle of barbaric tribes. At the present day, in the case of the civilized white man, it has become more and more the conscious, carefully directed attempt of the nation to fit itself to a continuously changing environment. The nation has to foresee how and where the struggle will be carried on; the maintenance of national position is becoming more and more a conscious preparation for changing conditions, an insight into the needs of coming environments. . . .

It may be as well now to sum up my position as far as I have yet developed it. I have asked you to look upon the nation as an organized whole in continual struggle with other nations, whether by force of arms or by force of trade and economic processes. I have asked you to look upon this struggle of either kind as a not wholly bad thing; it is the source of human progress throughout the world's history. But if a nation is to maintain its position in this struggle, it must be fully provided with trained brains in every department of national activity, from the government to the factory, and have, if possible, a *reserve of brain and physique* to fall back upon in times of national crisis. . . .

You will see that my view—and I think it may be called the scientific view of a nation—is that of an organized whole, kept up to a high pitch of internal efficiency by insuring that its numbers are substantially recruited from the better stocks, and kept up to a high pitch of external efficiency by contest, chiefly by way of war with inferior races, and with equal races by the struggle for trade-routes and for the sources of raw material and of food supply. This is the natural history view of mankind, and I do not think you can in its main features subvert it. Some of you may refuse to acknowledge it, but you cannot really study history and refuse to see its force. Some of you may realize it, and then despair of life; you may decline to admit any glory in a world where the superior race must either reject the inferior, or, mixing with it or even living alongside it, degenerate itself. What beauty can there be when the battle is to the stronger, and the weaker must suffer in the struggle of nations and in the struggle of individual men? You may say: Let us cease to struggle, let us leave the lands of the world to the races that cannot profit by them to the full, let us cease to compete in the markets of the world. Well, we could do it, if we were a small nation living on the produce of our own soil, and a soil so worthless that no other race envied it and sought to appropriate it. We should cease to advance; but then we should naturally give up progress as a good which comes through suffering. I say it is possible for a small rural community to stand apart from the world-contest and to stagnate, if no more powerful nation wants its possessions.

But are we such a community? Is it not a fact that the daily bread of our millions of workers depends on their having somebody to work for? that if we give up the contest for trade-routes and for free markets and for waste lands, we indirectly give up our food-supply? Is it not a fact that our strength depends on these and upon our colonies, and that our colonies have been won by the ejection of inferior races, and are maintained against equal races only by respect for the present power of our empire? . . .

We find that the law of the survival of the fitter is true of mankind, but that the struggle is that of the gregarious animal. A community not knit together by strong social instincts, by sympathy between man and man, and class and class, cannot face the external contest, the competition with other nations, by peace or by war, for the raw material of production and for its food supply. This struggle of tribe with tribe, and nation with nation, may have its mournful side; but we see as a result of it the gradual progress of mankind to higher intellectual and physical efficiency. It is idle to condemn it; we can only see that it exists and recognise what we have gained by it—civilization and social sympathy. But while the statesman has to watch this external struggle, . . . he must be very cautious that the nation is not silently rotting at its core. He must insure that the fertility of the inferior stocks is checked, and that of the superior stocks encouraged; he must regard with suspicion anything that tempts the physically and mentally fitter men and women to remain childless. . . .

The path of progress is strewn with the wrecks of nations; traces are everywhere to be seen of the hecatombs of inferior races, and of victims who found not the narrow way to perfection. Yet these dead people are, in very truth, the stepping stones on which mankind has arisen to the higher intellectual and deeper emotional life of today.

41. Letter to the English Ruler, 1839

Lin Tse-Hsu

As the British extended their interests in Asia during the nineteenth century native leaders in China and India were forced to cope with the demands of the Europeans. During the 1830s the English profited from an extensive trade in opium in China, and they wished to obtain political and diplomatic privileges and more economic concessions from the Chinese officials. Lin Tse-Hsu (1785–1850) was China's Imperial Commissioner at Canton. He waged a crusade against opium and wrote a letter to Queen Victoria in which he complained about the British support for the drug traffic into China. (See below for an excerpt.) Although the English were willing to make concessions on opium for the sake of improved relations and better trade opportunities overall, they refused to agree to Lin's demands for China's full control over the administration of justice in cases that involved Chinese and foreigners. Lin's strong stand resulted in a breakdown of negotiations and the outbreak of the first Anglo-Chinese war in 1839. The British easily routed the Chinese and further expanded their influence over the following decades. After this humiliating defeat Lin urged his superiors to adopt Western arms and means of warfare, but the officials ignored his advice.

QUESTIONS

1. What are the views of Lin Tse-Hsu on the emperor of China and his handling of the foreigners?
2. How does he assess the trade between China and other countries? To whom is the trade beneficial, and why?
3. How was China planning to stop the sale of opium? Why did its strategy fail?
4. What does Lin Tse-Hsu's letter tell us about the author?

A communication: magnificently our great emperor soothes and pacifies China and the foreign countries, regarding all with the same kindness. If there is profit, then he shares it with the peoples of the world; if there is harm, then he removes it on behalf of the world. This is because he takes the mind of Heaven and earth as his mind.

The kings of your honorable country by a tradition handed down from generation to generation have always been noted for their politeness and submissiveness. We have read your successive tributary memorials saying: "In general our countrymen who go to trade in China have always received His Majesty the Emperor's gracious treatment and equal justice," and so on. Privately we are delighted with the way in which the honorable rulers of your country deeply understand the grand principles and are grateful for the Celestial grace. For this reason the Celestial Court on soothing those from afar has redoubled its polite and kind treatment. The profit from trade has been enjoyed by

them continuously for two hundred years. This is the source from which your country has become known for its wealth.

But after a long period of commercial intercourse, there appear among the crowd of barbarians both good persons and bad, unevenly. Consequently there are those who smuggle opium to seduce the Chinese people and so cause the spread of the poison to all provinces. Such persons who only care for profit themselves, and disregard their harm to others, are not tolerated by the laws of Heaven and are unanimously hated by human beings. His Majesty the Emperor, upon hearing of this, is in a towering rage. He has especially sent me, his commissioner, to come to Kwangtung, and together with the governor-general and governor jointly to investigate and settle this matter.

All those people in China who sell opium or smoke opium should receive the death penalty. If we trace the crime of those barbarians who through the years have been selling opium, then the deep harm they have wrought and the great profit they have usurped should fundamentally justify their execution according to law. We take into consideration, however, the fact that the various barbarians have still known how to repent their crimes and return to their allegiance to us by taking the 20,183 chests of opium from their storeships and petitioning us, through their consular officer Elliot, to receive it. It has been entirely destroyed and this has been faithfully reported to the Throne in several memorials by this commissioner and his colleagues.

Fortunately we have received a specially extended favor from His Majesty the Emperor, who considers that for those who voluntarily surrender there are still some circumstances to palliate their crime, and so for the time being he has magnanimously excused them from punishment. But as for those who again violate the opium prohibition, it is difficult for the law to pardon them repeatedly. Having established new regulations, we presume that the ruler of your honorable country, who takes delight in our culture and whose disposition is inclined towards us, must be able to instruct the various barbarians to observe the law with care. It is only necessary to explain to them the advantages and disadvantages and then they will know that the legal code of the Celestial Court must be absolutely obeyed with awe.

We find that your country is sixty or seventy thousand *li* [three *li* make one mile, ordinarily] from China. Yet there are barbarian ships that strive to come here for trade for the purpose of making great profit. The wealth of China is used to profit the barbarians. That is to say, the great profit made by the barbarians is all taken from the rightful share of China. By what right do they then in return use the poisonous drug to injure the Chinese people? Even though the barbarians may not necessarily intend to do us

harm, yet in covering profit to an extreme, they have no regard for injuring others. Let us ask, where is your conscience? I have heard that the smoking of opium is very strictly forbidden by your country; that is because the harm caused by opium is clearly understood. Since it is not permitted to do harm to your own country, then even less should you let it be passed on to the harm of other countries—how much less to China! Of all that China exports to foreign countries, there is not a single thing that is not beneficial to people; they are of benefit when eaten, or of benefit when used, or of benefit when resold: all are beneficial. Is there a single article from China which has done harm to foreign countries? Take tea and rhubarb, for example; the foreign countries cannot get along for a single day without them. If China cuts off these benefits with no sympathy for those who are to suffer, then what can the barbarians rely upon to keep themselves alive? Moreover the woolens, camlets, and longells [i.e., textiles] of foreign countries cannot be woven unless they obtain Chinese silk. If China, again, cuts off this beneficial export, what profit can the barbarians expect to make? As for other foodstuffs, beginning with candy, ginger, cinnamon, and so forth, and articles for use, beginning with silk, satin, chinaware, and so on, all the things that must be had by foreign countries are innumerable. On the other hand, articles coming from the outside to China can only be used as toys. We can take them or get along without them. Since they are not needed by China, what difficulty would there be if we closed the frontier and stopped the trade? Nevertheless our Celestial Court lets tea, silk, and other goods be shipped without limit and circulated everywhere without begrudging it in the slightest. This is for no other reason but to share the benefit with the people of the world.

The goods from China carried away by your country not only supply your consumption and use, but also can be divided up and sold to other countries, producing a triple profit. Even if you do not sell opium, you still have this threefold profit. How can you bear to go further, selling products injurious to others in order to fulfill your insatiable desire?

Suppose there were people from another country who carried opium for sale to England and seduced your people into buying and smoking it; certainly your honorable ruler would deeply hate it and be bitterly aroused. We have heard heretofore that your honorable ruler is kind and benevolent. Naturally you would not wish to give unto others what you yourself do not want. We have also heard that the ships coming to Canton have all had regulations promulgated and given to them in which it is stated that it is not permitted to carry contraband goods. This indicates that the administrative orders of your honorable rule have been originally strict and clear. Only because the trading ships are numerous, heretofore perhaps they have not been examined with care. Now after this communication has been dispatched and you have clearly understood the strictness of the prohibitory laws of the Celestial Court, certainly you will not let your subjects dare again to violate the law.

We have further learned that in London, the capital of your honorable rule, and in Scotland (Ssu-ko-lan), Ireland (Ai-lun), and other places, originally no opium has been produced. Only in several places of India under your control such as Bengal, Madras, Bombay, Patna, Benares, and Malwa has opium been planted from hill to hill, and ponds have been opened for its manufacture. For months and years work is continued in order to accumulate the poison. The obnoxious odor ascends, irritating Heaven and frightening the spirits. Indeed you, O King, can eradicate the opium plant in these places, hoe over the fields entirely, and sow instead the five grains [i.e., millet, barley, wheat, etc.]. Anyone who dares again to attempt to plant and manufacture opium should be severely punished. This will really be a great, benevolent government policy that will increase the common weal and get rid of evil. For this, Heaven must support you and the spirits must bring you good fortune, prolonging your old age and extending your descendants. All will depend on this act.

As for the barbarian merchants who come to China, their food and drink and habitation are all received by the gracious favor of our Celestial Court. Their accumulated wealth is all benefit given with pleasure by our Celestial Court. They spend rather few days in their own country but more time in Canton. To digest clearly the legal penalties as an aid to instruction has been a valid principle in all ages. Suppose a man of another country comes to England to trade, he still had to obey the English laws; how much more should he obey in China the laws of the Celestial Dynasty?

Now we have set up regulations governing the Chinese people. He who sells opium shall receive the death penalty and he who smokes it also the death penalty. Now consider this: if the barbarians do not bring opium, then how can the Chinese people resell it, and how can they smoke it? The fact is that the wicked barbarians beguile the Chinese people into a death trap. How then can we grant life only to these barbarians? He who takes life of even one person must atone for it with his own life; yet is the harm done by opium limited to the taking of one life only? Therefore in the new regulations, in regard to those barbarians who bring opium to China, the penalty is fixed at decapitation or strangulation. This is what is called getting rid of a harmful thing on behalf of mankind.

Moreover we have found that in the middle of the second month of this year [April 9] Consul Elliot of your nation, because the opium prohibition law was very stern and severe, petitioned for an extension of the time limit. He requested a limit of five months for India and its adjacent harbors and related territories, and ten months for England proper, after which they would act in conformity with the new regulations. Now we, the commissioner and others, have memorialized and have received the extraordinary Celestial grace of His Majesty the Emperor, who has redoubled his consideration and compassion. All those who within the period of the coming one year (from England) or six months (from India) bring opium to China by mistake, but who voluntarily confess and completely surrender the opium, shall be exempt from their punishment. After this limit of time, if there are those who still bring opium to China then they will plainly have committed a willful violation and shall at once be executed according to law, with absolutely no clemency or pardon. This may be called the height of kindness and the perfection of justice.

Our Celestial Dynasty rules over and supervises the myriad states, and surely possesses unfathomable spiritual dignity. Yet the Emperor cannot bear to execute people without having first tried to reform them by instruction. Therefore he especially promulgates these fixed regulations. The barbarian merchants of your country, if they wish to do business for a prolonged period, are required to obey our statutes respectfully and to cut off permanently the source of opium. They must by no means try to test the effectiveness of the law with their own lives. May you, O King, check your wicked and sift out your vicious people before they come to China, in order to guarantee the peace of your nation, to show further the sincerity of your politeness and submissiveness, and to let the two countries enjoy together the blessings of peace. How fortunate, how fortunate indeed! After receiving this dispatch will you immediately give us a prompt reply regarding the details and circumstances of your cutting off the opium traffic. Be sure not to put this off. The above is what has to be communicated. [Vermilion endorsement:] This is appropriately worded and quite comprehensive (Te-t'i chou-tao).

42. Two Views of English Rule in India

While the British pursued a policy of "informal empire" in China, they exerted more direct control over India during these years. The economic and political reforms they introduced enriched England but yielded mixed results for the native peoples of the subcontinent. Dadabhai Naoroji (1825–1917) was the son of a Parsi priest and a founder of the Indian National Congress. Although he criticized the British for their economic exploitation of India, he also admired their political institutions, as the following selection from his presidential address suggests. From 1892 to 1895 he sat in Parliament as a Liberal representative from a London constituency. There he advanced the Indian cause and enjoyed support from Irish nationalists. In his later years he became more radical and less Anglophile and sought self-government but not independence for India. This document concludes with an excerpt from a speech by Bal Gangadhar Tilak (1856–1920). Born into a middle class Hindu family of Brahman caste, he was a strong nationalist who sought a Hindu revival and complete independence from England. A leader of the extremist wing of the Indian National Congress, he advocated boycotts of British goods and assassinations of British officials. He was imprisoned for advocating violent opposition to British rule and then formed his own Home Rule League in 1914. Ironically and symbolically, he died on the day Gandhi inaugurated his first campaign of nonviolent political action.

QUESTIONS

1. How does Naoroji view the pros and cons of English rule in India?
2. According to him, what attitude should Indians have toward England?
3. Does Tilak agree with Naoroji's assessment? According to him, what did happen to India under the English? What is he advising Indians to do to achieve freedom?

Dadabhai Naoroji

The Pros and Cons of British
Rule, 1871

To sum up the whole, the British rule has been—morally, a great blessing; politically peace and order on one hand, blunders on the other; materially, impoverishment (relieved as far as the railway and other loans go). The natives call the British system "Sakar ki Churi," the knife of sugar. This is to say there is no oppression, it is all smooth and sweet, but it is the knife, notwithstanding. I mention this that you should know these feelings. Our great misfortune is that you do not know our wants. When you will know our real wishes, I have not the least doubt that you would do justice. The genius and spirit of the British people is fair play and justice. The great problems before the English statesmen are two: 1) To make the foreign rule self-supporting, either by returning to India, in some shape or other, the wealth that has been, and is being, drawn from it, or by stopping that drain in some way till India is so far improved in its material condition as to be able to produce enough for its own ordinary wants and the extraordinary ones of costly distant rule. If you cannot feel yourself actuated by the high and noble ambition of the amelioration of 200,000,000 of human beings, let your self-interest suggest to you to take care of the bird that gives the golden-egg of £12,000,000 a year to your nation, and provisions to thousands of your people of all classes. In the name of humanity, I implore our rulers to make up their minds not to prevent the restoration of the equilibrium, after the continuous exhaustion by drain and by horrible famines. I do not in the least grudge any legitimate benefit England may derive for its rule in India. On the contrary, I am thankful for its invaluable moral benefits; but it is the further duty of England to give us such a government, and all the benefit of its power and credit, as to enable us to pay, without starving or dying by famine, the tribute or price for the rule; 2) How to satisfy reasonably the growing political aspirations and just rights of a people called British subjects to have a fair share in the administration and legislation of their own country. If the Select Committee solve these two problems, before which all other difficulties, financial or others, are as nothing, they will deserve the blessings of 200,000,000 of the human race.

The Blessings of British Rule, 1886

The assemblage of such a Congress is an event of the utmost importance in Indian History. I ask whether in the most glorious days of Hindu rule, in the days of the Rajahs like the great Vikram, you could imagine the possibility of a meeting of this kind, whether even Hindus of all different provinces of the kingdom could have collected and spoken as one nation. Coming down to the later Empire of our friends, the Mahomedans, who probably ruled over a larger territory at one time than any Hindu monarch, would it have been, even in the days of the great Akbar himself, possible for a meeting like this to assemble composed of all classes and communities, all speaking one language, and all having uniform and high aspirations of their own.

Well, then, what is it for which we are now met on this occasion? We all have assembled to consider the questions upon which our future, whether glorious or inglorious. It is our good fortune that we are under a rule which makes it possible for us to meet in this manner. (Cheers.) It is under the civilizing rule of the Queen and the people of England that we meet here together, hin-dered by none, and are freely allowed to speak our minds without the least fear and without the least hesitation. Such a thing is possible under British rule and British rule only. (Loud Cheers.) Then I put the question plainly: Is this Congress a nursery for sedition and rebellion against the British Government (cries of "No, no"); or is it another stone in the foundation of the stability of that government? (Cries of "Yes, yes".) There could be but one answer, and that you have already given, because we are thoroughly sensible of the numberless blessings conferred upon us, of which the very existence of this Congress is a proof in a nutshell. (Cheers.) Were it not for the blessings of British rule, I could not have come here, as I have done, without the least hesitation and without the least fear that my children might be robbed and killed in my absence; nor could you have come from every corner of the land, having performed, within a few days journeys, which in former days would have occupied as many months. (Cheers.) These simple facts bring home to us at once some of those great and numberless blessings which British rule has conferred upon us. But there remain even greater blessings for which we have to be grateful. It is to British rule that we owe the education we possess; the people of England were sincere in the declarations made more than a half century ago that India was a sacred charge entrusted to their care by Providence, and that they were bound to administer it for the good of India, to the glory of their own name, and the satisfaction of God. (Prolonged cheering.) When we have to acknowledge so many blessings as flowing from British rule,—and I could descant on them for hours, because it would simply be recounting to you the history of the British Empire in India—is it possible that an assembly like this, every one of whose members is fully impressed with the knowledge of these blessings, could meet for any purpose inimical to that rule to which we owe so much? (Cheers.)

The thing is absurd. Let us speak out like men and proclaim that we are loyal to the backbone (cheers); that we understand the benefits English rule has conferred upon us; that we thoroughly appreciate the education that has been given to us, the new light which has been poured upon us, turning us from darkness into light and teaching us the new lesson that kings are made for the people, not the peoples for their kings; and this new lesson we have learned amidst the darkness of Asiatic despotism only by the light of free English civilization.

Bal Gangadhar Tilak

The Tenets of the New Party
1906, 1907
. . . India is under foreign rule and Indians welcomed the change at one time. Then many races were the masters and they had no sympathy and hence the change was welcomed and that was the cause why the English succeeded in establishing an empire in India. The confusion which characterized native rule was in striking contrast with the constitutional laws of the British Government. The people had much hope in the British Government, but they were much disappointed in their anticipations. They hoped that their arts and industries would be fostered under British rule and they would gain much from their new rulers. But all those hopes had been falsified. The people were now compelled to adopt a new line, namely, to fight against the bureaucracy.

Hundred years ago it was said, and believed by the people, that they were socially inferior to their rulers and as soon as they were socially improved they would obtain their liberties and privileges. But subsequent events have shown that this was not based on sound logic. Fifty years ago Mr. Dadabhai Naoroji, the greatest statesman of India, thought that Government would grant them rights and privileges when they were properly educated, but that hope is gone. Now it might be said that they were not fitted to take part in the administration of the country owing to their defective education. But, I ask, whose fault it is. The Government has been imparting education to the people and hence the fault is not theirs but of the Government. The Government is imparting an education to make the people fit for some subordinate appointments. . . .

Protests are of no avail. Mere protest, not backed by self-reliance, will not help the people. Days of protests and prayers have gone. . . . Three P's—pray, please, and protest—will not do unless backed by solid force. Look to the examples of Ireland, Japan and Russia and follow their methods. . . .

Two new words have recently come into existence with regard to our politics, and they are *Moderates* and *Extremists*. These words have a specific relation to time, and they, therefore, will change with time. The Extremists of to-day will be the Moderates of to-morrow, just as the Moderates of to-day were the Extremists yesterday. When the National Congress was first started by Mr. Dadabhai's views, which now go for Moderates, were given to the public, he was styled an Extremist, so that you see that the term Extremist is an expression of progress. We are Extremists to-day and our sons will call themselves Extremists and us Moderates. Every new party begins as Extremists and ends as Moderates. The sphere of practical politics is not unlimited. We cannot say what will or will not happen 1,000 years hence—perhaps during that long period, the whole white race will be swept away in another glacial period. We must, therefore, study the present and work out a programme to meet the present condition.

It is impossible to go into details within the time at my disposal. One thing is granted, viz., that this Government does not suit us. As has been said by an eminent statesman—the government of one country by another can never be successful, and therefore, a permanent Government. There is no difference of opinion about this fundamental proposition between the Old and New schools. One fact is that this alien Government has ruined the country. In the beginning, all of us were taken by surprise. We were almost dazed. We thought that everything that the rulers did was for our good and that this English Government has descended from the clouds to save us from the invasions of Tamerlane and Chengis Khan, and, as they say, not only from foreign invasions but from internecine warfare, or the internal or external invasions, as they call it. We felt happy for a time, but it soon came to light that the peace which was established in this country did this, as Mr. Dadabhai has said in one place—that we were prevented from going at each other's throats, so that a foreigner might go at the throat of us all. *Pax Britannica* has been established in this country in order that a foreign government may exploit the country. That this is the effect of this *Pax Britannica* is being gradually realized in these days. It was an unhappy circumstance that it was not realised sooner. We believed in the benevolent intentions of the government, but in politics there is no benevolence. Benevolence is used to sugarcoat the declarations of self-interest and we were in those days deceived by the apparent benevolent institutions under which rampant self-interest was concealed. That was

our state then. But soon a change came over us. English education, growing poverty, and better familiarity with our rulers, opened our eyes and our leaders; especially, the venerable leader who presided over the recent Congress was the first to tell us that the drain from the country was ruining it, and if the drain was to continue, there was some great disaster awaiting us. So terribly convinced was he of this that he went over from here to England and spent twenty-five years of his life in trying to convince the English people of the injustice that is being done to us. He worked very hard. He had conversations and interviews with secretaries of states, with members of Parliament—and with what result? . . .

. . . Every Englishman knows that they are a mere handful in this country and it is the business of every one of them to befool you in believing that you are weak and they are strong. That is politics. We have been deceived by such a policy so long. What the New Party wants you to do is realise the fact that your future rests entirely in your own hands. If you mean to be free, you can be free; if you do not mean to be free, you will fall and be forever fallen. So many of you need not like arms; but if you have not the power of active resistance, have you not the power of self-denial and self-abstinence in such a way as not to assist this foreign Government to rule over you? This is boycott and this is what is meant when we say, boycott is a political weapon. We shall not give them assistance to collect revenue and keep peace. We shall not assist them in fighting beyond the frontiers or outside India with Indian blood or money. We shall not assist them in carrying on the administration of justice. We shall have our own courts, and when the time comes we shall not pay taxes. Can you do that by your united efforts? If you can, you are free from to-morrow.

43. The Manifesto of the Tongmeng Hui, 1905 [Revolutionary Alliance]

Sun Yat-sen

Dr. Sun Yat-sen (1866–1925) was a leader of the revolutionary movement which overthrew the Manchu dynasty in China and established a republican form of government for that nation in 1912. Born into a poor rural family in the Canton region, Sun attended a Christian mission school in Hawaii and later studied (but never practiced) medicine in Hong Kong. He was not well versed in the classics of Chinese literature and philosophy. As a young man he plotted to overthrow the Manchus and began to formulate a program for the political, economic, and social reconstruction of his country. In 1894 he issued the Manifesto of the Xingzhong Hui [Revive China Society], which condemned the corruption and weakness of the Chinese government and called for the revival of China against government repression and foreign interference. The document reprinted below presents a revolutionary program of land redistribution and a political process by which a provisional government would train the Chinese masses for eventual participation in a constitutional democracy. During Sun's later career he led the Chinese nationalist Kuomintang Party and served briefly as the President of the new Chinese republic in 1912. For the rest of his life he strove to unite China under a central government founded upon his "Three People's Principles": nationalism, democracy, and socialism.

QUESTIONS

1. According to Sun, how does the current revolutionary struggle differ from previous revolts?
2. What is Sun's view of the Manchu dynasty?
3. What general goals does he outline for China?
4. Summarize and explain the significance of his three-step program for China's political transformation.
5. Compare Sun's proposals with those of the leaders of the American, French, and Russian revolutions. Is he a westernizer or a restorer of tradition?

By order of the Military Government, on the——day,——month,——year of T'ien-yun, the Commander-in-Chief of the Chinese National Army proclaims the purposes and platform of the Military Government to the people of the nation:

Now the National Army has established the Military Government, which aims to cleanse away two hundred and sixty years of barbarous filth, restore our four-thousand-year-old fatherland, and plan for the welfare of the four hundred million people. Not only is this an unavoidable obligation of the Military Government, but all our fellow-nationals should also take it as their own responsibility. We recall that, since the beginning of our nation the Chinese have always ruled China; although at times alien peoples have usurped the rule, yet our ancestors were able to drive them out and restore Chinese sovereignty so that they could hand down the nation to posterity. Now the men of Han [i.e., the Chinese] have raised a righteous [or patriotic] army to exterminate the northern barbarians. This is a continuation of heroic deeds bequeathed to us by our predecessors, and a great righteous cause lies behind it; there is none among us Chinese who does not understand this. But the revolutions in former generations, such as the Ming Dynasty and the Taiping Heavenly Kingdom, were concerned only with the driving out of the barbarians and the restoration of Chinese rule. Aside from these they sought no other change. We today are different from people of former times. Besides the driving out of the barbarian dynasty and the restoration of China, it is necessary also to change the national polity and the people's livelihood. And though there are myriad ways and means to achieve this goal, the essential spirit that runs through them all is freedom, equality, and fraternity. Therefore in former days there were heroes' revolutions, but today we have a national revolution [*Kuo-min ko-ming*, lit., revolution of the people of the country]. "National revolution" means that all people in the nation will have the spirit of freedom, equality, and fraternity; that is, they will all bear the responsibility of the Military Government, and the achievements of the Military Government will be those of the people. With a cooperative mind and concerted effort, the Military Government and the people will thus perform their duty. Therefor we proclaim to the world in utmost sincerity the outline of the present revolution and the fundamental plan for the future administration of the nation.

1. *Drive out the Tartars*: The Manchus of today were originally the eastern barbarians beyond the Great Wall. They frequently caused border troubles during the Ming dynasty; then when China was in a disturbed state they came inside Shanhaikuan, conquered China, and enslaved our Chinese people. Those who opposed them were killed by the hundreds of thousands, and our Chinese have been a people without a nation for two hundred and sixty years. The extreme cruelties and tyrannies of the Manchu government have now reached their limit. With the righteous army poised against them, we will overthrow that government, and restore our sovereign rights. Those Manchu and Chinese military men who have a change of heart and come over to us will be granted amnesty, while those who dare to resist will be slaughtered without mercy. Chinese who act as traitors in the cause of the Manchu will be treated in the same way.

2. *Restore China*: China is the China of our Chinese. The government of China should be in the hands of the Chinese. After driving out the Tartars we must restore our national state. Those who dare to act like Shih Ching-t'ang or Wu San-kuei [both were traitors] will be attacked by the whole country.

3. *Establish the Republic*: Now our revolution is based on equality, in order to establish a republican government. All our people are equal and all enjoy political rights. The president will be publicly chosen by the people of the country. The parliament will be made up of members publicly chosen by the people of the country. A constitution of the Chinese Republic will be enacted, and every person must abide by it. Whoever dares to make himself a monarch shall be attacked by the whole country.

4. *Equalize land ownership*: The good fortune of civilization is to be shared equally by all the people of the nation. We should improve our social and economic organization, and assess the value of all the land in the country. Its present price shall be received by the owner, but all increases in value resulting from reform and social improvements after the revolution shall belong to the state, to be shared by all the people, in order to create a socialist state, where each family within the empire can be well supported, each person satisfied, and no one fail to secure employment. Those who dare to control the livelihood of the people through monopoly shall be ostracized.

The above four points will be carried out in three steps in due order. The first period is government by military law. When the righteous army has arisen, various places will join the cause. The common people of each locality will escape from the Manchu fetters. Those who come upon the enemy must unite in hatred of him, must join harmoniously with the compatriots within their ranks and suppress the enemy bandits. Both the armies and the people will be under the rule of military law. The armies will do their best in defeating the enemy on behalf of the people, and the people will supply the needs of the armies, and not do harm to their security. The local administration, in areas where the enemy has been either already defeated or not yet defeated, will be controlled in general by the Military Government, so that step by step the accumulated evils can be swept away. Evils like the oppression of the government, the greed and graft of the officials, the squeeze of government clerks and runners, the cruelty of tortures and penalties, the tyranny of tax collections, the humiliation of the queue— shall all be exterminated together with the Manchu rule. Evils in social customs, such as the keeping of slaves, the cruelty of footbinding, the spread of poison opium, the obstructions of geomancy (*feng-shui*) [a form of divination or fortune telling by supernatural means], should also all be prohibited. The time limit for each district (*hsien*) is three years. In those *hsien* where real results are achieved before the end of three years, the military law shall be lifted and a provisional constitution shall be enacted.

The second period is that of government by the provisional constitution. When military law is lifted in each *hsien,* the Military Government shall return the right of self-government to the local people. The members of local councils and local officials shall be elected by the people. All rights and duties of the Military Government toward the people and those of the people toward the government shall be regulated by the provisional constitution, which shall be observed by the Military Government, the local councils, and the people. Those who violate the law shall be held responsible. Six years after the securing of peace in the nation the provisional constitution shall be annulled and the constitution shall be promulgated.

The third period shall be government under the constitution. Six years after the provisional constitution has been enforced a constitution shall be made. The military and administrative powers of the Military Government shall be annulled; the people shall elect the president, and elect the members of parliament to organize the parliament. The administrative matters of the nation shall proceed according to the provisions of the constitution.

Of these three periods the first is the period in which the Military Government leads the people in eradicating all traditional evils and abuses; the second is the period in which the Military Government gives the power of local self-government to the people while retaining general control over national affairs under the constitution. It is hoped that our people will proceed in due order and cultivate their free and equal status; the foundation of the Chinese Republic will be entirely based on this.

44. King of Benin's Ambush of British Officers in Nigeria, 1897

The ambush described below and the punitive expedition that followed are typical of the imperialism of free trade. Benin was situated in the Oil Rivers Protectorate in Nigeria. In earlier centuries Benin had been a great kingdom, built up on the slave trade, and had exercised suzerainty in western Nigeria. Like other African societies, Benin offered armed resistance to foreign encroachment on its autonomy and way of life. Normally such resistance was futile. The particular event that provoked the ambush by King Duboar appears to have been actions by the British consul, J. B. Phillips, to stop human sacrifices in Benin; the punitive expedition later reported finding "the place of sacrifice reeking with blood." In the aftermath of the expedition, King Duboar was deposed, his palace destroyed, his kingdom not annexed but brought under indirect rule through a council of chiefs. Benin's royal art was confiscated and sold by the British government to help pay for the expedition; that too was typical of the imperialism of free trade. These sculptures in brass and wood glorified the king, his ancestors and predecessors, and heroic events in Benin's past. At first the art was condemned as the icons of a disgusting cult, but soon it came to be admired and found its way into the hands of collectors and museums. Some of these treasures may still be viewed at the British Museum.

QUESTIONS

1. What makes Gallwey so confident that order will be restored and the guilty punished? What actions have already been taken before the military and naval forces arrive? What does he propose be done?
2. Analyze this episode as an ethical issue: Who is morally correct? Morally wrong?
3. Is there any evidence in the account for Lord Salisbury's assertion: "Our object is not territiory, but facility for trade"?
4. What might explain the contrast between British imperial expansion being initiated by merchants and manufacturers and French and other nations whose soldiers took the initiative?

Vice-Consul Gallwey to Foreign Office.
Bonny, January 16, 1897

Received February 15

Sir,

I HAVE the honor to report, for [the Prime Minister and Foreign Secretary] Lord Salisbury's information, that, on arrival at Eberu in the Ibo country yesterday, I received news of the disaster that had happened in Benin. I proceeded on at once, reaching Bonny the following evening. I had been surveying the country between the New Calabar and Opobo Rivers. . . .

All particulars up to date have been given by cablegram. Benin not being a telegraph station, news takes a long time to reach Bonny and Brass. Launch communication has been started between Brass and Benin, but the round journey takes about 12 days or so. In addition to this, the water in the Niger is low.

I proceed today to Benin to learn full particulars from the two survivors, Captain Boisragon and Mr. Locke [and] will cable full details.

Acting Commissioner Gallwey to Foreign Office—(Received February 22.) *"Widegeon," at Benin, January 21, 1897.*

Sir,

IN continuation of my dispatch of the 18th instant, I have the honor to report, for the Marquess of Salisbury's information, that I have arrived in the Benin River on the 20th instant on board Her Majesty's ship "Widegeon."

2. I regret to state that, after interviewing the two surviving officers of the expedition, Captain Boisragon and Mr. Locke, and gaining all possible information from escaped carriers and messengers, and after holding a meeting of the leading Jakri Chiefs, no hope can be held out that any other officers have escaped.

Messrs. Boisragon and Locke are both wounded, not seriously; but wandering for five days and five nights in the forest seriously exaggerated the injuries received. Dr. d'Arcy Irvine has been most attentive in caring for these officers.

3. In brief extract, the following is an account of what actually happened, taken from statements of Messrs. Locke and Boisragon, and of several natives who accompanied the ill-fated expedition:—

The expedition left Sapele on the morning of the 2nd instant. It consisted of Messrs. Phillips [Consul-General], Copland, Crawford, Locke, Boisragon, Mailing, Campbell, Elliot and Lyon, also of two European traders—Mr. Gordon, belonging to the African Association at Sapele, and Mr. Powis, belonging to the firm of Messrs. Miller Brothers at Old Calabar. These gentlemen accompanied the expedition on Mr. Phillips' invitation. There were over 200 carriers, 2 Government interpreters, the Consul-General's chief clerk and cook, 2 orderlies, 1 store-keeper (from Sapele), and 1 servant to each officer, with the exception of Mr. Powis, who it appears had 4 boys with him. Mr. Phillips also took the drum-and-fife band of the Niger Coast Protectorate Force with him, but sent it back from Gwato, after being begged by the Kari natives not to take them.

The expedition anchored off Gilli-Gilli for the night. Mr. Phillips' messenger, whom he had sent to the King with a present a couple of days before, returned and reported that the King took the present, and expressed surprise at getting another present so soon.

The King further said that he had so much "custom" to make just now that he could not see the Acting Consul-General or any white man, but that in about a month's time he would send down and let the Acting Consul-General know when he was ready, and receive him and one big Jakri Chief only.

The messenger further stated, in private, that as he was leaving Benin City, the King of Benin gave orders for some of his soldiers to go to the different waterside towns. The messenger also told the Acting Consul-General quietly that the King had said to him, "If the white men are really coming, that he (the messenger) was to come on and let him know first of all."

This messenger is reported as being most intelligent, and was apparently an old friend of the King before the latter succeeded to the Throne, but this must be taken *cum grano salis* [with a grain of salt]. The messenger, however, had a personal interview with the King, so the King's message was "first-hand."

Mr. Phillips then sent the messenger back to the King to say he was coming. A Jakri messenger next arrived, and said that all the Jakris (the Benin River tribe—distinct and unconnected with the Binis, except in trade matters) were frightened, and were leaving the waterside towns on the Benin city side of Gwato Creek, as the Bini soldiers were coming down from the city. Mr. Phillips then sent this man to the Headman or Chief of Gwato next morning, and wanted accommodation for about 10 white men and 200 carriers. The next day the expedition reached Gwato—which is quite close to Gilli-Gilli—where they found all ready for them, the Chief having given up his own house to the white men. Three King's messengers then came and said they were sent to lead the expedition to the city.

Mr. Phillips explained that he had come as a friend to the King, who had taken his presents, that he had no wish nor intention of interfering with any of their customs, and that he wished to proceed on his way the following morning, as he had plenty of work to do elsewhere. Mr. Phillips then introduced each officer in turn, with his rank, to the King's messengers.

The messengers begged for a day's delay to give the King time to prepare. This was refused. The messengers then asked Mr. Phillips to give them a "token" to send to the King, to show that the expedition was really coming. Mr. Phillips sent a uniform cane belonging to Captain Boisragon. The messengers departed for Benin city.

After this, everything appeared to go most smoothly, and the Gwato people (subjects of the King) seemed very pleased to see the white men. One Benin city Chief, named Mary Boma, with several other people there, recognized with much evident pleasure Major Crawford and Mr. Maling, who had visited Gwato before.

The expedition went through the recognized custom of "feet washing" before entering Gwato town. That evening Mr. Phillips issued two or three orders, one of which was to the effect that he would lead the column with the guide and one interpreter, and another, that officers might carry revolvers if they so wished it, but that they were not to show them. As a matter of fact, no officers carried revolvers on their person.

The next morning (3rd instant) at 8 A.M., the expedition started from Gwato, Mr. Lyon returning to Sapele to take charge in Mr. Campbell's absence. Dr. d'Arcy Irvine had already relieved Dr. Elliot temporarily at Sapele. At 11 A.M. the expedition halted for breakfast. The natives seemed extremely pleased to see them. The road, although they could only walk comfortably in single file, was in excellent order (bearing from east-north-east to east). After breakfast the expedition pushed on, and somewhere near 4 o'clock in the afternoon it came to a small defile.

All the white men were walking in front, and when the head of the column got round a corner, they suddenly heard a fusillade of guns. At first, the officers of the expedition thought this was meant for a salute, but soon discovered they had been treacherously led into an ambush, and that the carriers were being massacred. The white men then ran back with a view to getting their revolvers out of their boxes, but failed in their efforts. Mr. Phillips, however, did not turn back, he being well round the corner at the head of the column. Then all went forward to close round Mr. Phillips but Major Crawford came back, saying, Mr. Phillips had just been shot dead. Mr. Phillips' orderly then came up and corroborated the statement. The remainder then fell back slowly along the route they had come. They were all unarmed, and the enemy were firing at them on both sides at very close quarters. Major Crawford was then badly hit, and Messrs. Locke, Mailing, Boisragon and Elliot tried to assist him along, as he, Major Crawford, had lost the entire use of his legs through the wound received. Major Crawford was almost immediately hit again, this time fatally; then Mr. Maling fell dead, as did Dr. Elliot shortly afterwards. Mr. Campbell doing his best to rally the carriers, with Messrs. Powis and Gordon, were all shot dead. Messrs. Boisragon and Locke, then seeing that all their companions were killed—they both being wounded—crept into the bush, and after wandering for five days and nights they reached a waterside market, called Ikoru, about twenty miles above Gwato, and were taken down stream in a canoe by a friendly Ijo man who happened to be there. On getting some way down the creek below Gwato they met Mr. Lyon in the steam-launch "Primrose," who was on the look-out for fugitives. Mr. Lyon brought them to the African Association factory in the Benin River, where they now are. During all the time they were wandering in the forest they went without food and drink, except what they could get by sucking the dew off the leaves. Dr. d'Arcy Irvine informed me that they could not have lived another day without food.

Both these officers go home by first opportunity. Mr. Locke has more than completed his year on the coast. They are both progressing very favorably, and out of all danger.

4. All property fell into the hands of the enemy, and those natives who were not shot or cut down were taken as prisoners to the city. I have this day issued an ultimatum to the King, which will be sent by a trustworthy messenger, demanding that all persons and property in his hands shall be given up at once. I have taken care to say nothing further, but issued the ultimatum in chance of saving some lives and recovering private property: whether the King complies or not will make no difference as to making any alteration in the punishment to be inflicted, which cannot be too severe.

5. I held a meeting of the leading Jakri Chiefs today, and thanked them for the loyalty they had shown in assisting the Government during the present crisis. I urged them to continue doing so, saying that all losses in carriers, etc., would be paid for, and their services properly noticed.

I am arranging for carriers and water transport with the Jakri Chiefs of Warri, Benin, and Sapele, so that when I meet Admiral Rawson at Brass, on or about the 30th instant, I can give him full information of carriers, etc., available; and I can also give him my views as to the best points of attack, etc., having a sketch, drawn up by Mr. District Commissioner Burrows, showing the three landing points of Ologbo, Ikuru, and Gwato. Great vigilance is being shown in the way of messengers and spies to report on the King's movements and plans.

6. Before coming here I thought that probably it would be wise to have the assistance of a column of West India troops, but I

am now of an opinion that the navy and Protectorate force are fully able to carry out the object of the expedition. The Bini is not a fighting man, and a great coward into the bargain.

7. . . . Mr. Burrows has done most useful work in surveying the water approaches to Ikuru and Ologbo. Before I arrived, and a few days after the facts of the expedition were known, he took a few men with him and burnt Ologbo. Since receiving your cable, no further forward action will be taken until Mr. Moor's arrival, and I have issued strict orders to that effect. . . .

8. I might add that the station of Sapele and the Benin River factories are perfectly safe. The Benis, not being watermen, cannot leave their mainland, and, in any case, they are too great cowards to do so had they the chance, so there is no fear of any offensive movement on the King's part.

9. I would add that the destruction of Benin city, the removal and punishment of the King, the punishment of the fetish priests, the opening up of the country, etc., will prove a wonderful impetus to trade in this part of the Protectorate, and at the same time do away with a reign of terror and all its accompanying horrors.

10. I proceed to Sapele tomorrow, and then on to Brass and Bonny, where I hope to meet Admiral Rawson about the 30th instant. . . .

11. I do not think the King will offer much resistance as far as actual fighting goes. The people (there being no regular army) are probably only fighting under pressure, and on the first reverse I fancy nearly the whole country will flock in and claim protection. The people live under a heavy yoke of oppression and starvation at times. They are badly armed—chiefly long danes. Captain Boisragon and Mr. Locke say that they saw no rifles on the day the expedition was attacked. If not already removed, the ivory at Benin city should fully pay the cost of the expedition.

I am, etc.

(Signed)   H. L. GALLWEY

Proclamation.

WHEREAS, by the orders of the King of Benin City and his Councillors, a peaceful party of Government officers, whilst proceeding to visit the King, unarmed and unescorted, have been attacked by the soldiery of the King, and seven Europeans and over 200 natives murdered:

Notice is hereby given that steps are about to be taken to punish the King and his people, and that the following rewards will be paid to any person or persons who may capture and hand over to Her Britannic Majesty's Government the persons hereafter mentioned:—

	Puncheons.
King Duboar	50
Ojomo	10
Okrigi	5
Head fetish priest	10
Five fetish priests, of whose importance I shall satisfy myself	5
	each.

45. The Monroe Doctrine, 1823

In his seventh annual message to Congress on the state of the union in December 1823 President James Monroe (1752–1831) announced that the United States was opposed to any expansion of European influence in the Western Hemisphere, either by further colonization or political interference. Two developments prompted this pronouncement. The first came in 1821 when Tsar Alexander I extended the Russian claim to the Pacific coast of northwest America to the 51st parallel and prohibited the ships of other countries from entering coastal waters north of that line. The second was the reaction in 1822 of the Quadruple Alliance (Austria, Russia, France, and Prussia) to the independence movements in Latin America. The rebellions (1810–1822) had broken up the Spanish Empire and had established republics in much of the region from the Rio Grande river to the Straits of Magellan. The Alliance contemplated sending an army to restore the area to Spain in the name of "legitimacy."

In 1823 the British foreign minister, George Canning, suggested to the American minister in London that the two countries issue a joint statement opposing any interference by the Alliance powers in South America. Canning also proposed that the United States and Britain agree not to annex any part of the old Spanish Empire and not recognize the new republics. The joint statement was tempting, but the United States had already recognized the new republics, had no wish to rule out future annexations and had no desire to assist the British in retaining their South American trade. Although former Presidents (and fellow Virginians) Thomas Jefferson and James Madison advised Monroe to accept a joint statement with Britain, the President decided instead to follow the recommendation of Secretary of State John Quincy Adams. Adams urged Monroe to act independently, and not "come in as a cockboat in the wake of the British man-of-war."

Both the short term and long term results of Monroe's decision proved to be favorable for the United States. The United States did not yet have the power to enforce its new policy, but fortunately no European power was interested in challenging it. Russia decided against colonizing North America and signed a treaty with the United States in 1824 which scaled back the Russian coastal claim to 54/40 north latitude and removed the restrictions on foreign shipping. The other European nations were busy building empires elsewhere in the world and chose not to compete with Great Britain or the United States for preeminence in Latin America.

QUESTIONS

1. According to this document, what is the policy of the United States toward European colonization of the western hemisphere?
2. What is Monroe's attitude toward the countries in Latin America that had recently broken away from European control? How does he view possible European intervention in those countries?

3. What are Monroe's views on American involvement in European politics and wars? Is his view consistent with previous American policy toward Europe?

. . . At the proposal of the Russian Imperial Government, made through the minister of the Emperor residing here, a full power and instructions have been transmitted to the minister of the United States at St. Petersburg to arrange by amicable negotiation the respective rights and interests of the two nations on the northwest coast of this continent. A similar proposal had been made by His Imperial Majesty to the Government of Great Britain, which has likewise been acceded to. The Government of the United States has been desirous by this friendly proceeding of manifesting the great value which they have invariably attached to the friendship of the Emperor and their solicitude to cultivate the best understanding with his Government. In the discussions to which this interest has given rise and in the arrangements by which they may terminate the occasion has been judged proper for asserting, as a principle in which the rights and interests of the United States are involved, that the American continents, by the free and independent condition which they have assumed and maintain, are henceforth not to be considered as subjects for future colonization by any European powers. . . .

In the West Indies and the Gulf of Mexico our naval force has been augmented by the addition of several small vessels provided for by the "act authorizing an additional naval force for the suppression of piracy," passed by Congress at their last session. That armament has been eminently successful in the accomplishment of its object. The piracies by which our commerce in the neighborhood of the Island of Cuba had been afflicted have been repressed and the confidence of our merchants in a great measure restored. . . .

It is a source of great satisfaction that we are always enabled to recur to the conduct of our Navy with pride and commendation. As a means of national defense it enjoys the public confidence, and is steadily assuming additional importance. . . .

A strong hope has been long entertained, founded on the heroic struggle of the Greeks, that they would succeed in their contest and resume their equal station among the nations of the earth. It is believed that the whole civilized world take a deep interest in their welfare. Although no power has declared in their favor, yet none, according to our information, has taken part against them. Their cause and their name have protected them from dangers which might ere this have overwhelmed any other people. The ordinary calculations of interest and acquisition with a view to aggrandizement, which mingles so much in the transactions of nations, seem to have had no effect in the regard to them. From the facts which have come to our knowledge there is good cause to believe that their enemy has lost forever all dominion over them; that Greece will become again an independent nation. That she may obtain that rank is the object of our most ardent wishes.

. . . Of the events in that quarter of the globe, with which we have so much intercourse and from which we derive our origin, we have always been anxious and interested spectators. The citizens of the United States cherish sentiments the most friendly in favor of liberty and happiness of their fellow men on that side of the Atlantic.

In the wars of the European powers in matters relating to themselves we have never taken any part, nor does it comport with our policy so to do. It is only when our rights are invaded or seriously menaced that we resent injuries or make preparation for our defence. With the movements in this hemisphere we are of necessity more immediately connected, and by causes which must be obvious to all enlightened and impartial observers. The political system of the allied powers is essentially different in this respect from that of America. This difference proceeds from that which exists in their respective Governments; and to the defence of our own, which has been achieved by the loss of so much blood and treasure, and matured by the wisdom of their most enlightened citizens, under which we have enjoyed unexampled felicity, this whole nation is devoted. We owe it, therefore, to candor and to the amicable relations existing between the United States and those powers to declare that we should consider any attempt on their part to extend their system to any portion of this hemisphere as dangerous to our peace and safety. With the existing colonies or dependencies of any European power we have not interfered and shall not interfere. But with the Governments who have declared their independence and maintained it, and whose independence we have, on great consideration and on just principles, acknowledged, we could not view any interposition for the purpose of oppressing them, or controlling in any other manner their destiny, by any European power in any other light than as the manifestation of an unfriendly disposition toward the United States. In the war between those new Governments and Spain we declared our neutrality at the time of their recognition, and to this we have adhered, and shall continue to adhere, provided no change shall occur which, in the judgment of the competent authorities of this Government, shall make a corresponding change on the part of the United States indispensable to their security.

The late events in Spain and Portugal show that Europe is still unsettled. Of this important fact no stronger proof can be adduced than that the allied powers should have thought it proper, on any principle satisfactory to themselves, to have interposed by force in the internal concerns of Spain. To what extent interposition may be carried, on the same principle, is a question in which all independent powers whose governments differ from theirs are interested, even those most remote, and surely none more so than the United States. Our policy in regard to Europe, which was adopted in the early stage of the wars which have so long agitated that quarter of the globe, nevertheless remains the same, which is; not to interfere with the internal concerns of any of its powers; to consider the government *de facto* as the legitimate government for us; to cultivate friendly relations with it, and to preserve those relations by a frank, firm, and manly policy, meeting in all instances the just claims of every power, submitting to injuries from none. But in regard to those continents circumstances are eminently and conspicuously different. It is impossible that the allied powers should extend their political system to any portion of either continent without endangering our peace and happiness; nor can anyone believe that our southern brethren, if left to themselves, would adopt it of their own accord. It is equally impossible, therefore, that we should behold such interposition in any form with indifference. If we look to the comparative strength and resources of Spain and those new Governments, and their distance from each other, it must be obvious that she can never subdue them. It is still the true policy of the United States to leave the parties to themselves in the hope that other powers will pursue the same course.

46. Message to Congress on War with Spain, 1898

William McKinley

Because of Cuba's proximity to the United States the political status of that Spanish colony had been a vital concern for American diplomats since the early nineteenth century. At the time of the announcement of the Monroe Doctrine Secretary of State John Quincy Adams had stated the opposition of the United States to any transfer of Cuba from Spain to any other European power. During the mid-1850s northern antislavery forces blocked President Franklin Pierce's attempt to acquire Cuba. After the Civil War a series of rebellions against Spanish rule created difficulties for the United States as violence on the island threatened American investments and lives. Although there was considerable sympathy in the United States for the cause of the revolutionaries, American officials were reluctant to intervene. A renewed Cuban crisis intensified during the mid-1890s. After President William McKinley (1843–1901) took office in 1897 he at first resisted public pressure for military action. But in the spring of 1898 he finally became convinced that the use of force by the United States would provide the only acceptable resolution for the problem of insurrection in Cuba. The following excerpts from his war message present his reasons for military intervention.

QUESTIONS

1. How does President McKinley justify American intervention in Cuba?
2. What is McKinley's attitude toward recognizing the independence of Cuba?
3. What is the meaning of his references to the sinking of the *Maine*? How does he make use of that incident to support his case for intervention?
4. What is McKinley's attitude toward the competency of the Spanish government?
5. Is there any indication that the Spanish government was on the brink of capitulating to American demands?

Our people have beheld a once prosperous community reduced to comparative want, its lucrative commerce virtually paralyzed, its exceptional productiveness diminished, its fields laid waste, its mills in ruins, and its people perishing by tens of thousands from hunger and destitution. We have found ourselves constrained, in the observance of that strict neutrality which our laws enjoin and which the law of nations commands, to police our own waters and watch our own seaports in prevention of any unlawful act in aid of the Cubans.

Our trade has suffered, the capital invested by our citizens in Cuba has been largely lost, and the temper and forbearance of our people have been so sorely tried as to beget a perilous unrest among our own citizens, which has inevitably found its expression from time to time in the National

Legislature, so that issues wholly external to our own body politic engross attention and stand in the way of that close devotion to domestic advancement that becomes a self-contained commonwealth whose primal maxim has been the avoidance of all foreign entanglements. All this must needs awaken, and has, indeed, aroused, the utmost concern on the part of this Government, as well during my predecessor's term as in my own. . . .

The efforts of Spain were increased, both by the dispatch of fresh levies to Cuba and by the addition to the horrors of the strife of a new and inhuman phase happily unprecedented in the modern history of civilized Christian peoples. The policy of devastation and concentration, inaugurated by the Captain-General's *bando* of October 21, 1896, in the province of Pinar del Rio was thence extended to embrace all of the island to which the power of the Spanish arms was able to reach by occupation or by military operations. The peasantry, including all dwelling in the open agricultural interior, were driven into the garrison towns or isolated places held by the troops.

The raising and movement of provisions of all kinds were interdicted. The fields were laid waste, dwellings unroofed and fired, mills destroyed, and, in short, everything that could desolate the land and render it unfit for human habitation or support was commanded by one or the other of the contending parties and executed by all the powers at their disposal. . . .

The agricultural population to the estimated number of 300,000 or more was herded within the towns and their immediate vicinage, deprived of the means of support, rendered destitute of shelter, left poorly clad, and exposed to the most unsanitary conditions. As the scarcity of food increased with the devastation of the depopulated areas of production, destitution and want became misery and starvation. Month by month the death rate increased in an alarming ratio. By March, 1897, according to conservative estimates from official Spanish sources, the mortality among the *reconcentrados* from starvation and the diseases thereto incident exceeded 50 percent of their total number.

The war in Cuba is of such nature that, short of subjugation or extermination, a final military victory for either side seems impracticable. The alternative lies in the physical exhaustion of one or the other party, or perhaps of both—a condition which in effect ended the ten years' war by the truce of Zanjon. The prospect of such a protraction and conclusion of the present strife is a contingency hardly to be contemplated with equanimity by the civilized world, and least of all by the United States, affected and injured as we are, deeply and intimately, by its very existence.

Realizing this, it appeared to be my duty, in a spirit of true friendliness, no less to Spain than to the Cubans, who have so much to lose by the prolongation of the struggle, to seek to bring about an immediate termination of the war. To this end I submitted on the 27th ultimo, as a result of much representation and correspondence, through the United States minister at Madrid, propositions to the Spanish Government looking to an armistice until October 1 for the negotiation of peace with the good offices of the President.

In addition I asked the immediate revocation of the order of reconcentration, so as to permit the people to return to their farms and the needy to be relieved with provisions and supplies from the United States, cooperating with the Spanish authorities, so as to afford full relief.

The reply of the Spanish cabinet was received on the night of the 31st ultimo. It offered, as the means to bring about peace in Cuba, to confide the preparation thereof to the insular parliament, inasmuch as the concurrence of that body would be necessary to reach a final result, it being, however, understood that the powers reserved by the constitution to the central Government are not lessened or diminished. As the Cuban parliament does not meet until the 4th of May next, the Spanish Government would not object for its part to accept at once a suspension of hostilities if asked for by the insurgents from the general in chief, to whom it would pertain in such case to determine the duration and conditions of the armistice. . . .

With this last overture in the direction of immediate peace, and its disappointing reception by Spain, the Executive is brought to the end of his effort. . . .

Nor from the standpoint of expediency do I think it would be wise or prudent for this Government to recognize at the present time the independence of the so-called Cuban Republic. Such recognition is not necessary in order to enable the United States to intervene and pacify the island. To commit this country now to the recognition of any particular government in Cuba might subject us to embarrassing conditions of international obligation toward the organization so recognized. In case of intervention our conduct would be subject to the approval or disapproval of such government. We would be required to submit to its direction and to assume to it the mere relation of a friendly ally.

When it shall appear hereafter that there is within the island a government capable of performing the duties and discharging the functions of a separate nation, and having as a matter of fact the proper forms and attributes of nationality, such government can be promptly and readily recognized and the relations and interests of the United States with such nation adjusted. . . .

The forcible intervention of the United States as a neutral to stop the war, according to the large dictates of humanity and following many historical precedents where neighboring states have interfered to check the hopeless sacrifices of life by internecine conflicts beyond their borders, is justifiable on rational grounds. It involves, however, hostile constraint upon both the parties to the contest, as well to enforce a truce as to guide the eventual settlement.

The grounds for such intervention may be briefly summarized as follows:

First. In the cause of humanity and to put an end to the barbarities, bloodshed, starvation, and horrible miseries now existing there, and which the parties of the conflict are either unable or unwilling to stop or mitigate. It is no answer to say this is all in another country, belonging to another nation, and is therefore none of our business. It is specially our duty, for it is right at our door.

Second. We owe it to our citizens in Cuba to afford them that protection and indemnity for life and property which no government there can or will afford, and to that end to terminate the conditions that deprive them of legal protection.

Third. The right to intervene may be justified by the very serious injury to the commerce, trade, and business of our people and by the wanton destruction of property and devastation of the island.

Fourth, and which is of the utmost importance, the present condition of affairs in Cuba is a constant menace to our peace and entails upon this Government an enormous expence. With such a conflict waged for years in an island so near us and with which our people have such trade and business relations; when the lives and liberty of our citizens are in constant danger and their property destroyed and themselves ruined; where our trading vessels are liable to seizure and are seized at our very door by war ships of a foreign nation; the expeditions of filibustering that we are powerless to prevent altogether, and the irritating questions and entanglements thus arising—all these others that I need not mention, with the resulting strained relations, are a constant menace to our peace and compel us to keep on a semi war footing with a nation with which we are at peace.

These elements of danger and disorder already pointed out have been strikingly illustrated by a tragic event which has deeply and justly moved the American people. I have already transmitted to Congress the report of the naval court of inquiry on the destruction of the battleship *Maine* in the harbor of Havana during the night of the 15th of February. The destruction of that noble vessel has filled the national heart with inexpressible horror. Two hundred and fifty-eight brave sailors and marines and two officers of our Navy, reposing in the fancied security of a friendly harbor, have been hurled to death, grief and want brought to their homes and sorrow to the nation.

The naval court of inquiry, which, it is needless to say, commands the unqualified confidence of the Government, was unanimous in its conclusion that the destruction of the *Maine* was caused by an exterior explosion—that of a submarine mine. It did not assume to place the responsibility. That remains to be fixed.

In any event, the destruction of the *Maine,* by whatever exterior cause, is a patent and impressive proof of a state of things in Cuba that is intolerable. That condition is thus shown to be such that the Spanish Government can not assure safety and security to a vessel of the American Navy in the harbor of Havana on a mission of peace, and rightfully there.

Further referring in this connection to recent diplomatic correspondence, a dispatch from our minister to Spain of the 26th ultimo contained the statement that the Spanish minister for foreign affairs assured

him positively that Spain will do all that the highest honor and justice require in the matter of the *Maine.* The reply above referred to, of the 31st ultimo, also contained an expression of the readiness of Spain to submit to an arbitration all the differences which can arise in this matter, which is subsequently explained by the note of the Spanish minister at Washington of the 10th instant, as follows:

"As to the question of the fact which springs from the diversity of views between the reports of the American and Spanish boards, Spain proposes that the facts be ascertained by an impartial investigation by experts, whose decision Spain accepts in advance."

To this I have made no reply. . . .

The long trial has proved that the object for which Spain has waged the war can not be obtained. The fire of insurrection may flame or may smolder with varying seasons, but it has not been and it is plain that it can not be extinguished by present methods. The only hope of relief and repose from a condition which can no longer be endured is the enforced pacification of Cuba. In the name of humanity, in the name of civilization, in the behalf of endangered American interests which give us the right and the duty to speak and to act, the war in Cuba must stop.

In view of these facts and of these considerations I ask the Congress to authorize and empower the President to take measures to secure a full and final termination of hostilities between the Government of Spain and the people of Cuba, and to secure in the island the establishment of a stable government, capable of maintaining order and observing its international obligations, as well as our own, and to use the military and naval forces of the United States as may be necessary for these purposes. . . .

Yesterday, and since the preparation of the foregoing message, official information was received by me that the latest decree of the Queen Regent of Spain directs General Blanco, in order to prepare and facilitate peace, to proclaim a suspension of hostilities, the duration and details of which have not yet been communicated to me.

This fact, with every other pertinent consideration, will, I am sure, have your just and careful attention in the solemn deliberations upon which you are about to enter. If this measure attains a successful result, then our aspirations as a Christian, peace-loving people will be realized. If it fails, it will be only another justification for our contemplated action.

47. Land and Liberty for Mexico, 1911

Emiliano Zapata

Emiliano Zapata (1877?–1919) was a Mexican revolutionary leader who championed agrarian reform for his country. Born in San Miguel Anenecuilco (now Anenecuilco de los Zapata) in Morelos State, he was a small landowner and local officeholder of Indian descent. In 1910 he recruited an army of Indians from local villages and haciendas and joined with Francisco Madero in a revolt against the Mexican president, Porfirio Díaz. Madero issued his Plan of San Luis Potosí, which called for political reforms, and became president of the nation in 1911. Zapata soon became disenchanted with Madero's policies, and that year he issued his Plan of Ayala, excerpts of which appear below. After Madero was murdered Zapata opposed the succeeding regimes of Victoriano Huerta and Venustiano Carranza. For a while he and his supporters controlled much of southern Mexico, and in 1914 he joined with Francisco (Pancho) Villa in a successful occupation of Mexico City. But during the following year he retreated to his home state of Morelos, where he was murdered by an agent of Carranza in 1919.

QUESTIONS

1. What precisely does Zapata propose in this plan? How does he justify it?
2. Compare his program with that of Sun Yat-sen. What do these manifestos suggest about common themes and differences in the Mexican and Chinese revolutions?

The Liberating Plan of the sons of the State of Morelos, members of the insurgent army that demands the fulfillment of the Plan of San Luis Potosí, as well as other reforms that it judges convenient and necessary for the welfare of the Mexican nation.

We, the undersigned, constituted as a Revolutionary Junta, in order to maintain and obtain the fulfillment of the promises made by the revolution of November 20, 1910, solemnly proclaim in the face of the civilized world . . . , so that it may judge us, the principles that we have formulated in order to destroy the tyranny that oppresses us. . . .

　1. . . . Considering that the President of the Republic, Señor Don Francisco I. Madero, has made a bloody mockery of Effective Suffrage by . . . entering into an infamous alliance with the *científicos* [professionals or business persons who believed in technological progress according to the U.S./European model], the *hacendados* [owners of large estates], the feudalists, and oppressive *caciques* [local political strongmen], enemies of the Revolution that he proclaimed, in order to forge the chains of a new dictatorship more hateful and terrible than that of Porfirio Díaz . . . : For these reasons we declare the said Francisco I. Madero unfit to carry out the promises of the Revolution of which he was the author. . . .

　4. The Revolutionary Junta of the State of Morelos formally proclaims to the Mexican people:

　That it endorses the Plan of San Luis Potosí with the additions stated below for the benefit of the oppressed peoples, and that it will defend its principles until victory or death. . . .

　As an additional part of the Plan we proclaim, be it known: that the lands, woods, and waters usurped by the *hacendados, científicos,* or *caciques* through tyranny and venal justice henceforth belong to the towns or citizens who have corresponding titles to these properties, of which they were despoiled by the bad faith of our oppressors. They shall retain possession of the said properties at all costs, arms in hand. The usurpers who think they have a right to the said lands may state their claims before special tribunals to be established upon the triumph of the Revolution. . . .

　7. Since the immense majority of Mexican towns and citizens own nothing but the ground on which they stand and endure a miserable existence, denied the opportunity to improve their social condition or to devote themselves to industry or agriculture because a few individuals monopolize the lands, woods, and waters—for these reasons the great estates shall be expropriated, with indemnification to the owners of one third of such monopolies, in order that the towns and citizens of Mexico may obtain *ejidos* [land owned communally by Indians from pre-Columbian times], colonies, town sites, and arable lands. Thus the welfare of the Mexican people shall be promoted in all respects.

　8. The properties of those *hacendados, científicos,* or *caciques* who directly or indirectly oppose the present Plan shall be seized by the nation, and two thirds of their value shall be used for war indemnities and pensions for the widows and orphans of the soldiers who may perish in the struggle for this Plan.

　9. In proceeding against the above properties there shall be applied the laws of disentail and nationalization, as may be convenient, using as our precept and example the laws enforced by the immortal [Benito] Juarez [1806–1872] against Church property [which outlawed church ownership of land]—laws that taught a painful lesson to the despots and conservatives who at all times have sought to fasten upon the people the yoke of oppression and backwardness.

INTRODUCTION TO UNIT FIVE

World War I and Its Aftermath

The outbreak of the Great War in the summer of 1914 proved to be one of the most momentous events in the history of Western civilization. Its causes were deeply rooted in the imperial and national rivalries and alliances of the late nineteenth and early twentieth centuries. Its political, social, and economic consequences were vast. The conflict lasted for more than four years, involving thirty sovereign states. Intermittent fighting continued in Eastern Europe, Russia, and the Near East after the Armistice of 1918; the peace-making process extended until 1923. The catastrophe destroyed four empires and gave birth to seven new nations. It marked the end of the age of innocence for Europe and the United States. The agreements that ended this struggle (particularly the Treaty of Versailles) were designed to ensure peace for generations to come, but within twenty years a second and even deadlier conflagration engulfed the world. The Great War was then renamed World War I. Today both world wars may be viewed as part of a continuing crisis which ultimately ended nearly five centuries of European hegemony around the globe.

In Europe during the early 1900s two heavily armed groups of nations faced each other amidst an atmosphere of tension. Germany, Austria-Hungary, and Italy (the Triple Alliance) squared off against the Triple Entente of France, Russia, and Britain. Any diplomatic incident tended to become a test of strength between the two alliances. Even minor conflicts threatened to escalate into full-scale war. In a sense, the alliance system was only a symptom of a deeper problem. Each European nation depended upon a global marketplace, but there was no worldwide political system that could guarantee fair participation for all nations. Each power had to look out for its own interests. The result was the drive for colonies and the quest for allies and binding alliances that would bolster security for each state.

While diplomatic historians tend to see foreign relations and alliances as paramount in bringing on the war, domestic policies and internal crises were also important factors in 1914. Since 1890 domestic tension had been rising concomitantly with international stresses, and the two forces had reacted upon each other in all of the nations that became belligerents in the Great War. Statesmen viewed foreign clashes as political conveniences which permitted them to rally their populations in patriotic union while distracting them from problems at home. Almost every European nation witnessed the erosion of the moderate, stabilizing center in politics with displacements to the ideological extremes of radicalism or reaction. The governments ranged from moderate liberal in Britain to reactionary in Germany and Russia, and all felt themselves to be under attack from socialist forces.

While many leaders saw war as the way out of their political predicament, some worried about its domestic consequences. Most conservatives and reactionaries viewed a short and victorious war as both the antidote to social revolution and the best means to thwart their neighbors from growing stronger. But others feared that a prolonged war would prove to be too strenuous for their brittle societies and fragile empires and would unleash the forces of change. Whereas moderates and liberals tended to see war as the catalyst of radicalism and revolution, democrats, radicals, and socialists were concerned that it would bring reaction and despotism.

In England a triple threat loomed in the summer of 1914. Labor leaders prepared for a massive general strike, rebellion and civil war over home rule threatened the peace in Ireland, and suffragettes staged relentless agitations and demonstrations demanding the right to vote for women. In France the government feared a socialist upheaval. In Germany a revolutionary situation had been ripening at least since 1912, when the Social Democrats became the largest single party in the Reichstag and pressed vigorously for a genuinely democratic constitution to replace traditions of despotism, aristocratic privilege, and militarism. A similar situation existed in Austria-Hungary, but there it was also confounded by the national demands for independence by Czechs, Poles, Serbs, and other nationalities within the Empire. In Russia the Tsar's regime was wracked by similar fears, industrial disturbances, and the memory of the Revolution of 1905. Nor was Italy immune: political insurgency and labor unrest culminated in the explosive strike of "Red Week," in June 1914.

The spark that set off the Great War came on June 28, 1914, when a Serbian revolutionary assassinated Archduke Francis Ferdinand, heir to the throne of Austria-Hungary. The killing occurred in Sarajevo, Bosnia, which was part of the Austro-Hungarian Empire. The Austrians, seeing an opportunity for a quick and easy triumph at home and abroad, blamed Serbia for the incident. Tragically, the alliance system magnified a local Balkan incident into a catastrophe within a few weeks. Russia supported the Serbs, while Germany backed Austria. For the German leaders the war offered an opportunity to secure their nation's borders and expand its political and economic power in both the west and the east (see Document 49). France joined the Russian side against Germany. After some hesitation and futile attempts at negotiation, Great Britain joined France and Russia. Italy held back and eventually joined the Allies in 1915, while the Ottoman Empire joined the Central Powers because of its traditional hostility toward Russia. The logic of the alliance system and internal pressures created a momentum toward world war which could not be stopped.

Never before had there been a struggle so gigantic, so deadly, and so costly. The leaders expected a short war, but instead they faced the horror of a nightmare as the opposing armies fought to a deadly stalemate in northern France. The alliance system itself guaranteed that the war would not be decided swiftly; victory would be earned by the side that could amass the greatest combination of military, financial, industrial, and technological resources. A century before in 1815 152,000 men had fought in the Battle of Waterloo; the first battle of the Marne in 1914 engaged over one million. At Verdun in 1916 German and French forces fought for 302 days, in what is still the most massive single battle in history, with casualties exceeding a million on each side. Estimates of the human costs of the entire war range from 8.5 to 10 million men killed in combat, 20–29 million wounded, captured, or missing, and millions of noncombatant deaths due to disease, privation, massacre, and revolution. Economically the direct cost of the war was 200 billion dollars; the indirect costs amounted to 150 billion dollars in interest payments, veterans' care, and related items.

Ultimately the outcome of the Great War hinged on the role of the United States, but in 1914 President Woodrow Wilson and congressional leaders agreed on a strategy of neutrality that was consistent with the nation's traditional policy of avoiding entanglements in European power politics. The conflict offered a golden opportunity for the United States to profit through trade with both sides. Americans insisted upon the rights of neutral carriers, but in practice the British dominance on the seas meant that most of the trade wound up in Allied ports. Moreover, when the Allies ran short of cash the United States extended liberal credit. That state of affairs infuriated the Central Powers, and before long German submarine attacks on British and French passenger and merchant ships created a crisis because of the loss of American lives on Allied ships that were sunk by German torpedoes. After repeated protests by the United States, Germany pledged that her submarines would observe the rules of warning and would visit and search all merchant vessels both within and outside war zones. But at the same time that nation insisted that the United States must force Britain to ease her blockade of Europe. Wilson and other leaders then attempted mediation to end the war, but the British refused to settle for his formula of "peace without victory." Early in 1917 Germany made the fateful decision to resume submarine attacks against all shipping, including vessels of the United States. That action led to Wilson's call in April for a declaration of war against Germany. American intervention supplied the Allies with an enormous psychological boost, but it took more than one year for the United States to mobilize its forces effectively in Europe. The added pressure of the American entry into the war took its toll, and after the failure of Germany's spring offensive, Germany surrendered at the eleventh hour of the eleventh day of the eleventh month, 1918.

When Wilson decided to ask Congress to declare war against Germany, he also dedicated himself and the United States to transform the struggle into a crusade to achieve a liberal and lasting peace program. In January 1918 he announced his Fourteen Points (see Document 51), in which he called for open diplomacy, freedom of the seas, free trade, disarmament, impartial settlement of colonial claims including consideration of the interests of inhabitants, and the creation of a League of Nations to guarantee security for all nations in the future. In 1919 he carried the hopes of liberals with him to Europe as he led the American delegation to Paris to negotiate the peace treaty that ended the Great War.

In preparing for the Paris Peace Conference, the heads of state studied the work and results of the Congress of Vienna of 1814–1815. In 1918–1919, as in 1814–1815, the diplomats sought to resolve a multilateral, limitless, ideological conflict and to redraw the map drastically and legitimize many new boundaries and new nation-states. They also wished to prevent the defeated aggressor from disturbing the peace again and to find new methods and institutions to preserve the general peace and the balance of power within a system of collective security. At the same time, of course, each power pursued its own national interest and political aims. The British delegation, led by David Lloyd George, was especially conscious of the parallels with 1814–1815. The American contingent, led by Wilson, rejected the validity of the Vienna settlement. Wilson viewed that accord as a work of reaction that restored monarchy and arbitrary government. He lobbied for a "New Diplomacy," which featured democratization and national self-determination as the proper goals of the conference.

The statesmen who gathered at Versailles struggled with problems that were enormous in scope and immensely complex. The Great War which had just concluded had been fought on a scale unprecedented in world history, and it had profoundly shaken the foundations of political, social, and economic life around the globe. One of the great differences between the two conferences at Paris and at Vienna was the power of mass public opinion in the modern era. Hence the statesmen at Versailles, quite unlike their predecessors, kept their attention focused as much on public opinion polls, newspaper editorials, and the activities of parliamentary opposition parties as on the traditional tasks of diplomacy in negotiating such matters as frontiers, reparations, colonies, the size of military forces, etc. Participants were profoundly conscious of the world crisis unleashed by the communist revolution in Russia, and they feared that it would spread to Germany and the new states carved out of the former Hapsburg empire. The diplomats wished to establish stable governments and societies on the sites of the defeated regimes. At the same time they aimed to punish the vanquished parties and to contain—and perhaps even overthrow by military force—the communist government of Lenin. The specter of Bolshevism haunted the conference; in an important sense, the policy of containment, the Cold War, and the division of the world into two ideological camps dates back not to the breakup of the World War II Allies, but to 1917–1919.

Under the pressure applied by his skilled European counterparts, who were guided by principles of power politics, Wilson was forced to compromise on a number of his Fourteen Points. In the end the Treaty of Versailles forced unilateral disarmament on Germany and also compelled her to give up some territory to allow Poland access to the sea and to restore Alsace-Lorraine to France.

The terms of the treaty also held Germany responsible for starting the war and imposed heavy penalties of indemnities and reparations. In addition, the Allies and Japan took control of Germany's colonies. Wilson conceded many points in the negotiations in exchange for the creation of the League of Nations. But although he expected that the new organization would resolve many of the remaining conflicts, his hopes for a new world order were dashed when the United States Senate refused to ratify the treaty (see Document 54).

Japan championed its own interests at the Paris Peace Conference, where it demanded a proclamation of racial equality, which was vetoed by the lone vote of the Australian representative. The Treaty of Versailles gave Japan predominance in China's Shantung peninsula, retention of similar claims in Manchuria and Mongolia, and, as League mandates, possession of the former German islands. This betrayed the Chinese, who had also declared war on Germany and who explained to the Peace Conference that the Japanese Twenty-One Demands of May 1915 were invalid since that ultimatum was forced on them (see Document 50). But those Chinese protests were to no avail. The Japanese had often taken satisfaction in explaining to the Americans that her Chinese policy was comparable to the Monroe Doctrine. Japan was thus the least scathed and most rewarded of the belligerents of World War I. Her Twenty-One Demands on China in 1915 set the stage for her aggression against that nation in the 1930s and her attacks on United States and British possessions in 1941.

The Great War had many domestic and foreign consequences. On the home fronts the wartime emergency compelled governments to take charge of production, and transportation and communications systems. In so doing they weakened traditional *laissez-faire* policies, and they established crucial precedents for future legislation during the next major crisis—the Great Depression. Furthermore, World War I also led directly to the final triumph of women's suffrage in many Western countries, especially Great Britain and the United States. In England, for example, by 1900 women had won significant gains in law, education, and employment (in teaching, nursing, and typing) as well as the right to vote and hold office on school boards and other local governmental bodies. But they were excluded from the parliamentary franchise and national politics, causing a great reservoir of frustration and animosity to be dammed up against the male world. English suffragists were part of a worldwide struggle for women's rights. They were buoyed up by female acquisition of the vote in some of the western states of the United States, Australian provinces, New Zealand, Finland, and Norway. As a result of their militancy plus the wartime demand for women's labor in critical industries, they finally achieved their goal (see Document 48). In Great Britain in 1918 an act enfranchised women over thirty, but with some property qualifications; in 1928 the "flapper franchise" gave women over twenty-one the vote on the same terms with men. In the United States the Nineteenth Amendment to the federal Constitution (ratified in 1920) secured that right for American women.

The Great War and the results of the Paris Peace Conference led directly to the collapse of the Austro-Hungarian, Ottoman, Russian, and German empires.

Charles I, the last Habsburg emperor of Austria, abdicated in November 1918. Austria and Hungary then became separate republics, and the new states of Czechoslovakia, Poland, Yugoslavia, and an enlarged Romania entered the family of nations. Thus in Central and Eastern Europe the principle of national self-determination for ethnic groups was at least partially realized. In the eastern Mediterranean and Near East, the Ottoman Empire disintegrated. Turkey emerged as a republic confined to Constantinople and Asia Minor, while Syria and Lebanon went to France as mandate states under the League of Nations. Great Britain held control over Palestine and Iraq under the same formula, and by the Balfour Declaration of 1917 had pledged to facilitate the restoration of the Jews to their ancient homeland.

The Great War offered a challenge that the tsarist government of Russia could not meet. As the old regime of Tsar Nicholas II toppled, a faction of moderate constitutionalists led by Alexander Kerensky took control in March 1917. That government struggled against socialist and communist revolutionaries for control of the country. A faction of Bolsheviks led by Vladimir I. Lenin defeated the rival groups and seized power in November 1917 (see Document 52). Lenin triumphed in large part because he offered desperate soldiers, peasant farmers, and workers "peace, land, and bread." Victories by the Germans over the Russians had contributed to the collapse of the tsarist government, and in the Treaty of Brest-Litovsk (March 1918) the Bolsheviks were forced to surrender control over the Baltic provinces, Poland, Transcaucasia, and Ukraine. The treaty was a humiliating diktat for the Russians.

The concessions granted to the Germans in 1918 proved to be only a temporary setback to the Bolsheviks. After the defeat of Germany in the West they moved quickly to crush domestic opposition and to launch a new empire, the Soviet Union, reconquering Ukraine but not Poland or the Baltic states. Over the next few years Lenin and his supporters defeated the Whites, a coalition of tsarist reactionaries, liberal democrats, and moderate socialists. Their tactics included the use of the Red Army; a terroristic campaign of mass executions conducted by their secret police, the Cheka; and a social and economic policy that featured nationalization of large industries and food requisitions. In 1922 the Bolsheviks reestablished control over Russia, Ukraine, Belarus, and Transcaucasia and proclaimed the creation of the Union of Soviet Socialist Republics. Although the communist leadership recognized the cultural autonomy of dozens of nationalities, they also established a totalitarian state that severely curtailed political rights in the new state (see Document 53).

The struggle that followed the death of Lenin brought Joseph Stalin to power. In 1928 he announced a Five-Year Plan of rapid industrialization that aimed at the modernization of the Soviet Union without dependency on foreign loans (see Document 55). His program required a reversal of the preceding policy of permitting private trading by small businesses and farmers. Now a severe plan of forced collectivization of agriculture led to great hardships and mass death through famine among the agrarian population, especially in Ukraine (see Document 56). During the 1930s Stalin tightened his control over the communist party and the nation through a series of brutal political purges. He arranged for the execution of many old revolutionaries, and his political and economic policies cost the lives of millions. After his death in 1953, the new leader of the Soviet Union exposed his crimes in a speech to a communist party meeting (see Document 57).

A final consequence of the Great War was the instability in Germany, which contributed to the outbreak of World War II in 1939. A revolution against Kaiser Wilhelm II had led to his abdication and the surrender of Germany in 1918. The new regime, the Weimar Republic, was a mildly socialist government which reluctantly signed the Treaty of Versailles. No one in Germany accepted the terms of that agreement as just or final, especially the war guilt clause and the heavy reparations required. Germany's new leaders now turned to better relations with the Soviet Union, but a ruinous inflation in 1923 threatened to send the nation into chaos. A new round of financial and diplomatic agreements gave the Weimar Republic a temporary reprieve, but the onset of a worldwide depression in the early 1930s doomed that experiment in democracy.

Adolf Hitler and his National Socialist Party came to power in 1933, and for the remaining years of the decade he and his fellow Nazis rebuilt Germany into a political, economic, diplomatic, and military powerhouse. On the domestic front he began a program of close cooperation between private industry and government that featured mass public works projects and large-scale rearmament. He also orchestrated a propaganda campaign that singled out Jews for special attacks and in which he glorified himself as the absolute leader of a totalitarian state. In addition, he stressed autarky (self-sufficiency) and economic nationalism and pressed for a foreign policy of expansion and war (see Document 58). After repudiating the treaties of Versailles and St. Germain, he prepared for a war that would reverse the humiliating defeat of the Great War and secure a new enlarged German empire. The non-aggression pact which he negotiated with the Soviet Union in 1939 was a death warrant for Poland that led directly to the invasion and joint occupation of that nation by both powers (see Document 59). The Second World War had begun.

48. My Own Story

Emmeline Pankhurst, 1914

The Pankhurst family of England led the fight for equal rights for women during the late nineteenth and early twentieth centuries. Emmeline (1858–1928) remembered that as a child she collected donations to assist the recently emancipated blacks in the United States, and she grew up in a household that was devoted to Irish home rule, the Labour Party, and the enfranchisement and equality of women. Her husband Richard (a friend of Mill) and their daughters

Christabel, Sylvia, and Adela, devoted themselves to these same causes. She served her apprenticeship for her lifelong career as reform activist in Manchester, England. There she toiled as a poor law guardian, registrar of births and deaths, and school board member, before founding and leading the Women's Social and Political Union in 1903, five years after she was widowed. From the start the WSPU was militant, independent and aloof from all of the political parties, admitted only women, and was dedicated to action, not mere words. She and Christabel (who had earned a law degree but as a woman was barred from practicing in the courts) had a combined genius for organization and eloquence, and public relations. Many tactics they devised became standard forms of protest and agitation. These included calling "women's parliaments," chaining themselves to fences and gates, conducting parades and petition-bearing processions, holding hunger strikes when held as prisoners, propagating their cause through numerous pamphlets and their own newspaper *The Suffragette,* and destroying property through arson, detonating bombs, breaking windows by throwing stones, marring works of art, pouring acid on golf greens, and cutting telegraph and telephone wires. They also boycotted and sabotaged the 1910 census, scrawling "No vote, No census" on the form, and proclaiming "since we don't count, don't count us"—a type of defiance for which there was no penalty under the law. In 1913 they took their petition directly to King George V; they secured seats adjoining the royal box in the opera house on a gala occasion when "Joan of Arc" was playing. After barricading themselves in, they used a megaphone to harangue George on how they, like Joan, were "tortured and done to death in the name of the King, in the name of the Church, and with the full knowledge and responsibility of established Government," until the door was finally broken down and the women ejected!

London newspapers minted the term "suffragettes" in 1906 to distinguish these militants from the moderate and traditional suffragists; epithets thrown at them ran from "mock martyrs" and "martyrettes" to "outragettes." They objected strongly: their action was intended to attain citizenship, not martyrdom, citing Mazzini "that the way to reform has always led through prison." They regarded the calculated martyrdom of the suffragette Emily Wilding Davison (who threw herself under the king's horse in the Derby race at Epsom Downs in 1913) as a tragic mistake. Although they destroyed much property, they were nonviolent in that they eschewed deadly weapons. "Oh, my tongue is weapon enough," one of them explained. Part of the double standard was, in their view, that men were permitted to resort to violence to gain political rights, while women were accused of turning themselves into harpies if they did. They proclaimed that violence was used against them, not by them.

Christabel, who thought all men were "monsters" and today would probably call herself a radical feminist, saw militancy as a war against the idea that "women are of value only because of their sex functions." The WSPU campaigned against prostitution, white slavery, and what Christabel called "the great scourge," the venereal infection which wives and mothers acquired from husbands who consorted with prostitutes. For her the way to end the scourge was to end the double standard, to hold men to the same moral standard as women. Her motto was "Votes for Women and Chastity for Men."

For the Pankhursts the camaraderie and vindication of womanhood was exhilarating. As Sylvia reported in recalling a major demonstration: "Throughout that great gathering there was a wonderful spirit of unity and not one woman there could wish in her heart, as so many millions have done, 'if I had only been a man.' No, they were rather like to pity those who were not women, and so could not join in this great fight, for to-day it was the woman's battle."

QUESTIONS

1. What were the WSPU's tactics and strategy in their campaign for the vote? Was this violent or nonviolent political action? Why was the WSPU not democratic?
2. Why did the government persist over a decade in rejecting women's claim to the vote? Did the militant campaign help or hinder attainment of the goal?
3. Did the government break the law? Is there any explanation why the prison doctors were "brutal" or could not desist from "cruelty"?
4. What arguments were advanced by the Pankhursts and the WSPU to justify votes for women?
5. Did women simply want the vote or a larger program? If so, what?
6. What traits of character does Emmeline Pankhurst show?

Now repeated experience had taught us that the only way to attain women's suffrage was to commit a Government to it. . . . We determined to address ourselves to those men who were likely to be in the Liberal Cabinet [after the 1906 election], demanding to know whether their reforms were going to include justice to women. We laid our plans to begin this work at a great meeting . . . with Sir Edward Grey as the principal speaker. . . .

Annie Kenney and my daughter Christabel were charged with the mission of questioning Sir Edward Grey. They sat quietly through the meeting, at the close of which questions were invited. Several questions were asked by men and were courteously answered. Then Annie Kenney arose and asked: "If the Liberal party is returned to power, will they take steps to give votes for women?" At the same time Christabel held aloft the little banner that everyone in the hall might understand the nature of the question. Sir Edward Grey returned no answer to Annie's question, and the men sitting near her forced her rudely into her seat, while a steward of the meeting pressed his hat over her face. A babel of shouts, cries and catcalls sounded from all over the hall. As soon as order was restored Christabel stood up and repeated the question. . . . Again Sir Edward Grey ignored the question, and again a perfect tumult of shouts and angry cries arose . . . and the meeting began to break up. Annie Kenney stood up in her chair and cried out over the noise of shuffling feet and murmurs of conversation: "Will the Liberal Government give votes to women?" Then the audience became a mob. They howled, they shouted and roared, shaking their fists fiercely at the woman who dared to intrude her question into a man's meeting. Hands were lifted to drag her out of her chair, but Christabel threw one arm about her as she stood, and with the other arm warded off the mob, who struck and scratched at her until her sleeve was red with blood. Still the girls held together and shouted over and over: "The question! The question! Answer the question!"

Six men, stewards of the meeting, seized Christabel and dragged her down the aisle, past the platform, other men following with Annie Kenney, both girls calling for an answer to their question. . . . Flung into the streets, the two girls staggered to their feet and began to address the crowds, and to tell them what had taken place in a Liberal meeting. Within five minutes they were arrested on a charge of obstruction and, in Christabel's case, of assaulting the police. Both were summoned to appear next morning in a police court, where, after a trial which was a mere farce, Annie Kenney was sentenced to pay a fine of five shillings, with an alternative of three days in prison, and Christabel Pankhurst was given a fine of ten shillings or a jail sentence of one week. Both girls promptly chose the prison sentence. . . . Of course the affair created a tremendous sensation . . . all over England. . . .

This, then, was our situation: the Government all-powerful and consistently hostile; the rank and file of legislators impotent; the country apathetic; the women divided in their interests. The Women's Political and Social Union was established to meet this situation, and to overcome it. . . . There was little formality about joining the Union. Any woman could become a member by paying a shilling, but at the same time she was required to sign a declaration of loyal adher-

ence to our policy and a pledge not to work for any political party until the women's vote was won. This is still our inflexible custom. Moreover, if at any time a member, or members, loses faith in our policy; if any one begins to suggest that some other policy ought to be substituted, or if she tries to confuse the issue by adding other policies, she ceases at once to be a member. Autocratic? Quite so. But, you may object, a suffrage organization ought to be democratic. Well, the members of the WSPU do not agree with you. We do not believe in the effectiveness of the ordinary suffrage organization. The WSPU is not hampered by a complexity of rules. We have no constitution and by-laws; nothing to be tinkered with or quarrelled over at an annual meeting. In fact, we have no annual meeting, no business sessions, no elections of officers. The WSPU is simply a suffrage army in the field. . . . We did not invent this policy. It was most successfully pursued by Mr. Parnell in his [Irish] Home Rule struggle more than thirty-five years ago. . . .

I think we began to be noticed in earnest after our first success in opposing a Liberal candidate. This was in a by-election held at Cockermouth in August 1906. . . . The verdict of a by-election is considered as either an indorsement or a censure of the manner in which the Government have fulfilled their pre-election pledges. So we went to Cockermouth. . . . How we were ridiculed! With what scorn the newspapers declared that "those wild women" could never turn a single vote. Yet when the election was over it was found that the Liberal candidate had lost. . . . Tremendously elated, we hustled our forces off to another by-election. . . . We devoted ourselves to the by-election work, sometimes actually defeating the Liberal candidate [e.g. Winston Churchill at Manchester in 1908], sometimes reducing the Liberal majority, and always raising a tremendous sensation and gaining hundreds of new members. . . .

We determined to organize a Hyde Park demonstration of at least 250,000 people. Sunday, June 21, 1908, was fixed for the date of this demonstration, and for many months we worked to make it a day notable in the history of the movement. . . . We spent, for advertising alone, over a thousand pounds. . . . We covered the hoardings of London and all the principal provincial cities with great posters bearing portraits of the women who were to preside at the twenty platforms from which speeches were to be made; a map of London, showing the routes by which the seven processions were to advance, and a plan of the Hyde Park meeting-place were also shown. London, of course, was thoroughly organized. For weeks a small army of women was busy chalking announcements on sidewalks, distributing handbills, canvassing from house to house, advertising the demonstration by posters and sandwich boards carried through the streets. We invited everybody to be present, including both Houses of Parliament. [Thirty special trains brought people up from all over the country.] . . .

What a day was Sunday, June 21st. . . . When I mounted my platform in Hyde Park, and surveyed the mighty throngs that waited there and the endless crowds that were still pouring into the park from all directions, I was filled with amazement. . . . Never had I imagined that so many people could be gathered together to share in a political demonstration. . . . The bugles sounded, and the speakers at each of the twenty platforms began their addresses, which could not have been heard by more than a half or a third of the vast audience. Notwithstanding this, they remained to the end. At five o'clock the bugles sounded again, the speaking ceased, and the resolutions calling upon the Government to bring in an official woman-suffrage bill without delay was carried at every platform, often without a dissenting vote. Then, with a three-times-repeated cry of "Votes for Women!" from the assembled multitude, the great meeting dispersed. . . . The London *Times* said next day [that half to three quarters of a million people had participated]. . . .

[In 1909 the suffragette] Miss Wallace Dunlop had been sent to prison for one month for stamping an extract from the [1689] Bill of Rights on the stone walls of St. Stephen's Hall [near Parliament]. On arriving at Holloway [prison] . . . she sent for the governor and demanded that she be treated as a political prisoner . . . [saying] that it was the unalterable resolution of the suffragettes never again to submit to the prison treatment given to ordinary offenders against the law. Therefore she should, if placed in the second division as a common criminal, refuse to touch food until the government yielded her point. . . . Several times daily the doctor came to feel her pulse and observe her growing weakness [until he] reported that she was rapidly reaching a point where death might at any time supervene. Hurried conferences were carried on between the prison and the Home Office, and that evening [she] was sent home, having served one-fourth of her sentence, and having ignored completely all the terms of her imprisonment.

On the day of her release the fourteen women who had been convicted of window breaking received their sentences, and learning of Miss Wallace Dunlop's act, they, as they were being taken to Holloway in the prison van, held a consultation and agreed to follow her example. . . . At the end of five days one of the women was reduced to such a condition that the Home Secretary ordered her released. The next day several more were released, and before the end of the week the last of the fourteen had gained their liberty.

The affair excited the greatest sympathy of all over England. . . . [And] after this each succeeding batch of suffragette prisoners, unless otherwise directed, followed the example of these heroic rebels. The prison officials, seeing their authority vanish, were panic stricken. Holloway and other women's prisons throughout the kingdom became perfect dens of violence and brutality. . . .

Several days later we were horrified to read in the newspapers that these prisoners [who had thrown stones at the prime minister's train] were being forcibly fed. . . . The Home Secretary reluctantly admitted that, in order to preserve the dignity of the government and at the same time save the lives of the prisoners, "hospital treatment" was being administered. "Hospital treatment" was the term used to draw attention [away] from one of the most disgusting and brutal expedients ever resorted to by prison authorities. No law allows it [forced feeding] except in the case of persons certified to be insane. . . .

Mrs. Leigh, the first victim . . . refused to touch the food that was brought to her, and three days after her arrival she was taken to the doctor's room. . . . The senior doctor spoke, saying: "Listen carefully to what I have to say. I have orders from my superior officers that you are not to be released even on medical grounds. If you still refrain from food I must take other measures to compel you to take it." Mrs. Leigh replied that she did still refuse, and she said further that she knew that she could not legally be forcibly fed. . . . Later two doctors and the wardresses appeared in her cell, forced Mrs. Leigh down to the bed and held her there. To her horror the doctors produced a rubber tube, two yards in length, and this he began to stuff up her nostril. The pain was so dreadful that she shrieked again and again. Three of the wardresses burst into tears and

the junior doctor begged the other to desist. Having had his orders from the government, the doctor persisted and the tube was pushed down into the stomach. One of the doctors, standing on a chair and holding the tube high poured liquid food through a funnel almost suffocating the poor victim. . . . In an almost fainting condition Mrs. Leigh was taken back to the punishment cell and laid on her plank bed. The ordeal was renewed day after day. The other prisoners suffered similar experiences.

The government, at their wits' end to cope with the hunger strikers, and to overcome a situation which had brought the laws of England into such scandalous disrepute, had recourse to a measure, surely the most savagely devised ever brought before a modern Parliament. . . . This measure, now universally known as the "Cat and Mouse Act," provided that when a hunger striking suffrage prisoner (the law was frankly admitted to apply only to suffrage prisoners) was certified by the prison doctors to be in danger of death, she could be ordered released on a sort of ticket of leave for the purpose of regaining strength enough to undergo the remainder of her sentence. Released, she was still a prisoner, . . . being kept under constant police surveillance. According to the terms of the bill the prisoner was released for a specific number of days, at the expiration of which she was supposed to return to prison on her own account. . . .

We don't want to use any weapons that are unnecessarily strong. Why should women go to Parliament Square [for demonstrations] and be battered about and insulted [by the police], and most important of all, produce less effect than when they throw stones? . . . After all, is not a woman's life, is not her health, and are not her limbs more valuable than panes of glass? There is no doubt of that, but most important of all, does not the breaking of glass produce more effect upon the government? If you are fighting a battle, that [is what] should dictate your choice of weapons. . . . I get letters from people who . . . implore me not to be reckless with human life. [But] the only recklessness the militant suffragists have shown about human life has been about their own lives. . . . Recklessly to endanger human life . . . is not the method of women. [However,] there is something that governments care far more for than human life, and that is the security of property, and so it is through property that we shall strike the enemy. . . .

[In pursuit of "our newer and stronger policy of aggression," the police] were utterly unable to calculate what we were going to do. We planned a demonstration for March 4th, and this one we announced. We planned another demonstration for March 1st, but this one we did not announce. Late in the afternoon of Friday, March 1st, I drove in a taxicab, accompanied by . . . other of our members, to No. 10 Downing Street, the official residence of the prime minister. It was exactly half past five when we alighted from the cab and threw our stones, four of them, through the window panes. As we expected we were promptly arrested and taken to Cannon Row police station. The hour that followed will long be remembered in London. At intervals of fifteen minutes relays of women who had volunteered for the demonstration did their work. The first smashing of glass occurred in the Haymarket and Piccadilly, and greatly startled and alarmed both pedestrians and police. A large number of the women were arrested, and everyone thought that ended the affair. But before the excited populace and the frustrated shop owners' first exclamations had died down, before the police had reached the station with their prisoners, the ominous crashing and splintering of plate glass began again, this time along both sides of Regent Street and the Strand. A furious rush of police and people towards the second scene of action ensued. While their attention was being taken up with occurrences in this quarter, the third relay of women began breaking the windows in Oxford Circus and Bond Street. . . . [On the 4th] a hundred or more women walked quietly into Knightsbridge and walking singly along the streets demolished nearly every pane of glass they passed. Taken by surprise the police arrested as many as they could reach, but most of the women escaped. . . .

[Arrested for inciting the rash of guerrilla attacks on property and sentenced to three years of hard labor, Pankhurst promptly refused all food.] No one who has not gone through the awful experience of the hunger strike can have any idea how great that misery is. . . . I generally suffer most on the second day. After that there is no very desperate craving for food. Weakness and mental depression take its place. Great disturbances of digestion divert the desire for food to a longing for relief from pain. Often there is intense dizziness, or slight delirium. Complete exhaustion and a feeling of isolation from earth mark the final stages of the ordeal. Recovery is often protracted, and entire recovery of normal health is sometimes discouragingly slow. . . . The hunger strike I have described as a dreadful ordeal, but it is a mild experience compared with the thirst strike, which is from beginning to end simple and unmitigated torture. Hunger striking reduces a prisoner's weight very quickly, but thirst striking reduces weight so alarmingly fast that prison doctors were at first thrown into absolute panic of fright. . . . When, at the end of the third day of my first strike, I was sent home I was in a condition of jaundice from which I have never completely recovered. So badly was I affected that the prison authorities made no attempt to arrest me for nearly a month after my release. . . . [Re-arrested] I added to this the sleep strike, which means that as far as was humanly possible I refused all sleep and rest. For two nights I sat or lay on the concrete floor, resolutely refusing the oft repeated offers of medical examination. "You are not a doctor," I told the man. "You are a government torturer, and all you want to do is satisfy yourself that I am not quite ready to die." . . . To the governor I made the simple announcement that I was ready to leave prison and that I intended to leave very soon, dead or alive. I told him that from that moment I should not even rest on the concrete floor, but should walk my cell until I was released or until I died of exhaustion. All day I kept to this resolution, pacing up and down the narrow cell, many times stumbling and falling, until the doctor came in at evening to tell me that I was ordered released on the following morning. [In this way Pankhurst, although she was re-arrested twelve times over the year, avoided all but one month of her three-year prison term.]

. . . Other histories of the militant movement will undoubtedly be written; in time to come when in all constitutional countries of the world, women's votes will be universally accepted as men's votes are now; when men and women occupy the world of industry on equal terms, as co-workers rather than as cut-throat competitors; when, in a word, all the dreadful and criminal discriminations which exist now between the sexes are abolished, as they must one day be abolished, the historian will be able to sit down in leisurely fashion and do full justice to the strange story of how the women of England took up arms against the blind and obstinate government of England and fought their way to political freedom. I should like to live long enough to read such a history, calmly considered, carefully analyzed, conscientiously set forth. It will be a better book to read than this one, written, as it were, in camp between battles. But perhaps this one, hastily prepared as it has been, will give the reader of the future a clearer impression of the strenuousness and the desperation of the conflict, and also something of the heretofore undreamed of courage and fighting strength of women, who, having learned the joy of battle, lose all sense of fear and continue their struggle up to and past the gates of death, never flinching at any step of the way.

49. German Aims in World War I, 1914

Chancellor Theobald Von Bethmann Hollweg's Program

The following document lists the demands put forward by the German chancellor in September 1914, before the strategic significance of the battle of the Marne was understood. It was considered to be a moderate program in contrast to the demands of the military leaders. Fritz Fischer, an expert on Germany's goals in World War I, has argued 1) that the German leadership knowingly initiated war by exploiting the crisis over the assassination of the Austro-Hungarian heir Archduke Franz Ferdinand in Sarajevo in order to escape what the leaders believed was a desperate impasse in domestic and foreign politics, and 2) that the German government fought on tenaciously and disastrously from 1914 to 1918 because the ruling class feared revolutionary upheaval by democrats and socialists. According to his view, German leaders believed that military successes, annexations, and national glory would vindicate and legitimize the regime of Hohenzollern absolutism and Junker aristocratic domination in the face of calls for democratization. The war thus became a proposition of all or nothing. Fischer also concluded that Germany vastly expanded its war aims following its defeat of Russia and its dictation of the Treaty of Brest-Litovsk to the new Bolshevik government in March 1918. When Germany launched its great offensive (March–July 1918) on the Western Front, it bid to decisively defeat France, Belgium, Britain and the United States, and become dominant in Europe and world-wide as "Imperium Germanicum." Reconsideration of the Fischer thesis nearly forty years after he propounded it confirms and also complicates the argument. V. R. Berghan concludes: "It was the men gathered at the Imperial Palace in Berlin who pushed Europe over the brink" of war in 1914, although they anticipated a localized, not a world war, a short rather than a long war, a victorious not a lost war.

QUESTIONS

1. What precisely were the German aims and ambitions at the beginning of World War I? Were they legitimate?
2. How did these aims compare with those of the other belligerents?
3. In what sense could it be said that the German government became the prisoner of its own war aims?
4. Does this document, together with the Treaty of Brest-Litovsk, put the Versailles treaty settlement in a new light?

[The] general aim of the war [is] security for the German Reich in west and east for all imaginable time. For this purpose France must be so weakened as to make her revival as a great power impossible for all time. Russia must be thrust back as far as possible from Germany's eastern frontier and her domination over the non-Russian vassal peoples broken.

1. *France*. The military to decide whether we should demand cession of Belfort and western slopes of the Vosges, razing of fortresses and cession of coastal strip from Dunkirk to Boulogne.

The ore-field of Briey, which is necessary for the supply of ore for our industry, to be ceded in any case.

Further, a war indemnity, to be paid in installments; it must be high enough to prevent France from spending any considerable sums on armaments in the next 15–20 years.

Furthermore: a commercial treaty which makes France economically dependent on Germany, secures the French market for our exports and makes it possible to exclude British commerce from France. This treaty must secure for us financial and industrial freedom of movement in France in such fashion that German enterprises can no longer receive different treatment from French.

2. *Belgium.* Liège and Verviers to be attached to Prussia, a frontier strip of the province of Luxemburg to Luxemburg.

Question whether Antwerp, with a corridor to Liège, should also be annexed remains open.

At any rate Belgium, even if allowed to continue to exist as a state, must be reduced to a vassal state, must allow us to occupy any militarily important ports, must place her coast at our disposal in military respects, must become economically a German province. Given such a solution, which offers the advantages of annexation without its inescapable domestic political disadvantages, French Flanders with Dunkirk, Calais and Boulogne, where most of the population is Flemish, can without danger be attached to this unaltered Belgium. The competent quarters will have to judge the military value of this position against England.

3. *Luxemburg.* Will become a German federal state and will receive a strip of the present Belgian province of Luxemburg and perhaps the corner of Longwy.

4. We must create a *central European economic association* through common customs treaties, to include France, Belgium, Holland, Denmark, Austria-Hungary, Poland [sic], and perhaps Italy, Sweden and Nor-

way. This association will not have any common constitutional supreme authority and all its members will be formally equal, but in practice will be under German leadership and must stabilize Germany's economic dominance over Mitteleuropa, [i.e., central Europe].

5. *The question of colonial acquisitions,* where the first aim is the creation of a continuous Central African colonial empire, will be considered later, as will that of the aims to be realized vis-a-vis Russia.

6. A short provisional formula suitable for a possible preliminary peace to be found for a basis for the economic agreements to be concluded with France and Belgium.

7. *Holland.* It will have to be considered by what means and methods Holland can be brought into closer relationship with the German Empire.

In view of the Dutch character, this closer relationship must leave them free of any feeling of compulsion, must alter nothing in the Dutch way of life, and must also subject them to no new military obligations. Holland, then, must be left independent in externals, but be made internally dependent on us. Possibly one might consider an offensive and defensive alliance, to cover the colonies; in any case a close customs association, perhaps the cession of Antwerp to Holland in return for the right to keep a German garrison in the fortress of Antwerp and at the mouth of the Scheldt.

50. Japan's Twenty-One Demands on China, 1915

By 1914 Japan had become a great power and sought to take full advantage in the Far East of Europe's embroilment in World War I. Japan sided with the Allies and soon declared war on Germany, looking to acquire German concessions in China and convert the "open door" policy into a Japanese monopoly. The war greatly stimulated the commercial and industrial growth of Japan and transformed her from a debtor to a creditor nation. The Twenty-One Demands of January 1915 (presented secretly but leaked to the American ambassador by President Yuan) looked to stake out all of China as a Japanese sphere of influence or protectorate. The goal was to establish Japanese preponderance in the Far East—invoked in Japanese imperial tradition as "The Whole World Under One Roof." The paper on which the Demands were presented, it was noted, bore the water mark of a machine gun! In the aftermath, with an uproar in China and in the West, Japan retreated somewhat, deciding to hold Part V in abeyance for "future discussion" and to water down Parts I–IV. In this form they were imposed as an ultimatum in May, which China felt helpless to resist. Meanwhile, Japan had acquired for itself German possessions and concessions, including a naval base on the Shantung peninsula, the strategically important railways in China to Manchuria and Korea, and German islands (the Carolines, Marianas, and Marshalls) in the Pacific. The Treaty of Versailles further strengthened Japan's position in Asia and the Pacific.

QUESTIONS

1. What kinds of demands are made by Japan on China in this document?
2. What significance attaches to all the references to railroads? Are they just means of transport?
3. Is this national criminal behavior or is it in character with the nature of the nation-state?
4. As a third-party witness to this episode, what would a contemporary draw as the lesson for Japan? For China? For the United States and Europe?
5. What were the sources of Japanese dynamism?

I.

The Japanese Government and the Chinese Government, being desirous of maintaining the general peace in Eastern Asia and further strengthening the friendly relations and good neighborhood existing between the two nations, agree to the following articles:—

Article 1. The Chinese Government engages to give full consent to all matters upon which the Japanese Government may hereafter agree with the German Government relating to the disposition of all rights, interests, and concessions, which Germany, by virtue of treaties or otherwise, possesses in relation to the Province of Shantung.

Article 2. The Chinese Government engages that within the Province of Shantung and along its coast no territory or island shall be ceded or leased to a third Power under any pretext.

Article 3. The Chinese Government consents to Japan's building a railway from Chefoo or Lung-kau to join the Kiao-chau-Tsinanfu Railway.

Article 4. The Chinese Government engages, in the interest of trade and for the residence of foreigners, to open by herself as soon as possible certain important cities and towns in the Province of Shantung as Commercial Ports. What places shall be opened are to be jointly decided upon in a separate agreement.

II.

The Japanese Government and the Chinese Government, since the Chinese Government has always acknowledged the special position enjoyed by Japan in South Manchuria and Eastern Inner Mongolia, agree to the following articles:

Article 1. The Two Contracting Parties mutually agree that the term of lease of Port Arthur and Dalney, and the term of lease of the South Manchurian Railway and the Antung-Mukden Railway, shall be extended to the period of ninety-nine years.

Article 2. Japanese subjects in South Manchuria and Eastern Inner Mongolia shall have the right to lease or own land required either for erecting suitable buildings for trade and manufacture or for farming.

Article 3. Japanese subjects shall be free to reside and travel in South Manchuria and Eastern Inner Mongolia, and to engage in business and in manufacture of any kind whatsoever.

Article 4. The Chinese Government agrees to grant to Japanese subjects the right of opening the mines in South Manchuria and Eastern Inner Mongolia. As regards what mines are to be opened, they shall be decided upon jointly.

Article 5. The Chinese Government agrees that in respect of the [two] cases mentioned herein below, the Japanese Government's consent shall be first obtained before action is taken:

a) Whenever permission is granted to the subject of a third Power to build a railway or to make a loan with a third Power for the purpose of building a railway in South Manchuria and Eastern Inner Mongolia.

b) Whenever a loan is to be made with a third Power pledging the local taxes of South Manchuria and Eastern Inner Mongolia as security.

Article 6. The Chinese Government agrees that if the Chinese Government employs political, financial, or military advisers or instructors in South Manchuria or Eastern Inner Mongolia, the Japanese Government shall first be consulted.

Article 7. The Chinese Government agrees that the control and management of the Kirin-Changchun Railway shall be handed over to the Japanese Government for a term of ninety-nine years, dating from the signing of this Agreement.

III.

The Japanese Government and the Chinese Government, seeing that Japanese financiers and the Hanyehping Company have close relations with each other at present, and desiring that the common interests of the two nations shall be advanced, agree to the following articles:

Article 1. The two Contracting Parties mutually agree that when the opportune moment arises the Hanyehping Company shall be made a joint concern of the two nations, and they further agree that, without the previous consent of Japan, China shall not by her own act dispose of the rights and property of whatsoever nature of the said Company, nor cause the said Company to dispose freely of the same.

Article 2. The Chinese Government agrees that all mines in the neighborhood of those owned by the Hanyehping Company shall not be permitted, without the consent of the said Company, to be worked by other persons outside of the said Company; and further agrees that if it is desired to carry out any undertaking which, it is apprehended, may directly or indirectly affect the interests of the said Company, the consent of the said Company shall first be obtained.

IV.

The Japanese Government and the Chinese Government, with the object of effectively preserving the territorial integrity of China, agree to the following special article:

The Chinese Government engages not to cede or lease to a third Power any harbor, or bay, or island along the coast of China.

V.

Article 1. The Chinese Central Government shall employ influential Japanese as advisers in political, financial and military affairs.

Article 2. Japanese hospitals, churches and schools in the interior of China shall be granted the right of owning land.

Article 3. Inasmuch as the Japanese Government and the Chinese Government have had many cases of dispute between Japanese and Chinese police to settle, cases which cause no little misunderstanding, it is for this reason necessary that the Police departments of important places [in China] shall be jointly administered by Japanese and Chinese, or that the police departments of these places shall employ numerous Japanese, so that they may at the same time help to plan for the improvement of the Chinese Police Service.

Article 4. China shall purchase from Japan a fixed amount of munitions of war (say 50 per cent. or more) of what is needed by the Chinese Government, or that there shall be established in China a Sino-Japanese jointly worked arsenal. Japanese technical experts are to be employed and Japanese material to be purchased.

Article 5. China agrees to grant to Japan the right of constructing a railway connecting Wuchang with Kiukiang and Nanchang, another line between Nanchung and Hanchow, and another between Nanchang and Chaochou.

Article 6. If China needs foreign capital to work mines, build railways, and construct harbor works (including dockyards) in the Province of Fukien, Japan shall be consulted.

Article 7. China agrees that Japanese subjects shall have the right of missionary propaganda in China.

51. Woodrow Wilson's Fourteen Points, 1918

The United States entered World War I in April of 1917—almost three years after it had begun. President Woodrow Wilson (1856–1924) committed the United States as an "Associate Power" to full-scale participation on the side of the Allies. Keenly aware of the war's devastation and its threat to civilization, Wilson tried hard to make America's role in the struggle worthy of the sacrifices that would be demanded of the American people. He wished to justify the effort as a "war to end war" and to make the world "safe for democracy."

On January 8, 1918 President Wilson delivered a speech to Congress in which he outlined fourteen points that he hoped would guide the war aims of all of the Allies. In stating his goals for a lasting world order in peacetime Wilson was attempting to counter the Russian Bolsheviks' publication of the Tsarist government's secret treaties with the Allies. The Bolshevik revolutionaries had contended that these agreements justified a Russian withdrawal from what they called an imperialistic war. Wilson and the Allies dreaded the Bolshevik decision to leave the war against the Central Powers. The President used this speech to demonstrate his commitment to a new style of diplomacy that would stress democracy, national self-determination, and international cooperation through a League of Nations.

QUESTIONS

1. Why, and under what circumstances, did Woodrow Wilson issue the Fourteen Points?
2. What is the significance of the words *should* and *must* in the Fourteen Points?
3. In order to gain the fourteenth point, did Wilson sacrifice all the others?
4. How do these war aims compare with those of Franklin Roosevelt, Harry Truman, and Lyndon Johnson?

We entered this war because violations of right had occurred which touched us to the quick and made the life of our people impossible unless they were corrected and the world secure once and for all against their recurrence. What we demand in this war, therefore, is nothing peculiar to ourselves. It is that the world be made fit and safe to live in, and particularly that it be made safe for every peace-loving nation which, like our own, wishes to live its own free life, determine its own institutions, be assured of justice and fair dealing by the other peoples of the world, as against force and selfish aggression. All the peoples of the world are in effect partners in this interest, and for our own part we see very clearly that unless justice be done to others it will not be done to us. The program of the world's peace, therefore, is our program, and the only possible program, as we see it, is this:

I. Open covenants of peace openly arrived at, after which there shall be no private international understandings of any kind, but diplomacy shall proceed always frankly and in public view.

II. Absolute freedom of navigation upon seas outside territorial waters alike in peace and in war, except that the seas may be closed in whole or in part by international action for the enforcement of international covenants.

III. The removal, so far as possible, of all economic barriers and the establishment of an equality of trade conditions among the nations consenting to the peace and associating themselves for its maintenance.

IV. Adequate guarantees given and taken that national armaments will be reduced to the lowest point consistent with domestic safety.

V. A free, open-minded, and absolutely impartial adjustment of all colonial claims based upon a strict observance of the principle that in determining all such questions of sovereignty the interests of the populations concerned must have equal weight with the equitable claims of the Government whose title is to be determined.

VI. The evacuation af all Russian territory, and such a settlement of all questions affecting Russia as will secure the best and freest cooperation of the other nations of the world in obtaining for her unhampered and unembarrassed opportunity for the independent determination of her own political development and national policy, and assure her of a sincere welcome into the society of free nations under institutions of her own choosing, and more than a welcome, assistance also of every kind that she may

need and may herself desire. The treatment accorded to Russia by her sister nations in the months to come will be the acid test of their good will, of their comprehension of her needs as distinguished from their own interests, and of their intelligent and unselfish sympathy.

VII. Belgium, the whole world will agree, must be evacuated and restored without any attempt to limit the sovereignty which she enjoys in common with all other free nations. No other single act will serve as this will serve to restore confidence among nations in the laws which they have themselves set and determined for the government of their relations with one another. Without this healing act the whole structure and validity of International Law is forever impaired.

VIII. All French territory should be freed, and the invaded portions restored, and the wrong done to France by Prussia in 1871 in the matter of Alsace-Lorraine, which has unsettled the peace of the world for nearly fifty years, should be righted in order that peace may once more be made secure in the interest of all.

IX. A readjustment of the frontiers of Italy should be effected along clearly recognizable lines of nationality.

X. The peoples of Austria-Hungary, whose place among the nations we wish to see safe-guarded and assured, should be accorded the freest opportunity for autonomous development.

XI. Rumania, Serbia, and Montenegro, should be evacuated, occupied territories restored, Serbia accorded free and secure access to the sea, and the relations of several Balkan States to one another determined by friendly counsel along historically established lines of allegiance and nationality, and international guarantees of the political and economic independence and territorial integrity of the several Balkan States should be entered into.

XII. The Turkish portions of the present Ottoman Empire should be assured a secure sovereignty, but the other nationalities which are now under Turkish rule should be assured an undoubted security of life and an absolutely unmolested opportunity of autonomous development, and the Dardanelles should be permanently opened as a free passage to the ships and commerce of all nations under international guarantees.

XIII. An independent Polish State should be erected which should include the territories inhabited by indisputably Polish populations, which should be assured a free and secure access to the sea, and whose political and economic independence and territorial integrity should be guaranteed by international covenant.

XIV. A general association of nations must be formed under specific covenants for the purpose of affording mutual guarantees of political independence and territorial integrity to great and small States alike.

In regard to these essential rectifications of wrong and assertions of right we feel ourselves to be intimate partners of all the Governments and peoples associated together against the Imperialists. We cannot be separated in interest or divided in purpose. We stand together until the end. . . .

52. The Tasks of the Proletariat in the Present Revolution, 1917

Lenin's April Theses

Vladimir Ilyich Lenin (Ulyanov) (1870–1924), the son of a school inspector, was educated at the Universities of Kazan and St. Petersburg. A professional revolutionary, he became one of the early Russian Marxists and was arrested and deported by the tsarist government. In 1903 the second congress of the Russian Social Democratic Labor Party split over such questions as the nature of party organization and political tactics. Lenin headed the militant faction that became known as the Bolsheviks. He spent most of the years between 1900 and 1917 in exile. After the March Revolution (1917) he returned to Petrograd, which was formerly St. Petersburg, and later Leningrad, and is now again named St. Petersburg. On his return journey to his homeland he traveled with other revolutionaries in a sealed train provided by the German General Staff, who were hoping that the Bolshevik radicals would disrupt the Russian war effort against the Central Powers. They were not disappointed. On the day following his arrival Lenin outlined his position in his "April Theses," which he presented to the caucus of Bolshevik members of the All-Russian Conference of Soviets. This document created considerable controversy when it was published in the party organ *Pravda*. A majority of his own party at first rejected his uncompromising views, maintaining that Lenin had lost touch with the realities of the Russian empire. But

Lenin fought back, scorning those who opposed him, and by mid-May the Bolsheviks endorsed his program.

QUESTIONS

1. What is the precise historical situation that Lenin addresses here?
2. What tactics does he propose in order to bring the communists to power?
3. What can you infer from this document about Lenin's qualities as a leader, his character and disposition, etc.?

I arrived in Petrograd only on the night of April 3, and I could therefore, of course, deliver a report at the meeting on April 4 on the tasks of the revolutionary proletariat only upon my own responsibility, and with reservations as to insufficient preparation.

The only thing I could do to facilitate matters for myself and for *honest* opponents was to prepare *written* theses. I read them, and gave the text to Comrade Tsereteli. I read them very slowly, *twice*; first at a meeting of Bolsheviks and then at a meeting of Bolsheviks and Mensheviks. . . .

1. In our attitude towards the war, which under the new government of Lvov and Co. unquestionably remains on Russia's part a predatory imperialist war owing to the capitalist nature of that government, not the slightest concession must be made to "revolutionary defencism."

The class-conscious proletariat could consent to a revolutionary war, which would really justify revolutionary defencism, only on condition: (a) that the power of government pass to the proletariat and the poorest sections of the peasantry bordering on the proletariat; (b) that all annexations be renounced in deed and not only in word; (c) that a complete and real break be effected in actual fact with all capitalist interests.

In view of the undoubted honesty of the broad strata of the mass believers in revolutionary defencism, who accept the war as a necessity only, and not as a means of conquest, in view of the fact that they are being deceived by the bourgeoisie, it is necessary very thoroughly, persistently and patiently to explain their error to them, to explain the inseparable connection between capital and the imperialist war, and to prove that *it is impossible* to end the war by a truly democratic, non-coercive peace without the overthrow of capital.

The most widespread propaganda of this view among the army on active service must be organized.

Fraternization.

2. The specific feature of the present situation in Russia is that it represents a *transition* from the first stage of the revolution—which, owing to the insufficient class-consciousness and organization of the proletariat, placed the power in the hands of the bourgeoisie—to the *second* stage, which must place the power in the hands of the proletariat and the poorer strata of the peasants.

This transition is characterized, on the one hand, by a maximum of freedom (Russia is *now* the freest of all the belligerent countries in the world); on the other, by the absence of violence in relation to the masses, and, finally, by the unreasoning confidence of the masses in the government of capitalists, the worst enemies of peace and Socialism.

This specific situation demands of us an ability to adapt ourselves to the *specific* requirements of Party work among unprecedentedly large masses of proletarians who have just awakened to political life.

3. No support must be given to the Provisional Government; the utter falsity of all its promises must be explained, particularly those relating to the renunciation of annexations. Exposure, and not the unpardonable ilusion-breeding "demand" that *this* government, a government of capitalists, should *cease* to be an imperialist government.

4. The fact must be recognized that in most of the Soviets of Workers' Deputies our Party is in a minority, so far a small minority, as against a *bloc* of all the petty-bourgeois opportunist elements, who have yielded to the influence of the bourgeoisie and convey its influence to the proletariat, from the Popular Socialists and the Socialist-Revolutionaries down to the Organization Committee (Chkheidze, Tsereteli, etc.), Steklov, etc., etc.

It must be explained to the masses that the Soviets of Workers' Deputies are the *only possible* form of revolutionary government, and that therefore our task is, as long as *this* government yields to the influence of the bourgeoisie, to present a patient, systematic and persistent *explanation* of the errors of their tactics, an explanation especially adapted to the practical needs of the masses.

As long as we are in the minority we carry on the work of criticizing and explaining errors and at the same time we preach the necessity of transferring the entire power of state to the Soviets of Workers' Deputies, so that the masses may by experience overcome their mistakes.

5. Not a parliamentary republic—to return to a parliamentary republic from the Soviets of Workers' Deputies would be a retrograde step—but a republic of Soviets of Workers', Agricultural Labourers' and Peasants' Deputies throughout the country, from top to bottom.

Abolition of the police, the army and the bureaucracy. (The standing army to be replaced by the universally armed people.)

The salaries of all officials, who are to be elected and to be subject to recall at any time, not to exceed the average wage of a competent worker.

6. In an agrarian program the emphasis must be laid on the Soviets of Agricultural Labourers' Deputies.

Confiscation of all landed estates.

Nationalization of *all* lands in the country, the disposal of the land to be put in the charge of the local Soviets of Agricultural Labourers' and Peasants' Deputies. The organization of separate Soviets of Deputies of Poor Peasants. The creation of model farms on each of the large estates (varying from 100 to 300 dessiatins, in accordance with local and other conditions, at the discretion of the local institutions) under the control of the Soviets of Agricultural Labourers' Deputies and for the public account.

7. The immediate amalgamation of all banks in the country into a single national bank, control over which shall be exercised by the Soviet of Workers' Deputies.

8. Our *immediate* task is not to "introduce" Socialism, but only to bring social production and the distribution of products at once under the *control* of the Soviets of Workers' Deputies.

9. Party tasks:
   a) Immediate summoning of a Party congress;
   b) Alteration of the Party Programme, mainly:

1) On the question of imperialism and the imperialist war;
2) On the question of our attitude towards the state and our demand for a "commune state";
3) Amendment of our antiquated minimum program.

c) A new name for the Party. Instead of "Social Democrats," whose official leaders *throughout* the world have betrayed socialism by deserting to the bourgeoisie (the "defencists" and the vacillating "Kautskyites"), we must call ourselves a *Communist Party.*

10. A new International. We must take the initiative in creating a revolutionary International, an International against the *social-chauvinists* and against the "Centre."

---

53. Declaration of the Rights of the Peoples of Russia, 1917

The Bolshevik armed coup in Petrograd of October 25/November 7, 1917 ended the seven-month rule of the Provisional Government of Russia, the successor to the tsarist regime. At that time, with the assistance of the left wing of the Socialist Revolutionaries, the Bolsheviks gained control of the Second all-Russian Congress of the Soviets. This Congress, which met between November 7–9, 1917, passed a Decree on Peace and a Decree on Land, and formed the first Bolshevik government—the fifteen member Council of Peoples Commissars, headed by Lenin. That Council (under the signature of Joseph Stalin, the Commissar of Nationalities) issued the Declaration of the Rights of the Peoples of Russia on November 15, 1917.

The following Declaration has to be viewed in the context of Bolshevik revolutionary strategy. Lenin and a majority of his followers supported the announcement of a right to national self-determination because they believed that such an action would promote a voluntary drawing together of nationalities. But the Bolsheviks also emphasized that actual national self-determination would have to be decided according to the merits of each case. They were particularly concerned about the effects of national self-determination on the larger cause of the proletarian revolution. After the Bolsheviks took power they disrupted the national movements of the non-Russian peoples and worked to undermine the establishment of their national states. When leaders in Finland and Ukraine took action to form independent states the Bolsheviks accused them of counterrevolutionary activity. They used tactics of subversion and all-out invasion in those cases, and this pattern was applied towards other non-Russian peoples as the Bolsheviks tried to assert control throughout the old Russian empire.

QUESTIONS

1. According to the Declaration, what was the tsarist policy toward nationalities of the Russian empire?
2. What rights does the Declaration recognize for the non-Russian peoples?

The October revolution of the workmen and peasants began under the common banner of emancipation.

The peasants are being emancipated from the power of the landowners, for there is no longer the landowner's property right in the land—it has been abolished. The soldiers and sailors are being emancipated from the power of autocratic generals, for generals will henceforth be elective and subject to recall. The workingmen are being emancipated from the whims of arbitrary will of the capitalists, for henceforth there will be established the control of the workers over mills and factories. Everything living and capable of life is being emancipated from the hateful shackles.

There remain only the peoples of Russia, who have suffered and are suffering oppression and arbitrariness, and whose emancipation must immediately be begun, whose liberation must be effected resolutely and definitely.

During the period of tsarism the peoples of Russia were systematically incited against one another. The results of such a policy are known: massacres and pogroms on the one hand, slavery of peoples on the other.

There can be and there must be no return to this disgraceful policy of instigation. Henceforth the policy of a voluntary and honest union of the peoples of Russia must be substituted.

In the period of imperialism, after the February/March revolution, when the power was transferred to the hands of the [Cadet party] bourgeoisie, the naked policy of instigation gave way to one of cowardly distrust of the peoples of Russia, to a policy of fault-finding and provocation, of "freedom" and "equality" of peoples. The results of such a policy are known: the growth of national enmity, the impairment of mutual trust.

An end must be put to this unworthy policy of falsehood and distrust, of fault-finding and provocation. Henceforth it must be replaced by an open and honest policy which leads to complete mutual trust of the peoples of Russia. Only as the result of such a trust can there be formed an honest and lasting union of the peoples of Russia. Only as the result of such a union can the workmen and peasants of the peoples of Russia be cemented into one revolutionary force able to resist all attempts on the part of the imperialist-annexationist bourgeoisie.

Starting with these assumptions, the first Congress of Soviets, in June of this year, proclaimed the right of the peoples of Russia to free self-determination.

The second Congress of Soviets, in October of this year, reaffirmed this inalienable right of the peoples of Russia more decisively and definitely.

The united will of these Congresses, the Council of the People's Commissars, resolved to base their activity upon the question of the nationalities of Russia, as expressed in the following principles:

1. The equality and sovereignty of the peoples of Russia.
2. The right of the peoples of Russia to free self-determination, even to the point of separation and the formation of a separate state.
3. The abolition of any and all national and national-religious privileges and disabilities.
4. The free development of national minorities and ethnographic groups inhabiting the territory of Russia.

The concrete decrees which follow will be framed immediately upon the formation of a commission for the affairs of nationalities.

54. The Treaty of Versailles, 1919

Historians have generally viewed the lengthy and complicated Treaty of Versailles as a badly flawed document that planted the dragon seeds of Nazism and fascism and that contributed greatly to the 1929 depression and World War II. Clemenceau, the leader of the host country of France, presided at the conference. The German delegation did not participate in the deliberations but were kept under a kind of house arrest and were permitted only to respond to treaty provisions in writing. Germany was not admitted to the League of Nations. Clemenceau sought revenge for the German defeat of France in the war of 1870–1871. He wanted to detach the Rhineland from Germany and either annex it to France or create a buffer state between the two mortal enemies. He also aimed to disarm Germany and to make it pay the full cost of the war in reparations. Wilson and Lloyd George induced him to renounce the claim to the Rhineland in return for a military guarantee of France's security; but when the U.S. refused to ratify the treaty, the guarantee collapsed, leaving the French very bitter. German resentment of and resistance to the treaty derived from its war aims and the belief that it had not been truly defeated. However, the German government had systematically lied to its people about war aims and the chances of victory, hence the 1918 defeat stunned the Germans and was quickly translated into charges of betrayal and subversion. The treaty was signed on 28 June 1919, the fifth anniversary of the assassination of the Archduke Francis Ferdinand, in the Hall of Mirrors of the Palace of Versailles, where in 1871 the victorious Germans had proclaimed their new empire. Only fifteen months had passed since the victorious Germans had dictated the much more severe treaty of Brest-Litovsk to the vanquished Russians.

QUESTIONS

1. How does Germany's treatment after World War I compare with France's treatment after the Napoleonic wars?
2. Is the Treaty of Versailles too harsh or too soft?
3. Discuss the section on reparations—especially Article 231.
4. What were the attitudes of the Allies toward the settlement? Could there have been a different peace?

**Part III—Political Clauses
for Europe**

Section III

Left Bank of the Rhine

Article 42. Germany is forbidden to maintain or construct any fortifications either on the left bank of the Rhine or on the right bank to the west of a line drawn 50 kilometres to the East of the Rhine.

Article 43. In the area defined above the maintenance and the assembly of armed forces, either permanently or temporarily, and military manoeuvres of any kind, as well as the upkeep of all permanent works for mobilization, are in the same way forbidden.

Article 44. In case Germany violates in any manner whatever the provisions of Articles 42 and 43, she shall be regarded as committing a hostile act against the Powers signatory of the present Treaty and as calculated to disturb the peace of the world.

Section IV

Saar Basin

Article 45. As compensation for the destruction of the coal mines in the north of France and as part payment towards the to-

tal reparation due from Germany for the damage resulting from the war, Germany cedes to France in full and absolute possession, with exclusive rights of exploitation, unencumbered and free from all debts and charges of any kind, the coal mines in the Saar Basin as defined in article 48. . . .

Article 49. Germany renounces in favour of the League of Nations, in the capacity of trustee, the government of the territory defined above.

At the end of fifteen years from the coming into force of the present Treaty the inhabitants of the said territory shall be called upon to indicate the sovereignty under which they desire to be placed.

Section V

Alsace-Lorraine

The High Contracting Parties, recognising the moral obligation to redress the wrong done by Germany in 1871 both to the rights of France and to the wishes of the population of Alsace and Lorraine, which were separated from their country in spite of the solemn protest of their representatives at the Assembly of Bordeaux, agree upon the following articles:

Article 51. The territories which were ceded to Germany in accordance with the

Preliminaries of Peace signed at Versailles on February 26, 1871, and the Treaty of Frankfort of May 10, 1871, are restored to French sovereignty as from the date of the Armistice of November 11, 1918.

The provisions of the Treaties establishing the delimitation of the frontiers before 1871 shall be restored. . . .

Section VI

Austria

Article 80. Germany acknowledges and will respect strictly the independence of Austria, within the frontiers which may be fixed in a Treaty between that State and the Principal Allied and Associated Powers; she agrees that this independence shall be inalienable, except with the consent of the Council of the League of Nations.

Section VII

Czecho-Slovak State

Article 81. Germany, in conformity with the action already taken by the Allied and Associated Powers, recognises the complete independence of the Czecho-Slovak State which will include the autonomous territory of the Ruthenians to the south of the Carpathians. Germany hereby recognises the frontiers of this State as determined by the Principal Allied and Associated Powers and other interested States. . . .

Section XIV

Russia and Russian States

Article 116. Germany acknowledges and agrees to respect as permanent and in-

alienable the independence of all territories which were part of the former Russian Empire on August 1, 1914.

. . . Germany accepts definitely the abrogation of the Brest-Litovsk Treaties and of all other treaties, conventions and agreements with the Maximalist [Bolshevik] Government in Russia.

The Allied and Associated Powers formally reserve the rights of Russia to obtain from Germany restitution and reparation based on the principles of the present Treaty. . . .

Part IV—German Rights and Interests Outside of Germany

Section I

German Colonies

Article 119. Germany renounces in favour of the Principal Allied and Associated Powers all her rights and titles over her oversea possessions. . . .

Section VIII

Shantung

Article 156. Germany renounces, in favour of Japan, all her rights, title and privileges—particularly those concerning the territory of Kiaochow, railways, mines and submarine cables—which she acquired in virtue of the Treaty concluded by her with China on March 5, 1898, and of all other arrangements relative to the Province of Shantung. . . .

Part V—Military, Naval, and Air Clauses

Section I

Military Clauses

Article 159. The German military forces shall be demobilised and reduced as prescribed hereinafter.

Article 160. (I) By a date which must be no later than March 31, 1920, the German Army must not comprise more than seven divisions of infantry and three divisions of cavalry.

After that date the total number of effectives in the Army of the States constituting Germany must not exceed one hundred thousand men, including officers and establishments of depots. The army shall be devoted exclusively to the maintenance of order within the territory and to control of the frontiers.

The total effective strength of officers, including the personnel of staffs, whatever their composition, must not exceed four thousand. . . .

Article 173. Universal compulsory military service shall be abolished in Germany.

The German Army may be constituted and recruited by means of voluntary enlistment. . . .

Section II—Naval Clauses

Article 181. After the expiration of a period of two months from the coming into force of the present Treaty the German naval forces in commission must not exceed:

6 battleships of the Deutschland or
    Lotheringen type,
6 light cruisers,
12 destroyers,
12 torpedo boats,

or an equal number of ships constructed to replace them as provided in Article 190.

No submarines are to be included.

All other warships, except where there is provision to the contrary in the present Treaty, must be placed in reserve or devoted to commercial purposes.

Section III—Air Clauses

Article 198. The armed forces of Germany must not include any military or naval air forces. . . .

Section IV—Inter-Allied Commissions of Control

Article 203. All the military, naval and air clauses contained in the present Treaty, for the execution of which a time-line is prescribed, shall be executed by Germany under the control of Inter-Allied Commissions specially appointed for this purpose by the Principal Allied and Associated Powers. . . .

Part VII—Penalties

Article 227. The Allied and Associated Powers publicly arraign William II of Hohenzollern, formerly German Emperor, for a supreme offence against international morality and the sanctity of treaties.

A special tribunal will be constituted to try the accused, thereby assuring him the guarantees essential to the right of defence. It will be composed of five judges, one appointed by each of the following Powers: namely, the United States of America, Great Britain, France, Italy and Japan.

Article 228. The German Government recognises the right of the Allied and Associated Powers to bring before military tribunals persons accused of having committed acts in violation of the laws and customs of war. . . .

Part VIII—Reparation

Section I—General Provisions

Article 231. The Allied and Associated Governments affirm and Germany accepts the responsibility of Germany and her allies for causing all the loss and damage to which the Allied and Associated Governments and their nationals have been subjected as a consequence of the war imposed upon them by the aggression of Germany and her allies.

Article 232. The Allied and Associated Governments recognise that the resources of Germany are not adequate, after taking into account permanent diminutions of such resources which will result from other provisions of the present Treaty, to make complete reparation for all such loss and damage.

The Allied and Associated Governments, however, require, and Germany undertakes, that she will make compensation for all damage done to the civilian population of the Allied and Associated Powers and to their property during the period of their belligerency of each as an Allied or Associated Power against Germany by such aggression by land, by sea and from the air, and in general all damage as defined in Annex I hereto. . . .

Article 233. The amount of the above damage for which compensation is to be made by Germany shall be determined by an Inter-Allied Commission, to be called the *Reparation Commission* and constituted in the form and with the powers set forth hereunder and in Annexes II to VII inclusive hereto.

This Commission shall consider the claims and give to the German Government a just opportunity to be heard. . . .

Article 235. In order to enable the Allied and Associated Powers to proceed at once to the restoration of their industrial and economic life, pending the full determination of their claims, Germany shall pay in such installments and in such manner (whether in gold, commodities, ships, securities or otherwise) as the Reparation Commission may fix, during 1919, 1920 and the first four months of 1921, the equivalent of 20,000,000,000 gold marks. Out of this sum the expenses of the armies of occupation subsequent to the Armistice of November 11, 1918, shall first be met, and such supplies of food and raw materials as may be judged by the Governments of the Principal Allied and Associated Powers to be essential to enable Germany to meet her obligations for reparation may also, with the approval of the said Governments, be paid for out of the above sum. The balance shall be reckoned towards liquidation of the amounts due for reparation. . . .

Part XIV—Guarantees

Section I—Western Europe

Article 428. As a guarantee for the execution of the present Treaty by Germany, the German territory situated to the west of the Rhine, together with the bridgeheads, will be occupied by Allied and Associated troops for a period of fifteen years from the coming into force of the present Treaty. . . .

Section II—Eastern Europe

Article 433. As a guarantee for the execution of the provisions of the present Treaty, by which Germany accepts definitely the abrogation of the Brest-Litovsk Treaty, and of all treaties, conventions, and agreements entered into by her with the Maximalist Government in Russia, and in order to ensure the restoration of peace and good government in the Baltic Provinces and Lithuania, all German troops at present in the said territories shall return to within the frontiers of Germany as soon as the Governments of the Principal Allied and Associated Powers shall think the moment suitable, having regard to the internal situation of these territories. These troops shall abstain from all requisitions and seizures and from any other coercive measures, with a view to obtaining supplies intended for Germany, and shall in no way interfere with such measures for national defence as may be adopted by the Provisional Governments of Estonia, Latvia and Lithuania. . . .

---

55. Speech to Managers of Socialist Industry, 1931

Joseph Stalin

Joseph V. Stalin (1879–1953) was born in Georgia in Transcaucasia and joined the Russian Social-Democratic Party in his youth. He was expelled from divinity school for his radicalism. When the Social Democrats split Stalin sided with the Bolsheviks, and as a professional revolutionary he rose to the highest ranks of the party. After Lenin's death the ambitious and unscrupulous Stalin exploited the divisions within the party in order to gain total control over both the organization and the entire Soviet Union. In 1928 he inaugurated the first Five Year Plan, which called for rapid industrialization and forced collectivization of agriculture. In the summer of 1929 the party's Central Committee and the Sixteenth Party Congress raised production quotas and designated the last three months of 1930 as the "shock quarter." The following excerpts from a speech Stalin delivered in 1931 illustrate the arguments he used to maintain a state of urgency in the Soviet Union.

QUESTIONS

1. Why did Joseph Stalin believe that rapid industrialization was essential for the Soviet Union?
2. What does Stalin mean by "our obligations, internal and international"?
3. What interpretation of Russian history underlies Stalin's speech? Was his analysis confirmed ten years later?

It is sometimes asked whether it is not possible to slow down the tempo a bit, to put a check on the movement. No, comrades, it is not possible! The tempo must not be reduced! On the contrary, we must increase it as much as is within our powers and possibilities. This is dictated to us by our obligations to the workers and peasants of the U.S.S.R. This is dictated to us by our obligations to the working class of the whole world.

To slacken the tempo would mean falling behind. And those who fall behind get beaten. But we do not want to be beaten. No, we refuse to be beaten! One feature of the history of old Russia was the continual beatings she suffered for falling behind, for her backwardness. She was beaten by the Mongol Khans. She was beaten by the Turkish beys. She was beaten by the Swedish feudal lords. She was beaten by the Polish and Lithuanian gentry. She was beaten by the British and French capitalists. She was beaten by the Japanese barons. All beat her—for her backwardness: for military backwardness, for cultural backwardness, for political backwardness, for industrial backwardness, for agricultural backwardness. She was beaten because to do so was profitable and could be done with impunity. Do you remember the words of the pre-revolutionary poet [Nikolai Nekrassov]: "You are poor and abundant, mighty and impotent, Mother Russia." These words of the old poet were well learned by those gentlemen. They beat her, saying: "You are abundant," so one can enrich oneself at your expense. They beat her, saying: "You are poor and impotent," so you can be beaten and plundered with impunity. Such is the law of the exploiters—to beat the backward and the weak. It is the jungle law of capitalism. You are backward, you are weak—therefore you are wrong; hence, you can be beaten and enslaved. You are mighty—

therefore you are right; hence, we must be wary of you.

That is why we must no longer lag behind.

In the past we had no fatherland, nor could we have one. But now that we have overthrown capitalism and power is in the hands of the working class, we have a fatherland, and we will defend its independence. Do you want our socialist fatherland to be beaten and to lose its independence? If you do not want this you must put an end to its backwardness in the shortest possible time and develop genuine Bolshevik tempo in building up its socialist system of economy. There is no other way. That is why Lenin said during the October Revolution: "Either perish, or overtake and outstrip the advanced capitalist countries."

We are fifty or a hundred years behind the advanced countries. We must make good this distance in ten years. Either we do it, or they crush us.

This is what our obligation to the workers and peasants of the U.S.S.R. dictates to us.

But we have other still more serious and more important obligations. They are our obligations to the world proletariat. They coincide with our obligations to the workers and peasants of the U.S.S.R. But we place them higher. The working class of the U.S.S.R. is part of the world working class. We achieved victory not only as a result of the efforts of the working class of the U.S.S.R., but also thanks to the support of the working class of the world. Without this support we would have been torn to pieces long ago. It is said that our country is the shock-brigade of the proletariat of all countries. This is well said. But this imposes very serious obligations upon us. Why does the international proletariat support us? How did we merit this support? By the fact that we were the first to establish a working class state, we were the first to start building socialism. By the fact that we are doing work which, if successful, will change the whole world and free the entire working class. But what is needed for success? The elimination of our backwardness, the development of a high Bolshevik tempo of construction. . . . Must we not justify the hopes of the world's working class, must we not fulfill our obligations to them? Yes, we must if we do not want utterly to disgrace ourselves.

Such are our obligations, internal and international. . . .

In ten years at most we must make good the distance we are lagging behind the advanced capitalist countries. We have all the "objective" opportunities for this. The only thing lacking is the ability to make proper use of these opportunities. And that depends on us. *Only* on us! It is time we learned to use these opportunities.

56. Execution by Hunger: The Ukrainian Famine, 1931–1933

Miron Dolot

The collectivization of agriculture constituted a part of the transformation of the U.S.S.R., during the so-called "second revolution" initiated in 1928 by the first Five Year Plan. It meant an extension of direct economic and political control by the party over the rural population. The initial Plan called for a limited program, but by the end of 1929 Stalin announced a forced mass collectivization of agriculture as well as the liquidation of the kulak class (well-to-do farmers or any peasants who opposed collectivization). This unleashed the all-out struggle against private farming. The government used party members and military units and recruited outsiders to crush peasant resistance. Since the peasants could not meet the high grain and other produce quotas imposed on them, the authorities used house-to-house searches to seize foodstuffs. That policy left the peasants without food for themselves and resulted in a severe famine. In Ukraine the suffering and starvation reached a massive scale. Recent estimates place the number of dead in this man-made famine in Ukraine at over six million people. In addition, the famine was accompanied by a wide-ranging destruction of Ukrainian cultural and religious life. Stalin's intention was to destroy private peasant agriculture in Ukraine, which provided the social foundation for Ukrainian nationalism. The following narrative was written by a survivor of this catastrophe, who used a pen name to tell his story.

QUESTIONS

1. The scenes depicted here are vignettes in what is known as a "man-made famine," in which the casualties ran into millions. What possible policy aims required suffering on such a scale?

2. What factors in the twentieth century generate such extreme devaluation of human life?
3. Can it happen here?

There was silence and the monotony of snow everywhere throughout the village. The only signs of life came from the chimneys here and there, with tiny streams of smoke rising in the sky. Many houses in our neighborhood did not have any smoke coming out of their chimneys. Hadn't the people inside made any fires? How could they possibly stay alive, we wondered, in subzero temperatures, without their houses being heated?

To find out for ourselves, we ran first to Dmytro's house which showed no signs of life. Dmytro had never returned home after he had been taken to the county center. His young wife Solomia was left alone with their daughter. She had gone to work in the collective farm, taking her little child with her. As the wife of a banished man, she too was considered an "enemy of the people," and her child was refused admission to the nursery. Later, Solomia was expelled from the collective farm, and thus forced to seek a job in the city. That was impossible, however, because she could not show a certificate of release from the collective farm. She found herself trapped in the circle of the Communist death ring. She had to return to the village.

When winter came, Solomia went from house to house, willing to work for just a piece of bread. She was too proud to beg. People were sympathetic and helped her as much as they could. However, as the famine worsened, and the villagers were no longer able to help her, she was not seen on her rounds any more.

We found the front door of Solomia's house open, but the entrance was blocked with snowdrifts, and it was hard to get inside. When we finally reached the living room, we saw a pitiful sight: Solomia was hanging from the ceiling in the middle of the room. She was dressed in her Ukrainian national costume, and at her breast hung a large cross. It was obvious that she had made preparations before committing suicide. Her hair was combed neatly in two braids hanging over her shoulders.

Frightened, we ran to fetch mother. We helped her take down Solomia's frozen body, and laid it on a bench, and covered it with a handmade blanket. It was only after we finished doing this that we noticed the dead body of her little daughter. The child was lying in a wooden tub in the corner under the icons, clean and dressed in her best clothes. Her little hands were folded across her chest.

On the table was a note:

Dear neighbors:

Please bury our bodies properly. I have to leave you, dear neighbors. I can bear this life no longer. There is no food in the house, and there is no sense in living without my little daughter who has starved to death, or my husband. If you ever see Dmytro, tell him about us. He will understand our plight, and he will forgive me. Please tell him that I died peacefully, thinking about him and our daughter.

I love you my dear neighbors, and I wish with all my heart that you somehow recover from this disaster. Forgive me for troubling you. Thank you for everything that you have done for me.

Solomia.

After reading the note, we stood there for a while, motionless and forlorn. Our mother tried to suppress the sound of her weeping, pressing the corner of her head scarf to her lips. Mykola gazed at the corpses in disbelief.

In my imagination I was recreating the agony of their dying: the child's hunger cries, and then the death convulsions of its exhausted little body.

How great must have been the sufferings of the mother. She had to listen helplessly to the pleas of her child for food, while she herself was near starvation. She must have felt great relief, I thought, when she saw her little daughter breathing for the last time. Then, in my imagination, I saw the mother attending to her lifeless child: dressing her in the best and cleanest clothing she had, praying on her knees near the body, and finally kissing her for the last time before her own suicide.

Mother interrupted my thoughts. We had to fulfill the last wishes of our dead neighbor and bury the two corpses properly. My mother always wanted to do everything correctly. But how could we do it this time. We were too weak to dig a grave in the snow-covered frozen ground, or even to take the bodies to the cemetery.

After realizing these facts, we decided to leave them in the house. For the time being, the cold prevented their decay, so we just laid the body of the child beside her mother on the sleeping bench, covered them both with the blanket, and left.

After this sad discovery, we could not sit idly at home. There were many other houses around us that had no smoke coming out of their chimneys. We realized that similar tragedies had taken place there too. My mother was especially concerned about Boris's family and also about a widow who lived with her crippled daughter in our neighborhood. She thought they might still be alive and in need of help.

Without losing much time, we went to Boris's house. He also had not returned from the village jail, but had been transferred to the county center, and no one has seen him since. His wife, Khymka, was living alone with their two children. We frequently visited her, helping the family as much as we could. Lately, during the heavy snowstorms, we had lost all contact with them.

When we reached the front of Khymka's house, we noticed a dark object protruding from underneath the snow. It was Khymka. Her body was completely frozen and covered with snow. We rushed into the house, anticipating the worst about her children: we were right. On the sleeping bench lay the corpse of Khymka's eldest son Trokhym. His hands were folded across his chest, his eyes were closed, and his frozen body was covered with an overcoat. At his head was a saucer with the remnants of a candle. Trokhym must have died before his mother. Then, in order to try and save the life of her other child, Khymka apparently left the house in search of help. But, too weakened by hunger, she collapsed a few steps in front of her house, and died in the snow.

We also found her youngest child, a boy of about eight years of age, in a bed. He was well covered with several pieces of old clothing and was miraculously still alive! He lay there totally exhausted by hunger and too weak to move. His body had stiffened and was apparently half-frozen.

We had to act immediately to try to save the glimmer of life still in this young boy. There was no time for contemplation and emotions. We brought Khymka's body back into the house and laid it alongside the body of her starved eldest son. It became clear to us that we had to take the youngest boy home with us, if we wanted to keep him alive, for his own house was freezing with not a trace of fuel for heating or food for survival. We carefully laid him on a sled and brought him home with us to revive him and care for him. Mother put him in bed, and told us with God's help, he might recover.

She then sent us with a sled to the widow's house to bring her and her crippled daughter with us if they were still alive. They lived close by, and it didn't take us long to reach her house.

The widow Shevchenko and her crippled daughter Lida were also victims of government policy. A few years earlier, her husband had clashed with a Party representative when the collectivization scheme was being instituted. The representative had come to our village to organize a collective farm, and during a heated argument, Shevchenko had dared to call him "a stupid parrot"! That was his end. He was accused of assailing the dignity of the Communist Party, and he was sent to the north for five years of "corrective labor." After a year or so, his wife had received an anonymous letter telling her that her husband had died while digging the Baltic Sea-White Sea Canal. His widow now lived all alone with their daughter, who had been crippled from birth and needed constant attention. Widow Shevchenko had twice as difficult a task as the other villagers in providing food and other necessities for the two of them. Being tied down at home by the daily care of her handicapped daughter, she could not go to work. She could not get any official help either, since she was the wife of an arrested "enemy of the people." She became a beggar, completely dependent upon the goodwill of her fellow villagers. When the whole village was struck by famine, her fate was sealed.

We found her house on a hill not far from ours, completely snowbound, with the front door blocked by the snow.

We had a hard time clearing it away, and when we finally opened the door, we found the poor widow dead, just as we feared, lying on the threshold halfway in the entrance hall. We carried her body into the living room and laid it on a bench. We found her daughter Lida, lying on a sleeping bench

wrapped in many layers of rags but still alive. We carefully laid her on our sled and rushed her back to our house.

At home, Mother was still occupied with Khymka's young son. She was rubbing his body with snow, and there was something cooking for him on the stove.

When we brought Lida indoors, Mother began administering to her needs, and we took over the care of the young boy. After making them as warm and comfortable as we could, we tried to feed them porridge and some homemade herb tea prepared by Mother, but our efforts to force some food and drink into them were all in vain. Except for the slow and spasmodic breathing, they didn't show any other signs of life, lying there completely motionless. When night fell, we witnessed their horrible death throes. At midnight, Lida died and the young boy followed shortly after.

Now we found ourselves in a peculiar situation. We had two corpses of people not related to us in our house. We could not keep them like that in our house too long, and burying them in the cemetery had certain risks.

It was dangerous to show sympathy to starving villagers, particularly to people who, like this boy and girl, were looked upon by the government officials as "enemies of the people." Trying to save the lives of these young people came as natural to us as trying to save our own lives, but the Communist Party looked upon such an act as high treason. Nevertheless, come what may, we decided to bury their bodies properly in the cemetery.

The next morning, Mykola and I loaded the bodies on our sled, covered them over, and started toward the village center where the cemetery was located. It was very hard for us to pull the sled with such a heavy load; we had very little strength for such a task, especially in the deep snow and the freezing cold. Moving along the main road, we saw a few more corpses, some of them we recognized as the remains of neighbors. There were also strangers among them who had probably come over from other villages in search of food. The fact that all the corpses were covered with heavy snow suggested to us that they had been lying on the road for quite some time.

As we came closer to the village center, we saw a pair of horses pulling up a sleigh and galloping toward us. We knew such a luxury was only afforded Party and government officials. The road was narrowed by the high snowdrifts, so we could not give way. The rearing horses stopped almost in front of us. At first we only heard swearing coming from the sleigh; then we were commanded to move aside. While we were trying to do this, our heavy loaded sled became firmly stuck into the snow. As we vainly attempted to push and pull our sled out, we inadvertently uncovered our cargo. The attention of the officials was instantly riveted to our sled. They dismounted and came over to us for a closer look.

There were two of them and both of them were strangers to us. They were warmly dressed and looked well fed and prosperous, as in olden days. One of them with a fur coat stepped forward and demanded what we were pulling in our sled.

"You see what we're pulling!" I replied, pointing to the corpses. The other stranger was eying us with curiosity.

"Who were they, and how did they die?" the man in the fur coat continued his interrogation.

What a superfluous and ridiculous question! I casually answered that the corpses were those of our neighbors. Then, instead of explaining to him the cause of their deaths, I pointed out that one could see many corpses on the road, and that there were many more dead and dying in their homes. He apparently must have been very displeased with my answer because he asked me angrily who we were and stepped closer to us.

"You certainly don't want to tell me that the entire population of the village died, or is about to die out do you?" he continued, raising his voice. Then hurling more insults and curses at us, he took a notebook out of his pocket and wrote down our names.

The other man watched the whole procedure silently. After the man in the fur coat put his notebook away, they both returned to their sleigh, and passed swiftly by. It was no small effort for us to finally extricate our sled from the deep snow.

It was quite a relief when we at last reached the cemetery, for we were very cold and exhausted. Here we found ourselves among dozens of corpses. They lay scattered on both sides of the road. Some of them were piled up into heaps probably all members of one family or of one neighborhood. Others were thrown all over in a haphazard fashion.

The cemetery was deathly quiet. No one was around. Nobody bothered to bury the remains of these miserable wretches.

57. Speech on De-Stalinization, 1956

Nikita S. Khrushchev

The gradual down-grading of Stalin was a part of the developing changes in the U.S.S.R. following his death in 1953. In particular the rivals who aspired to succeed him criticized his "cult of personality" and emphasized the necessity of "collective leadership." Nikita S. Khrushchev's secret speech, delivered at the 20th Congress of the Communist Party of the Soviet Union in February 1956, initiated the de-Stalinization process. Although Khrushchev (1894–1971) denounced Stalin's despotic absolutism, cruelty, and self-glorification, he did not ascribe these practices to the communist doctrine or the Soviet system which served as the basis of Stalinism. He insisted that Stalin departed from Leninism, and he refused to concede that in Stalinism there were policies and practices that were rooted in Lenin's term of power. In October 1961 Khrushchev attacked Stalin again, calling him a murderer, an abuser of power, and a violator of Leninism. The delegates to the 22nd Congress of the Communist Party then voted to remove Stalin's remains from the mausoleum on Red Square and to rebury him alongside the Kremlin Wall.

QUESTIONS

1. According to Khrushchev, how did Stalin misuse his power?
2. What distinctions did Khrushchev draw between the policies of Lenin and Stalin? Why did he stress those differences?
3. How did Stalin cultivate and promote his own reputation and image?
4. What does this document reveal about the Soviet political system in 1956?

Stalin acted not through persuasion, explanation, and patient cooperation with people, but by imposing his concepts and demanding absolute submission to his opinion. Whoever opposed this concept or tried to prove his viewpoint, and the correctness of his position, was doomed to removal from the leading collective and to subsequent moral and physical annihilation. This was especially true during the period following the XVIIth Party Congress, when many prominent Party leaders and rank-and-file Party workers, honest and dedi-

cated to the cause of Communism, fell victim to Stalin's despotism.

We must affirm that the party had fought a serious fight against the Trotskyites, rightists and bourgeois nationalists, and that it disarmed ideologically all the enemies of Leninism. This ideological fight was carried on successfully as a result of which the Party became strengthened and tempered. Here Stalin played a positive role. . . .

Stalin originated the concept "enemy of the people." This term automatically rendered it unnecessary that the ideological errors of a man or men engaged in a controversy be proven; this term made possible the usage of the most cruel repression, violating all norms of revolutionary legality, against anyone who in any way disagreed with Stalin, against those who were only suspected of hostile intent, against those who had bad reputations. This concept, "enemy of the people," actually eliminated the possibility of any kind of ideological fight or the making of one's views known on this or that issue, even those of a practical character. In the main, and in actuality, the only proof of guilt used, against all norms of current legal science, was the "confession" of the accused himself; and, as subsequent probing proved, "confessions" were acquired through physical pressures against the accused.

This led to glaring violations of revolutionary legality, and to the fact that many entirely innocent persons, who in the past had defended the Party line, became victims.

We must assert that, in regard to those persons who in their time had opposed the Party line, there were often no sufficiently serious reasons for their physical annihilation. The formula, "enemy of the people" was specifically introduced for the purpose of physically annihilating such individuals.

It is a fact that many persons, who were later annihilated as enemies of the Party [were] people [who] had worked with Lenin during his life. Some of these persons had made errors during Lenin's life, but, despite this, Lenin benefited by their work, he corrected them and he did everything possible to retain them in the ranks of the party; he induced them to follow him. . . .

An entirely different relationship with people characterized Stalin. Lenin's traits—patient work with people; stubborn and painstaking education of them; the ability to induce people to follow him without using compulsion, but rather through the ideological influence on them of the whole collective—were entirely foreign to Stalin. He [Stalin] discarded the Leninist method of convincing and educating; he abandoned the method of ideological struggle for that of administrative violence, mass repressions, and terror. He acted on an increasingly larger scale and more stubbornly through punitive organs, at the same time often violating all existing norms of morality and of Soviet laws.

Arbitrary behavior by one person encouraged and permitted arbitrariness in others. Mass arrests and deportations of many thousands of people, execution without trial and without normal investigation created conditions of insecurity, fear and even desperation.

This, of course, did not contribute toward unity of the Party ranks and of all strata of working people, but on the contrary brought about annihilation and the expulsion from the Party of workers who were loyal but inconvenient to Stalin. . . .

Lenin used severe methods only in the most necessary cases, when the exploiting classes were still in existence and were vigorously opposing the revolution, when the struggle for survival was decidedly assuming the sharpest forms, even including a civil war.

Stalin, on the other hand, used extreme methods and mass repression at a time when the revolution was already victorious, when the Soviet state was strengthened, when the exploiting classes were already liquified and Socialist relations were rooted solidly in all phases of national economy, when our Party was politically consolidated. . . .

. . . The Commission has presented to the Central Committee Presidium lengthy and documented material pertaining to mass repressions against the delegates to the XVIIth Party Congress and against members of the Central Committee elected at that Congress. These materials have been studied by the Presidium of the Central Committee.

It was determined that of the 139 members and candidates of the Party's Central Committee who were elected at the XVIIth Congress, 98 persons, i.e. 70 percent, were arrested and shot (mostly in 1937–1938). [Indignation in the hall.]

What was the composition of the delegates to the XVIIth Congress? It is known that 80 percent of the voting participants of the XVIIth Congress joined the party during the years of conspiracy before the Revolution and during the Civil War; this means before 1921. By social origin the basic mass of the delegates to the Congress were workers (60 percent of the voting members).

For this reason, it was inconceivable that a Congress so composed would have elected a Central Committee, a majority of whom would prove to be enemies of the Party. The only reason why 70 percent of Central Committee members and candidates elected at the XVIIth Congress were branded as enemies of the Party and of the people was because honest Communists were slandered, accusations against them were fabricated, and revolutionary legality was gravely undermined.

The same fate met not only the Central Committee members but also the majority of the delegates to the XVIIth Party Congress. Of 1,966 delegates with either voting or advisory rights, 1,108 persons were arrested on charges of anti-revolutionary crimes, i.e., decidedly more than the majority. This very fact shows how absurd, wild and contrary to common sense were the charges of counter-revolutionary crimes made out, as we now see, against a majority of participants at the XVIIth Congress. [Indignation in the hall.]

We should recall that the XVIIth Party Congress is historically known as the Congress of Victors. Delegates to the Congress were active participants in the building of our Socialist State; many of them suffered and fought for Party interests during the pre-revolutionary years in the conspiracy and at the Civil War fronts; they fought their enemies valiantly and often nervelessly looked into the face of death. How then can we believe that such people could prove to be "two-faced" and had joined the camps of the enemies of Socialism during the era after the political liquidation of Zinovievites, Trotskyites and rightists and after the great accomplishments of Socialist construction?

This was the result of the abuse of power by Stalin, who began to use mass terror against the Party cadres. . . .

Comrades! The cult of the individual acquired such monstrous size chiefly because Stalin himself, using all conceivable methods, supported the glorification of his own person. This is supported by numerous facts. One of the most characteristic examples of Stalin's self-glorification and of his lack of even elementary modesty is the edition of his *Short Biography*, which was published in 1948.

This book is an expression of the most dissolute flattery, an example of making a man into a godhead, of transforming him into an infallible sage, "the greatest leader," "sublime strategist of all times and nations." Finally no other words could be found with which to lift Stalin up to the heavens.

We need not give here examples of the loathsome adulation filling this book. All we need to add is that they all were approved and edited by Stalin personally and some of them were added in his own handwriting to the draft text of the book.

What did Stalin consider essential to write into this book? Did he want to cool the ardor of his flatterers who were composing his "Short Biography"? No! He marked the very places where he thought that the praise of his services was insufficient.

Here are some examples characterizing Stalin's activity, added in Stalin's own hand: . . .

"Although he performed his task of leader of the Party and the people with consummate skill and enjoyed the unreserved support of the entire Soviet people, Stalin never allowed his work to be marred by the slightest hint of vanity, conceit, or self-adulation."

Where and when could a leader so praise himself? Is this worthy of a leader of the Marxist-Leninist type? No. Precisely against this did Marx and Engels take such a strong position. This also was always sharply condemned by Vladimir Ilyich Lenin.

In the draft text of his book appeared the following sentence: "Stalin is the Lenin of today." This sentence appeared to Stalin to be too weak, so in his own handwriting he changed it to read: "Stalin is the worthy continuer of Lenin's work, or, as it is said in our Party, Stalin is the Lenin of today." You see how well it is said, not by the Nation but by Stalin himself.

It is possible to give many such self-praising appraisals written into the draft of that book in Stalin's hand. Especially generous does he endow himself with praises pertaining to his military genius, to his talent for strategy.

I will cite one more insertion made by Stalin concerning the theme of the Stalinist military genius.

"The advanced Soviet science of war received further development," he writes, "at Comrade Stalin's hands. Comrade Stalin elaborated the theory of the permanently operating factors that decide the issue of wars, of active defense and the laws of counter-offensive and offensive, of the co-operation of all services and arms in modern warfare, of the role of big tank masses and air forces in modern war, and of the artillery as the most formidable of the armed services. At the various stages of the war Stalin's genius found the correct solutions that took account of all the circumstances of the situation." [Movement in the hall.]

And further, writes Stalin:

"Stalin's military mastership was displayed both in defense and offense. Comrade Stalin's genius enabled him to divine the enemy's plans and defeat them. The battles in which Comrade Stalin directed the Soviet armies are brilliant examples of operational military skill."

In this manner was Stalin praised as a strategist. Who did this? Stalin himself, not in his role as a strategist but in the role of an author-editor, one of the main creators of his self-adulatory biography.

Such, comrades, are the facts. We should rather say shameful facts.

58. Mein Kampf, 1924

Adolf Hitler

Adolf Hitler (1889–1945) was the Austrian-born Nazi dictator of Germany from 1933–1945. His Thousand Year Reich ended with his suicide and German defeat in World War II. His father was a minor customs official who ill treated his son, but upon his death in 1903 Hitler's mother was able to maintain a comfortable middle class status. In 1907 she sent her son to study art in Vienna, where he saturated himself in racial ideology and national phobias. In 1913 he fled the Austrian draft to Munich. His youth and early manhood were miserable, the life of a drifter and failure but he was not plagued by the poverty he later pretended to have suffered. During his formative years he harbored an enormous hatred which resulted from his failures as an artist. As a soldier in World War I he won the Iron Cross for bravery, but his frustrations increased with Germany's defeat. After the war he became an army informer, and then he joined and took over the minuscule National Socialist German Workers Party (Nazi) and converted it into a mass movement. His attempt to overthrow the Bavarian government failed in the *putsch* of 1923, after which he was imprisoned a short time and wrote *Mein Kampf*. Thereafter he sought power by demonstrations and street fights, and he became one of history's great demagogues. A degree of prosperity and normality in Germany deprived him of much appeal until the 1929 Depression gave him the opportunity to come to power as chancellor by legal means. He capitalized on support from sympathetic industrialists and secret funds from the army that enabled him and the party to finance a newspaper, a paramilitary force, and election contests.

While there was nothing original about Hitler's ideology except his synthesis of ideas and his genius in promoting it, it is of fundamental importance as the controlling factor of all his actions and policies as party agitator, ruler of Germany, conqueror of Europe, or destroyer of the Jews. His ideology consisted of an impulse for war, conquest, destruction, nihilism, domination, and the will to power. It featured an intense nationalism and extreme racism that equated the Germans with the superior "Aryan" race and bestowed on them the right to conquer and rule. Hitler also promulgated the Führer principle, which is the totalitarian rule of one man, and a social ethos of discipline, heroism, military ideals and values, and willingness to sacrifice. An antisemitic phobia permeated his mind. He viewed Jews as "the people of Satan," who conspired to dominate and rule the world through communism, socialism, internationalism, democracy, pacifism, or disarmament. In short, Hitler equated the Jews with everything he feared, hated, and sought to destroy. If he had been no more than an ideological crank, Hitler would not have cut such a lethal swath in history. He had a devastating impact because he combined a fanatical belief in his own ideological system with a tactical genius and political demagoguery that enabled him to win and hold supreme power long enough to carry out his frightful program.

QUESTIONS

1. Summarize Adolf Hitler's views on the nature and proper use of propaganda. Explain his references to advertising and mass psychology.
2. Explain Hitler's concept of race. What characteristics does he attribute to Aryans? What does he view as the causes of cultural decline for races?
3. Does Hitler view the Jews as a race or a religion? According to him, what characteristics do the Jewish people display? What danger do they pose to other races?
4. How does Hitler prove his case against the Jews? What kind of arguments does he present? What traditions of antisemitism does he draw upon?
5. According to Hitler, what should be the foreign policy objectives of the German people? How does his recommendation for territorial expansion differ from previous German territorial goals? What means does he suggest for the implementation of his goals?
6. What assumptions and intentions lie behind Hitler's statement, "A state which in this age of racial poisoning dedicates itself to the care of its best racial elements must some day become lords of the earth"?

Propaganda

To whom has propaganda to appeal? To the scientific intelligentsia or to the less educated masses?

It has to appeal forever and only to the masses!

Propaganda is not for the intelligentsia or for those who unfortunately call themselves by that name today, but scientific teaching. But propaganda is in its contents as far from being science as perhaps a poster is art in its presentation as such. . . .

The task of propaganda lies not in a scientific training of the individual, but rather in directing the masses towards certain facts, events, necessities, etc., the purpose being to move their importance into the masses' field of vision.

The art now is exclusively to attack this so skillfully that a general conviction of the reality of a fact, of the necessity of an event, that something that is necessary is also right, etc., is created. But as it is not and cannot be science in itself, as its task consists of catching the masses' attention, just like that of the poster, and not in teaching one who is already scientifically experienced or is striving towards education and knowledge, its effect has always to be directed more and more towards the feeling, and only to a certain extent to so-called reason.

All propaganda has to be popular and has to adapt its spiritual level to the perception of the least intelligent of those towards whom it intends to direct itself. Therefore its spiritual level has to be screwed the lower, the greater the mass of people which one wants to attract. But if the problem involved, like the propaganda for carrying on a war, is to include an entire people in its field of action, the caution in avoiding too high spiritual assumptions cannot be too great. . . .

The great masses' receptive ability is only very limited, their understanding is small, but their forgetfulness is great. As a consequence of these facts, all effective propaganda has to limit itself only to a very few points and to use them like slogans until even the very last man is able to imagine what is intended by such a word. As soon as one sacrifices this basic principle and tries to become versatile, the effect will fritter away, as the masses are neither able to digest the material offered nor to retain it. Thus the result is weakened and finally eliminated.

The greater the line of its representation has to be, the more correctly from the psychological point of view will its tactics have to be outlined. . . .

What would one say about a poster, for instance, which was to advertise a new soap, and which nevertheless describes other soaps as also being 'good'?

At this one would certainly shake one's head.

Exactly the same is the case with political advertising.

Propaganda's task is for instance, not to evaluate the various rights, but far more to stress exclusively the one that is to be represented by it. It has not to search into truth as far as this is favorable to others, in order to present it then to the masses with doctrinary honesty, but it has rather to serve its own truth uninterruptedly. . . .

The great mass of a people is not composed of diplomats or even teachers of political law, nor even of purely reasonable individuals who are able to pass judgment, but of human beings who are as undecided as they are inclined towards doubts and uncertainty. As soon as by one's own propaganda even a glimpse of right on the other side is admitted, the cause for doubting one's own right is laid. The masses are not in a position to distinguish where the wrong of the others ends and their own begins. In this case they become uncertain and mistrusting, especially if the enemy does not produce the same nonsense, but, in turn, burdens their enemy with all and the whole guilt. . . .

The people, in an overwhelming majority, are so feminine in their nature and attitude that their activities and thoughts are motivated less by sober consideration than by feeling and sentiment.

This sentiment, however, is not complicated but very simple and complete. There are not many differentiations, but rather a positive or a negative; love or hate, right or wrong, truth or lie; but never half this and half that, or partially, etc. . . .

. . . propaganda will not lead to success unless a fundamental principle is considered with continually sharp attention; it has to confine itself to little and to repeat this eternally. Here, too, persistency, as in so many other things in this world, is the first and the most important condition for success. . . .

A change must never alter the content of what is being brought forth by propaganda, but in the end it always has to say the same. Thus the slogan has to be illuminated from various sides, but the end of every reflection has always and again to be the slogan itself. Only thus can and will propaganda have uniform and complete effect.

This great line alone, which one must never leave, brings the final success to maturity by continually regular and consistent emphasis. But then one will be able to determine with astonishment to what enormous and hardly understandable results such perseverance will lead.

All advertising, whether it lies in the field of business or of politics, will carry success by continuity and regular uniformity of application.

Here, too, the enemy's war propaganda [1914–1918] set a typical example. It was limited to a few points of view, calculated exclusively for the masses, and it was carried out with untiring persistency. Basic ideas and forms of execution which had once been recognized as being right were employed throughout the entire War, and never did one make even the slightest change. At the beginning it was apparently crazy in the impudence of its assertions, later it became disagreeable, and finally it was believed. After four and a half years a revolution broke out in Germany the slogan of which came from the enemy's war propaganda. . . .

Nation and Race

All great cultures of the past perished only because the originally creative race died off through blood-poisoning.

The ultimate cause of such a decline was always the forgetting that all culture depends on men and not the reverse; that means, that in order to save a certain culture the man who created it has to be saved. But the preservation is bound to the brazen law of necessity and of the right of the victory of the best and the strongest in this world.

He who wants to live should fight, therefore, and he who does not want to battle in this world of eternal struggle does not deserve to be alive.

Even if this were hard, this is the way things are. . . .

What we see before us of human culture today, the results of art, science, and techniques, is almost exclusively the creative product of the Aryan. But just this fact admits of the not unfounded conclusion that he alone was the founder of higher humanity as a whole, thus the prototype of what we understand by the word 'man.' . . .

If one were to divide mankind into three groups: culture-founders, culture-bearers, and culture-destroyers, then as representative of the first kind, only the Aryan would come in question. It is from him that the foundation and the walls of all human creations originate, and only the external form and color depend on the characteristics of the various peoples involved. He furnishes the gigantic building-stones and also the plans for all human progress, and only execution corresponds to the character of

the people and races in the various instances. . . .

Aryan tribes (often in a really ridiculously small number of their own people) subjugate foreign peoples, and now, stimulated by the special living conditions of the new territory (fertility, climatic conditions, etc.) and favored by the mass of the helping means in the form of people of inferior kind now at their disposal, they develop the mental and organizatory abilities, slumbering in them. Often, in the course of a few millenniums or even centuries, they create cultures which originally completely bear the inner features of their character, adapted to the already mentioned special qualities of the soil as well as of the subjected people. Finally, however, the conquerors deviate from the purity of their blood which they maintained originally, they begin to mix with the subjected inhabitants and thus they end their own existence; for the fall of man in Paradise has always been followed by expulsion from it. . . .

The blood-mixing, however, with the lowering of the racial level caused by it, is the sole cause of the dying-off of old cultures; for the people do not perish by lost wars, but by the loss of that force of resistance which is contained only in the pure blood.

All that is not race in this world is trash.

All world historical events, however, are only the expression of the races' instinct of self-preservation in its good or in its evil meaning. . . .

The Jew forms the strongest contrast to the Aryan. Hardly in any people of the world is the instinct of self-preservation more strongly developed than in the so-called 'chosen people.' . . .

For, even if the Jewish people's instinct of self-preservation is not smaller, but rather greater, than that of other nations, and even if his spiritual abilities very easily create the impression as though they were equal to the intellectual disposition of the other races, yet the most essential presumption for a cultured people is completely lacking, the idealistic disposition. . . .

. . . the Jewish people, with all its apparent intellectual qualities, is nevertheless without any true culture, especially without a culture of its own. For the sham culture which the Jew possesses today is the property of other peoples, and is mostly spoiled in his hands. When judging Jewry in its attitude towards the question of human culture, one has to keep before one's eye as an essential characteristic that there never has been and consequently that today also there is no Jewish art; that above all the two queens of all arts, architecture and music, owe nothing original to Jewry. What he achieves in the field of art is either bowdlerization or intellectual theft. With this, the Jew lacks those qualities which distinguish creatively and, with it, culturally blessed races. . . .

. . . the Jew possesses no culture-creating energy whatsoever, as the idealism, without which there can never exist a genuine development of man towards a higher level, does not and never did exist in him. His intellect, therefore, will never have a constructive effect, but only a destructive one, and in very rare cases it is perhaps stimulating, at the utmost. . . . Any progress of mankind takes place not through him but in spite of him.

As the Jew never possessed a State with definite territorial boundary, and as therefore he never called a culture his own, the conception arose that one had to deal with a people that had to be counted among the ranks of the *nomads*. . . .

But this has nothing to do with nomadism for the reason that the Jew does not think of leaving a territory he occupies, but he remains where he is sitting, and that

means so 'sedentary' that he may be expelled only with force and with great difficulty. His spreading to ever new countries takes place only in the moment when certain conditions for his existence are apparent there; without that he would (like the nomad) change his previous residence. He is and remains the typical parasite, a sponger who, like a harmful bacillus, spreads out more and more if only a favorable medium invites him to do so. But the effect of his existence resembles also that of parasites; where he appears the host people die out sooner or later. . . .

In the Jew's life as a parasite in the body of other nations and States, his characteristic is established which once caused Schopenhauer to pronounce the sentence . . . that the Jew is the 'great master of lying.' Life urges the Jew towards the lie, that is, to a perpetual lie, just as it forces the inhabitants of northern countries to wear warm clothes. . . .

The Jews were always a people with definite racial qualities and never a religion, only their progress made them probably look very early for a means which could divert disagreeable attention from their person. But what would have been more useful and at the same time more harmless than the 'purloining' of the appearance of being a religious community? For here, too, everything is purloined, or rather, stolen. But resulting from his own original nature the Jew cannot possess a religious institution for the very reason that he lacks all idealism in any form and that he also does not recognize any belief in the hereafter. But in the Aryan conception one cannot conceive of a religion which lacks the conviction of the continuation of life after death in some form. Indeed, the Talmud is then not a book for the preparation for the life to come, but rather for a practical and bearable life in this world. . . .

... [The Jew's] life is really only of this world, and his spirit is as alien to true Christianity, for instance, as his nature was two thousand years ago to the Sublime Founder of the new doctrine. Of course, the latter made no secret of His disposition towards the Jewish people, and when necessary He even took to the whip in order to drive out of the Lord's temple this adversary of all humanity, who even then as always saw in religion only a means for his business existence. But for this, of course, Christ was crucified, while our present party Christianity disgraces itself by begging for Jewish votes in the elections and later tries to conduct political wirepulling with atheistic Jewish parties, and this against their own nation.

Upon this first and greatest lie, that the Jew is not a race but simply a religion, further lies are then built up in necessary consequence. . . .

Now begins the great, final revolution. The Jew, by gaining the political power, casts off the few cloaks which he still wears. The democratic national Jew becomes the blood Jew and the people's tyrant. In the course of a few years he tries to eradicate the national supporters of intelligence, and, while he thus deprives the people of their natural spiritual leaders, he makes them ripe for the slave's destiny of permanent subjugation.

The most terrible example of this kind is offered by Russia where he killed or starved about thirty million people with a truly diabolic ferocity, under inhuman tortures, in order to secure to a crowd of Jewish scribblers and stock exchange robbers the rulership over a great people.

But the end is not only the end of the freedom of the peoples oppressed by the Jew, but also the end of these peoples' parasites themselves. With the death of the victim this peoples' vampire will also die sooner or later.

If we let all the causes of the German collapse [in 1918] pass before our eyes, there remains as the ultimate and decisive cause the non-recognition of the race problem and especially of the Jewish danger.

Eastern Policy

For Germany . . . the only possibility of carrying out a sound territorial policy was to be found in the acquisition of a new soil in Europe proper. Colonies cannot serve this purpose, since they do not appear suitable for settlement with Europeans on a large scale. But in the nineteenth century it was no longer possible to gain such colonial territories in a peaceful way. Such a colonial policy could only have been carried out by means of a hard struggle which would have been fought out more suitably, not for territories outside Europe, but rather for land in the home continent itself. . . .

The frontiers of the year 1914 signify nothing at all for the future of the German nation. They embodied neither a protection in the past, nor would they embody strength for the future. The German nation will neither maintain its internal integrity through them, nor will its sustenance be guaranteed by them, nor do these frontiers appear appropriate or even satisfactory from a military viewpoint, nor, finally, can they improve the relation in which, at the moment, we find ourselves with respect to the other world powers, or rather, the real world powers. The distance to England will not be shortened, the size of the Union not achieved; no, France will not even experience a material decrease in her world political importance.

Only one thing would be certain: even assuming a favorable outcome, such an attempt at re-establishing the frontiers of 1914 would lead to an additional bleeding of our national body, to an extent that no worthwhile blood reserve would be available for national life and for decisions and actions which would really insure the nation's future. On the contrary, in the intoxication of such a shallow success every added posing of goals would be the more readily abandoned, once the *'national honor'* had been restored and some doors reopened, at least for a time, to commercial development.

As opposed to this, we National Socialists must cling unflinchingly to our foreign-policy aims, that is to guarantee the *German nation the soil and territory to which it is entitled on this earth.* And this is the only action which, before God and our German posterity, would seem to justify an investment of blood: *before God,* since we are placed in this world on condition of an eternal struggle for daily bread, as beings to whom nothing shall be given and who owe their position as lords of the earth only to the genius and courage with which they know how to struggle for and defend it; before our German posterity, however, in so far as we spill no citizen's blood except that out of it a thousand others are bequeathed to posterity. The soil and territory on which a race of German peasants will some day be able to beget sons sanction the investment of the sons of today, and will some day acquit the responsible statesmen of blood and guilt and national sacrifice, even though they be persecuted by their contemporaries. . . .

Much as we all today recognize the necessity for a reckoning with France, it will remain largely ineffective if our foreign-policy aim is restricted thereto. It has and will retain significance if it provides the rear cover for an enlargement of our national domain of life in Europe. For we will find this question's solution not in colonial acquisitions, but exclusively in the winning of land for settlement which increases the area of the motherland itself, and thereby not only keeps the new settlers in the most intimate community with the land of origin, but insures to the total area those advantages deriving from its united magnitude. . . .

. . . what is involved is not some little Negro people or other, but the German mother of all life, which has given its cultural picture to the contemporary world. *Germany will be either a world power or will not be at all.* To be a world power, however, it requires that size which nowadays gives its necessary importance to such a power, and which gives life to its citizens.

With this, we National Socialists consciously draw a line through the foreign-policy trend of our pre-War period. We take up at the halting place of six hundred years ago. We terminate the endless German drive to the south and west of Europe, and direct our gaze towards the lands in the east. We finally terminate the colonial and trade policy of the pre-War period, and proceed to the territorial policy of the future.

But if we talk about new soil and territory in Europe today, we can think primarily only of *Russia* and its vassal border states.

59. Treaty of Non-Aggression Between Germany and the Union of Soviet Socialist Republics, 1939

In August 1939 several treaties were signed between Germany and the Soviet Union. The combined agreements are commonly known as the Nazi–Soviet Pact. The published terms included a trade agreement and mutual pledges of neutrality and non-aggression that were designated to last for ten years. A secret protocol divided Eastern Europe into German and Russian spheres of influence.

The Nazi–Soviet Pact was in reality an aggression pact. On September 1, 1939 Germany attacked Poland, thus beginning World War II. Sixteen days later, the Soviet Union invaded Poland to secure its treaty-allotted portions of that country. Poland was defeated and within a year Eastern Europe was overrun by the two totalitarian powers. Strategically the non-aggression agreement enabled Germany to avoid a war on two fronts (as it had fought in World War I) and concentrate its forces on the western offensive that led to the rapid fall of France in June 1940. By the following September Germany, its Axis partners, and a cooperative Soviet Union dominated the Eurasian land mass.

The Nazi–Soviet Pact surprised and shocked the world. The two powers were odd international bed-fellows. Before August 1939 they had been enemies and had vigorously denounced each other. That summer they set aside their ideological differences for the sake of their common aggressive designs. The treaty was not destined to last. Friction developed between the two powers over southeastern Europe, and when Germany was unable to defeat Great Britain in 1940 Hitler ordered the invasion of the Soviet Union on June 22, 1941. The Soviet Union continued to claim the territorial gains secured under the Nazi–Soviet Pact after it joined with Great Britain and the United States in the alliance that would ultimately defeat Germany.

QUESTIONS

1. On the surface, what is odd about this alliance between Hitler and Stalin?
2. Whose death warrant was signed here?
3. What might Stalin have expected to gain from this agreement?

The Government of the German Reich and the Government of the Union of Soviet Socialist Republics, desirous of strengthening the cause of peace between Germany and the U.S.S.R., and proceeding from the fundamental provisions of the Treaty of Neutrality, which was concluded between Germany and the U.S.S.R. in April 1926, have reached the following agreement:

Article I

Both High Contracting Parties obligate themselves to desist from any act of violence, any aggressive action, and any attack on each other, either individually or jointly with other powers.

Article II

Should one of the High Contracting Parties become the object of belligerent action by a third Power, the other High Contracting Power shall in no manner lend its support to this third Power.

Article III

The Governments of the two High Contracting Parties shall in the future maintain continual contact with one another for the purpose of consultation in order to exchange information on problems affecting their common interests.

Article IV

Neither of the two High Contracting Parties will join any grouping of Powers whatsoever that is directly or indirectly aimed at the other Party.

Article V

Should disputes or conflicts arise between the High Contracting Parties over problems of one other kind or another, both parties shall settle these disputes or conflicts exclusively through friendly exchange of opinion or, if necessary, through the establishment of arbitration commissions.

Article VI

The present Treaty is concluded for a period of ten years, with the proviso that, in so far as one of the High Contracting Parties does not denounce it one year prior to the expiration of this period, the validity of this Treaty shall automatically be extended for another five years.

Article VII

The present Treaty shall be ratified within the shortest possible time. The instruments of ratification will be exchanged in Berlin. The Treaty shall enter into force as soon as it is signed.

Done in duplicate in the German and Russian languages.

Moscow, August 23, 1939.

| For the Government of the German Reich: v. Ribbentrop | With the full power of the Government of the U.S.S.R.: V. Molotov |

Secret Additional Protocol

On the occasion of the signature of the Non-Aggression Pact between the German Reich and the Union of Soviet Socialist Republics, the undersigned plenipotentiaries of each of the two Parties discussed in strictly confidential conversations the question of the boundary of their respective spheres of interest in Eastern Europe. These conversations led to the following result:

1. In the event of territorial and political rearrangement in the areas belonging to the Baltic States (Finland, Estonia, Latvia, Lithuania), the northern boundary of Lithuania shall represent the boundary of the

spheres of influence of Germany and the U.S.S.R. In this connection the interest of Lithuania in the Vilna area is recognized by each party.

2. In the event of a territorial and political rearrangement of the areas belonging to the Polish State the spheres of interest of Germany and the U.S.S.R. shall be bounded approximately by the line of the rivers Narev, Vistula, and San.

The question of whether the interests of both Parties make desirable the maintenance of an independent Polish State and how such a state should be bounded can only be definitely determined in the course of further political developments.

In any event both Governments will resolve this question by means of a friendly agreement.

3. With regard to Southeastern Europe attention is called by the Soviet side to its interest in Bessarabia. The German side declares complete political disinterestedness in these areas.

4. This Protocol shall be treated by both parties as strictly secret.

Moscow, August 23, 1939.

| For the Government of the German Reich: v. Ribbentrop | With full power of the Government of the U.S.S.R.: V. Molotov |

INTRODUCTION TO UNIT SIX

World War II
and Its Consequences

Twenty years after the Paris Peace Conference that concluded World War I, a second and far greater struggle began in Europe that soon engulfed the globe. In retrospect the Second World War may be viewed as a continuation of the Great War of 1914–1918, separated by an interlude of brief prosperity followed by economic crisis, depression, and the rise of totalitarianism in the Soviet Union, Germany, Italy, and Japan. When the catastrophe ended in 1945, the Western European nations that had dominated world history since the Age of Exploration lay in ruins. Two new superpowers took their place—the Soviet Union to the east and the United States to the west. Three new trends would mark the postwar period: the threat of nuclear destruction from new weapons; the Cold War confrontration between communism and democracy; and decolonization and the emergence of dozens of new nations in the so-called Third World of Africa, Asia, and Latin America.

The era of the Western European appeasement of Hitler ended on September 1, 1939, when Germany invaded Poland. On September 3, Britain and France, followed by all the British dominions (but not Ireland), declared war on Germany. On behalf of India, war was declared by the Viceroy. For a few months after the fall of Poland there were no major military actions in Western Europe. The two defensive systems, the French Maginot Line and the German Siegfried Line, confronted one another. Soon, this period became popularly known as the "Phony War" or the "Sitzkrieg."

But on the eastern front the German conquest of Poland proceeded rapidly, thanks to the success of their "blitzkrieg" (lightning war) tactics, which mobilized tanks, trucks, and airplanes to speed up the pace of the attack. On September 17, Soviet troops crossed the border, advancing into Poland from the east, taking their share of territory promised by the Nazi-Soviet Pact. Before the end of September the war with Poland was over. While Germany engaged in actions at sea and prepared for its planned conquests in the following year, the Soviet Union established military bases in the Baltic states and seized some territories from Finland and Romania. On April 9, 1940, the Germans launched a campaign that quickly gave them control of Denmark and Norway. A month later, they invaded Holland, Belgium, Luxembourg, and France. The first three of these nations fell to Nazi rule by the end of May; on June 22, 1940, the French accepted Germany's terms of armistice.

On the day Germany invaded the Netherlands, Winston Churchill succeeded the inept Neville Chamberlain as Prime Minister of Great Britain. In his stirring speeches he dramatically spelled out the challenge that faced Great Britain as he bolstered his people's resolve (see Document 61). Thanks in part to his forceful leadership and the skill of the Royal Air Force, Hitler failed to win the Battle of Britain and postponed indefinitely operation "Sea Lion"—his plan for an invasion of England.

On September 27, 1940, Germany, Italy, and Japan (the Axis Powers) signed the Tripartite Pact. In this they recognized one another's role in their respective spheres and promised to give assistance to each other if one of them was attacked by a power not yet involved in the European or Pacific wars. During the fall of 1940 and the spring of 1941, Germany brought most of the Balkan states into the Tripartite Pact. On June 22, 1941, Hitler broke his pact with Stalin and invaded the Soviet Union through Operation Barbarossa. He revealed his policy toward the national aspirations of the republics of the Soviet Union when the Germans suppressed the Ukrainian attempt to reestablish their independent state. The Nazis then imprisoned thousands in concentration camps (see Document 64).

As the war expanded, President Roosevelt, Prime Minister Churchill, and their Chiefs of Staff met in August 1941 and issued the Atlantic Charter, which expressed their ideals and war aims (see Document 62). They disavowed any ambitions for conquering territory and subscribed to principles of self-determination and free trade throughout the world. They also aimed to establish some new system of general security that would avoid the horror of a third world war. The United States was still technically a neutral country, but by then President Franklin D. Roosevelt had persuaded Congress to offer direct aid to the Allies who were fighting the Axis powers. The Japanese attack on Pearl Harbor on December 7 and the German declaration of war shortly thereafter turned the United States into a belligerent nation.

In the first phase of the war Germany conquered most of Europe and a large portion of northern Africa. In the occupied countries of Eastern and Central Europe, Hitler drove for "living space" and the establishment of an imperial Third Reich. He then introduced a policy of annihilation of Jews and other peoples that he considered racially undesirable. His program of the "Final Solution" aimed to destroy European Jewry to the last man, woman, and child.

The Holocaust or "Shoah" stands apart as unique among many examples of genocide in history (see Document 63). Other exterminations of populations include the Armenians at the hands of the Turks, Cambodians by the Khmer Rouge, Biafrans by Nigeria, Stalin's numerous massacres, and the Gulag Archipelago. But in these other instances total annihilation was not sought and it was possible for many to escape by conversion, capitulation, bribery, or refuge else-where. No such ways out were possible for the Jews, however, because they were the object of an age-old religious hatred and racial ideology. Over two mil-lennia Christian antisemitism made the Jews guilty of "deicide," usurious ex-ploiters of the poor, agents of Satan and armed with his superhuman powers. That fear was reinforced and secularized by the nationalist-racist doctrines that developed in the nineteenth century. This long, complex evolution meant that Jews were perceived as everyone's enemy and scapegoats for every imaginable and unimaginable reason and fantasy. Hence with rare exceptions witnesses and bystanders, the subject peoples who were themselves victims, the Allies, and the neutral states all ignored the plight of the Jews. Paradoxical as it is to us but liter-ally true at the time, the Germans feared the Jews and believed they had to de-stroy the Jews before the Jews destroyed them. Hence the destructive process went on to the end of the war, despite its enormous cost to the war effort, e.g., in preempting railway rolling stock to ship millions of Jews to the death camps in-stead of war material to the fronts.

There are two broad interpretations of the "Shoah". Scholars of the "inten-tionalist" school contend that Hitler consistently stated his determination to an-nihilate the Jews in his writings and speeches from *Mein Kampf* on, and that he simply waited until he had the power, the apparatus of destruction, and the cover provided by total war to effect it. Other historians support the "functional-ist" viewpoint, which traces a series of attempts to "solve the Jewish problem" by bureaucratic expedients that were frustrated until the only solution possible was literal annihilation. To some historians, the decision to annihilate turned on the exhilarating victories over the U.S.S.R. in the summer of 1941, which made it unnecessary to preserve the Jews as a reservoir of skilled labor. To others, it was the frustration of the offensive at Moscow in December 1941 and the prospect of the war lost that triggered the decision.

While Germany and Italy were tightening their hold over much of Europe, Japan was expanding its empire in East and Southeast Asia. In the Far East World War II had actually begun as early as 1931, when Japan intervened in Manchuria. Japanese leaders were ambitious to extend their power in Asia and were worried about the possibility of a stronger China united under the leader-ship of nationalist leader Chiang Kai-shek. After Japan occupied eastern China during the late 1930s, the United States decided to resist this challenge to the Open Door policy by placing an embargo on oil and scrap iron. Japan's leaders then acted boldly to assure themselves of a sufficient supply of oil by destroying the American Pacific fleet at Pearl Harbor and by seizing the Dutch East Indies (Indonesia). The empire of the Rising Sun then tried to launch their "Co-Prosper-ity Sphere" by rallying the people of Asia to their side with their slogan "Asia for the Asians" (see Document 60). While the European and Asian conquerors found some collaborators, there was growing resistance in many forms from simple disruptions to guerrilla warfare.

During the conflict Japanese war crimes were on such a scale that an Inter-national Military Tribunal convened in Tokyo between 1946 and 1948 to try twenty-eight Japanese leaders, including the wartime prime minister, General Hideki Tojo. These judgments were comparable to the trials of the principal German war criminals at Nuremberg during 1945 and 1946. The Tribunal concluded that the Japanese atrocities were on a very large scale, were conducted almost entirely by the Japanese Imperial Army in all theaters of war, followed a common pattern, and were, therefore, the centrally directed and sanctioned policy of the Japanese government and high command. The atrocities included "the rape of Nanking" of 1937–1938, where a quarter to a third of a million Chinese civilians and POWs were massacred within six weeks of the Japanese capture of the city. By 1945 China had suffered a minimum of ten million and as many as thirty million casualties at Japanese hands. By 1942 the Japanese army had carried out at least twenty-six large-scale massacres of civilian populations, and it had also inflicted the most appalling kind of slave labor, with wanton beatings and starvation diets. Like the German SS doctors, the Japanese carried out massive medical experiments and germ warfare and poison gas tests, inflicting terrible suffering on POWs and civilians. Atrocious "death marches" and POW camps took a high death toll of Allied POWs (27 percent in Japanese compared to 4 percent in German and Italian POW camps). The Kempi Tai military police, equivalent to the Nazi SS except that they were an integral part of the army, carried out much of the murder and torture, justifying their brutish violence by invocation of the ancient Knights of Bushido and the Samurai tradition.

In a surprising contrast with their German allies, the Japanese did not persecute the Jews, but, rather, sought to give refuge to as many as a million European Jews in a "Manchurian Israel." Although Japanese ideologists shared many of the traditional antisemitic beliefs of the West, they did not fear the Jews as an enemy and danger that had to be destroyed. Rather, they sought to "ally" themselves with the Jews and "use" the supposed Jewish power, wealth, and influence to fulfill Japan's ambition for its "Greater East Asia Co-Prosperity Sphere." While few of these grandiose plans were implemented, there were no massacres or persecutions of Jews, and perhaps 60,000 mostly German and Austrian Jews found safety in Japan's empire, about one-third of them in a famous settlement at Shanghai.

The Allies, the Western democracies, and the Soviet Union gradually turned the tide of the war. In the Pacific the Americans were victorious in the battles of the Coral Sea and of Midway in May and June 1942. In North Africa the British were successful in the battle of Alamein in October 1942. The surrender of the encircled German army at Stalingrad at the beginning of February 1943 marked the turning point in the Soviet Union. By the spring of 1943 the Allies controlled Africa and in the summer landed in Italy. On June 6, 1944, their forces landed in Normandy, France, while the Soviet army was advancing into the Baltics, Poland, and the Balkans. Approaching from opposite sides, American and Soviet troops made their first contact on the banks of the Elbe River in Germany in April 1945. On May 2, 1945, Berlin was occupied and on May 7 a German delegation agreed to unconditional surrender at the headquarters of

General Eisenhower at Reims. Two days later, the ceremony was repeated at the Soviet headquarters in Berlin.

The war with Japan continued until mid-August. The dropping of the atomic bomb on August 6 on Hiroshima and on August 9 on Nagasaki and the entry of the Soviet Union into the Pacific war forced the Japanese government to accept the terms of surrender on August 14, 1945. The signing of the document took place aboard the battleship "Missouri" on September 2, 1945 in Tokyo Bay (see Document 66). The dropping of the two bombs which ended the war also marked the beginning of a new era. The large-scale release of atomic energy had far-reaching implications. It became, on the one hand, a source of hope, and on the other, an instrument of terror.

As Roosevelt, Churchill, and Stalin and their aides met during the war to formulate and coordinate military and political policies, tensions began to appear among the Allies. While disagreements did surface between Roosevelt and Churchill (especially concerning the ending of colonialism), the most serious friction occurred between the leaders of the Western democracies and Stalin. In particular, the Soviet leader was deeply disturbed over the delay in launching the cross–English Channel invasion that was planned to restore the second front in France and thus relieve German pressure in the east. Stalin also expected territorial concessions from his Allies in Eastern and Central Europe. In addition, he demanded increased supplies from the United States. The three leaders met for the first time at Teheran (November 28 to December 1, 1943), where they addressed military matters, of which the most important was the cross-channel invasion and the establishment of the second front. The other discussions, dealing with long-range political questions, were mostly of a tentative nature. Some of those problems received further attention at the conference of the "Big Three" at Yalta (February 4–11, 1945), the most controversial of the war conferences, since Stalin was able to secure most, if not all, of what he wanted. The decisions reached there addressed such issues as membership and veto power in the new international organization, the United Nations, and some aspects of their policy toward Germany. The question of Poland was resolved with a border adjustment and a vague statement which promised democratic procedures and free elections but which in fact permitted the consolidation of Soviet control and a communist regime in that nation. A separate agreement was concluded which gave the Soviet Union territory and rights in the Far East in exchange for her participation in the war against Japan (see Document 65).

As the war ended in Europe at the beginning of May, and in Asia in mid-August, a new world order began to take shape. Fifty nations gathered in San Francisco to form the United Nations, which dedicated itself to promote peace, trade, and human rights around the world (see Document 71). But before long new political developments generated new conflicts among the most powerful nations. The Soviet Union extended its control over Eastern Europe, and made substantial gains in the Far East, at the expense of China and Japan. At the same time, the international position of the Western European states declined and they became dependent on the United States, which emerged as the major global power among the capitalist nations.

The growing disagreements among the wartime allies (already evident among President Harry Truman, Prime Minister Clement Attlee, and Stalin at the Potsdam Conference, July 17–August 2, 1945) led to the development of two opposing blocs, the Western democracies led by the United States and the Eastern communist regimes headed by the Soviet Union. The victory of the Allies further enhanced Stalin's power in the Soviet Union, as he declared the outcome a triumph for the Soviet military, economic, and social system (see Document 67). Before long Churchill (now out of office) warned of an "iron curtain" that was descending across Central Europe (see Document 68).

The different underlying political and socioeconomic philosophies and conflicts over the postwar goals of the two blocs soon led to the Cold War. Disagreements over the treatment of Germany and the Soviet blockade of Berlin resulted in the split into West Germany, the Federal Republic, associated with the West, and East Germany, the Democratic Republic dominated by the Soviet Union. East-West relations were aggravated by the consolidation of Soviet control, disguised as "people's democracies" over Eastern Europe, and Soviet attempts to extend its power to the south (Turkey, Greece, and Iran). These Soviet actions led to the adoption, as the expression of United States containment policy, of the Truman Doctrine (see Document 69). Because of the danger that the economic deterioration in Western Europe might lead to communist takeovers in Italy, France, and other nations, the United States initiated a recovery program—the Marshall Plan. The Soviet Union rejected the Western approach to the question of economic assistance and proceeded to establish the Cominform (see Document 70), and, as a counterprogram to the Marshall Plan, formed in 1949, the Comecon (CMEA). The initial activities of the Comecon were minimal, and only after the death of Stalin in 1953 did Khrushchev use this organization to tie the economies of the communist states closer to that of the Soviet Union.

By establishing the North Atlantic Treaty Organization (NATO) in 1949 the Western European countries, the United States, and Canada formed a common defense system, based on the principles, as stated in Article 5 of the treaty, that ". . . an armed attack against one or more of them in Europe or North America shall be considered an attack against all of them." In 1955 the Soviet Union and the Eastern European countries signed the mutual assistance treaty, the Warsaw Pact, which placed their armies under Red Army command. Until that time, the Soviet Union directed the military policy of the communist bloc through bilateral arrangements with each of its satellite states. The communist bloc gained considerably with the victory of Mao Tse-tung's party in China in late 1949.

The colonial awakening in the Third World goes back at least to the nineteenth century. The struggle against imperialism took various forms, including, as in India, the passive resistance tactics of Mohandas Gandhi (see Document 72). It was not until after World War II that the most extensive disintegration of the European colonial empires took place. Weakened by the war and preoccupied by their domestic problems, the colonial powers were on the retreat. The international anticolonial mood helped the process of liberation. There were only fourteen nation-states in 1871, but there were twenty in 1914, twenty-six in 1924, and over sixty in 1945. In the two decades following the war, more than fifty countries gained independence in Asia, the Middle East, and Africa (see Document 73). By 1991 there were more than one hundred and sixty.

The emergence of so many states had an increasingly major impact on international relations. Some of the Third World countries tried to use the rivalries between the two blocs for their benefit. At the same time, the leading powers of the two blocs were active in the Third World promoting their own interests. Thus decolonization and the disintegration of the British, French, and other European colonial empires after 1945 did not bring peace and harmony to the world. That was largely because a number of the new nation-states were ferocious in their political rivalry and economic competition. Neither the League of Nations earlier nor the United Nations was able to counterbalance the sovereign nation-state.

Furthermore, some of these states, imbued with imperial ambitions, have not been hospitable to minorities. Jealous of their sovereignty, they have been reluctant to diminish it by conferring local or national autonomy on minorities. Instead, they have preferred to nationalize the minorities by inducing or compelling them to assimilate themselves to the whole. In retrospect, the recasting of the world's political geography along national lines, which began in 1776 with that shot heard round the world and goes on with no prospect of being concluded, has been at a tremendous cost of blood and treasure. The success of one submerged nationality is a signal to others to make the try, and at any cost.

The death of Stalin brought some relaxation in the Soviet Union, the communist bloc, and a slight easing of tensions in international relations. As Nikita Khrushchev rose to power, he denounced Stalin (see Document 57), spoke of different roads to communism, and kept proclaiming the policy of "peaceful coexistence" between communist and capitalist states. But when Poland and Hungary attempted to embark on their own roads to communism, they were stopped—in the case of Hungary, with Soviet tanks. Communist China, on the other hand, was able to assert its own position and to challenge Soviet leadership in the communist bloc. It was during the Khrushchev era, though, that the Soviet Union extended its influence and also introduced communist systems to some countries in other parts of the world, especially Africa and Latin America. Following that, Khrushchev decided on a bold step, introducing missiles to Cuba in 1962. This led to the greatest crisis of the Cold War, in which the wills of the two sides were tested and Moscow faltered.

During the postwar years the countries of Asia also emerged as an important factor in the world's political and economic relationships. Communist China, after its break with the Soviet Union, ultimately established diplomatic relations with the United States and became a member of the United Nations and its powerful body, the Security Council. Japan, with its economic expansion and worldwide interests, became one of the leading states. Even relatively small countries such as South Korea established economic relations with many countries of the world. A generation after the end of World War II, the Cold War still dominated world politics, but new nations and new forces were poised to inaugurate a new era as the tumultuous twentieth century entered its final decades.

60. Japan's Justifications and Goals for War, 1930s–1942

What the Japanese called the Great East Asia War began in 1931 in China and over the next decade was extended to all of East Asia and the Pacific Basin. By mid-1942 Japan had gained a huge empire that stretched from the borders of India east toward Hawaii, and from Australia north to Siberia. The theoretical basis for the expansion was expounded by Japanese nationalists and militarists (such as Okawa Shumei and Hashimoto Kingoro) during the 1930s and early 1940s. Excerpts from their writings follow.

In establishing an administrative structure for this new empire, Japan divided the area into an inner zone, made up of countries considered essential to its national defense, and an outer zone, comprising nations that would be more loosely connected to the core. Japan was to be the dominant political and cultural influence throughout this union, called the Greater East Asia Co-Prosperity Sphere (see the draft of the basic plan that follows). All European and American imperialism was to be rooted out and hostile indigenous Asian groups eliminated. Independence, equality, and self-government were supposed to follow in the wake of Japanese conquests of lands previously governed by westerners. It was to be Asia for the Asians, but in keeping with the Japanese Imperial Way— *Hakko Ichiu*—a form of government that combined social, economic, and political life in one. Hakko Ichiu traced its origin to the Japanese Emperor Jimmu, who, in the seventh century A.D., decreed laws, built a palace, and proposed to extend the capital until it covered "all eight corners of the world under one imperial roof." The Japanese leaders now aimed to apply this ancient tradition to the world of the twentieth century.

The peoples of Asia soon discovered that Japanese rule was to be more onerous than that of the West. Rebellious movements broke out in satellite states, weakening the overall Japanese war effort. The Co-Prosperity Sphere, along with the Japanese Empire, collapsed with Japan's defeat in August 1945.

QUESTIONS

1. Explain and discuss Okawa Shumei's interpretation of the conflict between Japan and the Western powers.

2. According to Hashimoto Kingoro, what alternatives did Japan's leaders consider as possible solutions to the problem of their nation's expanding population? What strategy does he propose? Explain and discuss his views of European expansion and imperialism. Compare his ideas with those of Adolf Hitler.
3. What is the underlying philosophy behind Japan's plan for establishing a Greater East Asia Co-Prosperity Sphere? What are its short- and long-term military, political, and economic objectives? What is its view of Western political and cultural influence in Asia? What does it require of the peoples of Asia?

The Way of Japan and the Japanese

Okawa Shumei

Asia's stubborn efforts to remain faithful to spiritual values, and Europe's honest and rigorous speculative thought, are both worthy of admiration, and both have made miraculous achievements. Yet today it is no longer possible for these two to exist apart from each other. The way of Asia and the way of Europe have both been traveled to the end. World history shows us that these two must be united; when we look at that history up to now we see that this unification is being achieved only through war. Mohammed said that "Heaven lies in the shadow of the sword," and I am afraid that a struggle between the great powers of the East and the West which will decide their existence is at present, as in the past, absolutely inevitable if a new world is to come about. The words "East-West struggle," however, simply state a concept and it does not follow from this that a united Asia will be pitted against a united Europe. Actually there will be one country acting as the champion of Asia and one country acting as the champion of Europe, and it is these who must fight in order that a new world may be realized. It is my belief that Heaven has decided on Japan as its choice for the champion of the East. Has not this been the purpose of our three thousand long years of preparation? It must be said that this is a truly grand and magnificent mission. We must develop a strong spirit of morality in order to carry out this solemn mission, and realize that spirit in the life of the individual and of the nation.

The Need for Emigration and Expansion

Hashimoto Kingoro

We have already said that there are only three ways left to Japan to escape from the pressure of surplus population. We are like a great crowd of people packed into a small and narrow room, and there are only three doors through which we might escape, namely emigration, advance into world markets, and expansion of territory. The first door, emigration, has been barred to us by the anti-Japanese immigration policies of other countries. The second door, advance into world markets, is being pushed shut by tariff barriers and the abrogation of commercial treaties. What should Japan do when two of the three doors have been closed against her?

It is quite natural that Japan should rush upon the last remaining door.

It may sound dangerous when we speak of territorial expansion, but the territorial expansion of which we speak does not in any sense of the word involve the occupation or the possession of other countries, the planting of the Japanese flag thereon, and the declaration of their annexation to Japan. It is just that since the Powers have suppressed the circulation of Japanese materials and merchandise abroad, we are looking for some place overseas where Japanese capital, Japanese skills, and Japanese labor can have free play, free from the oppression of the white race.

We would be satisfied with just this much. What moral right do the world powers who have themselves closed to us the two doors of emigration and advance into world markets have to criticize Japan's attempt to rush out of the third and last door?

If they do not approve of this, they should open the doors which they have closed against us and permit the free movement overseas of Japanese emigrants and merchandise. . . .

At the time of the Manchurian incident [1931], the entire world joined in criticism of Japan. They said that Japan was an untrustworthy nation. They said that she had recklessly brought cannon and machine guns into Manchuria, which was the territory of another country, flown airplanes over it, and finally occupied it. But the military action taken by Japan was not in the least a selfish one. Moreover, we do not recall ever having taken so much as an inch of territory belonging to another nation. The result of this incident was the establishment of the splendid new nation of Manchuria. The Powers are still discussing whether or not to recognize this new nation, but regardless of whether or not other nations recognize her, the Manchurian empire has already been established, and now, seven years after its creation, the empire is further consolidating its foundations with the aid of its friend, Japan.

And if it is still protested that our actions in Manchuria were excessively violent, we may wish to ask the white race just which country it was that sent warships and troops to India, South Africa, and Australia and slaughtered innocent natives, bound their hands and feet with iron chains, lashed their backs with iron whips, proclaimed these territories as their own, and still continues to hold them to this very day?

They will invariably reply, these were all lands inhabited by untamed savages. These people did not know how to develop the abundant resources of their land for the benefit of mankind. Therefore it was the wish of God, who created heaven and earth for mankind, for us to develop these undeveloped lands and to promote the happiness of mankind in their stead. God wills it.

This is quite a convenient argument for them. Let us take it at face value. Then there is another question that we must ask them.

Suppose that there is still on this earth land endowed with abundant natural resources that have not been developed at all by the white race. Would it not then be God's will and the will of Providence that Japan go there and develop those resources for the benefit of mankind?

And there still remain many such lands of this earth.

Draft of Basic Plan for Establishment of Greater East Asia Co-Prosperity Sphere, 1942

Part I. Outline of Construction

The Plan. The Japanese empire is a manifestation of morality and its special characteristic is the propagation of the Imperial Way. It strives but for the achievement of *Hakko Ichiu,* the spirit of its founding. . . . It is necessary to foster the increased power of the empire, to cause East Asia to return to its original form of independence and co-prosperity by shaking off the yoke of Europe and America, and to let its countries and peoples develop their respective abilities in peaceful cooperation and secure livelihood.

The Form of East Asiatic Independence and Co-Prosperity. The states, their citizens, and resources, comprised in those areas pertaining to the Pacific, Central Asia, and the Indian Oceans formed into one general union are to be established as an autonomous zone of peaceful living and common prosperity on behalf of the people of the nations of East Asia. The area including Japan, Manchuria, North China, lower Yangtze River, and the Russian Maritime Province, forms the nucleus of the East Asiatic Union.

The above purpose presupposes the inevitable emancipation or independence of Eastern Siberia, China, Indo-China, the South Seas, Australia, and India.

Regional Division in the East Asiatic Union and the National Defense Sphere for the Japanese Empire. In the Union of East Asia, the Japanese empire is at once the stabilizing power and the leading influence. To enable the empire actually to become the central influence in East Asia, the first necessity is the consolidation of the inner belt of East Asia; and the East Asiatic Sphere shall be divided as follows for this purpose:

The Inner Sphere—the vital sphere for the empire—includes Japan, Manchuria, North China, the lower Yangtze Area and the Russian Maritime area.

The Smaller Co-Prosperity Sphere— the smaller self-supplying sphere of East Asia—includes the inner sphere plus East-

ern Siberia, China, Indo-China and the South Seas.

The Greater Co-Prosperity Sphere— the larger self-supplying sphere of East Asia—includes the smaller co-prosperity sphere, plus Australia, India, and island groups in the Pacific. . . .

For the present, the smaller co-prosperity sphere shall be the zone in which the construction of East Asia and the stabilization of national defense are to be aimed at. After their completion there shall be a gradual expansion toward the construction of the Greater Co-Prosperity Sphere.

Outline of East Asiatic Administration. It is intended that the unification of Japan, Manchoukuo, and China in Neighborly friendship be realized by the settlement of the Sino-Japanese problems through the crushing of hostile influences in the Chinese interior, and through the construction of a new China in tune with the rapid construction of the Inner Sphere. Aggressive American and British influence in East Asia shall be driven out of the area of Indo-China and the South Seas, and this area shall be brought into our defense sphere. The war with Britain and America shall be prosecuted for that purpose.

The Russian aggressive influence in East Asia will be driven out. Eastern Siberia shall be cut off from the Soviet regime and included in our defense sphere. For this purpose, a war with the Soviets is expected. It is considered possible that this Northern problem may break out before the general settlement of the present Sino-Japanese and the Southern problems if the situation renders this unavoidable. Next the independence of Australia, India, etc. shall gradually be brought about. For this purpose, a recurrence of war with Britain and her allies is expected. The construction of the Smaller Co-Prosperity Sphere is expected to require at least twenty years from the present time.

The Building of the National Strength.
Since the Japanese empire is the center and pioneer of Oriental moral and cultural reconstruction, the officials and people of this country must return to the spirit of the Orient and acquire a thorough understanding of the spirit of the national moral character.

In the economic construction of the country, Japanese and Manchurian national power shall first be consolidated, then the unification of Japan, Manchoukuo and China, shall be effected. . . . Thus a central industry will be constructed in East Asia, and the necessary relations established with the Southern Seas.

The standard for the construction of the national power and its military force, so as to meet the various situations that might affect the stages of East Asiatic administration and the national defense sphere, shall be so set as to be capable of driving off any British, American, Soviet or Chinese counterinfluence in the future. . . .

Chapter 3. Political Construction

Basic Plan. The realization of the great ideal of constructing Greater East Asia Co-Prosperity requires not only the complete prosecution of the current Greater East Asia War but also presupposes another great war in the future. Therefore, the following two points must be made the primary starting points for the political construction of East Asia during the course of the next twenty years: 1) Preparation for war with the other spheres of the world; and 2) Unification and construction of the East Asia Smaller Co-Prosperity Sphere.

The following are the basic principles for the political construction of East Asia, when the above two points are taken into consideration:

a. The politically dominant influence of European and American countries in the Smaller Co-Prosperity Sphere shall be gradually driven out and the area shall enjoy its liberation from the shackles hitherto forced upon it.

b. The desires of the peoples in the sphere for their independence shall be respected and endeavors shall be made for their fulfillment, but proper and suitable forms of government shall be decided for them in consideration of military and economic requirements and of the historical, political and cultural elements peculiar to each area.

It must also be noted that the independence of various peoples of East Asia should be based upon the idea of constructing East Asia as "independent countries existing within the New Order of East Asia" and that this conception differs from an independence based on the idea of liberalism and national self-determination.

c. During the course of construction, military unification is deemed particularly important, and the military zones and key points necessary for defense shall be directly or indirectly under the control of our country.

d. The peoples of the sphere shall obtain their proper positions, the unity of the people's minds shall be effected and the unification of the sphere shall be realized with the empire as its center. . . .

Chapter 4 . Thought and Cultural Construction

General Aim in Thought. The ultimate aim in thought construction in East Asia is to make East Asiatic peoples revere the imperial influence by propagating the Imperial Way based on the spirit of construction and to establish the belief that uniting solely under this influence is the one and only way to the eternal growth and development of East Asia.

And during the next twenty years (the period during which the above ideal is to be reached) it is necessary to make the nations and peoples of East Asia realize the historical significance of the establishment of the New Order in East Asia, and in the common consciousness of East Asiatic unity, to liberate East Asia from the shackles of Europe and America and to establish the common conviction of constructing a New Order based on East Asiatic morality.

Occidental individualism and materialism shall be rejected and a moral world view, the basic principle of whose morality shall be the Imperial Way, shall be established. The ultimate object to be achieved is not exploitation but co-prosperity and mutual help, not competitive conflict but mutual assistance and mild peace, not a formal view of equality but a view of order based on righteous classification, not an idea of rights but an idea of service, and not several world views but one unified world view.

General Aim in Culture.   The essence of the traditional culture of the Orient shall be developed and manifested. And, casting off the negative and conservative cultural characteristics of the continents (India and China) on the one hand, and taking in the good points of Western culture on the other, an Oriental culture and morality, on a grand scale and subtly refined, shall be created.

---

61. Excerpts from Speeches, 1940

Winston Churchill

Grandson of the duke of Marlborough, the son of a cabinet minister and an American mother ("Half-American but all British"), Winston Churchill (1874–1965) was, as he liked to think, the epitome of the English-speaking world. Destined for a life in politics, his career culminated in his leadership of Britain as prime minister in World War II. Self-educated, he was a voracious reader who possessed great courage, soaring imagination, tremendous intellect, unrelenting energy, and grand eloquence in speech and writing. Compassionate and sensitive to the poor, the deprived, and the victims of war, he could also be overbearingly impatient. A human dynamo, he held a seat in Parliament for more than half a century, beginning in 1901. He was also an outstanding historian and author of the multi-volume series, *The Second World War.*

During the interwar period he remained an imperialist of the late nineteenth-century type and relentlessly opposed Gandhi and independence for India. His brilliant and prophetic analysis of the Nazi menace went unheeded until the German invasion of Poland in September 1939, when he was reluctantly taken into the Cabinet as head of the Admiralty. Ironically, he was chiefly responsible for the fiasco resulting from an ill-prepared expedition to Norway, but the blame fell to Neville Chamberlain, the prime minister and architect of appeasement, who was forced to resign. On the day that Hitler invaded France and the Netherlands, Churchill became prime minister and formed a coalition government. Excerpts from Churchill's stirring speeches in that time of danger and crisis appear below. He devoted an enormous amount of preparation to these addresses, which he memorized and recited by heart.

QUESTIONS

1. What was Winston Churchill's view of the consequences of a Nazi victory for Europe and the United States?
2. Summarize Churchill's interpretation of the nature and significance of the Battle of Britain. To whom does he give credit for the success in repelling German attacks?
3. What is Churchill's attitude toward the involvement of the United States in the fight against Germany?

Blood, Toil, Tears, Sweat, May 13, 1940

I say to the House, as I said to the Ministers who have joined this Government, I have nothing to offer but blood and toil and tears and sweat. We have before all of us an ordeal of the most grievous kind. We have before us many, many long months of struggle and of suffering. If you ask what is our policy I will say it is to wage war—(cheers),—war by air, land, and sea, war with all our might and with all the strength that God can give us, and to wage war against a monstrous tyranny never surpassed in the dark and lamentable catalogue of human crime. That is our policy. If you ask us, "What is your aim?" I can answer in one word—victory—(loud cheers)—victory however long and hard the road may be. For without victory there is no survival—and let that be realised—no survival for the British Empire, no survival for all that the British Empire has stood for, no survival for the urge and impulse of the ages that mankind shall move forward towards its goal.

I take up my task in buoyancy and hope. I feel sure that our cause will not be suffered to fail among men. I feel entitled at this juncture and at this time to claim the aid of all, and I say, "Come, then, let us go forward together in our united strength."

Dunkirk, June 4, 1940

. . . I have said that this vast armoured scythe stroke almost reached Dunkirk. . . . When, a week ago, I asked the House to fix this afternoon for a statement, I feared it would be my hard lot to announce from this box the greatest military disaster in our long history. I thought . . . that perhaps from [only] 20,000 to 30,000 men might be re-embarked. . . .

The enemy attacked in great strength on all sides, and their main power—the power of their far more numerous Air Force—was thrown into the battle or concentrated upon Dunkirk and the beaches. Pressing in on the narrow exits both from the east and west, the enemy began to fire with cannon along the beaches by which alone shipping could approach or depart. They set magnetic mines in the channels and the seas, they sent repeated waves of hostile aircraft, sometimes more than a hundred strong in one formation, to cast their bombs upon the single pier that remained and the sand dunes upon which the British troops were trying to take shelter. Meanwhile the Royal Navy, with the willing help of the Merchant Navy and craft of all kinds, strained every nerve to embark the British and Allied troops. Over 200 light warships and more than 650 other vessels were engaged. They had to operate upon a difficult coast and often under adverse weather conditions, and under an almost ceaseless hail of enemy bombers and increasing concentration of artillery fire. Nor were the seas themselves free from mines or torpedoes. . . .

This struggle was protracted and fierce. Now, suddenly, the scene is clear and the crash and thunder has, if only for a moment, died away. A miracle of deliverance has been achieved by valour, perseverance, perfect discipline, and faultless service. The skill, resource, and unconquerable fidelity is manifest to us all. The enemy is hurled back by the retreating British and French troops.

It was so roughly handled that it dare not molest their departure. Our Air Force decisively defeated the main strength of the enemy Air Force and inflicted upon the enemy losses of at least four to one. The Navy, using nearly 1,000 ships carried our 335,000 men, French and British, out of the jaws of death back to their native land, and to the tasks which lie immediately before them. (Loud cheers.)

We must be very careful not to assign to this deliverance the attributes of a victory. Wars are not won by evacuation, but there was a victory inside this deliverance which should be noted. . . . But our losses in material are enormous . . . nearly 1,000 guns and all our transport and all the armed vehicles that were with the Army in the North. This loss will impose a further delay on the expansion of our military strength. That ex-

pansion had not been proceeding as fast as we had hoped. The best of all we had to give have gone with the B.E.F. and, although they had not the number of tanks, they were a very well and finely equipped army. They had the first fruits of all our industry had to give, and that is gone.

Now there is this further delay. How long will it be? How long it will last depends upon the exertions we make in this island. An effort the like of which has never been seen in our records is now being made. . . . Nevertheless, our thankfulness at the escape of our army and of so many men, loved ones who have passed through an agonizing week—our thankfulness must not blind us to the fact that what has happened in France and Belgium is a colossal military disaster. . . . We cannot flag or fail. We shall go on to the end.

We shall fight in France, we shall fight on the seas and oceans; we shall fight with growing confidence and growing strength in the air. We shall defend our island whatever the cost may be. We shall fight on the beaches, we shall fight on the landing grounds, in the fields, in the streets, and in the hills. We shall never surrender, and even if—which I do not for a moment believe—this island or a large part of it were subjugated and starving, then our Empire beyond the seas, armed and guarded by the British fleet, will carry on the struggle until, in God's good time, the New World with all its power and might sets forth to the liberation and rescue of the Old.

Finest Hour, June 18, 1940

. . . the "Battle of France" is over. I expect that the "Battle of Britain" is about to begin. Upon this battle depends the survival of the Christian civilisation. Upon it depends our own British life and the long-continued history of our institutions and our Empire. The whole fury and might of the enemy must very soon be turned on us. Hitler knows that he will have to break us on this island or lose the war.

If we can stand up to him all Europe may be free, and the life of the world may move forward into broad and sunlit uplands. If we fail, then the whole world, including the United States—and all that we have known and cared for, will sink into the abyss of a new dark age, made more sinister and more prolonged by the light of a perverted science. Let us therefore do our duty and so bear ourselves that if the British Commonwealth and Empire lasts a thousand years men will still say: "This was their finest hour."

The Royal Air Force, August 20, 1940

The great air battle which has been in progress over this island for the past few weeks has recently attained a high intensity. It is too soon to attempt to assign limits either to its scale or its duration. We must certainly expect that greater efforts will be made by the enemy than any he has so far put forth. . . . On the other hand, the conditions and course of the fighting have so far been favourable to us. I told the House two months ago that whereas in France our fighter aircraft were wont to inflict a loss of two or three to one upon the Germans and in the fighting at Dunkirk, which was a kind of no-man's-land, a loss of about three or four to one, we expected that in an attack on this island we should achieve a larger ratio. This has certainly come true. (Cheers.)

It must also be remembered that all the enemy machines and pilots which are shot down over our island, or over the seas which surround it, are either destroyed or captured, whereas a considerable propor-

tion of our machines and also of our pilots are saved, and many of them soon again come into action. A vast and admirable system of salvage, directed by the Ministry of Aircraft Production, ensures the speediest return to the fighting line of damaged machines. At the same time [there is] the splendid, nay, astounding, increase in the output and repair of British aircraft and engines. . . .

The gratitude of every home in our island, in our Empire, and indeed throughout the world except in the abodes of the guilty goes out to the British airmen who, undaunted by odds, unwearied by their constant challenge and mortal danger, are turning the tide of world war by their prowess and their devotion.

Never in the field of human conflict was so much owed by so many to so few. (Prolonged cheers.) All hearts go out to the fighter pilots, whose brilliant actions we see with our own eyes day after day. . . .

On no part of the Royal Air Force does the weight of the war fall more heavily than on the daylight bombers, who will play an invaluable part in the case of an invasion and whose unflinching zeal it has been necessary in the meantime on numerous occasions to restrain. I have no hesitation in saying that the process of bombing the military industries and communications of Germany and the air bases and storage depots from which we are attacked, which will continue on an ever increasing scale until the end of the war and may in another year attain dimensions hitherto undreamed of, assures one at least of the most certain, if not the shortest, of all the roads to victory. Even if the Nazi legions stood triumphant on the Black Sea or indeed upon the Caspian, even if Hitler was at the gates of India, it would profit him nothing if at the same time the entire economic and scientific apparatus of German war power lay shattered and pulverised at home. (Cheers.)

Some months ago we came to the conclusion that the interests of the United States and of the British Empire both required that the United States should have facilities for the naval and air defence of the western hemisphere against the attack of a Nazi power which might have acquired temporary but lengthy control of a large part of Western Europe and its formidable resources. . . . Undoubtedly this process means that these two great organizations of the English-speaking democracies, the British Empire and the United States, will have to be somewhat mixed up together in some of their affairs for mutual and general advantage. (Cheers.) For my own part, looking out upon the future, I do not view the process with any misgivings. (Cheers.) I do not want to stop it. No one can stop it. Like the Mississippi, it just keeps rolling along. Let it roll. Let it roll on full flood, inexorable, irresistible, benignant, to broader lands and better days. (Loud cheers.)

---

62. The Atlantic Charter, 1941

In August 1941 President Franklin D. Roosevelt (1882–1945) met secretly with Prime Minister Winston Churchill (1874–1965) in Argentia Bay off the coast of Newfoundland. At the conclusion of their meetings the two leaders issued a joint statement of principles that they hoped would govern both the war effort and also the postwar world. This document, the Atlantic Charter, contained eight points that reflected both Woodrow Wilson's Fourteen Points and Roosevelt's domestic New Deal philosophy. When the Atlantic Charter was issued the United States was not yet at war, while Great Britain had been fighting the Axis Powers for nearly two years. For the United States this document marked another step away from neutrality and towards an alliance of the two leading English-speaking nations.

On January 1, 1942, a few weeks after America's entry into World War II, twenty-six nations (including the Soviet Union) that were fighting the Axis Powers endorsed the Atlantic Charter (some with reservations). It was reaffirmed at the Yalta Conference in February 1945. Although it stirred the hopes of many peoples around the globe, Great Britain and the Soviet Union did not support the fulfillment of all of its points in their own empires. Yet despite its generality of language and limited implementation, the Atlantic Charter did serve as an idealistic guide for the postwar world.

QUESTIONS

1. According to this statement, what were the most important goals of the Americans and the British as they prepared to defeat the Axis powers?

2. Did the fulfillment of these goals conflict with previous traditions and policies of either the United States or Great Britain?
3. Which of these goals created the greatest tensions with other World War II allies, especially China and the Soviet Union?
4. To what extent were these goals achieved after World War II?

Joint declaration of the President of the United States of America and the Prime Minister, Mr. Churchill, representing His Majesty's Government in the United Kingdom, being met together, deem it right to make known certain common principles in the national policies of their respective countries on which they base their hopes for a better future for the world.

First, their countries seek no aggrandizement, territorial or other;

Second, they desire to see no territorial changes that do not accord with the freely expressed wishes of the people concerned;

Third, they respect the right of all peoples to choose the form of government under which they will live; and they wish to see sovereign rights and self government restored to those who have been forcibly deprived of them;

Fourth, they will endeavor, with due respect for their existing obligations, to further the enjoyment by all States, great or small, victor or vanquished, of access, on equal terms, to the trade and to the raw materials of the world which are needed for their economic prosperity;

Fifth, they desire to bring about the fullest collaboration between all nations in the economic field with the object of securing, for all, improved labor standards, economic advancement, and social security.

Sixth, after the final destruction of the Nazi Tyranny, they hope to see established peace which will afford to all nations the means of dwelling in safety within their own boundaries, and which will afford assurance that all men in all the lands may live out their lives in freedom from fear and want;

Seventh, such a peace should enable all men to traverse the high seas and oceans without hindrance;

Eighth, they believe that all of the nations of the world, for realistic as well as spiritual reasons must come to the abandonment of the use of force. Since no future peace can be maintained on land, sea or air if armaments continue to be employed by nations which threaten, or may threaten, aggression outside of their frontiers, they believe, pending the establishment of a wider and permanent system of general security, that the disarmament of such nations is essential. They will likewise aid and encourage all other practicable measures which will lighten for peace-loving peoples the crushing burden of armaments.

63. The Shoah (Holocaust)

Responsibility for the Holocaust (or "Shoah," the Hebrew word for destruction) lies with the Nazi regime and its willing agents at home and throughout Hitler-dominated Europe. Historians generally agree that the Christian churches did not ordain and implement the "Shoah," but that without the support and justification provided by two millennia of Christian antisemitism in thought and deed it would not have been possible. Other peoples suffered terribly under the totalitarian regime, but since they were not "dangerous" they did not have to be destroyed. Rather, they could be exploited in the most ferocious manner for the benefit of the German economy and war effort. In the Third Reich Slavic peoples and others had some "justification for existence," but the Jews had none. The closest parallel to the Jews was the Gypsies, that is Sinti and Romani, who were also slated for annihilation. The number of casualties calculated by historians and statisticians runs from 4.2 to 6.9 million, or about two-thirds of European Jewry and one-third of world Jewry. The casualties among Soviet Jews were much higher than estimated heretofore, more than 2.2 million rather than .75 to 1 million. Total Soviet casualties in the war may have reached 40 million, far more than the long-standing estimate of 20 million.

The German war on the Jews was the work of the civil service, the Nazi party and SS, the armed forces, and the business, industrial, and financial sector working harmoniously together. The process began with bureaucratic definition of who was a Jew (in terms of religious affiliation and descent). Next came a series of decrees that subjected them to expropriation, dismissal from public employment and the professions, confiscation of property by forced sales and liquidations, forfeiture of all citizenship rights, compulsory marking of homes, papers, and clothing with the Jewish Star of David, and all kinds of vexations and humiliations intended to badger Jews into emigration. These procedures were developed and applied in Germany, Austria, and the area (Reich-Protektorat) annexed from Czechoslovakia in the 1930s; they were subsequently extended and adapted throughout the whole of German-dominated Europe, either by the Germans directly or by their allies and satellites (Romania, Croatia, Vichy France, etc.) where the Germans could exploit a combination of native antisemitism and greed to loot Jewish property. Initially the Hitler regime aimed at the "solution of the Jewish question" by emigration outside the German sphere (e.g. to the island of Madagascar), but failure and frustration of such schemes led on to more drastic solutions. With the fall of Poland, the next stage, concentration, was undertaken. After having lost most of their property to confiscations and seizure, Jews were deported to ghettos. Many were also dragooned into slave labor exploitation, and exposed to starvation and epidemic diseases. With the 1941 invasion of Soviet Russia another stage was reached, that of the mobile killing bands of *Einsatzgruppen* and *Sonderkommandos* that operated in the front lines, flanks, and rear areas as the German army advanced. With the help of local recruits and auxiliaries these forces murdered Jews and destroyed communities like Mrs. Yosselevscka's before they could flee. They also killed prisoners of war. The resounding success of the Russian invasion probably induced a new phase. All further emigration was blocked and the decision to annihilate all the Jews of Europe was taken. Its implementation and planning are the subject of the Wannsee conference. Auschwitz and five other death camps were fed by a system of railway operations from every part of Hitler's Europe, to which was added Mussolini's domain when he was overthrown in 1943, and Hungary when it was occupied in 1944. The process of destruction continued to practically the last hour of the war.

The "Shoah" presents a tremendous problem of historical interpretation: it represents a rebuttal of every value and ideal of Western civilization, whether in its religious guise or secular manifestations since the Enlightenment. Its hallmarks, the application of science and technology as well as efficient administration and bureaucratic rationality to mass murder, are also the hallmarks of our civilization and the sources of some of its greatest and most characteristic achievements. The "Shoah" is a unique, incomprehensible, and unapproachable event—in a sense outside history and beyond the historian's ken. Yet it is one of the pivotal events of the twentieth century and a watershed of Western civilization.

QUESTIONS

1. Summarize the various stages in the Nazi policy toward the Jews.
2. Did the Nazis make any distinctions among the various groups in the Jewish population?
3. What is your reaction to the description of the annihilation described by Mrs. Yosselevscka? Why did she survive?

I. Reaching a Decision to Destroy

A. SS-Major R. H. Höppner to Adolf Eichmann, July 16, 1941

Dear Comrade Eichmann,

Enclosed is a memorandum on the results of various discussions held locally in the office of the Reich Governor. I would be grateful to have your reactions sometime. These things sound in part fantastic, but in my view are thoroughly feasible.

Subject: Solution of the Jewish question

During discussions of the office of the Reich Governor various groups broached the solution of the Jewish question in Warthe province. The following solution is being proposed.

1. All the Jews of Warthe province will be taken to a camp for 300,000 Jews which will be erected in barracks form as close as possible to the coal precincts and which will contain barracks-like installations for economic enterprises, tailor shops, shoe manufacturing plants, etc.

2. All Jews of Warthe province will be brought into this camp. Jews capable of labor may be constituted into labor columns as needed and drawn from the camp.

3. In my view, a camp of this type may be guarded . . . with substantially fewer police forces than are required now. Furthermore, the danger of epidemics, which always exists in the Lodz and other ghettos for the surrounding population, will be minimized.

4. This winter there is a danger that not all of the Jews can be fed anymore. One should weigh honestly, if the most humane solution might not be to finish off those of the Jews who are not employable by means of some quick-working device. At any rate,

that would be more pleasant than to let them starve to death.

5. For the rest, the proposal was made that in this camp all the Jewish women, from whom one could still expect children, should be sterilized so that the Jewish problem may actually be solved completely with this generation. . . .

B. Reich Marshal Hermann Göring to SS-Lieutenant General Reinhard Heydrich, July 31, 1941

Complementing the task already assigned to you in the decree of January 24, 1939, to undertake, by emigration or evacuation, a solution of the Jewish question as advantageous as possible under the conditions at the time, I hereby charge you with making all necessary organizational, functional, and material preparations for a complete solution of the Jewish question in the German sphere of influence in Europe.

In so far as the jurisdiction of other central agencies may be touched thereby, they are to be involved.

I charge you furthermore with submitting to me in the near future an overall plan of the organizational, functional, and material measures to be taken in preparing for the implementation of the aspired final solution of the Jewish question.

C. Minutes of Wannsee Conference, Berlin, January 20, 1942, taken by Adolf Eichmann:

Meeting of 15 representatives of SS, Nazi Party, ministries of Interior, Justice, Foreign Office, "Race and Resettlement Headquarters," etc.

II. Chief of Security Police and Security Service, SS-Lieutenant General Heydrich, opened the meeting by informing everyone

that the Reich Marshal [Göring] had placed him in charge of preparations for the final solution of the Jewish question, and that the invitations to this conference had been issued to obtain clarity in fundamental questions. The Reich Marshal's wish to have a draft submitted to him on the organizational, functional, and material considerations aimed at a final solution of the European Jewish question requires that all of the central agencies, which are directly concerned with these problems, first join together with a view to parallelizing their lines of action.

The implementation of the final solution of the Jewish question is to be guided centrally without regard to the geographic boundaries from the office of the Reichsführer-SS and Chief of the German Police (Chief of Security Police and Security Service).

The chief of Security Police and Security Service then reviewed briefly the battle fought thus far against these opponents. The principal stages constituted

a) Forcing the Jews out of individual sectors of life [*Lebensgebiete*] of the German people
b) Forcing the Jews out of the living space [*Lebensraum*] of the German people

In pursuance of this endeavor, a systematic and concentrated effort was made to accelerate Jewish immigration from Reich territory as the only temporary solution possibility.

On instructions of the Reich Marshal, a Reich Central Office for Jewish Emigration was established in January, 1939, and its direction was entrusted to the Chief of the Security Police and Security Service. In particular the office had the task of

a) taking every step to prepare for a larger volume of Jewish emigration,
b) steering the flow of emigration,
c) expediting emigration in individual cases.

The goal of the task was to cleanse the German living space of Jews in a legal manner.

The disadvantages brought forth by such forcing of emigration were clear to every agency. In the meantime, however, they had to be accepted for the lack of any other solution possibility.

The migration work in the ensuing period was not only a German problem, but also one that concerned the offices of the countries of destination and immigration. Financial difficulties, such as increasingly demanding regulations on the part of various foreign governments for money to be shown by the immigrant or to be paid by him on landing, insufficient berths on ships, constantly increasing immigration restrictions and suspensions—all this placed extraordinary burdens on emigration efforts. In spite of these difficulties, some 537,000 Jews were moved out from the day of the seizure of power to October 31, 1941. Of this total

from January 30, 1933 out of the Old Reich . . . ca. 360,000
from March 15, 1938 out of Austria . . . . ca. 147,000
from March 15, 1939 out of the Protectorate Bohemia and Moravia . . . ca. 30,000-7

The emigration was financed by the Jews (or Jewish political organizations) themselves. In order to avoid having a residue of proletarianized Jews, the Jews with means had to finance the departure of the Jews without means; an appropriate assessment and emigration tax were used to finance the payments of debts owed by the poor Jews in the course of their emigration.

In addition to this levy in Reichsmark, foreign currencies were required for showing or payment on landing. In order to spare German foreign currency reserves, the Jewish financial institutions abroad were called upon by Jewish organizations at home to take care of the collection of an appropriate foreign currency pile. In this manner about $9,500,000 were made available through these foreign Jews as gifts to October 30, 1941.

Meanwhile, in view of the dangers of emigration in time of war and in view of the possibilities in the east, the Reichsführer-SS and Chief of the German Police [Himmler] has forbidden the emigration of Jews.

III. In lieu of emigration, the evacuation of the Jews to the east has emerged, after an appropriate prior authorization by the Führer [Hitler], as a further solution possibility.

While these actions are to be regarded solely as temporary measures, practical experiences are already being gathered here which will be of great importance during the coming final solution of the Jewish question.

Around 11 million Jews are involved in this final solution of the Jewish question. They are distributed as follows among individual countries:

A.		
Old Reich		131,800
Austria		43,700
Eastern Territories [Poland]		420,000
General government [Poland]		2,284,000
Bialystok [Poland]		400,000
Protectorate of Bohemia and Moravia		74,000
Estonia—Free of Jews		
Latvia		3,500
Lithuania		34,000
Belgium		43,000
Denmark		5,600
France, occupied territory		165,000
France, unoccupied territory		700,000
Greece		69,600
Netherlands		160,800

	Norway	1,300
B.	Bulgaria	48,000
	England	330,000
	Finland	2,300
	Ireland	4,000
	Italy, including Sardinia	58,000
	Albania	200
	Croatia	40,000
	Portugal	3,000
	Romania, including	
	Bessarabia	342,000
	Sweden	8,000
	Switzerland	18,000
	Serbia	10,000
	Slovakia	88,000
	Spain	6,000
	Turkey (European portion)	55,300
	Hungary	742,000
	USSR	5,000,000*
	Ukraine	2,994,685*
	White Russia	
	(excluding Bialystok)	446,484

Total	over	11,000,000

* [these figures are exaggerated, but recent German research estimates 4.7 million in U.S.S.R.]

So far as the Jews of the various foreign countries are concerned, the numbers listed include only Jews by religion, since definitions of Jews according to racial principles are in part still lacking there. Given prevailing attitudes and conceptions, the treatment of the problem in individual countries will encounter certain difficulties, especially in Hungary and Romania. For example, even today a Jew in Romania can buy for cash appropriate documents officially certifying him in a foreign nationality.

The pervasive influence of Jewry in the USSR is known. The European area contains some 5 million, the Asian barely a half million Jews.

The occupation distribution of Jewry in the European area of the USSR was approximately as follows:

agriculture	09.1%
urban workers	14.8%
trade	20.0%
state employees	23.4%
private professionals— medical, press, theater and so forth	32.7%

In the course of the final solution, the Jews should be brought under appropriate direction in a suitable manner to the east for labor utilization. Separated by sex, the Jews capable of work will be led into these areas in large labor columns to build roads, whereby doubtless a large part will fall away through natural reduction.

The inevitable final remainder which doubtless constitutes the toughest element will have to be dealt with appropriately, since it represents a natural selection which upon liberation is to be regarded as a germ cell of a new Jewish development. (See the lesson of history.)

In the course of the practical implementation of the final solution, Europe will be combed from west to east. If only because of the apartment shortage and other sociopolitical necessities, the Reich area—including the Protectorate of Bohemia and Moravia—will have to be placed ahead of the line.

For the moment, the evacuated Jews will be brought bit by bit to so-called transit ghettos from where they will be transported farther to the east. . . .

It is intended not to evacuate Jews over 65, but to transfer them to an old people's ghetto (the plans call for Theresienstadt).

In addition to these age groups—some 30% of the 280,000 Jews who lived in the Old Reich and Austria on October 1, 1941, are over 65—the old people's ghetto will receive badly invalided Jewish war veterans and Jews with war decorations (Iron Cross First Class). Many intercessions will be eliminated in one blow by means of this purposeful solution.

The start of major individual evacuation operations will depend in large measure on military developments. With regard to the treatment of the final solution in European areas occupied or influenced by us, it was proposed that the appropriate specialists of the Foreign Office get together with the experts having jurisdiction in these matters within the Security Police and Security Service.

In Slovakia and Croatia the situation is no longer all that difficult, since the essential key questions there have already been resolved. Meanwhile, the Romanian government has already appointed a plenipotentiary for Jewish affairs. To settle the matter in Hungary, it will be necessary before long to impose upon the Hungarian government an adviser on Jewish questions.

Regarding a start of preparations in Italy, SS-Lieutenant General Heydrich considers it appropriate to contact the Police Chief for liason.

In occupied and unoccupied France, the seizure of Jews for evacuation should in all probablility proceed without major difficulty.

Assistant Secretary Luther [Foreign Office] then pointed out that with a deeply penetrating treatment of these problems in some countries, such as the Nordic states, difficulties would emerge and that meanwhile it would therefore be best to hold these countries in abeyance. In view of the insignificant number of Jews involved there, the postponement would not amount to a substantial restriction. On the other hand, the Foreign Office sees no major difficulties in southeastern and western Europe.

SS-Major General Hofmann intends to dispatch a specialist of the Race and Resettlement Office for general orientation to Hungary as soon as the Chief of Security Police and Security Service is about to tackle the situation over there. It was decided that temporarily the specialist of the Race and Resettlement Office—who is not to become active—should be officially attached as an assistant to the Police Attaché.

IV. The [1935 racialist] Nuremberg Laws should constitute the basis, so to speak, of the final solution project, while a solution of the mixed marriage and mixed parentage questions is a prerequisite for the complete purification of the problem [for which the conferees urged sterilization].

II. Carrying Out the Decision of Annihilation

A. SS Open Air Shootings in Russia by Einsatzkommandos

Testimony of Mrs. Rivka Yosselevscka at the Eichmann trial, Jerusalem, May 8, 1961.

[The witness was born in Zagrodski, a town containing some five hundred Jewish families, in the Pinsk district. Her father, owner of a leather goods shop, was considered a notable there. Mrs. Yosselevscka was married in 1934, and when the Germans arrived she had one child. The events she describes took place in mid-August 1942.]

Attorney-General: Do you remember the Sabbath at the beginning of the Hebrew month of Ellul, 1942?

A. I remember that day very well. Jews were not allowed to go to pray, yet they would risk their lives and go into a cellar in the ghetto . . . the only Jews left in the ghetto would endanger their very lives to go into the cellar to pray—very early, before dawn. On that night, there was too much commotion in the ghetto. There was always noise in the ghetto. Germans would be coming in and leaving the ghetto during all hours of the night. But the commotion and noise on that night was not customary, and we felt something in the air. . . .

And we asked—why so many Germans in the ghetto? They told us that there was a partisan woman trying to get into the ghetto and mix with us. . . . This was the first day of the month. I remember very well—this was the first day of the New Year. We were told to leave the houses—to take with us only the children. We were always used to leave the ghetto at short order, because very often they would take us all out for a roll-call. Then we would all appear. But we felt and realized that this was not an ordinary roll-call, but something very special. As if the Angel of Death was in charge. The place was swarming with Germans. Some four to five Germans to every Jew.

We were left standing in the ghetto. They began saying that he who wishes to save his life could do so with money, jewels and valuable things. This would be ransom, and he would be spared. Thus we were held until the late afternoon, before evening came.

Presiding Judge: And did the Jews hand over jewels and so on?

Witness: We did not. We had nothing to hand over. They already took all we had before. And . . . the children screamed. They wanted food, water. This was not the first time. But we took nothing with us. We had no food and no water, and we did not know the reason. The children were hungry and thirsty. We were held this way for 24 hours while they were searching the houses all the time—searching for valuables.

In the meantime, the gates of the ghetto were opened. A large truck appeared and all of us were put onto the truck—either thrown, or went up himself.

Q. Now—they filled up this truck. And what happened to the people for whom there was no room in the truck?

A. Those for whom there was no room in the truck were ordered to run after the truck. I had my daughter in my arms and ran after the truck. There were mothers who had two or three children and held them in their arms—running after the truck. We ran all the way. There were those who fell—we were not allowed to help them rise. They were shot—right there—whenever they fell. All my family was amongst them. When we all reached the destination, the people from the truck were already down and they were undressed—all lined up. All my family was there—undressed, lined up. The people from the truck, those who arrived before us. There was a kind of hillock. At the foot of this little hill, there was a dugout. We were ordered to stand at the top of the hillock and the four devils shot us—each one of us separately. They were SS men—the four of them. They were armed to the teeth. They were real messengers of the Devil and the Angel of Death.

When I came up to the place—we saw people naked lined up. But we were still hoping this was only torture. Maybe there is Hope—hope of living. One could not leave the line, but I wished to see—what are they doing on the hillock? Is there anyone down below? I turned my head and saw that some three or four rows were already killed—on the ground. There were some twelve people amongst the dead. I also want to mention that my child said while we were lined up in the Ghetto, she said, "Mother, why did you make me wear the Shabbat dress; we are being taken to be shot"; and when we stood near the dug-out, near the grave, she said, "Mother, why are we waiting, let us run!" Some of the young people tried to run, but they were caught immediately, and they were shot right there. It was difficult to hold on to the children. We took all children not ours, and we carried—we were anxious to get it all over—the suffering of the children was difficult; we all trudged along to come nearer to the place and to come nearer to the end of the torture of the children. The children were taking leave of their parents and parents of their elder people.

Presiding Judge: How did you survive through all this? . . .

Witness: We were driven; we were already undressed, the clothes were removed and taken away; our father did not want to undress; he remained in his underwear. We were driven up to the grave, this shallow. . . . When it came to our turn, our father was beaten. We prayed, we begged with my father to undress, but he would not undress, he wanted to keep his underclothes. He did not want to stand naked. Then they tore off the clothing of the old man and he was shot. I saw it with my own eyes. And then they took my mother, and she said, let us go before her; but they caught mother and shot her too; and then there was my grandmother, my father's mother, standing there; she was eighty years old and she had two children in her arms. And then there was my father's sister. She also had children in her arms and she was shot on the spot with the babies in her arms. There was my younger sister, and she wanted to leave, she prayed with the Germans; she asked to run, naked; she went up to the Germans with one of her friends; they were embracing each other; and she asked to be spared, standing there naked. He looked into her eyes and shot the two of them. They fell together in their embrace, the two young girls, my sister and her young friend. Then my second sister was shot and then my turn did come.

Q. Were you asked anything? A.: We turned towards the grave and then he turned around and asked "Whom shall I shoot first?" We were already facing the grave. The German asked "Who do you

want me to shoot first?" I did not answer. I felt him take the child from my arms. The child cried out and was shot immediately. And then he aimed at me. First he held on to my hair and turned my head around; I stayed standing; I heard a shot, but I continued to stand and then he turned my head again and he aimed the revolver at me and ordered me to watch and then turned my head around and shot at me. Then I fell to the ground into the pit amongst bodies; but I felt nothing. The moment I did feel I felt a sort of heaviness and then I thought maybe I am not alive anymore, but I feel something after I died. I thought I was dead, that this was the feeling which comes after death. Then I felt that I was choking; people falling all over me. I tried to move and felt that I was alive and that I could rise. I was strangling, but I tried to save myself, to find some air to breathe, and then I felt that I was climbing towards the top of the grave of bodies. I rose, and I felt bodies pulling at me down, down. And yet with my last strength I came up on top of the grave, and when I did I did not know the place, so many bodies were lying all over, dead people; I wanted to see the end of this stretch of dead bodies but I could not. It was impossible. They were lying, all dying, suffering; not all of them dead, but in their last sufferings; naked; shot, but not dead. Children crying "Mother," "Father"; I could not stand on my feet. . . . The Germans were gone. There was nobody there. No-one standing up. I was naked, covered with blood, dirty from the other bodies, with the excrement from other bodies which was poured onto me.

Q.: What did you have in your head? A.: When I was shot I was wounded in the head. Q.: Was it in the back of the head?

A.: I have a scar to this day from the shot by the Germans; and yet, somehow I did come out of the grave. This was something I thought I would never live to recount. I was searching among the dead for my little girl, and I cried for her—Merkele was her name—Merkele! There were children crying "Mother!" "Father!"—but they were all smeared with blood and one could not recognize the children. I cried for my daughter. From afar I saw two women standing. I went up to them. They did not know me, I did not know them, and then I said who I was, and then they said, "So you survived." And there was another woman crying "Pull me out from amongst the corpses, I am alive, help!" We removed the corpses and the dying people who held onto her and continued to bite. She asked us to take her out, to free her, but we did not have the strength.

Attorney-General: It is very difficult to relate, I am sure, it is difficult to listen to, but we must proceed. Please tell us now: After that you hid?

A.: And thus we were there all night, fighting for our lives, listening to the cries and the screams and all of a sudden we saw Germans, mounted Germans. We did not notice them coming in because of the screamings and the shoutings from the bodies around us. The Germans ordered that all the corpses be heaped together into one big heap and with shovels they were heaped together, all the corpses, amongst them many still alive, children running about the place. I saw them. I saw the children. They were running after me, hanging onto me. Then I sat down in the field and remained sitting with the children around me. The children who got up from the heap of corpses. Then the Germans came and were going around the place. We were ordered to collect all the children, but they did not approach me, and I sat there watching how they collected the children. They gave a few shots and the children were dead, and this . . . woman pleaded with the Germans to be spared, but they shot her.

They all left—the Germans and the non-Jews from around the place. They removed the machine guns and they took the trucks. I saw that they all left, and the four of us, we went onto the grave, praying to fall into the grave, even alive, envying those who were dead already and thinking what to do now. I was praying for death to come. I was praying for the grave to be opened and to swallow me alive. Blood was spurting from the grave in many places, like a well of water, and whenever I pass a spring now, I remember the blood which spurted from the ground, from that grave. I dug with my fingernails, trying to join the dead in that grave. I dug with my fingernails, but the grave would not open. I did not have enough strength. I cried out to my mother, to my father, "Why did they not kill me? What was my sin? I have no one to go to. I saw them all being killed. Why was I spared? Why was I not killed?"

And I remained there, stretched out on the grave, three days and three nights. I saw no one. Not a farmer passed by. After three days, shepherds drove their herd onto the field. At night, the herds were taken back and during the day they threw stones believing that either it was a dead woman or a mad woman. They wanted me to rise, to answer. But I did not move. I hid near the grave. A farmer passed by, after a number of weeks.

Q.: He took pity on you, he fed you, and he helped you join a group of Jews in the forest, and you spent time until the summer of '44 with this group, until the Soviets came.

A.: I was with them until the very end. Q.: And now you are married and you have two children? A.: Yes.

Presiding Judge: Please, quiet in the courtroom. Some respect, please. Thank you, Mrs. Yosselevscka.

64. Ebensee: Nazi Concentration Camp

Petro Mirchuk

Germany's invasion of the U.S.S.R. and its occupation of Ukrainian territories prompted Ukrainian nationalists to proclaim the re-establishment of an independent Ukrainian state on June 30, 1941. Taken by surprise, German authorities at first attempted to persuade nationalist leaders to renounce this proclamation and to disband their government. When these demands were refused the Germans arrested the Ukrainian leaders on September 15, 1941 and then incarcerated them in the concentration camp of Sachsenhausen. On the same day, the Germans launched a well coordinated campaign of mass arrests of Ukrainian nationalists. Among those arrested was the author of the following narrative. At the time of his arrest he was employed by the Institute of Education. He survived imprisonment in several concentration camps and was liberated by the American Army on May 6, 1945.

QUESTIONS

1. How can you explain the conditions described in this concentration camp? Do they indicate any concern for human life?
2. Does this selection indicate any change in the treatment of the prisoners as the end of the war approached?
3. As the war was ending, what were the chief concerns of the prisoners?
4. What is the Austrian myth that is exploded here?

Late in the afternoon of our fourth day of marching we passed the little town of Ebensee [in Austria] and went to a small concentration camp by the same name located on top of the hill some miles outside the town.

The small camp consisted of twenty wooden barracks built in a forest. The only brick building was the crematorium, and actually only a part of it was brick. The other part, used for keeping corpses, was wooden. The rectangle, as in all other cases, was surrounded by double electrified wire and a high wall with towers for the SS guards and their machine guns. In front of the gate was a place for the roll call. We went through the normal procedure, but after we had showered and had come into the barracks there was not enough clothing available. Only a part received all items of prisoner's clothing; the others received some of the items. The last group received no clothing at all and had to wait a few days naked. I was in this last group and had only a blanket to ward off the cold.

The next day the prisoners were ordered to go to work, but only those who had clothing could do that. The others had to remain in the blocks. One group of prisoners was sent to repair the bombed railroad and when the administration saw that there were not enough fully dressed prisoners, they began to collect others from among those who had only one piece of clothing to complete the group of one hundred.

Prisoners began to hide what they had—shirt or pants—on the beds. This was discovered and about one hundred needed prisoners were sent to the work with full sets of clothing made up from pieces found on the beds. Those who had to remain in the block were brought outside for punishment exercises. We were taken back into the blocks, but the windows were opened and there we had to remain for two or three hours as punishment for trying to hide our pieces of clothing.

On the third day I received a shirt and on the fifth day I was given pants and a coat and was sent to the work. The basic work here was the same as it was in Melk—to build tunnels and rooms for underground industry.

In the bed I was assigned I found a hidden pullover, but since it was too dangerous to wear it in the normal way, I decided to use it to replace the underwear I did not have and wore it under my pants.

After I received my pants and coat I was added to a "kommando" [group] working in the construction of tunnels. The kommando was called Holzmann-Polensky.

KZ Ebensee was one of the branches of concentration camp Mauthausen, but we met something new here—a real famine. In all concentration camps the prisoners received a starvation portion of food, but always there was the chance to organize something additional, and the prisoners were given at least one-third of what a regular worker would need to survive. Here the situation was totally different. We received virtually no food. In the morning when we had to go to work, we were given only tea or coffee. It wasn't real tea or coffee, just a drink made from tree leaves or something else. It was at least hot. There was nothing more than that in the morning.

At noon we were given a portion of "soup." However, in other camps what we were given was really soup, but here it was only the hot water in which the potatoes for the SS guards had been boiled. After the potatoes were ready, they were taken out for the SS and the prisoners received only this hot water with sometimes a piece of potato in it. That was our entire lunch.

Between 6:00 and 7:00 P.M. there was again one portion of coffee or tea and a portion of bread. A one-kilogram loaf was divided among twelve prisoners. It was made from extremely bad ingredients. It was impossible to cut it into twelve pieces, so they cut it into four. The prisoners were divided into groups of three. One got the one-quarter loaf and had to divide it for himself and the other two prisoners in his group. The prisoners had no knife, but even if they had had a very good knife, the bread still would have beeen impossible to cut. However, as we had done in the prison at Montelupich, we of the Ukrainian group tried to divide it evenly. In the other groups, though, usually the strongest prisoner would take the whole portion and run away and eat it all himself. The two others would not receive even this small portion of bread. As a result, an average of five hundred prisoners died each day from starvation.

There was a "schonungsblock," a recuperation section of the hospital, meant for prisoners too ill or exhausted to work. There they were to stay until they had recuperated enough to return to the work, but actually it was the place where the prisoners finished their lives. It was one of the wooden barracks where there were no beds. The prisoners brought by others were placed on the floor. Here they remained until they died.

They lay on the floor unable to stand and received the same portion of food as all the others—almost nothing, so there was no chance for recovery. When one died, the portion of bread that was to have been his was given to the "stubendienst" or "block altester," so that often they did not take the dead out for three or four days and continued to report them as alive during that time.

This was the last concentration camp in the territory still in operation at that time—the others had already been liberated by the American or English armies in the west and north or by the Russian army in the east. From all camps the prisoners who had been evacuated before the camps were liberated were brought here. As a result, at least five hundred new prisoners were brought in to replace the five hundred who had died from starvation and perhaps two hundred more who had died during the work.

In Mauthausen, after evacuation from Auschwitz, our Ukrainian group was separated. Only a part was sent to Melk. The others were sent to other branches of Mauthausen. One group had been sent immediately to Ebensee. Now we found them mostly in the "schonungsblock," only a few were still able to work and many had already died.

A good friend of mine was in the "schonungsblock," so I visited him after work. He was lying on the floor, unable to even lift his head to greet me. He only glanced at me and told me that he would not ever leave, that he would die in the next hour. He begged me to ask the administration to remove the prisoners on either side of him who had been dead for three and four days. I asked the "stubendienst," but he told my friend to be patient for a few more hours; he would soon join them so it shouldn't make any differ-

ence to him that there were dead men beside him. . . .

Here also, as in Melk, were the civilian "meisters." They interfered here, also, in the work of the prisoners, kicking and beating them with obvious pleasure.

In the "kommando" where I worked there was a man called Meister Barany. I heard his name when another meister called him Herr Barany. Very often during the work we experienced a blackout because the lighting was only temporary and when someone touched the wires it caused a blackout. So once when we had a long blackout, Herr Barany was near me in the darkness. I took advantage of the fact that he could not see us and said, "We are just as human as you and the others. Here is a former French general, and here is a priest, here is a former Polish professor, I have a higher education, too, and there are intelligent people from all over Europe in this group. Why do you keep on torturing, persecuting, and beating us? The war is almost over. Can you not be human even for this short time?"

He answered, "Well, you are right, but I am not responsible for all that is going on. You must realize that I am an Austrian and Austria is occupied by Germany as are your countries. I am not responsible for National Socialistic Germany and I will be glad, too, when Austria is liberated. I never had anything against non-German people."

Then the light came on, and as soon as there was light in our section he shouted to us, "An die arbeit!" This means "To the work." He began hitting the prisoners with his stick once more. What he had said in the darkness was only a trick because he was afraid that one of the prisoners might take advantage of the darkness to kill him. Actually, even though he was Austrian, he was just as sadistic and brutal to the non-German prisoners as were the Germans themselves.

The terrible hunger forced the prisoners to try to eat grass and charcoal. This had already been done in Auschwitz, but here it took place much more often. It was the general belief that German margarine was extracted from charcoal chemically. This meant that in charcoal there was a percentage of margarine and if one ate some charcoal one might force the stomach to do what the specialists did in making it margarine. Almost all the prisoners brought to the "schonungsblock" had black lips from eating charcoal. Of course, this didn't work and only caused additional suffering and stomach pains.

One Russian prisoner working in my kommando told me that he and three of the other prisoners, one Polish and two French, decided to eat the flesh of one of the new prisoners. During the night they killed him and ate his flesh. The result was that they had stomach convulsions. He survived, but the other three had died. He said he would never try eating human flesh again.

Two of the prisoners in my kommando were Hungarian Jews. One of them told me that they had been students before they were arrested. They both spoke fluent German. Only one now talked; the other didn't react to anything. When the forabeiter and meister were in another part of the corridor and couldn't see us, we stopped working to conserve our energy. The other young Jewish prisoner continued to work. I tried to tell him that he should not continue because he would soon fall down from exhaustion. There was absolutely no reaction. Then I told him that for his work he would get nothing additional to eat. "Eat, eat," he said. "Yes," I said. "The small portion of bread will not get any larger." "Bread, bread!" he shouted. I found out that only when he

heard the words connected with food did he react. Otherwise, he showed no awareness of what was going on around him.

Every day when we returned from the work, at least one-quarter of the kommando were delivered as dead to the crematorium or to the "schonungsblock," starved and exhausted. They were replaced the next morning by others, since bringing of prisoners from the other camps continued. . . .

One of the new prisoners, a young Polish political prisoner, told me an interesting story about his experiences in Gardelegen. During the evacuation of the concentration camp where he was a prisoner they were walking in different directions because of the confusion caused by the military operations. In the second week of April, 1945 they came to a village, Gardelegen, near Magdeburg. The kommandant of the transport, along with the mayor of the town, ordered all prisoners to go into a wooden barn. About one thousand prisoners were crowded into the barn, then the doors were locked and the wooden building set on fire. The prisoners tried to break down the door, but most of them were soon suffocated by the smoke. Only a few were able to break through the doors or wooden walls, but when they tried to run out they were met with machine guns. Not more than ten from a group of more than a thousand escaped. After one day, since they were in prison dress, they were caught by villagers and reported to German authorities. Since another transport was then passing the place, they were added to the new transport and taken to Ebensee. He also told us about the conditions in the camp where they had been before, and especially about the SS guard Ziereis. He was the moral double of Palitsch in Auschwitz. He liked to torture the prisoners, and so, when his fourteen-year-old son had a birthday, he gave him a special birthday gift. He gave him a gun and forty prisoners. The forty victims were taken to an orchard and bound to the trees for the fourteen-year-old boy to use for target practice. After the war, during the trial of this beast, his son was a witness and admitted that this had actually happened. . . .

We Ukrainian political prisoners had something additional to worry about. If the camp were liberated before the Germans annihilated all prisoners, who would liberate Ebensee? Would it be the Americans or English from the south or the Russians from the east? If the English or Americans came, we would be safe; if the Russians liberated the camp we knew the Ukrainian political prisoners would be sent to Russian concentration camps or be executed—we were their political enemies, too. We were political enemies of Communist Russia as well as Nazi Germany.

During the first week of May, 1945 the news spread that Hitler was dead. Someone who had managed to get a German newspaper told us that the Führer had fallen in heavy battle against the Russians in Berlin. True or untrue, the news brought none of the expected changes. Everything continued as it had for the next two or three days.

On the morning of May 4 the roll call was different. The kommandant of the camp and the SS guards were absent. In their place was a civilian who introduced himself to us as the mayor of the town of Ebensee. He told us that the war was over, we were free, and were under the protection of the International Red Cross. He said that he was responsible for us. He also told us that there was some danger that some diehard Nazis might decide to make a last stand here in the only part of Germany not occupied by the Allies. In that case, he told us, we would be in danger since the camp might be strafed. He suggested that we all take cover in the tunnels we had built for two or three days

until an allied army would come to take charge of us.

We all reacted suspiciously and nervously to his suggestion. Only a few days earlier we had been ordered to bring bags of dynamite and put them on both sides of the entrance to the tunnels. Many bags were placed in other places inside the tunnels. Therefore, we feared that what the mayor was suggesting was nothing more than a trick — that when we were all in the tunnels we would be buried there by the explosion of the dynamite. We told him that if we had to die, we would die where we were.

To our surprise, the mayor didn't insist, but told us that it was only his idea for our well-being. . . .

After the roll call we were not sent to work, but were allowed to stay in the camp and do whatever we wanted.

We saw that there were no longer any SS guards at the towers. In their places were members of the Volkssturm, the militia. The gate was locked. None of the prisoners were permitted to leave the camp. We were informed that these regulations had been imposed by the International Red Cross which had a representative who would come to the camp soon and take it over.

At noon, instead of the usual hot water, we were given real soup, a gruel. This was the first we had had in three weeks. Then we had to wait until night.

For part of the time I walked around, but that was not so easy because I, also, was totally exhausted. However, I wanted to see those from my group who were still alive to find out what we should do. I met some of them and we decided that as soon as the gates were opened, we would leave and find out what our true situation was. In case it was not possible for us to leave the camp, we would all pretend to be Polish, Czech, or Russian from the first moment until we were sure we were out of reach of the Russian NKVD.

For supper, between 5:00 and 6:00 P.M., we received another bowl of real soup. There was no other roll call that day or thereafter. For breakfast the next morning we were given some coffee and some real bread. At noon and again at supper we were given bowls of real soup. . . .

On Sunday, May 6, 1945, about 10:00 A.M., a shouting came from the prisoners who were looking through the gate. They shouted that a tank was coming. Soon a tank appeared on the narrow road, broke down the gate, and came into the camp. On top of the tank were two or three soldiers waving and smiling at the prisoners. From all sides the prisoners jumped on the tank, shouting happily, thanking them for our liberation, kissing the soldier and the tank. I did not know then that the Americans, too, used a five-pointed star, and so I thought that it was a Russian tank. So I decided to take advantage of the open gate and I left the camp quickly.

Other prisoners were streaming through the gate toward the barracks where the kitchen for the SS had been located. The prisoners broke into the building and went looking for food. In chaos everyone tried to get whatever he could find. I got an onion which I ate whole, then found a piece of bread and ate that, too. A barrel of butter was opened, and I, along with many others, tried to put my hand in the barrel. One tried to cut out some butter with a knife he had found and wounded many prisoners in the process. In only a few moments the barrel was empty. When everything had been eaten, the prisoners went back to the camp, counting on the help of the liberators.

I met another Ukrainian prisoner and we decided to try to get to the next town. When we came out on the road which led to the town of Ebensee, we were passed by a girl on a bicycle. We stopped her, asking for something to eat. She was frightened and told us that she had only a piece of bread, opened her bag, and gave it to us. She left quickly, happy that we had let her go. When we examined the bread, we were surprised to find that it looked exactly like Paska, a kind of bread prepared by Ukrainians for Easter. My friend said that the day was Sunday, Easter according to the Ukrainian calendar. We thought perhaps that the girl was a Ukrainian working as a slave somewhere in the neighborhood in German industry. At any rate we happily consumed the Paska, looked at the concentration camp behind us, and recalled the words of the Ukrainian poet, Iwan Franko. In his poem about the abolition of serfdom he wrote, "Oh, Lord, since the world existed, there never was such a happy Easter."

We were quite overcome with happiness, realizing that we had survived four years in a Nazi concentration camp and all this inferno was now behind us. The Nazi German Empire which, according to Goebbels, was to have lasted one thousand years, had ceased to exist and we who were to have been annihilated had outlived the "thousand-year Nazi empire."

During the time we were looking for food in the SS kitchen, I had found some big scales. I checked my weight and found that I weighed 70 pounds, a little less than half my regular weight of 155 to 160 pounds. It didn't matter now, however, for the important thing was that I was alive, the war was over and the concentration camp was behind.

After walking for about an hour, we decided to rest, and sat down on some rocks. About an hour later we were joined by a third Ukrainian prisoner who had left the camp alone. We three continued to walk to Gmunden, the next large town.

65. Yalta Conference, 1945

As World War II came closer to its end the Big Three—Franklin D. Roosevelt, Winston Churchill, and Joseph Stalin—met at Yalta in the Crimea from February 4–11, 1945 to discuss postwar political and diplomatic issues. Most of the attention of the delegates focused on the problems of launching the United Nations and the future of Germany and Poland. Churchill permitted Roosevelt and Stalin to decide matters of the Far East, and in the end Stalin received everything he asked for in exchange for his promise to enter the war against Japan. The Yalta conference's declaration on Poland and the secret protocol on the Far East are reprinted below.

QUESTIONS

1. Summarize the main points of the political and territorial agreements on Poland. Why did this declaration become a source of friction between the United States and the Soviet Union after the defeat of Germany?
2. Who is giving or getting what in this poker game regarding Japan, and what factors might explain the terms offered or insisted upon? Who is the better poker player?
3. What were the "treacherous" events of 1904? Why are they so central to this document? Are they formative of the Soviet outlook on foreign affairs?
4. Can you see the seeds of future developments planted here?

Poland

A new situation has been created in Poland as a result of her complete liberation by the Red Army. This calls for the establishment of a Polish provisional government which can be more broadly based than was possible before the recent liberation of the western part of Poland. The provisional government which is now functioning in Poland should therefore be reorganized on a broader democratic basis with the inclusion of democratic leaders from Poland itself and from Poles abroad. This new government should then be called the Polish Provisional Government of National Unity.

Mr. Molotov, Mr. Harriman and Sir A. Clark Kerr are authorized as a commission to consult in the first instance in Moscow with members of the present provisional government and with other Polish democratic leaders from within Poland and from abroad, with a view to the reorganization of the present government along the above lines. This Polish Provisional Government of National Unity shall be pledged to the holding of free and unfettered elections as soon as possible on the basis of universal suffrage and secret ballot. In these elections all democratic and anti-Nazi parties shall have the right to take part and to put forward candidates.

When a Polish Provisional Government of National Unity has been properly formed in conformity with the above, the Government of the U.S.S.R., which now maintains diplomatic relations with the present Provisional Government of Poland and the Government of the United Kingdom and the Government of the United States of America will establish diplomatic relations with the new Polish Provisional Government of National Unity, and will exchange Ambassadors by whose reports the respective governments will be kept informed about the situation in Poland.

The three heads of government consider that the eastern frontier of Poland should follow the Curzon Line with some digressions from it in some regions of five to eight kilometers in favor of Poland. They recognize that Poland must receive substantial accessions of territory in the north and west. They feel that the opinion of the new Polish Provisional Government of National Unity should be sought in due course of the extent of the accessions and that the final delimitation of the western frontier of Poland should thereafter await the peace conference. . . .

Provisions on the Far East

The leaders of the three great powers—the Soviet Union, the United States of America and Great Britain—have agreed that in two or three months after Germany has surrendered and the war in Europe has terminated, the Soviet Union shall enter into the war against Japan on the side of the Allies on condition that:

1. The status quo in Outer Mongolia (the Mongolian People's Republic) shall be preserved;
2. The former rights of Russia violated by the treacherous attack of Japan in 1904 shall be restored, viz:
    A. The southern part of Sakhalin as well as the islands adjacent to it shall be returned to the Soviet Union;
    B. The commercial port of Dairen shall be internationalized, the preeminent interests of the Soviet Union in this port are being safeguarded and the lease of Port Arthur as a naval base of the U.S.S.R. restored;
    C. The Chinese-Eastern Railroad and the South Manchurian Railroad, which provides an outlet to Dairen, shall be jointly operated by the establishment of a joint Soviet-Chinese company, it being understood that the preeminent interests of the Soviet Union shall be safeguarded and that China shall retain full sovereignty in Manchuria;
3. The Kurile Islands shall be handed over to the Soviet Union.

It is understood that the agreement concerning Outer Mongolia and the ports and railroads referred to above will require concurrence of Generalissimo Chiang Kai-Shek. The President [Roosevelt] will take measures in order to obtain this concurrence on advice from Marshal Stalin.

The heads of the three great powers have agreed that these claims of the Soviet Union shall be unquestionably fulfilled after Japan has been defeated.

For its part, the Soviet Union expresses its readiness to conclude with the National Government of China a pact of friendship and alliance between the U.S.S.R. and China with its armed forces for the purpose of liberating China from the Japanese yoke.

JOSEPH V. STALIN
FRANKLIN D. ROOSEVELT
WINSTON S. CHURCHILL

February 11, 1945

66. The Surrender of Japan, 1945

General Douglas MacArthur

General Douglas MacArthur (1880–1964), Supreme Commander of Allied Forces, graduated from West Point in 1903 and served with distinction in a military career that spanned the time between the use of bows and arrows in battle and atomic weapons. On September 2, 1945 he accepted the formal surrender of Japan on the battleship *Missouri* in Tokyo Bay. The ceremony lasted eighteen minutes. The ritual was filled with symbolism. The American flag which had flown over the Capitol in Washington, D.C. on December 7, 1941 now flew over the *Missouri*. MacArthur signed the capitulation document with five pens. The first he gave to General Jonathan Wainwright, who had surrendered Corregidor; the second, to General Arthur Percival, who had surrendered Singapore; the third and fourth went to West Point and Annapolis, respectively; the fifth, he saved for his son, Arthur. World War II ended as MacArthur announced that the proceedings were closed and prayed that God would preserve the peace of the world. But he intended to conquer the peace as well. In a broadcast address to the American people he began planning for a benign but revolutionary approach toward the reconstruction of Japan. The following selection includes MacArthur's remarks prior to the signing of the document and his final speech.

QUESTIONS

1. What did MacArthur mean when he said, "We have had our last chance"?
2. What is the meaning of his reference to Commodore Perry?
3. What does he envision for the future of Japan?

We are gathered here, representatives of the major warring powers, to conclude a solemn agreement whereby peace may be restored. The issues, involving divergent ideals and ideologies, have been determined on the battlefields of the world and hence are not for our discussion or debate. Nor is it for us here to meet, representing as we do a majority of the people on the earth, in a spirit of distrust, malice or hatred. But rather it is for us, both victors and vanquished, to rise to that higher dignity which alone befits the sacred purposes we are about to serve, committing all our people unreservedly to faithful compliance with the obligation they are here formally to assume.

It is my earnest hope and indeed the hope of all mankind that from this solemn occasion a better world shall emerge out of the blood and carnage of the past—a world founded upon faith and understanding—a world dedicated to the dignity of man and the fulfillment of his most cherished wish—for freedom, tolerance and justice.

The terms and conditions upon which the surrender of the Japanese Imperial Forces is here to be given and accepted are contained in the instrument of surrender now before you.

As Supreme Commander for the Allied Powers, I announce it my firm purpose, in the tradition of the countries that I represent, to proceed in the discharge of my responsibilities with justice and tolerance, while taking all necessary dispositions to ensure that the terms of surrender are fully, promptly, and faithfully complied with. . . .

Today the guns are silent. A great tragedy has ended. A great victory has been won. The skies no longer rain death—the seas bear only commerce—men everywhere walk upright in the sunlight. The entire world is quietly at peace. The deadly mission has been completed. And in reporting this to you, the people, I speak for the thousands of silent lips, forever stilled among the jungles and the beaches and in the deep waters of the Pacific which marked the way. I speak for the unmentioned brave millions homeward bound to take up the challenge of that future which they did so much to salvage from the brink of disaster.

As I look back on the long, tortuous trail from those grim days of Bataan and Corregidor, when an entire world lived in fear, when democracy was on the defensive everywhere, when modern civilization trembled in the balance, I thank a merciful God that He has given us the faith, the courage and the power from which to mould victory. We have known the bitterness of defeat and the exultation of triumph, and from both we have learned there can be no turning back. We must go forward to preserve in peace what we have won in war.

A new era is upon us. Even the lesson of victory itself brings with it profound concern, both for our future security and the survival of civilization. The destructiveness of the war potential, through progressive advances in scientific discovery, has in fact now reached a point which revises the traditional concept of war.

Men since the beginning of time have sought peace. Various methods through the ages have attempted to devise an international process to prevent or settle disputes between nations. From the very start workable methods were found insofar as individual citizens were concerned, but the mechanics of an instrumentality of larger international scope have never been successful. Military alliances, balances of power, leagues of nations, all in turn failed, leaving the only path to be by way of the crucible of war. The utter destructiveness of war now blots out this alternative. We have had our last chance. If we do not now devise some greater and more equitable system, Armageddon will be at our door. The problem basically is theological and involves a spiritual recrudescence and improvement of human character that will synchronize with our almost matchless advances in science, art, literature, and all material and cultural developments of the past two thousand years. It must be of the spirit if we are to save the flesh.

We stand in Tokyo today reminiscent of our countryman, Commodore Perry, ninety-two years ago. His purpose was to bring to Japan an era of enlightenment and progress, by lifting the veil of isolation to the friendship, trade, and commerce of the world. But alas the knowledge thereby gained of Western science was forged into an instrument of oppression and human enslavement. Freedom of expression, freedom of action, even freedom of thought were denied through appeal to superstition, and through the application of force. We are committed by the Potsdam Declaration of principles to see that the Japanese people are liberated from this condition of slavery. It is my purpose to implement this commitment just as rapidly as the armed forces are demobilized and other essential steps taken to neutralize the war potential.

The energy of the Japanese race, if properly directed, will enable expansion vertically rather than horizontally. If the talents of the race are turned into constructive channels, the country can lift itself from its present deplorable state into a position of dignity.

To the Pacific basin has come the vista of a new emancipated world. Today, freedom is on the offensive, democracy is on the march. Today, in Asia as well as in Europe, unshackled peoples are tasting the full sweetness of liberty, the relief from fear.

In the Philippines, America has evolved a model for this new free world of Asia. In the Philippines, America has demonstrated that peoples of the East and peoples of the West may walk side by side in mutual respect and with mutual benefit. The history of our sovereignty there has now the full confidence of the East.

And so, my fellow countrymen, today I report to you that your sons and daughters have served you well and faithfully with the calm, deliberate, determined fighting spirit of the American soldier and sailor, based upon a tradition of historical truth as against the fanaticism of an enemy supported only by mythological fiction. Their spiritual strength and power has brought us through to victory. They are homeward bound—take care of them.

67. Election Speech, 1946

Joseph Stalin

The wartime alliance of Great Britain, the United States, and the Soviet Union deteriorated as their policies clashed over numerous postwar problems. Their ideological differences had a profound impact on East-West relations. Stalin's election speech, delivered in a radio address on February 9, 1946, illustrated the ideological temper of the times. On one hand he asserted that the capitalist system exhibited chronic crisis and conflict, and that Western powers were responsible for the two world wars. On the other hand, he extolled the Soviet system and attributed the victory over the Axis powers to the superiority of communism. Soon after he gave this speech Stalin launched a full-scale campaign which stressed Russian nationalism and ideological purity and which condemned Western ideas. The hardening of his policy toward the West marked a new stage in the escalating tensions between the Soviet Union and the capitalist nations. The Cold War had begun.

QUESTIONS

1. According to Stalin, what causes brought on the Second World War?
2. What are Stalin's views on the capitalist countries? Cold War phobias?

3. How seriously can we take Stalin's accusations against the fascist states in the light of domestic policies in the Soviet Union?
4. According to Stalin, how did World War II differ from World War I?
5. How does Stalin evaluate the results of World War II for the Western nations? for the Soviet Union?
6. What is Stalin *not* telling about collectivization of agriculture in the Soviet Union?
7. What evidence does this speech afford of the Stalinist "cult of personality"?

COMRADES!

Eight years have lapsed since the last election to the Supreme Soviet. This was a period abounding in events of decisive moment. The first four years passed in intensive effort on the part of Soviet people to fulfill the Third Five-Year Plan. The second four years embrace the events of the war against the German and Japanese aggressors, the events of the Second World War. There is no doubt that the war was the principal event in the past period.

It would be wrong to think that the Second World War was a casual occurrence or the result of mistakes of any particular statesmen, though mistakes undoubtedly were made. Actually, the war was the inevitable result of the development of world economic and political forces on the basis of modern monopoly capitalism. Marxists have declared more than once that the capitalist system of world economy harbours elements of general crises and armed conflicts and that, hence, the development of world capitalism in our time proceeds not in the form of smooth and balanced progress but through crises and military catastrophes.

The fact is, that the unevenness of development of the capitalist countries usually leads in time to violent disturbance of equilibrium in the world system of capitalism. Moreover that group of capitalist countries which considers itself less adequately provided than others with raw materials and markets usually makes attempts to alter the situation and repartition the "spheres of influence" in its favor by armed force. The result is a splitting of the capitalist world into two hostile camps and war between them. . . .

Thus the First World War was the result of the first crises of the capitalist system of world economy, and the Second World War was the result of the second crises. . . . The Second World War differs essentially from the First in its nature. It must be borne in mind that before attacking the Allied countries the principal fascist states—Germany, Japan, and Italy—destroyed the last vestiges of bourgeois democratic liberties at home, established a brutal terrorist regime in their own countries, rode roughshod over the principles of sovereignty and free development of small countries, proclaimed a policy of seizure of foreign territories as their own policy and declared for all to hear that they were striving for world domination and the establishment of a fascist regime throughout the world.

Moreover, by the seizure of Czechoslovakia and of the central regions of China, the Axis states showed that they were prepared to carry out their threat of enslaving all freedom-loving nations. In view of this, unlike the First World War, the Second World War against the Axis states from the very outset assumed the character of an anti-fascist war, a war of liberation, one aim of which was also the restoration of democratic liberties. The entry of the Soviet Union into the war against the Axis states could only enhance, and indeed did enhance, the anti-fascist and liberation character of the Second World War.

Thus was organized the anti-fascist coalition consisting of the Soviet Union, the United States of America, Great Britain, and other freedom-loving states which played the decisive role in destroying the armed forces of the Axis powers.

That is how matters stand as regards the origin and character of the Second World War.

By now I should think that everyone admits that the war really was not and could not have been an accident in the life of nations, that actually this war became the war of nations for their very existence, and that for this reason it could not be a quick lightning affair.

As regards our country, for it this war was the most bitter and arduous of all wars in the history of our Motherland.

But the war was not only a curse. It was at the same time a great school that tried and tested all the forces of the people. The war laid bare all facts and events in the rear and at the front; it pitilessly tore off all veils and coverings which had concealed the true faces of the states, governments, and parties and exposed them to view without a mask or embellishment, with all their shortcomings and merits.

The war was something like an examination of our Soviet system, for our state, for our government, for our Communist Party. . . .

There is one basic result in which all other results have their source. The result is that in the upshot of the war our enemies were defeated and we, together with our Allies, emerged as victors. We concluded the war with complete victory over the enemies.

That is the basic result of war. But that result is too general and we cannot stop at that. Of course, to crush an enemy in a war like the Second World War, for which the history of mankind knew no parallel, meant to achieve a world historic victory. All that is true. But still, it is only a general result and we cannot rest content with that. In order to grasp the great historic importance of our victory we must examine the thing more concretely.

And so, how is our victory over our enemies to be understood? What is the significance of this victory as regards the development of the internal forces of our country?

Our victory means, first of all, that our Soviet *social* system has triumphed, that the Soviet social system has successfully passed the ordeal in the fire of war and has proved its unquestionable vitality.

As you know, it was claimed more than once in the foreign press that the Soviet social system was a "risky experiment" doomed to failure, that the Soviet system was a "house of cards" which has no roots in real life and had been imposed upon the people by the Cheka [secret police], and that a slight push from without was enough for the "house of cards" to collapse.

Now we can say that the war refuted all these assertions of the foreign press as groundless. The war showed that the Soviet social system is a truly popular system springing from the depths of the people and enjoying their mighty support, that the Soviet social system is a form of organization of society which is perfectly stable and capable of enduring.

More than that. There is no longer any question today whether the Soviet social system is or is not capable of enduring, for after the object lessons of war none of the skeptics ventures any longer to voice doubts as to the vitality of the Soviet social system. The point now is that the Soviet social system has shown itself more stable and capable of enduring than a non-Soviet social system, that the Soviet social system is a form of organization, a society superior to any non- Soviet social system.

Second, our victory means that our Soviet *state* system has triumphed, that our multinational Soviet state has stood all the trials of war and has proved its vitality.

As you know, prominent foreign press men have more than once gone on the record to the effect that the Soviet multinational state was an "artificial, non-viable structure," that in the event of any complications, the disintegration of the Soviet Union would be inevitable, and that the fate of Austria-Hungary awaited the Soviet Union.

Today we can say that the war refuted these assertions of the foreign press as totally unfounded. The war showed that the Soviet multinational state system passed the test successfully, that it grew even stronger during the war and proved itself as the state system perfectly capable of enduring. These gentlemen did not understand that the parallel with Austria-Hungary did not apply, for our multinational state has not grown up on a bourgeois foundation which stimulates sentiments of national distrust and national animosity, but on the Soviet foundation which on the contrary cultivates the sentiments of friendship and fraternal collaboration among the peoples of our state.

As a matter of fact, after the lessons of the war, these gentlemen no longer venture to deny that the Soviet state system is capable of enduring. Today it is no longer a question of the vitality of the Soviet state system, for the vitality can no longer be doubted. The point now is that the Soviet state system has proved itself a model for a multinational state, has proved that the Soviet state system is a system of state organization in which the national question and the problem of collaboration among nations has been settled better than in any other multinational state. . . .

Third, our victory means that the Soviet armed forces have triumphed, that our Red Army has triumphed, that the Red Army bore up heroically under all the trials of war, utterly routed the armies of our enemies and came out of the war as a victor. [Voice from floor: "Under the leadership of Comrade Stalin!" All rise—stormy, prolonged applause, rising to an ovation.]

Now everyone, friend as well as foe, admits that the Red Army proved equal to its great tasks. But this was not the case some six years ago during the prewar period. As you know, prominent men from the foreign press and many recognized military authorities abroad declared more than once that the condition of the Red Army gave rise to grave doubts, that the Red Army was poorly armed and had no proper commanding personnel, that its morale was beneath all criticism, that while it might be of some use in defense, it was useless for an offensive, and that if the German forces should strike the Red Army was bound to crumble like a "colossus with feet of clay." Statements like these were made not only in Germany, but in France, Great Britain and in America as well. . . .

It would be a mistake to think that such a historic victory could have been won if the whole country had not prepared beforehand for active defense. . . . To meet the blow of such an enemy, to repulse him and then to inflict utter defeat upon him required, in addition to the matchless gallantry of our troops, fully up-to-date armaments and adequate quantities of them as well as well-organized supplies in sufficient amounts— such elementary things as *metal* for the manufacture of armaments, equipment and machinery for factories, *fuel* to keep the factories and transport going, *cotton* for the manufacture of uniforms and grain for supplying the Army.

Can it be claimed that before entering the Second World War our country already commanded the necessary minimum material potentialities for satisfying all these requirements in the main? I think it can. In order to prepare for this tremendous job we had to carry out three Five-Year Plans that helped us to create these material potentialities. At any rate, our country's position in this respect before the Second World War, in 1940, was several times better than it was before the First World War, in 1913. . . .

This historic transformation was accomplished in the course of three Five-Year Plan periods, beginning with 1928, the first year of the First Five-Year Plan. . . . we find that it took only about 13 years to transform our country from an agrarian into an industrial one. It cannot but be admitted that 13 years is an incredibly short period for the accomplishment of such an immense task. . . .

By what policy did the Communist Party succeed in providing material potentialities in the country in such a short time?

First of all, by the Soviet policy of industrializing the country.

The Soviet method of industrializing the country differs radically from the capitalist method of industrialization. . . . that is a lengthy process requiring an extensive period of several decades, in the course of which these countries have to wait until light industry has developed and must make shift without heavy industry. Naturally, the Communist Party could not take this course. The Party knew that war was looming, that the country could not be defended without heavy industry, that the development of heavy industry must be undertaken as soon as possible, that to be behind with this would mean to lose out. The Party remembered Lenin's words to the effect that without heavy industry it would be impossible to uphold the country's independence, that without it the Soviet system might perish. Accordingly, the Communist Party of our country rejected the "usual"

course of industrialization and began the work of industrializing the country by developing heavy industry. It was very difficult, but not impossible. A valuable aid in this work was the nationalization of industry, and banking, which made possible the rapid accumulation and transfer of funds to heavy industry. There can be no doubt that without this it would have been impossible to secure our country's transformation into an industrial country in such a short time.

Second, by a policy of collectivization of agriculture.

In order to do away with our backwardness in agriculture and to provide the country with greater quantities of marketable grain, cotton, and so forth, it was essential to pass from small-scale peasant farming to large-scale farming, for only large-scale farming can make use of new technology, apply all the achievements of agronomical science and yield greater quantities of marketable produce. There are, however, two kinds of large farms—capitalist and collective. The Communist Party could not adopt the capitalist path of development of agriculture. . . . Therefore, the Communist Party took the path of collectivization of agriculture, the path of creating large-scale farming by uniting peasant farms into collective farms. The method of collectivization proved a highly progressive method not only because it did not cause the ruin of the peasants but especially because it permitted them, within a few years, to cover the entire country with large collective farms which are able to use new technology, take advantage of all the achievements of agronomic science and give the country greater quantities of marketable produce. There is no doubt that without a collectivization policy we could not in such a short time have done away with the age-old backwardness of our agriculture.

It cannot be said that the Party's policy encountered no resistance. Not only backward people, who always decry anything new, but many prominent members of the Party as well, systematically dragged the Party backward and tried by every possible means to divert it on the "usual" capitalist path of development. All the anti-Party machinations of the Trotskyites and the Rightists, all their "activities" in sabotaging the measures of our government, had one single aim: to frustrate the Party's policy and to obstruct the work of industrialization and collectivization. But the Party did not yield. . . . There can be no doubt that without such firmness and tenacity the Communist Party could not have upheld the policy of industrializing the country and collectivizing agriculture.

Was the Communist Party able to make proper use of the material potentialities thus created in order to develop war production and provide the Red Army with the weapons it needed? I think that it was able to do so and with maximum success. . . .

There is a saying that victors are not judged [laughter, applause], that they should not be criticized and checked upon. That is incorrect. Victors should and must be judged [laughter, applause]; they should and must be criticized and checked upon.

This is essential not only for the process but for the victors themselves [laughter, applause]. There will be less conceitedness and more modesty [laughter, applause]. I consider that in the election campaign the electors are sitting in judgment on the Communist Party as the ruling party. And the election returns will constitute the electors' verdict [laughter, applause]. The Communist Party of our country would not be worth much if it feared to be criticized and checked upon. The Communist Party is prepared to accept the electors' verdict. [Stormy applause.]

In conclusion, allow me to thank you for the confidence you have shown me [prolonged, unabating applause. Shout from the audience: "Hurrah for the great leader of all victories, Comrade Stalin!"] in nominating me to the Supreme Soviet. You need not doubt that I shall do my best to justify your trust. [All rise. Prolonged, unabating applause turning into an ovation. From all parts of the hall come cheers: "Long live our great Stalin!" "Hurrah!" "Hurrah for the great leader of the peoples!" "Glory to the great Stalin!" "Long live comrade Stalin, the candidate of the entire nation! Glory to Comrade Stalin, the Creator of all victories!"]

---

68. The Iron Curtain, 1946

Winston Churchill

Winston Churchill was a keen student of military history and strategy, and he was profoundly steeped in the history of Europe. Those attributes greatly affected his leadership and shaped his policies and diplomacy. He was among the first to perceive the danger of an expansionist Soviet Russia. Surprisingly, he and his party were overwhelmingly defeated by Labour in the July 1945 election. Forgotten were his pre-1914 social reforms; remembered were several episodes earlier in his political career when he opposed the demands of laboring men. He was thus seen as the enemy of the workers, but even his fellow Tories distrusted the impatient, flamboyant, pugnacious Churchill as a renegade. He was out of touch with the nation on domestic affairs and was not very effective as Leader of the Opposition. During the immediate postwar era he devoted himself to public speeches. Below is an excerpt from an address he delivered in 1946 at Fulton, Missouri, in which he championed Western unity, European unification, the "special relationship" with the U.S., and the holding of summit conferences to check Cold War phobias. Again prime minister, 1951–1955, he suffered a stroke, but compelled himself to go on and to complete the multi-volumed work he had begun before the war, *A History of the English-Speaking Peoples.* A monument using pieces from the Berlin Wall has been erected at Fulton, designed by Churchill's granddaughter, a sculptress. In May 1992 Mikhail Gorbachev, also out of power and office, came to Fulton to acknowledge the pivotal importance of Churchill's speech, and to declare that the Iron Curtain had rusted away and the Cold War was a matter of history.

QUESTIONS

1. According to Churchill, what common political values and traditions are shared by the peoples of Great Britain and the United States?
2. What countries did Churchill believe were most threatened by totalitarian governments? What tactics did he believe the Russians were using to expand their influence in those nations?
3. What is Churchill's view of the current situation in Germany?
4. What policies did Churchill suggest to stop Soviet expansionism?

The United States stands at this time at the pinnacle of world power. It is a solemn moment for the American democracy. With primacy in power is also joined an awe-inspiring accountability to the future. As you look around you, you must feel not only the sense of duty done but also feel anxiety lest you fall below the level of achievement. Opportunity is here now, clear and shining, for both our countries. To reject it or ignore it or fritter it away will bring upon us all the long reproaches of the after-time.

It is necessary that constancy of mind, persistency of purpose and the grand simplicity of decision shall rule and guide the conduct of the English-speaking peoples in peace as they did in war. We must and I believe we shall prove ourselves equal to this severe requirement. . . .

We cannot be blind to the fact that the liberties enjoyed by individual citizens throughout the British Empire are not valid in a considerable number of countries, some of which are very powerful. In these states, control is enforced upon the common people by various kinds of all-embracing police governments, to a degree which is overwhelming and contrary to every principle of democracy. The power of the state is exercised without restraint, either by dictators or by compact oligarchies operating through a privileged party and a political police.

It is not our duty at this time, when difficulties are so numerous, to interfere forcibly in the internal affairs of countries which we have not conquered in war, but we must never cease to proclaim in fearless tones the great principles of freedom and the rights of man, which are the joint inheritance of the English-speaking world and which, through Magna Carta, the Bill of Rights, the habeas corpus, trial by jury and the English common law find their most famous expression in the American Declaration of Independence.

All this means that the people of any country have the right and should have the power by constitutional action, by free, unfettered elections, with secret ballot, to choose or change the character or form of government under which they dwell, that freedom of speech and thought should reign, that courts of justice independent of the executive, unbiased by any party, should administer laws which have received the broad assent of large majorities or are consecrated by time and custom. Here are the title deeds of freedom, which should lie in every cottage home. Here is the message of the British and American peoples to mankind. Let me preach what we practice, let us practice what we preach. . . .

A shadow has fallen upon the scenes so lately lighted by the Allied victory. Nobody knows what Soviet Russia and its Communist international organization intends to do in the immediate future, or what are the limits, if any, to their expansive and proselytizing tendencies.

I have a strong admiration and regard for the valiant Russian people and for my wartime comrade, Marshal Stalin. There is sympathy and good will in Britain—and I doubt not here also—toward the people of all the Russias and a resolve to persevere through many differences and rebuffs in establishing lasting friendships.

We understand the Russians need to be secure on her western frontiers from all renewal of German aggression. We welcome her to her rightful place among the leading nations of the world. Above all we welcome constant, frequent and growing contacts between the Russian people and our own people on both sides of the Atlantic.

It is my duty, however, and I am sure you would not wish me not to state the facts as I see them to you, it is my duty to place before you certain facts about the present position in Europe.

From Stettin in the Baltic to Triest in the Adriatic, an iron curtain has descended across the Continent. Behind that line lie all the capitals of ancient states of central and eastern Europe. Warsaw, Berlin, Prague, Vienna, Budapest, Belgrade, Bucharest and Sofia, all these famous cities and the populations around them lie in the Soviet sphere and all are subject in one form or another, not only to Soviet influence but to a very high and increasing measure of control from Moscow.

Police governments are pervading from Moscow. But Athens alone, with its immortal glories, is free to decide its future at an election under British, American and French observation.

The Russian-dominated Polish government has been encouraged to make enormous and wrongful inroads upon Germany, and mass expulsions of millions of Germans on a scale grievous and undreamed of are now taking place.

The Communist parties, which were very small in all these eastern states of Europe, have been raised to pre-eminence and power far beyond their numbers and are seeking everywhere to obtain totalitarian control.

Police governments are prevailing in nearly every case, and so far, except in Czechoslovakia, there is no true democracy.

Turkey and Persia are both profoundly alarmed and disturbed at the claims which are made upon them and at the pressure being exerted by the Moscow government.

An attempt is being made by the Russians in Berlin to build up a quasi-Communist party in their zone of occupied Germany by showing special favors to groups of Left-Wing German leaders. At the end of the fighting last June the American and British armies withdrew westward, in accordance with an earlier agreement, to a depth at some points of 150 miles upon a front of nearly 400 miles, in order to allow our Russian allies to occupy this vast expanse of territory which the western democracies had conquered.

If now the Soviet Government tries, by separate action, to build up a pro-Communist Germany in their areas this will cause new serious difficulties in the American and British zones, and will give the defeated Germans the power of putting themselves up to auction between the Soviets and the Western democracies. Whatever conclusions may be drawn from these facts—and facts they are—this is certainly not the liberated Europe we fought to build up. Nor is it one

which contains the essentials of permanent peace. . . .

What we have to consider here today while time remains, is the permanent prevention of war and the establishment of conditions of freedom and democracy as rapidly as possible in all countries. Our difficulties and dangers will not be removed by mere waiting to see what happens; nor will they be relieved by a policy of appeasement.

What is needed is a settlement and the longer this is delayed the more difficult it will be and the greater our dangers will become.

From what I have seen of our Russian friends and allies during the war, I am convinced that there is nothing they admire so much as strength, and there is nothing for which they have less respect than for military weakness. . . .

If the western democracies stand together in strict adherence to the principles of the United Nations Charter, their influence for furthering these principles will be immense and no one is likely to molest them. If, however, they become divided or falter in their duty, and if these all-important years are allowed to slip away, then indeed catastrophe may overwhelm us all.

---

69. The Truman Doctrine, 1947

Harry S Truman (1884–1972) became President of the United States when Franklin D. Roosevelt died on April 12, 1945. He took the oath of office at a critical moment in world history. The "hot war" against the Axis powers was concluding, but the "cold war" against the Soviet Union and communism was already underway. Truman was a strong-willed Missouri Democrat who was much less inclined than his predecessor to engage in diplomatic shadow-boxing with "Uncle Joe" Stalin. Early in 1947 Truman feared that insurgent movements against the governments of Greece and Turkey would result in communist regimes for those two strategically important nations. Great Britain was weakened by years of war and her leaders informed Truman that it could no longer provide economic assistance to those countries. The President then delivered the following address to Congress on March 12, 1947. Congress approved Truman's historic call for economic and military assistance to Greece and Turkey by votes of 67 to 23 in the Senate and 287 to 107 in the House. Although the Truman Doctrine was originally limited to Greece and Turkey, its principles were soon extended to many other countries which were threatened by communist movements around the globe.

QUESTIONS

1. If this is the American declaration of Cold War, what were the causes of that war? What were the means to be used in pursuing it? What were its goals?
2. In what way can Truman be said to apply the lessons of appeasement from the 1930s?
3. What vision does Truman have of the world at large? What sense of the American mission does he exemplify?
4. On the basis of his assessment of the situation and of his proposals for resolving it, comment on Truman's policy with regard to Korea in the 1950s; speculate what his policy toward Vietnam would have been in the 1960s.

The gravity of the situation which confronts the world today necessitates my appearance before a joint session of the Congress. The foreign policy and the national security of this country are involved. . . .

The United States has received from the Greek government an urgent appeal for financial and economic assistance. Preliminary reports from the American Economic Mission now in Greece and reports from the American Ambassador in Greece corroborate the statement of the Greek government that assistance is imperative if Greece is to survive as a free nation. . . .

Since 1940, this industrious, peace-loving country has suffered invasion, four years of cruel enemy occupation, and bitter internal strife.

When forces of liberation entered Greece they found that the retreating Germans had destroyed virtually all the railroads, ports, port facilities, communications, and merchant marine. More than a thousand villages were burned. Eighty-five percent of the children were tubercular. Livestock, poultry and draft animals had almost disappeared. Inflation had wiped out practically all savings.

As a result of these tragic conditions, a militant minority, exploiting human want and misery, was able to create political chaos which, until now, has made economic recovery impossible. . . .

The very existence of the Greek state is today threatened by the terrorist activities of several thousand men, led by Communists, who defy the government's authority at a number of points, particularly along the northern boundaries. A commission appointed by the United Nations Security Council is at present investigating disturbed conditions in Northern Greece and alleged border violations along the frontiers between Greece on the one hand and Albania, Bulgaria, and Yugoslavia on the other.

Meanwhile, the Greek government is unable to cope with the situation. The Greek army is small and poorly equipped. . . .

Greece must have assistance if it is to become a self-supporting and self-respecting democracy. The United States must supply that assistance. . . . There is no other country to which democratic Greece can turn. . . .

We have considered how the United Nations might assist in this crisis. But the situation is an urgent one requiring immediate action, and the United Nations and its related organizations are not in a position to extend help of the kind that is required. . . .

No government is perfect. One of the chief virtues of a democracy, however, is that its defects are always visible and under democratic processes can be pointed out and corrected. The government of Greece is not perfect. Nevertheless, it represents 85 percent of the members of the Greek Parliament who were chosen in an election last year. Foreign observers, including 692 Americans, considered this election to be a fair expression of the views of the Greek people.

The Greek government has been operating in an atmosphere of chaos and extremism. It has made mistakes. The extension of aid by this country does not mean that the United States condones everything the Greek government has done or will do. We have condemned in the past, and we condemn now, extremist measures of the right or left. We have in the past advised tolerance, and we advise tolerance now.

Greece's neighbor, Turkey, also deserves our attention. The future of Turkey as an independent and economically sound state is clearly no less important to the free-dom-loving peoples of the world than the future of Greece. . . .

Since the war Turkey has sought financial assistance from Great Britain and the United States for the purpose of effecting that modernization necessary for the maintenance of its national integrity. That integrity is essential to the preservation of order in the Middle East.

The British Government has informed us that, owing to its own difficulties, it can no longer extend financial or economic aid to Turkey. As in the case of Greece, if Turkey is to have the assistance it needs, the United States must supply it. We are the only country able to provide that help.

I am fully aware of the broad implications involved if the United States extends assistance to Greece and Turkey, and I shall discuss these implications with you at this time.

One of the primary objects of the foreign policy of the United States is the creation of conditions in which we and other nations will be able to work out a way of life free from coercion. This was a fundamental issue in the war with Germany and Japan. Our victory was won over countries which sought to impose their will, and their way of life, upon other nations.

To ensure the peaceful development of nations, free from coercion, the United States has taken a leading part in establishing the United Nations. The United Nations is designed to make possible lasting freedom and independence for all its members. We shall not realize our objectives, however, unless we are willing to help free peoples to maintain their free institutions and their national integrity against aggressive movements that seek to impose upon them totalitarian regimes. This is no more than a frank recognition that totalitarian regimes imposed on free peoples, by direct or indirect aggression, undermine the foundations of international peace and hence the security of the United States.

The people of a number of countries of the world have recently had totalitarian regimes forced upon them against their will. The government of the United States has made frequent protests against coercion and intimidation, in violation of the Yalta Agreement, in Poland, Rumania, and Bulgaria. I must also state that in a number of other countries there have been similar developments.

At the present moment in world history nearly every nation must choose between alternative ways of life. The choice is too often not a free one.

One way of life is based upon the will of the majority, and is distinguished by free institutions, representative government, free elections, guarantees of individual liberty, freedom of speech and religion, and freedom from political oppression.

The second way of life is based upon the will of a minority forcibly imposed upon the majority. It relies upon terror and oppression, a controlled press and radio, fixed elections, and the suppression of personal freedoms.

I believe it must be the policy of the United States to support free peoples who are resisting attempted subjugation by armed minorities or by outside pressures.

I believe that we must assist free peoples to work out their own destinies in their own way.

I believe that our help should be primarily through economic and financial aid which is essential to economic stability and orderly political processes.

The world is not static, and the status quo is not sacred. But we cannot allow changes in the status quo in violation of the charter of the United Nations by such methods as coercion, or by such subterfuges as political infiltration. . . .

It is necessary only to glance at a map to realize that the survival and integrity of the Greek nation are of grave importance in a much wider situation. If Greece should fall under the control of an armed minority, the effect upon its neighbor, Turkey, would be immediate and serious. Confusion and disorder might well spread throughout the entire Middle East.

Moreover, the disappearance of Greece as an independent state would have a profound effect upon those countries of Europe whose peoples are struggling against great difficulties to maintain their freedoms and their independence while they repair the damages of war. . . .

Should we fail to aid Greece and Turkey in this fateful hour, the effect will be far reaching to the west as well as to the east. We must take immediate and resolute action.

I therefore ask the Congress to provide authority for assistance to Greece and Turkey in the amount of $400,000,000 for the period ending June 30, 1948. . . .

In addition to funds, I ask the Congress to authorize the detail of American civilian and military personnel to Greece and Turkey, at the request of those countries, to assist in the tasks of reconstruction, and for the purpose of supervising the use of such financial and material assistance as may be furnished. I recommend that authority also be provided for the instruction and training of selected Greek and Turkish personnel. . . .

The seeds of totalitarian regimes are nurtured by misery and want. They spread and grow in the evil soil of poverty and strife. They reach their full growth when the hope of a people for a better life has died. We must keep that hope alive. The free peoples of the world look to us for support in maintaining their freedoms.

If we falter in our leadership, we may endanger the peace of the world—and we shall surely endanger the welfare of our own nation.

Great responsibilities have been placed upon us by the swift movement of events. I am confident that the Congress will face these responsibilities squarely.

70. Founding of the Cominform, 1947

Andrei Zhdanov

Andrei A. Zhdanov (1896–1948) was a Russian communist leader and a loyal supporter and chief aide of Stalin. During the early postwar period he played a prominent role in Soviet ideological reindoctrination programs. He was also instrumental in imposing intellectual and ideological conformity and the years of his domination became known as "Zhdanovshchina." He headed the Soviet delegation to the meeting of the six satellite parties in addition to those of France and Italy that was held in Poland on September 22–23, 1947. The document below is an excerpt from his opening address in which he presented Moscow's analysis of the current world situation. The participants at this conference (from the Soviet Union, Poland, Yugoslavia, Hungary, Romania, Bulgaria, Czechoslovakia, Italy and France) formed a Communist Information Bureau, or Cominform, which established its headquarters in Belgrade. That organization was created to facilitate the cooperation of the communist parties of the member nations.

QUESTIONS

1. According to Zhdanov, what impact did the Second World War have on the great Western powers? On the Soviet Union?
2. How did the war affect Great Britain? The U.S.A.?
3. What goals was the U.S.A. pursuing in the post-World War II years? What kind of arguments does Zhdanov make against the U.S.A.?
4. How convincing is Zhdanov's description of the two post-World War II opposing camps?

I. The Post-War Situation

The war immensely enhanced the international significance and prestige of the USSR. The USSR was the leading force and the guiding spirit in the military defeat of Germany and Japan. The progressive democratic forces of the whole world rallied around the Soviet Union. The socialist state successfully stood the strenuous test of the war and emerged victorious from the mortal struggle with a most powerful enemy. Instead of being enfeebled, the USSR became stronger.

The capitalist world has also undergone a substantial change. Of the six so-called great imperialist powers (Germany, Japan, Great Britain, the U.S.A., France and Italy), three have been eliminated by military defeat (Germany, Italy and Japan). France has also been weakened and has lost its significance as a great power. As a result, only two great imperialist world powers remain—the United States and Great Britain. But the position of one of them, Great Britain, has been undermined. The war revealed that militarily and politically British imperialism was not so strong as it had been. In Europe, Britain was helpless against Germany's aggression. In Asia, Britain, one of the biggest of imperialist powers, was unable to retain hold of her colonial possessions without outside aid. Temporarily cut off from the colonies that supplied her with food and raw materials and absorbed a large part of her industrial products, Britain found herself dependent militarily and economically upon American supplies of food and manufactured goods. After the war, Britain became increasingly dependent, financially and economically, on the United States. Although she succeeded in recovering her colonies after the war, Britain found herself faced there with the enhanced influence of American imperialism, which during the war had invaded all the regions that before the war had been regarded as exclusive spheres of influence of British capital (the Arab East, Southeast Asia). America has also increased her influence in the British dominions and in South America, where the former role of Britain is very largely and to an ever increasing extent passing to the United States.

World War II aggravated the crises of the colonial system, as expressed in the rise of a powerful movement for national liberation of the colonies and dependencies. This has placed the rear of the capitalist system in jeopardy. The peoples of the colonies no longer wish to live in the old way. The ruling classes of the metropolitan countries can no longer govern the colonies on the old lines. Attempts to crush the national liberation movement by military force now increasingly encounter armed resistance on the part of the colonial peoples and lead to protracted colonial war (Holland-Indonesia, France-Viet Nam).

The war—itself a product of the unevenness of capitalist development in the different countries—still further intensified this unevenness. Of all the capitalist powers, only one—the United States—emerged from the war not only unweakened, but even considerably stronger economically and militarily. The war greatly enriched the American capitalists. The American people, on the other hand, did not experience the privations that accompany war, the hardship of occupation, or aerial bombardment; and since America entered the war practically in its concluding stage, when the issue was already decided, her human casualties were relatively small. For the U.S.A., the war was primarily and chiefly a spur to extensive industrial development and to a substantial increase of her exports (principally to Europe).

But the end of the war confronted the United States with a number of new problems. The capitalist monopolies were anxious to maintain their profits at the former high level, and accordingly pressed hard to prevent a reduction of the wartime volume of deliveries. But this meant that the United States must retain the foreign markets which had absorbed American products during the war, and moreover, acquire new markets inasmuch as the war had substantially lowered the purchasing power of most of the countries. The financial and economic dependence of these countries on the U.S.A. had likewise increased. The United States extended credits abroad to a sum of 19,000 million dollars, not counting investments on the International Bank and the International Currency Fund. America's principal competitors, Germany and Japan, have disappeared from the world market, and this has opened up new and considerable opportunities for the United States. Whereas before World War II the more influential reactionary circles of American imperialism had adhered to an isolationist policy and had refrained from active interference in the affairs of Europe and Asia, in the new, postwar conditions the Wall Street bosses adopted a new policy. They advanced a program of utilizing America's military and economic might, not only to retain and consolidate the positions won abroad during the war, but to expand them to the maximum and to replace Germany, Japan and Italy in the world market. The sharp decline of the economic power of the other capitalist states makes it possible to speculate on the postwar economic difficulties of Great Britain, which makes it easier to bring these countries under American control. The United States proclaimed a new frankly predatory and expansionist course.

The purpose of this new, frankly expansionist course is to establish the world supremacy of American imperialism. With a view to consolidating America's monopoly position in the markets gained as a result of the disappearance of her two biggest competitors, Germany and Japan, and the weakening of her capitalist partners, Great Britain and France, the new course of the United States policy envisages a broad program of military, economic and political measures, designed to establish United States political and economic domination in all countries marked out for American expansion, to reduce these countries to the status of satellites of the United States and to set up regimes within them which would eliminate all obstacles on the part of labor and democratic movement to the exploitation of these countries by American capital. The United States is now endeavoring to extend this new line of policy not only to its enemies in the war and to neutral countries, but in an increasing degree to its wartime allies.

Special attention is being paid to the exploitation of the economic difficulties of Great Britain, which is not only America's ally but also a long-standing capitalist rival and competitor. It is the design of America's expansionist policy not only to prevent Britain from escaping from the vise of economic dependence on the United States in which she was gripped during the war, but, on the contrary, to increase the pressure, with a view of gradually depriving her of control over her colonies, ousting her from her spheres of influence, and reducing her to the status of a vassal state.

Thus the new policy of the United States is designed to consolidate its monopoly position and to reduce its capitalist partners to the state of subordination and dependence on America.

But America's aspiration to world supremacy encounters an obstacle in the USSR, the stronghold of anti-imperialist and anti-fascist policy, and its growing international influence, in the new democracies which have escaped the control of Britain and American imperialism, and in the workers of all countries, including America itself, who do not want a new war for the supremacy of their oppressors. Accordingly, the new expansionist and reactionary policy of the United States envisages a struggle against the USSR, against the labor movement in all countries, including the United States, and against the emancipationist, anti-imperialist forces in all countries.

Alarmed by the achievements of Socialism in the USSR, by the achievements of the new democracies, and by the post-war growth of the labor and democratic movement in all countries, the American reactionaries are disposed to take upon themselves the mission of "saviors" of the capital system from Communism.

The frank expansionist program of the United States is therefore highly reminiscent of the reckless program, which failed so ignominiously, of the fascist aggressors, who, as we know, also made a bid for world supremacy.

Just as the Hitlerites, when they were making their preparations for piratical aggression, adopted the camouflage of anti-Communism in order to make it possible to oppress and enslave all peoples and primarily and chiefly their own people, America's present day ruling circles mask their expansionist policy, and even their offensive against the vital interests of the weaker imperialist rival, Great Britain, by fictitious considerations of the defense against Communism. The feverish piling up of armaments, the construction of new military bases and the creation of bridgeheads for the American armed forces in all parts of the world is justified on the false and pharisaical grounds of "defense" against an imaginary threat of war on the part of the USSR. With the help of intimidation, bribery and chicanery, American diplomacy finds it easy to extort from other capitalist countries, and primarily from Great Britain, consent to the legitimization of America's superior position in Europe and Asia—in the Western Zones of Germany, in Austria, Italy, Greece, Turkey, Egypt, Iran, Afghanistan, China, Japan, and so forth.

The American imperialists regard themselves as the principal force opposed to the USSR, the new democracies of labor and democratic movement in all countries of the world, as the bulwark of the reactionary, anti-democratic forces in all parts of the globe. Accordingly, literally on the day following the conclusion of World War II, they set to work to build up a front hostile to the USSR, and world democracy, and to encourage the anti-popular reactionary forces—collaborationists and former capitalist stooges—in the European countries which had been liberated from the Nazi yoke and which were beginning to arrange their affairs according to their own choice.

The more malignant and unbalanced imperialist politicians followed the lead of Churchill in hatching plans for the speedy launching of a preventive war against the USSR and openly called for the employment of America's temporary monopoly of the atomic weapon against the Soviet people. The new warmongers are trying to intimidate and browbeat not only the USSR, but other countries as well, notably China and India, by libelously depicting the USSR as a potential aggressor, while they themselves pose as "friends" of China and India, as "saviors" from the Communist peril, their mission being to "help" the weak. By these means they are seeking to keep India and China under the sway of imperialism and in continued political and economic bondage.

II. The New Post-War Alignment of Political Forces and the Formation of Two Camps: The Imperialist and Anti-Democratic Camp, and the Anti-Imperialist and Democratic One

The fundamental changes caused by the war on the international scene and in the position of individual countries has entirely changed the political landscape of the world. A new alignment of political forces has arisen. The more the war recedes into the past, the more distinct become two major trends of postwar international policy, corresponding to the division of the political forces operating on the international arena into two major camps: the imperialist and anti-democratic camp, on the one hand, and the anti-imperialist and democratic camp, on the other. The principal driving force of the imperialist camp is the U.S.A. Allied with it are Great Britain and France. The existence of the Atlee-Bevin Labor Government in Britain and the Ramadier Socialist Government in France does not hinder these countries from playing the part of satellites of the United States and following the lead of its imperialist policy on all major questions. The imperialist camp is also supported by colony-owning countries, such as Belgium and Holland, by countries with reactionary anti-democratic regimes, such as Turkey and Greece, and by countries politically and economically dependent on the United States, such as Near-Eastern and South American countries and China.

The cardinal purpose of the imperialist camp is to strengthen imperialism, to hatch a new imperialist war, to combat Socialism and democracy, and to support reactionary and anti-democratic pro-fascist regimes and movements everywhere.

In the pursuit of these ends the imperialist camp is prepared to rely on reactionary and anti-democratic forces in all countries, and to support its former adversaries in the war against its wartime allies.

The anti-fascist forces comprise the second camp. This camp is based on the U.S.S.R. and the new democracies. It also includes countries that have broken with imperialism and have firmly set foot on the path of democratic development, such as Romania, Hungary and Finland. Indonesia and Viet Nam are associated with it; it has the sympathy of India, Egypt and Syria. The anti-imperialist camp is backed by the labour and democratic movement and by the fraternal Communist parties in all countries, by the fighters for national liberation in the colonies and dependencies, by all progressive and democratic forces in every country. The purpose of this camp is to resist the threat of new wars and imperialist expansion, to strengthen democracy and to extirpate the vestiges of fascism.

---

71. United Nations Universal Declaration of Human Rights and Genocide Convention, 1948

The name United Nations was minted by President Roosevelt in 1941. Its official use for the countries fighting the Axis dates from the first day of 1942. At the Yalta conference the Big Three agreed that a United Nations Organization should be established as soon as possible; representatives of the 46 nations fighting the Axis (some rushed to declare war in order to be invited) met in San Francisco in the spring of 1945 and, in two months—despite many fundamental disagreements—they hammered out a draft that was signed by 50 nations in June. While there was none of the enthusiasm that accompanied the proclamation of the League of Nations in 1919, there was considerable confidence that weaknesses in the League's constitution had been avoided and that this time neither the United States nor Soviet Russia would stand aside. One of the UN's areas of concern has been human rights, as in the Declaration below, which was adopted unanimously although the Soviet bloc, South Africa, and Saudi Arabia abstained. Since 1948 several newly independent nations have incorporated the Declaration in their constitutions; adherence to the Declaration or to human rights in a more general way is more and more insisted upon in political agreements and diplomatic negotiations. The UN has also concerned itself with the rights of women and children.

The term genocide was minted by Raphael Lemkin, who described several forms of it—political, social, cultural, economic, biological, physical, religious—in his 1944 book *Axis Rule in Occupied Europe.* The Convention (treaty) on Genocide clearly reflects the shock at the atrocities committed during World War II and has been ratified by about 90 nations; President Truman was among the first signers but it was not ratified by the US Senate until 1986 and the necessary (under Article V) modifications in the Criminal Code were not enacted until 1989. It took nearly two years before agreement could be reached on the Convention (all the while that the Nuremberg trials were proceeding) and not until, at the insistence of Soviet Russia, its satellites, Iran, Egypt, and Argentina, the category of *political* groups was dropped from Article II; it might be noted that political groups were among the first victims of Hitler, Stalin, Peron, etc.

QUESTIONS

1. Compare the Universal Declaration of Human Rights with the English Bill of Rights, the Bill of Rights in the United States Constitution, and the French Declaration of Rights of Man and of Citizen.
2. How would the interpretation of this document differ in capitalist, communist, and Third World countries?
3. What demands do the rights listed under Articles 22 to 26 of the United Nations declaration make on a country's society and government?
4. What was the definition of genocide, according to the United Nations convention of 1948?

The Universal Declaration of Human Rights

Preamble   Whereas recognition of the inherent dignity and of the equal and inalienable rights of all members of the human family is the foundation of freedom, justice and peace in the world,

Whereas disregard and contempt for human rights have resulted in barbarous acts which have outraged the conscience of mankind, and the advent of a world in which human beings shall enjoy freedom of speech and belief and freedom from fear and want has been proclaimed as the highest aspiration of the common people,

Whereas it is essential, if man is not compelled to have recourse, as a last resort, to rebellion against tyranny and oppression, that human rights should be protected by the rule of law,

Whereas it is essential to promote the development of friendly relations between nations,

Whereas the people of the United Nations have in the Charter reaffirmed their faith in fundamental human rights, in the dignity and worth of the human person and in the equal rights of men and women and have determined to promote social progress and better standards of life in larger freedom,

Whereas Member States have pledged themselves to achieve, in cooperation with the United Nations, the promotion of universal respect for and observance of human rights and fundamental freedoms,

Whereas, as common understanding of these rights and freedoms is of the greatest importance for the full realization of this pledge,

Now, therefore, The General Assembly,

Proclaims this Universal Declaration of Human Rights, as a common standard of achievement for all peoples and all nations, to the end that every individual and every organ of society, keeping this Declaration constantly in mind, shall strive by teaching and education to promote respect for these rights and freedoms and by progressive measures, national and international, to secure their universal and effective recognition among the peoples of Member States themselves and among the peoples of territories under their jurisdiction.

Article 1. All human beings are born free and equal in dignity and rights. They are endowed with reason and conscience and should act towards one another in a spirit of brotherhood.

Article 2. Everyone is entitled to all the rights and freedoms set forth in this Declaration, without distinction of any kind, such as race, colour, sex, language, religion, political or other opinion, national or social origin, property, birth or other status.

Furthermore, no distinction shall be made on the basis of the political, jurisdictional or international status of the country or territory to which a person belongs, whether it be independent, trust, non-self-governing or under any other limitation of sovereignty.

Article 3. Everyone has the right to life, liberty and the security of person.

Article 4. No one shall be held in slavery or servitude; slavery and the slave trade shall be prohibited in all their forms.

Article 5. No one shall be subjected to torture or to cruel, inhuman or degrading treatment or punishment.

Article 6. Everyone has the right to recognition everywhere as a person before the law.

Article 7. All are equal before the law and are entitled without any discrimination to equal protection of the law. All are entitled to equal protection against any discrimination in violation of this Declaration and against any incitement to such discrimination.

Article 8. Everyone has the right to an effective remedy by the competent national tribunals for acts violating the fundamental rights granted him by the constitution or by law.

Article 9. No one shall be subjected to arbitrary arrest, detention or exile.

Article 10.   Everyone is entitled in full equality to a fair and public hearing by an independent and impartial tribunal, in the determination of his rights and obligations and of any criminal charge against him.

Article 11.   1. Everyone charged with a penal offense has the right to be presumed innocent until proved guilty according to law in a public trial at which he has had all the guarantees necessary for his defence.
2. No one shall be held guilty of any penal offense on account of any act or omission which did not constitute a penal offence, under national or international law, at the time when it was committed. Nor shall a heavier penalty be imposed than the one that was applicable at the time the penal offence was committed.

Article 12.   No one shall be subjected to arbitrary interference with his privacy, family home or correspondence, nor to attacks upon his honour and reputation. Everyone has the right to the protection of the law against such interference or attacks.

Article 13.   1. Everyone has the right to freedom of movement and residence within the borders of each State.
2. Everyone has the right to leave any country including his own, and to return to his country.

Article 14.   1. Everyone has the right to seek and to enjoy in other countries asylum from persecution.
2. This right may not be invoked in the case of prosecutions genuinely rising from non-political crimes or from acts contrary to the purposes and principles of the United Nations.

Article 15.   1. Everyone has the right to a nationality.

2. No one shall be arbitrarily deprived of his nationality nor denied the right to change his nationality.

Article 16.   1. Men and women of full age, without any limitation due to race, nationality or religion, have the right to marry and to found a family. They are entitled to equal rights as to marriage and at its dissolution.
2. Marriage shall be entered into only with the free and full consent of the intending spouses.
3. The family is the natural and fundamental group unit of society and is entitled to protection by society and the State.

Article 17.   1. Everyone has the right to own property alone as well as in association with others.
2. No one shall be arbitrarily deprived of his property.

Article 18.   Everyone has the right to freedom of thought, conscience and religion; this right includes freedom to change his religion or belief, and freedom, either alone or in a community with others and in public or private, to manifest his religion or belief in teaching, practice, worship and observance.

Article 19.   Everyone has the right to freedom of opinion and expression; this right includes freedom to hold opinions without interference and to seek, receive and impart information and ideas through any media and regardless of frontiers.

Article 20.   1. Everyone has the right to freedom of peaceful assembly and association.
2. No one may be compelled to belong to an association.

Article 21.   1. Everyone has the right to take part in the government of his country, directly or through freely chosen representatives.

2. Everyone has the right to equal access to public service in his country.

3. The will of the people shall be the basis of authority of government; this will shall be expressed in periodic and genuine elections which shall be by universal and equal suffrage and shall be held by secret vote or by equivalent free voting procedures.

Article 22.   Everyone, as a member of society, has the right to social security and is entitled to realization, through national effort and international cooperation and in accordance with the organization and resources of each State, of the economic, social and cultural rights indispensable for his dignity and the free development of his personality.

Article 23.   1. Everyone has the right to work, to free choice of employment, to just and favourable conditions of work and to protection against unemployment.

2. Everyone, without any discrimination, has the right to equal pay for equal work.

3. Everyone who works has the right to just and favourable remuneration ensuring for himself and his family an existence worthy of human dignity, and supplemented, if necessary, by other means of social protection.

4. Everyone has the right to form and to join trade unions for the protection of his interests.

Article 24.   Everyone has the right to rest and leisure, including reasonable limitation of working hours and periodic holidays with pay.

Article 25.   1. Everyone has the right to a standard of living adequate for the health and well-being of himself and of his family, including food, clothing, housing and medical care and necessary social services, and the right to security in the event of unemployment, sickness, disability, widowhood, old age or other lack of livelihood in circumstances beyond his control.

2. Motherhood and childhood are entitled to special care and assistance. All children, whether born in or out of wedlock, shall enjoy the same social protection.

Article 26.   1. Everyone has the right to education. Education shall be free, at least in the elementary and fundamental stages. Elementary education shall be compulsory. Technical and professional education shall be made generally available and higher education shall be equally accessible to all on the basis of merit.

2. Education shall be directed to the full development of the human personality and to the strengthening of respect for human rights and fundamental freedoms. It shall promote understanding, tolerance and friendship among all nations, racial or religious groups, and shall further the activities of the United Nations for the maintenance of peace.

3. Parents have a prior right to choose the kind of education that shall be given to their children.

Article 27.   1. Everyone has the right freely to participate in the cultural life of the community, to enjoy the arts and to share in scientific advancement and its benefits.

2. Everyone has the right to the protection of the moral and material interests resulting from any scientific, literary or artistic production of which he is the author.

Article 28.   Everyone is entitled to a social and international order in which the rights and freedoms set forth in this Declaration can be fully realized.

Article 29. 1. Everyone has duties to the community in which alone the free and full development of his personality is possible.

2. In the exercise of his rights and freedoms, everyone shall be subject only to such limitations as are determined by law solely for the purpose of securing due recognition and respect for the rights and freedoms of others and of meeting the just requirements of morality, public order and the general welfare in a democratic society.

3. These rights and freedoms may in no case be exercised contrary to the purposes and principles of the United Nations.

Article 30. Nothing in this Declaration may be interpreted as implying for any State, group or person any right to engage in any activity or to perform any act aimed at the destruction of any of the rights and freedoms set forth herein.

The United Nations Genocide Convention

The Contracting Parties

Having considered the declaration made by the General Assembly of the United Nations in its resolution 96 (1) dated 11 December 1946 that genocide is a crime under international law, contrary to the spirit and aims of the United Nations and condemned by the civilized world;

Recognizing that at all periods of history genocide has inflicted great losses on humanity; and

Being convinced that, in order to liberate mankind from such an odious scourge, international cooperation is required;

Hereby agree as hereinafter provided.

Article I. The Contracting Parties confirm that genocide whether in time of peace or in time of war, is a crime under international law which they undertake to prevent and to punish.

Article II. In the present Convention, genocide means any of the following acts committed with intent to destroy, in whole or in part, a national, ethnical, racial or religious group, as such: (a) Killing members of the group; (b) Causing serious bodily or mental harm to members of the group; (c) Deliberately inflicting on the group conditions of life calculated to bring about its physical destruction in whole or in part; (d) Imposing measures intended to prevent births within the group; (e) Forcibly transferring children of the group to another group.

Article III. The following acts shall be punishable: (a) Genocide; (b) Conspiracy to commit genocide; (c) Direct and public incitement to commit genocide; (d) Attempt to commit genocide; (e) Complicity in genocide.

Article IV. Persons committing genocide or any of the other acts enumerated in article III shall be punished, whether they are constitutionally responsible rulers, public officials or private individuals.

Article V. The Contracting Parties undertake to enact, in accordance with their respective Constitutions, the necessary legislation to give effect to the present Convention and, in particular, to provide effective penalties for persons guilty of genocide or any of the other acts enumerated under article III.

Article VI. Persons charged with genocide or any of the acts enumerated in article III shall be tried by a competent tribunal of the State in the territory of which the act was committed, or by such international penal tribunal as may have jurisdiction with respect to those Contracting Parties which shall have accepted its jurisdiction.

Article VII.   Genocide and other acts enumerated in article III shall not be considered as political crimes for the purposes of extradition. The Contracting Parties pledge themselves in such cases to grant extradition in accordance with their laws and treaties in force.

Article VIII.   Any Contracting Party may call upon the competent organs of the United Nations to take action under the Charter of the United Nations as they consider appropriate for the prevention and suppression of acts of genocide or any of the other acts enumerated in article III.

72. Indian Home Rule: Passive Resistance, c. 1910

Mohandas K. Gandhi

Mohandas Gandhi, the Mahatma (holy man) (1869–1948), was born into the *Bania* or merchant caste of India. His father and grandfather were lawyers and served as prime minister in the small west India state where he was born. Engaged at seven and married at fourteen, he was educated in India and from 1888 to 1891 he studied law and other subjects at the Inner Temple in London. In the contemptuous term of the time, he became a "Western Oriented Gentleman," adopting aristocratic English speech, manners, and dress. As a young man he worked in South Africa as attorney to an Indian business firm. For the next twenty years he was a successful lawyer, politician, and journalist-editor. A victim of notorious racial discrimination, Gandhi then formulated his concept of *Satyagraha* (truth—or soul-force). In a prolonged anti-discrimination campaign, he deployed the weapons of the spirit: nonviolence, passive resistance, civil disobedience, boycott, and fasting. Thus came into being the "moral equivalent of war," in which the aim was not the destruction but the "conversion" of the enemy. Poverty and an ascetic life were his means of disciplining body and spirit. Gandhi nurtured himself and fashioned his tactics on the writings of Henry David Thoreau, Leo Tolstoy, the New Testament, the tradition of nonviolent political action in Ireland, and most of all on the classic of Hindu scripture, the *Bhagavad Gita.*

Gandhi spent World War I in India, where he supported the British side in the war. He turned against British rule in India only when the imperial government did not abolish wartime abridgments of civil rights and liberties, and took harsh reprisals against Indian resistance, most notably in the infamous Amritsar massacre of 1919. He then organized the *Satyagraha* campaign across India against British rule, utilizing the boycott of British imports, but also pursuing a "constructive program" to induce each household to be self-sufficient in making its own clothes. The spinning wheel became one of his emblems. A famous example of successful civil disobedience was his Great Salt March of 1930, protesting the British tax and monopoly on that necessity of life. He organized consumer cooperative societies and was frequently arrested, spending 2,338 days of his life in jail. Often he managed to get released by fasting. While in many respects a traditional Hindu, he nevertheless struggled to extinguish the category of Untouchables, calling them instead *Harijan*, "Children of God." He also strove mightily for Hindu-Moslem-Sikh understanding and tolerance. During World War II he condemned Hitler and Nazism but without supporting the British cause since India remained a colony. He strongly opposed the partition of India in 1947 after independence was finally won in large part owing to his mobilization of the nation. When he was assassinated by a Hindu fanatic, Gandhi was typically engaged in organizing, praying, and fasting for peace and mutual acceptance among Hindus and Moslems.

QUESTIONS

1. What justification did Mohandas Gandhi offer for passive resistance and "soul-force"?
2. How did Gandhi believe that home rule (or independence) could be achieved?
3. What was Gandhi's reply to the objection that passive resistance is suited only to the weaker party in any conflict?
4. What attributes did Gandhi believe were essential to those who wished to become passive resisters?

Reader: I cannot follow this. There seems little doubt that we shall have to expel the English by force of arms. So long as they are in the country we cannot rest. . . .

Editor: . . . I believe that you want the millions of India to be happy, not that you [merely] want the reins of government in your hands. If that be so, we have to consider only one thing: how can the millions obtain self-rule? You will admit that people under several Indian princes are being ground down. The latter mercilessly crush them. Their tyranny is greater than that of the English, and if you want such tyranny in India, then we shall never agree. My patriotism does not teach me that I am to allow people to be crushed under the heel of Indian princes if only the English retire. If I have power, I should resist the tyranny of Indian princes just as much as that of the English. By patriotism I mean the welfare of the whole people, and if I could secure it at the hands of the English, I should bow down my head to them. If any Englishman dedicated his life to securing the freedom of India, resisting tyranny, and serving the land, I should welcome that Englishman as an Indian.

Again [you say that] India can fight . . . only when she has arms. You have not considered this problem at all. The English are splendidly armed; that does not frighten me, but it is clear that, to pit ourselves against them in arms, thousands of Indians must be armed. If such a thing be possible, how many years will it take? Moreover, to arm India on a large scale is to Europeanize it. Then her condition will be just as pitiable as that of Europe. This means, in short that India must accept European civilization, and if that is what we want, the best thing is that we have among us those who are so well trained in that civilization. We will then fight for a few rights, will get what we can and so pass our days. But the fact is that the Indian nation will not adopt arms, and it is well that it does not. . . .

Thousands, indeed tens of thousands, depend for their existence on a very active working of this [soul] force. Little quarrels of millions of families in their daily lives disappear before the exercise of this force. Hundreds of nations live in peace. History does not and cannot take note of this fact. History is really a record of every interruption of the even working of the force of love or of the soul. Two brothers quarrel; one of them repents and reawakens the love that was lying dormant in him. The two again begin to live in peace; nobody takes note of this. But if the two brothers, through the intervention of solicitors or some other reason, take up arms or go to law—which is another form of the exhibition of brute force—their doings would be immediately noticed in the press, they would be the talk of their neighbors and would probably go down to history. And what is true of families and communities is true of nations. There is no reason to believe that there is one law for families and another for nations. History, then, is a record of an interruption of the course of nature. Soul-force, being natural, is not noted in history.

Reader: According to what you say, it is plain that instances of this kind of passive resistance are not to be found in history. It is necessary to understand this passive resistance more fully. It will be better, therefore, if you enlarge upon it.

Editor: Passive resistance is a method of securing rights by personal suffering; it is the reverse of resistance by arms. When I refuse to do a thing that is repug-

nant to my conscience, I use soul-force. For instance, the Government of the day has passed a law which is applicable to me. I do not like it. If, by using violence, I force the government to repeal the law I am employing what may be termed body-force. If I do not obey the law and accept the penalty for its breach, I use soul-force. It involves sacrifice of self.

Everybody admits that sacrifice of self is infinitely superior to sacrifice of others. Moreover, if this kind of force is used in a cause that is unjust, only the person using it suffers. He does not make others suffer for his mistakes. Men have before now done many things which were subsequently found to have been wrong. No man can claim to be absolutely in the right or that a particular thing is wrong because he thinks so, but it is wrong for him so long as it is his deliberate judgement. It is therefore meet that he should not do that which he knows to be wrong, and suffer the consequence whatever it may be. This is the key to the use of soul-force.

Reader: You would then disregard laws—this is rank disloyalty. We have always been considered a law-abiding nation. You seem to be going even beyond the extremist. They say that we must obey the laws that have been passed but that if the laws be bad, we must drive out the lawgivers even by force.

Editor: Whether I go beyond them or whether I do not is a matter of no consequence to either of us. We simply want to find out what is right and to act accordingly. The real meaning of the statement that we are a law-abiding nation is that we are passive resisters. When we do not like certain laws, we do not break the heads of lawgivers but we suffer and do not submit to the laws. That we should obey laws whether good or bad is a new-fangled notion. There was no such thing in former days. The people disregarded those laws they did not like and suffered the penalties for their breach. It is contrary to our conscience. Such teaching is opposed to religion and means slavery. If the Government were to ask us to go about without any clothing, should we do so? If I were a passive resister I would say to them that I would have nothing to do with their law. But we have so forgotten ourselves and become so compliant, that we do not mind any degrading law.

A man who has realized his manhood, who fears only God, will fear no one else. Man-made laws are not necessarily binding on him. Even the Government do not expect any such thing from us. They do not say: "You must do such and such a thing," but they say: "If you do not do it, we will punish you." We are sunk so low, that we fancy that it is our duty and our religion to do what the law lays down. If man will only realise that it is unmanly to obey laws that are unjust, no man's tyranny will enslave him. This is the key to self-rule or home-rule.

It is a superstition and an ungodly thing to believe that an act of a majority binds a minority. Many examples can be given in which acts of majorities will be found to have been wrong and those of minorities to have been right. All reforms owe their origin to the initiation of minorities in opposition to majorities. If among a band of robbers, a knowledge of robbing is obligatory, is a pious man to accept the obligation? So long as the superstition that men should obey unjust laws exists, so long will their slavery exist. And a passive resister alone can remove such a superstition.

To use brute-force, to use gun-powder is contrary to passive resistance, for it means that we want our opponent to do by force that which we desire but he does not. And, if such a use of force is unjustifiable, surely he is entitled to do likewise by us. And so we should never come to an agreement. We may simply fancy, like the blind horse moving in a circle around a mill, that we are making progress. Those who believe that they are not bound to obey laws which are repugnant to their conscience have only the remedy of passive resistance open to them. Any other must lead to disaster.

Reader: From what you say, I deduce that passive resistance is a splendid weapon of the weak, but that when they are strong they may take up arms.

Editor: This is gross ignorance. Passive resistance, that is, soul-force, is matchless. It is superior to the force of arms. How, then, can it be considered only a weapon of the weak? Physical-force men are strangers to the courage that is requisite in a passive resister. Do you believe that a coward can ever disobey a law that he dislikes? Extremists are considered to be advocates of brute force. Why do they, then, talk about obeying laws? I do not blame them. They can say nothing else. When they succeed in driving out the English and they themselves become governors, they will want you and me to obey the laws. And that is a fitting thing for their constitution. But a passive resister will say he will not obey a law that is against his conscience, even though he may be blown to pieces at the mouth of a cannon.

What do you think? Wherein is courage required—in blowing others to pieces from behind a cannon or with a smiling face to approach a cannon to be blown to pieces? Who is the true warrior—he who keeps death always as a bosom-friend, or he who controls the death of others? Believe me that a man devoid of courage and manhood can never be a passive resister.

This, however, I will admit: that even a man weak in body is capable of offering this resistance. One man can offer it just as well as millions. Both men and women can indulge in it. It does not require the training of an army; it needs no Jiu-jitsu. Control over the mind is alone necessary and, when that is attained, man is free like the king of the forest and his very glance withers the enemy.

Passive resistance is an all-sided sword; it can be used anyhow; it blesses him who uses it and him against whom it is used. Without drawing a drop of blood it produces far-reaching results. It never rusts and cannot be stolen. Competition between passive resisters does not exhaust. The sword of passive resistance does not require a scabbard. It is strange indeed that you should consider such a weapon to be a weapon merely of the weak.

Reader: You have said that passive resistance is a specialty of India. Have cannons never been used in India?

Editor: Evidently, in your opinion, India means its few princes. To me it means its teeming millions on whom depends the existence of its princes and our own.

Kings will always use their kingly weapons. To use force is bred in them. They want to command, but those who have to obey commands do not want guns: and these are in a majority throughout the world. They have to learn either body-force or soul-force. Where they learn the former, both the rulers and the ruled become like so many madmen; but where they learn soul-force, the commands of the rulers do not go beyond the point of their swords, for true men disregard unjust commands. Peasants have never been subdued by the sword, and never will be. They do not know the use of the sword, and they are not frightened by the use of it by others. That nation is great which rests its head upon death as its pil-

low. Those who defy death are free from all fear. For those who are laboring under the delusive charms of brute-force, this picture is not overdrawn. The fact is that, in India, the nation at large has generally used passive resistance in all departments of life. We cease to cooperate with our rulers when they displease us. This is passive resistance. . . .

Reader: Then you will say that it is not at all necessary for us to train the body?

Editor: I will certainly not say any such thing. It is difficult to become a passive resister unless the body is trained. As a rule, the mind, residing in a body that has become weakened by pampering, is also weak, and where there is no strength of mind there can be no strength of soul. We shall have to improve our physique by getting rid of infant marriages and luxurious living. If I were to ask a man with a shattered body to face a cannon's mouth I should make a laughing-stock of myself.

Reader: From what you say, then, it would appear that it is not a small thing to become a passive resister and, if that is so, I would like you to explain how a man may become a passive resister.

Editor: To become a passive resister is easy enough but it is also equally difficult. I have known a lad of fourteen years become a passive resister; I have known also sick people doing likewise; and I have also known physically strong and otherwise happy people being unable to take up passive resistance. After a great deal of experience it seems to me that those who want to become passive resisters for the service of the country have to observe perfect chastity, adopt poverty, follow truth, and cultivate fearlessness.

Chastity is one of the greatest disciplines without which the mind cannot attain requisite firmness. A man who is unchaste loses stamina, becomes emasculated and cowardly. He whose mind is given over to animal passions is not capable of any great effort. This can be proved by innumerable instances. What, then, is a married man to do is the question that arises naturally; and yet it need not. When a husband and wife gratify the passions, it is no less an animal indulgence on that acount. Such an indulgence, except for perpetuating the race, is strictly prohibited. But a passive resister has to avoid even that very limited indulgence because he can have no desire for progeny. A married man, therefore, can observe perfect chastity. . . .

Just as there is necessity for chastity, so is there for poverty. Pecuniary ambition and passive resistance cannot well go together. Those who have money are not expected to throw it away, but they are expected to be indifferent about it. They must be prepared to lose every penny rather than give up passive resistance.

Passive resistance has been described in the course of our discussion as truth-force. Truth, therefore, has necessarily to be followed and that at any cost. . . .

Passive resistance cannot proceed a step without fearlessness. Those alone can follow the path of passive resistance who are free from fear, whether as to their possessions, false honor, their relatives, the government, bodily injuries or death.

73. Declaration of Independence in Vietnam, 1945

Ho Chi Minh

After World War II nationalist and anticolonial movements swept through the Third World countries of Africa, Asia, and Latin America. In Southeast Asia Ho Chi Minh (1890–1969) led a revolution against French rule in Vietnam which began in 1945 and ended with the defeat of French forces in 1954. Born Nguyen Van Thanh, he embraced communism in 1920 and contributed to the founding of the French Communist Party. Leader of the communist Vietminh party, he became President of North Vietnam after a peace conference held in Geneva in 1954 divided Vietnam into two nations. Elections that were supposed to lead to reunification of North and South Vietnam in 1956 were never held. Instead, the United States replaced France as the major western power in South Vietnam. During the late 1950s and 1960s he and his North Vietnamese government assisted the Viet Cong, the rebel forces in South Vietnam. After his death the United States agreed to a peace settlement in Vietnam and withdrew most of its troops from the region. South Vietnam fell to communist forces in 1975.

QUESTIONS

1. Explain the significance of Ho Chi Minh's references to the Declaration of Independence and the French Declaration of the Rights of Man and of Citizen.
2. On what grounds did Ho Chi Minh claim independence for Vietnam?
3. How does he depict the French colonial regime and the occupation by the Japanese during World War II?

"All men are created equal. They are endowed by their Creator with certain inalienable rights, among these are Life, Liberty, and the Pursuit of Happiness."

This immortal statement was made in the Declaration of Independence of the United States of America in 1776. Now if we enlarge the sphere of our thoughts, this statement conveys another meaning: All the peoples on earth are equal from birth, all the peoples have a right to live, be happy and free.

The Declaration of the Rights of Man and of the Citizen of the French Revolution in 1791 also states: "All men are born free and have equal rights, and must always be free and have equal rights."

Those are undeniable truths.

Nevertheless for more than eighty years, the French imperialists deceitfully raising the standard of Liberty, Equality, and Fraternity, have violated our fatherland and oppressed our fellow citizens. They have acted contrarily to the ideals of humanity and justice.

In the province of politics, they have deprived our people of every liberty.

They have enforced inhuman laws; to ruin our unity and national consciousness, they have carried out three different policies in the North, the Center and the South of Vietnam.

They have founded more prisons than schools. They have mercilessly slain our patriots; they have deluged our revolutionary areas with innocent blood. They have fettered public opinion; they have promoted illiteracy.

To weaken our race they have forced us to use their manufactured opium and alcohol.

In the province of economics, they have stripped our fellow-citizens of everything they possessed, impoverishing the individual and devastating the land.

They have robbed us of our rice fields, our mines, our forests, our raw materials. They have monopolized the printing of bank-notes, the import and export trade; they have invented numbers of unlawful taxes, reducing our people, especially our countryfolk, to a state of extreme poverty.

They have stood in the way of our businessmen and stifled all their undertakings; they have extorted our working class in a most savage way.

In the autumn of the year 1940, when the Japanese fascists violated Indochina's territory to get one more foothold in their fight against the Allies, the French imperialists fell on their knees and surrendered, handing over our country to the Japanese, adding Japanese fetters to the French ones. From that day on, the Vietnamese people suffered hardships yet unknown in the history of mankind. The result of this double oppression was terrific: from Quangtri to the northern border two million people were starved to death in the early months of 1945.

On the 9th of March, 1945, the French troops were disarmed by the Japanese. Once more the French either fled, or surrendered unconditionally, showing thus that not only were they incapable of "protecting" us, but that they twice sold out to the Japanese.

Yet, many times before the month of March, the Vietminh had urged the French to ally with them against the Japanese. The French colonists never answered. On the contrary, they intensified their terrorizing policy. Before taking to flight, they even killed a great number of our patriots who had been imprisoned at Yenbay and Cao-bang.

Nevertheless, towards the French people our fellow citizens have always manifested an attitude pervaded with toleration and humanity. Even after the Japanese putsch of March 1945 the Vietminh have helped many Frenchmen to reach the frontier, have delivered some of them from the Japanese jails, and never failed to protect their lives and properties.

The truth is that since the Autumn of 1940 our country had ceased to be a French colony and had become a Japanese outpost. After the Japanese had surrendered to the Allies our whole people rose to conquer political power and institute the Republic of Vietnam.

The truth is that we have wrested our independence from the Japanese and not from the French. The French have fled, the Japanese have capitulated. Emperor Bao Dai has abdicated, our people has broken the fetters which for over a century have tied us down; our people has at the same time over-thrown the monarchic constitution that had reigned supreme for so many centuries and instead has established the present Republican Government.

For these reasons, we, members of the Provisional Government, representing the whole population of Vietnam, have declared and renew here our declaration that we break off all relations with the French people and abolish all the special rights the French have unlawfully acquired on our Fatherland.

The whole population of Vietnam is united in common allegiance to the republican government and is linked by a common will, which is to annihilate the dark aims of the French imperialists.

We are convinced that the Allied nations which have acknowledged at Teheran and San Francisco the principles of self-determination and equality of status will not refuse to acknowledge the independence of Vietnam.

A people that has courageously opposed French domination for more than eighty years, a people that has fought by the Allies' side these last years against the fascists, such a people must be free, such a people must be independent.

For these reasons, we, members of the Provisional Government of Vietnam, declare to the world that Vietnam has the right to be free and independent, and has in fact become a free and independent country. We also declare that the Vietnamese people are determined to make the heaviest sacrifices to maintain its independence and its liberty.

Hanoi Sept. 2nd 1945

INTRODUCTION TO UNIT SEVEN

The New World Order

As the twentieth century draws to a close, the peoples of the world face dramatically new conditions of life. Over the past few decades political changes and powerful new economic and social forces have transformed the experiences of both westerners and inhabitants of less developed regions of the globe. In a series of stunning events, the Soviet Union disintegrated, communist regimes toppled in Eastern Europe, Germany reunited, South Africans launched a new government dedicated to racial equality, and Islamic revolutionaries deposed the Shah of Iran and threatened other governments in the Middle East. Meanwhile, citizens of all nations had to cope with the cumulative effects of the population explosion; revolutions in communications, finance, agriculture, and industry; the rise of powerful multinational corporations; the advent of biotechnology and robotics; and unprecedented threats to the environment. The final unit of this volume concentrates on a few of the leading issues which present critical challenges for the men and women of all nations as they approach the end of the second millennium A.D.

During this period the Western European states enjoyed economic growth and prosperity, which resulted in large part from their effective economic cooperation in the Common Market, established by the Treaty of Rome in 1957. The new system worked so well that plans were made to further the unification of the member states which, in time, doubled from the initial six to twelve. As the European states collectively became more independent politically and economically, they adopted a more confident foreign policy. France, for example, in asserting its international position, left NATO, and West Germany formulated its own policy toward the East, the "Ostpolitik," that was a new approach in its relations with the Soviet Union, Poland, East Germany, and other countries of the Soviet bloc.

The Treaty of Maastricht (Netherlands) marked the next major step in the long process of the integration of Western Europe. Signed in February 1992, it spelled out the basic principles of a new European Union. It was founded to promote economic and social progress, personal rights, and common security among the member nations and their peoples. It aimed to eliminate internal frontiers, establish a common currency and citizenship, develop closer cooperation on justice and domestic matters, and implement joint security and defense policies. Although it suffered an early setback when Danish voters rejected it, by the fall of 1993 all twelve members (Belgium, Denmark, Germany, Greece, Spain, France, Ireland, Italy, Luxembourg, Netherlands, Portugal, and Great Britain) approved the treaty. Although the degree of cooperation among the member states in the European Union remains in doubt, it appears that the countries of Western Europe are moving toward greater ties, setting a model for the rest of the world.

While the political turmoil in the Soviet Union during the 1980s contributed greatly to the end of communism in Central and Eastern Europe, the groundwork for that outcome had already been laid in August 1975, when the European nations, the United States, and Canada signed the Final Act of the Conference for Security and Cooperation in Europe (CSCE), also known as the Helsinki Accords. Although those agreements did not actually constitute a peace settlement for World War II, they did finally recognize the political outcome of that conflict in Europe. They established principles for European security, recognized boundaries set at the end of the war, and provided measures designed to reduce conflicts and promote economic cooperation and respect for human rights (see Document 76). The signing of the Helsinki Accords began a new political process which continued with conferences at Belgrade (1977–1978), Madrid (1980–1983), and Vienna (1986–1989). Although the guarantees of rights were unenforceable, they had, nevertheless, immense moral power and they greatly encouraged dissidents in Eastern Europe and the Soviet Union.

The developments in the Soviet Union in the late 1980s and the early 1990s proved to be of extraordinary historic significance, with a great impact on international affairs as well as on the domestic policies of many countries. During the neo-Stalinist era of Leonid Brezhnev, Yuri Andropov, and Konstantin Chernenko, the Soviet Union preserved and strengthened its status as a military superpower, but its economy fell into a deepening crisis. The attempts to suppress dissent and opposition failed in the Soviet Union and in the Soviet bloc countries.

When Mikhail S. Gorbachev succeeded Chernenko in power in 1985, he embarked on a policy of reform, summed up in the slogans of "glasnost" and "perestroika"—that is, a policy of openness and the introduction of economic reforms (restructuring). It soon became evident that the extent of reforms that Gorbachev had in mind was limited, since he intended to have the communist party retain its privileged position. But, under pressure from various segments of the society, the limits of "openness" constantly expanded. And the plans for economic reforms continuously trailed behind what the people needed and demanded. In particular, a strong challenge emerged to the Soviet imperial power, especially in East Central Europe. By the end of 1989 all states in that region had asserted their independence from the Soviet Union and from communist control.

Within the Soviet Union, however, Gorbachev, while willing to pass more authority to the republics, was determined to preserve the union. The collapse of the hard-liners' coup of August 19–21, 1991, in which they attempted in part to prevent any loosening of the union, further strengthened the opponents of the Soviet empire. The Baltic states of Latvia, Lithuania, and Estonia left the union, and the other republics, following Ukraine's lead, also proclaimed their own sovereignty. Gorbachev's desperate attempts to save some kind of a union failed, a fact made clear in the Ukrainian referendum of December 1, 1991, when over 90 percent expressed support for independence. Russia, Ukraine, and Belarus then established the Commonwealth of Independent States (CIS) on December 8, 1991, which most of the other republics subsequently joined. The resignation of Gorbachev from the presidency of the Soviet Union on December 25, 1991 formally confirmed the already existing reality—the end of the Soviet Union (see Document 77).

The continuing crisis underlay the rise to power of Boris Yeltsin, who faced down the reactionaries in Moscow, outlawed the communist party, and demolished much of the apparatus and institutions of Soviet control and domination. Although Yeltsin was the first popularly elected president in Russian history, in 1993 he still had to fight off a serious challenge from leaders of the new Russian Parliament, many of whom had grave doubts about his reform policies. In a controversial action he crushed the revolt with the help of the military, but he was still not completely in command. While a new constitution (ratified in December 1993) strictly limited parliamentary authority and gave the president more powers, both Yeltsin and the new Russian republic faced an uncertain future.

The disintegration of the Soviet empire provides an excellent illustration of the underlying forces that have shaped the last half century. In the first place, its decline may be traced to economic problems brought on by the immense costs of waging the Cold War. The socialist system in the U.S.S.R. could not simultaneously bear the escalating price of foreign intervention, new weapons, and domestic needs. In addition, these years were marked by the struggle for self-determination of nations and for the full rights of the individual that brought democracy to countries all over the world—including the republics of the Soviet Union. The future of that part of the world will be determined, in large part, by whether Russia chooses to either once again manifest its imperial character (as in its suppression of the Chechen revolt in 1994–1996 and its efforts to dominate the CIS), or join the peaceful community of democratic states. The disintegration of the Soviet empire, along with the rise to power of Germany and Japan, points to the need for a new structure for international relations, particularly in regard to the role of the United Nations.

In Germany the events of the late 1980s proved to be truly momentous. They marked the end of an age that opened in 1914 with war on two fronts and continued in a state of crisis until reunification was achieved in 1990. In August-September 1989 the Hungarian and Czechoslovak governments ended their restrictions on travel to Western European states and brought about the final crisis of the Soviet empire in Eastern Europe. Although the German Democratic Republic (GDR) had the highest per capita income in the Soviet bloc, it was less than half that of the capitalist Federal Republic of Germany. With the gates to the west open, many thousands of East Germans made their way to West German embassies and consulates in Czechoslovakia and Hungary to take advantage of the welcome, bonus, and citizenship that the Federal Republic held out. The exodus sparked demonstrations in Berlin and other East German cities, which culminated on November 9 (the anniversary of many historic events in German annals), when the Berlin wall was breached. The East German elections in March 1990 (the first free elections in that country's brief history) gave a majority to the Christian Democratic Party, which was affiliated with the ruling Christian Democratic Union Party in West Germany; that outcome signified the end of communist rule and the end of the GDR itself. In July 1990 the two Germanies agreed to monetary, economic, and social union; in September the "Treaty on the Final Settlement with Respect to Germany" (so called to emphasize that it was achieved *in peace* rather than negotiated to end war) was concluded. In this pact Britain, France, the United States, and the U.S.S.R. renounced all their rights in the Germanies and cleared the way for the political and territorial union that followed in October. Although many countries (especially Poland and the Soviet Union) feared that the new Germany would become economically dominant on the continent, possibly turning into a "Fourth Reich," they did not want to remain prisoners of the past. Because West Germany had been an exemplary democracy for forty years and was closely integrated with the rest of Western Europe, they took a chance on a united Germany in a united Europe.

During these years Eastern Europe experienced equally dramatic events. A visit by Pope John Paul II to his native Poland sparked an upsurge in nationalism that contributed to the formation of Solidarity, the federation of Polish trade unions. Outlawed in 1981, it resurfaced in 1989 to participate in the first relatively free elections in Eastern Europe since World War II. These elections resulted in the appointment of the first noncommunist premier (Tadeusz Mazowiecki) in the history of the now crumbling Soviet bloc. Soon the Republic of Poland was resurrected, and the communist regime went down the historical drainpipe.

The revolutions in Poland and Germany had a major impact on the rest of Eastern Europe, thanks in good measure to instant replay on television. The presence of huge numbers of East German refugees in their capital cities was the final element in the collapse of the communist regimes in Czechoslovakia and Hungary, while in Bulgaria communist party insiders overthrew the hardline dictator, Todor Zhivkov, who had ruled for thirty-five years, and recreated their party as a reformist, socialist movement. Romania, the last Soviet puppet to fall, alone experienced violence in a bloody rebellion in December 1989, which ended the brutal Ceaucescu regime but did not unseat the entrenched party apparatus. Even Albania got on the bandwagon, partly to avoid a Romanian bloodbath.

All of these upheavals had a profound impact on East-West relations between the superpowers. The changing atmosphere led presidents George Bush of the United States and Mikhail Gorbachev of the Soviet Union to announce the end of the Cold War at their meeting in Malta in December 1989. The CSCE summit conference in Paris in November 1990 inaugurated what Bush called "The New World Order."

While all the discredited regimes were overthrown and the communist parties lost their monopoly of power, the state bureaucracies and party apparatus they left behind have proven to be grave obstacles to the new democratic or would-be democratic governments. In the heroic days of resistance to the dictatorial regimes, the opposition was generally united. After the hated regime was toppled, these movements lost the glue which had held them together, and they fell into their component parts. For some countries, such as Romania and Bulgaria, this provided the opportunity for the former communists to return to power.

In all of the newly democratic countries, political parties declared their commitment to European integration, pluralism, democracy, and "modernization," a suitably vague term for economic policy. They generally refrained from going capitalist full throttle, apprehensive that it would bring unemployment, plummeting productivity, hyperinflation, or other dislocations. After all, freedom from unemployment was the one promise that the "socialist" regimes had kept, even though "socialism" was a taboo word associated with economic failure and political repression. As a frequently heard joke had it, "Socialism is the road from capitalism to capitalism." The widespread concern for human welfare, strong labor unions, an egalitarian or homogeneous society, much public investment, and restrictions on foreign investment and profiting are reminiscent of the "Swedish model" and of the social democracy of prewar Eastern Europe. This "third way" smacks too much of discredited socialism, however, and it has been undermined in recent years, even in Sweden, and by the procapitalist policies of Great Britain and the United States.

Nationalism is, far and away, the most powerful political and social force in the new Eastern Europe, with boundaries, now as in the past, a potent source of conflict. Just as poverty and economic backwardness fuel nationalist antipathies and ambitions, prosperity and economic growth will go far to diminish them. Shortly after the overthrow of the hated communist regimes, the ugly cloud of nationalist intolerance and barbarity reappeared. Within days of the East German revolution, skinheads and neo-Nazi hoodlums made their debut, and celebrations of the overthrow of the Ceaucescu police-state tyranny in Romania had barely ended before bloodshed between Romanians and Hungarians broke out in the contested province of Transylvania. While the Ceaucescu regime in Romania had persecuted the Hungarian minority there, Hungary's harsh attitude toward its eight minorities undermines its claim to be the guardian of the Hungarians in Transylvania and Slovakia. Even Czechoslovakia, seemingly the most stable country in the region, split into two independent republics in a "velvet divorce" opposed by most of the population in both areas. While the new Czech Republic seems en route to becoming a successful democratic state with a strong and diversified economic base, the emergent Slovakia appears economically weak and backward, dependent on agriculture, intolerant, and undemocratic.

The first severe setback on the road to freedom in the region came in August 1991, when war between Serbs and Croats tore the Yugoslav federation apart. Distracted by the attempted coup against Gorbachev in the U.S.S.R., the western powers at first remained aloof from the conflict. The Yugoslav imbroglio intensified as Catholic Croats, Eastern Orthodox Serbs, and Bosnian Muslims engaged in "ethnic cleansing" and fought for territory. It seemed too much to hope for that Slovenia, Croatia, and Bosnia-Herzegovina might form a viable federal state separated by the old Habsburg frontier from a workable federal state of Serbia, Montenegro, Kosovo, and Macedonia, in an age of irreconcilable nationalism and imperialism. However, in December 1995 the contending parties reached an agreement in Dayton, Ohio. This treaty was implemented by NATO, with the United States contributing 20,000 out of a total of 60,000 troops to enforce the peace.

The political turmoil during these decades was not confined to Europe, as conflicts and transformations swept through Africa, the Middle East, and Asia. By 1980 most of the European colonies in Africa had achieved independence and black majority rule through peaceful means. In a few cases (especially Kenya and Northern and Southern Rhodesia) white settlers resisted independence movements that were designed to bring black African governments into power. Black guerrilla movements fought white minority groups in those regions, while violence also broke out in Angola and Namibia.

The Republic of South Africa was the scene of a particularly bloody and bitter struggle over human rights, because by 1991 it was the only African nation still controlled by a white minority. In that state the Africaners (descendants of Dutch settlers, the Boers) maintained their system of apartheid (racial segregation) and white dominance. Many nations demanded that the South African government grant equal rights to its black population. The white officials responded by creating several black African homelands and by giving Asians and people of mixed ancestry some limited political rights. But these token reforms did not satisfy international opinion or activists in the African National Congress. When violence escalated in black townships, foreign governments increased the pressure by applying economic sanctions. In addition, Nelson Mandela and other opponents of white minority rule used a variety of violent and peaceful tactics to gain equal rights and political power for blacks. After prolonged struggle the white leaders capitulated. In 1994 Mandela and his ANC party won a general election and brought black majority rule to South Africa (see Document 74).

In the Middle East a revolution in Iran disturbed world peace. In 1979 rebel forces overthrew the government of Shah Reza Pahlavi and paved the way for the establishment of a theocratic Islamic state under the rule of Shi'ite clergy. The chief religious and political architect for the revolutionary movement was

Ruhollah al-Musavi al-Khomeini. The Shah had been a determined westernizer and ally of capitalist nations, and his downfall dealt a severe blow to United States interests in the region. The presidency of Jimmy Carter also suffered a humiliating setback when fundamentalist revolutionaries captured the American Embassy in Teheran and seized dozens of hostages. Khomeini exploited the taking of the Americans to mobilize domestic support, dramatize abroad the Iranian revolution, and attack the nation he called the "Great Satan"—the United States. But even as he lashed out at the capitalist Western powers, he also denounced communism, and especially the Soviet Union, which had recently launched an invasion of Afghanistan (see Document 78). The Iranian revolution in turn led to a long war throughout most of the 1980s between Iran and Iraq. But the conclusion of those hostilities did not bring peace to the region for very long, because in 1990 Saddam Hussein, the leader of Iraq, attacked and occupied Kuwait. United Nations forces (which included a heavy representation from the United States) defeated Iraq with relative ease in 1991, but instability remained in the region.

In Asia the great liberating wave also swept through communist China, although the outcome proved to be quite different from that of Eastern Europe and the Soviet Union. In 1989 a democratic reform movement led by students, professionals, and some middle-class followers challenged the communist party. But the ruling officials suppressed their demonstrations in a bloody rout on Tiananmen Square on June 4. Although China continued on the path of economic liberalization and greater participation in the market economy at home and abroad, communist leaders have tenaciously held their power and have fought movements for democracy and national autonomy (for example, in Tibet). Unlike its counterparts in Eastern Europe, the Chinese communist party retained the allegiance of the army and most of the population (especially the peasantry). However, relentless social and economic change and the passing of the aging rulers must eventually shift the balance of power toward democratic forces and advocates of rights for national minorities within the Chinese nation.

While political and diplomatic developments occupy the attention of statesmen and the masses who are directly involved in world crises, demographic, economic, social, and cultural forces have an immense impact on all of the peoples of the globe. Perhaps the best place to begin is with population trends. In 1825, as Thomas Malthus completed his studies, the world numbered about one billion souls. The total grew to two billion in 1925, four billion in 1976, and five and a half billion in 1993. While birth rates are decreasing in certain nations (as in Italy and Germany), so are the death rates. Projections for 2025 range from seven and a half to nine and a half billion, stabilizing in 2050 at ten to eleven billion but perhaps as high as fourteen to fifteen billion.

The crux of the problem is the unequal rate of population growth, with the most rapid growth concentrated in the developing countries, such as Mexico, India, Nigeria, and Syria. By 2025 95 percent of the population growth is expected to occur in those lands which are least able to provide food, shelter, and clothing. They are agricultural societies in which medicine, public health, pesticides in food production, and some industrialization have brought the death rate down dramatically. The population glut tends to concentrate in the cities, there being a rural exodus in almost all the developing countries. The resulting "megacit-ies"—huge shanty towns of squalor, poverty, hunger, disease, and resentment—will total twenty by 2000, seventeen in the developing world, with Mexico City and São Paulo in the lead. Provision of jobs, housing, transportation, sanitation, education, and food will be problematic. AIDS, the incidence of which is highest in the developing countries and most notably in Asia and Africa (where the dis-ease originated), might reverse the population explosion entirely and cause a shrinkage, as did the Black Plague in Europe from 1348 to 1475. Migration will not solve the problem; the doors of many Western nations are closed or are being closed to outsiders. In contrast to the nineteenth century when most of the mi-gration was from modernizing to less developed societies, today the flow is re-versed and is much resisted and resented in Europe and the United States. After half a century of economic growth unprecedented in world history, at least one billion people live in utter poverty and degradation, and another two billion struggle in the middle range. If the gap becomes more extreme between the de-veloping countries and the one-sixth of the population that is industrialized and consumes five-sixths of the world's wealth, these pockets of prosperity might come under siege or attack by migrants and refugees seeking to escape Malthu-sian misery.

While this great and uneven surge in global prosperity was going on, the multinational corporation has come into its own. It is not new. The Rothschild bank, utilizing the nineteenth-century revolution in communication, the tele-graph, is an example, as is Lloyd's of London. But the number and size of the multinationals are extraordinary. Their growth was facilitated by deregulation worldwide; freer trade in goods, capital, technology, and movement of people; and by the creation of instant communications through computers, software, fiber-optic cables, and satellites. Instant communication is not confined to eco-nomic information and financial transactions, but includes political, cultural, and social news flashed among the many thousands of monitors and stations of a global network. Within this nexus and largely because of it, many companies attempt to achieve international status, which enables them to reach a world market, enjoy the benefits of large-scale production, operate where costs are lowest, and sell where profits are highest. Multinational corporations seek to maximize profit; they have no loyalties, allegiances, or attachments to people (certainly not employees), nations, or communities. Globalization has mixed matters up so thoroughly that the day may come when no product is made in one place or country, and so, for example, a machine, car, or other manufactured item could not be called "American." In a borderless world no one is in control except the directors of the multinational corporations or their shareholders.

Recent revolutions in agriculture and industry have also sent shock waves around the world. Between 1950 and 1984 world production of grain, fish, meat, and vegetables rose by a multiple of two to three and kept ahead of population growth. Such gains came out of the "green revolution," the utilization of new land and farm machinery, better fertilizer and irrigation, crop rotation, and new genetic strains of plants, such as wheat and "miracle rice" (the production of which nearly doubled from 1965 to 1985). In the last ten years increases continue but at a slower pace and are nullified by the population spiral. Cropland diminishes owing to erosion, drought, salinization, and road building. About one billion people in the world suffer from malnutrition and hunger. In the West, owing to efficiency, farm subsidies, and agricultural protection, there are food surpluses, some of which are donated to famine areas or sold abroad. Such practices tend to make the recipient dependent or drain away precious resources to pay for food imports. Programs to expand production by additional croplands or other conventional means are not very promising, since there is very little virgin land to bring under the plough; most of it is marginal; and further destruction of forests, tropical rain forests in particular, brings calamities like global warming in their wake. Such prospects have focused attention on biotechnology, defined as "any technique that uses living organisms or processes to create or modify products, to improve plants or animals, or to develop microorganisms for special purposes" in medicine and agriculture.

In the industrial sector a new technology has emerged which threatens to replace the traditional factory and labor systems with machines—robots controlled by computers. The word *robot* comes from the Czech word for serf, robotnik, and suggests the possibility of new industrial serfs to replace the old ones, Marx's "wage slaves." The factory of the future has already appeared in Japan: entirely run by robots, it is faster and more efficient, dispenses with heating and air conditioning, can run in the dark, does not get tired or sloppy or slipshod, can be reprogrammed more quickly than workers can be retrained, wastes fewer materials (one quarter less in spray painting), and does not need health and accident insurance or paid vacations and maternity or paternity leave. If these trends continue, they could result in a cumulative increase in the quality of production and efficiency of the country that applies them, in this case Japan and perhaps Germany, and inaugurate a second industrial revolution, one of factories without workers paralleling agriculture without land or farmers. If such a trend were to continue, there would likely be a global economic shift, and with it a military shift, from Britain, Western Europe, and the United States to Japan and Germany, the losers in World War II.

The complex factors enumerated above are all relevant to environmental problems. Nor are such dilemmas new, although new and revolutionary in scale. There is no escaping massive pollution of air, water, and land, which is, therefore, of universal concern. The developing countries, burdened as most of them are by heavy foreign debt, are reluctant to attempt much about the environment, because they cannot spare the resources and are doing all they can to modernize and industrialize. They seek to have the same standard of living as anyone else and make the correct argument that when the advanced economies were industrializing a century ago they were prodigal and indifferent to ecology. The U.S.S.R. and the Soviet bloc after 1945 were bent on catching up fast and developed heavy industry, chemicals, and atomic power with little regard for ecology or public health and safety. The result was fishless lakes and streams, the Danube turned into "a deadly sump," smog that kills forests, and the nuclear disaster at Chernobyl. The patterns duplicate themselves in China, India, and elsewhere: great quantities of carbon and sulfur dioxide belch from the factory chimneys, poisoning the air of Beijing, New Delhi, Ankara, Teheran, Mexico City, and a growing number of cities. Owing to population growth, industrialization, lack of sewage and water purification, irrigation, and the use of pesticides, the water supply is both polluted and used up. Water tables drop and aquifers shrink. Environmentalists and "green" parties in the United States and Europe have pressed with some success for reforestation, control of industrial and auto emissions, cleansing and restocking of fishing streams and lakes, cleanup of environmental disasters and dumping sites, recycling, and waste treatment (see Document 79).

The gravest environmental problem foreseeable in the future is global warming through the greenhouse effect. Since the Ice Age, carbon dioxide levels have been rising in the upper atmosphere, where the particles form a mirror that reflects more heat back to earth. The average temperature then (40,000 to 50,000 years ago) was c. $5°C$; today it is c. $15°C$; it is projected to rise to c. $17°$ to c. $19.5°C$ in 2050. There is much disagreement as to whether this would be good or bad. Some economists say that warmer temperatures mean longer growing seasons and rises in production, that what is lost in the torrid zone would be more than made up in the temperate and frigid zones. Scientists say sea levels will rise: oceans would be warmer and therefore expand in volume, the Arctic and Antarctica glaciers and snow would melt. There is no agreement on how much the sea level would rise but a prevalent view is that small rises would make a great difference. It is calculated that a one-meter rise in sea level would cause the shoreline to contract a hundred meters, that hurricanes and such storms would thrust more water farther inland, that salt water would penetrate inland and up-river to contaminate fresh water, that warmer weather might mean more pests and insects rather than greater yields of crops. Reassessments in 1995 by 2,500 scientists working under U.N. auspices concluded that global warming was occurring and that it was more likely to result in deleterious than beneficial outcomes for the environment and economic and social conditions. For many developing countries the prospect is more ominous. Egypt, Bangladesh, Gambia, the Maldive Islands (the highest point of which is six or seven feet), Mozambique, Indonesia, Pakistan, Senegal, Surinam, and Thailand are the most threatened: all have rapidly rising populations and shrinking lands menaced by flooding, and all lack the resources to deal with the problem or to relocate population.

Since World War II women's rights activists such as Simone de Beauvoir have argued for greater equality and opportunity for females in a world traditionally dominated by men (see Document 75). In Western Europe and North America women have achieved impressive gains in political rights and economic power, especially since the revival of more militant forms of feminism since the 1970s. But even in wealthier nations women have not achieved political or financial parity with men, and their work continues to be undervalued and underpaid compared to their male counterparts. Women in underdeveloped countries tend to be poorer than men because of traditions of gender which bind them to family and home obligations, excluding them from access to education and jobs in the modern sectors of the economy. In certain parts of the world (especially the Middle East), the growing popularity of militant fundamentalist religious movements makes it very difficult for women to follow the example of Western feminist movements.

Finally, the nation-state is the principal instrument available to cope with all of these transnational changes and issues. In some ways it is too big and clumsy, in others too small and ineffective. Also the 180+ nation-states in the United Nations are very unequal in every way; they are as different in size, location, and resources as they are in their histories, social structures, cultural values, and attitudes. Some judge the nation-state to be obsolete and point to the proliferation of multinational corporations as proof of its eclipse. On the other hand, nationalism is the most powerful social/moral force acting in the world today—witness its dismemberment of ex-Yugoslavia and ex-U.S.S.R. and reunification of Germany. The two world wars went far to discredit the national-imperialist state, and were followed by attempts to provide for international cooperation and collective security, first through the League of Nations and then the United Nations. The United Nations expanded its efforts to resolve international crises through its involvement in peacekeeping operations in such places as Cambodia, Lebanon, Somalia, and Bosnia, although not always successfully. It is also linked with a great many social and economic institutions. The end of the Cold War has reduced military rivalries and arms races but it has also shifted national energies toward economic rivalries, technology races, and trade wars. The weakness, slowness, and inefficaciousness of the nation-state in dealing with transnational problems and issues have given rise to "relocations of authority," such as the multinational corporations and banks and the global communications network, which are largely independent of governments. There are also regional commercial organizations, which involve some erosion of national power and sovereignty. "Relocation of authority downward" into smaller units than the nation-state for purposes of trade and technology development may be seen in the American states and cities (like New York City) that send out their "missions" to conclude agreements in Tokyo, Brussels, or South Africa; and in Russian cities like St. Petersburg that have declared themselves a free trade zone. Such relocations downward in societies where ethnic rivalries and boundary disputes fuel regional antagonisms, as in ex-Yugoslavia, ex-U.S.S.R., Africa (where most boundaries were drawn by nineteenth-century empires and make no geographical, ethnic, or historical sense), and possibly China, can be disruptive of the nation-state. How far these relocations upward and downward proceed, and whether to the demise of the nation-state, only time will tell. As historians have often commented, the only thing certain about the future is that it will astonish even those who have seen into it the farthest! This anthology concludes with two reflective pieces on the course of Western civilization—where humankind has been, where it might go, and how it might end (see Document 80).

74. I Am Prepared to Die, 1964

Testimony of Nelson Mandela

Nelson Mandela, the President of South Africa and a political leader of the African National Congress, played a primary role in ending racial discrimination and apartheid in his native country. Born in the Transkei territory of South Africa in 1918, he was the son of a Xhosa tribal chief. Trained as a lawyer, in 1944 he joined the African National Congress, a civil rights organization, and later, liberation movement, which had been founded in 1912 to fight for equal rights for Africans. During the 1950s and 1960s Mandela and other members of the ANC struggled with a number of critical issues. These questions concerned the meaning of democracy in South Africa, and especially what rights the black majority, the white minority, and people of mixed and Asian ancestry should have in the country. They also debated the desirability of applying socialist approaches to the economy, the significance of class and national considerations as compared to race matters, the role of external assistance in their efforts, and the appropriate strategies and tactics they should apply in striving for their goals.

In 1961 Mandela was acquitted of charges of treason, but the following year he was arrested again for his role in sabotage and conspiracy against the white supremacist government. The selection below presents excerpts from his testimony at his trial, at which he was sentenced to life imprisonment. While in jail he became a symbol of the crusade to end apartheid in South Africa. After his release in 1990 he was elected president of the ANC. Shortly thereafter he participated in negotiations with the white State President and leader of the Afrikaner-dominated National Party of South Africa, Frederik Willem de Klerk; those talks led to a new constitution that provided for South Africa's first democratic national elections in April 1994, in which Africans and other people of color were permitted to vote. After a triumphal election campaign the ANC won two thirds of the popular vote and Nelson Mandela was sworn in as executive president of South Africa on May 10, 1994.

QUESTIONS

1. According to Mandela, what tactics did the ANC apply during its struggle against the government of South Africa? What is his evaluation of the results of peaceful actions?
2. Explain his definitions and distinctions among various forms of violence. How does he justify the use of violence?
3. According to Mandela, what do South Africans want from their government?

I am the First Accused.

I hold a Bachelor's Degree in Arts and practiced as an attorney in Johannesburg for a number of years in partnership with Oliver Tambo. I am a convicted prisoner serving five years for leaving the country without a permit and for inciting people to go on strike at the end of May 1961.

. . . I have done whatever I did both as an individual and as a leader of my people, because of my experience in South Africa. . . .

In my youth in the Transkei, I listened to the elders of my tribe telling stories of the old days. Among the tales they related to me were those of the wars fought by our ancestors in defense of the fatherland. . . . I hoped then that life might offer me the opportunity to serve my people and make my own humble contribution to their freedom struggle. This is what has motivated me in all that I have done in relation to the charges made against me in this case.

Having said this, I must deal immediately and at some length with the question of violence. Some of the things so far told to the court are true and some are untrue. I do not, however, deny that I planned sabotage. I did not plan it in a spirit of recklessness, nor because I have any love of violence. I planned it as a result of a calm and sober assessment of the political situation that had arisen after many years of tyranny, exploitation, and oppression of my people by the whites.

I admit immediately that I was one of the persons who helped to form Umkonto we Sizwe [the military arm of the ANC], and that I played a prominent role in its affairs until I was arrested in August 1962.

In the statement which I am about to make I shall correct false impressions which have been created by State witnesses.

. . . I have already mentioned that I was one of the persons who helped to form Umkonto. I, and the others who started the organization, did it for two reasons. Firstly, we believed that as a result of the government policy, violence by the African people had become inevitable, and that unless responsible leadership was given to canalize and control the feelings of our people, there would be outbreaks of terrorism which would produce an intensity of bitterness and hostility between the various races of this country which is not produced even by war. Secondly, we felt that without violence there would be no way open to the African people to succeed in their struggle against the principle of white supremacy. All lawful modes of expressing opposition to this principle had been closed by legislation, and we were placed in a position in which we had either to accept a permanent state of inferiority, or to defy the government. We chose to defy the law. We first broke the law in a way which avoided any recourse to violence; when this form was legislated against, and when the government resorted to a show of force to crush opposition to its policies, only then did we decide to answer violence with violence.

But the violence which we chose to adopt was not terrorism. We who formed Umkonto were all members of the African National Congress, and had behind us the ANC tradition of nonviolence and negotiation as a means of solving political disputes. . . .

The African National Congress was formed in 1912 to defend the rights of the African people which had been seriously curtailed by the South African Act, and which were then being threatened by the Native Land Act. For thirty-seven years—that is until 1949—it adhered strictly to a constitutional struggle. It put forward demands and resolutions; it sent delegations to the government in the belief that African grievances could be settled through peaceful discussion and that Africans could advance gradually to full political rights. But white governments remained unmoved, and the rights of Africans became less instead of becoming greater. . . .

In 1960, there was the shooting at Sharpeville, which resulted in the proclamation of a state of emergency and the declaration of the ANC as an unlawful organization. My colleagues and I, after careful consideration, decided that we would not obey this decree. The African people were not part of the government and did not make the laws by which they were governed. We believed in the words of the Universal Declaration of Human Rights, that "the will of the people shall be the basis of authority of the government," and for us to accept the banning was equivalent to accepting the silencing of the Africans for all time. The ANC refused to dissolve, but instead went underground. We believed it was our duty to preserve this organization which had been built up with almost fifty years of unremitting toil.

. . . In 1960, the government held a referendum which led to the establishment of the Republic. Africans, who constituted approximately 70 percent of the population of South Africa, were not entitled to vote, and were not even consulted about the proposed constitutional change. All of us were apprehensive of our future under the proposed white republic, and a resolution was taken to hold an All-In African Conference to call for a National Convention, and to organize mass demonstrations on the eve of the unwanted Republic, if the government failed to call a Convention. The conference was attended by Africans of various political persuasions. I was the Secretary of the conference and undertook to be responsible for organizing the national stay-at-home which was subsequently called to coincide with the declaration of the Republic. As all strikes by Africans are illegal, the person organizing such a strike must avoid arrest. I was chosen to be this person, and consequently I had to leave my home and family and my practice and go into hiding to avoid arrest.

The stay-at-home, in accordance with ANC policy, was to be a peaceful demonstration. Careful instructions were given to organizers and members to avoid any recourse to violence. The government's answer was to introduce new and harsher laws, to mobilize its armed forces, and to send saracens, armed vehicles, and soldiers into townships in a massive show of force designed to intimidate the people. This was an indication that the government had decided to rule by force alone, and this decision was a milestone on the road to Umkonto.

. . . We had no doubt that we had to continue the fight. Anything else would have been abject surrender. Our problem was not whether to fight, but was how to continue the fight. We of the ANC had always stood for a nonracial democracy, and we shrank from any action which might drive the races further apart than they already were. But the hard facts were that fifty years of nonviolence had brought the African people nothing but more and more repressive legislation, and fewer rights. It may not be easy for this Court to understand, but it is a fact that for a long time the people had been talking of violence—of the day when they would fight the white man and win back their country—and we, the leaders of the ANC, had nevertheless always prevailed upon them to avoid violence and to pursue peaceful methods. When some of us discussed this in May and June of 1961, it could not be denied that our policy to achieve a nonracial State by nonviolence had achieved nothing, and that our followers were beginning to lose confidence in this policy and were developing disturbing ideas of terrorism.

It must not be forgotten that by this time violence had, in fact, become a feature of the South African political scene. There had been violence in 1957 when the women of Zeerust were ordered to carry passes; there was violence in 1958 with the enforcement of cattle culling in Sekhukhuniland; there was violence in 1959 when the people of Cato Manor protested against pass raids; there was violence in 1960 when the government attempted to impose Bantu Authorities in Pondoland. Thirty-nine Africans died in these disturbances. In 1961 there had been riots in Warmbaths, and all this time the Transkei had been a seething mass of unrest. Each disturbance pointed clearly to the inevitable growth among Africans of the belief that violence was the only way out—it showed that a government which uses force to maintain its rule teaches the oppressed to use force to oppose it. Already small groups had arisen in the urban areas and were spontaneously making plans for violent forms of political struggle. There now arose a danger that these groups would adopt terrorism against Africans, as well as whites, if not properly directed. Particularly disturbing was the type of violence engendered in places such as Zeerust, Sekhukhuniland, and Pondoland amongst Africans. It was increasingly taking the form, not of struggle against the government—though this is what prompted it—but of civil strife amongst themselves, conducted in such a way that it could not hope to achieve anything other than a loss of life and bitterness.

At the beginning of June 1961, after a long and anxious assessment of the South African situation, I, and some colleagues came to the conclusion that as violence in this country was inevitable, it would be unrealistic and wrong for African leaders to continue preaching peace and nonviolence at a time when the government met our peaceful demands with force.

. . . the decision was made to embark on violent forms of political struggle, and to form Umkonto we Sizwe. In the Manifesto of Umkonto published on December 16, 1961, we said:

"The time comes in the life of any nation when there remain two choices—submit or fight. That time has now come to South Africa. We shall not submit and we have no choice but to hit back by all means of our power in defence of our people, our future, and our freedom."

The avoidance of civil war had dominated our thinking for many years, but when we decided to adopt violence as part of our policy, we realized that we might one day have to face the prospect of such a war. This had to be taken into account in formulating our plans. We required a plan which was flexible and which permitted us to act in accordance with the needs of the times; above all, the plan had to be one which recognized civil war as the last resort, and left the decision on this question to the future. We did not want to be committed to civil war, but we wanted to be ready if it became inevitable.

Four forms of violence were possible. There is sabotage, there is guerrilla warfare, there is terrorism, and there is open revolution. We chose to adopt the first method and to exhaust it before taking any other decision.

In the light of our political background, the choice was a logical one. Sabotage did not involve loss of life, and it offered the best hope for future race relations. Bitterness would be kept to a minimum and, if the policy bore fruit, democratic government could become a reality. . . .

The initial plan was based on a careful analysis of the political and economic situation of our country. We believed that South

Africa depended to a large extent on foreign capital and foreign trade. We felt that planned destruction of power plants, and interference with rail and telephone communications, would tend to scare away capital from the country, make it more difficult for goods from the industrial areas to reach the seaports on schedule, and would in the long run be a heavy drain on the economic life of the country, thus compelling the voters of the country to reconsider their position.

Attacks on the economic life lines of the country were to be linked with sabotage on government buildings and other symbols of apartheid. These attacks would serve as a source of inspiration to our people. In addition, they would provide an outlet for those people who were urging the adoption of violent methods and would enable us to give concrete proof to our followers that we had adopted a stronger line and were fighting back against government violence.

In addition, if mass action were successfully organized, and mass reprisals taken, we felt that sympathy for our cause would be roused in other countries, and that greater pressure would be brought to bear on the South African government. . . .

The Manifesto of Umkonto was issued on the day that operations commenced. The response to our actions and Manifesto among the white population was characteristically violent. . . .

In contrast, the response of the Africans was one of encouragement. Suddenly there was hope again. Things were happening. People in the townships became eager for political news. A great deal of enthusiasm was generated by the initial successes, and people began to speculate on how soon freedom would be obtained.

But we in Umkonto weighed up the white response with anxiety. The lines were being drawn. The whites and blacks were moving into separate camps, and the prospects of avoiding a civil war were made less. The white newspapers carried reports that sabotage would be punished by death. If this was so, how could we continue to keep Africans away from terrorism.

Already scores of Africans had died as a result of racial friction. In 1920, when the famous leader, Masabala, was held in Port Elizabeth jail, twenty-four of a group of Africans who had gathered to demand his release were killed by the police and white civilians. In 1921, more than one hundred Africans died in the Bulhoek affair. In 1924, over two hundred Africans were killed when the Administrator of South West Africa led a force against a group which had rebelled against the imposition of a dog tax. On May 1, 1950, eighteen Africans died as a result of police shooting during the strike. On March 21, 1960, sixty-nine unarmed Africans died at Sharpeville.

How many more Sharpevilles would there be in the history of our country? And how many more Sharpevilles could the country stand without violence and terror becoming the order of the day? And what would happen to our people when that stage was reached? In the long run we felt certain we must succeed, but at what cost to ourselves and the rest of the country? And if this happened, how could black and white ever live together again in peace and harmony? These were the problems that faced us, and these were our decisions.

Experience convinced us that rebellion would offer the government limitless opportunities for the indiscriminate slaughter of our people. But it was precisely because the soil of South Africa is already drenched with the blood of innocent Africans that we feel it our duty to make preparations as a long-term undertaking to use force in order to defend ourselves against force. If war were inevitable, we wanted the fight to be conducted on terms most favorable to our people. The fight which held out prospects best for us and the least risk of life to both sides was guerrilla warfare. We decided, therefore, in our preparations for the future, to make provision for the possibility of guerrilla warfare.

All whites undergo compulsory military training, but no such training was given to Africans. It was in our view essential to build up a nucleus of trained men who would be able to provide the leadership which would be required if guerrilla warfare started. . . . It was also necessary to build up a nucleus of men trained in civil administration and other professions, so that Africans would be equipped to participate in the government of this country as soon as they were allowed to do so. . . .

I was completely objective. The Court will see that I attempted to examine all types of authority on the subject—from the East and the West, going back to the classic work of Clausewitz, and covering such a variety as Mao Tse-tung and Che Guevara on the one hand, and the writings on the Anglo-Boer War [1899–1902] on the other.

. . . I also made arrangements to undergo military training. . . . I consequently obtained the permission of the ANC in South Africa to do this. To this extent then there was a departure from the original decision of the ANC, but it applied outside South Africa only. The first batch of recruits actually arrived in Tanganyika when I was passing through that country on my way back to South Africa.

I returned to South Africa and reported to my colleagues on the results of my trip. It was decided to go ahead with the plans for military training because of the fact that it would take many years to build up a sufficient nucleus of trained soldiers to start

a guerrilla campaign, and whatever happened the training would be of value. . . .

Africans want to be paid a living wage. Africans want to perform work which they are capable of doing, and not work which the government declares them to be capable of. Africans want to be allowed to live where they obtain work, and not be endorsed out of an area because they were not born there. Africans want to be allowed to own land in places where they work, and not to be obliged to live in rented houses which they can never call their own. Africans want to be part of the general population, and not confined to living in their own ghettoes. African men want to have their wives and children to live with them where they work, and not forced into an unnatural existence in men's hostels. African women want to be with their menfolk and not be left permanently widowed in the Reserves. Africans want to be allowed out after eleven o'clock at night and not to be confined to their rooms like little children. Africans want to be allowed to travel in their own country and to seek work where they want to and not where the Labor Bureau tells them to. Africans want a just share in the whole of South Africa; they want security and a stake in society.

Above all, we want equal political rights, because without them our disabilities will be permanent. I know this sounds revolutionary to the whites in this country, because the majority of voters will be Africans. This makes the white man fear democracy.

But this fear cannot be allowed to stand in the way of the only solution which will guarantee racial harmony and freedom for all. It is not true that the enfranchisement of all will result in racial domination. Political division, based on color, is entirely artificial and, when it disappears, so will the domination of one color group by another. The ANC has spent half a century fighting against racialism. When it triumphs it will not change that policy.

This then is what the ANC is fighting. Their struggle is a truly national one. It is a struggle of the African people, inspired by their own suffering and their own experience. It is a struggle for the right to live.

During my lifetime, I have dedicated myself to this struggle of the African people. I have fought against white domination, and I have fought against black domination. I have cherished the ideal of a democratic and free society in which all persons live together in harmony and with equal opportunities. It is an ideal which I hope to live for and to achieve. But if needs be, it is an ideal for which I am prepared to die.

75. The Second Sex, 1949

Simone de Beauvoir

Simone de Beauvoir (1908–1986) was a French novelist, autobiographer, and moral and political essayist. Through her writings and political activity she became a prominent rebel and a leftist witness of contemporary affairs and events, student of social problems, indefatigable protester against injustice, and pioneer of modern feminism. Born into the haute bourgeoisie, her father's family came from the fringes of the aristocracy but had lost its fortune. Her mother was a devout Catholic who reared her children in convent schools and in an air of piety. The family's political and social allegiances were conservative and reactionary. Her father leaned toward militarism and fascism and supported the Vichy regime that collaborated with the Nazis during World War II. De Beauvoir rebelled against all of that: the "bourgeoisie" and "capitalism" represented everything she loathed. She relentlessly dedicated herself to the literal extinction of the class and all its values. Her rebellion began in the 1920s at the Sorbonne, where she was a brilliant student of philosophy. There she met Jean-Paul Sartre, 1905–1980, the existentialist philosopher with whom she maintained a "special relationship" through many vicissitudes for 50 years until his death. It was an intellectual partnership as much as a sexual liaison; whether it was a relationship of equals has been doubted. Her critics have charged that in her personal life she did not practice what she preached in her feminist writings. A possible explanation of that inconsistency appears in the excerpt from *The Second Sex* that is reprinted below. She admired the Soviet Union, believing "a new species of mankind" was being created there, and was quite oblivious of Stalin's repressive policies. She was highly critical of the United States as the citadel of capitalism and "imperialism" in Vietnam and throughout the world. Characteristically, she differed vehemently from two other students of the women's movement, her older contemporary, the historian Mary R. Beard, and her younger contemporary, Betty Friedan, the leading writer on women's liberation in the U.S.

QUESTIONS

1. Explain what Simone de Beauvoir means when she writes that "the woman problem has always been a man's problem"?
2. What is her view of the institution of marriage?
3. What changes does she see in the status of women in society?
4. According to Beauvoir, what problems face the independent woman? What does she have to say in particular about women who are doctors and actresses?

If we cast a general glance over this history, we see several conclusions that stand out from it. And this one first of all: the whole of feminine history has been man-made. Just as in America there is no Negro problem, but rather a white problem; just as anti-semitism is not a Jewish problem: it is our problem; so the woman problem has always been a man's problem. We have seen why men had moral prestige along with physical strength from the start; they created values, mores, religions; never have women disputed this empire with them. Some isolated individuals—Sappho, Christine de Pisan, Mary Wollstonecraft, Olympe de Gouges— have protested against the harshness of their destiny, and occasionally mass demonstrations have been made; but neither the Roman matrons uniting against the Opian law nor the Anglo-Saxon suffragettes could have succeeded with their pressure unless the men had been quite disposed to submit to it. Men have always held the lot of woman in their hands; and they have determined what it should be, not according to her interest, but rather with regard to their own projects, their fears, and their needs. . . .

Woman has always been man's dependant, if not his slave; the two sexes have never shared the world in equality. And even today woman is heavily handicapped,

though her situation is beginning to change. Almost nowhere is her legal status the same as man's, and frequently it is much to her disadvantage. Even when her rights are legally recognized in the abstract, long-standing custom prevents their full expression in the mores. In the economic sphere men and women can almost be said to make up two castes; other things being equal, the former hold the better jobs, get higher wages, and have more opportunity for success than their new competitors. In industry and politics men have a great many more positions and they monopolize the most important posts. In addition to all this, they enjoy a traditional prestige that the education of children tends in every way to support, for the present enshrines the past—and in the past all history has been made by men. At the present time, when women are beginning to take part in the affairs of the world, it is still a world that belongs to men—they have no doubt of it at all and women have scarcely any. To decline to be the Other, to refuse to be a party to the deal—this would be for women to renounce all the advantages conferred upon them by their alliance with the superior caste. Man-the-sovereign will provide woman-the-liege with material protection and will undertake the moral justification of her existence; thus she can evade at once both economic risk and the metaphysical risk of a liberty in which ends and aims must be contrived without assistance. Indeed, along with the ethical urge of each individual to affirm his subjective existence, there is also the temptation to forgo liberty and become a thing. This is an inauspicious road, for he who takes it—passive, lost, ruined—becomes henceforth, the creature of another's will, frustrated in his transcendence and deprived of every value. But it is an easy road; on it one avoids the strain involved in undertaking an authentic existence. When man makes of woman the **Other,** he may, then, expect to manifest deep-seated tendencies towards complicity. Thus, woman may fail to lay claim to the status of subject because she lacks definite resources, because she feels the necessary bond that ties her to man regardless of reciprocity, and because she is often very well pleased with her role as the **Other**. . . .

Marriage is the destiny traditionally offered to women by society. It is still true that most women are married, or have been, or plan to be, or suffer from not being. The celibate woman is to be explained and defined with reference to marriage, whether she is frustrated, rebellious, or even indifferent in regard to that institution. We must therefore continue this study by analyzing marriage.

Economic evolution in woman's situation is in process of upsetting the institution of marriage: it is becoming a union freely entered upon by the consent of two independent persons; the obligations of the two contracting parties are personal and reciprocal; adultery is for both a breach of contract; divorce is obtainable by the one or the other on the same conditions. Woman is no longer limited to the reproductive function, which has lost in large part its character as natural servitude and has come to be regarded as a function to be voluntarily assumed; and it is compatible with productive labour, since, in many cases, the time off required by a pregnancy is taken by the mother at the expense of the State or the employer. In the Soviet Union marriage was for some years a contract between individuals based upon the complete liberty of the husband and wife; but it would seem that it is now a duty that the State imposes upon them both. Which of these tendencies will prevail in the world of tomorrow will depend upon the general structure of society, but in any case male guardianship of woman is disappearing. Nevertheless, the epoch in which we are living is still, from the feminist point of view, a period of transition. Only a part of the female population is still engaged in production, and even those who are belong to a society in which ancient forms and antique values survive. Modern marriage can be understood only in the light of a past that it tends to perpetuate in part.

Marriage has always been a very different thing for man and for woman. The two sexes are necessary to each other, but this necessity has never brought about a condition of reciprocity between them; women, as we have seen, have never constituted a caste making exchanges and contracts with the male caste upon a footing of equality. A man is a social and independent and complete individual; he is regarded first of all as a producer whose existence is justified by the work he does for the group: we have seen why it is that the reproductive and domestic role to which the woman is confined has not guaranteed her an equal dignity. Certainly the male needs her; in some primitive groups it may happen that the bachelor, unable to manage his existence by himself, becomes a kind of outcast; in agricultural societies a woman co-worker is essential to the peasant; and for most men it is of advantage to unload certain drudgery upon a mate; the individual wants a regular sex life and posterity, and the State requires him to contribute to its perpetuation. But man does not make his appeal directly to woman herself; it is the men's group that allows each of its members to find self-fulfillment as husband and father; woman, as slave or vassal, is integrated within families dominated by fathers and brothers, and she has always been given in marriage by certain males to other males. In primitive societies the paternal clan, the gens, disposed of woman almost like a thing: she was included in deals agreed upon by the two groups. The situation is not much modified when marriage assumes a contractual form in the course of its evolution; when dowered or having her share in inheritance, woman would seem to have civil standing as a person, but dowry and inheritance still enslave her to her family. During a long period the contracts were made between father-in-law and son-in-law, not between wife and husband; only widows then enjoyed economic independence. The young girl's freedom of choice has always been much restricted; and celibacy—apart from the rare cases in which it bears a sacred character—reduced her to the rank of parasite and pariah; marriage is her only means of support and the sole justification of her existence. It is enjoined upon her for two reasons.

The first reason is that she must provide the society with children; only rarely—as in Sparta and to some extent under the Nazi regime—does the State take woman under direct guardianship and ask only that she be a mother. But even the primitive societies that are not aware of the paternal generative role demand that woman have a husband, for the second reason why marriage is enjoined is that woman's function is also to satisfy a male's sexual needs and to take care of his household. These duties placed upon woman by society are regarded as a **service** rendered to her spouse: in return he is supposed to give her presents, or a marriage settlement, and to support her. Through him as intermediary, society discharges its debt to the woman it turns over to him. The rights obtained by the wife in fulfilling her duties are represented in obligations that the male must assume. He cannot break the conjugal bond at his pleasure; he can repudiate or divorce his wife only when the public authorities so decide, and even then the husband sometimes owes her compensation in money; the practice even becomes an abuse in Egypt under Bocchoris or, as the demand for alimony, in the United States today. Polygamy has always been more or less openly tolerated: man may bed with slaves, concubines, mistresses, prostitutes, but he is required to respect certain privileges of his legitimate wife. If she is maltreated or wronged, she has the right—more or less definitely guaranteed—of going back to her family and herself obtaining a separation or divorce.

Thus for both parties marriage is at the same time a burden and a benefit; but there is no symmetry in the situations of the two sexes; for girls marriage is the only means of integration in the community, and if they remain unwanted, they are, socially viewed, so much wastage. This is why mothers have always eagerly sought to arrange marriage for them. . . .

It must be said that the independent woman is justifiably disturbed by the idea that people do not have confidence in her. As a general rule, the superior caste is hostile to newcomers from the inferior caste: white people will not consult a Negro physician, nor males a woman doctor; but individuals of the inferior caste, imbued with a sense of their specific inferiority and often full of resentment towards one of their kind who has risen above their usual lot, will also prefer to turn to the masters. Most women, in particular, steeped in adoration for man, eagerly seek him out in person of the doctor, the lawyer, the office manager, and so on. Neither men nor women like to be under a woman's orders. Her superiors, even if they esteem her highly, will always be somewhat condescending; to be a woman, if not a defect, is at least a peculiarity. Woman must constantly win the confidence that is not at first accorded her: at the start she is suspect, she has to prove herself. If she has worth she will pass the tests, so they say. But worth is not a given essence, it is the outcome of a successful development. To feel the weight of an unfavourable prejudice against one is only on very rare occasions a help in overcoming it. The initial inferiority complex ordinarily leads to a defence reaction in the form of an exaggerated affection of authority.

Most women doctors, for example, have much too much or too little of the air of authority. If they act naturally, they fail to take control, for their life as a whole disposes them rather to seduce than to command; the patient who likes to be dominated will be disappointed by plain advice simply given. Aware of this fact, the woman doctor assumes a grave accent, a peremptory tone; but then she lacks the bluff good nature that is the charm of the medical man who is sure of himself.

Man is accustomed to asserting himself; his clients believe in his competence; he can act naturally; he infallibly makes an impression. Woman does not inspire the same feeling of security; she affects a lofty air, she drops it, she makes too much of it. In business, in administrative work, she is precise, fussy, quick to show aggressiveness. As in her studies, she lacks ease, dash, audacity. In the effort to achieve she gets tense. Her activity is a succession of challenges and self-affirmations. This is the great defect that lack of assurance engenders: the subject cannot forget himself. He does not aim gal-

lantly towards some goal: he seeks rather to make good in prescribed ways. In boldly setting out towards ends, one risks disappointments; but one also obtains unhoped-for results; caution condemns to mediocrity.

We rarely encounter in the independent woman a taste for adventure and for experience for its own sake, or a disinterested curiosity; she seeks "to have a career" as other women build a nest of happiness; she remains dominated, surrounded, by the male universe, she lacks the audacity to break through its ceiling, she does not passionately lose herself in her projects. She still regards her life as an immanent enterprise: her aim is not at an objective but, through the objective, at her subjective success. This is a very conspicuous attitude, for example, among American women; they like having a job and proving to themselves that they are capable of handling it properly; but they are not passionately concerned with the **content** of their tasks. Woman similarly has a tendency to attach too much importance to minor setbacks and modest successes; she is turn by turn discouraged or puffed up with vanity. When a success has been anticipated, one takes it calmly; but it becomes an intoxicating triumph when one has been doubtful of obtaining it. This is the excuse when women become addled with importance and plume themselves ostentatiously over their least accomplishments. They are forever looking back to see how far they have come, and that interrupts their progress. By this procedure they can have honourable careers, but not accomplish great things. It must be added that many men are also unable to build any but mediocre careers. It is only in comparison with the best of them that woman—save for very rare exceptions—seems to us to be trailing behind. The reasons I have given are sufficient explanation, and in no way mortgage the future. What woman essentially lacks today for doing great things is forgetfulness of herself; but to forget oneself it is first of all necessary to be firmly assured that now and for the future one has found oneself. Newly come into the world of men, poorly seconded by them, woman is still too busily occupied to search for herself.

There is one category of women to whom these remarks do not apply because their careers, far from hindering the affirmation of their femininity, reinforce it. These are women who seek through artistic expression to transcend their given characteristics; they are the actresses, dancers, and singers. For three centuries they have been almost the only women to maintain a concrete independence in the midst of society, and at the present time they still occupy a privileged place in it. Formerly actresses were anathema to the Church, and the very excessiveness of that severity has always authorized a great freedom of behavior on their part. They often skirt the sphere of gallantry and like courtesans, they spend a

great deal of their time in the company of men; but making their own living and finding the meaning of their lives in their work, they escape the yoke of men. Their great advantage is that their professional successes—like those of men—contribute to their sexual valuation; in their self-realization, their validation of themselves as human beings, they find self-fulfillment as women: they are not torn between contradictory aspirations. On the contrary, they find in their occupations a justification of their narcissism; dress, beauty care, charm, form a part of their professional duties. It is a great satisfaction for a woman in love with her own image to *do* something in simply exhibiting what she *is*; and this exhibition at the same time demands enough study and artifice to appear to be, as Georgette Leblanc said, a substitute for action. A great actress will aim higher yet: she will go beyond the given by the way she expresses it; she will be truly an artist, a creator, who gives meaning to her life by lending meaning to the world.

76. Helsinki Accords, 1975

On August 1, 1975 in Helsinki, Finland, statesmen from thirty-five nations from Europe and North America signed the Final Act of the Conference for Security and Co-operation in Europe (CSCE). The Helsinki Accords contain three sections, known as "baskets." The following document presents ten principles from the first "basket." The second "basket" deals with economic, technological, and environmental cooperation and tourism. "Basket" three treats the area of human relations, contacts, family reunions, freedom of information, and cultural and educational exchanges. The signing of this agreement led to the formation of groups in various republics in the USSR and in Eastern European countries which monitored human rights violations in their homelands. They then passed their findings to western nations for publication. These organizations persisted despite arrests of some of their members, and their activities contributed to the disintegration of communist systems in their countries. During the political upheavals of the late 1980s and early 1990s the membership in the CSCE grew to 53 nations, and on January 1, 1995 it changed its name to the Organization for Security and Cooperation in Europe (OSCE).

One of the main consequences of the Helsinki Accords was the Treaty on the Final Settlement with Respect to Germany, signed in September 1990. It reaffirmed German boundaries as left by the outcome of World War II and specified the withdrawal of Soviet troops from the former GDR by the end of 1994. The reunited Germany acknowledged that it "has no territorial claims against other states and shall not assert any in the future"; renounced the production or possession of nuclear, biological, and chemical weapons; agreed to the reduction in personnel of its armed forces to 370,000; and pledged "that only peace will emanate from German soil." Shortly thereafter, in November, the CSCE proclaimed the "Charter of Paris for a New Europe," by which the Ten Principles of the Helsinki Accords were reiterated and extended in both letter and spirit.

QUESTIONS

1. Compare the Helsinki Accords with the United Nations Universal Declaration of Human Rights.
2. Discuss the impact of the Helsinki Accords on the communist governments of the USSR. and the Eastern European countries during the late 1970s and 1980s.
3. What significance and applications does this treaty have for present-day conditions in Europe?

Declaration on Principles Guiding Relations Between Participating States

I. Sovereign Equality, Respect for the Rights Inherent in Sovereignty

The participating States will respect each other's sovereign equality and individuality as well as all the rights inherent in and encompassed by its sovereignty, including in particular the right of every State to juridicial equality, to territorial integrity and to freedom and political independence. They will also respect each other's right freely to choose and develop its political, social, economic and cultural systems as well as its right to determine its laws and regulations.

Within the framework of international law, all the participating States have equal rights and duties. They will respect each other's right to define and conduct as it wishes its relations with other States in accordance with international law and in the spirit of the present Declaration. They consider that their frontiers can be changed, in accordance with international law, by peaceful means and by agreement. They also have the right to belong or not to be a party to bilateral or multilateral treaties including the right to be or not to be a party of treaties of alliance; they also have the right to neutrality.

II. Refraining from the Threat or Use of Force

The participating States will refrain in their mutual relations, as well as in their international relations in general, from the threat or use of force against the territorial integrity or political independence of any State, or in any other manner inconsistent with the purposes of the United Nations and with the present Declaration. No consideration may be invoked to serve to warrant resort to the threat or use of force in contravention of this principle.

Accordingly, the participating States will refrain from any acts constituting a threat of force or direct or indirect use of force for the purpose of including another participating State to renounce the full exercise of its sovereign rights. Likewise they will also refrain in their mutual relations from any act of reprisal by force.

No such threat or use of force will be employed as a means of settling disputes or questions likely to give rise to disputes, between them.

III. Inviolability of Frontiers

The participating States regard as inviolable all one another's frontiers as well as the frontiers of all States in Europe and therefore they will refrain now and in the future from assaulting these frontiers.

Accordingly, they will also refrain from any demand for, or act of, seizure and usurpation of part or all of the territory of any participating State.

IV. Territorial Integrity of States

The participating States will respect the territorial integrity of each of the participating States.

Accordingly, they will refrain from any action inconsistent with the purposes and principles of the Charter of the United Nations against territorial integrity, political independence or the unity of any participating State, and in particular from any such action constituting a threat or use of force.

The participating States will likewise refrain from making each other's territory the object of military occupation or other direct or indirect measures of force in contravention of international law, or the object of acquisition by means of such measures or the threat of them. No such occupation or acquisition will be recognized as legal.

V. Peaceful Settlement of Disputes

The participating States will settle disputes among them by peaceful means in such a manner as not to endanger international peace and security, and justice.

They will endeavour in good faith and a spirit of co-operation to reach a rapid and equitable solution on the basis of international law.

For this purpose they will use such means as negotiation, enquiry, mediation, conciliation, arbitration, judicial settlement or other peaceful means of their own choice including any settlement procedure agreed to in advance of disputes to which they are parties.

In the event of failure to reach a solution by any of the above peaceful means, the parties to a dispute will continue to seek a mutually agreed way to settle the dispute peacefully.

Participating States, parties to a dispute among them, as well as other participating States, will refrain from any action which might aggravate the situation to such a degree as to endanger the maintenance of international peace and security and thereby make a peaceful settlement of the dispute more difficult.

VI. Non-Intervention in Internal Affairs

The participating States will refrain from any intervention, direct or indirect, individual or collective, in the internal or external affairs falling within the domestic jurisdiction of another participating State, regardless of their mutual relations.

They will accordingly refrain from any form of armed intervention or threat of such intervention against another participating State.

They will likewise in all circumstances refrain from any other act of military, or of political, economic or other coercion designed to subordinate to their own interest the exercise by another participating State of the rights inherent in its sovereignty and thus to secure advantages of any kind.

Accordingly, they will, inter alia, refrain from direct or indirect assistance to terrorist activities, or to subversive or other activities directed towards the violent overthrow of the regime of another participating State.

VII. Respect for Human Rights and Fundamental Freedoms, including the Freedom of Thought, Conscience, Religion or Belief

The participating States will respect human rights and fundamental freedoms, including the freedom of thought, conscience, religion or belief, for all without distinction as to race, sex, language or religion.

They will promote and encourage the effective exercise of civil, political, economic, social, cultural and other rights and freedoms all of which derive from the inherent dignity of the human person and are essential for his free and full development.

Within this framework the participating States will recognize and respect the freedom of the individual to profess and practise, alone or in community with others, religion or belief acting in accordance with the dictates of his own conscience.

The participating States on whose territory national minorities exist will respect the right of persons belonging to such minorities to equality before the law, will afford them the full opportunity for the actual enjoyment of human rights and fundamental freedoms and will, in this manner, protect their legitimate interests in this sphere.

The participating States recognize the universal significance of human rights and fundamental freedoms, respect for which is an essential factor for the peace, justice and well-being necessary to ensure the development of friendly relations and co-operation among themselves as among all States.

They will constantly respect these rights and freedoms in their mutual relations and will endeavour jointly and separately, including in co-operation with the United Nations, to promote universal and effective respect for them.

They confirm the right of the individual to know and act upon his rights and duties in this field.

In the field of human rights and fundamental freedoms, the participating States will act in conformity with the purposes and principles of the Charter of the United Nations and with the Universal Declaration of Human Rights. They will also fulfill their obligations as set forth in the international declarations and agreements in this field, including inter alia the International Covenants on Human Rights, by which they may be bound.

VIII. Equal Rights and Self-Determination of Peoples

The participating States will respect the equal rights of peoples and their right to self-determination, acting at all times in conformity with the purposes and principles of the Charter of the United Nations and with the relevant norms of international law, including those relating to territorial integrity of States.

By virtue of the principle of equal rights and self-determination of peoples, all peoples always have the right, in full freedom, to determine, when and as they wish, their internal and external political status, without external interference, and to pursue as they wish their political, economic, social and cultural development.

The participating States reaffirm the universal significance of respect for and effective exercise of equal rights and self-determination of peoples for the development of friendly relations among themselves as among all States; they also recall the importance of the elimination of any form of violation of this principle.

IX. Co-Operation Among States

The participating States will develop their co-operation with one another and with all States in all fields in accordance with the purposes and principles of the Charter of the United Nations. In developing their co-operation the participating States will place special emphasis on the fields as set forth within the framework of the Conference on Security and Co-operation in Europe, with each of them making contributions in conditions of full equality.

They will endeavour, in developing their co-operation as equals, to promote mutual understanding and confidence, friendly and good-neighborly relations among themselves, international peace, security and justice. They will equally endeavour, in developing their co-operation, to improve the well-being of peoples and contribute to the fulfillment of their aspirations through, inter alia, the benefits resulting from increased mutual knowledge and from progress and achievement in the economic development, and in particular the interest of developing countries throughout the world.

They confirm that governments, institutions, organizations and persons have a relevant and positive role to play in contributing toward the achievement of these aims of their co-operation.

They will strive, in increasing their co-operation as set forth above, to develop closer relations among themselves on an improved and more enduring basis for the benefit of peoples.

X. Fulfillment in Good Faith of Obligations Under International Law

The participating States will fulfil in good faith their obligations under international law, both those obligations from the generally recognized principles and rules of international law and those obligations arising from treaties or other agreements, in conformity with international law, to which they are parties.

In exercising their sovereign rights, including the right to determine their laws and regulations, they will conform with their legal obligations under international law; they will furthermore pay due regard to and implement the provisions in the Final

Act of the Conference on Security and Co-operation in Europe.

The participating States confirm that in the event of a conflict between the obligations of the members of the United Nations under the Charter of the United Nations and their obligations under any other treaty or other international agreement, their obli-gations under the Charter will prevail, in accordance with Article 103 of the Charter of the United Nations.

All the principles set forth above are of primary significance and, accordingly, they will be equally and unreservedly applied, each of them being interpreted taking into account the others. . . .

---

77. The Fall of the Soviet Union, 1991

Mikhail S. Gorbachev was born in 1931 in the Stavropol province in the north Caucasus, U.S.S.R. He studied law at Moscow State University, graduating with honors in 1955. Gorbachev began his political career, rising to the position of chief of his provincial communist party. In 1971 he was named to the Central Committee of the Communist Party of the Soviet Union and in 1980 he became a full member of the Politburo. Following the death of K. Chernenko in March 1985 he became General Secretary of the Communist Party. As he consolidated his power he promoted a number of younger men, both in the party and the government, thereby inaugurating significant reforms. He aimed to transform the Soviet system while retaining its basic tenets and the dominant position of the Communist Party (see A); but this proved to be unattainable. The openness that he promoted revealed the atrocities of the Stalin era and the oppression and stagnation of recent times. He then faced growing demands for more fundamental changes. Contrary to liberal demands, he also strengthened the position of the presidency and elevated a number of men from the conservative wing of the party. In light of these developments his close associate and Foreign Minister E. Shevardnadze resigned, warning about the possibility of a dictatorship.

The foremost challenge that Gorbachev faced was the increasing assertion of national self-determination of the peoples of the U.S.S.R. In his attempts to prevent the disintegration of the Soviet Union Gorbachev was ready to reorganize it by granting a broad autonomy to the republics. Some of the republics insisted on complete independence, while others consented to sign an accord for a new relationship, which was to take effect on August 20, 1991. This was the last straw for the hard-liners, who attempted to seize power on August 19. On that day they announced the ousting of Gorbachev and the formation of a "State Committee for the State Emergency in the U.S.S.R." The collapse of the putsch after only two days in power brought the end to the Communist Party and facilitated the disintegration of the empire. The Baltic states took the opportunity to make a final break from the Union, and then on August 24, 1991 Ukraine proclaimed its independence, which was later confirmed by an overwhelming vote of approval in a referendum (see B). By the fall of 1991 it had become clear that there was no realistic base for a new federation or even a confederation. On December 8, 1991 Belarus, Russia, and Ukraine signed an accord on a Commonwealth of Independent States and declared the Soviet Union dead. They were joined on December 21, 1991 by eight more republics, leaving Gorbachev without a country (see C).

QUESTIONS

1. Summarize Mikhail Gorbachev's defense of his policy of perestroika. Does he blame the founders of Marxism for the problems of the Soviet Union? What role does he envisage for the communist party in reforming the Soviet system?
2. Compare the Ukrainian Declaration of Independence with the American Declaration of Independence and also the Declaration of the Rights of the Peoples of Russia.
3. Summarize the main principles of the Declaration of the Commonwealth of Independent States. How does the new commonwealth differ from the former Soviet Union?

A. The Socialist Idea and Revolutionary Perestroika

Mikhail S. Gorbachev, 1989

Some people try to reproach us that we have no clear-cut, detailed plan to realize the concept of perestroika.

One can hardly agree with the way the question is put. I believe that we would have made a theoretical error if we began to impose ready-made schemes on society again, or tried to squeeze actual life into schemes. This was the characteristic feature of Stalinism with which we have parted ways. . . .

Opinions are now being voiced increasingly often that the socialist idea is an artificial, abstract construction and therefore is devoid of a future, and that the theory of Marxism that expressed and substantiated it has not justified itself because it is responsible for the crisis state of our society.

The founders of Marxism never engaged in inventing specific forms and mechanisms for the development of a new society. They developed the socialist idea, relying on actual social life and the practice of the revolutionary working-class movement of their time.

It is clear that the founders of Marxism and the theory they created cannot bear responsibility for the deformations of socialism over the years, of the personality cult and stagnation, and for the erroneous actions of some political figures—and not only because a century-long period separates the emergence of the theory and those events, but also due to the substance of the matter. . . .

We now take a wider, deeper and more realistic view of socialism than in the recent past. We view it as a world process in which, along with socialist countries with different stages of socioeconomic and political development, there are also various currents of socialist thought in the rest of the world and some social movements different in their composition and motivation. . . .

Notions of a new aspect of socialism form naturally in the process of identifying and theoretically comprehending the basic requirements and interests of people nowadays. On this basis, it is possible to work out goals and programs adequate to the present-day reality but at the same time oriented toward the future.

A special role in the new social organism belongs to the Communist Party, which is called upon to be the political vanguard of Soviet society. The destiny of perestroika and the attainment of a qualitatively new state of society and a new aspect of socialism depend on the party's activities immensely if not decisively. . . .

At the present complex stage, the interests of the consolidation of society and the concentration of all its sound forces on the accomplishment of the difficult tasks of perestroika prompt the advisability of keeping the one-party system.

And in this case, the party will promote the development of opinions in society and the broadening of glasnost in the interests of democracy and the people. In the efforts to renew socialism, the party may not concede the initiative to either populist demagoguery, nationalist or chauvinistic currents or to the spontaneity of group interests.

B. Act of Declaration of the Independence of the Ukraine, 1991

In view of the mortal danger surrounding Ukraine in connection with the state coup in the USSR on August 19, 1991,

* continuing the thousand-year tradition of state building in Ukraine,

* based on the right of a nation to self-determination in accordance with the Charter of the United Nations and other international legal documents, and

* realizing the Declaration on State Sovereignty of Ukraine, the Supreme Soviet solemnly

DECLARES THE INDEPENDENCE
OF UKRAINE AND THE CREATION
OF AN INDEPENDENT UKRAINIAN
STATE — UKRAINE.

The territory of Ukraine is indivisible and inviolable.

From this day forward, on the territory of Ukraine only the Constitution and laws of Ukraine are valid.

This act becomes effective at the moment of its approval.

Supreme Soviet of Ukraine
August 24, 1991

C. Text of Declaration of the Commonwealth of Independent States 1991

THE INDEPENDENT STATES—The Azerbaijani Republic, the Republic of Armenia, the Republic of Byelorussia, the Republic of Kazakhstan, the Republic of Kirghizia, the Republic of Moldavia, the Russian Federation, the Republic of Tadzhiskistan, Turkmania, the Republic of Uzbekistan and Ukraine,

SEEKING to build democratic law-governed states, the relations between which will develop on the basis of mutual recognition and respect for state sovereignty and sovereign equality, the inalienable right to self-determination, principles of equality and non-interference in internal affairs, the rejection of the use of force, the threat of force and economic and any other methods of pressure, a peaceful settlement of disputes, respect for human rights and freedoms, including the rights of national minorities, a conscientious fulfillment of commitments and other generally recognized principles and standards of international law;

RECOGNIZING   and respecting each other's territorial integrity and the inviolability of the existing borders;

BELIEVING   that the strengthening of the relations of friendship, good neighborliness and mutually advantageous cooperation, which has deep historical roots, meets the basic interests of nations and promotes the cause of peace and security;

BEING   aware of their responsibility for the preservation of civilian peace and inter-ethnic accord;

BEING   loyal to the objectives and principles of the agreement on the creation of the Commonwealth of Independent States;

ARE MAKING   the following statement:

Cooperation between members of the commonwealth will be carried out in accordance with the principle of equality through coordinating institutions formed on a parity basis and operating in the way established by the agreements between members of the commonwealth, which is neither a state nor a superstate structure.

In order to insure international strategic stability and security, allied command of the military-strategic forces and a single control over nuclear weapons will be preserved, the sides will respect each other's desire to attain the status of a non-nuclear or neutral state.

The commonwealth of independent states is open, with the agreement of all its participants, for other states to join—members of the former Soviet Union as well as other states sharing the goals and principles of the commonwealth.

The allegiance to cooperation in the formation and development of the common economic space, and all-European and Eurasian markets is being confirmed.

With the formation of the Commonwealth of Independent States, the Union of Soviet Socialist Republics ceases to exist.

Member states of the commonwealth guarantee, in accordance with their constitutional procedures, the fulfillment of international obligations stemming from the treaties and agreements of the former U.S.S.R.

Member states of the commonwealth pledge to observe strictly the principles of this declaration.

---

78. New Year's Message, 1980

Ruhollah Khomeini

Ruhollah al-Musavi al-Khomeini (1902–1989) was born in the desert town of Khomein, south of Teheran. During the 1920s he became a disciple of a prominent teacher of Islam and began a long career as a religious scholar of the Shi'ite sect. The author of more than twenty books on Islamic subjects, he achieved the rank of "Ayatollah" (Farsi for "sign of God"). An active critic of the Pahlavi dynasty which ruled Iran, he was arrested in 1963. He was exiled to Turkey and then Iraq, where he settled in 1964. Iraqi authorities banished him from their country in 1978, but he found refuge in a Parisian suburb. From France he intensified his attack on the Shah of Iran, through radio messages and tape recordings which were smuggled into Iran and broadcast via short-wave radio. He returned to his homeland after the overthrow of the Shah in early 1979, and in December of that year the new constitution of the Iranian Islamic republic named him supreme leader for life. He continued to preach internal revolution to counter the effects of what he deemed "western decadence" on his country's people.

Khomeini exerted an enormous influence on the establishment of a theocratic parliamentary government system in Iran. In Islam the concept of separation of church and state is unknown. Even the most secular government of a country with a Muslim majority must make some reference to *shari'a* (Quranic law, eternal and immutable) in its constitution. Contemporary Iran has the most "religious" constitution of any Muslim parliamentary government. In addition, Iran's Muslim population is primarily Shi'ite. Members of that sect believe in the five basic tenets of Islam: the Oneness of God and the authority of the Prophet Muhammad; prayer; alms for the poor; the Fast of Ramadan; and pilgrimage to Mecca. They differ with the majority of Muslims on the identity of the Caliph or successor to the Prophet. According to their view, until the emergence of the proper Caliph (or "Imam"), who is to come from the Prophet's family in Shi'ite belief, Shi' ite Islam is guided by men who attain the rank of "Ayatollah." Khomeini was one of the many ayatollahs who live at any one time.

QUESTIONS

1. According to Khomeini, who are the enemies of the Iranian people? What does he mean by his references to "the interests of the East and the West"?
2. What are the main points of his program for domestic reform?
3. What is his special message for students, intellectuals, and religious scholars?
4. What is his position on free speech and mass communications?

I OFFER MY CONGRATULATIONS to all the oppressed and to the noble people of Iran on the occasion of the New Year, which coincides with the completion of the pillars of the new Islamic Republic.

God Almighty has willed—and all thanks are due Him—that this noble nation be delivered from the oppression and crimes inflicted on it by a tyrannical government and from the domination of the oppressive powers, especially America, the global plunderer, and that the flag of Islamic justice wave over our beloved land. It is our duty to stand firm against the superpowers, as we are indeed able to do, on condition that the intellectuals stop following and imitating either the West or the East, and adhere instead to the straight path of Islam and the nation. We are at war with international communism no less than we are struggling against the global plunderers of the West, headed by America, Zionism, and Israel.

Dear friends! Be fully aware that the danger represented by the communist powers is no less than that of America; the danger that America poses is so great that if you commit the smallest oversight, you will be destroyed. Both superpowers are intent on destroying the oppressed nations of the world, and it is our duty to defend those nations.

We must strive to export our Revolution throughout the world, and must abandon all idea of not doing so, for not only does Islam refuse to recognize any difference between Muslim countries, it is the champion of all oppressed people. Moreover, all the powers are intent on destroying us, and if we remain surrounded in a closed circle, we shall certainly be defeated. We must make plain our stance toward the powers and the superpowers and demonstrate to them that despite the arduous problems that burden us, our attitude to the world is dictated by our beliefs.

Beloved youths, it is in you that I place my hopes. With the Qur'an [Koran] in one hand and a gun in the other, defend your dignity and honor so well that your adversaries will be unable even to think of conspiring against you. At the same time, be so compassionate toward your friends that you will not hesitate to sacrifice everything you possess for their sake. Know well that the world today belongs to the oppressed, and sooner or later they will triumph. They will inherit the earth and build the government of God.

Once again, I declare my support for all movements and groups that are fighting to gain liberation from the superpowers of the left and the right. I declare my support for the people of Occupied Palestine and Lebanon. I vehemently condemn once more the savage occupation of Afghanistan by the aggressive plunderers of the East, and I hope that the noble Muslim people of Afghanistan will achieve victory and true independence as soon as possible, and be delivered from the clutches of the so-called champions of the working class.

The noble people should be aware that all our victories have been attained by the will of God Almighty, as manifested in the transformation that has occurred throughout the country, together with the spirit of belief and Islamic commitment and cooperation that motivate the overwhelming majority of our people.

The basis of our victory has been our orientation to God Almighty and our unity of purpose. But if we forget this secret of our success, deviate from the sacred ordinances of Islam, and embark on the path of division and disagreement, it is to be feared that God Almighty will withdraw His grace from us and the path will be open again for the tyrants to drag our people back into slavery by means of their satanic tricks and stratagems. Then the pure blood that has been spilled for the sake of independence and freedom, and the sufferings endured by old and young alike, would be in vain; the fate of our Islamic land would remain for all eternity what it was under the tyrannical regime of the Shah; and those who were defeated by our Islamic Revolution would treat us in the same way that they treat all the oppressed people of the world.

It is my God-given and religious duty, therefore, to impress certain things upon you and to assign to the President of the Republic, the Council of the Revolution, the government, and the security forces the responsibility for carrying them out. At the same time, I request the entire nation not to withhold from them all their wholehearted and ungrudging support, in accordance with their commitment to the Islam we all cherish.

I see that satanic counterrevolutionary conspiracies, aiming at promoting the interests of the East and the West, are on the rise; it is the God-given human and national duty of both the government and the people to frustrate those conspiracies with all the powers at their command. I wish to draw particular attention to several points.

1. This is the year in which security must return to Iran so that our noble people can pursue their lives in utter tranquillity. I declare once again my complete support for the honorable Iranian army. I stress that the army of the Islamic Republic must fully observe military discipline and regulations. It is the duty of the President of the Republic, whom I have appointed Commander-in-Chief of the Armed Forces, to admonish severely all those, irrespective of rank, who foment disorder in the army, incite strikes, neglect their duties, ignore military discipline and regulations, or disobey military commands. If they are proven to have committed any of these offenses, they should be immediately expelled from the army and prosecuted.

I can no longer tolerate any form of disorder in the army. Anyone who incites disorder in the army will immediately be denounced to the people as a counterrevolutionary, so that the nation may settle its accounts with any remaining vestiges of the criminal Shah's army. . . .

2. I declare once again my support for the Corps of Revolutionary Guards. I wish to impress upon them and their commanders that the slightest laxity in the fulfillment of their duties is a punishable offense. If they act (God forbid) in such a way as to disturb the order of the Corps, they will immediately be expelled, and what I have said concerning the army applies equally to them. Revolutionary sons of mine, take heed that your conduct toward each other be inspired by affection and Islamic ethics.

3. The police and gendarmerie must also observe discipline. I have been informed that a remarkable laziness prevails in the police stations. The past record of the police is not good; they should therefore do their utmost to establish harmonious relations with the people, maintaining order throughout the country and regarding themselves as an integral part of society. A basic reorganization of the gendarmerie and police is envisaged for the future. In the meantime, the security forces must regard themselves as being at the service of Islam and the Muslims. . . .

4. The Revolutionary Courts throughout Iran must be a model of the implementation of God's laws. They must try not to deviate in the slightest from the ordinances of God Almighty; observing the utmost caution, they must display revolutionary patience in fulfilling the judicial tasks entrusted to them. The Courts do not have the right to maintain their own armed forces, and they must act in accordance with the Constitution. An Islamic judicial system will gradually assume the responsibilities now fulfilled by the Revolutionary Courts, and in the meantime, judges must do their best to prevent all irregularities. If any judge (God forbid) deviates from the commands

of God, he will immediately be exposed to the people and punished.

5. It is the duty of the government to provide the workers and laborers with all they need for productive labor. For their part, the workers should be aware that strikes and slowdowns not only tend to strengthen the superpowers in their hostility to the Revolution, but also tend to transform into despair the hopes now placed in us by the oppressed of the world, who have risen in revolt in both Muslim and non-Muslim countries. As soon as the people learn that a strike is taking place at a factory in their town, they should proceed there immediately and investigate, identifying and exposing to the people all counterrevolutionary forces. There is no reason for the noble people of Iran to pay wages to a handful of godless individuals. . . .

6. I do not know why the government has failed to proceed with its suspended plans for promoting the welfare of the people. It must immediately implement existing plans and adopt new ones in order to remedy the economic situation in our country.

7. Everyone must obey governmental authorities in government offices, and stern action is to be taken against those who fail to do so. Anyone who wishes to create a disturbance in any government office must immediately be expelled and denounced to the people. I am amazed at the failure of the government to appreciate the power of the people. The people are able to settle their accounts with counterrevolutionaries themselves and to disgrace them.

8. Confiscation of the property of miscreants by an unauthorized individual or courts lacking the proper competence is to be severely condemned. All confiscations must take place in accordance with the *shari'a* and after a warrant has been obtained from a prosecutor or judge. No one has the right to intervene in these matters, and anyone who does so will be severely punished.

9. Land must be distributed according to the criteria of the *shari'a,* and only the competent courts have the right to sequester land after due investigation. No one else has the right to encroach on anyone's land or orchards. Unauthorized persons in general have no right to intervene in these affairs. They may place at the disposal of the competent authorities, however, any information they may have concerning the land, orchards, or buildings belonging to persons associated with the old regime who usurped the property of the people. Anyone who acts in defiance of Islamic and legal criteria will be subject to severe prosecution. . . .

10. A fundamental revolution must take place in all the universities across the country, so that professors with links to the East or the West may be purged, and the university may provide a healthy atmosphere for cultivation of the Islamic sciences. The evil form of instruction imposed by the previous regime must be stopped, because all the miseries of society during the reign of that father and that son were ultimately caused by such evil instruction. If a proper method of education had been followed in the universities, we would never have had a class of university-educated intellectuals choose to engage in factionalism and dispute, in total isolation from the people and at a time of intense crisis for the country; they overlooked the sufferings of the people so completely that it was as if they were living abroad. All of our backwardness has been due to the failure of most university-educated intellectuals to acquire correct knowledge of Iranian Islamic society, and unfortunately, this is still the case. Most of the blows our society has sustained have been inflicted on it precisely by these university-educated intellectuals, who, with

their inflated notions of themselves, speak in a manner only their fellow so-called intellectuals can understand; if the people at large cannot understand them, too bad! Because the people do not even exist in the eyes of these intellectuals; only they themselves exist. The evil form of instruction practiced in the universities during the time of the Shah educated intellectuals in such a way that they paid no regard to the oppressed and exploited people, and unfortunately, they still fail to do so.

Committed, responsible intellectuals! Abandon your factionalism and separation and show some concern for the people, for the salvation of this heroic population that has offered so many martyrs. Rid yourselves of the "isms" of the East and the West; stand on your own feet and stop relying on foreigners. The students of the religious sciences as well as the university students must take care that their studies are entirely based on Islamic foundations. They must abandon the slogans of deviant groups and replace all incorrect forms of thought with the true Islam that we cherish. Let both groups of students be aware that Isalm is an autonomous, rich school of thought that has no need of borrowings from any other school. Furthermore, let everyone be aware that to adopt a syncretic ideology is a great act of treason toward Islam and the Muslims, the bitter fruits of which will become apparent in the years ahead. Unfortunately, we see that because of a failure to understand certain aspects of Islam correctly and precisely, these aspects have been mixed with elements taken from Marxism, so that a melange has come into being that is totally incompatible with the progressive laws of Islam.

Beloved students, do not follow the wrong path of university intellectuals who have no commitment to the people! Do not separate yourself from the people!

11. Another matter is that of the press and the mass communications media. Once again, I request the press throughout the country to collaborate, to write freely whatever they wish, but not to engage in conspiracies. I have said repeatedly that the press must be independent and free, but unfortunately, I see some newspapers engaged on a course designed to serve the evil aims of the right and the left in Iran. In all countries, the press plays a fundamental role in creating an atmosphere that is either healthy or unhealthy. It is to be hoped that in Iran, the press will enter the service of God and the people.

Radio and television must also be free and independent, and they must broadcast all forms of criticism with complete impartiality, so that we do not again witness the kind of radio and television we had under the deposed Shah. Radio and television must be purged of all pro-Shah and deviant elements.

12. These days, the agents and supporters of the Shah are unleashing a campaign against the beloved religious scholars who were among the most militant segments of society in both the time of the deposed Shah and that of his father: they staged numerous uprisings against the corrupt regime to expose its true nature, continuously led the just struggles of our noble people, and guided them to victory. When the religious scholars embarked on their determined struggle against the treacherous Shah in the years 1341 and 1342 [1962 and 1963], he labelled our committed and responsible religious leaders "Black Reaction," because the militant religious scholars, with their deep roots in the souls of the nation, represented the only serious danger to him and his monarchy. Now, too, in order to crush the religious leadership, which is the very foundation of the independence and freedom of our country, the agents of the Shah are putting the word "reaction" in the mouths of

some of our young people who are unaware of the true situation.

My beloved, revolutionary children! Insulting and attempting to weaken the religious leadership strikes a blow against our freedom and independence and against Islam. It is an act of treason to imitate the treacherous Shah and apply the word "reaction" to this respectable class of our population that has always refused to submit to either East or West.

Beloved sisters and brothers! Understand that anyone who regards the religious scholars as reactionaries is following the path of the Shah and America. By supporting the true and committed religious leaders, who have always guarded and protected this land, the noble nation of Iran is paying its debt to Islam and frustrating the covetous designs entertained on our country by historical oppressors.

At the same time, I wish to draw the attention of the respected religious scholars throughout the country to the possibility that the devils hostile to our Revolution may be spreading malicious propaganda among them against our beloved youth, particularly the university students. They should realize that it is our common duty today to ensure that all segments of society—particularly the university students and the religious leaders, who together constitute the intellectual resources of our nation—unite against satanic and tyrannical forces, advance our Islamic movement in unison with each other, and guard our independence and freedom as jealously as they would their own lives. In the time of the tyrannical regime of the Shah, it was the plan of the world-plunderers and their agents to create a division between these two important classes. Unfortunately, they succeeded, and the country was ruined as a result. Now they wish to implement the same plan again, and the slightest lack of vigilance on our part will lead to the ruin of our country again. It is my hope that in the year that is now beginning, all classes of the nation, in particular these two respected classes, will be fully conscious of the stratagems and conspiracies that are directed against us and frustrate those evil plans with their unity of purpose.

Finally, at the beginning of this new year, I seek God's mercy for the martyrs of the Islamic Revolution, and express my gratitude for the sacrifices they made. . . .

79. Silent Spring, 1962

Rachel Carson

Rachel Carson (1907–1964) was an American marine biologist and author of several influential books on the natural life of the seas and the environment. Born in Springdale, Pennsylvania, she earned an undergraduate degree from the Pennsylvania College for Women and a Masters from Johns Hopkins University. She began her career in 1931 as a zoology professor at the University of Maryland. From 1936 to 1952 she was an aquatic biologist at the U.S. Bureau of Fisheries and the Fish and Wildlife Service. Her ideas gained national attention in 1951 after the publication of *The Sea Around Us,* which won the National Book Award for Nonfiction. The following selection presents excerpts from her last book, *Silent Spring,* in which she warned about the dangers of pesticides to plants, animals, and human beings. One of the pioneers of the modern environmentalist movement, she did not live to see the fruits of her labors realized in such federal legislation as the National Environmental Protection Act, the Clean Air Act, and the Clean Water Act.

QUESTIONS

1. What was Carson's purpose in beginning her book with "A Fable for Tomorrow"?
2. According to this fable, what are the "strange blight" and the "evil spell" which had settled on the community? Who and what was in danger?
3. Who does she believe is responsible for these threats?

A Fable for Tomorrow

THERE WAS ONCE a town in the heart of America where all life seemed to live in harmony with its surroundings. The town lay in the midst of a checkerboard of prosperous farms, with fields of grain and hillsides of orchards where, in spring, white clouds of bloom drifted above the green fields. In autumn, oak and maple and birch set up a blaze of color that flamed and flickered across a backdrop of pines. Then foxes barked in the hills and deer silently crossed the fields, half hidden in the mists of the fall mornings.

Along the roads, laurel, viburnum and alder, great ferns and wildflowers delighted the traveler's eye through much of the year. Even in winter the roadsides were places of beauty, where countless birds came to feed on the berries and on the seed heads of the dried weeds rising above the snow. The countryside was, in fact, famous for the abundance and variety of its bird life, and when the flood of migrants was pouring through in spring and fall people traveled from great distances to observe them. Others came to fish the streams, which flowed clear and cold out of the hills and contained shady pools where trout lay. So it had been from the days many years ago when the first settlers raised their houses, sank their wells, and built their barns.

Then a strange blight crept over the area and everything began to change. Some evil spell had settled on the community: mysterious maladies swept the flocks of chickens; the cattle and sheep sickened and died. Everywhere was a shadow of death. The farmers spoke of much illness among their families. In the town the doctors had become more and more puzzled by new kinds of sickness appearing among their patients. There had been several sudden and unexplained deaths, not only among adults but even among children, who would be stricken suddenly while at play and die within a few hours.

There was a strange stillness. The birds, for example—where had they gone? Many people spoke of them, puzzled and disturbed. The feeding stations in the backyards were deserted. The few birds seen anywhere were moribund; they trembled violently and could not fly. It was a spring without voices. On the mornings that had once throbbed with the dawn chorus of robins, catbirds, doves, jays, wrens, and scores of other bird voices there was now no sound; only silence lay over the fields and woods and marsh.

On the farms the hens brooded, but no chicks hatched. The farmers complained that they were unable to raise any pigs—the litters were small and the young survived only a few days. The apple trees were coming into bloom but no bees droned among the blossoms, so there was no pollination and there would be no fruit.

The roadsides, once so attractive, were now lined with browned and withered vegetation as though swept by fire. These, too, were silent, deserted by all living things. Even the streams were now lifeless. Anglers no longer visited them, for all the fish had died.

In the gutters under the eaves and between the shingles of the roofs, a white granular powder still showed a few patches; some weeks before it had fallen like snow upon the roofs and the lawns, the fields and streams.

No witchcraft, no enemy action had silenced the rebirth of new life in this stricken world. The people had done it themselves.

This town does not actually exist, but it might easily have a thousand counterparts in America or elsewhere in the world. I know of no community that has experienced all the misfortunes I describe. Yet every one of these disasters has actually happened somewhere, and many real communities have already suffered a substantial number of them. A grim specter has crept upon us almost unnoticed, and this imagined tragedy may easily become a stark reality we all shall know.

What has already silenced the voices of spring in countless towns in America? This book is an attempt to explain.

---

80. Two Reflections on the Legacy of Western Civilization

The first part of this document is by Arnold J. Toynbee (1889–1975), an English classical scholar and historian, educated at Oxford. After a few years at Oxford as a tutor in Greek and Roman history, he pursued a variety of careers as a professor at London University, author, editor, and director of the Royal Institute of International Affairs and the Foreign Office Research Department. Author of an immense number of books, Toynbee is best known for *A Study of History*, a twelve-volume work written between 1930 and 1961. For Toynbee the driving force of history is human and environmental "challenge and response," his formulation of a non-materialist, anti-deterministic explanation of historical change. He believed that the Western world was passing through a crisis similar to that of Greece at the time of the Peloponnesian war as interpreted by Thucydides. His *Study* analyzes and compares every civilization (by his reckoning there were about 23) and religion, past and present. In the course of the work he focused on religion as "the chief business" of the historian. He thus came under an avalanche of criticism, as many commentators thought that he had ceased to be an historian and had become a "prophet." While professional historians shot holes in his grand synthesis, the public was fascinated by his answers to the eternal questions of human destiny. The *Study* became a best seller, as did many of his other grand and controversial works. It was the time when the Cold War was at its height and the general public was greatly concerned about the prospects of the West and about Western civilization's moral worth. While his system has been largely discredited and his writings are no longer in favor among academics and the general public, he did teach the world and the historical profession that our approach to history can no longer be provincial but must be ecumenical. Part of his legacy is the recognition today that while specialized monographs and national histories still have their value, an understanding of the contemporary world requires an appreciation of the big picture, comprising world history, encounters between cultures and civilizations, and a global perspective. In a sense, then, Toynbee is the creator of the course in which you the student are enrolled; the proliferation of such college courses testifies to his enduring significance.

The second part of this document is by Bernard Lewis, an author who is Cleveland E. Dodge Professor of Near Eastern Studies Emeritus at Princeton University. The excerpts which appear below present some of his thoughts on the long term significance of Western culture for the peoples of the globe.

QUESTIONS

1. What does Arnold Toynbee see as the most serious "man-made menaces" to mankind's survival?
2. According to Toynbee, how do recent political trends around the world differ from technological, cultural, and economic trends? What disturbs him about that state of affairs?
3. For Toynbee, what is the most important cause of political disunity? What is his view of modern nationalism?
4. Does Toynbee end his essay on an optimistic or pessimistic note? Discuss the significance of recent events for his argument.
5. Summarize Bernard Lewis's defense of Western civilization. What does he see as the negative and positive effects of the West on the world?
6. Explain and discuss his interpretation of the meaning of "multiculturalism."

A. For the First Time in 30,000 Years, 1972

Arnold Toynbee

Till now, mankind has either taken it as a matter of course that it is going to survive, or, alternatively, assumed that its destiny will be decided by forces beyond human control: the gods or God or Nature. We have now woken up to the truth that, today, we are in greater danger of extinction than we have been at any time since the date—perhaps 30,000 years ago—at which our ancestors gained the upper hand over all other forms of life on this planet except microbes and viruses. In the present age we have discovered and conquered the microbes, and we have hopes of getting the better of the viruses. But our recent victories over non-human menaces to human life are far outweighed by new threats to us from ourselves. These threats have no precedents; for man, armed with the power of science applied to technology, is a vastly more formidable enemy for man than any non-human enemy that man has yet encountered.

The present human threats to mankind's survival are notorious. The three principal current man-made menaces are nuclear weapons, the pollution of mankind's habitat on this planet, together with the using up of the planet's irreplaceable natural resources, and the population explosion produced by a reduction in the death-rate without a simultaneously corresponding reduction in the birth-rate. . . .

The technological unification of our habitat is now an accomplished fact. Its economic unification is hardly less complete, and even its social and cultural unification has been accomplished at some levels. This is the result of the global radiation during the last five centuries of West European technology, trade, investment, government, population, institutions, ideas, and ideals. . . .

The present situation and, still more, the current tendency on the political plane presents a disturbing contrast to the situation and tendency on other planes of human activity. On these other planes, the history of human affairs during the last five hundred years has resulted in at least a beginning of the process of unification which is the outcome that we should expect. On the political plane, on the other hand, there has been so far little discernible progress toward unification.

Indeed, there has been quite a marked accentuation of political disunity, both in fact and feeling. This increasing disharmony between politics and other human activities has now reached a degree at which it is manifestly threatening mankind with catastrophe. Why are we exposing ourselves to this fearful risk? Why, in our political life, are we so allergic to the unifying tendency which has prevailed in other fields? It is important to try to identify and understand the causes of this political misfit. To lay bare the causes is the most promising first step toward finding a cure.

The most obvious cause is the persistent disunity of the Western civilization, since it is the Western peoples who, within the last five hundred years, have initiated the global unification of mankind on a number of non-political planes. Since the collapse of the Roman Empire in its western provinces in the fifth century, the new Western civilization that has sprung up out of the Roman Empire's ruins has been disunited politically, though united culturally, technologically and to some extent also economically. . . .

This political division of the modern Westerners into a number of mutually hostile nation-states has now been imitated by the non-Western majority of mankind. During the two centuries and a half that ended in the two world wars, the West was manifestly dominant in the world. Consequently, Western institutions acquired prestige. Non-Western peoples who revolted against Western domination adopted the Western political ideology of nationalism because they believed this had been the source of the West's strength. The dissolution of the West European national states' colonial empires during and since the Second World War has resulted in a doubling of the number of the world's local sovereign independent states. Each formerly subject territory that has recovered its political independence has set itself up as a national state in imitation of the Western national state whose rule it has shaken off.

The tendency to increase the number and to reduce the average size of local sovereign states has been stimulated, both in the West and elsewhere, by the nineteenth-century Western political doctrine of self-determination. . . .

Nationalism is the most potent of the causes of the political disunity of the present-day world. . . .

What are the prospects of the present tug-o'-war between the forces of political fission versus those of political consolidation? . . .

We have to ask ourselves whether the global political unification which is the alternative to a catastrophe is likely to be helped or hindered by partial political unifications on a less than global scale. . . .

In most previous cases, political unity has been imposed eventually by military conquest. The cost, psychological as well as physical, of this barbarous method of unification has proved, again and again, to be prohibitively high. Unification by conquest has sometimes postponed the dissolution of a civilization, but it has seldom averted it and, insofar as the dissolution of forcibly unified civilization has been postponed, the civilization has been preserved in most

cases only in a state of petrification. However, in the age of atomic weapons by which mankind has now been overtaken, the traditional violent method of unification is no longer practicable anyway. A world war fought with atomic weapons could not unify mankind; it would only annihilate it. In the atomic age, the only possible method of unification is some form of voluntary association.

It has been noted already that since 1945—the year in which the Second World War culminated and ended in the invention and use of atomic weaponry—some of the sovereign national states of Western Europe have taken the radically new departure of entering into a voluntary association in the E.E.C. This is a good augury, considering how deeply ingrained is nationalism in the tradition of the Western European peoples and how often one or other of them has tried to subjugate the rest by force. If the Western European peoples can unite with each other voluntarily, as they are now demonstrating they can, a voluntary union of all mankind, on a global scale, is not a utopian objective.

The objective is not utopian, but will it be achieved? That is to say, will it be achieved in time to avert the catastrophe which is the alternative to it? This question will be answered by the three present superpowers [United States, Soviet Union, and China]; their answer is still unknown—probably even to themselves. Will the superpowers' governments and peoples recognize in time that the winning of successes in their competition with each other is not the paramount interest of any one of them? Will they recognize that their paramount interest is the preservation of the human race; that this interest is common to them all and also to the rest of mankind; and that the pursuit of this objective is not only their interest but their duty, both to themselves and to their fellow men? If and when the views and intentions of the superpowers become clear, we shall be better able than we are today to forecast the future of mankind. Today we know only that mankind's future is once again in doubt for the first time, perhaps, within the last 30,000 years.

B. Eurocentrism Revisited, 1994

Bernard Lewis

Europe, Asia, and Africa are the three continents into which, by ancient tradition, the world was divided. . . .

. . . the inhabitants of Asia and Africa . . . were as unaware of being Asians and Africans as the inhabitants of pre-Columbian America were unaware of being Americans. They first became aware of this classification when it was brought to them—and at some times and in some places imposed on them—by Europeans. . . .

Europe became Europe. Europe discovered and in a sense created America, since every polity in the western hemisphere, from the Arctic to the Antarctic, was founded on a European model and expresses itself in a European language. But Europe neither created nor discovered Asia and Africa. It invented them, and it is a supreme irony of our own time that in a wave of revolt against Eurocentrism, so many non-Europeans have adopted this ultimately Eurocentric view of the world, and defined themselves by the identity which Europeans imposed on them. . . .

The oceanic voyages of the European explorers around Africa to Asia, across the Atlantic to the Americas, created, for the first time in history, a new unity among all the continents, bringing all of them into contact with one another and preparing the way for a global interchange of foodstuffs and commodities, plants and domestic animals, knowledge and ideas.

There was also a negative side. These new intercontinental lines of communication made possible an interchange of diseases between the eastern and western hemispheres, sometimes leading to the emergence of virulent new strains, calling for new diagnoses and remedies. These could be social as well as medical, such as, for example, the new strain of slavery added to the numerous and widespread slave institutions of both the Old and the New Worlds.

Although it was known in medieval Europe, slavery was of minor importance there, far less significant in the social and economic life of Europe than it was in pre-Columbian America or in Muslim and non-Muslim Africa. The meeting of all these different cultures gave rise to a new variant—that known as colonial slavery. The inventiveness and cupidity of Europe, learning from and drawing on the plantation systems and the slave trade of Africa and the Islamic world, developed this variant. Colonial slavery and the seaborne slave trade became major factors in the crisscrossing interchanges among the four shores of the Atlantic—Western Europe, Western Africa, North America, South America.

But it was Europe and its daughters, too, that first decided to set the slaves free—at home, then in the colonies, finally in all the world. Western technology made slavery unnecessary; Western ideas made it intolerable. There have been many slaveries; there was only one abolition, which eventually shattered even the rooted and ramified slave systems of the Old World.

In all this, as in much else, the discovery of America, for better or for worse, was a turning point in human history, and an essential part of the transition to a modernity that began in Europe and was carried all over the world by European discoverers, conquerors, missionaries, colonists, and, let us not forget, refugees. Far more than the final Christian reconquest of Muslim Spain under Ferdinand and Isabella, the contemporary discovery of America ensured, in the long run, the triumph of Europe over its enemies.

The mines of the New World gave European Christendom gold and silver to finance its trade, its wars, and its inventions. The fields and plantations of the Americas gave it new resources and commodities, and enabled Europeans, for the first time, to trade with the Muslims and others as equals, and ultimately, as superiors. And the very encounter with strange lands and peoples, unknown to history and scripture alike, contributed mightily to the breaking of intellectual molds, and the freeing of the human mind and spirit.

Why then did the peoples of Europe embark on this vast expansion and, by conquest, conversion, and colonization, attempt to create a Eurocentric world. Was it, as some believe, because of some deep-seated, perhaps hereditary vice—some profound moral flaw?

The question is unanswerable because it is wrongly posed. In setting out to conquer, subjugate, and despoil other peoples, the Europeans were merely following the example set them by their neighbors and predecessors, and indeed conforming to the common practice of mankind. In particular, their attack on the neighboring lands of Islam in Africa and Asia was a clear case of be-done-by-as-you-did. The interesting questions are not why they tried, but why they succeeded—and then why, having succeeded, they repented of their success as a sin. The success was unique in modern times; the repentance, in all of recorded history.

The attempt was due to their common humanity; their success to some special qualities inherent in the civilization of Europe and its daughters and deficient or lacking in others. No doubt the Europeans had the mixture of appetite, ferocity, smugness, and sense of mission which are essential to the imperial mood, and which they shared with their various imperial predecessors. But they also had something else, which today both the former conquerors, and those whom they conquered and then relinquished, might find useful to examine. . . .

. . . It has now become customary to designate the larger civilization of which Europe is the source and America the leader as "the West." In addition to its obvious geographical denotation, this word originally had two overlapping but somewhat different meanings. In its first meaning, the word denoted a military alliance against the Soviet Union, an alliance that included some countries sharing few or none of the basic values of the West and linked to it only by strategic necessity; in its second, the world denoted a comity of like-minded nations sharing certain basic values concerning freedom and decency and human rights, and including neutrals who wished no part of the anti-Soviet alliance.

Today, with the collapse of the Soviet Union and the end of the cold war, a new, larger, and perhaps even greater Europe may emerge. The West, no longer hemmed in by military needs and constraints, may also aspire to yet greater achievements. But for the moment, among the Europeans and among their children and disciples, especially in North America, the mood of greed and self-confidence has given way to one of satiety, guilt, and doubt.

Doubt is good and, indeed, is one of the mainsprings of Western civilization. It undermines the certitudes that in other civilizations and in earlier stages of our own have fettered thought, weakened or ended tolerance, and prevented the emergence of that cooperation of opponents that we call democracy. It leads to questioning and thus to discoveries, and to new achievements and new knowledge, including the knowledge of other civilizations.

On the other hand, guilt in the modern sense—not a legal decision, but a mental condition—is corrosive and destructive, and is an extreme form of that arrogant self-indulgence that is the deepest and most characteristic flaw of our Western civilization. To claim responsibility for all the ills of the world is a new version of the "white man's burden," no less flattering to ourselves, no less condescending to others, than that of our imperial predecessors, who with equal vanity and absurdity claimed to be the source of all that was good.

A word that is much heard nowadays is "multiculturalism." Indeed, all cultures have their achievements—their art and music, philosophy and science, literature and styles of life, and other contributions to the advancement of humankind—and there can be no doubt that knowledge of these would benefit us and enrich our lives. The recognition of this infinite human variety, and of the need to study and learn from it, is indeed one of the West's most creative innovations. For it is only the West that has developed this curiosity about other cultures, this willingness to learn their languages and study their ways, to appreciate and to respect their achievements.

The other great civilizations known to history have all, without exception, seen themselves as self-sufficient, and regarded the outside, and even the subculture or low-status insider, with contempt, as barbarians, Gentiles, untouchables, unbelievers, foreign devils, and other more intimate, less formal terms of opprobrium. Only under the pressure of conquest and domination did they make the effort to learn the languages of other civilizations and, in self-defense, try to understand the ideas and the ways of the current rulers of the world. They would learn, in other words, from those whom they were constrained to recognize as their masters, in either sense or both, as rulers or as teachers. By contrast, the special combination of unconstrained curiosity concerning the Other, and unforced respect for his otherness, remains a distinctive feature of Western and Westernized cultures, and is still regarded with bafflement and anger by those who neither share nor understand it.

We of the West have often failed catastrophically in respect for those who differ from us, as our dismal record of wars and persecutions may attest. But such respect is something for which we have striven as an ideal, and in which we have achieved some success, both in practicing it ourselves and in imparting it to others. It is surely significant that in the late 1970s and 1980s refugees fleeing from Vietnam made for the crowded island of Hong Kong—the one spot in all East Asia where a Western government still ruled, and where they could therefore count on the certainty of public scrutiny and concern, and the consequent hope, however slight, of help.

Imperialism, sexism, and *racism* are words of Western coinage—not because the West invented these evils, which are, alas, universal, but because the West recognized and named and condemned them as evils and struggled mightily, and not entirely in vain, to weaken their hold and to help their victims. If, to borrow a phrase, Western culture does indeed "go," imperialism, sexism, and racism will not go with it. More likely casualties will be the freedom to denounce them and the effort to end them.

It may be that Western culture will indeed go: the lack of conviction of many of those who should be its defenders, the passionate intensity of its accusers, may well join to complete its destruction. But if it does go, the men and women of all the continents will thereby be impoverished and endangered.

Credits

Page 6: From "The Broken Spears" by Miguel Leon-Portilla. Copyright © 1962, 1990 by Beacon Press. Reprinted by permission of Beacon Press.

Page 21: Copyright © 1970 Oxford University Press. Reprinted from "A View of the Present State of Ireland" by Edmund Spenser, edited by W. L. Kenwick (1970) by permission of Oxford University Press.

Page 36: Excerpts from Louis Gallagher, S. J., trans., *China in the Sixteenth Century* (Random House, 1970). Reprinted by permission of Random House, Inc.

Page 42: Excerpts from Basil Dmytryshyn, E. A. P. Crownhurt-Vaughan, and Thomas Vaughan, eds., *Russia's Conquest of Siberia, 1558–1700,* Vol. I (Oregon Historical Society Press, 1985). Reprinted by permission of the Oregon Historical Society Press.

Page 47: Excerpt from C. R. Boxer *The Christian Century in Japan, 1549–1650* (University of California Press, 1979). Reprinted by permission of Carcanet Press, Ltd.

Page 86: Excerpts from a *Documentary Survey of the French Revolution* by Stewart, John Hall. Copyright © 1951 by permission of Prentice Hall Inc. Upper Saddle River, New Jersey.

Page 90: Excerpts from *A Documentary Survey of the French Revolution* by Stewart, John Hall. Copyright © 1951 by permission of Prentice Hall Inc. Upper Saddle River, New Jersey.

Page 94: Excerpts from *A Documentary Survey of the French Revolution* by Stewart, John Hall. Copyright © 1951 by permission of Prentice Hall Inc. Upper Saddle River, New Jersey.

Page 95: From *European Women—A Documentary History, 1789–1945* by Eleanor S. Riemer & John C. Fout, editors. Copyright © 1980 by Schocken Books, Inc. Reprinted by permission of Schocken Books, published by Pantheon Books, a division of Random House, Inc.

Page 97: Excerpts from *A Documentary Survey of the French Revolution* by Stewart, John Hall. Copyright © 1951 by permission of Prentice Hall Inc. Upper Saddle River, New Jersey.

Page 102: Excerpts from *A Documentary Survey of the French Revolution* by Stewart, John Hall. Copyright © 1951 by permission of Prentice Hall Inc. Upper Saddle River, New Jersey.

Page 105: Excerpts from *Robespierre* edited by George Rudé (Prentice Hall, 1967). Copyright © 1967 Prentice Hall. Used by permission of the publisher, Prentice Hall/A division of Simon & Schuster, Upper Saddle River, New Jersey.

Page 107: Excerpts from Vincent Lecuna and Harold Bierck, eds., Lewis Bertrand trans., *Selected Writings of Bolivar* Vol. I, 1810–1822. (Banco de Venezuela, Colonial Press, N. Y., 1951).

Page 117: From *Sources of Japanese Tradition* by William Theodore de Bary. Copyright © 1958 by Columbia University Press. Reprinted by permission of Columbia University Press.

Page 145: From *Documents of European Economic History*, Vol. I by Pollard/Holmes. Copyright © S. Pollard & C. Holmes. Reprinted with permission of St. Martin's Press, Inc.

Page 172: From *Latin American Civilization: History and Society, 1492 to the Present* edited by Benjamin Keen, 4th ed. Copyright © 1986 by Westview Press. Reprinted by permission of Westview Press.

Page 184: From *J. G. Herder on Social and Political Culture* edited by F. M. Barnard. Copyright © 1969 by Cambridge University Press. Reprinted by permission of Cambridge University Press and F. M. Barnard.

Page 206: From *Arab Rediscovery of Europe* by Ibrahim Abu-Lughood. Copyright © 1963 by Princeton University Press. Reprinted by permission of Princeton University Press.

Page 210: From *Cecil Rhodes* by John Flint. Copyright © 1974 by John Flint. Reprinted by permission of Little, Brown and Company.

Page 213: Excerpts reprinted from *Problems in Western Civilization, The Challenge of History*, Vol. II by Ludwig Frederick Schafer, David Fowler, Jacob Ernest Cooke. Copyright ©1968 by Charles Scribner's Sons. Used by permission of Prentice Hall/A division of Simon & Schuster, Upper Saddle River, New Jersey.

Page 219: From *China's Response to the West: A Documentary Survey, 1839–1923* by Ssu-yu-Teng and John King Fairbank. Copyright © 1954, 1979 by the President and Fellows of Harvard College. Reprinted by permission of Harvard University Press.

Page 223: From *Sources of Indian Tradition* by William Theodore de Bary. Copyright © 1964 by Columbia University Press. Reprinted by permission of Columbia University Press.

Page 228: From *China's Response to the West: A Documentary Survey, 1839–1923* by Ssu-yu-Teng and John King Fairbank. Copyright © 1954, 1979 by the President and Fellows of Harvard College. Reprinted by permission of Harvard University Press.

Page 243: From *Latin American Civilization: History and Society, 1492 to the Present*, 4th ed. edited by Benjamin Keen. Copyright © 1986 by Westview Press. Reprinted by permission of Westview Press.

Page 258: From *Germany's Aim in the First World War* by Fritz Fischer. Copyright © 1961 by Droste Verlag und Druckerei GmbH, Dusseldorf. English translation copyright © 1967 by W. W. Norton & Company, Inc. Reprinted by permission of W. W. Norton & Company, Inc.

Page 276: From Joseph Stalin, *Leninism: Selected Writings*. Copyright © 1942 by International Publishers Co. Reprinted by permission of International Publishers, Co.

Page 278: From *Execution By Hunger: The Hidden Holocaust* by Miron Dolot. Copyright © 1985 by Miron Dolot. Reprinted by permission of W. W. Norton & Company, Inc.

Page 283: From *Anti-Stalin Campaign and International Communism* by the Russian Institute. Copyright © 1956 by Columbia University Press. Reprinted with permission of Columbia University Press.

Page 287: Excerpts from *Mein Kampf* by Adolf Hitler, translated by Ralph Manheim. Copyright © 1943, renewed 1971 by Houghton Mifflin Co. Reprinted by permission of Houghton Mifflin Co. All rights reserved.

Page 304: From *Sources of Japanese Tradition* by William Theodore de Bary. Copyright © 1958 by Columbia University Press. Reprinted by permission of Columbia University Press.

Page 314: Excerpts from Raul Hilberg, ed. *Documents of Destruction, Germany and Jewry, 1933–1945* (Quadrangle Books, 1971). Reprinted by permission of Raul Hilberg.

Page 324: Excerpts from Petro Mirchuk, *In the German Mills of Death, 1941–45* (Vantage Press, 1976). Reprinted by permission of Petro Mirchuk.

Page 332: From speeches by General Douglas MacArthur, 9/2/45. Copyright © 1945 by The New York Times Company. Reprinted by permission of The New York Times.

Page 334: From *U.S.S.R.: A Concise History* 4th ed. by Basil Dmytryshyn, (Charles Scribner's Sons, 1984). Reprinted by permission of Basil Dmytryshyn.

Page 339: From speeches by Winston Churchill, 3/4/46. Copyright © 1946 by The New York Times Company. Reprinted by permission of The New York Times.

Page 350: From *Yearbook of the United Nations*. Copyright © 1950 by Columbia University Press. Reprinted with permission of Columbia University Press.

Page 356: From *Sources of Indian Tradition* by William de Bary. Copyright © 1964 by Columbia University Press. Reprinted with permission of Columbia University Press.

Page 361: Excerpted from *Conflict in Indo-China and International Repercussions: A Documentary History, 1945–1955,* ed. Alan B. Cole. Copyright © 1956 by The Fletcher School of Law and Diplomacy. Used by permission of the publisher, Cornell University Press.

Page 376: From *The Struggle is My Life* by Nelson Mandela. Copyright © 1990 by Pathfinder Press. Reprinted by permission of Pathfinder Press.

Page 382: From *The Second Sex* by Simone de Beauvoir, trans., H. M. Parshley. Copyright © 1952 and renewed 1980 by Alfred A. Knopf, Inc. Reprinted by permission of the publisher, Alfred A. Knopf, Inc.